ALIVE IN CHRIST

GRADE 7 TEACHER EDITION

Jesus Christ and the New Testament

aliveinchrist.osv.com

OurSundayVisitor

The Subcommittee on the Catechism, United States Conference of Catholic Bishops, has found the doctrinal content of this manual, copyright 2014, to be in conformity with the *Catechism of the Catholic Church.*

Nihil Obstat
Rev. Fr. Jeremiah L. Payne, S.Th.L.
Censor Librorum, Diocese of Orlando

Imprimatur
✠ Most Rev. John Noonan
Bishop of Orlando
May 15, 2014

Alive in Christ School Grade 7 Teacher Edition
ISBN: 978-1-61278-035-1
Item Number: CU5123
1 2 3 4 5 6 7 8 015016 17 16 15 14
Webcrafters, Inc., Madison, WI, USA; August 2014; Job #113694

Table of Contents

Vision and Philosophy

❝ I am the way and the truth and the life… I am the resurrection and the life. ❞

John 14:6, 11:25

❝ Jesus Christ not only transmits the word of God: he *is* the Word of God. Catechesis is therefore completely tied to him. Thus what must characterize the message transmitted by catechesis is, above all, its 'christocentricity'. ❞

General Directory for Catechesis, 98

Jesus Christ at the Center

Welcome to *Alive in Christ*. Christ is at the center of our faith, our Church, our catechesis. *Alive in Christ* is intentional in its focus on the life, mission, and saving work of Jesus Christ. This lays a foundation for a relationship with Jesus, who continually leads us to his Father's love and calls us through the Spirit to share in the divine life through his Church (see *Catechism of the Catholic Church*, 426).

Mirroring the Divine Pedagogy

The catechetical process of *Alive in Christ* mirrors the divine pedagogy—the gradual and relational way God teaches us so that we can know him and his truth, be guided by the Holy Spirit to respond with faith and love, and accept the gift of new life in Christ.

In this unique and effective pedagogy, each lesson encourages a personal and ongoing relationship with God, beginning with God's invitation through Sacred Scripture and leading students to reflect on his Word, deepen their understanding of our Sacred Tradition, and respond with a lived faith within the home and among friends, within the Church and in the community.

Building Knowledge of, and Reverence for, Sacred Scripture

Sacred Scripture from the *New American Bible Revised Edition* is foundational to every lesson in *Alive in Christ*. Scripture from both the Old Testament and New Testament is presented in a variety of ways that encourage students to listen to the voice of God in his written Word and learn about the people and stories of the Bible. Each lesson offers several distinct encounters with Sacred Scripture, giving students the opportunity to pray with, reflect on, study, and apply God's Word to their lives and helping form Catholllic identity.

Comprehensive Presentation of Catholic Teaching

Alive in Christ provides an authentic and comprehensive presentation of the essentials of the Catholic faith and has been found by the United States Conference of Catholic Bishops' Subcommittee on the Catechism to be in conformity with the *Catechism of the Catholic Church*.

Following a systematically organized scope and sequence, key themes of Catholic teaching are repeated each year, through a grade-level focus, building on the student's knowledge of the faith at each developmental stage. This presentation of Catholic teaching—coupled with a purposeful emphasis on Catholic practices, images, and models of faith—promotes a common language of faith and builds a vibrant Catholic identity.

Developmentally Responsive and Appropriate

Created by a team of experts in catechesis, theology, and child psychology, *Alive in Christ* incorporates the most trusted research on how children learn and communicate. Definitions, activities, questions, and reading passages have been reviewed for developmental appropriateness. Targeted on-page interactions help students more effectively learn or reinforce lesson content.

Topics are presented at important developmental "windows"—ages when research in child development tells us that learning about a particular topic would be most effective. Illustrations, Catholic art, and photos emphasize Scripture and visually present the chapter objectives in ways students can understand and relate to.

Complete and Purposeful Approach to Prayer and Worship

Every grade level intentionally incorporates each of the five forms of prayer mentioned in the *Catechism*—blessing and adoration, petition, intercession, thanksgiving, and praise (see CCC, 2626–2643). Students learn about and pray these basic prayer forms and are introduced to traditional prayers and devotions. They are taught how to talk with God in their own words and listen silently as he speaks to them. Each grade level also presents many opportunities to deepen students' understanding of the feasts and seasons of the Church year and how we celebrate the Paschal Mystery through them.

Putting Faith into Practice

Alive in Christ presents and effectively implements the six fundamental tasks of catechesis (see *General Directory for Catechesis*, 84–85). Exercises, features, and questions throughout the text prompt students to relate knowledge of our Catholic faith with their life experience. Every chapter has on-page activities for immediate application as well as concrete suggestions for students to live out the faith at school, at their parish, and in their homes and communities.

Each lesson's Our Catholic Life section provides practical examples of the ways we worship, live, pray, and serve together. It introduces students to Catholic figures who stand as models of heroic virtue in everyday life. Every lesson has connections to the Catholic social tradition, and each grade level provides catechesis on the seven themes of Catholic Social Teaching.

Practical Ways to Involve Families in Their Children's Faith Formation

It is vitally important, and equally challenging, to maintain communication with parents of students this age. The *Alive in Christ* website provides information teachers and administrators can share with parents via email, on class websites, or by sending it home with the students. Parents will gain insight into their children's developmental understanding of chapter topics, discussion prompts, and resources for family prayer. Taking into consideration the aims of the New Evangelization, parents are provided opportunities for adult reflection on their own relationship with Jesus and the Church. Online multimedia resources foster family interaction and reinforce the lesson.

A Commitment to Support Both New and Experienced Catechists

Alive in Christ Teacher Editions empower teachers with easy-to-use and effective tools for lesson planning, teaching, and reinforcing faith concepts, and growing in their own relationship with Christ and his Church.

The key concepts and chapter objectives are fully explained and conveniently located at the beginning of each lesson along with background information to strengthen teacher understanding and nurture personal faith.

A clear, concise, wraparound lesson plan leads the teacher page-by-page through the effective three-step process with integrated background on Sacred Scripture and doctrine, teaching tips, and connections to music, liturgy, and Catholic Social Teaching.

Extensive Online Resources for Teachers and Families

Alive in Christ provides teachers, principals, and religion coordinators comprehensive program level resources and unit, chapter, and seasonal specific tools and activities. Online support includes lesson planning tools, teacher formation for their role as catechist, custom test building and eAssessments, connections to the Sunday readings, and the option to share lesson plans via social media.

This extensive site provides students and families access to web-based assessments, interactive games and reviews, and resources targeted specifically to adults—all to support faith sharing and continued learning.

Age-Appropriate Music that Enhances Learning

With the knowledge that music is a means for forming students in Sacred Scripture, Church teachings, and Catholic Identity, *Alive in Christ* utilizes a variety of traditional and contemporary music from Oregon Catholic Press. Many prayer pages feature a song to be used within the prayer service. Music can be sampled and downloaded from **aliveinchrist.osv.com**.

Alive in Christ Development Team

  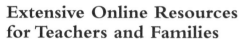

| **Greg Erlandson** | **Beth McNamara** | **Sabrina Magnuson** |
| President and Publisher | General Manager | Associate Publisher |

Dr. Jo Ann Paradise   Dr. Joseph White

Ana Arista   Heidi Busse   David Dziena   Dr. Hosffman Ospino   Denise Utter

Alive in Christ Structural Framework

Alive in Christ follows a systematic Scope and Sequence organized around key themes of Catholic teaching that repeat each year within a grade-level focus, building on the student's knowledge of the faith at each developmental stage.

This organizational structure takes into account research in child development that tells us at which age learning about a particular topic is most effective. These developmental "windows" help us to understand when the spiritual, cognitive, emotional, sociological, moral, and physical abilities of a child are "ripe" for learning. Included in the sequence, then, is a sensitivity to when students are ready to learn. A grade level focus based within the structural framework of the seven essential themes allows for optimal learning.

The seven essential, foundational themes of the faith— Revelation, Trinity, Jesus, The Church, Sacraments, Morality, and Kingdom of God—provide the structural framework that organizes the content of the grade. Progressing from first to eighth grade, the student deepens understanding as he or she is presented content that is theologically precise and developmentally appropriate.

As you study the Scope and Sequence, you will see how the objectives across grades move the learner to examine and appropriate a greater knowledge of our Catholic faith and how those objectives help to form a vibrant Catholic identity.

Grade Level Focus	
1: Jesus Christ	"For through faith you are all children of God in Christ Jesus." **Galatians 3:26**
2: Sacraments of Penance and the Eucharist	"This is my body, which will be given for you; do this in memory of me." **Luke 22:19**
3: The Church	"I am the vine, you are the branches. Whoever remains in me and I in him will bear much fruit…" **John 15:5**
4: The Moral Life	"This is my commandment: love one another as I love you." **John 15:12**
5: The Seven Sacraments	"The water I shall give will become in him a spring of water welling up to eternal life." **John 4:14**
6: The Word of God in the Old Testament	"Your word is a lamp for my feet,\ a light for my path." **Psalm 119:105**
7: Jesus Christ and the New Testament	"Whoever wishes to come after me must deny himself, take up his cross, and follow me." **Matthew 16:24**
8: The Church	"Come after me, and I will make you fishers of men." **Mark 1:17**

Go to **aliveinchrist.osv.com** for an overview of the developmental windows for each grade level focus and a full program Scope and Sequence.

Program Scope and Sequence

This graphic gives a visual image of the scope and sequence as a seventh grader in your class will experience it. The circles name the foundational themes that are the framework (unit structure) for every grade level. The snapshots below show key developmental factors or "windows" that lead to the grade level focus (for more on this, see page TE34). No matter what unit you are teaching, some component of the grade level focus is being treated.

| Unit 1 Revelation | Unit 2 Trinity | Unit 3 Jesus Christ | Unit 4 The Church | Unit 5 Morality | Unit 6 Sacraments | Unit 7 Kingdom of God |

Snapshot of Developmental Factors
Seventh Grade—Jesus Christ and the New Testament

- The physical growth and change of the middle school years leads to questions and concerns about identity. It is an excellent time to talk about discipleship—following Jesus, as he offers us a pattern for living, showing us what it looks like to be fully human.

- Seventh graders are often preoccupied with their own identity. Encourage them to think of their future goals, and discuss choices together as a group.

Snapshot of Developmental Factors
Eighth Grade—The Church

- Young people this age have grown in their abstract reasoning ability. They can imagine hypothetical situations and better understand symbols and signs. This can help them dive deeper into their faith and learn the meaning behind some of the things they have previously learned.

- Eighth graders want to belong. Peers are very important at this age. Their experience of Church should be one of inclusion and welcome.

Student Book Structure

With the systematic Scope and Sequence as the foundation, each grade level's Student Book has four sections:

- **Church Feasts and Seasons:** In these eight lessons, students learn about special days and times of the Church year that celebrate Jesus and honor Mary and the Saints.

- **Core Chapters:** Each unit begins with a Unit Preview that forecasts main chapter emphases and concludes with a three-page Unit Review. Also, each chapter begins with a preview of chapter objectives and pre-assessment activities and concludes with a Chapter Review.

- **Catholic Social Teaching/Live Your Faith:** This section covers the seven themes of Catholic Social Teaching, and connects them to both core and seasonal lessons.

These pages introduce students to important teachings of Jesus and the Church that help us live Jesus' New Commandment to love as he loved.

- **Church History Timeline/Our Catholic Tradition:** These reference sections present information on important events in Church history, as well as our Creeds, Sacraments, prayers, and practices of our Catholic faith.

Within this structure, *Alive in Christ* School Edition offers helpful and important features that support the unique needs of Catholic schools.

Each seasonal lesson has a Fruits of the Holy Spirit feature as part of the lesson. Each seasonal lesson focuses on one of the Fruits of the Holy Spirit and how that quality is expressed when students allow the grace of the Holy Spirit to work in their hearts. The same **Fruit of the Holy Spirit** is introduced in each of the seasonal lessons across the different grade levels. For example, the Advent seasonal lesson focuses on "patience," making the students more aware and connected to the gifts that God has offered.

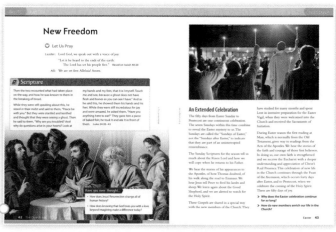

Seasonal Lessons: Seasonal lessons catechize and celebrate the Church year in a liturgically focused way. Eight complete seasonal lessons introduce children to the themes and Scripture of feasts and seasons of the Church year. Each four-page lesson follows a three-step catechetical process and is intended for a one- or two-day implementation.

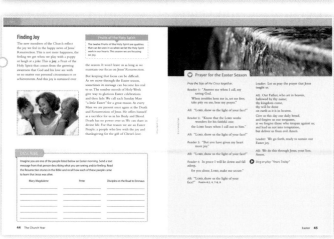

Fruits of the Holy Spirit

The twelve **Fruits of the Holy Spirit** are qualities that can be seen in us when we let the Holy Spirit work in our hearts. This season we are focusing on **faithfulness.**

The **Big Question** ties directly to chapter objectives and demonstrates the intentionality of the *Alive in Christ* scope and sequence. The students will be able to answer this question by the time they complete the three chapters of the unit.

Unit Preview: The **Unit Opener** includes a Church History Timeline connection and a bulleted list for both **Our Catholic Tradition** and **Our Catholic Life**, which forecast the foundational Catholic beliefs, teachings, and practices presented in the chapters of each unit.

Unit Review: Using the closing points from Days 2–4 in each chapter, each Unit Review highlights the lesson concepts taught in a particular unit.

Pre-assessment: Within the **Invite Step** (Day 1 of a five-day lesson plan, see page TE21), after the opening Scripture reflection, a two-page spread previews the main topics and vocabulary of the chapter, and helps teachers gauge the students' prior knowledge and exposure to concepts. This "pre-assessment" is done using developmentally appropriate graphic organizers that the students complete.

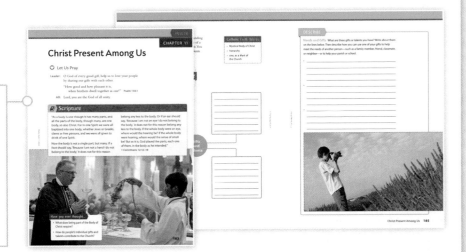

Our Catholic Tradition: This reference section presents information on our Creeds, Sacraments, prayers, and practices of our Catholic faith.

Church History Timeline: At the back of each Student Book, a **Church History Timeline** presents key people, places, and events in the Church's life, along with secular events that affected the course of Church history.

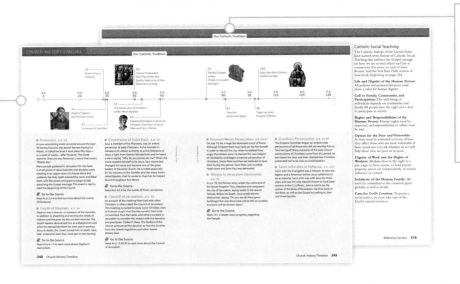

Alive in Christ School Edition Program Components

Student Books Grades 1–8

Student Books follow a seven-unit structure with a grade level focus on a foundational topic in our Catholic faith. They are the perfect tool to teach students to know, love, and live their Catholic faith through Sacred Scripture, doctrine, prayer, practices of the faith, and seasonal celebrations.

Teacher Editions Grades 1–8

The Teacher Editions help to build confident, capable, and successful teachers with comprehensive background and lesson preparation pages, timed wrap around lesson plans, optional activities, and point of use information. They are spiral bound and conveniently sized to match the Student Book.

People of Faith Collection Grades 1–6

This beautifully illustrated collection of Saints, Blesseds, and Venerables are connected to specific chapters. Students will learn about models of our Catholic faith while deepening their relationship with God and the Church.

Music Resources

Teachers are provided options for developmentally appropriate music that enhances learning. *Alive in Christ* integrates music for grades 1–8 into each lesson. A variety of music from Oregon Catholic Press is tied to chapter objectives and themes.

A unique, all new music component for Grades 1–6, *Songs of Scripture: Deepening Children's Understanding of God's Word*, features songs by John Burland and Dr. Jo Ann Paradise, that teach, reinforce, and unfold the meaning of Scripture stories presented in the Student Book.

📶 Go to **aliveinchrist.osv.com** to download hands-on activities related to *Songs of Scripture*.

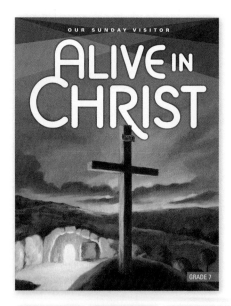
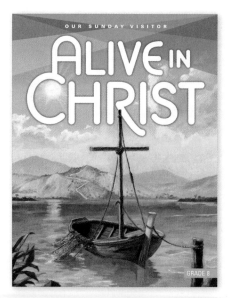

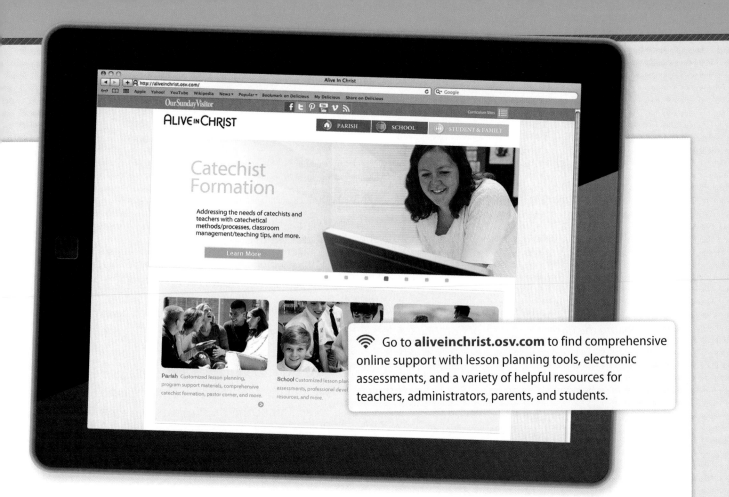

Go to **aliveinchrist.osv.com** to find comprehensive online support with lesson planning tools, electronic assessments, and a variety of helpful resources for teachers, administrators, parents, and students.

Online Resources for the Teacher

- Online lesson planning helps teachers to plan using chapter, seasonal, or Catholic Social Teaching lessons

- Share lesson plans via social media such as Facebook & Twitter

- Unit- and chapter-specific tools, assessments, activities, and multimedia resources

- Build a Custom Test allows teachers to build, print, and distribute tests using a bank of multiple choice, matching, fill in the blank, and long answer questions

- Assign eAssessments to students for completion online

- Catechetical formation and professional development tools are designed to help teachers hone their skills and grow in the knowledge of God's love

- Sample and download chapter-specific music to enhance catechetical learning or for prayer

- Download unit-specific cross-curricular activities that reinforce the chapter objectives of *Alive in Christ*

Online Resources for the Student & Family

- Interactive Reviews offer students an opportunity for web-based assessment, preparation, and practice

- At-home faith formation resources for all ages help reinforce Catholic identity

- Faith-sharing features and resources geared to parents, students, and families encourage continued learning at home via games, multimedia activities, Lectionary-connected resources, social media interaction, and topical articles

- Sample and download chapter-specific music to enhance catechetical learning or for prayer

Online Resources for the Religion Coordinator

- Program-level tools and resources provide principals, administrators, and religion coordinators with higher-level materials from correlations to in-service models

- Sample and download chapter-specific music to enhance catechetical learning or for prayer

Call of the Teacher as Catechist

Responding to Your Vocation

"We must remember that teachers and educators fulfill a specific Christian vocation and share an equally specific participation in the mission of the Church, to the extent that 'it depends chiefly on them whether the Catholic school achieves its purpose.' (25)"
— *The Catholic School on the Threshold of the Third Millennium, 19*

Teachers and administrators play an important role in enhancing the Catholic identity of Catholic schools. Do you reflect on why you have chosen to teach in a Catholic school? Why did the added responsibilities of being a Catholic school teacher stir your heart? Who are the teachers and catechists in your life that were role models for you? Catholic schools are vital to the life of the Church, and a vibrant school can be the lifeblood of a parish. They foster Catholic identity in their students and can help make Christ the center of their family life. For it is through education and formation that schools form future Church leaders and laypeople.

No matter the circumstances regarding how you became a religion teacher, it was Christ who called you. And by the power of the Holy Spirit, you, like Mary, responded, "Yes!" The vocation to catechesis, like all vocations, first comes from the grace of Baptism, is strengthened in Confirmation, and is sustained by the Eucharist and Penance. "The person of each individual human being, in his or her material and spiritual needs, is at the heart of Christ's teaching: this is why the promotion of the human person is the goal of the Catholic school" (Pope Saint John Paul II, *Address to the National Meeting of the Catholic School in Italy, "L'Osservatore Romano,"* 24 November 1991, p. 4).

You have been called by Christ and been given the mission by his Church to be instruments of his work. Take a moment and ponder that statement. With so many responsibilities and demands on our time, we might sometimes lose sight of this, and being a catechist becomes just one of the many things we must do each week. This cannot be so. Every time you gather with your students, you take your place in the long line of those who have for 2,000 years held the sacred duty of bringing others into "communion, in intimacy, with Jesus Christ" (*Catechesi Tradendae*, 5).

Your Role as Catechist

To support and nurture your students in their baptismal call to a lifetime of growing closer to and more like Jesus, the Church sets out some essential instructions. In order to provide a presentation of the "entire treasure of the Christian message"[2] while adapting it to the "capacity of those being catechized" (GDC, 112), a teacher must do several things.

Teach the comprehensive course of study outlined by the United States Conference of Catholic Bishops' Subcommittee on the Catechism. In *Alive in Christ*, you find these doctrines and practices presented in the objectives of the lesson. (See GDC, 112.)

Respect the developmental level of your students by understanding how they learn. (See GDC, 112.)

Use various methods as they are a "sign of life and richness"[3] that will address multiple learning styles and special needs (GDC, 148).

Model a Catholic life through your own behaviors and practices, for the "charism given to [the teacher] by the Spirit, a solid spirituality and transparent witness of life, constitutes the soul of every method" (GDC, 156).

Proclaim with joy and enthusiasm that "God so loved the world that he gave his only Son" (John 3:16). In the words of Pope Benedict XVI, "Today too, there is a need… to rediscover the joy of believing and the enthusiasm for communicating the faith" (*Porta Fidei*, 7).

As you accept this sacred and challenging vocation, be assured that the Holy Spirit will lead and guide you in handing on our Catholic faith to the next generation. Let the love of God pour through so that they see in you the image and heart of our loving God.

The Task of Catechesis

As Jesus Formed His Disciples

There are six fundamental tasks in the ministry of catechesis. These six tasks are named and treated in the *General Directory for Catechesis* (see GDC, 85), and later in the *National Directory for Catechesis* (see NDC, 20). Each of these tasks corresponds to an aspect of faith in Jesus. The following are the six tasks of catechesis.

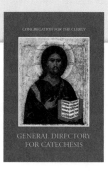

General
Directory
for Catechesis

Promoting Knowledge of the Faith

We cannot live a faith we do not know. For this reason, studying the teachings of Jesus and his Church is an essential task of catechesis. The U.S. Bishops' Subcommittee on the Catechism and the conformity review process direct what is to be contained in this comprehensive presentation of the faith. According to the *National Directory for Catechesis*, this task of catechesis is a response to the individual's desire that God plants in the heart of every person to know. This desire comes naturally when individuals have had opportunities to encounter Christ and his message and have experienced an initial conversion. *Alive in Christ* begins each lesson by giving students an opportunity to meet God in his Word and to wonder about his life and love, followed by a process of helping them to know more about him through Sacred Tradition—the teaching of the Church. In this way, we help students frame questions that drive their desire to know more.

Liturgical Education

This task relates to learning about the ways in which the Church worships and celebrates, including the Seven Sacraments, the Order of Mass, and the liturgical year. According to the *General Directory for Catechesis*, liturgical education includes teaching about the form and the meaning of liturgical celebrations, but also means helping individuals prepare their minds and hearts to enter into these mysteries of our faith. As you use *Alive in Christ*, you will teach your students about the liturgy both through the doctrine presented in the core chapters as well as through seasonal activities and prayerful experiences that echo the words and rhythms of our liturgical celebrations.

Moral Formation

This task of catechesis involves forming the consciences of learners through the moral teachings of Jesus and his Church and fostering understanding of what it means to live these teachings in one's daily life. Morality in the Christian life involves standards and guidelines, but it is more than learning a list of rules. Morality is about discipleship. As you use *Alive in Christ*, you will find opportunities to challenge students to apply what they have learned about the Ten Commandments, Jesus' command to love as he has loved, and the Beatitudes to situations at home and school and in the community.

Teaching to Pray

"When catechesis is permeated by a climate of prayer, the assimilation of the entire Christian life reaches its summit" (GDC, 85). The "climate of prayer" in catechesis invites individuals into an ever deeper relationship with God. Teaching to pray is more than merely "teaching prayers"; it involves fostering an understanding of prayer as conversation with God—helping students learn how to talk with God in their own words as well as how to listen to God.

This task of catechesis involves teaching the traditional prayers of the Church and the various forms and expressions of prayer mentioned in the *Catechism of the Catholic Church*. *Alive in Christ* incorporates experiences of all five forms of prayer. You will also have opportunities to help students speak to God in their own words.

Education for Community Life

This task of catechesis relates to developing an understanding of what it means to be a part of the Christian community, including respecting the authority and structure of the Church, as well as living out Jesus' New Commandment to love one another as he has loved us. "Catechesis prepares the Christian to live in community and to participate actively in the life and mission of the Church" (GDC, 86). Catechesis should prepare us to live and work with one another, both within the Church and in society as a whole. The

bishops write that catechesis should encourage a spirit of simplicity and humility, a special concern for the poor, particular care for the alienated, a sense of fraternal correction, common prayer, mutual forgiveness, and a fraternal love that embraces all these attitudes. (See GDC, 86.) Various chapter features, as well as the Live Your Faith sections on Catholic Social Teaching will assist you in this task of catechesis.

Missionary Initiation

While only some may be called to other lands to minister in Christ's name, by Baptism, all are called to live in such a way that we serve as witnesses of the faith to those who are around us. This task of catechesis prepares the learner to share his or her faith with others. *Alive in Christ* helps to form students in the language of the Catholic faith and the behaviors and practices of the faith. Forming them in a vibrant Catholic identity gives them the skills necessary to be strong witnesses of the faith. This is reinforced in the tools we provide the parents in the Family + Faith page, as it equips the parents to talk about faith with their children.

Our bishops state, "all efforts in evangelization and catechesis should incorporate these tasks" (NDC, 20). In this way, we pay attention to several different dimensions of faith, with the ultimate goal of helping students grow into deeper communion with Christ so that they live as disciples in faith, word, and deed.

The Divine Pedagogy

As teachers, we always hold two realities: the "what" and the "how" of catechesis. What do we want our students to know and love about our faith and how do we best communicate the treasure of our faith?

We use the word *pedagogy* to speak about the art, science, or profession of teaching. In other words, pedagogy is the "how" of faith formation. We are called to hand on the truths of our faith by echoing God's own way of teaching us his truths. The *General Directory for Catechesis* tells us that,

> 66 Catechesis, as communication of divine Revelation, is radically inspired by the pedagogy of God, as displayed in Christ and in the Church. [It is the Church's mission to be] a visible and actual continuation of the pedagogy of the Father and of the Son. 99
>
> GDC, 143, 141

Each lesson in *Alive in Christ* mirrors the divine pedagogy—the gradual and relational way God teaches us so that we can know him and his truth, be guided by the Holy Spirit to respond with faith and love, and accept the gift of new life in Christ. Even as we teach others, God remains active in their hearts, bringing growth to the seeds of faith that are planted there.

Here are five important characteristics of the divine pedagogy that are at the heart of each lesson of *Alive in Christ*.

The pedagogy of God is invitational and person-centered.

God initiates a relationship with each person. He does so by first creating us with a desire to know him and the capacity to respond to him. The ultimate invitation to relationship comes in Jesus. Pope Saint John Paul II tells us that the purpose of all catechesis is to bring people into intimacy with Jesus.

As God enters into dialogue with us, we are called to follow this example by providing catechesis that it is rooted in interpersonal relationships and involves a process of dialogue. (See GDC, 143.) God also meets us where we are and accommodates for our particular needs. Therefore, effective catechesis should be developmentally appropriate and should make allowances for adapting to special needs.

God's pedagogy is incarnational.

Dei Verbum points out the "inner unity" of deeds and words in God's plan of revelation: "the deeds wrought by God in the history of salvation manifest and confirm the teaching and realities signified by the words, while the words proclaim the deeds and clarify the mystery contained in them" (2).

Jesus the Teacher

From speaking the universe into existence, to his promise to Noah and his covenants with Abraham and Moses, to the Word made flesh in Jesus Christ, it is evident that God's Word becomes action.

An effective pedagogy should make the faith come to life through hands-on activities and applications and multisensory teaching methodologies. It should give learners clear ways to go out and live the Gospel they have received.

The pedagogy of God is familial and communal.
God reveals himself as a communion of Persons—Father, Son, and Holy Spirit—and creates human beings to be in communion with one another.

Effective catechesis should build community among the students, involve parents and families as primary catechists, and connect students to the larger parish community. Connecting the families to the life of the parish, particularly through participation in the Sunday Eucharist, is vital in building up the Body of Christ.

God's pedagogy is structured and comprehensive.
In salvation history, God reveals himself to humanity gradually as people are able to understand. One revelation builds upon the next, until Revelation reaches its fullness in the Person of Jesus Christ. Effective catechesis also presents key truths of the faith gradually as the learner is able to receive them.

The pedagogy of God is perpetual.
We read in **Isaiah 55:11**, "So shall my word be\ that goes forth from my mouth;\ It shall not return to me empty,\ but shall do what pleases me,\ achieving the end for which I sent it." God's truths are handed on through the generations in the forms of Sacred Scripture and Sacred Tradition, which is the living memory of the Church. God's covenants do not end, but come to greater fulfillment and realization.

A catechesis based on the divine pedagogy prepares the learner to share the Gospel with others, in word and deed, so that the Good News of salvation is handed on to others and to future generations.

The Catechetical Process and the Five–Day Lesson Plan

Alive in Christ's catechetical methodology mirrors the divine pedagogy by following a three-step process of **Invite**, **Discover**, and **Live**. Unfolding over a five-day lesson plan, this process encourages a personal and ongoing relationship with the Holy Trinity.

Catechetical Process

1. **Day 1: The Invite Step** begins the lesson with God's invitation through Sacred Scripture. Students open their minds and hearts to what God is saying to them in Scripture and reflect on it. Uniquely created for the *Alive in Christ* School Edition, pre-assessment of Catholic Faith Words and chapter concepts are then presented and serve as a transition to the Discover step and chapter objectives.

2. **Days 2–4: The Discover Step** helps form Catholic identity through the study of Scripture, knowledge of Church teaching, and an understanding of Catholic practices. It presents the doctrine of the lesson in developmentally appropriate language and images. Charts, on-page questions, and activities noted by asterisks prompt students to interact directly with the page, and aid in understanding and retention. With large on-page activities, students are given the opportunity to process and reinforce what they have learned and apply it to their own lives and the experience of the Church.

3. **Day 5: The Live Step** helps students relate knowledge of the faith and the ways we worship, live, pray, and serve together as Catholics. Students are given the tools to connect their faith to everyday life and to deepen their relationship with God and the Church through the prayer experiences at the end of each lesson.

Teaching Method

The three-step catechetical process unfolds over five sessions of approximately 30–40 minutes each. Each session's self-contained structure **Open**, **Build**, **Close** provides teachers with a natural daily lesson arc while keeping the three-step catechetical process intact.

Open: Includes an introduction, prayer, and discussion questions.

Build: Provides the instruction for the heart of the day's lesson and includes Scripture, activities, and Catholic Faith Words.

Close: May include an activity or a song, but always wraps up each day's lesson by reinforcing the day's objectives.

If you follow this three-step process, you will in fact mirror the divine pedagogy by offering your students the opportunity to know God and his truth through Sacred Scripture and Sacred Tradition. You will inspire them to be open to the Holy Spirit so that they will respond in faith and love and accept the gift of new life in Christ!

As a teacher, during the **Invite** step you:

- Call the students together to begin in **prayer**.
- Prepare the students to hear the **Word of God**.
- Guide the students through the **Scripture reflection** process, proclaiming God's Word and inviting quiet thought. (See TE28 for a full description of the Scripture reflection process.)
- After proclamation of the Scripture, allow time (governed by what is developmentally appropriate) for sacred **silence**.
- Invite the students **to share** what they have experienced, what they felt God was saying to them or what he wanted them to know in a special way today. Assure them sharing is voluntary.
- Prompt continued thought about God's Word and move to chapter objectives by using the "**Have you ever thought**" questions.

Present chapter highlights by indicating prior knowledge of chapter concepts and vocabulary.

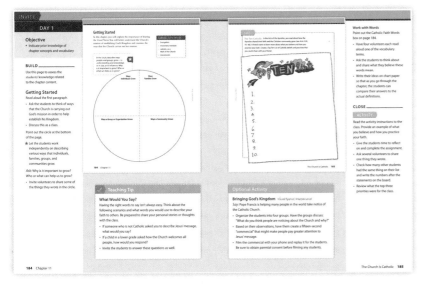

- **Opening Paragraph:** Introduces the main points of the chapter.
- **Graphic Organizer:** This chapter preview feature includes cluster diagrams, basic timelines, Venn diagrams, and more.
- **Pre-assessment Activity:** Provides activities that focus on pre-assessment rather than teaching.
- **Preview of the Catholic Faith Words:** Assesses a student's prior knowledge of the terms presented in a chapter.

Unique and Effective Pedagogy

As a teacher, during the **Discover** step you:

- Teach the **objectives** of the lesson, which are identified in the Teacher Edition in two places: the overview Lesson Plan in the teacher background section and in the top left-hand corner of each Discover spread.

- Follow the **instruction** in the vertical side columns, which walks you through the entire lesson. Note that the activities are an integral part of the lesson. They emphasize the essential elements of Church teaching and help the students apply those truths to worship, prayer, and daily life.

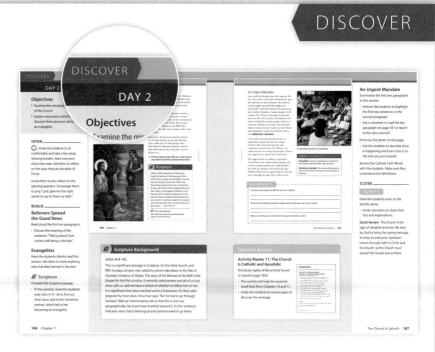

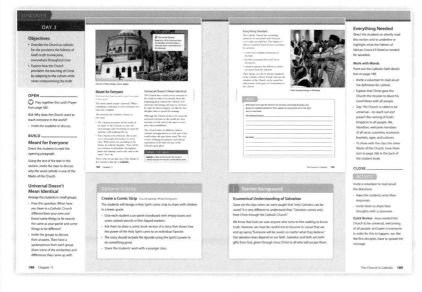

- Present the **Catholic Faith Words**, which are highlighted in the text and called out in separate boxes. These words build a common language of faith and are explained with precise theological language that is developmentally appropriate.

- Use the **boxes** at the bottom of the page that provide additional Scripture and doctrinal background, optional activities, teaching tips, ways to adapt lessons for special needs, suggestions for including music, and more.

- Guide the students through a review of the **In Summary** section to reiterate the chapter's key concept and wrap up with the main summary points.

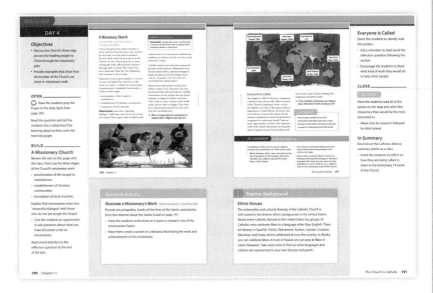

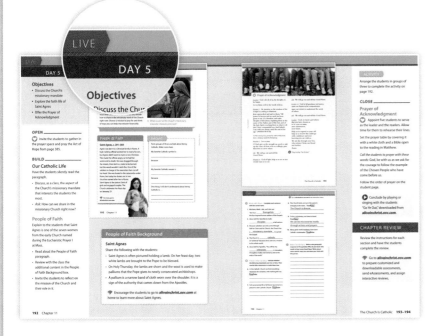

As a teacher, during the **Live** step you:

- Reflect on a practice of **Our Catholic Faith** and introduce the students to a **Saint**, **Blessed**, or **Venerable** whose life exemplifies the content of the lesson.

- Use a closing **activity** to help the students relate their knowledge of the faith to their lives, and to commit more deeply to what it means to be Catholic.

- Lead the **prayer celebration** and have the students complete the **Chapter Review**.

Unique and Effective Pedagogy

Chapter Background

Alive in Christ Teacher Editions give you everything you need for lesson planning, teaching and reinforcing faith concepts, and growing in your own relationship with Christ and his Church.

Each chapter has teacher-specific content provided in the planning and background pages. These are the seven pages that provide scriptural, doctrinal, and methodological background and formation. You will also find pages that address the different ways students process, understand, and learn lesson content at any given grade level.

Key Concept for each lesson is clearly stated at the start of each chapter. **Doctrinal Content** correlates to paragraphs from the *Catechism of the Catholic Church*.

How Grade Level Children Understand offers insight on the relationship between the lesson objectives and the students' developmental level of understanding.

Teacher's Prayer offers a moment of reflection for the teacher before planning each lesson.

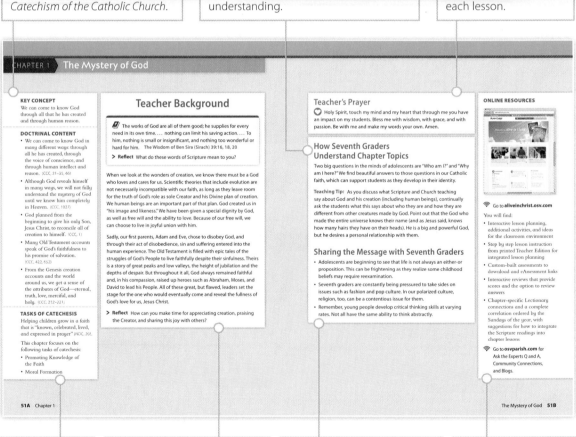

Tasks of Catechesis relate lesson components to one of the six Tasks of Catechesis as outlined in the *National Directory for Catechesis*.

Teacher Background gives easy-to-understand theological background on the chapter content with questions to help teachers connect concepts to their own experience.

Sharing the Message provides background on where students this age typically are in terms of cognitive, social, spiritual, and emotional development.

Online Resources are clearly labeled throughout the Teacher Edition and direct you to downloads, lesson planning tools, interactive reviews, eAssessments, and more.

Chapter Planner

The Chapter Planner presents objectives and step-by-step instructions for a five-day lesson plan, with flexibility for alternative pacing and inclusion of review and multiple options for assessment.

Open Column points out the Invite Scripture, prayers, and discussion questions for each session.

Build Column provides Scripture, activities, instructions, and Catholic Faith Words for the lesson.

Close Column indicates activities, closing points, and songs that complete each day's session.

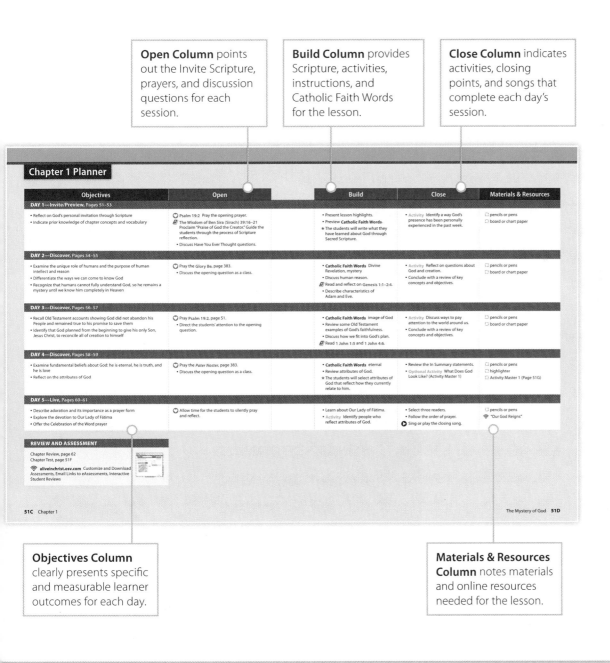

Objectives Column clearly presents specific and measurable learner outcomes for each day.

Materials & Resources Column notes materials and online resources needed for the lesson.

Unique and Effective Pedagogy

Chapter Connections

This page references ways to connect the chapter content to other sections of the Student Book, as with one of the features on Catholic Social Teaching, as well as to web-specific content, such as cross-curricular activities and music. It also highlights the correlation between chapter content and independent assessment tools from NCEA.

NCEA IFG: ACRE Edition correlates the lesson objectives to the domains of *NCEA Information for Growth: Assessment of Children/Youth Religious Education* (2013) and helps teachers measure students' understanding and appropriation of lesson content.

Catholic Social Teaching identifies which principles of Catholic Social Teaching/Live Your Faith pieces connect to this chapter and provides direction for how to integrate them into the Live step of the process. In the seasonal lessons, these connections are noted at point of use in the bottom band of the lesson plan.

Music Options are provided to enhance catechetical learning and the prayer celebration.

Forming Catholic Identity across the Curriculum Each chapter contains a unique feature for forming Catholic identity across the curriculum. This feature identifies the connection between chapter objectives and other disciplines. These are designed to reinforce the learning in other disciplines and help make a connection to what is being taught in religion class.

Chapter Reproducibles

Each chapter of the Teacher Edition includes a reproducible Chapter Test
and Chapter Activity Master for assessment and extension opportunities.

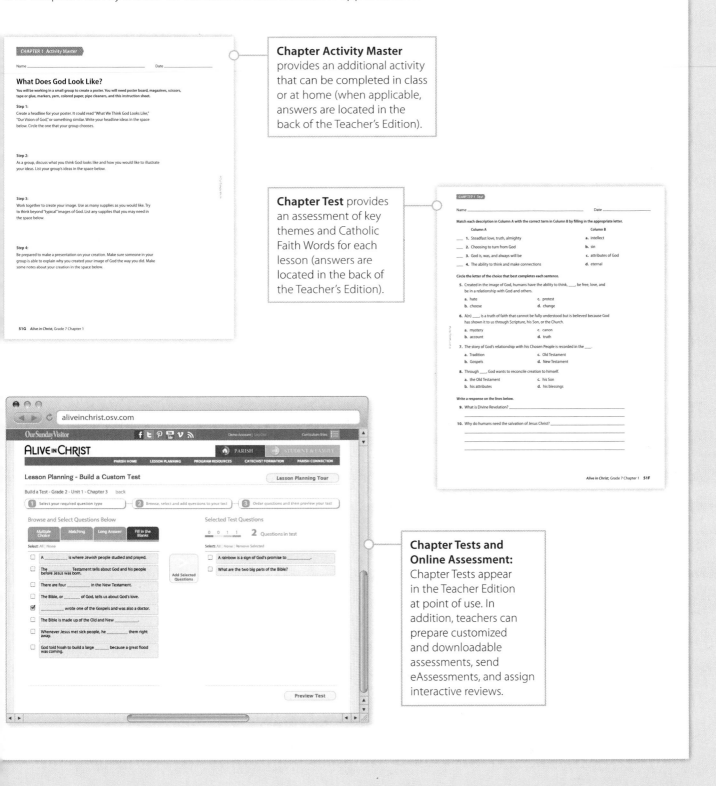

Chapter Activity Master
provides an additional activity
that can be completed in class
or at home (when applicable,
answers are located in the
back of the Teacher's Edition).

Chapter Test provides
an assessment of key
themes and Catholic
Faith Words for each
lesson (answers are
located in the back of
the Teacher's Edition).

**Chapter Tests and
Online Assessment:**
Chapter Tests appear
in the Teacher Edition
at point of use. In
addition, teachers can
prepare customized
and downloadable
assessments, send
eAssessments, and assign
interactive reviews.

Sacred Scripture

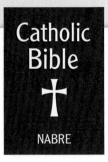

Catholic Bible

✝

NABRE

New American Bible Revised Edition

> " For in the sacred books, the Father who is in heaven meets His children with great love and speaks with them; and the force and power in the word of God is so great that it stands as the support and energy of the Church…. "

Dei Verbum, 21

Sacred Scripture from both the Old Testament and New Testament is at the heart of *Alive in Christ*. The students are invited to understand the importance of Sacred Scripture, as a font of Divine Revelation and the guide for their lives. The Word is always given prominent visual importance to highlight its significance, with a parchment background, an icon, and a logo. Students are led to know, love, and be formed by God's Word.

Scripture in the Catechetical Process

The students always **pray** with Scripture in the opening prayer of the Invite step and often in the prayer experience in the Live step.

The practice of Scripture **reflection** is an essential element in the Invite step of every lesson and the means by which we enter into the divine pedagogy.

By following the simple process noted in the Invite bottom band box, the students are formed by the practice of reflecting on Scripture and being open to the Word of God that is personally speaking to them. Listening with the ear of the heart and reflecting on Scripture prepares students for practices such as *Lectio Divina*.

Sacred Scripture is **studied** in the Discover step as students learn about God's action throughout salvation history and see how Scripture is a source of Church teaching. Key Scripture accounts are presented in multiple grade levels to encourage biblical literacy, familiarity, and understanding.

Throughout the Discover and Live steps, the students **apply** the Word of God to their lived experience and acquire the behaviors and practices of a Catholic life.

Go to the Source

Scripture is foundational to each chapter, and passages are contained within each chapter. In addition, throughout the Discover step of the chapters, **Go to the Source** features prompt students to go directly to Scripture itself for reading, reflection, and activities.

Some **Go to the Source** references appear directly below a Scripture passage included in the Student Book. Students see the context of the included passage and can go deeper into God's message revealed there.

In other instances, the **Go to the Source** is independent of Scripture contained in the Student Book. Students may be searching for parables or accounts with a similar message, looking for a biblical connection to a doctrine included in their books, or reflecting in a personal way on Jesus' life, teachings, and actions.

Go to the Source
Read Matthew 6:2–4 to find out more of what Jesus had to say about good deeds.

When making a choice, you have to consider all three elements: what is the action or object itself; why are you doing it, or not doing it; and what are the pressures, environment, or issues surrounding it that might be affecting your judgment.

> Why is the brother's action described earlier a morally good act?

Consider This

A good intention—such as wanting to help your sister—does not make an object or behavior that is morally wrong—such as lying to your parents—good. A bad intention—such as the desire to boast—can make an object or behavior that is good—such as donating money or time to a worthy cause—morally bad. As Jesus said, "[But] take care not to perform righteous deeds in order that people might see them" (Matthew 6:1).

Saint Thomas Aquinas argued that whether

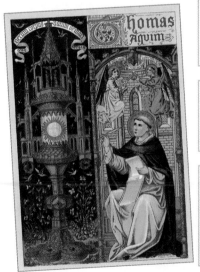

The circumstances of an action can increase or decrease the moral goodness of the action. Factors such as fear, ignorance, and pressure are some examples. But circumstances cannot change whether an act is morally good or not, only the degree of its goodness

Sacred Tradition

What is necessary for the students to know so that they will develop a vibrant Catholic identity and be able to express their faith with competence, understanding, and love?

The Church guides us, teaching that the catechetical message has "a 'comprehensive hierarchical character,'[4] which constitutes a vital synthesis of the faith" (GDC, 114). The truths of the faith are organized in a hierarchy around the mystery of the most Holy Trinity, in a Christ-centered (or *Christocentric*) perspective.

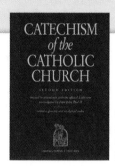

Catechism of the Catholic Church

> 66 The mutual connections between dogmas, and their coherence, can be found in the whole of the Revelation of the mystery of Christ.[5] 'In Catholic doctrine there exists an order or "hierarchy" of truths, since they vary in their relation to the foundation of the Christian faith.'[6] 99
>
> CCC, 90

In other words, some truths are so basic and foundational to what we believe as Catholics that they must be presented first, and then other related truths can be better understood.

To help us know what is basic and foundational, the USCCB's Subcommittee on the Catechism has identified the truths of the faith deemed essential to the formation of students. *Alive in Christ* has been found to be in conformity with the *Catechism of the Catholic Church.*

In salvation history, God has revealed himself to people in a systematic and gradual way, showing us more of himself as we are capable of understanding. (See GDC, 38 and CCC 54–65.) Our catechesis models this divine pedagogy and includes all of the foundational elements of the faith, presenting them in a gradual and systematic way as the learner is ready to hear them.

Alive in Christ organizes the foundational truths around seven key themes of Catholic teaching that repeat each year within a grade level focus.

Systematic and Comprehensive

The content of Sacred Scripture and Sacred Tradition are systematically presented in precise theological language in the **lesson objectives** of each lesson. The objectives are found on your Lesson Planner and at point of use where they are presented to the students.

Important **Catholic Faith Words** are highlighted in every chapter with definitions that grow as students' understanding does, and their repetition across grades helps to promote the common language of faith.

Each **Unit Opener** summarizes key concepts being presented and identifies *Catechism of the Catholic Church* references for each of these faith statements. A Big Question allows for discussion around an essential aspect of each unit.

At the back of each Student Book, the **Our Catholic Tradition** reference section reinforces the faith basics presented in the lessons. It is referenced in your lesson plan with specific instructions on how to integrate the content into the lesson.

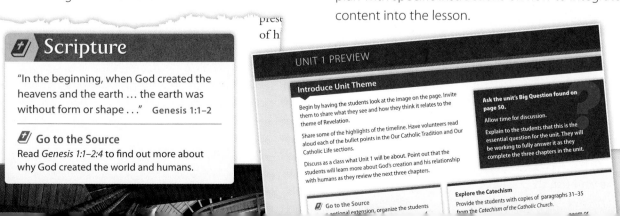

📖 Scripture

"In the beginning, when God created the heavens and the earth … the earth was without form or shape . . ."   Genesis 1:1–2

___

📖 Go to the Source
Read *Genesis 1:1–2:4* to find out more about why God created the world and humans.

UNIT 1 PREVIEW

Introduce Unit Theme

Begin by having the students look at the image on the page. Invite them to share what they see and how they think it relates to the theme of Revelation.

Share some of the highlights of the timeline. Have volunteers read aloud each of the bullet points in the Our Catholic Tradition and Our Catholic Life sections.

Discuss as a class what Unit 1 will be about. Point out that the students will learn more about God's creation and his relationship with humans as they review the next three chapters.

Ask the unit's Big Question found on page 50.

Allow time for discussion.

Explain to the students that this is the essential question for the unit. They will be working to fully answer it as they complete the three chapters in the unit.

📖 Go to the Source

Explore the Catechism
Provide the students with copies of paragraphs 31–35 from the *Catechism of the Catholic Church.*

Developmental Appropriateness

The Theory Behind It

At one point or another in your family life and your ministry as a teacher, you've likely found yourself explaining to a student, "It's not just what you say, it's how you say it." The message is as important as the delivery. You can't separate the *what* from the *how*. Similarly, doctrine and method are not two ends of a spectrum. They are interdependent. In catechesis, you can't have one without the other. And it goes a step further, for it's not just *what* we teach, and how we teach it, but *how* the learner receives it.

"Consequently catechesis starts out with…the integral structure of the Christian message, and proceeds to explain it in a manner adapted to the capacity of those being catechized" (GDC, 112).

When we teach things in a theologically accurate way, and in a manner sensitive to where the students are developmentally, we provide the best chance that they will appropriate the content—process and understand it in a way that has meaning to them so that they can then apply it to their own lives.

According to the National Association for the Education of Young Children (NAEYC), *developmental appropriateness* includes multiple components.

1. It is important to know how young people develop and learn at particular ages and stages and to create learning environments that are responsive to these general needs.
2. Because every person is unique, knowing the individual youth and how they learn best is essential.
3. It is important to know what is culturally appropriate for different ages and stages of development.

The Practice of It

Alive in Christ provides you with carefully selected topics and activities that meet the developmental level of the students you are teaching as well as tips for addressing individual needs. The program includes

Presentation of Text

- Information is sequenced and organized in smaller "chunks" to make reading and understanding faster and easier.
- Fonts and type sizes are set with consideration given to the reading level of the student across all eight grades.
- Words are defined consistently at point-of-use and highlighted for easy identification.
- Terms and concepts are introduced, reinforced, and then further defined in advanced ways as they develop across grades.

prayers, Saints, and activities that represent the diversity of cultures found in our Church and introduces these traditions at developmentally appropriate times.

Alive in Christ takes into account the experience level of today's students with various topics and how they are used to receiving and processing those topics. So, the series is developmentally appropriate not just in what students learn at particular ages, but how they learn it.

As a teacher, you can feel confident that you are giving the students the most precise presentation of Church teaching in the most developmentally appropriate way. That's what excellent catechesis is all about.

Use of Visuals

- Fine art, illustrations, and photos advance in detail and sophistication as grades progress.
- Graphic organizers, charts, and call outs are used to present content in easy to track and access formats.
- Captions are used to aid in learning, and the content and purpose of captions advance as the grades do.
- The text-to-art ratio is intentional and customized for each grade level.

Teaching Strategies

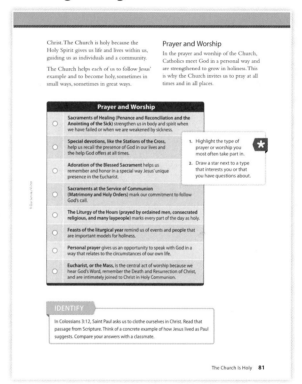

- Questions focus reading, prompt reflection, and reinforce learning.
- On-page activities and teaching strategies incorporate dynamic, interactive learning methods.
- Chapter reviews use multiple formats to accommodate different learning styles.
- The Teacher Edition includes a Teaching This Grade page that gives details on how students at this age might understand lesson objectives.
- Ideas for customizing content are found in the Reaching All Learners boxes in some chapters.

The Use of Images

" In order to communicate the message entrusted to her by Christ, the Church needs art. "

—*Letter of Pope Saint John Paul II to Artists* (1999), 12

While educational research assures us that students make meaning through the interplay of text and images (Carney and Levine, 2002), any adult who has spent time with young people knows that verbal and visual both tell the story. For hundreds of years, the Church has used sacred art and stained glass windows to teach Catholic doctrine and provide a physical presentation of the truths of our faith. Jesus often used images when he preached, giving his disciples a glimpse into his Father's mystery and the Kingdom.

Alive in Christ mirrors the divine pedagogy through its use of photos, illustrations, and images of fine art, stained glass, and statues—each one specifically selected for this program.

Educational research (Carney and Levine, 2002) and our own experience tells us that photos, illustrations, and art closely tied to text

- improve the reader's learning and recall
- direct their attention to what's most important on the page
- make the text more understandable and memorable
- help them connect and apply what's been learned to their lived experience.

In *Alive in Christ* lessons, developmentally appropriate visuals—Scripture illustration, fine art, stained glass, statues, icons, photos, and accompanying captions—meet lesson objectives and build Catholic identity.

Reaching All Learners

"Growth in faith is related to human development and passes through stages. Individuals develop as human beings and faithful followers of Christ in different ways and according to their own pace…The Church's catechesis—and even more so, the catechist—must take into consideration all the human factors of a particular age level in order to present the Gospel message in a vital and compelling way."

NDC, 48

Benefitting from the work of educators in the past decades, religious educators now have new tools in providing young people the fullness of the faith in developmentally appropriate ways.

Not only must we teach the faith related to young people's level of human development, we must also meet the individual needs of our students. When working with any group of youth, it does not take long to realize that they learn in different ways. Many have written about how to best provide strategies to address different learning styles. Dr. Howard Gardner's research on Multiple Intelligences provides particular insight. His theory looks at eight different ways people learn. Applying his theory to your planning will help you reach each student with the Good News of salvation.

Throughout *Alive in Christ*, a variety of teaching strategies are employed within the lesson process. Working with words and reading Scripture (Verbal/Linguistic), using photos and illustrations to prompt discussion (Visual/Spatial), and listening to, singing, and reflecting on songs (Musical) are just a few examples. Additional features, such as Reaching All Learners and Optional Activities, address various methods to help students with different learning styles and abilities connect with the lessons.

Multiple Intelligences	
Verbal/ Linguistic	This learning occurs best through reading, writing, telling stories, and discussing ideas.
Logical/ Mathematical	This learning occurs best through problem solving, analyzing, and applying logic.
Musical	This learning occurs best through singing, listening to music, and remembering melodies.
Bodily/ Kinesthetic	This learning occurs best through physically moving, dancing, acting, and making things.
Visual/Spatial	This learning occurs best through looking at pictures, drawing, and creating.
Interpersonal	This learning occurs best through sharing about one's feelings, talking with others, and collaborating with others on tasks.
Intrapersonal	This learning occurs best through working alone and reflecting.
Naturalist	This learning occurs best through exploring nature and living things.

Go to **aliveinchrist.osv.com** for additional resources on meeting the challenges of providing for special needs in your religion classroom.

Developmental Appropriateness

Teaching Seventh and Eighth Graders

Cognitive Development

In seventh and eighth grades, young people have reached a period of cognitive development in which they should be more able to take the perspective of others and understand what others are feeling. This may at times be compromised by the young adolescent's own defensiveness. For example, they may have difficulty seeing their parent's point of view if they are being told no about something.

Students this age are also more adept at abstract reasoning. They can imagine hypothetical situations and better understand symbols and signs. This can help them dive deeper into their faith and learn the meaning behind some of the things they have previously learned.

Identity Development

The physical growth and change of the middle school years lead to questions and concerns about identity. Young people may be very self-conscious, wondering if they look okay or act "cool enough." They might even appear to try on different personalities, roles, and looks. At this age, they are realizing that they are becoming young men and young women, and this naturally leads to thoughts of what sort of people they are and will be as they get older.

It is an excellent time to talk about discipleship—following Jesus as he offers us a pattern for living, showing us what it looks like to be fully human. Emphasize that, while we don't always know what will make us happy, God does. He created us and knows what he made us to be. Following God's plan for our lives will lead to our ultimate happiness, even if we must make some sacrifices along the way.

Moral Development

Seventh and eighth graders are still impulsive at times, acting without thinking things through. However, they have entered a stage of life in which their actions can have more serious consequences. Some choices could profoundly affect their lives.

Recent research has suggested that there are some things we can do to help seventh and eighth graders make responsible choices and avoid risky ones. One is to encourage them to think of their future goals—where do they wish to see themselves in five, ten, or fifteen years? What choices can they make now that will get them closer to these goals? What choices would get them further away? Discussing choices in a group setting with peers can also be helpful for young people this age, provided an adult moderates the discussion.

Social Development and Belonging

Seventh and eighth graders want to belong. Peers are very important at this age, and we should be concerned when young people are socially isolated or have trouble getting along with peers. Some conflict is expected. Boys can sometimes be rough with one another as they try to appear tough or strong. Girls are more likely to use name-calling or social isolation as ways to find their place in the social order. Be sensitive to students who may be being teased or bullied, and set limits on this behavior when you see it. Work to create environments in which everyone feels he or she has a place. Some students may need help understanding and appreciating the effect of their actions on others.

Living and Learning Together

In the *General Directory for Catechesis* we are told that the "childhood religious awakening which takes place in the family is irreplaceable"[7] (226). The role of the principal, religion coordinator, and the teacher in the school is to help form and support families in this sacred journey.

The *Alive in Christ* website provides information teachers and administrators can share with parents via email, on class websites, or by sending it home with students. These resources are invaluable in providing adults the practical help they need to grow in faith themselves and to nurture the faith of their children.

Catholic Social Teaching

Pope Saint John Paul II reminded us that one of the fundamental tasks of the Christian family is to remember that the family is always at the service of God's Kingdom. While the family is to "guard, reveal, and communicate love," it does so knowing that their love is not only to be shared within itself, but meant to be shared with the world (*Familiaris Consortio*, 17). We are called to reach out past our family to build relationships of love and justice in our neighborhoods, communities, and beyond.

Each grade level of *Alive in Christ*, presents the seven principles of Catholic Social Teaching, articulated by the United States Conference of Catholic Bishops. In this **Live Your Faith** component, the scriptural and doctrinal foundations of the principles help the students connect their faith to a life of peace and justice. While peace and justice are taught in many of the core chapters, the seven principles are intentionally treated in Live Your Faith.

You can use these Catholic Social Teaching features in a variety of ways. Every core chapter and seasonal lesson has a Catholic Social Teaching connection integrated into the lesson plan. Combining this component with the seasonal lessons can help your students connect how Catholics worship with how Catholics live.

Your principal or religion coordinator may choose to schedule these components so that all the students will be focusing on the same principle at the same time. If you schedule your own lessons, you may choose to combine several of the principles and present them at one time.

This presentation of Catholic teaching builds a vibrant Catholic identity and prepares us to evangelize the world through faith and action as we work in service of God's Kingdom.

Church Community

Connecting to the Church Community

Alive in Christ grades 7 and 8 Student Books include features that draw students into the historical, geographical, and cultural context of the Church. As seventh and eighth graders are searching for a deeper sense of belonging, these features highlight where we have been and how we are living as the Church today.

Church History Timeline

At the back of each Student Book, a Church History Timeline presents key people, places, and events in the Church's growth and development, along with major secular events that affected the course of Church history and the life and work of Catholics around the world. Grade seven spans from the death of Christ to 1085, the period surrounding the Great Schism. Grade eight spans from 1085 to the present day.

Timeline Span Each two-page spread presents a continuous timeline covering 135 years from left to right. The timeline is broken down into 15-year segments, as noted by the vertical lines.

Graphic Representations Some entries include visuals—such as portraits, artifacts, statues, and modern geographical indicators—to give a greater frame of reference for understanding the event, person, or place noted on the timeline.

Entry Specifics Each entry on the timeline includes a title and date (or range of dates) to promote viewing singular events within the context of a broader historical picture.

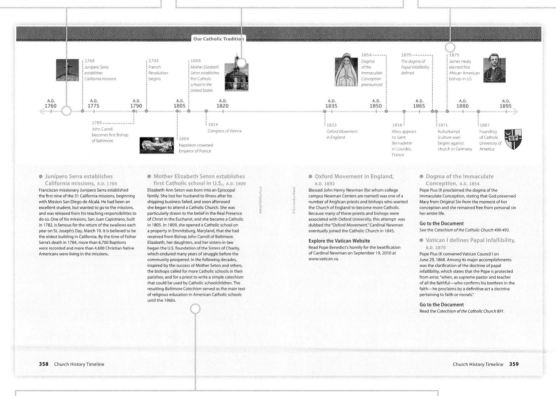

Extended Descriptions Located below the timeline, students will find more information regarding selected entries along with an opportunity to research more about the importance and implications of that entry on the whole of the Church.

Catholics Today

This feature introduces students to customs, practices, and devotions of our Church as experienced and celebrated throughout the world.

CATHOLICS TODAY

Every year, Catholics end the Easter Season by celebrating the Feast of Pentecost, remembering the day the Holy Spirit came to the Apostles in the form of fire and wind, filling them with the courage to go out and spread the news of salvation in Jesus Christ. That day, no matter what language they spoke, everyone who heard the Apostles understood them!

On Pentecost, the Church celebrates the Gifts of the Holy Spirit given to us at Baptism and Confirmation. Those gifts help us build unity in the Catholic faith, grow in moral and spiritual well-being, and give us strength to witness to the Risen Lord in our lives. On Pentecost, the Church gives thanks by renewing her commitment to spread the Word.

Where It Happened

This feature makes geographical and historical connections with scriptural accounts, events in Church history, and Catholic figures addressed in the presentation of a chapter's objectives. In some instances, images are used to provide visual context on the geographical and cultural connections.

WHERE IT HAPPENED

Why is the Nicene Creed so much longer than the Apostles' Creed? At the time the Nicene Creed was written (A.D. 325), there were heresies (false teachings) being spread that Jesus was not really a man, but was God who made himself look like a man, and did not already exist as the second Divine Person of the Holy Trinity before he was born on Earth.

The Pope and bishops met together in several councils at Nicaea and Constantinople expressly to answer these heresies. They declared that Jesus Christ is both true God and true man. The councils wrote the Nicene Creed with very clearly defined details, which stated this belief once and for all.

Iznik, Turkey, formerly Nicaea

Grade 7 Scope and Sequence

		Chapter	Lesson Concepts
1 **REVELATION**	1	The Mystery of God	• We can come to know God in many different ways: through all he has created, through the voice of conscience, and through human intellect and reason. • Although God reveals himself in many ways, we will not fully understand the mystery of God until we know him completely in Heaven. • God planned from the beginning to give his only Son, Jesus Christ, to reconcile all of creation to himself. • Many Old Testament accounts speak of God's faithfulness to his promise of salvation. • From the Genesis creation accounts and the world around us, we get a sense of the attributes of God—eternal, truth, love, merciful, and holy.
	2	The Word of God in Sacred Scripture	• God is the author and inspiration of the Sacred Scripture that humans have recorded under his guidance and direction. • Scripture can be read and interpreted in a literal sense and a spiritual sense, providing a richness to the living reading of Scripture in the Church. • The Gospels are the center of the Bible because they record the truth of the life and ministry of Jesus. • God continues to speak to us through the Scriptures, as we proclaim them at Mass, reflect on them personally, and study them to learn more about Jesus. • Moral conscience is present at the heart of every person, but we must assimilate it through the Word of God.
	3	Jesus, Sign of God's Love	• Jesus is the fulfillment of the Law; he perfectly reveals God the Father to us. • God showed the depth of his love when he made a new covenant in Jesus Christ. This covenant is made present in the world today through the Eucharist. • Being baptized in Christ gives us a share in his Divine life as sisters and brothers of Christ. • Natural moral law and God's revealed law in the Ten Commandments direct us to live in right relationship with him and with one another.
2 **TRINITY**	4	God Is Trinity	• Trusting in God's presence leads us to look for guidance in his Word. • God the Father sent his Son and the Holy Spirit to help us know him and guide us to him. • The love among members of the Trinity is a model for human affection and bonds and is the source of God's loving plan. • The total union of the Trinity is a mystery that can never be totally understood by the human mind, but can be approached through faith. • Grace is a loving gift from God and a sharing in his Divine life.
	5	Jesus, Word of God	• The Son of God has existed for all time, and through the Incarnation, became fully man while remaining fully God. • Through the Incarnation, God the Father speaks directly to us through his Son. • Through the work of the Holy Spirit, the Son of God was born to Mary; her trust and discipleship serves as a model for our own journey of faith. • Jesus showed that he was Divine in many ways, particularly through the working of miracles, which also gave us a glimpse into his human nature and emotions.
	6	Holy Spirit, Comforter and Guide	• Jesus sent us the Holy Spirit to be our Guide and Comforter and the source of our gifts and talents. • The members of the Catholic Church are called to be the hands and feet of Jesus; we are the Body of Christ in the world. • Just as the Saints often prayed to God for help, we call on the Saints to pray or intercede for us. • The Holy Spirit guides the Church in her Sacred Tradition and her prayer. The Holy Spirit helps us pray in different ways and in different circumstances.
3 **JESUS CHRIST**	7	The Way	• Jesus, the Son of God, became man to show us how to live and to share his divinity with us. Because he is true God and true man, Jesus Christ is "the way" to the Father. • Jesus is the Substantial Image of the Father because he is a visible image of the true nature of God. • When we seek the Lord and live as disciples of Christ, following his example, we will experience the fullness of life. Happiness comes from becoming the people God created us to be.

Sacred Scripture	Catechism of the Catholic Church	Tasks of Catechesis	Catholic Faith Words	People of Faith	Catholic Social Teaching
Praise of God the Creator Wisdom of Ben Sira (Sirach) 39:16–21; The Story of Creation Genesis 1:1–2	31–35, 46, 1027, 1, 422, 652, 212–221	Promoting Knowledge of the Faith, Moral Formation	Divine Revelation, eternal, mystery, image of God	Our Lady of Fátima	Rights and Responsibilities of the Human Person, Care for God's Creation
The Sabbath Rest Hebrews 4:12; The Similes of Salt and Light Matthew 5:14–16	105, 106, 115–117, 75–76, 81, 1153, 1776–1782, 1802	Promoting Knowledge of the Faith, Moral Formation	Sacred Scripture, Divine Inspiration, canon of Scripture, Gospel, Evangelists	St. Matthew	Rights and Responsibilities of the Human Person, Option for the Poor and Vulnerable
The Servant of the Lord Isaiah 42:1–3, 6–7	73, 240, 66, 1113, 1213, 1271, 1954–1960	Promoting Knowledge of the Faith, Moral Formation	covenant, *abba*, natural moral law, New Commandment, Ten Commandments	St. Maria Goretti	Life and Dignity of the Human Person, Rights and Responsibilities of the Human Person
The Prayer of Jesus John 17:24–26	215–216, 238–248, 261, 221, 255–260, 253–254, 263, 759, 1999	Promoting Knowledge of the Faith, Education for Community Life	faith, Holy Trinity, grace	St. Frances of Rome	Call to Family, Community, and Participation, Solidarity of the Human Family
Plea for Unity and Humility Philippians 2:9–11; In the Beginning Was the Word John 1:1–2	461, 464, 480, 51–53, 238–242, 967, 2030, 547–550, 1503	Promoting Knowledge of the Faith, Teaching to Pray	Incarnation, Emmanuel, Annunciation, miracle	Sts. Maria, Rosa, and Mary Zhao	Life and Dignity of the Human Person, Care for God's Creation
Faith, Hope, and Love Romans 5:1–5; The Advocate John 14:15–17	243, 1830–1832, 776–780, 956, 2683, 2625–2649, 2661	Promoting Knowledge of the Faith, Teaching to Pray	Advocate, Saints, intercession	St. Rafqa (Rebecca)	Call to Family, Community, and Participation, Rights and Responsibilities of the Human Person
Plea for Unity and Humility Philippians 2:5–8; Last Supper Discourses John 14:6; Prayer and Conduct 1 Timothy 2:5–6	456–460, 480, 467, 604, 605, 27–30	Promoting Knowledge of the Faith, Moral Formation	Visitation, Mediator	St. Maximilian Kolbe	Rights and Responsibilities of the Human Person, Solidarity of the Human Family

Grade 7 Scope and Sequence

		Chapter	Lesson Concepts
JESUS CHRIST 3	8	Model of Wisdom	• Jesus' wisdom came from being the Son of God; he looked at the world with that perspective and challenged some of the commonly accepted understandings of his time. • Jesus taught through his words and actions. He used parables to teach us about the coming of God's Kingdom. • In his Sermon on the Mount, Jesus gave specific directions for living, honoring God, and making our actions reflect our beliefs. • The Beatitudes challenge us to live by the values of God's Kingdom and to understand that true happiness comes from the hope of eternal life with God.
	9	Christ Our Savior	• Sin and suffering came into the world because of human action, but God sent leaders, prophets, and, ultimately, his Son to guide us back to him. • Jesus is sometimes called the new Adam, because his saving action is the only means by which we are saved from the Original Sin of Adam and Eve and our own personal sin. • The Paschal Mystery is Christ's work of Redemption through his Passion, Death, Resurrection, and Ascension. • Jesus' saving actions continue through his Church. We can experience new life in Christ in the Seven Sacraments.
THE CHURCH 4	10	Disciples in Community	• Saint John the Baptist proclaimed the coming of Christ and led people to Jesus. • The Apostles played a critical role in the continuation of Jesus' work and ministry. • Just as Jesus sent the first disciples out to spread the Good News, he wants us to be a sign of the Kingdom of God and to follow Church teachings. • We must have a personal relationship with God nourished by prayer in order to answer our call to bring his love and truth to others.
	11	Christ Present Among Us	• The Church is both visible and spiritual. We call the spiritual part the Mystical Body of Christ. • The Church is the Body of Christ; she is one because she acknowledges one Lord, confesses one faith, and is born of one Baptism. • Each individual member is united with all members as part of Christ's Body. When members of the Church live in communion with the Holy Spirit and with one another, harmony results. • The Church needs the diverse gifts of all members to be a sign of God's Kingdom here on Earth.
	12	Source of Life	• God created us with free will. He helps us learn to use it to choose that which is good. • We receive new life in the gift of salvation that Jesus, the Mediator, offers us in Baptism. • The Church is catholic—for all people at all times and in all places, and, through the actions of her members, people come to know God and share in his life. • Purgatory is the process of purification we experience after death, before we enter complete communion with the Holy Trinity. • Prayer is an important means of communion with God, and an important part of the call to live a life of love and truth.
MORALITY 5	13	Freedom and Responsibility	• God made us with a free will, an intellect, and a soul; our conscience works with these gifts to help us choose good and avoid sin. • The distinction between mortal and venial sin is part of the tradition of the Church. Mortal sin and venial sin both affect a sinner's relationship with God, but in different ways. • Morally good actions require that their object, intention, and circumstance be good; the end does not justify the means. • A well-formed conscience—and the help of Christ's teachings, the Church, the Holy Spirit, prayer, and wise people—will guide us to do what is right and good.
	14	Respecting Life	• All human life is sacred and a gift from God. All people possess the human dignity that comes from being made in God's image. • The Fifth Commandment forbids direct and intentional killing as gravely sinful. If anger reaches the point of a deliberate desire to kill or seriously wound a neighbor, it is a mortal sin. • The Church teaches about and advocates the right to life of every person. We have a responsibility to honor and protect life at all stages, from conception to old age. • We respect the dignity of the human person by respecting the rights of others, taking care of ourselves physically and emotionally, not abusing ourselves or others, and by not leading others into sin.
	15	Being Virtuous	• Virtues are strong habits of doing good that help us make moral decisions and contribute to how we become the people God created us to be. • The Theological Virtues are gifts from God that help us believe in him, trust in his plan for us, and love him as he loves us. • The Cardinal Virtues of prudence, justice, fortitude, and temperance can help us respect ourselves and others and act with integrity. • The Eighth Commandment forbids misrepresenting the truth in our relationships with others. This sin damages our integrity and character, but by practicing the virtues and avoiding sin, we can live truthful and faith-filled lives.

Sacred Scripture	Catechism of the Catholic Church	Tasks of Catechesis	Catholic Faith Words	People of Faith	Catholic Social Teaching
The Boy Jesus in the Temple Luke 2:46–52; Nicodemus John 3:2	574–576, 546, 1966–1971, 1716–1719	Moral Formation, Teaching to Pray	wisdom, Kingdom of God, parable, Sermon on the Mount, Beatitudes	St. Gerard Majella	Life and Dignity of the Human Person, Option for the Poor and Vulnerable
The Preeminence of Christ Colossians 1:15, 19–22; God's Love and Christian Life John 4:10–11	218, 402–406, 410, 411, 430–431, 517, 1708, 738–740, 1136–1139	Promoting Knowledge of the Faith, Missionary Initiation	Original Holiness, Original Sin, personal sin, salvation, Paschal Mystery	St. Madeleine Sophie Barat	Call to Family, Community, and Participation, Rights and Responsibilities of the Human Person
Counsel to Timothy 1 Timothy 4:6, 12; The First Disciples John 1:45–46; The Light of the World John 8:12	523, 719, 75–77, 935, 942, 3	Promoting Knowledge of the Faith, Teaching to Pray	disciples; Apostles; Church; apostolic, as a Mark of the Church; doctrine	St. Théodora (Anne-Thérèse Guérin)	The Dignity of Work and the Rights of Workers, Solidarity of the Human Family
One Body, Many Parts 1 Corinthians 12:12–18; Saul's Conversion Acts 9:1–5; The Vine and the Branches John 15:4–5	771, 779, 813–816, 866, 341, 752, 791, 814	Education for Community Life, Missionary Initiation	Mystical Body of Christ; hierarchy; one, as a Mark of the Church	St. John Bosco	Call to Family, Community, and Participation, Solidarity of the Human Family
The Coming of the Spirit Acts 2:1–7; The Commissioning of the Disciples Matthew 28:19–20	302, 1730, 771, 1257, 831, 1030, 1031, 3, 2559	Teaching to Pray, Missionary Initiation	free will; Baptism; eternal life; catholic, as a Mark of the Church	St. Lorenzo Ruiz	Call to Family, Community, and Participation, Option for the Poor and Vulnerable
Free Will The Wisdom of Ben Sira (Sirach) 15:14–17; The Golden Rule Matthew 7:12	1705, 1706, 1711, 1854–1863, 1750–1754, 1783–1785	Promoting Knowledge of the Faith, Moral Formation	soul, intellect, conscience, mortal sin, venial sin	Bl. Aloysius Stepinac	Rights and Responsibilities of the Human Person, Solidarity of the Human Family
The Choice Before Israel Deuteronomy 30:19–20	2258, 2268, 2302, 2270, 2319, 2288–2290	Promoting Knowledge of the Faith, Moral Formation	human dignity, murder, abortion, euthanasia, scandal	St. Martin de Tours	Life and Dignity of the Human Person, Rights and Responsibilities of the Human Person
Renunciation of Vice Colossians 3:12–15; Joy and Peace Philippians 4:8	1803–1804, 1812–1813, 1805–1809, 2464, 2468	Promoting Knowledge of the Faith, Moral Formation	virtue, Theological Virtues, Cardinal Virtues	St. Margaret Ward	Life and Dignity of the Human Person, Solidarity of the Human Family

Grade 7 Scope and Sequence

		Chapter	Lesson Concepts
6 SACRAMENTS	16	God's Masterworks	• Every sacramental celebration is a meeting between God's children and their Father, a dialogue in the form of actions and words, a celebration woven from signs and symbols. • Jesus himself is a Sacrament because he makes God known to us; he is a visible sign of the mystery of the Holy Trinity. • The Holy Spirit works with the Church in making Jesus' saving work present in the Sacraments. • The Catholic teaching that Jesus is really and truly with us in the Eucharist—Body, Blood, Soul, and Divinity—is called Real Presence.
	17	Sacraments of Initiation	• We are welcomed to the Church though the Sacraments of Initiation. • Confirmation is the Sacrament of Initiation through which the spiritual life, received in Baptism, is strengthened and the person is sealed with the Gifts of the Holy Spirit. • Transubstantiation is the process by which, through the power of the Holy Spirit and the words and actions of the priest, the bread and wine are transformed into the Body and Blood of Christ. • In the Eucharist, we are fed with the Body and Blood of Christ and are brought closer to Christ and one another.
	18	Sacraments of Healing	• Jesus shows us that God is compassionate, always willing to forgive and care for those who turn to him and believe. God heals us spiritually, emotionally, and sometimes physically in the Sacraments of Healing. • Conversion happens when we desire to change and are open to God's help. • In the Sacrament of Penance and Reconciliation, those who are truly sorry for their sins receive God's forgiveness and are reconciled with him and the Church. • In the Sacrament of the Anointing of the Sick, those who are seriously ill or suffering from old age receive God's grace to be strong, courageous, and hopeful in their trials.
7 KINGDOM OF GOD	19	Called by God	• The Catholic family is a domestic Church—a holy community of love, grace, and prayer. Our families help teach us to hear God's call and respond to him in faith and love. • Whether married, single, ordained, or consecrated, we are called to share our time, talent, and treasure through our vocation in order to serve the Church. • Discernment is the process by which we reflect, discuss, pray, and are ultimately drawn toward our vocation. • Whether we choose to be ordained, enter consecrated religious life, or remain a member of the laity, we are all called to faith and to continue the mission of Jesus.
	20	Act with Justice	• We can work together with God as he builds his Kingdom by choosing to believe, having faith, and making the necessary changes in our lives to work toward what is just, peaceful, and loving. • Justice is giving what is due to God and what is due to others as children of God made in his image and possessing equal human dignity. • The Tenth Commandment focuses on the intentions of our heart. To live right, we must rely on God, trust in his care, and have the right attitude toward money and things. • Society does not always support the values of God's Kingdom, so we must stand together in solidarity with those who need our help.
	21	Our Reason for Hope	• The raising of Lazarus showed that Jesus had power over death. Jesus' Resurrection makes it possible for us to have a life with God forever and gives us hope for our future. • We will be judged at our death based upon the ways we have accepted and acted on God's grace in our lives. • At the end of time, Jesus will come to judge both the living and the dead and to bring the Kingdom of God in its full glory. • The Corporal and Spiritual Works of Mercy are actions that are expected of us as members of the Church and disciples of Christ.

Sacred Scripture	Catechism of the Catholic Church	Tasks of Catechesis	Catholic Faith Words	People of Faith	Catholic Social Teaching
Prayer for the Readers Ephesians 3:14–21	1145, 1153, 1114–1115, 2812, 1116–1118, 1380, 1381	Promoting Knowledge of the Faith, Liturgical Education	Seven Sacraments, Sacraments of Initiation, Sacraments of Healing, Sacraments at the Service of Communion, Real Presence	St. Ludmilla	Life and Dignity of the Human Person, Solidarity of the Human Family
Freedom from Sin; Life in God Romans 6:1–4, 8	1275, 1121, 1285, 1376, 1377, 1382, 1416	Promoting Knowledge of the Faith, Liturgical Education	Confirmation, Gifts of the Holy Spirit, Eucharist, transubstantiation	St. Catherine of Genoa	Call to Family, Community, and Participation, Care for God's Creation
The Ministry of Reconciliation 2 Corinthians 5:17–21; The Compassion of Jesus Matthew 9:35–36	1421, 1503–1508, 1989, 1424, 1440–1445, 1520–1522	Liturgical Education, Moral Formation	contrition, Penance and Reconciliation, penance, absolution, Anointing of the Sick	Bl. Carlos Manuel Cecilio Rodriguez Santiago	Rights and Responsibilities of the Human Person, Solidarity of the Human Family
The Call of Samuel 1 Samuel 3:4–10; The Mission of the Seventy-Two Luke 10:2	1656–1657, 2685, 871–873, 2226, 2232, 1, 542–543	Education for Community Life, Missionary Initiation	domestic Church, laity, vocation, discernment, consecrated religious life	St. Anthony of Padua	Call to Family, Community, and Participation, The Dignity of Work and the Rights of Workers
Thanksgiving for Victory and Prayer for Justice Psalm 9:8–11, 10:14, 18; Parable of the Mustard Seed Matthew 13:31–32	2819–2820, 1929–1931, 2534–2536, 2548, 1939–1942	Promoting Knowledge of the Faith, Moral Formation	justice, peace, solidarity	Pope Leo XIII	Life and Dignity of the Human Person, Option for the Poor and Vulnerable
Destiny of Glory Romans 8:22–25, 28, The Raising of Lazarus John 11:1–44	988–991, 1021, 1051, 1036, 1038–1042, 1473, 2447	Promoting Knowledge of the Faith, Moral Formation	Heaven, Hell, Particular Judgment, Purgatory, Last Judgment, Works of Mercy	St. Francis de Sales	Life and Dignity of the Human Person, Care for God's Creation

Grade 8 Scope and Sequence

		Chapter	Lesson Concepts
1 REVELATION	1	In God's Image	• God made humans in his image and likeness so we could be in relationship with him. • With a soul, reason, and free will, humans can set their priority and direction in life toward friendship with God. Jesus is the model for living out this relationship. • Through the accounts of creation and the establishment of the covenant, we learn that God is faithful to all humans, even when they sin. • Natural and revealed law helps us live out the covenant and grow closer to God.
	2	Faith and Tradition	• God's revelation is contained in his written word of Scripture and in the Sacred Tradition of the Church passed down from Jesus; entrusted to the Apostles; and safeguarded by them and their successors, the bishops. Together, they make up one source of Divine Revelation. • Faith is both a gift from God and a free human choice and action. It is an individual act and an act of the Church; the faith of the Church nourishes and strengthens the faith of each of us. • The three Theological Virtues help us to believe in God, trust in his plan for us, and love him as he loves us.
	3	The Church Is Holy	• God created humans to share in his glory, to be holy, and to be joined fully with him. • Angels have been present since creation and throughout the history of salvation. They are spiritual beings that praise God and serve him as messengers to help people understand God's plan or to keep them safe from harm. • As the perfect and complete revelation of God, Jesus shows God's holiness. It is in the Church that Christ fulfills and reveals his own mystery as the purpose of God's plan. • The Church is the Body of Christ and a sign of the holiness of God. She helps us grow in holiness, especially through prayer and worship.
2 TRINITY	4	The Trinity Made Known	• Jesus' Transfiguration revealed his Divine glory as the Son of God, and shows us God the Father, God the Son, and God the Holy Spirit. • The Church is part of God's plan for all people to come to know him, love him, and glorify him. • The Holy Spirit is alive and active in the Church, uniting her and guiding her and each of us to help further God's work on Earth. • Grace is the free, loving gift of God's own life, which he offers to us, his adopted sons and daughters. • Our prayer reflects the way we understand and know God—Father, Son, and Holy Spirit.
	5	We Are Christ's People	• God invites everyone to be part of his family, the Church. All Church members have an important relationship with God. • We belong to the People of God through Baptism and belief in Christ, which matures as we grow, learn, and experience more. • The Church exists to spread the Good News of Jesus Christ. God uses each member's gifts and talents in the Church to help others come to know and love him. • Through Baptism, each of us shares in Christ's mission as priest, prophet, and king. We offer our lives and prayer to God, show others the Good News through our words and actions, and serve others with joy as we lead them to Christ.
	6	Temple of the Holy Spirit	• As temples of the Holy Spirit, we need to take care of our souls like we take care of our bodies. • Baptism and Confirmation strengthen us to be witnesses for Christ. • The Gifts of the Holy Spirit help us to live as faithful disciples. Opening our hearts to the Gifts of the Holy Spirit will help us grow into mature faith. • The Church is both a visible, structured organization and the Mystical Body of Christ, in which the Holy Spirit lives uniting the Church, guiding her and each of us, and giving us life.
3 JESUS CHRIST	7	Encountering Christ	• Jesus met many people in different circumstances. He welcomed them, urged them to believe, and encouraged them to change their lives. • As the Apostles' friendship with Jesus deepened, so did their understanding of who he was and what he taught them. • After Jesus' Ascension and then Pentecost, the early Christians gained the courage to witness to others. • The first members of the Church demonstrated Christian friendship in how they worshipped together, followed Jesus' example, and cared for each other.

Sacred Scripture	Catechism of the Catholic Church	Tasks of Catechesis	Catholic Faith Words	People of Faith	Catholic Social Teaching
The Story of Creation Genesis 1:27–28, 31; Dependence on God Matthew 6:26–33	35, 45, 356, 357, 346, 1954–1974	Promoting Knowledge of the Faith, Moral Formation	soul, free will, covenant, Ten Commandments, Decalogue	St. Marcella	Rights and Responsibilities of the Human Person, Solidarity of the Human Family
Faith and Works James 2:14–17; Prayer and Conduct 1 Timothy 2:3–4; Saying of Faith Luke 17:5–6	75–80, 84, 153, 176, 181, 1812–1813	Promoting Knowledge of the Faith, Moral Formation	Sacred Tradition, faith, Church, councils, virtue, Theological Virtues	St. Thomas	Call to Family, Community, and Participation, Option for the Poor and Vulnerable
Dependence on God Luke 12:22–23, 31–34; Divine Majesty and Human Dignity Psalm 8:4–7	357, 2013, 331–333, 772–773, 823–829	Moral Formation, Teaching to Pray	holiness, angel, holy, Marks of the Church	Bl. Miguel Pro	Life and Dignity of the Human Person, Rights and Responsibilities of the Human Person
Praise of the Father Luke 10:21–22	554–556, 824, 851, 747, 845, 1996–1999, 2564–2565	Promoting Knowledge of the Faith, Teaching to Pray	Transfiguration, Pentecost, grace, Holy Trinity, Creed	St. Lucy	Rights and Responsibilities of the Human Person, The Dignity of Work and the Rights of Workers
The Parable of the Tenants Matthew 21:42; God's House and People 1 Peter 2:9–10	1, 4, 851, 752, 1937, 783, 1546–1547	Education for Community Life, Missionary Initiation	salvation, *ekklesia*, domestic Church, offices of Christ	St. Angela Merici	Call to Family, Community, and Participation, Option for the Poor and Vulnerable
The Advocate John 14:24–27; Sexual Immorality 1 Corinthians 6:19–20; Call to Holiness 2 Corinthians 6:16–18	364–365, 1303–1304, 1830–1832, 791, 1396	Promoting Knowledge of the Faith, Liturgical Education	Temple of the Holy Spirit, character, Gifts of the Holy Spirit, Fruits of the Holy Spirit, Mystical Body of Christ	Bl. Cyprian Michael Iwene Tansi	Life and Dignity of the Human Person, Solidarity of the Human Family
The Prayer of Jesus John 17:20–24; The Call of Levi Mark 2:16; The Blind Bartimaeus Mark 10:51; The Pardon of the Sinful Woman Luke 7:47	871, 787, 788, 126, 1226, 751, 849	Promoting Knowledge of the Faith, Education for Community Life	disciple, Apostles, Ascension	Sts. Prisca and Aquila	Call to Family, Community, and Participation, Rights and Responsibilities of the Human Person

Grade 8 Scope and Sequence

		Chapter	Lesson Concepts
JESUS CHRIST **3**	8	Life in Christ	• Jesus is the Light of the World, who offers eternal life to those who accept God's grace and follow Jesus, our model of holiness in faith. • Justification is the forgiveness of sins and the return to the goodness for which humans were created. • Baptism offers us a share in the Divine Life, to live in "right" relationship with God because of the sacrifice of Jesus and the power of the Holy Spirit. We respond to the life that Jesus offers by doing what is just and right. • Conversion is a continual turning away from sin and the things that keep us from growing in God's love. The Sacrament of Penance and Reconciliation is an experience of conversion.
	9	One in Christ	• The Church is apostolic because her teaching authority comes directly from Jesus and his Apostles to the bishops of the Church who are their direct successors. • Roman Catholics and Eastern Catholics celebrate some Rites in different ways, but they are united by a common Creed, the Seven Sacraments, and the Pope's leadership. • The Church of Christ subsists in the Catholic Church. Catholics pray, hope, and work toward unity among all Christian (ecclesial) communities.
THE CHURCH **4**	10	The Church Is Apostolic	• Sacred Tradition is the teaching handed on to us from Jesus and his Apostles. It is one source of the Word of God. • The Apostles and their successors were empowered by Jesus to act in his name. Apostolic Succession is the authority to lead and teach the Church that can be traced through the centuries from the Apostles to their successors, the bishops. • The Church continues to teach the truth of Christ through the Magisterium—the Pope, and bishops in union with him, guided by the Holy Spirit. • The Nicene Creed and Apostles' Creed contain the foundational truths of our faith that express our oneness of belief.
	11	The Church Is Catholic	• The missionary mandate of the Church is that salvation can only come through faith in Christ and his Church. • Every baptized Catholic is called to share in the missionary work of the Church and to be evangelists, to spread Christ's message of salvation to people who have not yet come to know and believe in Jesus. • The Church is catholic, or universal, for she proclaims the fullness of God's truth to everyone, everywhere throughout time, welcoming people of all cultures and ages. • The Church proclaims the teaching of Christ by respectfully adapting to the culture while never compromising the truth.
	12	The Christian Faithful	• All baptized Catholics are called to share in Jesus' mission as priest, prophet, and king to serve the mission of the Church. • All lay people are called to be "like leaven" in the world. Lay people support the life of the parish community and the parish's mission to serve others in Christ's name. • The evangelical counsels are chastity, poverty, and obedience. Those in consecrated religious life take vows to live the evangelical counsels and serve an important role in the Church's mission.
MORALITY **5**	13	Honoring God	• God made a covenant with his Chosen People, the Israelites. The Ten Commandments are the laws of that covenant. These laws still hold true today. • The First Commandment calls us to put God first in our lives. Attitudes and behaviors that are not in accord with the First Commandment can lead us away from God. • Faith, hope, and charity are the Theological Virtues. Idolatry keeps us from experiencing true faith, hope, and charity. • The Second Commandment states that God's name is holy and we should always refer to his name with respect and reverence.
	14	Honoring the Family	• The Fourth Commandment calls us to honor our parents. • The love, honor, and respect found in the Holy Family is a model for our own families. • Within the family, we develop personal character, grow in our understanding of right and wrong, and learn what's truly important. • We have a moral obligation to form and follow a well-formed conscience to help us in judging what is right or wrong.
	15	The Dignity of All	• The common good is the Christian principle that all people, either in groups or as individuals, are given opportunities to reach the fullness of their God-given humanity. • The Church works to make sure that public and political authority acts with truth, justice, freedom, and solidarity. • The New Commandment not only guides our personal lives but that of organizations and nations. Solidarity compels us to work for the rights of others. • Our individual actions to promote Catholic Social Teaching, peace, and love begin close to home.

Sacred Scripture	Catechism of the Catholic Church	Tasks of Catechesis	Catholic Faith Words	People of Faith	Catholic Social Teaching
The Rejection at Nazareth Luke 4:18–19; Duty to Live in the Light Ephesians 5:8–9; Faith, Hope, and Love Romans 5:1	458, 459, 1987–1995, 1226, 1227, 1778, 1426–1429	Promoting Knowledge of the Faith, Moral Formation	justification, eternal life, righteous, conversion	Bl. Victoria Rasoamanarivo	Life and Dignity of the Human Person, Solidarity of the Human Family
Unity and Variety 1 Corinthians 12:4–11; The Prayer of Jesus John 17:20–26	857, 185–190, 1297–1301, 818–822, 874	Promoting Knowledge of the Faith, Education for Community Life	Apostles' Creed, apostolic (Mark of the Church), one (Mark of the Church), ecumenism	St. Peregrine Laziosi	Rights and Responsibilities of the Human Person, Solidarity of the Human Family
The Communal Life Acts 2:42–43; Peter's Confession about Jesus Matthew 16:18–19; Righteousness Based on Faith Romans 10:13–15	84, 873, 1209, 889–892, 2302–2306, 198–200	Promoting Knowledge of the Faith, Education for Community Life	Pope, Apostolic Succession, Magisterium, infallible, Nicene Creed	St. Peter Damian	Call to Family, Community, and Participation, Rights and Responsibilities of the Human Person
Peter's Speech at Pentecost Acts 2:39, 44–45; The Samaritan Woman John 4:13–26, 39–42	849–850, 905, 942, 831, 868, 814, 854	Education for Community Life, Missionary Initiation	Evangelists, missionary mandate, catholic (Mark of the Church), missionaries	St. Agnes	Life and Dignity of the Human Person, Solidarity of the Human Family
The Similes of Salt and Light Matthew 5:13–16	783, 1591, 898–906, 871–873, 915–916	Promoting Knowledge of the Faith, Missionary Initiation	clergy, laity, consecrated religious life, evangelical counsels	Bl. Edmund Ignatius Rice	Option for the Poor and Vulnerable, Care for God's Creation
The Greatest Commandment Mark 12:28–30; Matthew 22:34-40; Divine Majesty and Human Dignity Psalm 8:1; Teaching about Oaths Matthew 5:33–35, 37	781, 2086–2087, 1812–1813, 2113–2114, 2143–2144, 2161–2162	Promoting Knowledge of the Faith, Moral Formation	Great Commandment, idolatry, blasphemy, perjury	St. Blaise	Rights and Responsibilities of the Human Person, Care for God's Creation
Responsibilities to Parents The Wisdom of Ben Sirach (Sirach) 3:1–6; The Boy Jesus in the Temple Luke 2:49–52	2197–2200, 564, 1657, 2203–2208, 1776–1781	Promoting Knowledge of the Faith, Education for Community Life	filial respect, Feast of the Holy Family, conscience, informed conscience	St. Helena	Call to Family, Community, and Participation, Solidarity of the Human Family
Life in the Christian Community Acts 4:32–35	1924, 1929–1933, 2419, 2420, 1910–1912, 1939–1942, 1926	Moral Formation, Education for Community Life	common good, New Commandment, solidarity, personal sin, social sin	St. John Chrysostom	Life and Dignity of the Human Person, The Dignity of Work and the Rights of Workers

Grade 8 Scope and Sequence

		Chapter	Lesson Concepts
SACRAMENTS	**6**	16 — **Worship and Grace**	• The signs, symbols, and rituals of the liturgy form us in prayer, communicate God's gift of life, and show us the deeper meanings of the mystery. • Even outside of the Mass, we show adoration and veneration for the Real Presence of Christ in the Eucharist. • Our spiritual life—God's grace in us, the celebration of the liturgy, and our participation in the Seven Sacraments—strengthens our moral life—how we live by Jesus' example, his teachings, and the Precepts of the Church. • The Third Commandment required the people of the Old Law to observe the Sabbath. As Catholics we observe the Lord's Day on Sunday.
		17 — **Faithful Living**	• The Sacrament of Matrimony strengthens a couple to live out their promises to be true and faithful and open to the gift of children. • Living out the marriage covenant requires the couple to follow the Sixth and Ninth Commandments. • Holy Orders is the Sacrament in which a baptized man is ordained to teach the faithful, lead divine worship, and govern the Church. • All people are called to the virtues of modesty and chastity. The grace of the Eucharist and Reconciliation can strengthen all of us in our desire to be pure and self-respecting.
		18 — **The Liturgical Year**	• The Church celebrates the Paschal Mystery through a yearly cycle of seasons and feasts, which connect us more closely to Jesus. • Because we are different each year, we enter into the Church's seasons and feasts with different needs, hopes, and relationships with God and others. • The Eucharist is at the heart of what it means to be Catholic. Participation in Sunday Mass and our own regular personal prayer help us live the life of Christ. • In the liturgy, the three Divine Persons of the Holy Trinity are present and active in our worship. We are transformed by the liturgy to become more like Christ.
KINGDOM OF GOD	**7**	19 — **The Communion of Saints**	• The Communion of Saints is everyone who believes in and follows Jesus: Church members here on Earth, souls being purified in Purgatory, and the blessed already in Heaven. • We pray during every Mass for those who have died. We show our communion with all Church members when we support one another through prayer and sacrifice. • Sacramentals are holy objects, prayers, and practices that help us respond to God's grace and bring us closer to him. • Religious art, especially icons, helps Catholics honor the Saints and glorify God.
		20 — **Examples for Living**	• Mary lived a life of faithful obedience to God. She said "yes" to God and became the Mother of his Son and of all those who believe in him. • The Catholic Church teaches that, at the end of her life, Mary, body and soul, was "taken up" (assumed) into Heaven. • The Church honors Mary as the preeminent member of the Communion of Saints and honors her with many feast days and devotions. • Saints are role models for us. We are all called to be Saints and to accept God's friendship, which leads us to a life of service.
		21 — **From Age to Age**	• The Church grew from a persecuted, illegal religion to the religion of the Roman Empire. Many Saints and Popes promoted freedom of religion and helped believers keep their faith despite political and social situations. • Within the Catholic Church, there may be diversity in ministry but we have a unity of mission. • The Council of Trent worked to make Church teachings clearer and to reform perceived abuses. • The Church continues to address the needs of the poor and the oppressed. The documents and decisions from the Second Vatican Council invite all the members of the Church to give a Catholic response to the challenges we face in the modern world.

Sacred Scripture	Catechism of the Catholic Church	Tasks of Catechesis	Catholic Faith Words	People of Faith	Catholic Social Teaching
Communal Life Acts 2:46–47	1145–1155, 1378, 1803, 2177–2182	Liturgical Education, Moral Formation	liturgy, Seven Sacraments, Blessed Sacrament, Tabernacle, Precepts of the Church, sanctifying grace, actual grace	St. Thomas Becket	Rights and Responsibilities of the Human Person, The Dignity of Work and the Rights of Workers
Counsel to Timothy 1 Timothy 4:12	1602, 1624, 2514–2516, 2380, 1547–1553, 2348, 2533	Liturgical Education, Moral Formation	Matrimony, fidelity, vows, Holy Orders, *in persona Christi*	St. Benedict the Black	Call to Family, Community, and Participation, Option for the Poor and Vulnerable
Praise of God the Creator The Wisdom of Ben Sira (Sirach) 39:16, 21, 33–35; No One Can Determine the Right Time to Act Ecclesiastes 3:1–8	1163–1165, 1168, 1194, 1404, 1110–1112	Promoting Knowledge of the Faith, Liturgical Education	liturgical year, consecration, Saints, Liturgy of the Hours, Holy Days of Obligation	St. Maria del Transito de Jesus Sacramentado	Solidarity of the Human Family, Care for God's Creation
Freedom from Sin; Life in God Romans 6:3–9, 11; The Ten Commandments Exodus 20:2–5	946, 1475, 1032, 1670, 1677, 1678, 2501–2503	Liturgical Education, Teaching to Pray	Communion of Saints, sacramentals, Stations of the Cross, Paschal Candle, icons	St. André Bessette	Call to Family, Community, and Participation, Solidarity of the Human Family
The Beatitudes Matthew 5:2–12; Announcement of the Birth of Jesus Luke 1:26–38; The Vine and the Branches John 15:12–13	148, 149, 964, 966, 1195, 828	Promoting Knowledge of the Faith, Education for Community Life	Assumption, devotions, Immaculate Conception, canonization, beatification	Bl. Mariam Thresia Chiramel Mankidiyan	Rights and Responsibilities of the Human Person, Option for the Poor and Vulnerable
Trial of Persecution 1 Peter 4:12–14; 5:10–11; The Commissioning of the Disciples Matthew 28:16–20	2104–2109, 873, 1376, 2443, 2444	Moral Formation, Missionary Initiation	martyr, monastery	St. Marianne Cope	Life and Dignity of the Human Person, Care for God's Creation

Endnotes:

1. Cf. CCC 426–429; CT 5–6; DCG (1971) 40.

2. DCG (1971) 38a.

3. Cf. CT 31, 52, 59.

4. Cf. CT, 31; CT 31 which expounds the integrity and organization of the message; cf. DCG (1971) 39 and 43.

5. Cf. Vatican Council I: DS 3016: nexus mysteriorum; LG 25.

6. UR 11.

7. CT 68.

Feasts and Seasons at a Glance

KEY CONCEPT

The key concept for each lesson is clearly stated at the start of each chapter.

DOCTRINAL CONTENT

- The doctrinal content for each chapter will be found in this section. It will show how the chapter correlates to paragraphs from the *Catechism of the Catholic Church*.

TASKS OF CATECHESIS

The six tasks of catechesis are outlined in the *National Directory for Catechesis*. The relevant tasks of catechesis for a chapter will be found in this section.

Helping children grow in a faith that is "known, celebrated, lived, and expressed in prayer" (NDC, 20).

This chapter focuses on the following tasks of catechesis:

- Promoting Knowledge of the Faith
- Moral Formation

Teacher Background

📖 For by grace you have been saved through faith, and this is not from you; it is the gift of God; it is not from works, so no one may boast. For we are his handiwork, created in Christ Jesus for the good works that God has prepared in advance, that we should live in them.   Ephesians 2:8–10

> **Reflect** How has God's grace affected me and the way I live?

The Teacher Background includes a short essay that provides easy-to-understand theological background on the chapter content for both novice and experienced teachers.

The catechetical process of **Alive in Christ** mirrors the divine pedagogy—the gradual and relational way God teaches us so that we can know him in his truth, be guided by the Holy Spirit to respond with faith and love, and accept the gift of new life in Christ. Each lesson encourages this personal and ongoing relationship, beginning with God's invitation through Sacred Scripture. This leads the students to reflect on his Word, deepen their understanding of our Sacred Tradition, and respond with a lived faith within the home and in the community.

Alive in Christ incorporates the most trusted research on how children learn and communicate. Topics are presented at important developmental "windows"—ages when research in child development tells us that learning about a particular topic would be most effective. For example, the physical growth and change of the middle school years leads to questions and concerns about identity. It is an excellent time to talk about discipleship—following Jesus, as he offers us a pattern for living, showing us what it looks like to be fully human.

> **Reflect** How has God invited you to know him and love him?

Teacher's Prayer

💙 Lord, thank you for calling me to the ministry of catechesis. It is a great privilege and an awesome responsibility to echo your Word to others. Draw me closer to you, so that I may teach your wisdom and mirror your love by word and example. Amen.

A New Year

 Let Us Pray

Leader: O, Lord, you have given us so much, in the gifts of creation; the stars, the planets, and life on Earth. Help us understand what it means to be alive in you and for you.

"O Lord, our Lord, how awesome is your name through all the earth! I will sing of your majesty above the heavens"
Psalms 8:2

All: Help us be alive in you, Lord. Amen.

 Scripture

But God, who is rich in mercy, because of the great love he had for us, even when we were dead in our trangressions, brought us to life with Christ … raised us up with him in the heavens in Christ Jesus, that in the ages to come he might show us the immeasurable riches of his grace in his kindness to us in Christ Jesus. For by grace you have been saved through faith, and this is not from you; it is the gift of God; it is not from works, so no one may boast. For we are his handiwork, created in Christ Jesus for the good works that God has prepared in advance, that we should live in them.
Ephesians 2:4–10

Have you ever thought...

• What does your Catholic faith mean to you?

• How do you stay connected to Christ?

A New Year **1**

© Our Sunday Visitor

Objective

• Reflect on God's personal invitation through Scripture

OPEN

 Let Us Pray

Introduce the students to the prayer space and invite them into it. Lead them in the Sign of the Cross. Read aloud the leader's prayer and the Psalm or Scripture verse. Prompt the group's response. Note that this content will vary in that sometimes a volunteer will pray the Psalm verse or lead the prayer.

 Scripture

Guide the students through the process of Scripture reflection (see the Scripture Background box below).

Have you ever thought…

• Read aloud the questions and invite the students to respond to them.

• Point out the photo and ask the students to describe what is happening in it. Explain that we can stay connected to Christ through nature and Christian fellowship.

 Scripture Background

Scripture Reflection Process

Invite the students to be still, close their eyes, and focus on their breathing. Encourage them to open their minds and hearts to what God is saying to them.

• Proclaim the Scripture and have the students sit in silence.

• *Ask:* What did you hear God say to you today?

• Allow volunteers to share.

 You may play instrumental music to begin the reflection.

A New Year **1**

DAY 1

Objective

- Preview chapter concepts and vocabulary

BUILD _____

Use this page to assess the students' knowledge related to the chapter content.

Getting Started

After the opening Scripture reflection (see page 1), the Invite section continues with a two-page spread, which previews the main topics and vocabulary of the chapter, and helps you gauge the students' prior knowledge and exposure to concepts. This "pre-assessment" is done using developmentally appropriate charts, webs, cluster diagrams, timelines, and other graphic organizers that the students complete.

- Sometimes you will have the students work independently on these graphic organizers; other times you might have them work in pairs or small groups.
- Still other times, you might have the students return to these pages to add more information as they work through the chapter.

What I've Learned

Read aloud the text and point out the chart at the bottom of the page.

★ Direct the students to fill in the chart with some things they have already learned about the Catholic Church.

- Allow volunteers to share some of the things they wrote with the class.

Getting Started

Every chapter in your book begins with a Getting Started section that introduces you to the topics that will be covered in the chapter. You'll discover important points about Jesus, Sacred Scripture, Sacred Tradition, and Church history. In this section you will also complete charts, webs, tables, and other graphic organizers with information you have already learned about chapter topics. Sometimes you will return to these pages to complete the charts as you work through the chapters.

> In this box you will find direction for completing the graphic organizers and charts.
>
> Fill in the chart with some things you know about the Catholic Church. One example has been provided for you.

The Church celebrates Seven Sacraments.

What I've Learned

✔ Teaching Tip

Lesson Structure

Alive in Christ's catechetical methodology mirrors the divine pedagogy by following a three-step process that encourages a personal and ongoing relationship with the Holy Trinity.

- **Day 1:** The *Invite Step* begins the lesson with God's invitation through Sacred Scripture.
- **Days 2–4:** The *Discover Step* helps form Catholic identity through the study of Scripture, knowledge of Church teaching, and an understanding of Catholic practices.
- **Day 5:** The *Live Step* helps students relate knowledge of the faith and the ways we worship, live, pray, and serve together as Catholics.

ACTIVITY

The Church and My Life Today As a member of the Catholic Church and a disciple of Christ, your relationship with Jesus and the Church is a part of your life every day. Our faith is connected to who we are and therefore to everything we do. Place a check mark next to the statements that most apply to you. Draw a star next to things you have questions about.

- ◯ I take time to pray and read the Bible.
- ◯ I think about the teachings of Jesus and the Church when I'm making decisions.
- ◯ I've stood up for what I believe, even when it's been hard.
- ◯ My relationship with Jesus influences my life.
- ◯ I participate in Mass every week.
- ◯ I've told someone outside of my Church about my faith.
- ◯ I trust that God has a plan for my life.
- ◯ I think it's part of my responsibility as a Catholic to serve others.

What is one thing from the list above that you want to work on this year?

_____

_____

_____

_____

_____

_____

_____

Who or what do you think will help you do this?

_____

_____

_____

_____

_____

_____

_____

A New Year **3**

Reaching All Learners

Focus on Seventh Graders

Alive in Christ follows a systematic Scope and Sequence organized around key themes of Catholic teaching that repeat each year within a grade level focus.

- The grade seven focus is on Jesus Christ and the New Testament.
- This year's lessons have been designed to address the students' increased awareness of the connection between choices and consequences. It is an excellent time to talk about discipleship—following Jesus as he offers us a pattern for living.
- For more information on the abilities and perspectives of the students you are teaching, see pages TE9 and TE34.

Work with Words

Each chapter contains Catholic Faith Words, important vocabulary terms that help the students better understand core Catholic teachings—the "what" and "why" of our faith. These terms are highlighted and defined throughout the book.

- The Catholic Faith Words box will appear on either the left or right page of this spread (not shown here but can be found in each of the core chapters).
- Strategies will be provided to help you assess the students' prior knowledge of the terms presented in the chapter.
- Tell the students that they will learn more about these words as they study the rest of the chapter.

CLOSE

ACTIVITY

Activities on this page focus on pre-assessment and life experience rather than teaching. Use various methods to present the activity instructions.

- Let the students work with a partner when it makes sense to do so.
- Have them work independently when the activity requires a more personal reflection.
- Allow volunteers to share with the class.

Objectives

- Chapter objectives relating to the section are clearly stated here

OPEN

Each Discover spread (Days 2–4) will begin with a prayer. Often there will also be a reference to an opening question that helps the students begin to focus on the topic.

BUILD

Seventh Grade

Point out that the Discover pages in this book will help the students learn about their faith and deepen their relationship with God.

- Review the content of this page with the class, explaining the icons/symbols.

Say: Where you see a star on the page, you are given directions to help you interact with chapter content and better understand your Catholic faith. You may be asked to complete an activity, underline text, answer questions, or initiate a discussion.

Scripture/ Go to the Source

Applicable Scripture is studied in the Discover step as students learn about God's actions throughout salvation history and see Scripture as a source of Church teaching. Go to the Source features prompt the students to go directly to the Bible itself for reading, reflection, and activities relevant to the chapter.

Seventh Grade

Where will this year take you?

A new year is ahead of you. Your book will guide you on your journey in life and faith this year as you discover more about your connection with Jesus Christ and learn how to make it stronger.

This symbol lets you know that the reading that follows is from **Sacred Scripture**. In every chapter you will spend time with God's Word, meeting Jesus in a different and exciting way. You'll get to know him through his closest friends and followers. You'll find out what was important to him and why those things are still important to us today.

© Our Sunday Visitor

> ### Scripture
>
> Thus faith comes from what is heard, and what is heard comes through the word of Christ.   Romans 10:17
>
> Go to the Source
> Read *Romans 10:14–17* to learn what Saint Paul says about the importance of spreading the Good News.

You'll ask questions about topics that matter to you, and discover what Jesus and the Church have to say about them. You'll also have opportunities to Go to the Source—to read more about certain passages of Scripture and their background and apply it to what you have learned, and to your life today.

 Each chapter in your book begins and ends with prayer. Every time you start class,

you will have the chance to thank God, ask for his help, pray for others, and praise God just for being who he is. You'll learn about different prayer forms—prayers of praise and adoration, blessing, intercession, petition, and thanksgiving—and how to practice these forms in personal prayer and devotional practices.

Every chapter also includes tools to help you interact with chapter content and better understand what you're learning. You may be underlining, highlighting, completing thoughts, or more.

Each chapter also contains Catholic Faith Words, like Sacred Scripture referenced above, important vocabulary terms that help you better understand core Catholic teachings—the "what" and "why" of your faith. These terms are highlighted and defined throughout your book.

4   Opening Lesson

Teacher Background

Where It Happened

When a Where It Happened box appears on the student page, you will sometimes find an additional box at the bottom of the teacher page that will provide you with more background information on the location being discussed.

- In the Student Book, this feature makes geographical and historical connections with scriptural accounts, events in Church history, and Catholic figures addressed within the chapter.

- In some instances, images are also used to provide visual context on the geographical and cultural connections.

Your book also contains features such as Where It Happened, which explains the location and context of events in biblical or Church history. You'll see photographs from historical sites as they appear today, often as special places of pilgrimage for people of all Christian communities.

The Catholics Today feature connects you to that Church history and how your faith is still in action right now. You'll learn about how Catholics all over the world live their faith by the ways we pray and worship, how we serve others, and the choices we make.

At the end of each chapter you will find a Catholics Believe section, which summarizes what you have learned about Church teachings, and how Catholics put the core doctrines of our faith into practice.

The Our Catholic Tradition section in the back of your book provides valuable information on Sacred Scripture, Sacred Tradition, prayer, devotions, and other

reference material. There is also a Church History timeline to help you visualize the growth of the Catholic Church from her very beginning.

In the back of your book you will also find the Catholic Social Teaching: Live Your Faith section. This reference material explains the core principles that connect Catholics to all people through how we care about and for others because of our common human dignity, given by God. You'll learn about how the Catholic Church and her members respond to the needs of people—especially through the Corporal and Spiritual Works of Mercy—and what the Church has to say and share about the issues facing everyone around the world today.

© Our Sunday Visitor

Catholic Faith Words

Sacred Scripture the Word of God written by humans acting under the Holy Spirit's inspiration and guidance; another name for the Bible

LIST AND DISCUSS

List three things you want to find out about who Jesus is and what it means to follow him.

_____
_____
_____

Compare your thoughts with a classmate you haven't met before. Then work in small groups to find out what your class is wondering about.

_____
_____
_____

Scripture Background

Sacred Scripture

Throughout the text, the students are invited to understand the importance of Sacred Scripture, as a font of Divine Revelation and the guide for their lives. Students are led to know, love, and be formed by God's Word. For more on Sacred Scripture, see page TE28.

- The Word is always given prominent visual importance to highlight its significance, with a parchment background, an icon, and a logo.

- The students are given opportunities to pray with Scripture, study biblical references, and reflect on and apply the Word of God to their lives.

Seventh Grade, *continued*

Have the students read this section to learn about more valuable resources that they will find in their books.

- **Catholics Today** highlights where we have been and how we live as the Church today.

- **Catholics Believe** summarizes what the students have learned about Church teachings, and how Catholics put the core doctrines of our faith into practice.

- **Our Catholic Tradition** provides information on Sacred Scripture and Sacred Tradition, prayer, devotions, and other materials.

- **Church History Timeline** presents key people, places, and events in the Church's growth and development, along with major secular events that impacted the course of Church history.

Work with Words

- **Catholic Faith Words** are highlighted in the text. These words build a common language of faith using developmentally appropriate, precise theological language.

CLOSE _____

ACTIVITY

Point out the activity.

- Explain that this feature and others like it will help the students think about their faith and what it means to follow Jesus.

Quick Review End with a summation of the lesson from these two Discover pages.

DAY 3

Objectives

- Identify the Bible as the inspired Word of God written by humans
- Discover that the Catholic Church's official collection of inspired books is called the canon of Scripture

OPEN

Begin each Discover section with prayer. The content of the day will drive the prayer selections.

BUILD

Jesus in Sacred Scripture

Summarize the first two paragraphs.

- Tell the students that the Church's canon, the complete list of inspired books included in Sacred Scripture, contains seventy-three books.
- Remind them that we cannot read and understand the New Testament without the background of the Old Testament.

Invite two volunteers to read aloud the next two paragraphs, describing the content of both the Old Testament and the New Testament.

Share the definition of *canon of Scripture* from the Catholic Faith Words box.

Ask a student to read aloud the caption that goes with the image on this page.

Detail from a Desis mosaic image of Jesus in the Hagia Sophia (Holy Wisdom) church in Istanbul, Turkey. The Hagia Sophia was a central church of Christianity for over nine hundred years.

Jesus in Sacred Scripture

You have already learned that the Bible is made up of two parts: the Old Testament and the New Testament. Together, they make up what we call Sacred Scripture, and their unity comes from the unity of God's plan of salvation for all people. That plan and God's truth are recorded in both Testaments as our salvation history.

The Catholic **canon of Scripture**, or the Church's complete list of inspired books included in Sacred Scripture, contains seventy-three books. Forty-six books make up the Old Testament, and twenty-seven books can be found in the New Testament. We cannot read and understand the New Testament without the background of the Old Testament, or the other way around!

The Old Testament tells about God the Father's relationship with the Hebrew people before the birth of Jesus, his presence in their lives, and the covenant, or sacred agreement, he made with them. The Old Testament includes the laws, history, and stories of God's Chosen People.

The New Testament is about the birth, life, ministry, teachings, suffering, Death, and Resurrection of Jesus Christ. Jesus was a Jew who preached about the Kingdom of God to his fellow Jews at the time. Jesus fulfilled the promise of the Old Testament prophets

Catholic Faith Words

canon of Scripture the Church's complete list of inspired books included in Sacred Scripture

6 Opening Lesson

Optional Activity

Explore the Student Book *Verbal/Linguistic, Interpersonal*

In addition to what is presented in this opening lesson, there are many other features that help you present the Catholic faith to the students. Ask them to find the following features in their books.

- The Church Year: Invite the students to share some of the Church feasts and seasons covered in this section.
- Unit Previews: Preview the doctrinal theme with photos and art that convey the richness of our Catholic Tradition. Ask the unit's Big Question.
- Catholic Social Teaching/Live Your Faith: Introduce the students to important teachings of Jesus and the Church that help us live Jesus' New Commandment to love as he loved.

of a Messiah. He also fulfilled the Law of Moses as explained in the Old Testament, by giving the people a new law of love. He taught that God's covenant of love is for everyone, not just the Chosen People.

In the New Testament we discover accounts, stories, and parables that tell of God's love through Jesus and the Holy Spirit. The Gospels according to Matthew, Mark, Luke, and John proclaim the Good News of Jesus today, just as they did to the early followers of Christ. The Gospels were formed in three stages; first, in the life and teaching of Jesus, then through the oral tradition of storytelling and preaching, and then in the written Gospels themselves. You can discover more about the formation of the Gospels in the New Testament on page 364 in the Our Catholic Tradition section of your book.

When we study the Scriptures—in the Old Testament and the New Testament—we learn not only about God's past saving actions, but also about how he is still saving us today. Jesus in present in the Seven Sacraments, and in the Church's liturgy and worship.

You will come to better know Jesus and his teachings through studying the New Testament and seeing how he accomplished his mission during his time on Earth. You will come to realize in a deeper way how Christ's actions and the Word of God in Scripture and Tradition continue to guide and strengthen Catholics in the present time. You are connected to the early Christian followers, and God is calling you to be part of your parish and school community and part of the greater Catholic community.

> **What is one thing you would like to know about Jesus in the New Testament?**

© Our Sunday Visitor

IDENTIFY

Identify three times when you have connected with the Word of God through Sacred Scripture, in Church, in school, or in your own reading.

1. _____

2. _____

3. _____

A New Year **7**

Jesus in Sacred Scripture, *continued*

Arrange the students in three groups. Assign each group one of the paragraphs on this page.

- Invite the groups to review their paragraph together and to discuss the key points being made.

- Have a spokesperson from each group teach the rest of the class what they learned from their paragraph.

- Encourage the students to ask questions to clarify their understanding of the text.

- Ask the question at the end of this section and invite the students to respond.

CLOSE _____

ACTIVITY

Explain the activity.

- Have the students work independently to complete it.

- Invite volunteers to share their experiences.

Quick Review The Old Testament and New Testament make up Sacred Scripture. When we study Scripture, we learn not only about God's past saving actions, but also about how he is still saving us today.

DAY 4

Objectives

- Examine the constancy of our Triune God, who never changes
- Discover that the Blessed Trinity guides and strengthens us to be Christ's disciples

OPEN

Ask the students to stand and make the Sign of the Cross. Pray together the Glory Be from page 383.

Point out the photo at the bottom of the page. See if anyone can identify what the symbol represents. Throughout the book, you will discover many examples of Scripture illustration, fine art, stained glass, statues, icons, and photos that connect to each lesson.

BUILD

Jesus Christ, the Catholic Church, and You

Have the students silently read the text on this page. Encourage them to highlight the topic sentence in each paragraph

- *Ask:* What three things will always be there for us? God's wisdom, his Church, and his love

Alive in Christ takes into account the experience level of today's students with various topics and how they are used to receiving and processing those topics. So, the series is developmentally appropriate not just in what students learn at particular ages, but how they learn it and are formed in faith.

Jesus Christ, the Catholic Church, and You

Have you ever looked back at pictures of yourself as a young child and wondered how you could ever have been that small? Have you ever read something you wrote last year in class or in a journal and wondered what you were thinking at the time?

Sometimes it can feel like we grow into entirely new people in just one year. This time in your life is like that. You have learned a lot about yourself over the last few years, but the person you see in the mirror might feel like a stranger to you sometimes.

So many things in your life are changing. But there is one thing you can count on to remain the same: the love of God, who never changes. His wisdom, his Church, and his love will always be there for you. Your family

and school and parish are also there to help you as you continue your faith journey.

We live in a world where everything changes all the time, and not always for the better. There are few things we can depend on to help us no matter what. That's why our Catholic faith is so important. Things are different, and better, when you let the **Holy Trinity**—God the Father, his Son, Jesus, and the Holy Spirit—into your life. Learning about the Trinity will help you through the ups and downs in your life, and give you the strength to become who God wants you to be: someone who is Alive in Christ.

> **Catholic** Faith Words
>
> **Holy Trinity** the mystery of one God in three Divine Persons: Father, Son, and Holy Spirit

8 Opening Lesson

i Teacher Background

Church History Timeline

At the back of each Student Book, a Church History Timeline presents key people, places, and events in the Church's life, along with secular events that affected the course of the Church.

- The grade seven timeline spans from the death of Christ to 1085, the period surrounding the Great Schism (with the last entry noted on 1054). The grade eight timeline begins on 1085 (with the first entry on 1093) and covers up to the present day.
- Each Unit Preview includes a Church History Timeline connection. For more information on the Church History Timelines, refer to page TE36.

Are You Ready?

Jesus loves you for who you are right now. He calls you to begin this next part of your life with hope, trusting in the Father's plan for you. As you move through this book and study Christ's words and life in the New Testament, he speaks to you and asks you to live as his disciple. He wants to get to know you, to spend time with you, to strengthen you, and to challenge you to be the person God made you to be.

Fill in the chart with your thoughts about the next year. As you work through your book over the next few months, come back and update your chart with your progress or how your thoughts have changed. ✱

The Next Year	
What I know about Jesus:	
What I know about the Bible:	
My goals for the coming year:	
My faith helps my goals by:	
How is Christ alive in me now?	
How can I be alive in Christ?	

A New Year **9**

🌐 Catholic Social Teaching

Live Your Faith Component

Each grade level of *Alive in Christ* presents the seven principles of Catholic Social Teaching, articulated by the United States Conference of Catholic Bishops. In this Live Your Faith component, the scriptural and doctrinal foundations of the principles help the students connect their faith to a life of peace and justice.

Every core chapter and seasonal lesson has a Catholic Social Teaching connection integrated into the lesson plan. Combining this component with the seasonal lessons can help your students connect how Catholics worship with how Catholics live.

Are You Ready?

Say: As you move through this book and study Jesus' words and life in the New Testament, he speaks to you and asks you to live as his disciple.

Ask: Are you up to the challenge?

The Next Year

Point out the chart at the bottom of the page.

✱ Direct the students to fill in the chart with their thoughts about next year. Remind them that they can always come back to the chart later in the year to check their progress or update the information.

• When the students have completed their charts, initiate a class discussion by connecting the last question "How can I be alive in Christ?" with the principles of Catholic Social Teaching. For more information on each of the seven principles, turn to pages TE56 and TE57.

CLOSE _____

In Summary

The last page of the Discover section will always end with an In Summary section (not shown here but can be found in each of the core chapters) that shares the key concept and main summary points made in the chapter about what Catholics Believe.

A New Year **9**

DAY 5

Objective

- Learn about different forms of prayer and how to be an active member of the Church

OPEN _____

Begin this portion of the lesson with prayer. The students will either stand at their seats or move to the prayer space. Encourage them on occasion to pray in their own words.

BUILD _____

Our Catholic Life

Point out the *Live* heading on the page.

- Explain that each chapter in this book has a section that will help the students learn to live as good Catholics.
- Have the students read this section and reflect on the question at the end.
- Invite those who wish to do so to share their responses with the class.

People of Faith

Ask a volunteer to read aloud this paragraph.

- Tell the students that in this feature, they will learn about Saints and other holy people from all periods of Church history. They will also be encouraged to go online at home to learn more about the person of faith they read about.

Our Catholic Life

Each chapter in your book has an Our Catholic Life section. It builds on what you have read in the chapter and focuses in a special way on what it means to be Catholic. Text, images, and an activity will help you better understand how to grow closer to **God, Jesus, and the Church.** Topics covered will include learning more about the Catholic faith, background on the meaning and celebration of the Seven Sacraments, discovering how to live as Christ calls us to, understanding different forms of prayer, advice on how to be an active member of your Church, and ways to help others come to know Jesus Christ through our own words and actions.

> What are you looking forward to learning most this year?

© Our Sunday Visitor

People of Faith

Holy Men and Women

You will also be introduced to People of Faith, men and women of all ages who loved God and did his work to help build the Kingdom on Earth. Some were figures of Church history such as the Apostles, some were men and women religious—priest, monks, religious sisters—and some served as part of the laity, without taking vows or being ordained. They are officially recognized by the Catholic Church as Venerables, Blesseds, and Saints. You will learn about their lives and some of the people they met, influenced, or were influenced by, and discover how their lives changed as they accepted God's grace and made a commitment to live a Christian life.

📶 For more, go to **aliveinchrist.osv.com**

IDENTIFY

Think of someone you know who has been a role model of Catholic faith for you. This person could be a priest, a teacher, or someone in your community, even a good friend. Explain how they share their faith and are an example to you on the lines below.

_____
_____
_____
_____
_____
_____
_____
_____
_____
_____

10 Opening Lesson

People of Faith Background

Holy Men and Women

Introduce the students to a Saint, Blessed, or Venerable whose life exemplifies the content of the lesson. The box on the bottom of this page will often provide additional details about the person of faith to assist you in presenting this section. Sometimes it will contain information about an event in history this person participated in or was affected by. Other times you will find interesting facts about a location relevant to the People of Faith you are learning about. This feature offers yet another way that you can help the students connect to the Church community.

♥ Celebration of the Word

Leader: Let us take time, here and now, to gather for prayer, in the name of the One who calls us to "come and follow."

Jesus said, "I am the light of the world. Whoever follows me will not walk in darkness, but will have the light of life" **John 8:12.**

Reader 1: Lord Jesus, I want to be alive in you and your Word.

Help me to trust you and know you will show me how to love.

Let your light shine in me for friends who are searching,

and for all who are lost and can't find the way.

All: Let us be alive in you, Jesus Christ.

Leader: Jesus called to Peter and Andrew as they sat in their boats, "Come after me, and I will make you fishers of men" **Mark 1:17.**

Reader 2: Lord Jesus, I want to be alive in you and your Word.

Let me be ready when you cast your net.

Send me in search of the others you call to.

Help me to lead all the lost ones to you.

All: Let us be alive in you, Jesus Christ.

Leader: Jesus said, "Whoever serves me must follow me" **John 12:26.**

Reader 3: Lord Jesus, I want to follow.

Help me to stand by the things that I say.

Remind me that actions speak louder than words.

Give me a mission to go out and serve all that I can.

Send me as witness to all your Good News.

All: Let us be alive in you, Jesus Christ.

© Our Sunday Visitor

A New Year **11**

♥ Liturgy Link

Connecting to the Prayer

Sometimes a Liturgy Link box will appear on the bottom of a page in the core chapters or seasonal lessons. Some boxes will tie in to the time of year or the color of the season. Others will help you talk about a Psalm, Scripture reading, or a part of the Mass. Still others provide background information, ideas for conversations with the students, or important liturgical references to help you connect the students more deeply to the Church's worship.

📶 Go to **aliveinchrist.osv.com** for Sunday readings, Scripture background, questions of the week, and seasonal resources.

Use a closing activity to help the students relate their knowledge of the faith to their lives, and to commit more deeply to what it means to be Catholic.

- *Ask:* Who has been a role model of Catholic faith for you?
- Allow the students to share their thoughts with a classmate.

CLOSE _____

Celebration of the Word

♥ Explain that every chapter will end with prayer.

Sometimes you will be the prayer leader. In other cases, you will assign leaders and/or readers or arrange the class into two sides, and allow the students to practice their lines.

Gather the students in the prayer space.

Follow the order of prayer on the student page.

Pray a closing prayer when indicated.

▶ Conclude by playing the song and having the students reflect on it, or singing with the students a song that was downloaded from **aliveinchrist.osv.com**.

Prayer celebrations will usually conclude with the song, but at times you may also end with sharing the sign of peace or praying the Lord's Prayer.

About the Pre-Test

As you begin the year, you may be asked to complete the Pre-Test that starts on the next page. The Pre-Test corresponds with major concepts you will learn this year, and your teacher will use the results to determine individual and class knowledge related to the topics. This Pre-Test and the Post-Test at the end of the year will help your teacher assess your knowledge and understanding of Catholic teachings, beliefs, and practices.

Circle the letter of the response that correctly completes the statement.

1. God is ___, which means he always was, is now, and always will be.
   a. faithful
   b. eternal (circled)
   c. holy
   d. love

2. The Church's complete list of inspired books included in Sacred Scripture is called ___.
   a. the canon of Scripture (circled)
   b. Sacred Tradition
   c. Church doctrine
   d. natural law

3. Through ___, God promised to remain in a relationship with his People.
   a. his law
   b. his grace
   c. the covenant (circled)
   d. the spiritualities

4. ___ is the free, loving gift of God's life and help.
   a. Solidarity
   b. Inspiration
   c. Grace (circled)
   d. Conscience

5. The ___ is the term for the mystery surrounding the Son of God taking on human nature.
   a. Annunciation
   b. Nativity
   c. Miracle
   d. Incarnation (circled)

6. A prayer that acclaims God for his nature is a prayer of ___.
   a. intercession
   b. thanksgiving
   c. blessing
   d. praise (circled)

7. Jesus' ___ teach us about the meaning and path to true happiness and the ways to live in the Kingdom of God.
   a. Ten Commandments
   b. miracles
   c. Beatitudes (circled)
   d. first books of the Bible

8. The Paschal Mystery refers to ___.
   a. Jesus' Incarnation and birth
   b. Jesus' Death and Resurrection (circled)
   c. Jesus' teachings to the Apostles
   d. both a and b

9. Jesus instructed the Apostles to travel in such a way that they ___.
   a. would meet with important people
   b. could gather monetary treasures for the Church
   c. would trust in God to provide for them (circled)
   d. could leave a place quickly if they were persecuted

10. The Church is organized into ___ that has different levels of leadership and membership.
    a. a hierarchy (circled)
    b. the Magisterium
    c. a canon
    d. an encyclical

Have the students complete the Pre-Test pages. Review the responses provided by the students to assess class performance and identify areas of strengths and weaknesses. Use the results from the Pre-Test to help you determine where you may need to spend additional time as you teach each chapter.

On page 13, instruct the students to circle the letter of the response that best completes each statement.

On pages 14–15, instruct the students to circle the letter of the response that best completes each statement.

11. Contemplative prayer is ___.
   a. based on songs
   b. group prayer
   c. part of the Mass
   d. wordless prayer

12. You are obliged to form your ___ well, so that it will lead you to what is truthful and just.
   a. education
   b. free will
   c. conscience
   d. soul

13. The deliberate ending of a pregnancy by killing the unborn child is known as ___.
   a. suicide
   b. scandal
   c. abortion
   d. euthanasia

14. The Cardinal Virtues include all of the following except ___.
   a. prudence
   b. justice
   c. charity
   d. fortitude

15. Much of Catholic liturgy has its roots in the ___ traditions that Jesus took part in as he grew up.
   a. Jewish
   b. Roman
   c. Apostolic
   d. Gentile

16. The process by which, through the power of the Holy Spirit and the words and actions of the priest, the bread and wine are transformed into the Body and Blood of Christ is known as ___.
   a. discernment
   b. conversion
   c. transubstantiation
   d. transfiguration

17. We show our ___ when we are sorry for our sins and pledge to try to not sin again.
   a. contrition
   b. forgiveness
   c. suffering
   d. confession

18. A ___ is the purpose for which God made us and the particular way to answer and live out his call.
   a. spirituality
   b. vocation
   c. reparation
   d. covenant

19. When we act with ___, we give God and our neighbor what is due to them.
   a. prudence
   b. hope
   c. justice
   d. temperance

20. A soul that is in Purgatory is in the process of being ___.
   a. judged
   b. punished
   c. rewarded
   d. cleansed

21. ___ is the God-given ability that helps individuals judge whether actions are right or wrong.
    a. Free will
    b. Conscience
    c. Reason
    d. Judgment

22. The ___ Commandment instructs us not to kill another person.
    a. First
    b. Tenth
    c. Third
    d. Fifth

23. When we attempt to indirectly correct the damage caused by sin, we are making ___.
    a. reparation
    b. contrition
    c. conscience formation
    d. reconciliation

24. ___ is the courage to do what is right even if others disagree with or challenge you.
    a. Justice
    b. Temperance
    c. Fortitude
    d. Prudence

25. The ___ Commandment identifies lying as a sin that damages our character and integrity.
    a. Tenth
    b. Eighth
    c. Fourth
    d. Sixth

26. The ___ is the event of the Angel Gabriel telling Mary she would be the Mother of God.
    a. Assumption
    b. Annunciation
    c. Ascension
    d. Attribution

27. The name ___ means "God is with us."
    a. Jesus
    b. Mediator
    c. Christ
    d. Emmanuel

28. Jesus told ___, or stories that taught moral or spiritual truths.
    a. passages
    b. parables
    c. poems
    d. pastiches

29. Jesus told the Beatitudes during the ___.
    a. Last Supper
    b. Journey to Jerusalem
    c. Sermon on the Mount
    d. wedding at Cana

30. Letters from the Pope to the Church community are known as ___.
    a. spiritual treasury
    b. encyclicals
    c. evangelical counsels
    d. spiritualities

© Our Sunday Visitor

On pages 16 and 17, point out that the students will be writing a short answer to the statements and questions. Explain that even though these are short answer responses, they need to be sure that they fully answer the questions.

Respond to the following items.

Name the three Divine Persons of the Holy Trinity.

31. First Person: God the Father

32. Second Person: God the Son (Jesus)

33. Third Person: God the Holy Spirit

Name the Marks of the Church that we profess in the Creed.

34. one

35. holy

36. catholic

37. apostolic

Think about the following images of Jesus. Describe what each means.

38. Light of the World

Responses will vary, but may include that Jesus is light, and with him we don't walk in darkness or confusion.

39. Bread of Life

Responses will vary, but may include that Jesus gives us eternal life, we are fed by Jesus in the Eucharist, as we remember the Last Supper.

40. Vine

Responses will vary, but may include that we must remain attached to Jesus to live.

41. Jesus used parables about nature and everyday life to describe the Kingdom of God. How would you describe the Kingdom of God?

Responses will vary.

42. What are the Sacraments?

Effective signs of God's grace, instituted by Christ and given to his Church.

43. What is the Paschal Mystery?

<u>The Paschal Mystery is Jesus' work of redemption through his life,</u>
<u>Passion, Death, Resurrection, and Ascension.</u>

44. Name the Seven Sacraments.

<u>Baptism, Confirmation, Eucharist, Penance and Reconciliation,</u>
<u>Anointing of the Sick, Holy Orders, Matrimony</u>

45. What is the mission of the Catholic Church?

<u>Responses will vary, but may include that the Church's mission is to</u>
<u>proclaim the Gospel to all people and to be an example of Jesus' love</u>
<u>to the world.</u>

46. What are some steps in making good decisions?

<u>Responses will vary, but may include thinking about possible options,</u>
<u>comparing options to Jesus' teachings, talking to someone you can</u>
<u>trust, praying for guidance, and acting on your choice.</u>

47. Which four books of the New Testament are the Gospels?

<u>The Gospels according to Matthew, Mark, Luke, and John.</u>

48. Name two parables Jesus told in the Gospels.

<u>Responses will vary, but may include the Parable of the Good</u>
<u>Samaritan, the Parable of the Mustard Seed, the Parable of the</u>
<u>Prodigal Son, or others.</u>

49. Describe how the Church is the Body of Christ.

<u>Responses will vary, but may include that Jesus is the head of the</u>
<u>Church, and her members work together as his Body, bringing his love</u>
<u>to the world through her work.</u>

50. Who are the Saints and why are they important to us?

<u>Responses will vary, but may include that Saints are models of faith</u>
<u>who led holy lives, are in Heaven, intercede for us, and help us know</u>
<u>how to live as disciples.</u>

LESSON OBJECTIVES

- Discuss the Kingship of Christ
- Relate faithfulness to anticipating Christ's coming as our King
- Examine Scripture verses on faithfulness

ENVIRONMENT

Green cloth
Crucifix
Candle
Bible or Lectionary

- Place the prayer table in a central location.
- Set the prayer table with the green cloth, crucifix, candle, and Bible or Lectionary.
- Light the candle before beginning.
- Allow plenty of space around the prayer table for the students to gather.

🎧 MUSIC OPTION

Go to **aliveinchrist.osv.com** to sample and download, "Mighty King"

🌐 CATHOLIC SOCIAL TEACHING

- **Rights and Responsibilities of the Human Person**
  Pages 338–339
- **The Dignity of Work and the Rights of Workers**
  Pages 342–343

Teacher Background

> 📖 "You say I am a king. For this I was born and for this I came into the world, to testify to the truth. Everyone who belongs to the truth listens to my voice." **John 18:37**
>
> **> Reflect** In what ways do you help God bring about his Kingdom on Earth?

If you were to paint a picture of the perfect world, what would it look like? For those who seek the Kingdom of God (see Luke 12:3–31), the perfect world is a world transformed by Jesus Christ, the King. Jesus, in his many parables about the Kingdom of God, shares his Father's intentions for the world—a world in which the Reign of God is at hand, a world in which everyone has what they need (justice) because we are willing to share. Justice becomes the pathway to peace.

With eyes of faith, we celebrate Christ the King every day when we witness to the presence and power of God in our lives. We proclaim Christ as King when we work with God to transform the world in our own time and place through the little ways (and the big ways) we point people to God. We believe with faith that the Kingdom of God grows and will continue to grow until Jesus comes again in glory at the end of time. Meanwhile, where love and life are, there God's Reign is. The key question then is, how do we work together with God as he builds his Kingdom?

> **> Reflect** What evidence do you see of Christ's Kingdom?

Teacher's Prayer

💟 Christ, my King, I praise and bless you! Help me see with the eyes of faith the Kingdom of God at hand around me. Help me work with you to transform the world … thy kingdom come, thy will be done … every day. Amen.

Name _____   Date _____

Serving Others

We celebrate Christ the King to remind us that Jesus' power is not the temporary controlling kind found on Earth. The everlasting power of Christ comes from truth and love. To live the Paschal Mystery, we must die to the way the world defines power and rise to Jesus' understanding of power as loving and serving others.

The crossword puzzle below will help you to remember the Corporal and Spiritual works of Mercy. They are a sign of the Kingdom of God. (Turn to page 374 in the Our Catholic Tradition reference section to check your answers.)

ACROSS

2. Give ___ to the thirsty

4. ___ the naked

5. Teach the ___

6. ___ the sinner

8. ___ the doubtful

9. ___ the sorrowful

11. Feed the ___

12. Actions that address the needs of the heart, mind, and soul are the ___ Works of Mercy

13. ___ for the living and the dead

14. ___ the sick and imprisoned

DOWN

1. Bear ___ patiently

3. Shelter the ___

4. Actions that are for the physical needs of others are the ___ Works of Mercy

7. ___ injuries

10. ___ the dead

 Let Us Pray

Choose one of the students to be the Leader. Invite the students to gather in the prayer space and make the Sign of the Cross. Ask the leader to proclaim the opening prayer and Psalm verse, and lead the class in the response.

Have the students move out of the prayer space and back to their seats.

Say: Let's listen to God's Word and learn about the truth that only Jesus can provide.

Scripture

Guide the students through the process of Scripture reflection (see the Scripture Background box below).

Have your ever thought...

Say: Jesus' Kingdom is not of this world. When he spoke to Pilate, Jesus was speaking about the Kingdom of God.

- Invite the students to respond to the questions.

The King Returns

Let Us Pray

Leader: Jesus, our Lord,

Your throne stands firm from of old;
    you are from everlasting.
Your decrees are firmly established;
    holiness befits your house, LORD,
    for all the length of days.   Psalm 93:2, 5

All: You are from everlasting, O Lord! Amen.

Scripture

Pilate said to Jesus, "Are you the King of the Jews?" Jesus answered, "Do you say this on your own or have others told you about me?" Pilate answered, "I am not a Jew, am I? Your own nation and the chief priests handed you over to me. What have you done?" Jesus answered, "My kingdom does not belong to this world. If my kingdom did belong to this world, my attendants [would] be fighting to keep me from being handed over to the Jews. But as it is, my kingdom is not here." So Pilate said to him, "Then you are a king?" Jesus answered, "You say I am a king. For this I was born and for this I came into the world, to testify to the truth. Everyone who belongs to the truth listens to my voice."   John 18:33b–37

Have you ever thought...

- What happens when people do not accept the truth of Jesus?
- Why did Jesus, the King, spend so much time serving the needs of others?

18   The Church Year

Scripture Background

Scripture Reflection Process

Invite the students to be still, close their eyes, and focus on their breathing. Encourage them to open their minds and hearts to what God is saying to them.

- Proclaim the Scripture and have the students sit in silence.
- *Ask:* What did you hear God say to you today?
- Allow volunteers to share.

 You may play instrumental music to begin the reflection.

Marking the End and a New Beginning

The Church celebrates the life and ministry of Jesus as the focus of the season of Ordinary Time. The Feast of Christ the King marks the end of the liturgical year. As the last Sunday in Ordinary Time, it falls on the Sunday before Advent begins.

The feast recalls that by Pilate's order Jesus was called "King of the Jews" when he was on the Cross. During his life on Earth, Jesus never pursued political power. That was not his goal. By rejecting political gains, he was the very opposite of the common image of the king who goes to war or maintains armies to gain or preserve power. His new focus was on being the king of our hearts, the Prince of Peace. He is the king of God's Kingdom, which is not of this world.

The Feast of Christ the King looks forward, too. It predicts the end time, when Jesus will come in glory to gather the faithful to himself and give them the fullness of life they longed for on Earth—a life in union with his Father in Heaven. This feast reflects the richness of the Kingdom of God, where good and faithful servants will be reunited with one another. We will join with the angels in praising God. The righteous, those who seek God sincerely and respond to his grace, will reign with God forever. The feast makes us want to change our behavior, so that we will be known as good and faithful servants.

> Why would Jesus have avoided gaining political power?

> How should longing for God's Kingdom change our behavior on Earth?

Ordinary Time **19**

Catholic Social Teaching

Lesson Connections

To integrate Catholic Social Teaching into your lesson, choose one of the following features: Rights and Responsibilities of the Human Person, pages 338–339; or The Dignity of Work and the Rights of Workers, pages 342–343.

- To expand the lesson, complete pages 19–20, then move to the Catholic Social Teaching feature.
- Return to the prayer on page 21.

Marking the End and a New Beginning

Introduce the lesson with a summary of the first paragraph. Reinforce the fact that the Feast of Christ the King is the last Sunday in the liturgical year.

Select a volunteer to read the second paragraph.

- Link the content of the paragraph with the Gospel reading from page 18.
- Discuss what Jesus meant when he said that his Kingdom "does not belong to this world."
- *Ask:* Why was Jesus different from other kings of his time? He never pursued political power or war because he was focused on bringing peace and the Kingdom of God.

Read aloud the last paragraph.

- Challenge the students to describe what God's Kingdom will be like when it comes in its fullness.
- *Ask:* How does the Feast of Christ the King look forward? It predicts the end time; it reflects the richness of God's Kingdom.

Invite the students to silently read the reflection questions.

- Allow time for them to think about their feelings; ask volunteers to share their thoughts.

Faithfulness to Our King

Review that the Fruits of the Holy Spirit show how open we are to the work of the Holy Spirit within us.

Summarize the first paragraph.

- Talk about how people show loyalty and faithfulness.
- *Ask*: How does faithfulness connect us to others? helps build trustworthy relationships

Ask a volunteer to read aloud the second paragraph.

- Point out that faithfulness requires us to be steadfast over a long period of time.
- *Ask*: Why is faithfulness sometimes a challenge?

Summarize the third paragraph.

- Discuss examples of faithfulness from current events or movies.
- Emphasize that being faithful in small things, like showing up when we've promised, helps us develop faithfulness for more challenging occasions.

Make Bibles available to the students. Have them work in small groups to complete the activity.

- Discuss their explanations.

For your own use, here are the Bible references with brief reminders about their content: Matthew 8:23–26, Jesus calms the storm; Matthew 9:18–25, healing of the woman with a hemorrhage and the official's daughter; Revelation 2:9–10, encouragement to the people of Smyrna to be steadfast despite difficulties because they will be given "the crown of life."

Faithfulness to Our King

The Feast of Christ the King invites us to be faithful to Church teachings. **Faithfulness** helps us to keep our promises and follow through on our commitments. Being faithful to God and others is about being loyal and trustworthy, so people can count on us to do what we say we will.

It's easy to focus on God's desire for us to be with him forever in eternal glory. What is difficult is persevering in doing what is good and turning away from sin and evil, so that through the grace of God, we can be in God's presence forever. This perseverance, or steadfastness, is faithfulness. A faithful person is dedicated to his or her task of bringing glory to God.

We cultivate faithfulness by hanging on through troubled times, by constantly maintaining that vision of our goal. We nurture this Fruit of the Holy Spirit by being faithful in small things, such as a promise to a friend, saying daily prayers, or helping with household tasks without being asked. Like every Fruit of the Holy Spirit, faithfulness will deepen with practice and as we remain responsive to God's grace in the Sacraments and our lives.

© Our Sunday Visitor

Fruits of the Holy Spirit

The twelve Fruits of the Holy Spirit are qualities that can be seen in us when we let the Holy Spirit work in our hearts. This season we are focusing on faithfulness.

EXPLAIN

Look up these Scripture verses on faithfulness. Which passage gives you the best advice or inspiration to be faithful? Explain your answer below.

Matthew 8:23–26   Matthew 9:18–25   Revelation 2:9–10

_____

_____

_____

_____

_____

_____

_____

Fruits of the Holy Spirit

Faithfulness: Fidelity of God

Help the students examine some of God's faithful promises to us through nature.

- Begin by talking about how we can see God's faithfulness through creation. Talk about how the sun rises each morning and how the seasons turn each year.
- Ask the students for other examples in nature of how things return to a location over and over, such as migratory birds or salmon returning to spawn.
- Explain that God speaks to us of his faithfulness in many ways, and one of those ways is through his creation.

♥ A Prayer of Praise

Pray the Sign of the Cross together.

Reader 1: Today we honor Christ the King with these words from the Book of Revelation:

From Jesus Christ, the faithful witness, the firstborn of the dead and ruler of the kings of the earth.
To him who loves us and has freed us from our sins by his blood,
who has made us into a kingdom, priests for his God and Father,
to him be glory and power forever [and ever]. Amen.

All: To him be glory and power forever and ever. Amen.

Reader 2: Behold, he is coming amid the clouds,
and every eye will see him,
even those who pierced him.
All the peoples of the earth will lament him.
Yes. Amen.

All: To him be glory and power forever and ever. Amen.

Reader 3: "I am the Alpha and the Omega," says the Lord God,
"the one who is and who was and who is to come, the almighty."

All: To him be glory and power forever and ever. Amen.   **Revelation 1:5–8**

Leader: Let us now go forth to faithfully serve God.

All: God, grant us faithfulness. Amen.

▶ *Sing or play "Mighty King"*

A Prayer of Praise

♥ Choose three readers from the group and assign their roles. Allow time for the readers to become familiar with their parts.

Gather the students in the prayer space. Pray the Sign of the Cross together and signal to the first reader to begin.

Follow the order of prayer on the student page.

▶ Conclude by inviting the students to sing or reflect on the song "Mighty King," downloaded from **aliveinchrist.osv.com**.

Optional Activity

Ordinary Time Activity Master: Serving Others

Distribute copies of the activity found on teacher page 18B.

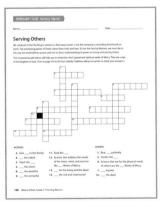

- The seasonal activity masters have been developed to help illustrate how we participate in the Paschal Mystery of Christ through the liturgical seasons.
- In this activity, the students will review the Corporal and Spiritual Works of Mercy.

LESSON OBJECTIVES

- Identify how Advent renews our faith and helps us anticipate the coming of Jesus
- Explain why developing a more intentional practice of patience is suited to the season of Advent
- Explore how to cultivate patience in specific situations

ENVIRONMENT

Prayer table
Purple cloth
Advent wreath
Candle
Bible or Lectionary

- Place the prayer table in a central location.
- Set the prayer table with the purple cloth, Advent wreath, candle, and Bible or Lectionary.
- Light the candle before beginning.
- Allow plenty of space around the prayer table for the students.

🛜 MUSIC OPTIONS

Go to **aliveinchrist.osv.com** to sample and download, "O Come O Come Emmanuel" "To You, O God"

🌐 CATHOLIC SOCIAL TEACHING

- **Option for the Poor and Vulnerable**, Pages 340–341
- **Solidarity of the Human Family**, Pages 344–345

Teacher Background

> 📖 Beware that your hearts do not become drowsy from … the anxieties of daily life… Be vigilant at all times and pray that you have the strength to escape the tribulations that are imminent and to stand before the Son of Man. **Luke 21:34, 36**
>
> **> Reflect** What are you doing to prepare for standing before the "Son of Man"?

A three-year old struggling to grasp the concept of time asked his mother, "Is tomorrow today?" Although he didn't realize it, he was describing the season of Advent. Do not wait to welcome Jesus into your heart and live his Word. Make room for God now.

During Advent, the Church asks us to take a good, hard look at how we are living now, precisely because Jesus is returning at any moment to take us with him and to experience the realization of God's Kingdom. During Advent we prepare our hearts and minds to learn from Jesus and to grow closer to him. The Gospels challenge us to examine our lives and discover what needs changing.

Time flies. Life is busy. Everything travels at high-speed—cable, phone networks, computers. Advent is the opportunity to move outside of our time into God's time to review our priorities. Whom and what do we need to make room for in our schedules? Is there "room at the inn" for the people in our lives who really need us right now? Is there room for prayer, for the Seven Sacraments, for reaching out in service?

The Lord who has already come once as our Messiah, is coming again at the end of time. During Advent we pray and prepare, and wait patiently for the Lord. Tomorrow is today.

> Reflect What can you do to make more time for God this Advent?

Teacher's Prayer

❤️ Lord, you who are beyond time, awaken me to your presence in every area of my life. May I share with my students your grace and light. Amen.

Name _____ Date _____

Preparing for Christmas

So much of the world's focus in preparing for Christmas is centered on gifts that are things. Living the Paschal Mystery in this season reminds us that we must die to the understanding that the gifts God has given us are only for our own benefit. We must rise to the understanding that the gifts God gives us, he gives to be shared with others.

**On each of the gift bags below write the name of one of the gifts that God has given you.
For instance, it may be your sense of humor or your athletic or musical ability.
On the lines under each bag, write who can benefit or be served by your gift.**

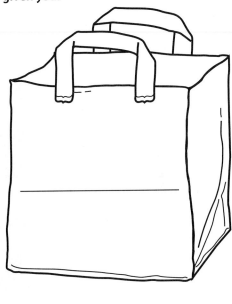

 Let Us Pray

Invite the students to gather in the prayer space and make the Sign of the Cross. Pray the Leader line. Have a few students read aloud the Psalm verse. Prompt the response from the rest of the class.

Music Option: Play or sing "To You, O God," downloaded from **aliveinchrist.osv.com**.

Have the students move out of the prayer space and back to their seats.

Say: Let's listen to God's Word and see how we must always be ready for the coming of Christ.

Scripture

Guide the students through the process of Scripture reflection (see the Scripture Background box below).

Have your ever thought...

Say: There will always be tribulations in this life. But God can bring clarity to a stressful or challenging situation.

- Invite the students to respond to the questions.

Being Ready

Let Us Pray

Leader: Lord Jesus, we want to see your face.

"O Shepherd of Israel, lend an ear ...
Seated upon the cherubim, shine forth. ...
Stir up your power, and come to save us." Psalm 80:2–3

We ask this in your name, O Lord.

All: Lord, rouse your power and come to save us. Amen.

Scripture

Beware that your hearts do not become drowsy from carousing and drunkenness and the anxieties of daily life, and that day catch you by surprise like a trap. For that day will assault everyone who lives on the face of the earth. Be vigilant at all times and pray that you have the strength to escape the tribulations that are imminent and to stand before the Son of Man.
Luke 21:34-36

Have you ever thought...
- What are the anxieties in your life?
- How does Advent prepare us to think about our own redemption?

22 The Church Year

Scripture Background

Scripture Reflection Process

Invite the students to be still, close their eyes, and focus on their breathing. Encourage them to open their minds and hearts to what God is saying to them.

- Proclaim the Scripture and have the students sit in silence.
- *Ask:* What did you hear God say to you today?
- Allow volunteers to share.

 You may play instrumental music to begin the reflection.

Art of a Jesse Tree, which symbolizes Jesus as the root of the tree of Jesse, the father of the biblical King David.

Awaiting Jesus

We often use the word "advent" to mean "the coming of" or "the onset," as in the phrase, "the advent of the internet age." But with a capital "A," the term can only mean one thing: the time when we anticipate the coming of Jesus.

Advent is the four weeks at the beginning of the liturgical year, leading up to the Christmas season. During Advent, the priest wears purple vestments at Mass, and churches are also decorated in purple to remind us to repent and remember that Christ is our King. We begin the Church year with hope and anticipation. We renew ourselves with the age-old story of God redeeming his People.

Throughout Advent, we gather with other Christians and listen to the prophets telling us to prepare for the coming of the Lord. We recall the story of the Incarnation, Jesus becoming man, and we hear the teachings of John the Baptist. We also pray before the Advent wreath and make small acts of sacrifice and penance, and celebrate the feast days of the Solemnity of the Immaculate Conception, Our Lady of Guadalupe, Saint Nicholas, and others.

These days, we are in a second Advent. We are waiting for Jesus to come again. He came once as our Messiah, our Savior, and he will come again at the end of the world. We must prepare our hearts and minds for that time when Jesus Christ comes again. In the meantime, we must have patience and wait.

> How can we anticipate the coming of Jesus now?

> What hopes do you have for the new liturgical year?

Advent **23**

Catholic Social Teaching

Lesson Connections

To integrate Catholic Social Teaching into your lesson, choose one of the following features: Option for the Poor and Vulnerable, pages 340–341; or Solidarity of the Human Family, pages 344–345.

- To expand the lesson, complete pages 23–24, then move to the Catholic Social Teaching feature.

- Return to the prayer on page 25.

Awaiting Jesus

Summarize the first two paragraphs of the text, being certain to define the season of Advent.

- Point out that Advent is a time of penitence and renewal for us personally and for the Church as a whole.

Invite a volunteer to read the third paragraph.

- Emphasize that the students are becoming more mature in their faith, and that they should understand that Advent has more than one purpose.

- Prompt the students to consider how the art in the photo on this page connects with the reading.

- *Ask:* Why are readings from the Old Testament prophets included in Mass during Advent? because they foretell of Christ's coming

Read aloud the last paragraph.

- Point out that we are again in a time of Advent, but we are not just waiting for December 25. We are preparing for Jesus' Second Coming.

- *Ask:* What is the purpose of celebrating Advent? to prepare our hearts and minds for Jesus' Second Coming

Modeling Patience

Summarize the first paragraph.

- Point out that everyone— especially parents—can sometimes feel rushed and confused during this season.
- *Ask:* What are some things that can keep us from concentrating on Jesus during Advent?

Create a definition of *patience* with the class. Write the students' suggestions on the board or on chart paper. Compare this definition to the definition of *patience* in the second paragraph.

- Highlight the concept that patience will help us focus on what is important during Advent.
- *Ask:* What is the most important thing to do during Advent? to prepare and make space for Christ in our lives

Invite a student to read aloud the third paragraph.

- Reinforce the link between our waiting and the Jewish people's wait for the Messiah.
- Emphasize that their patience can be our model for perseverance.

ACTIVITY

Suggest that the students work in small groups to brainstorm how we can be more patient as we wait for something and for someone.

- Allow time for groups to complete the activity. Invite them to share their ideas with the class.

Modeling Patience

Advent can be a very trying time. Too many things wrestle for our attention: tests at school, presents to buy or make, Christmas plays and concerts to prepare for and attend, caroling parties and tree decorating.

One Fruit of the Holy Spirit that will sustain us through this season is **patience**. Patience provides steadfastness in the face of difficulties because we trust God is with us and will somehow make things good and right. Patience helps us keep our focus on what is important rather than on distractions. The focus of Advent is preparing ourselves for Christ, making space for him in our lives.

We need to model ourselves after the Jewish people, who waited thousands of years for the Messiah. What sustained them in the storm of wandering and persecutions was trusting that the Messiah would come, that the prophecies would be fulfilled. They prepared the way for the Lord. During Advent we hear the words of the prophets calling us to be active in our anticipation, to prepare, through our words and deeds, as we wait.

Fruits of the Holy Spirit

The twelve **Fruits of the Holy Spirit** are qualities that can be seen in us when we let the Holy Spirit work in our hearts. This season we are focusing on patience.

CONSIDER

There's a difference between waiting for something and waiting for someone. Name one situation in each category and describe what our impatience might look like and how we might become more patient.

_____

_____

_____

_____

_____

_____

_____

_____

_____

24 The Church Year

Fruits of the Holy Spirit

Patience Isn't Easy!

Patience is one of the Gifts of the Holy Spirit that is challenging because in order to learn it, we have to be in situations that try our patience.

- Give each student about twenty playing cards.
- Ask them to try to build a two-story house with the cards.
- Discuss how sometimes things can be easy and other times we must exercise patience and keep trying before we succeed.

If someone has an easy time with a two-story creation, challenge them to try for three or more. A little frustration is the goal here!

A Waiting Prayer

Pray the Sign of the Cross together.

Leader: Make known to me your ways, LORD;
 teach me your paths.

Guide me by your fidelity and teach me,
 for you are God my savior,
 for you I wait all the day long.

All: To you, O Lord, I lift my soul.

Leader: Good and upright is the LORD;
 therefore he shows sinners the way.

He guides the humble in righteousness,
 and teaches the humble his way.

All: To you, O Lord, I lift my soul.

Leader: All the paths of the LORD are mercy
and truth
 toward those who honor his covenant and
 his decrees.

The counsel of the LORD belongs to those
who fear him;
 and his covenant instructs them.

All: To you, O Lord, I lift my soul.
Psalm 25:4–5, 8–9, 10, 14

Leader: Let us go forth with patience to
celebrate Advent.

All: We ask this through Jesus Christ. Amen.

▶ *Sing or play "O Come O Come Emmanuel"*

Advent **25**

A Waiting Prayer

♥ Appoint a leader and give this student time to become familiar with his or her part of the prayer.

Have all of the students move into the prayer space.

Signal the leader to begin. Then follow the order of prayer on the student page.

▶ Play or sing with the students the song "O Come O Come Emmanuel," downloaded from **aliveinchrist.osv.com**.

Close with a moment of silence.

Alternate Music Option:
"To You, O God"

Advent Activity Master: Preparing for Christmas

Distribute copies of the activity found on teacher page 22B.

- The seasonal activity masters have been developed to help illustrate how we participate in the Paschal Mystery of Christ through the liturgical seasons.
- This activity will help the students explore how we can use our gifts for the good of others.

LESSON OBJECTIVES

- Explore how the Incarnation transformed our existence
- Identify how God models the fullness of generosity in the gift of his Son, Jesus, to us
- List ways of cultivating and practicing generosity

ENVIRONMENT

Prayer table
White and/or gold cloth
Nativity scene
Candle
Bible or Lectionary

- Place the prayer table in a central location.
- Set the prayer table with the white or gold cloth, Nativity scene, candle, and Bible or Lectionary.
- Light the candle before beginning.
- Allow plenty of space around the prayer table for the students.

🎧 MUSIC OPTION

Go to **aliveinchrist.osv.com** to sample and download, "O Come All Ye Faithful"

🌐 CATHOLIC SOCIAL TEACHING

- **Life and Dignity of the Human Person** Pages 334–335
- **Call to Family, Community, and Participation** Pages 336–337

Teacher Background

📖 [The shepherds] made known the message that had been told them about this child. … And Mary kept all these things, reflecting on them in her heart. Then the shepherds returned, glorifying and praising God for all they had heard and seen, just as it had been told to them.   Luke 2:17, 19–20

> **Reflect** What are some of the daily distractions that you must look past to hear God?

The Gospels according to Matthew and Luke begin with stories of Jesus' birth and the events surrounding it. These accounts are referred to as the Infancy Narratives. They tell us that Jesus, like all human beings, was born of a woman after having been carried in her womb. These narratives, by paying attention to Jesus' birth, give special emphasis to the fact that he participated in the human condition. The Infancy Narratives tell us that Jesus was not simply a human being. He was fully man, but also fully God. The Gospels announce Jesus' unique identity. They tell of Jesus' conception through the power of the Holy Spirit. Both accounts show Jesus' unique relationship with God the Father and God the Holy Spirit.

What had begun nine months earlier in the womb of Mary came to be— the birth of Jesus, Emmanuel, Savior … a person like us in all things—all things, except sin. What a wondrous feast it is, the Feast of Christmas. God, fully present, fully human, takes up residence with us!

> **Reflect** What are some of the ordinary (and extraordinary) ways God's presence has been revealed to you?

Teacher's Prayer

💙 Jesus Christ, you are the Light of the World. Help me to know you as Savior and Lord. Let your glory fill the whole world. Rule all nations with mercy and justice. Fill my heart with joy. Help me bring your joy to this class. Jesus Christ, you are the Light of the world. Bring me your peace. Amen.

Name _____ Date _____

Season of Love

Many people look forward to the Christmas season because it is a season of love. Families and friends make efforts to celebrate the love that connects them. As disciples, we are being called to die to the thinking that our love for each other is not connected to God's love, and rise to knowing with certainty that *all* love begins in God. We receive God's love and share it with others.

Create titles for three new Christmas carols that might help people understand that their love for each other begins in the heart of God.

Let Us Pray

Invite the students to gather in the prayer space and make the Sign of the Cross. Pray the prayer, including the Psalm verse. Prompt the group's response.

Have the students move out of the prayer space and back to their seats.

Say: Let's listen to God's Word and hear how the shepherds came to find Jesus.

Scripture

Guide the students through the process of Scripture reflection (see the Scripture Background box below).

Have your ever thought...

Say: The coming of Jesus Christ, known as the Incarnation, is God's greatest gift to us.

- Invite the students to respond to the questions.

Our Gift

Let Us Pray

Leader: Lord Jesus, Let it be said of us, your people,

"Let the heavens be glad and the earth rejoice ...
before the LORD who comes,
who comes to govern the earth.
To govern the world with justice
and the peoples with his faithfulness." **Psalm 96:13**

All: Let us exult before the Lord. Amen.

Scripture

When the angels went away from them to heaven, the shepherds said to one another, "Let us go, then, to Bethlehem to see this thing that has taken place, which the Lord has made known to us." So they went in haste and found Mary and Joseph, and the infant lying in the manger. When they saw this, they made known the message that had been told them about this child.

All who heard it were amazed by what had been told them by the shepherds. And Mary kept all these things, reflecting on them in her heart. Then the shepherds returned, glorifying and praising God for all they had heard and seen, just as it had been told to them.   **Luke 2:15–20**

Have you ever thought...
- Why did Jesus come to Earth?
- How can God the Father be so generous that he offered us his Son?

Scripture Background

Scripture Reflection Process

Invite the students to be still, close their eyes, and focus on their breathing. Encourage them to open their minds and hearts to what God is saying to them.

- Proclaim the Scripture and have the students sit in silence.
- *Ask:* What did you hear God say to you today?
- Allow volunteers to share.

 You may play instrumental music to begin the reflection.

God With Us

Christmas—the word carries many images: gifts, decorations, music, and favorite foods. While these are all part of the celebration of Christmas, it is easy to lose sight of the heart of this season, which we celebrate from the Christmas Eve Vigil until the Feast of the Baptism of the Lord. Christmas is the day Christians all over the world remember and give thanks for God's greatest gift—the gift of his Son. At Christmas we celebrate the Incarnation, the sacred mystery of God becoming man, Jesus. Jesus Christ, the Second Divine Person of the Holy Trinity, chose to enter our world as a human being. "For God so loved the world," Saint John says, "that he gave his only Son" (John 3:16). Jesus, God made man, entered our human existence to save us from sin and death. That is the miracle of Christmas. That is why we celebrate with customs and traditions that remind us of this incredible gift.

It is a challenge to keep focused on the meaning of Christmas in the midst of so many distractions. You must make a choice to take the time to sift through all those distractions. You can do that by making time to pray and to read from Scripture. Allowing yourself the time and quiet to hear God's voice will help you to appreciate more deeply God's love and generosity. Jesus is the Father's gift to the world. He is the Father's gift to you. Open your heart to receive what God is offering you.

> **What can you do during the Christmas season to more clearly hear God's voice?**

> **What does it mean to you to say that while God offers us the gift of salvation, we must choose to receive it?**

Christmas **27**

![globe icon]

Catholic Social Teaching

Lesson Connections

To integrate Catholic Social Teaching into your lesson, choose one of the following features: Life and Dignity of the Human Person, pages 334–335; or Call to Family, Community, and Participation, pages 336–337.

- To expand the lesson, complete pages 27–28, then move to the Catholic Social Teaching feature.
- Return to the prayer on page 29.

God with Us

Invite the students to share images that they associate with Christmas.

Summarize the first paragraph of the text as you point out that many non-religious activities are associated with this holiday.

- *Ask:* What is the true message of the Christmas season? giving thanks to God for his greatest gift to us, Jesus

Read aloud the second paragraph.

- Emphasize the tranquil nature of Christmas, and help the students see that they can get to a peaceful place if they try hard enough.
- Invite the students to discuss how the image on this page connects to the idea of keeping the right focus during this season.
- *Ask:* In what ways do we allow ourselves to be distracted by what is unnecessary this time of year?

Invite the students to silently read the reflection questions.

- Allow time for them to consider their answers to the questions and then write their answers in paragraph form on a separate piece of paper.
- Encourage the students to reread their answers occasionally to help them keep their focus on the true meaning of the season.

True Generosity

Read aloud the text in the Fruits of the Holy Spirit box. Then ask a volunteer to read the first paragraph.

- Tell the students to think about the best present that they ever received.

- Invite them to share their thoughts on why it was such a wonderful gift.

- *Ask:* Does a present have to be expensive to be precious? Why or why not?

Discuss the generosity of God in sending Jesus, his Son, to save us, as well as Mary's own generosity and openness in saying "yes" to God's plan.

- *Ask:* How does a person feel when he or she gives generously?

Read aloud the last paragraph.

- Emphasize that the best presents will help the giver and the receiver know God better. The best presents are based on God's generosity to us at Christmas.

Have the students work individually to consider small acts of generosity they can perform in certain situations.

- Encourage them to be on the lookout for small acts of generosity that they can implement during this season and through the year.

True Generosity

During the Christmas season, we can't help but think of gifts. We are preoccupied with what others might want, and we are constantly quizzed about what we want. We sometimes fail to see that we have already received the greatest gift of all: God's Son.

As we celebrate Christmas, God is our model for generosity. He gave us his only Son as a tiny, dependent baby. **Generosity** is one of the Fruits of the Holy Spirit. We live generously when we share our gifts (talents), time, and possessions with others out of gratitude for God.

Mary is a model of generosity, too, in the way that she shared Jesus with others. She welcomed the shepherds and the Magi. She took Jesus to the Temple, to see Simeon and Anna.

We tend to give temporary pleasures, such as clothes and electronics, as gifts. To be truly generous, we need to give of ourselves, to find a way to share Christmas peace and joy with others. Then we will be more like God and Mary, our models of generosity.

Fruits of the Holy Spirit

The twelve Fruits of the Holy Spirit are qualities that can be seen in us when we let the Holy Spirit work in our hearts. This season we are focusing on generosity.

LIST AND IDENTIFY

Name small acts of generosity that you can take in each of these situations.

For an extended family member who might be lonely: _____
_____

For a family who is homeless: _____
_____

For a classmate who seems unhappy: _____
_____

For a single parent of one of your friends: _____
_____

For a teacher who is facing his or her first holiday without a loved one: _____
_____

28 The Church Year

Fruits of the Holy Spirit

Generosity: You Can "Bank" on It

We sometimes think of almsgiving as something we do only during Lent, but by starting an alms jar now, when Lent comes, the students will have some money available to perform acts of charity.

- Discuss the value of being generous. Invite the students to begin saving money in a special "alms" jar, but don't make this mandatory.

- Talk about what it means to tithe, and how the people of Jesus' time would bring the best of their flocks or crops to honor God.

- Set a goal for the class for something they would like to use the money to purchase (e.g., art supplies for a family mission), and keep track of how close you are from week to week.

An Adoration Prayer

Pray the Sign of the Cross together.

Leader: The people who walked in darkness
   have seen a great light;
Upon those who dwelt in the land of gloom
   a light has shone.

All: You have brought them abundant joy
   and great rejoicing;
They rejoice before you as people rejoice
at harvest, as they exult when dividing the
spoils.

Leader: For a child is born to us,
a son is given us;
   upon his shoulder dominion rests.

They name him Wonder-Counselor,
God-Hero,
   Father-Forever, Prince of Peace.

All: His dominion is vast
   and forever peaceful,
Upon David's throne, and over his kingdom,
   which he confirms and sustains
By judgment and justice,
   both now and forever.
The zeal of the LORD of hosts
will do this!   *Isaiah 9:1-6*

Leader: Glory to God in the highest,
and on earth peace to people of good will.

All: We praise you,
we bless you,
we adore you,
we glorify you,
we give you thanks for your great glory,
Lord God, heavenly King,
O God, almighty Father.

Lord Jesus Christ, Only Begotten Son,
Lord God, Lamb of God, Son of the Father,
you take away the sins of the world,
   have mercy on us;

you take away the sings of the world,
   receive our prayer;

you are seated at the right hand of the Father,
   have mercy on us.

For you alone are the Holy one,
you alone are the Most High,
Jesus Christ,
with the Holy Spirit,
in the glory of God the Father.
Amen.

Leader: Go forth and live generously to
honor Christ, our newborn King.

All: We thank God for this gift. Amen.

Sing or play "O Come All Ye Faithful"

An Adoration Prayer

Appoint a student leader. Allow time for the leader to become familiar with his or her part.

Gather the students around the prayer table.

Signal the leader to begin. Then follow the order of prayer on the student page.

Conclude by inviting the students to sing or reflect on the song "O Come All Ye Faithful," downloaded from **aliveinchrist.osv.com**.

Optional Activity

Christmas Activity Master: Season of Love

Distribute copies of the activity found on teacher page 26B.

- The seasonal activity masters have been developed to help illustrate how we participate in the Paschal Mystery of Christ through the liturgical seasons.

- This activity will help the students recognize that all love begins in God.

LESSON OBJECTIVES

- Discuss how Mary's willingness to be Jesus' mother served all of humanity
- Explain how Mary is a model of goodness
- Relate goodness to a life of discipleship

ENVIRONMENT

Prayer table
Purple cloth
Marian statue
Candle
Bible or Lectionary

- Place the prayer table in a central location.
- Set the prayer table with the purple cloth, a Marian statue, candle, and Bible or Lectionary.
- Light the candle before beginning.
- Allow plenty of space around the prayer table for the students.

 **MUSIC OPTION**

Go to **aliveinchrist.osv.com** to sample and download, "O Sanctissima"

CATHOLIC SOCIAL TEACHING

- **Call to Family, Community, and Participation**
  Pages 336–337
- **Care for God's Creation**
  Pages 346–347

Teacher Background

[Gabriel] said, "Hail, favored one! The Lord is with you. … Do not be afraid, Mary, for you have found favor with God. Behold, you will conceive in your womb and bear a son, and you shall name him Jesus. He will be great and will be called Son of the Most High … and of his kingdom there will be no end." Luke 1:28, 30–33

> **Reflect** What can you learn from Mary's response to God's plan?

Catholics regard Mary, the Mother of Jesus, as the perfect disciple, and the first Saint. Mary is venerated as a preeminent member of the Church because the work of redemption has been fully realized in both her body and soul. When she pronounced her fiat, her wholehearted "yes" at the Annunciation, "Mary was already collaborating with the whole work her Son was to accomplish…" (CCC, 973). Mary's is an exceptional faith; she made an unwavering, steadfast commitment to Jesus' mission. She endured the struggle that characterizes all human life, but her response and cooperation with the work of the Holy Spirit is a model of faith for us all. As the perfect disciple, Mary always points other disciples to her Son.

What a profound message the Angel Gabriel brought to Mary: "You," the angel told her, "are full of God's grace." In her response to the news that she was to become the Mother of God, Mary embodies what it means to be a disciple in the fullest, most complete sense of the word. Her response of "May it be done to me" (Luke 1:38), indicates a complete and obedient faithfulness to God, a faithfulness powered by the presence of God's Spirit. On the Feast of the Annunciation, we celebrate that "nothing will be impossible for God" (Luke 1:37).

> **Reflect** In what area of your life do you need to trust in and apply the phrase "nothing will be impossible for God"?

Teacher's Prayer

Holy Mary, Mother of God, blessed are you! May I follow your example of total awareness of God's presence and complete trust in his goodness. Pray that I live God's Word as you did. Amen.

Name _____ Date _____

Choosing to Do What's Right

Saying "yes" to following the will of God means saying "no" to the things that are not part of his plan. In other words, we must die to the temptation to look for an easy way out or ways to get out of doing the hard work of being a disciple and rise to putting in the effort it takes to share the Good News with others.

In the notes page on the first phone, write three situations in which someone your age might be tempted to "bend" a little because doing the right thing might be hard. (Example: Copying homework—because you don't "get" the material and it's not like it's a test.) In the text message boxes on the second phone, write two texts you could send to yourself to help you remember to do what is right.

 Let Us Pray

Invite the students to gather in the prayer space and make the Sign of the Cross. Read aloud the Psalm verse. Prompt the group's response.

Have the students move out of the prayer space and back to their seats.

Say: Let's listen to God's Word and remember how God chose Mary to be the Mother of the Son of God.

Scripture

Guide the students through the process of Scripture reflection (see the Scripture Background box below).

Have your ever thought...

Say: Mary's "yes" is an example of how we should be open to the will of God in our own lives.

- Invite the students to respond to the questions.

The Annunciation

 Let Us Pray

Leader: Lord God, Help us be like Mary. Help us say, as she did,

"I delight to do your will, my God;
your law is in my inner being!"   **Psalm 40:9**

All: May we come to do your will, just as Mary did. Amen.

Scripture

The angel Gabriel was sent from God to Nazareth, to a virgin named Mary. And coming to her, he said, "Hail, favored one! The Lord is with you." But she was greatly troubled at what was said and pondered what sort of greeting this might be. Then the angel said to her, "Do not be afraid, Mary, for you have found favor with God. Behold, you will conceive in your womb and bear a son, and you shall name him Jesus. He will be great and will be called Son of the Most High … and of his kingdom there will be no end." But Mary said to the angel, "How can this be, since I have no relations with a man?" And the angel said to her in reply, "The holy Spirit will come upon you, and the power of the Most High will overshadow you. Therefore the child to be born will be called holy, the Son of God." … Mary said, "Behold, I am the handmaid of the Lord. May it be done to me according to your word."   **Luke 1:26–35, 38**

Have you ever thought...

- How does someone become open to doing God's will?

- Can I be like Mary?

30

Scripture Background

Scripture Reflection Process

Invite the students to be still, close their eyes, and focus on their breathing. Encourage them to open their minds and hearts to what God is saying to them.

- Proclaim the Scripture and have the students sit in silence.

- *Ask:* What did you hear God say to you today?

- Allow volunteers to share.

  ▶ You may play instrumental music to begin the reflection.

Mary as Jesus' Mother

The season of Lent includes the Feast day on which the Church remembers Mary's "yes" to God's plan for her life. This day is known as the Feast of the Annunciation, and occurs on March 25. The feast is timed so that nine months elapse between it and Jesus' birth on December 25. On this feast day, and others devoted to Mary, the priest wears white vestments.

In the moment when Mary agreed to be Jesus' mother, everything changed. With her words and through the power of the Holy Spirit, Jesus became man. God became one of us, taking on human form while still maintaining his divinity. The world went from being in Old Testament times into the the time of the new covenant, the era of God with us. In a way that had never been before, God came for all people.

In this moment, Mary responded faithfully despite the many emotions that must have been going through her mind and heart. She was troubled by the Angel Gabriel's greeting, and she expressed confusion over how God's will would be done. Despite this, she didn't falter in her agreement.

The Church honors Mary above all other Saints because her "yes" set the example for all Christian believers. She was willing to serve God by bringing Jesus into the world. Her deed of goodness served all humanity.

> How did Mary's "yes" change the world?
> Why is Mary a model for us?

Mary with the infant Jesus

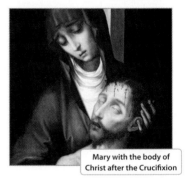
Mary with Jesus at the Wedding at Cana

Mary with the body of Christ after the Crucifixion

Lent **31**

Catholic Social Teaching

Lesson Connections

To integrate Catholic Social Teaching into your lesson, choose one of the following features: Call to Family, Community, and Participation, pages 336–337; or Care for God's Creation, pages 346–347.

- To expand the lesson, complete pages 31–32, then move to the Catholic Social Teaching feature.
- Return to the prayer on page 33.

Mary as Jesus' Mother

Summarize the content of the first paragraph. Note that when the Feast of the Annunciation falls during Holy Week, it is celebrated after Easter.

Invite a volunteer to read the second paragraph.

- Discuss with the students how Mary must have felt when Gabriel approached her with God's news.
- *Ask:* What does it mean when we say that the world went from being in Old Testament times into the new covenant era? We enter into a closer, more personal relationship with God through Jesus.

Select another student to read the last paragraph.

- Elaborate on the text by pointing out that tradition tells us that Mary's parents dedicated her to God at an early age.
- *Ask:* How would growing up in a Jewish household have prepared Mary for her role as Jesus' Mother? It helped her become familiar with the teachings of the Jewish religion and the promise of a Messiah.
- Call attention to the beautiful art depicting some of Mary's many relationships with Jesus.

Invite the students to read the reflection questions to themselves. Allow time for them to think about Mary's dedication to God's plan.

- Ask the students to share their insights about Mary.

The Annunciation **31**

Mary's Goodness

Select a student to read the first paragraph.

- Encourage the class to think about Mary's willingness to be the Mother of God.
- *Ask:* How did Mary show her goodness? by her willingness to participate in God's plan
- Invite the students to share their thoughts.

Summarize the content of the second paragraph.

- Reinforce the definition of goodness as showing love and honor to God. Because God is our creator and is good, we are good. Goodness is desiring and doing what is best for another person.

Read aloud the third paragraph.

- Emphasize that Mary is a model of goodness for us all.
- *Ask:* How can goodness change the world? Our actions can be signs that point others toward the Messiah.

Make Bibles available for student use. Allow the students to work in pairs to complete the exercise.

- Invite the pairs to share their insights into the Scripture passages.

For your own use, here are the Bible references with brief reminders about their content: Luke 1:39–56, Visitation; Luke 2:21–35, Presentation in the Temple; Luke 2:41–52, Finding Jesus in the Temple; John 2:1–11, Wedding at Cana.

Mary's Goodness

Mary's willingness to participate in God's plan showed her goodness. She could have refused, because, as he did for all of us, God gave her the gift of free will. She could have chosen an easier life than that of being the Messiah's mother, with the sorrows and cares that would come with it. She chose, however, to be part of our redemption, and that shows goodness on her part.

Goodness is one of the Fruits of the Holy Spirit. It is one of the qualities that show that the Holy Spirit is working in our hearts. Because God is our creator and is good, we are good. Goodness is showing love and honor to God. It is desiring and doing what is best for another person. When Mary agreed to be Jesus' mother, she knew that she was doing something good. She knew it would bring her troubles and sorrows, yet she still agreed.

We are invited to be models of goodness for others, just as Mary was a model of goodness. We can choose to do the right thing, even when making that choice leads to difficulties for us. Our actions can be signs that point others toward the Messiah.

© Our Sunday Visitor

Fruits of the Holy Spirit

The twelve Fruits of the Holy Spirit are qualities that can be seen in us when we let the Holy Spirit work in our hearts. This season we are focusing on goodness.

SUMMARIZE

Work with a classmate to look up these Scripture accounts of Mary and summarize each passage to each other. Then choose one account and explain how it shows Mary's goodness.

Luke 1:39–56   Luke 2:21–35   Luke 2:41–52   John 2:1–11

_____

_____

_____

_____

_____

_____

Fruits of the Holy Spirit

The Goodness of God

Provide the students with a list of Scripture verses about God's goodness. Psalm 25:8, Nahum 1:7, Isaiah 51:6, Psalm 31:19, and Psalm 27:13 are good places to start.

- Ask them to read the Scriptures and choose their favorite four verses.
- Give each student a piece of construction paper and direct them to draw a full-length image of themselves, writing one verse on each of their hands and feet.

Remind the students that we are God's "hands and feet" and that we are called on to be the goodness in the world that we want to see.

A Marian Prayer

Pray the Sign of the Cross together.

Leader: A reading from the Book of Isaiah.

"The Lord himself will give you a sign: the young woman, pregnant and about to bear a son, shall name him Emmanuel."
Isaiah 7:14

The word of the Lord.

All: Thanks be to God.

Leader: To celebrate the Annunciation, the feast that commemorates Mary's agreement to be Jesus' mother, we pray for her to show her goodness by helping us.

All: Mary, please help us grow in goodness.

Leader: Let us end our celebration of the Annunciation by reciting the prayer inspired by this feast.

All: Hail, Mary, full of grace,
the Lord is with thee.
Blessed art thou among women
and blessed is the fruit of thy womb, Jesus.
Holy Mary, Mother of God,
pray for us sinners,
now and at the hour of our death.
Amen.

Leader: Go forth and show your goodness, just as Mary did.

All: Amen.

Sing or play "O Sanctissima"

A Marian Prayer

Select a leader from the class. Allow time for this student to become familiar with his or her part of the prayer.

Point out that the prayer service includes the Hail Mary. Discuss with the students why this is an appropriate prayer for an Annunciation celebration.

Invite the students into the prayer space and signal the leader to begin.

Follow the order of prayer on the student page.

Conclude by inviting the students to sing or reflect on the song "O Sanctissima," downloaded from **aliveinchrist.osv.com**.

Optional Activity

Lent Activity Master: Choosing to Do What's Right

Distribute copies of the activity found on teacher page 30B.

- The seasonal activity masters have been developed to help illustrate how we participate in the Paschal Mystery of Christ through the liturgical seasons.

- This activity will help the students understand that being a disciple is not always easy.

LESSON OBJECTIVES

- Identify ways to resist temptation
- Recognize Jesus as the perfect model of self-control
- Describe ways to acquire self-control

ENVIRONMENT

Prayer table
Purple cloth
Crucifix
Candle
Bible or Lectionary

- Place the prayer table in a central location.
- Set the prayer table with the purple cloth, crucifix, candle, and Bible or Lectionary.
- Light the candle before beginning.
- Allow plenty of space around the prayer table for the students.

🛜 MUSIC OPTION

Go to **aliveinchrist.osv.com** to sample and download, "Create in Me"

🌐 CATHOLIC SOCIAL TEACHING

- **Rights and Responsibilities of the Human Person** Pages 338–339
- **Option for the Poor and Vulnerable** Pages 340–341

Teacher Background

> ✝ Jesus said to him, "Get away, Satan! It is written: 'The Lord, your God, shall you worship and him alone shall you serve.'" Then the devil left him and, behold, angels came and ministered to him. Matthew 4:10–11
>
> > **Reflect** Where do you find the strength to resist worldly temptations?

After being tempted by the devil, Jesus came out of the desert and began his ministry in Galilee. As we read further in the Gospel according to Luke, we learn that the call of the disciples was among the first actions of Jesus' ministry. What did he require of these men? A conversion of heart, a turning away from whatever temptations they faced that kept them from hearing the call of God was necessary to be a true disciple.

Each of us is called to be a disciple, but the temptations that tug at us can keep us from hearing God's call. During Lent, the Church graces us with the opportunity to take a look at and resist those things that keep us from growing in God's ways. When we resist the temptation to be unfaithful to family and friends, we become more faithful. When we are tempted to participate in a culture that often ridicules lives of virtue, we are called to be virtuous and resist this temptation. When we keep from abandoning time for prayer due to the many distractions and false idols around us, God's presence is strengthened in our daily lives.

Discipleship calls us to turn away from the temptation to think first of our own needs. Instead, it calls us to participate in Works of Mercy and justice for others. Lent is a time to turn back to God and to rediscover the discipleship to which we are called.

> **Reflect** What is the particular discipleship challenge that Jesus is asking of you this Lenten season?

Teacher's Prayer

💗 Jesus, help me to trust in your mercy and love. Teach me, lead me, so that I am worthy to share your Good News with others. Amen.

Name _____   Date _____

A Person for Others

When we see a small child in a store throwing a temper tantrum because the child is not getting what he or she wants, we understand that part of being a child is thinking that "it's all about me."

Lent is the season that helps us to remember that we must die to that kind of thinking so that we can rise to becoming a person who cares for others. Think of it like a walnut. The hard shell on the outside has to be crushed in order to get to the nut, or good stuff, inside. Scripture says it this way:

"From their bodies I will remove the hearts of stone, and give them hearts of flesh…"
—Ezekiel 11:19

On the shells of the nuts below, write some of the "it's all about me" thinking that has to diminish in you. For example, you might write "My brother should give me the video game right now" or "I don't care how much it costs, everyone else has one." During Lent, become aware of all the ways you act like the child in the store and ask God to help you as you begin to concern yourself more with the needs of others.

 Let Us Pray

Choose one of the students to be the Leader. Invite the class to gather in the prayer space and make the Sign of the Cross. Ask the Leader to proclaim the opening prayer and Psalm verse, and lead the class in the response.

Have the students move out of the prayer space and back to their seats.

Say: Let's listen to God's Word and learn how Jesus overcame many temptations.

📖 Scripture

Guide the students through the process of Scripture reflection (see the Scripture Background box below).

Have your ever thought...

Say: While temptation is all around us, by opening ourselves to God's grace we can resist temptation and do God's will.

- Invite the students to respond to the questions.

Conquering Temptation

💙 Let Us Pray

Leader: We gather to ask for God's help in avoiding sin, for

"Truly, I love your commandments
more than gold, more than the finest gold.
Thus, I follow all your precepts;
every wrong way I hate." Psalm 119:127–128

All: We ask for God's guidance. Amen.

📖 Scripture

Then Jesus was led by the Spirit into the desert to be tempted by the devil. ... the devil took him to the holy city, and made him stand on the parapet of the temple, and said to him, "If you are the Son of God, throw yourself down. For it is written:

"'He will command his angels concerning you'
and 'with their hands they will support you,
lest you dash your foot against a stone.'"

Jesus answered him, "Again it is written, 'You shall not put the Lord, your God, to the test.'"

Then the devil took him up to a very high mountain, and showed him all the kingdoms of the world in their magnificence, and he said to him, "All these I shall give to you, if you will prostrate yourself and worship me."

At this, Jesus said to him, "Get away, Satan! It is written:

'The Lord, your God, shall you worship
and him alone shall you serve.'"

Then the devil left him and, behold, angels came and ministered to him.   Matthew 4:1–11

Have you ever thought...
- What makes human beings so open to temptations?
- How do people overcome temptation?

34

© Our Sunday Visitor

📖 Scripture Background

Scripture Reflection Process

Invite the students to be still, close their eyes, and focus on their breathing. Encourage them to open their minds and hearts to what God is saying to them.

- Proclaim the Scripture and have the students sit in silence.
- *Ask:* What did you hear God say to you today?
- Allow volunteers to share.

 You may play instrumental music to begin the reflection.

Becoming Strong

Lent is forty days of work. For Catholics who live in the Northern hemisphere, it begins in winter, with long nights yielding a few more precious minutes of light to each successive day as spring approaches. With the added sun comes the warmth that wakens the dormant earth, stirring plants to flower and reveal God's glory as Easter arrives.

We are like the natural world: we have lots of growing to do between winter's barrenness and Easter's brightness. We have to examine ourselves to determine what keeps us from growing in God's ways. Once we recognize those things, we must find ways to help us die to sin in order that we would grow in grace. Often, the problem is temptation. This can come from within us, as envy or false pride. It can come from outside of us, from a world that holds up consumerism and selfishness as the good. Much of Lent focuses on growing the virtues that will help us fight temptation. As we grow closer to God, everything else falls into the right order.

Lenten practices such as fasting, doing works of penance, and almsgiving to people who are poor or who are in need help us remember Jesus' sacrifice and build our strength, too.

Prayer is also a vital practice during Lent. During the season we pray for faith to appreciate the gift of life, for the generosity of spirit that will help us give to others, and for hope to conquer obstacles in our lives. We also pray on behalf of others, asking Jesus to give them strength. We pray especially for those preparing for Baptism and joining the Catholic Church.

> What kind of growth do you want to achieve this Lent?

> Which temptations do you find especially difficult to overcome?

Lent **35**

Catholic Social Teaching

Lesson Connections

To integrate Catholic Social Teaching into your lesson, choose one of the following features: Rights and Responsibilities of the Human Person, pages 338–339; or Option for the Poor and Vulnerable, pages 340–341.

- To expand the lesson, complete pages 35–36, then move to the Catholic Social Teaching feature.
- Return to the prayer on page 37.

Becoming Strong

Summarize the first paragraph of the text.

- Point out that Lent spans over seven weeks of the year, beginning on Ash Wednesday and lasting for forty days.

Invite a volunteer to read the second paragraph.

- Talk with the students about what sorts of things keep them from growing spiritually.
- *Ask:* How can you measure your growth in holiness?
- Ask for examples of temptations that originate inside of a person as well as those that begin from the outside.

Read aloud the third paragraph.

- *Ask:* What are three Lenten practices? fasting, doing works of penance, almsgiving

Summarize the information in the fourth paragraph.

- *Ask:* How can you open yourself to God's grace in ways that will help you overcome temptation?

Invite the students to read the reflection questions to themselves.

- Allow time for the students to think about ways that they want to grow in holiness during Lent.

Focusing on Self-Control

Summarize Lenten practices and activities that might help the students overcome temptation.

- Invite them to share their ideas of ways to counter temptation.

Read aloud the second paragraph.

- Define *self-control* as striving to overcome temptation and do God's will. When we cooperate with God's grace to focus on his will for us, then we are more easily able to resist those things that keep us from helping to build his Kingdom.

- *Ask:* What examples of self-control have you seen in Saints or others you admire?

Invite a volunteer to read the third paragraph.

- Emphasize that Jesus' response to temptation is a model for us.

- *Ask:* How can you encourage others to develop self-control?

ACTIVITY

Have the students identify problem areas regarding temptations for people their age. Then have them identify ways that faith can help people overcome that temptation.

- *Say:* Jesus comes to you where you are and invites you to hand these temptations to him. He will, in turn, hand you something—the strength to face temptations. With Jesus' help you can resist those temptations that cause you harm.

Focusing on Self-Control

Lent provides us with many opportunities to counter temptation. The readings at Mass ask God to help us, because we are all sinners. Many parishes schedule additional times for us to take part in the Sacrament of Penance and Reconciliation, the Sacrament that helps us receive God's forgiveness and grace after we have examined our consciences and become aware of sin.

On a personal level, many people give up favorite things until Easter. Others try to change a bad habit into a good one. With these simple practices, they are developing **self-control**, one of the Fruits of the Holy Spirit. Self-control is about striving to overcome temptation and do God's will. It is cooperating with God's grace to focus on what's important and resist the things that keep us from becoming the people he wants us to be.

The Gospel reading at the beginning of this lesson shows how Jesus handled temptation with self-control. His responses to the devil's tempting words focus on living out God's instructions to us. Jesus showed us how to be in the world, yet keep the things of this world in proper order and not be deceived or distracted by the power of evil.

© Our Sunday Visitor

Fruits of the Holy Spirit

The twelve Fruits of the Holy Spirit are qualities that can be seen in us when we let the Holy Spirit work in our hearts. This season we are focusing on self-control.

IDENTIFY AND PLAN

In the space below, identify areas where you feel people your age need to grow in self-control. Next to each problem area, write a way that faith can help people overcome the temptation.

Problem Area	How It Can Be Addressed
_____	_____
_____	_____
_____	_____
_____	_____
_____	_____

36 The Church Year

Fruits of the Holy Spirit

Self-Control: Give It Up

Remind the students that Lent is the time we can practice self-control by denying ourselves something we enjoy.

- Ask them to talk about what they find hard to resist. For example, texting friends, being on social media sites, and eating junk food.
- Suggest that they choose one activity to give up/reduce during Lent.
- Each Friday during Lent, set aside a few minutes to talk about the challenges they are facing in their sacrifice.

Remind them that even if they falter, they can always start over. Lent calls us to continually work toward the goal of becoming better people, even (and especially) when we have fallen short.

A Prayer of Petition

Pray the Sign of the Cross together.

Leader: Have mercy on me, O God, in your goodness;
in the greatness of your compassion wipe out my offense.
Thoroughly wash me from my guilt and of my sin cleanse me.

All: Create a clean heart in me, O God.

Reader 1: A clean heart create for me, O God,
and a steadfast spirit renew within me.
Cast me not out from your presence,
and your Holy Spirit take not from me.

All: Create a clean heart in me, O God.

Reader 2: Give me back the joy of your salvation,
and a willing spirit sustain in me.
I will teach transgressors your ways,
and sinners shall return to you.

All: Create a clean heart in me, O God.
Based on Psalm 51:3–4, 12–13, 14–15

Leader: Let us go forth to fight temptation with self-control.

All: Our Father, who art in heaven,
hallowed be thy name;
thy kingdom come,
thy will be done
on earth as it is in heaven.
Give us this day our daily bread,
and forgive us our trespasses,
as we forgive those who trespass against us;
and lead us not into temptation,
but deliver us from evil. Amen.

Sing or play "Create in Me"

© Our Sunday Visitor

Lent **37**

A Prayer of Petition

Select two readers from the group. Allow time for them to become familiar with their parts.

Gather the students around the prayer table in the prayer space.

Begin with the Sign of the Cross.

Follow the order of prayer on the student page.

Conclude by playing or singing with the students the song "Create in Me," downloaded from **aliveinchrist.osv.com**.

Optional Activity

Lent Activity Master: A Person for Others

Distribute copies of the activity found on teacher page 34B.

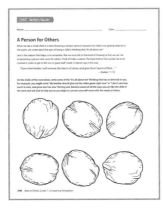

- The seasonal activity masters have been developed to help illustrate how we participate in the Paschal Mystery of Christ through the liturgical seasons.
- This activity will help the students reflect on giving up selfish ways.

LESSON OBJECTIVES

- Explore the great sacrifice of Jesus' life on Good Friday
- Relate the events of Holy Week with self-emptying love
- Express how to live a life of charity that reflects Jesus' great love

ENVIRONMENT

Prayer table
White or gold cloth
Crucifix
Palm branches
Candle
Bible or Lectionary

- Place the prayer table in a central location.
- Set the prayer table with the white or gold cloth, crucifix, palm branches, candle, and Bible or Lectionary.
- Light the candle before beginning.
- Allow plenty of space around the prayer table for the students.

 **MUSIC OPTION**
Go to **aliveinchrist.osv.com** to sample and download, "Take Up Our Cross"

CATHOLIC SOCIAL TEACHING

- **Call to Family, Community, and Participation** Pages 336–337
- **Solidarity of the Human Family** Pages 344–345

Teacher Background

> For we do not have a high priest who is unable to sympathize with our weaknesses, but one who has similarly been tested in every way, yet without sin. So let us confidently approach the throne of grace to receive mercy and to find grace for timely help.
> Hebrews 4:15–16
>
> **> Reflect** How can you show your appreciation for Jesus' sacrifice?

Each Memorial Acclamation we pray during the Liturgy of the Eucharist proclaims the central belief of our faith in the Paschal Mystery of Christ. Among other responses, we proclaim "Save us, Savior of the world, for by your Cross and Resurrection you have set us free," or, "We proclaim your Death, O Lord, and profess your Resurrection until you come again."

The Paschal Mystery of Christ's Death and Resurrection is at the heart of the Good News. In the redemptive Death of Jesus Christ, God's saving plan was accomplished "once for all" (see CCC, 571). Jesus' Death was his final testimony to his trust in the faithful, loving Father he had revealed. It was also an act of love, made evident through the gift of himself to God the Father and to us all.

Laying down his life for his friends was Jesus' ultimate sacrifice. In so doing, he identified with human sufferings by freely allowing himself to suffer and be put to Death. He loved so completely that he gave his very self—Body, Blood, soul, and divinity—on the Cross. His Death opens the possibility of salvation for all people. His Death frees us to live in a totally new way—as sons and daughters of God who are forgiven and loved unconditionally. Jesus' Death on the Cross is a verification of God's love and forgiveness, of God's longing to save us from sin and death. His ultimate sacrifice teaches us the way to God and how to live our lives.

> Reflect How does your experience of Holy Week and the Church's commemoration of Jesus' Passion and Death teach you how to live?

Teacher's Prayer

I adore you O Christ, and I bless you, because by your Holy Cross you have redeemed the world. Thank you for your love and sacrifice.

Name _____ Date _____

Bringing New Life

Each year during Holy Week, but especially on Holy Thursday, Good Friday, and Holy Saturday, we remember Jesus' Death—his perfect sacrifice of love for us. Entering into these sacred days reminds us that we must die to a life of sin and rise with Jesus to newness of life. On the cross, you will see a list of social sins.

In the empty tomb, following the same order as the social sins listed on the cross, write one way we can act for the good and bring new life to the situation. (Example: Children are starving in many impoverished areas in the world—help raise money for an organization that reaches out to these communities.)

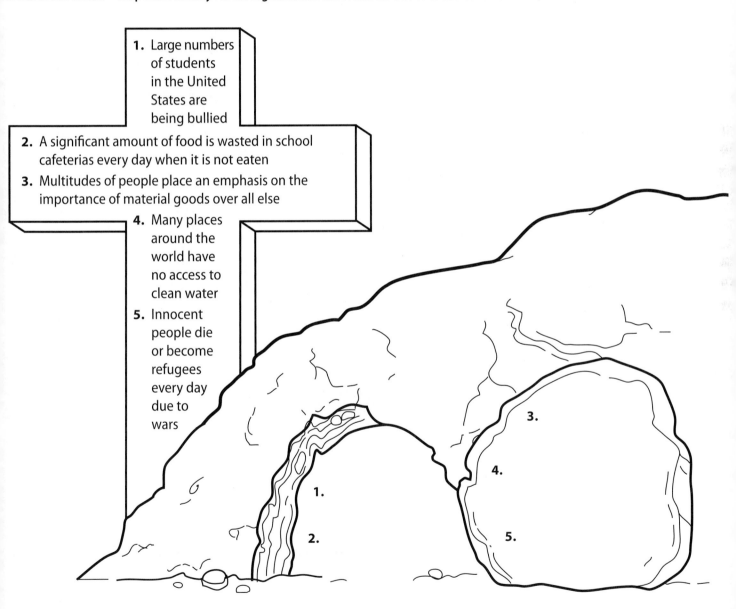

1. Large numbers of students in the United States are being bullied

2. A significant amount of food is wasted in school cafeterias every day when it is not eaten

3. Multitudes of people place an emphasis on the importance of material goods over all else

4. Many places around the world have no access to clean water

5. Innocent people die or become refugees every day due to wars

♥ Let Us Pray

Invite the students to gather in the prayer space and make the Sign of the Cross. Select a few students to read aloud the leader prayer, including the verse from Isaiah. Prompt the response from the remainder of the group.

Have the students move out of the prayer space and back to their seats.

Say: Let's listen to God's Word and learn about God's mercy and grace.

📖 Scripture

Guide the students through the process of Scripture reflection (see the Scripture Background box below).

Have your ever thought...

Say: Our hearts can hardly hold a love that is so great it is willing to sacrifice everything for us.

- Invite the students to respond to the questions.

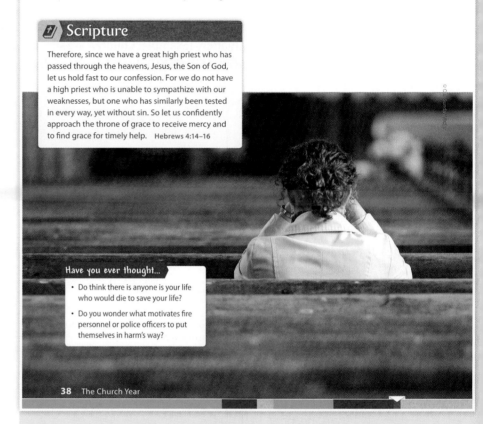

Triduum

♥ Let Us Pray

Leader: Lord God, during Holy Week we honor the Passion and Death of your Son. The prophet Isaiah wrote,

"[He] bore the sins of many,
    and interceded for the transgressors."   Isaiah 53:12

All: May he win pardon for our sins. Amen.

📖 Scripture

Therefore, since we have a great high priest who has passed through the heavens, Jesus, the Son of God, let us hold fast to our confession. For we do not have a high priest who is unable to sympathize with our weaknesses, but one who has similarly been tested in every way, yet without sin. So let us confidently approach the throne of grace to receive mercy and to find grace for timely help.   Hebrews 4:14–16

Have you ever thought...

- Do think there is anyone is your life who would die to save your life?
- Do you wonder what motivates fire personnel or police officers to put themselves in harm's way?

38   The Church Year

📖 Scripture Background

Scripture Reflection Process

Invite the students to be still, close their eyes, and focus on their breathing. Encourage them to open their minds and hearts to what God is saying to them.

- Proclaim the Scripture and have the students sit in silence.
- *Ask:* What did you hear God say to you today?
- Allow volunteers to share.

 You may play instrumental music to begin the reflection.

Jesus Suffers for Us

Holy Week is the most solemn week of the year. During the seven days from Passion (or Palm) Sunday to Easter, we remember Jesus' triumphant arrival in Jerusalem, the institution of the Holy Eucharist, and Jesus' Death and burial. The week ends with the Easter Vigil, when we celebrate our Savior's triumph over death. It is an intense week in the Church.

On Good Friday we recognize the depth of our Savior's sacrifice. Just hours after celebrating Passover with his companions, he is deserted by his friends. He is handed over to officials who have him scourged. His own people shout a death sentence for him. He carries his Cross up a hill, meeting his mother and other women on the way. He falls several times, to the point where Simon is pressed into service to help him.

At the top of the hill, Christ is nailed to the Cross and hoisted up between two criminals. He also says to those who have persecuted him, "Father, forgive them, they know not what they do" (Luke 23:34). He even tells a criminal being crucified by his side that he will be welcomed in Heaven. Finally, Jesus gives up his spirit, and a soldier pierces his side with a lance. The body is taken down and placed in a tomb.

The accumulated effect of these events is hard to imagine. What sort of love would sustain a person through these trials? Only a love that comes from God. Only a love that is meant to redeem others.

> How does Jesus model God's mercy and forgiveness?

> What could you do to be merciful and forgiving?

Easter **39**

Catholic Social Teaching

Lesson Connections

To integrate Catholic Social Teaching into your lesson, choose one of the following features: Call to Family, Community, and Participation, pages 336–337; or Solidarity of the Human Family, pages 344–345.

- To expand the lesson, complete pages 39–40, then move to the Catholic Social Teaching feature.
- Return to the prayer on page 41.

Jesus Suffers for Us

Invite a volunteer to read the first paragraph.

- On the board or on chart paper, make a Holy Week timeline. Invite the students to fill in the names of the days and what each day commemorates. Use the timeline to clarify any student questions.
- *Ask:* Why is it important to remember the events of Holy Week? These events help us to understand the depth of God's love for us and teach us about sacrifice, mercy, and forgiveness.

Read aloud the second and third paragraphs. Pause a moment for the students to reflect on Jesus' sacrifice.

- Point out the photo at the top of the page. Invite the students to describe what they see and connect it to the paragraphs that were just read.
- *Ask:* Why would Jesus allow himself to be sacrificed in such a manner? because he loves us and knew that through his sacrifice, we would be given new life

Summarize the content of the last paragraph.

- Reinforce that love was the motivation for Jesus' sacrifice.

Read aloud the reflection questions.

- Discuss the first question as a class.
- Allow time for the students to silently reflect on the second question.

Triduum **39**

Ultimate Charity

Read aloud the first paragraph.

- Define *charity* as the unselfish love we return to God and share with others.
- Invite the students to share their thoughts on their obligation to act with charity toward others.
- *Ask:* Why are we forever in Jesus' debt? Jesus gave up his life to redeem us.

Recall the Great Commandment with the students.

Summarize the second paragraph.

- Discuss why we should act with charity or love.
- *Ask:* Why is charity the foundation of all other virtues? It is an unselfish love that leads us to good spiritual habits.

Invite a volunteer to read the last paragraph of the text.

- *Ask:* Why do acts of charity make others feel loved, but also make the giver happy, as well?
- Use the image on the page to spark a discussion on inventive ways to be charitable and spread Jesus Good News to others.

Explain the activity.

- Allow the students to work alone. If they wish to share, permit them to do so, but remind them that sharing is not required.

Ultimate Charity

Good Friday is the day when we witness Jesus' ultimate act of love for us, his Death upon the Cross. We are forever in his debt for this redemption. Our best way of showing that we appreciate his selfless love for us is to pass that love on to others. We do that when we follow his teachings and act with love, or **charity**, toward one another.

© Our Sunday Visitor

Fruits of the Holy Spirit
The twelve Fruits of the Holy Spirit are qualities that can be seen in us when we let the Holy Spirit work in our hearts. This season we are focusing on charity.

The Great Commandment points us toward charity. It directs us to love God above all, and to love our neighbors as we love ourselves. Charity, both a fruit of the Holy Spirit and a Theological Virtue, is the foundation of all other virtues. It is the unselfish love we return to God and share with others.

Jesus asks us to love as he did. Although we might not be asked to give our very lives, as Jesus did, this means giving of ourselves to other. We can spend time with others, observe the Corporal and Spiritual Works of Mercy, and find other ways to selflessly give of ourselves.

WRITE

Write a short meditation on the ways that Jesus showed charity throughout his life. Include a sentence or two about how you intend to follow his lead. Read the meditation often during Holy Week.

_____
_____
_____
_____
_____
_____
_____
_____
_____

40 The Church Year

Fruits of the Holy Spirit

Charity: Love Makes the World Go Round

Use contemporary music as a way to talk about what love is and isn't.

- Ask each student to write down the lyrics to their favorite "love song." Have them read the lyrics aloud (after you ensure they are inoffensive).
- As a class, talk about the qualities of "love" that are expressed in the songs and list them on the board. Discuss that what we sometimes call "love" in today's world isn't really love, but control, lust, or sex.
- Explain that authentic love is a love that mirrors the same characteristics of God's love: freely given, unconditional, eternal, life-giving, and sacrificial. Remind the students that many of the messages we receive about love aren't authentic to its true meaning.

A Prayer of Mercy

Pray the Sign of the Cross together.

Leader: In you, O Lord, I take refuge;
let me never be put to shame.
In your justice rescue me.

Into your hands I commend my spirit;
you will redeem me, O Lord, O faithful
God.

All: Father, into your hands I commend my
spirit.

Leader: For all my foes I am an object of
reproach,
a laughingstock to my neighbors, and a
dread to my friends;
they who see me abroad flee from me.

I am forgotten like the unremembered dead;
I am like a dish that is broken.

All: Father, into your hands I commend
my spirit.

Leader: But my trust is in you, O Lord;
I say, "You are my God.

In your hands is my destiny; rescue me
from the clutches of my enemies and my
persecutors."

All: Father, into your hands I commend
my spirit.

Leader: Let your face shine upon your
servant;
save me in your kindness.

Take courage and be stouthearted,
all you who hope in the Lord.

All: Father, into your hands I commend
my spirit. **Based on Psalm 31:2, 6, 12–13, 15–16,
17, 25; Luke 23:46**

Leader: We go forth to honor Jesus' sacrifice
by following his teachings of love.

All: We shall follow his teachings of love.
Amen.

▶ *Sing or play "Take Up Our Cross"*

A Prayer of Mercy

♥ You will serve as the leader
for this prayer.

Gather around the prayer table
with the students.

Pray the Sign of the Cross. Then
follow the order of prayer on the
student page.

▶ Conclude by playing or
singing with the students "Take
Up Our Cross," downloaded from
aliveinchrist.osv.com.

Optional Activity

Easter Activity Master: Bringing New Life

Distribute copies of the activity found
on teacher page 38B.

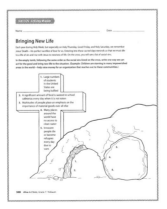

- The seasonal activity masters have
  been developed to help illustrate
  how we participate in the Paschal
  Mystery of Christ through the
  liturgical seasons.
- This activity will help the students
  grow in their understanding of how
  they can act for the good of all.

LESSON OBJECTIVES

- Identify Easter as the celebration of the entirety of the Paschal Mystery
- Relate Easter to the joy of serving God and others with love
- Express all that leads a person to experience Easter joy

ENVIRONMENT

Prayer table
White cloth
Crucifix
Holy water
Candle
Bible or Lectionary

- Place the prayer table in a central location.
- Set the prayer table with the white cloth, crucifix, holy water, candle, and Bible or Lectionary.
- Light the candle before beginning.
- Allow plenty of space around the prayer table for the students.

🎵 MUSIC OPTION

Go to **aliveinchrist.osv.com** to sample and download, "Come to the Water" "Put On Christ"

🌐 CATHOLIC SOCIAL TEACHING

- **Option for the Poor and Vulnerable** Pages 340–341
- **The Dignity of Work and the Rights of Workers** Pages 342–343

Teacher Background

> 📖 … [H]e is the one appointed by God as judge of the living and the dead. To him all the prophets bear witness, that everyone who believes in him will receive forgiveness of sins through his name.
> Acts 10:42–43

> **Reflect** How does Jesus' Resurrection give you confidence as a follower of Jesus and as a catechist?

The Paschal Mystery, as the Catechism reminds us, has two aspects: "by his death, Christ liberates us from sin, by his Resurrection, he opens for us the way to a new life. This new life is above all justification that reinstates us in God's grace, 'so that as Christ was raised from the dead by the glory of the Father, we too might walk in newness of life'" (CCC, 654).

Our belief in the Resurrection is central to our faith. All of our other beliefs hinge on the Resurrection. It is through the power of the Holy Spirit that we come to understand and live out our new life in Christ. Because Jesus rose from the dead, our life is changed both on Earth and into eternity. We now know that we are beloved children of God. We know that we are invited to live in a relationship of covenant love with God forever. We know that if we are faithful to this call we will act lovingly toward all people we meet, trying, in both our words and our actions, to be faithful witnesses to the Good News of Jesus Christ. We know that earthly death is not the end of our existence. Just as Jesus rose from the dead, so will we.

During the Easter season, we celebrate in a special way Christ's Resurrection and our new life in him. We are renewed as a people of hope who seek out and share Christ's presence in this life and the next.

> **Reflect** How do you celebrate the joys of the Easter season?

Teacher's Prayer

💗 This is the day the Lord has made! I rejoice and am glad. Christ is risen. Alleluia!

Name _____   Date _____

God Conquers All

Easter is the season when we celebrate that God can conquer all evil—even death. It is the season where we die to the thought that evil is more powerful than God. When we trust in the power of God's love even in the midst of great darkness, we rise to understanding that God can bring good from the evil.

You have most likely heard people reflect on the good that has come even after serious tragedies. When someone experiences a fire that consumes their home, you might hear, "Our town held a fundraiser for us. We never knew people could care so much." Or, after getting over the initial shock, someone who lost their job might say, "I didn't realize how my job was negatively affecting our family."

Think of an example you have heard on the news, Internet, or within your own family where good has triumphed over evil. Write down your example in the space provided below. As you write, be aware that it is our willingness to be open to God's grace that can change our hearts and help us to live in joy.

Let Us Pray

Invite the students to gather in the prayer space and make the Sign of the Cross. Read aloud the Psalm verse and prompt the response from the students.

▶ Music Option: Conclude with "Put On Christ" downloaded from **aliveinchrist.osv.com**.

Have the students move out of the prayer space and back to their seats.

Say: Let's listen to what God has to tell us about life.

📖 Scripture

Guide the students through the process of Scripture reflection (see the Scripture Background box below).

Have your ever thought...

Say: Jesus brought us new life through his Passion, Death, Resurrection, and Ascension.

- Invite the students to respond to the questions.

Meeting Jesus with Joy

Let Us Pray

Leader: Lord Jesus, by your Cross and Resurrection, you have set us free. You enable us to say,

"God indeed is my salvation,
I am confident and unafraid." Isaiah 12:2–3

All: I am confident, Lord. Amen.

📖 Scripture

Peter proceeded to speak and said: "You know what has happened all over Judea, beginning in Galilee after the baptism that John preached, how God anointed Jesus of Nazareth with the Holy Spirit and power. He went about doing good and healing all those oppressed by the devil, for God was with him. We are witnesses of all that he did both in the country of the Jews and in Jerusalem.

They put him to death by hanging him on a tree. This man God raised on the third day and granted that he be visible, not to all the people, but to us, the witnesses chosen by God in advance, who ate and drank with him after he rose from the dead.

He commissioned us to preach to the people and testify that he is the one appointed by God as judge of the living and the dead. To him all the prophets bear witness, that everyone who believes in him will receive forgiveness of sins through his name." Acts 10:34a, 37–43

© Our Sunday Visitor

Have you ever thought...

- Why does Jesus' Resurrection take away our biggest fear?
- How does believing in eternal life change the way you live this life?

42 The Church Year

📖 Scripture Background

Scripture Reflection Process

Invite the students to be still, close their eyes, and focus on their breathing. Encourage them to open their minds and hearts to what God is saying to them.

- Proclaim the Scripture and have the students sit in silence.
- *Ask:* What did you hear God say to you today?
- Allow volunteers to share.

 You may play instrumental music to begin the reflection.

Catholics gather as the processional begins during an Easter Sunrise Mass

The Center of Our Beliefs

When you were younger, you probably considered Christmas the primary religious holiday. It was easy for you to understand the happiness that came with the birth of a baby, and the traditions that came with the holiday made it even more memorable.

Now that you are older, you can understand why the Easter season, which runs from Easter to Pentecost, is the primary season of the liturgical year. Yes, it is important that God became man in Jesus Christ. What the Easter season celebrates, though, is the entirety of the Paschal Mystery: that Jesus suffered, died, rose, and ascended to Heaven.

When we celebrate Easter, we see the Risen Lord, who is glorified after his horrible suffering for our sake. We celebrate that he has returned from the dead and that he will teach us for a little longer. We recognize that he must return to his Father. We are happy that he sends the Spirit to sustain our faith. He tells the disciples, and us, "Peace be with you" (John 20:19).

During this season, we sing "Alleluia!" often. It is one way we express the joy we find in the risen Christ.

> How does an appreciation for Easter reflect a more mature view of your faith?

> What does "Alleluia!" mean to you?

Easter **43**

Catholic Social Teaching

Lesson Connections

To integrate Catholic Social Teaching into your lesson, choose one of the following features: Option for the Poor and Vulnerable, pages 340–341; or The Dignity of Work and the Rights of Workers, pages 342–343.

- To expand the lesson, complete pages 43–44, then move to the Catholic Social Teaching feature.
- Return to the prayer on page 45.

The Center of Our Beliefs

Select a student to read the first paragraph.

- Reinforce the idea that as the students mature, they will understand more about their religion.
- Explain that everyone who continues to study God's Word learns and understands more about our faith.
- Encourage the students to discuss how their views of Church holidays have changed as they have grown older.

Read aloud the rest of this section.

- Use the image on this page to spark a discussion on the importance and focus of the Easter season.
- Emphasize that the Easter season encompasses the time from Easter to Pentecost and that it is a time to deepen our appreciation for the Paschal Mystery.
- *Ask:* Which feast from the Easter season is your favorite? Why?

Have the students discuss the questions with a classmate.

- Ask various partners to share their thoughts with the class.

Our Reason for Joy

Challenge the students to think about things that make them joyful. Invite them to share their thoughts.

Summarize the first paragraph.

- Suggest that joy comes from the growing awareness that God and his love are with us no matter our personal circumstances or achievements.

Ask a volunteer to read aloud the second paragraph.

- Have the students reflect on their feelings about their Lenten disciplines.

Invite another volunteer to read the rest of the text.

- Ask the students to recognize the challenge stated in the the last paragraph.
- *Ask:* In what ways do you want to share Easter joy with others?

Have the students work alone on writing their reflection. After allowing the students the amount of time they need to complete the activity, ask volunteers to share their reflections with the group.

Our Reason for Joy

There is much to be joyful about at Easter. All of nature echoes the joy of the season, with greenery, blossoms, and new life. If we quietly contemplate the season, we will experience inner **joy** as well.

If we have been diligent during Lent and Triduum, we have been serving God and our fellow humans with love. We have denied ourselves pleasures in order to develop self-control. We have given alms and time to worthwhile causes to increase our charity to others. Those self-giving acts have opened us up to Christ's sacrifice and the Easter joy of his presence in our lives.

Joy is a Fruit of the Holy Spirit. It comes from the growing awareness that God and his love are with us no matter our personal circumstances or achievements.

Now that we are in the habit of serving with love, we will want to continue to share Christ's joy with others. Then it will grow even more.

Fruits of the Holy Spirit

The twelve Fruits of the Holy Spirit are qualities that can be seen in us when we let the Holy Spirit work in our hearts. This season we are focusing on joy.

WRITE

Write a short reflection on your own reasons for feeling Easter joy. Include observations on nature, your relationships, or ways you have changed for the better during Lent.

_____

_____

_____

_____

44   The Church Year

Fruits of the Holy Spirit

Joy to the World

Joy is often very personal, but when we see what brings other people joy, we can expand our feelings of joy as well.

- Hang a large sheet of paper or a felt banner at the front of the classroom with the letters J-O-Y at the top.
- Ask each student to bring something that represents "joy" to them to hang on the banner. This might include things such as family pictures, artwork, or poetry.
- As they decorate the banner, play "Joy to the World," "Down in my Heart," or another traditional Christian song about joy.

A Prayer of Praise

A Prayer of Praise

Pray the Sign of the Cross together.

Leader: We give thanks as we joyfully celebrate Christ's victory over death.

All: Alleluia!

Leader: Give thanks to the LORD, for he is good,
for his mercy endures forever.
Let the house of Israel say,
"His mercy endures forever."

All: This is the day the Lord has made;
let us rejoice and be glad.

Leader: In danger I called on the LORD;
the LORD answered and set me free.
The LORD is with me; I am not afraid;
what can mortals do against me?

All: This is the day the Lord has made;
let us rejoice and be glad.

Leader: "The right hand of the LORD has struck with power;
the right hand of the LORD is exalted.
I shall not die, but live,
and declare the works of the LORD."

All: This is the day the Lord has made;
let us rejoice and be glad.

Leader: The stone which the builders rejected
has become the cornerstone.
By the LORD has this been done;
it is wonderful in our eyes.

All: This is the day the Lord has made;
let us rejoice and be glad.
Based on Psalm 118:1-2, 16-17, 22-23, 24

Leader: Let us go forth to celebrate the Easter Season with joy.

All: Alleluia! Amen.

▶ *Sing or play "Come to the Water"*

Easter **45**

© Our Sunday Visitor

A Prayer of Praise

♡ Choose a leader from the group. Allow time for the leader to review his/her lines.

Gather in the prayer space with the students.

Make the Sign of the Cross and signal the leader to begin.

Follow the order of prayer on the student page.

▶ Conclude by inviting the students to sing or reflect on the song "Come to the Water," downloaded from **aliveinchrist.osv.com**.

Alternate Music Option:
"Put On Christ"

Easter Activity Master: God Conquers All

Distribute copies of the activity found on teacher page 42B.

- The seasonal activity masters have been developed to help illustrate how we participate in the Paschal Mystery of Christ through the liturgical seasons.
- This activity will help the students understand that God can bring good from evil.

Meeting Jesus with Joy **45**

LESSON OBJECTIVES

- Identify why the Ascension challenges Christians to be faithful disciples
- Express that maintaining the peace of Christ helps us with our mission
- Explore Scripture passages that deepen the understanding of the peace that comes from Christ

ENVIRONMENT

Prayer table
White cloth
Crucifix
Candle
Bible or Lectionary

- Place the prayer table in a central location.
- Set the prayer table with the white cloth, crucifix, candle, and Bible or Lectionary.
- Light the candle before beginning.
- Allow plenty of space around the prayer table for the students.

🎵 MUSIC OPTIONS

Go to **aliveinchrist.osv.com** to sample and download, "Go Ye Out" "Rise Up with Him"

🌐 CATHOLIC SOCIAL TEACHING YEAR

- **Call to Family, Community, and Participation** Pages 336–337
- **The Dignity of Work and the Rights of Workers** Pages 342–343

Teacher Background

📖 [The two men dressed in white garments] said, "Men of Galilee, why are you standing there looking at the sky? This Jesus who has been taken up from you into heaven will return in the same way as you have seen him going into heaven." **Acts 1:11**

> **Reflect** Why do you think the feast of the Ascension is so important to the Church?

Jesus did his best to prepare his disciples for the fact that he would be leaving them to return to his Father. In the Gospel of John (see John 14:1–17), he uses the image of his Father's house with many rooms. Jesus speaks of a special place that he will prepare for them, but they don't understand. Thomas asks Jesus to show them the way to get there (as if he was expecting a map) and Philip simply asks Jesus to show them the Father.

Thomas and Philip are a lot like we are; sometimes we just don't get it. So Jesus tells them, "I will ask the Father, and he will give you another Advocate to be with you always, the Spirit of truth…" (**John 14:16**). Jesus promises to send a helper; he knows we need help figuring it all out, on our own way to the Father.

The Feast of the Ascension celebrates Jesus' return home to God the Father. Jesus reminds his disciples to have faith. All who have faith in this world can rest their hearts in God's heavenly home. It will be ready and waiting for us.

> **Reflect** What steps can you take to ensure that you remain faithful to Jesus every day?

Teacher's Prayer

💗 Jesus, help me remain faithful to you. Let me never doubt your love for me and for the students in my care. Amen.

Name _____   Date _____

His Loving Presence

The Feast of the Ascension celebrates Jesus' return home to God the Father. Jesus reminds his disciples to have faith. Can you imagine how they must have felt? First, Jesus was with them. Then he died. Then he rose, and now he was leaving again. The disciples must have been confused, anxious, and afraid. Yet, Jesus asks them to have faith—to trust that if you live as his disciple, you will have a peace that only he can give. The Ascension reminds us that we must die to worrying and anxiousness and rise to trusting that God is always present; he is always with us.

On the slips of paper below, write some of the things you worry about that you need to "die to"—the things you need to hand over to Jesus so that he can give you peace. After you write down your thoughts, imagine closing the lid on the box and handing it and its contents over to Jesus.

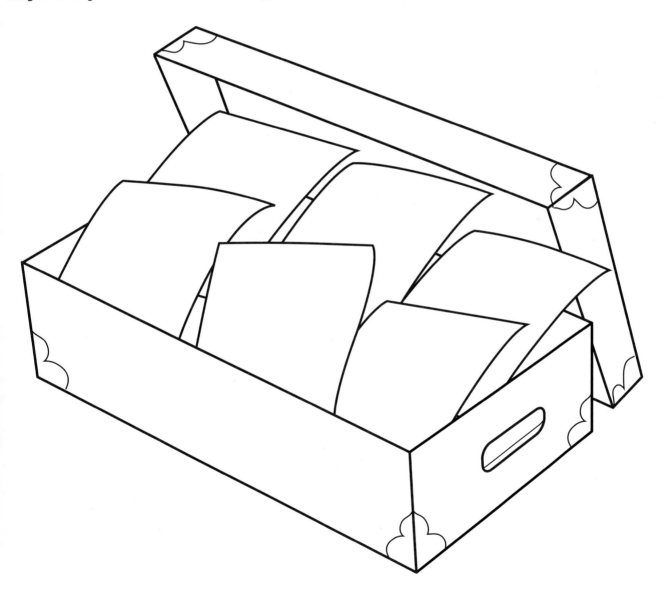

♡ Let Us Pray

Choose one of the students to be the Leader. Invite the students to gather in the prayer space and make the Sign of the Cross. Ask the Leader to proclaim the opening prayer and Psalm verse, and lead the class in the response.

▶ Music Option: Conclude the prayer with "Rise Up with Him" downloaded from **aliveinchrist.osv.com**.

Have the students move out of the prayer space and back to their seats.

Say: Let's listen to God's Word and hear what Jesus says to his disciples as he leaves this Earth.

📖 Scripture

Guide the students through the process of Scripture reflection (see the Scripture Background box below).

Have your ever thought...

Say: Jesus returns to his Father in Heaven and gives his disciples, and all of us, a mission.

- Invite the students to respond to the questions.

Ascension

♡ Let Us Pray

Leader: Lord Jesus, you returned to your Father. Of you it is said, "God has gone up with a shout." Psalm 47:6

All: We give you thanks for your great glory. Amen.

📖 Scripture

When they had gathered together they asked him, "Lord, are you at this time going to restore the kingdom to Israel?" He answered them, "It is not for you to know the times or seasons that the Father has established by his own authority. But you will receive power when the holy Spirit comes upon you, and you will be my witnesses in Jerusalem, throughout Judea and Samaria, and to the ends of the earth."

When he had said this, as they were looking on, he was lifted up, and a cloud took him from their sight. While they were looking intently at the sky as he was going, suddenly two men dressed in white garments stood beside them. They said, "Men of Galilee, why are you standing there looking at the sky? This Jesus who has been taken up from you into heaven will return in the same way as you have seen him going into heaven." Acts 1:6-11

Have you ever thought...
- Was Jesus sad to leave his disciples?
- Was Jesus worried that his disciples would be lost without him?

46

📖 Scripture Background

Scripture Reflection Process

Invite the students to be still, close their eyes, and focus on their breathing. Encourage them to open their minds and hearts to what God is saying to them.

- Proclaim the Scripture and have the students sit in silence.
- *Ask:* What did you hear God say to you today?
- Allow volunteers to share.

 You may play instrumental music to begin the reflection.

Changes for Us All

The Ascension celebrates a major transition for Jesus—and for us. For most of Jesus' ministry, he had been with us on Earth. For a few brief days—Good Friday evening to Easter Sunday morning—he was out of our presence. Then he returned and taught for another forty days.

But then, things changed. His teaching was done, and he was returning to the Father. The Gospels don't tell us how much notice Jesus gave his followers that this would happen. Clearly, they were astonished as he ascended and disappeared from sight. They were so surprised that two men dressed in white had to interrupt their gazing and explain that Jesus had gone up into Heaven. There is a second part to their message, too. They told us that he would also return to us.

The Ascension challenges Catholics to be faithful. It shows us what Jesus has left us: the Holy Spirit, his teachings, the Church, and one another. We are to make use of all of these resources as we wait in hope for his return.

After the Ascension, the early Church community was left with the promise of the coming of the Holy Spirit, who would strengthen them to continue the work of Christ, to spread the Good News and build the Kingdom of God. The Holy Spirit did come to Jesus' followers at Pentecost, and in the Sacraments of Baptism and Confirmation, Catholics receive the Holy Spirit as well. We are strengthened by the Spirit to bring the Good News to others through evangelization: talking to others

Study for a mural of the Ascension,
Hans Felbusch

about our faith, sharing how our faith influences us, using our gifts and talents to help others, and sharing what we have with those who are in need.

In the United States, Ascension Thursday is a Holy Day of Obligation. On the Feast of the Ascension, the priest wears white vestments to signify it is a feast of Jesus. The Church as a whole is reminded on this day of her mission to serve the world.

> What important lesson do we learn from the Ascension?

> What can you do to prepare for Jesus' return?

⊕ Catholic Social Teaching

Lesson Connections

To integrate Catholic Social Teaching into your lesson, choose one of the following features: Call to Family, Community, and Participation, pages 336–337; or The Dignity of Work and the Rights of Workers, pages 342–343.

- To expand the lesson, complete pages 47–48, then move to the Catholic Social Teaching feature.
- Return to the prayer on page 49.

Changes for Us All

Invite a volunteer to read the first paragraph of the text.

- On chart paper, make a brief timeline indicating Jesus' life, his time away from us between Good Friday and Easter Sunday morning, the forty days after Easter, the Ascension, and Pentecost. Review the timeline with the students.

- *Ask:* Why would Jesus' departure—his Ascension—be a major change for his followers? because he would no longer be physically there to teach them and lead them

Point out the artwork on this page. Ask the students to describe what they see in the painting.

Summarize the second paragraph.

- Link the paragraph content to the reading from the beginning of the lesson.

- *Ask:* Why should the message from the two men dressed in white garments be reassuring to us? these two men were angels

Read aloud the last three paragraphs.

- Invite the students to reflect on the resources Jesus has given us. Link them to specific people and organizations in your parish and community.

Allow time for the students to meet in small groups to discuss the reflection questions.

- Have each group report its ideas to the class.

Peace from Within

Summarize the first paragraph.

- Refer to the timeline on your chart paper to show where the Feast of the Ascension is relative to the end of the Easter season.

- *Ask:* Why would we have a sense of completeness at this point in the Church year? Why do we call ourselves an "Easter people"?

Select a student volunteer to read the second paragraph.

- Define peace as a time when we experience freedom from worry allowing God's love to fill our hearts as we strive toward following Christ's example.

- Link our peace on Earth with the peace of Christ we will achieve at the end of time.

- *Say:* The peace of Christ, a peace that the world cannot give, happens when we surrender ourselves to God and allow him to work through us. Everything necessary for peace to happen begins in the heart of God.

Read aloud the third paragraph.

- Ask the students for examples of ways that we can help others desire Christ's peace.

ACTIVITY

Have the students work in small groups to complete the activity.

- Note: Some examples include, we must be willing to forgive; meet basic needs; selfishness and greed must end; we should show respect for the dignity of others.

- Have each group explain to the class the idea that they chose and what Jesus taught about it.

Peace from Within

The Easter Season is almost over when we celebrate the feast of the Ascension, but we live as an Easter people all year long. Christ's Death and Resurrection are made present at every celebration of the Eucharist. He is present with us always, even though he has returned to his Father in Heaven.

We are at **peace**, the Fruit of the Holy Spirit in which we experience freedom from worry as God's love fills our hearts. We strive to act as Christ, resolving conflicts respectfully and with kindness. It gives us a sense of calm, but not of complacency. It provides resolve and a sense of mission.

And we do still have a mission to fulfill. Jesus has returned to Heaven, but we are still on Earth. We are here to do his work. It is our responsibility to help prepare the world for his Second Coming. We do that by sharing the Gospel, and by encouraging everyone to long for and share with others the peace of Christ. We do that by being good models of virtue for younger children. We do that by living in peace—trusting in our inner calm and letting the world know that calm comes from living God's will.

Fruits of the Holy Spirit

The twelve Fruits of the Holy Spirit are qualities that can be seen in us when we let the Holy Spirit work in our hearts. This season we are focusing on peace.

BRAINSTORM

Work in groups to identify what is necessary for peace in our homes, schools, community, and world. Record your top 5 ideas here. Then choose one thing necessary for peace and describe what Jesus teaches us about it.

1. _____
2. _____
3. _____
4. _____
5. _____

Fruits of the Holy Spirit

War and Peace

Use contemporary news to highlight the need for peace in the world.

- Ask the students to research areas in the world that are at war or in conflict.

- Set a globe in the center of a box of sand, with room to place votive candles around it.

- As the students name an area of conflict, point out that area on the globe and then light a candle and pray for peace.

Suggest the class adopt one war-torn region of the world and remember the children in that area each day during their prayers.

A Prayer for Peace

Pray the Sign of the Cross together.

Reader 1: Brothers and sisters,

I, a prisoner for the Lord, urge you to live in a manner worthy of the call you have received,

with all humility and gentleness, with patience, bearing with one another through love,

striving to preserve the unity of the spirit through the bond of peace: one body and one Spirit, as you were also called to the one hope of your call;

one Lord, one faith, one baptism; one God and Father of all, who is over all and through all and in all.

Reader 2: But grace was given to each of us according to the measure of Christ's gift. Therefore, it says:

He ascended on high and took prisoners captive; he gave gifts to men.

What does "he ascended" mean except that he also descended into the lower regions of the earth?

The one who descended is also the one who ascended far above all the heavens, that he might fill all things.

All: And he gave some as apostles, others as prophets, others as evangelists, others as pastors and teachers, to equip the holy ones for the work of ministry, for building up the body of Christ, until we all attain to the unity of faith and knowledge of the Son of God, to mature manhood, to the extent of the full stature of Christ. **Ephesians 4:1–13**

Leader: May we use our gifts to bring peace to all people and to lead them to Christ.

All: Our Father …

Leader: Let us offer each other the sign of peace.

Sing or play "Go Ye Out"

Easter **49**

A Prayer for Peace

Select two readers from the group. Allow time for the readers to become familiar with their parts.

Gather the students around the prayer table.

Begin with the Sign of the Cross.

Follow the order of prayer on the student page.

Conclude by inviting the students to sing or reflect on the song "Go Ye Out," downloaded from **aliveinchrist.osv.com**.

Alternate Music Option: "Rise Up with Him"

Optional Activity

Easter Activity Master: His Loving Presence

Distribute copies of the activity found on teacher page 46B.

- The seasonal activity masters have been developed to help illustrate how we participate in the Paschal Mystery of Christ through the liturgical seasons.
- The students will consider how to turn their worries and anxieties over to God.

Ascension **49**

Units at a Glance

REVELATION

How does Divine Revelation help us live as children of God?

CHURCH HISTORY TIMELINE

70	The first Gospels written
400	Saint Jerome publishes Vulgate Latin Bible
1455	Johannes Gutenberg prints Bible on newly invented press
1545	Council of Trent convenes to consider matters of faith

Go to page 348 for more

Our Catholic Tradition

- Out of nothing, God created the heavens and the earth, and made humans in his image and likeness. We can come to know God through all that he has created and through human reason. (CCC, 46)

- God speaks to us and tells us about himself and his plan for us. God is the author and inspiration of the sacred words of Scripture that humans have recorded under his guidance and direction. (CCC, 134–136)

- Jesus is the fulfillment of the law, and he perfectly reveals God the Father to us. He has a close and intimate relationship with the Father, and invites us to share in that relationship as God's sons and daughters. (CCC, 65)

Our Catholic Life

- The creation accounts in Genesis reveal a number of truths about God and his creation, including that he created the world from its beginning, for humans to live in harmony and to oversee his gifts of creation. (CCC, 306–307)

- Scripture has an important role in our lives, as God's Word is proclaimed in the liturgy, read and studied personally and in religion class, turned to for wisdom and guidance, and prayed. (CCC, 132–133)

- The many titles of Jesus teach us about him, his mission, and his relationship with God and each of us. (CCC, 429)

Introduce Unit Theme

Begin by having the students look at the image on the page. Invite them to share what they see and how they think it relates to the theme of Revelation.

Share some of the highlights of the timeline. Have volunteers read aloud each of the bullet points in the Our Catholic Tradition and Our Catholic Life sections.

Discuss as a class what Unit 1 will be about. Point out that the students will learn more about God's creation and his relationship with humans as they review the next three chapters.

Ask the unit's Big Question found on page 50.

Allow time for discussion.

Explain to the students that this is the essential question for the unit. They will be working to fully answer it as they complete the three chapters in the unit.

📖 Go to the Source

As an optional extension, organize the students into three groups, assigning each group one of the main Scripture passages found in this unit.

- Chapter 1: The Wisdom of Ben Sira 39:16–21
- Chapter 2: Hebrews 4:12
- Chapter 3: Isaiah 42:1–3, 6–7

Have each group read its passage and then give a dramatic reading (narrator with silent actors), create a visual representation, or write down one question they would ask God about the passage.

Reading the verses directly from the Bible will familiarize students with the sequence of the canon of Sacred Scripture.

Explore the Catechism

Provide the students with copies of paragraphs 31–35 from the *Catechism of the Catholic Church*.

- Have the students make a drawing or write a poem or paragraph about some aspect of the physical world that teaches us about God (e.g., something from nature, such as an animal, a mountain, the ocean, etc.).
- *Ask:* What does this part of God's creation teach us about the one who made it?

Reading the paragraphs directly from the *Catechism* will help the students learn where to find key teachings from the Sacred Tradition of the Church.

CHURCH HISTORY TIMELINE BACKGROUND

Refer the students to the Church History Timeline on pages 348–363 to learn more about important Church events and figures through A.D. 1085.

First-Ever Bible is Printed

After inventing the movable-type printing press in 1440, Johannes Gutenberg printed poems, calendars, and other smaller items before producing the first printed book in 1455: a Bible. The Latin text was printed in Mainz, Germany, and approximately two hundred copies were printed. Only twenty-two copies are now known to exist. Today, the Bible is the best-selling and most largely distributed book in the world.

The Council of Trent Convenes

The Council of Trent convened on December 13, 1545, and ended on December 4, 1563. At the fourth session of the Council, held in 1546, two decrees were debated and adopted by the Church Fathers. The first declared that in matters of faith, the Tradition of the Church, together with Sacred Scripture, is the standard of supernatural Revelation. It also declared the Vulgate edition of the Bible to be the authentic text for sermons and disputations.

KEY CONCEPT

We can come to know God through all that he has created and through human reason.

DOCTRINAL CONTENT

- We can come to know God in many different ways: through all he has created, through the voice of conscience, and through human intellect and reason. (CCC, 31–35, 46)

- Although God reveals himself in many ways, we will not fully understand the mystery of God until we know him completely in Heaven. (CCC, 1027)

- God planned from the beginning to give his only Son, Jesus Christ, to reconcile all of creation to himself. (CCC, 1)

- Many Old Testament accounts speak of God's faithfulness to his promise of salvation. (CCC, 422, 652)

- From the Genesis creation accounts and the world around us, we get a sense of the attributes of God—eternal, truth, love, merciful, and holy. (CCC, 212–221)

TASKS OF CATECHESIS

Helping children grow in a faith that is "known, celebrated, lived, and expressed in prayer" (NDC, 20).

This chapter focuses on the following tasks of catechesis:

- Promoting Knowledge of the Faith

- Moral Formation

Teacher Background

> 📖 The works of God are all of them good; he supplies for every need in its own time. . . . nothing can limit his saving action. . . . To him, nothing is small or insignificant, and nothing too wonderful or hard for him. **The Wisdom of Ben Sira (Sirach) 39:16, 18, 20**
>
> **> Reflect** What do these words of Scripture mean to you?

When we look at the wonders of creation, we know there must be a God who loves and cares for us. Scientific theories that include evolution are not necessarily incompatible with our faith, as long as they leave room for the truth of God's role as sole Creator and his Divine plan of creation. We human beings are an important part of that plan. God created us in "his image and likeness." We have been given a special dignity by God, as well as free will and the ability to love. Because of our free will, we can choose to live in joyful union with him.

Sadly, our first parents, Adam and Eve, chose to disobey God, and through their act of disobedience, sin and suffering entered into the human experience. The Old Testament is filled with epic tales of the struggles of God's People to live faithfully despite their sinfulness. Theirs is a story of great peaks and low valleys, the height of jubilation and the depths of despair. But throughout it all, God always remained faithful and, in his compassion, raised up heroes such as Abraham, Moses, and David to lead his People. All of these great, but flawed, leaders set the stage for the one who would eventually come and reveal the fullness of God's love for us, Jesus Christ.

> **> Reflect** How can you make time for appreciating creation, praising the Creator, and sharing this joy with others?

Teacher's Prayer

 Holy Spirit, touch my mind and my heart that through me you have an impact on my students. Bless me with wisdom, with grace, and with passion. Be with me and make my words your own. Amen.

How Seventh Graders Understand Chapter Topics

Two big questions in the minds of adolescents are "Who am I?" and "Why am I here?" We find beautiful answers to those questions in our Catholic faith, which can support students as they develop in their identity.

Teaching Tip: As you discuss what Scripture and Church teaching say about God and his creation (including human beings), continually ask the students what this says about who they are and how they are different from other creatures made by God. Point out that the God who made the entire universe knows their name (and as Jesus said, knows how many hairs they have on their heads). He is a big and powerful God, but he desires a personal relationship with them.

Sharing the Message with Seventh Graders

- Adolescents are beginning to see that life is not always an either-or proposition. This can be frightening as they realize some childhood beliefs may require reexamination.
- Seventh graders are constantly being pressured to take sides on issues such as fashion and pop culture. In our polarized culture, religion, too, can be a contentious issue for them.
- Remember, young people develop critical thinking skills at varying rates. Not all have the same ability to think abstractly.

Chapter 1 Planner

Objectives	Open

DAY 1—Invite/Preview, Pages 51–53

* Reflect on God's personal invitation through Scripture
* Indicate prior knowledge of chapter concepts and vocabulary

❤ **Psalm 19:2** Pray the opening prayer.

📖 **The Wisdom of Ben Sira (Sirach) 39:16–21** Proclaim "Praise of God the Creator." Guide the students through the process of Scripture reflection.

* Discuss Have You Ever Thought questions.

DAY 2—Discover, Pages 54–55

* Examine the unique role of humans and the purpose of human intellect and reason
* Differentiate the ways we can come to know God
* Recognize that humans cannot fully understand God, so he remains a mystery until we know him completely in Heaven

❤ Pray the **Glory Be**, page 383.

* Discuss the opening question as a class.

DAY 3—Discover, Pages 56–57

* Recall Old Testament accounts showing God did not abandon his People and remained true to his promise to save them
* Identify that God planned from the beginning to give his only Son, Jesus Christ, to reconcile all of creation to himself

❤ Pray **Psalm 19:2**, page 51.

* Direct the students' attention to the opening question.

DAY 4—Discover, Pages 58–59

* Examine fundamental beliefs about God: he is eternal, he is truth, and he is love
* Reflect on the attributes of God

❤ Pray the *Pater Noster*, page 383.

* Discuss the opening question as a class.

DAY 5—Live, Pages 60–61

* Describe adoration and its importance as a prayer form
* Explore the devotion to Our Lady of Fátima
* Offer the Celebration of the Word prayer

❤ Allow time for the students to silently pray and reflect.

REVIEW AND ASSESSMENT

Chapter Review, page 62
Chapter Test, page 51F

📶 **aliveinchrist.osv.com** Customize and Download Assessments, Email Links to eAssessments, Interactive Student Reviews

Build	Close	Materials & Resources
• Present lesson highlights. • Preview **Catholic Faith Words**. ★ The students will write what they have learned about God through Sacred Scripture.	• *Activity* Identify a way God's presence has been personally experienced in the past week.	☐ pencils or pens ☐ board or chart paper
• **Catholic Faith Words** Divine Revelation, mystery • Discuss human reason. 📖 Read and reflect on **Genesis 1:1–2:4**. • Describe characteristics of Adam and Eve.	• *Activity* Reflect on questions about God and creation. • Conclude with a review of key concepts and objectives.	☐ pencils or pens ☐ board or chart paper
• **Catholic Faith Words** image of God • Review some Old Testament examples of God's faithfulness. • Discuss how we fit into God's plan. 📖 Read **1 John 1:5** and **1 John 4:6**.	• *Activity* Discuss ways to pay attention to the world around us. • Conclude with a review of key concepts and objectives.	☐ pencils or pens ☐ board or chart paper
• **Catholic Faith Words** eternal • Review attributes of God. ★ The students will select attributes of God that reflect how they currently relate to him.	• Review the In Summary statements. • *Optional Activity* What Does God Look Like? (Activity Master 1)	☐ pencils or pens ☐ highlighter ☐ Activity Master 1 (Page 51G)
• Learn about Our Lady of Fátima. • *Activity* Identify people who reflect attributes of God.	• Select three readers. • Follow the order of prayer. ▶ Sing or play the closing song.	☐ pencils or pens 📶 "Our God Reigns"

Chapter Connections

FORMING CATHOLIC IDENTITY ACROSS THE CURRICULUM

To integrate the Catholic faith in all aspects of curriculum, this chapter's objectives can be reinforced and applied in the instruction of other disciplines.

Go to **aliveinchrist.osv.com** for cross-curricular activities and projects linked to the doctrinal content discussed in this unit. Activities are available from among the following knowledge categories and content areas:

Language Arts

- Integration of Knowledge
- Literacy
- Speaking and Listening
- Writing Skills

Math

- Algebraic Thinking
- Geometry
- Measurement and Data
- Numbers and Operations

Science

- Earth Science
- Life Science
- Physical Science
- Technology

Social Studies

- Civics
- Economics
- Geography
- History

NCEA IFG: ACRE Edition

Knowledge of the Faith

- **Objective:** To know and understand basic Catholic teaching about the Incarnate Word Jesus Christ as the way, truth, and life

Moral Formation

- **Objective:** To be knowledgeable about the teachings of Jesus and the Church as the basis of Christian morality and to understand Catholic Social Teaching

Catholic Faith Literacy

Abraham, Creator, mystery

Catholic Social Teaching

To integrate Catholic Social Teaching into your lesson, choose one of the following features: Rights and Responsibilities of the Human Person, pages 338–339; or Care for God's Creation, pages 346–347.

- Start the Live step of the process by talking about Our Lady of Fátima on page 60. Then move directly to the Catholic Social Teaching feature.
- Or, to expand the lesson, complete page 60, then move to the Catholic Social Teaching feature.
- Return to Chapter 1 for the prayer on page 61.

Music Option

Use the following song to enhance catechetical learning or for prayer.

- "Our God Reigns," Day 5, Page 61

Name _____   Date _____

Match each description in Column A with the correct term in Column B by filling in the appropriate letter.

Column A

____ **1.** Steadfast love, truth, almighty

____ **2.** Choosing to turn from God

____ **3.** God is, was, and always will be

____ **4.** The ability to think and make connections

Column B

a. intellect

b. sin

c. attributes of God

d. eternal

Circle the letter of the choice that best completes each sentence.

5. Created in the image of God, humans have the ability to think, ____, be free, love, and be in a relationship with God and others.

   a. hate   **c.** protest

   b. choose   **d.** change

6. A(n) ____, is a truth of faith that cannot be fully understood but is believed because God has shown it to us through Scripture, his Son, or the Church.

   a. mystery   **c.** canon

   b. account   **d.** truth

7. The story of God's relationship with his Chosen People is recorded in the ____.

   a. Tradition   **c.** Old Testament

   b. Gospels   **d.** New Testament

8. Through ____, God wants to reconcile creation to himself.

   a. the Old Testament   **c.** his Son

   b. his attributes   **d.** his blessings

Write a response on the lines below.

9. What is Divine Revelation? _____

_____

10. Why do humans need the salvation of Jesus Christ? _____

_____

_____

_____

Name _____ Date _____

What Does God Look Like?

You will be working in a small group to create a poster. You will need poster board, magazines, scissors, tape or glue, markers, yarn, colored paper, pipe cleaners, and this instruction sheet.

Step 1:

Create a headline for your poster. It could read "What We Think God Looks Like," "Our Vision of God," or something similar. Write your headline ideas in the space below. Circle the one that your group chooses.

Step 2:

As a group, discuss what you think God looks like and how you would like to illustrate your ideas. List your group's ideas in the space below.

Step 3:

Work together to create your image. Use as many supplies as you would like. Try to think beyond "typical" images of God. List any supplies that you may need in the space below.

Step 4:

Be prepared to make a presentation on your creation. Make sure someone in your group is able to explain why you created your image of God the way you did. Make some notes about your creation in the space below.

The Mystery of God

 Let Us Pray

Leader: Your wonderful works surround us, O God. All creation praises you.

> "The heavens declare the glory of God;
> the firmament proclaims the works of
> his hands." **Psalm 19:2**

All: God our Father, you have given us so much. We are a grateful people.

Scripture

The works of God are all of them good;
he supplies for every need in its own time.

At his word the waters become still as in a
flask; he had but to speak and the reservoirs
were made.

He has but to command and his will is done;
nothing can limit his saving action.

The works of all humankind are present to him;
nothing is hidden from his eyes.

His gaze spans all the ages:
is there any limit to his saving action?

To him, nothing is small or insignificant,
and nothing too wonderful or hard for him.

No cause then to say: "What is the purpose
of this?"
Everything is chosen to satisfy a need.
The Wisdom of Ben Sira (Sirach) 39:16–21

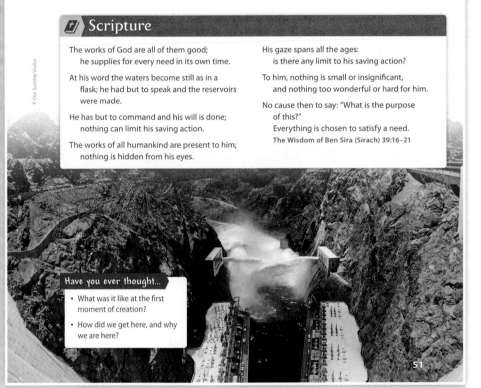

© Our Sunday Visitor

Have you ever thought...

- What was it like at the first moment of creation?
- How did we get here, and why we are here?

51

Scripture Background

Scripture Reflection Process

Invite the students to be still, close their eyes, and focus on their breathing. Encourage them to open their minds and hearts to what God is saying to them.

- Proclaim the Scripture and have the students sit in silence.
- *Ask:* What did you hear God say to you today?
- Allow volunteers to share.

▶ You may play instrumental music to begin the reflection.

Objective

- Reflect on God's personal invitation through Scripture

OPEN

Let Us Pray

Invite the students to gather in the prayer space and make the Sign of the Cross. Pray the leader prayer. Invite a student to read aloud the Psalm verse. Prompt the group's response.

Have the students move from the prayer space back to their seats.

Say: God created everything that we see and hear, especially each of us. Everything God created is good. Let's listen to what the Bible tells us about God's plan.

Scripture

Guide the students through the process of Scripture reflection (see the Scripture Background box below).

- Remember, this is a spiritual discipline that takes practice. The students will grow in their capacity to sit in silence. Throughout the year, build to four minutes.

Have you ever thought…

Say: All creation gives glory to God—including each one of us. When you care for creation, you share in God's plan.

- Invite the students to respond to the questions.

DAY 1

Objective

- Indicate prior knowledge of chapter concepts and vocabulary

BUILD _____

Use this page to assess the students' knowledge related to the chapter content.

Getting Started

Have a volunteer read aloud the first paragraph.

- *Ask:* How does God make himself known to us?
- Allow volunteers to respond.
- Write their answers on the board or on chart paper.

What I've Learned

Arrange the class into groups of four to work together and complete the graphic organizer.

- ★ Encourage the students to write in some ways that they have learned about God through Sacred Scripture. If they recall a particular Scripture passage, have them include it.
- Allow the students to discuss some of the things they have learned with their small groups.
- Reassemble the class and have the groups report back on how they completed the organizer.

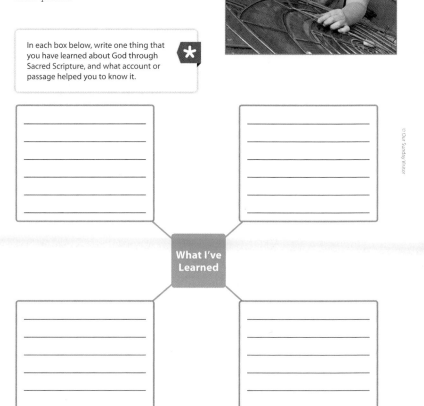

Getting Started

In this chapter, you will learn about how we come to know God and how we are made in his image and likeness, and how we fit into his plan. You will also explore some of the things we do know about God and about how he makes it possible for us to know him and share in his qualities.

In each box below, write one thing that you have learned about God through Sacred Scripture, and what account or passage helped you to know it.

What I've Learned

52 Chapter 1

✓ Teaching Tip

The Invite Experience

The students' experience with the Invite pages in this first chapter can set the tone for the opening prayers throughout the year, and even for the students' prayer lives for years to come.

- Through your prayerful facilitation, you have the opportunity to share how very much alive Scripture is, and how connected it is to our life experiences.
- By introducing your students to this prayerful process of reflection on God's Word, you are helping them to learn how to listen for God's invitation to them. This is a very personal journey and it may take some time for the students to become comfortable with it.

Catholic Faith Words

- Divine Revelation
- mystery
- image of God
- eternal

IDENTIFY

ID a Creation Connection Take a few minutes to reflect on the past couple of weeks. Choose two days and identify a simple "creation connection" for each. Write about one way you experienced God's presence. Where or when did you experience a connection with God's creation? For example, perhaps you saw evidence of the "works of God" (The Wisdom of Ben Sira [Sirach] 39:16) when you saw the sun rise or went for a walk. Be sure to explain how you gave praise to God.

_____
_____
_____
_____
_____
_____
_____
_____
_____
_____
_____
_____
_____
_____
_____
_____

The Mystery of God **53**

Optional Activity

God's Love for Creation _Visual/Spatial, Intrapersonal_

Help the students remember that God loves and cares for all creation.

- Throughout the year, invite the class to give thanks for the gifts of creation—family members, pets, or even places they have visited.
- Devote a bulletin board or poster area to pictures of ordinary objects and events for which the students are grateful.
- Encourage the students to frequently bring in pictures to add to the board, and to spend some time reflecting on the wonder of creation and our wonderful Creator.

Work with Words

Read aloud the vocabulary words at the top of this page.

- Ask the students to put a check mark next to words they have heard before and circle any words they are unfamiliar with.
- Invite volunteers to share the definitions of the words they know.
- Explain that the class will learn about all of these Catholic Faith Words as they complete the chapter.

CLOSE

ACTIVITY

Introduce the activity. Remind the students that God reveals himself to us through his creation every day. Being aware of and remembering God's presence throughout the moments of our days are profoundly spiritual acts.

- Tell the students that remembering God's presence is a spiritual habit that they will nurture during the year.
- Have the students work independently to identify some simple "creation connections" that they recently experienced.
- Provide time for reflection.
- Allow volunteers to share their responses with the class.

DAY 2

Objectives

- Examine the unique role of humans and the purpose of human intellect and reason

- Differentiate the ways we can come to know God

- Recognize that humans cannot fully understand God, so he remains a mystery until we know him completely in Heaven

OPEN

 Have the students pray the Glory Be from page 383.

As a class, discuss the question at the top of the page.

BUILD

Coming to Know God

Have a student read aloud the text.

- Explain that God has given us the ability to recognize his presence through all of creation.

Seeing God in the Works of Creation

Read aloud the text.

- Ask the students to describe the word *reason* in their own words.

- Have them discuss the questions in small groups.

Scripture

Invite a student to read the Scripture quote.

- Send the students directly to the source, Genesis 1:1—2:4, to find out more about why God created the world and humans.

Coming to Know God

How do we come to know who God is?

Most people can't help but have a sense of awe and wonder at the beauty and order of the stars, planets, and galaxies, especially when they look at some amazing satellite images. Looking at pictures of the universe can sometimes make us aware of how human beings are a part of "the big picture." And at some point in our lives, most of us ask ourselves what's the reason for it all, and what role do we play in that bigger picture.

The creation accounts in the Book of Genesis tell us something wonderful: Even though humans are a small part of the universe, they have a special place in the eyes of God. And God shows that he wants all humans to know and love him.

Scripture

"In the beginning, when God created the heavens and the earth … the earth was without form or shape …" Genesis 1:1–2

Go to the Source

Read *Genesis 1:1–2:4* to find out more about why God created the world and humans.

Seeing God in the Works of Creation

From the beginning of our time on Earth, the natural world has helped humans recognize and acknowledge God. People felt God's power in the forces of wind, fire, and water. They saw God's beauty in the trees and flowers. They got a sense of God's generosity as he gave them the responsibility to be caretakers of his many gifts of creation.

Adam and Eve were able to see these aspects of God because he had given them the gift of human reason. Like all of us, they were given an intellect—the ability to think and make connections. With this gift, we can grow in knowledge and search for the meaning of the things we experience. When we use reason, we discover the power and presence of God even in the most basic parts of his created world.

> What aspects of nature help you see God as the Creator?

> How do you experience God's presence in the world?

The Vatican Observatory at Castel Gandolfo, Lazio, Italy

54

Scripture Background

Genesis 1:1—2:25

The full texts of the Genesis creation accounts reflect the Hebrew people's search for an ultimate answer to some of life's fundamental questions: Who made humans, and why? Where did we come from, and where are we heading?

- Both accounts in Genesis reveal the religious truth that humans are creatures of God and are reliant upon him for life, love, and happiness.

- The Bible and science do not contradict one another regarding creation. Science addresses how various things in the world came to be. Genesis reveals who created the world and why.

Beyond Words

The works of creation are only one way people can learn about God. We can discover more of who God is through the ways he acts in the world and in our lives. Some things we can only come to know because he chooses to reveal them, or make them known to us. We call the process of God gradually revealing himself to us, **Divine Revelation**. In creating Adam and Eve, also referred to as our first parents, God showed his great generosity and love. He made them in his own image so that they could be like him, free to think and choose, able to love, and experience friendship. Out of love God made himself known to them.

Although he shows himself in so many ways through creation and through his relationship with people, God cannot be fully or completely known. Whether we see God in creation or in relation to a human person, what we see is only a small aspect of who God is.

This is why we call God a **mystery**, because the depth of who God is cannot be seen or fully understood by humans. Human expressions of God are limited because we are human. We will never know all about God's nature while on Earth. We will only know God completely when we know him in Heaven.

Catholic Faith Words

Divine Revelation the process by which God makes himself known. The chief sources of revelation are Sacred Scripture and Sacred Tradition.

mystery a truth of faith that cannot be fully understood but that is believed because God has shown it in Scripture, in the life of Jesus, or in the teachings of the Church

---

REFLECT

List some ways we come to know God. What are some questions you have about God and creation?

_____

_____

_____

_____

Who or what do you think can help you answer your questions?

_____

_____

_____

_____

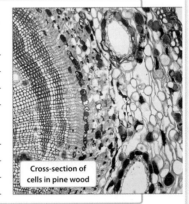

Cross-section of cells in pine wood

Optional Activity

Works of Creation   *Visual/Spatial, Interpersonal*

We can discover more about who God is through his works of creation, like the animals in the world around us.

- In the second creation account, God brings the animals he created to Adam to name them (see Genesis 2:19–20).
- Have the students "create" a new animal, illustrate it, and name it.
- Invite them to share their creation with a classmate.

Beyond Words

Invite a volunteer to read aloud the first paragraph.

- Remind the students that we learn from the creation accounts that God made humans in his image and likeness.
- Ask them to describe some of the characteristics of Adam and Eve that reflect God in them. Possible responses: ability to think, make choices, have feelings, and so on

Have the students silently read the last two paragraphs.

- Explain that despite the gifts God has given us, we still cannot understand him completely.

Work with Words

Write the Catholic Faith Words on the board or on chart paper.

- Ask the students to explain what these two terms mean, based on what they read in the text.
- Have a volunteer read aloud the definitions from the box.

CLOSE _____

ACTIVITY

Allow the students time to reflect on the questions. Then have them complete the activity individually.

- Invite volunteers to share their questions. Doing so can allow for a variety of answers.

Quick Review God makes himself known to us, out of love, through Sacred Scripture and Sacred Tradition. We will not fully know or understand God until we get to Heaven.

DAY 3

Objectives

- Recall Old Testament accounts showing God did not abandon his People and remained true to his promise to save them
- Identify that God planned from the beginning to give his only Son, Jesus Christ, to reconcile all of creation to himself

OPEN

Ask the students to stand and quiet themselves. Together read aloud Psalm 19:2, page 51.

Ask a volunteer to read aloud the question at the top of the page. Write the students' answers on the board or on chart paper.

BUILD

God's Plan for Us

Review the content of this section with the students. Have volunteers read aloud the bullet points.

- Allow the students to comment or ask questions after each paragraph or bullet point.

📖 Go to the Source

You may want to send the students directly to the Bible, 1 John 4:6 and 1 John 1:5, to read for themselves how John speaks about God.

- When you mention the Bible, tell the students they can read more about Sacred Scripture on page 364.

God's Plan for Us

How do humans fit into God's plan?

Our first parents reflected the goodness and glory of God. They were created in harmony with one another and with God. And when they freely chose to turn from God and to sin, God did not abandon them. Humans did not completely lose what made them like God—their ability to be good, to love, to be holy, to think, and to be free. In fact, we are each created in the **image of God**, his Divine likeness. Human nature remained basically good, but weakened, inclined to sin.

God remained with humans and promised to restore, or bring back, the human family to its original glory so that all can once again share life fully with him.

- The accounts in Genesis show that God wanted to lead all people to know his love.

- With Noah, God made a lasting covenant, or sacred, binding agreement, to bring all creation back to the harmony he had originally intended it to have. (See Genesis 9:1–17.)
- God made Abraham the "father of all nations," and promised that through Abraham's descendants, all nations would be blessed. (See Genesis 15:1–21.)
- In spite of her old age, God blessed Sarah with a son. She and her husband Abraham shared in God's blessing and promise. (See Genesis 17:15–19; 21:1–3.)

God planned from the beginning of creation to give his only Son, Jesus Christ, to the world so that humans would be restored to the place that they enjoyed originally. The promise of salvation was planted in the hearts of the Israelites, God's Chosen People. This hope gave them the courage to face hardship and even exile.

📖 **Go to the Source**
Read 1 John 4:6 and 1 John 1:5 to see how John speaks about God, who is Truth and Light.

56 Chapter 1

© Our Sunday Visitor

✝ Scripture Background

Love One Another

The three letters of John (1 John, 2 John, 3 John) reveal the conflict within a Christian community. Feelings of betrayal, mistrust, bitterness, and sadness are evident.

- The writer of the letters had once belonged to the community and is saddened and angry at its division. It is clear that there can be profoundly different understandings among Christians.
- The author expresses intense religious conviction using simple truths to remind the community that truly loving God also means truly loving one another.

Moses crossing the Red Sea, artist unknown

The story of God's relationship with the Israelites is recorded in the Old Testament. Throughout their history, God's Chosen People had indications of the salvation that would one day be brought into the world by Christ. For example, when the Israelites fled from slavery in Egypt, God helped them navigate their way across the Red Sea (see Exodus 14:21–31). This liberation foreshadowed, or prefigured, the salvation that Christ would bring us, helping us navigate our way toward the plan God the Father has for all humans. We see in this example how the Jewish faith, unlike other non-Christian faiths, is a response to God's Revelation in the old covenant.

> What do you think God's plan has to do with you?

> What signs of God's plan exist in the world?

Catholic Faith Words

image of God the Divine likeness in all human beings that comes from being made by God and includes the ability to think, choose, be free, love, and be in relationship with God and others

NOTICE, CONNECT, PRAY

How do you pay attention to the world around you?

- Name two things that surprise you as being signs of God's presence or his action in our lives.

  1. _____

  2. _____

- What could you do with your friends, class, or family to connect to what you've noticed, such as taking care, showing other people, using it?

- What do you want to say to or ask from God because of this? Compare your answer with a classmate.

The Mystery of God **57**

✓ **Teaching Tip**

Recognizing God's Presence

Faith is a gift that moves us to seek out God and recognize him in the world around us. The more an individual can have faith in God's presence through truth, beauty, and love, the easier it becomes to discover God in everyday life and to rely on him in hardship or sadness.

- Explain to the students that part of the skill of recognizing God's presence involves filtering out the "noise" in our lives that prevents us from listening to the gentle voice of God.

- Invite them to list three things that make it hard to recognize God's voice. Then have them list two things of beauty that have helped them experience God's presence.

God's Plan for Us, *continued*

Read aloud the paragraph.

- Point out the illustration at the top of the page and its connection to the text.

- Facilitate a discussion of the questions at the end of the text.

- Ask the students to brainstorm a list of the signs of God's plan.

Call the students' attention to the meaning of *image of God* in the Catholic Faith Words box. Have them silently read the definition.

- Invite them to share their understanding of what being created in the "image of God" means to them.

CLOSE _____

ACTIVITY

Read aloud the question and the first bullet.

- Have the students write their responses.

- Invite them to share their thoughts with a classmate.

- Continue by reading the second and third bullets, pausing after reading each one to allow time for class discussion.

Quick Review God planned from the beginning of creation to give his only Son, Jesus Christ, to the world. Through Christ, God reconciled all of his creation to himself so that the human race would be restored to the fullness of the life he created us for.

DAY 4

Objectives

- Examine fundamental beliefs about God: he is eternal, he is truth, and he is love
- Reflect on the attributes of God

OPEN

♥ Have the students stand and pray the *Pater Noster*, page 383, as an echo prayer, repeating each line after you.

- Point out that the *Pater Noster* is the Latin version of the Lord's Prayer. Explain that Latin is the official language of the Catholic Church.

Tell the class that this section will focus on some things we know about God.

BUILD

Revealed Truths

Have the students read the two paragraphs in silence.

- Explain that both nature and our own humanness make it possible to know God.
- Point out some things we can know about God: God is eternal, God is truth, God is love.
- Call the students' attention to the meaning of *eternal* in the Catholic Faith Words box.

God Is Truth

Read aloud the paragraph.

- Invite a class discussion on the questions at the end of the text.

Jesus said "I go and prepare a place for you.... Where I am going, you know the way" (John 14:3–4).

Revealed Truths

What are some of the things that we know about God?

Because of the way humans think, it's hard to understand anything that does not have a beginning or origin that can be easily explained. Yet, the accounts of creation show us that "God is" and "has always been," even before the beginning of time, and will be forever. This is what it means to say that God is **eternal**.

God alone created the Heavens and the Earth. He didn't need to create anything at all, not the Heavens and Earth or any human persons. He is complete in himself. He isn't lonely. Yet God chose freely to show himself by creating out of nothing all that we see around us today.

58   Chapter 1

God Is Truth

God is Truth itself. He will never deceive us or lead us in the wrong direction. Whatever God makes known about himself is true, and the words that he speaks are always true. God is faithful to his Word. His promise to bring salvation to all people is a promise that we can count on.

> When have you counted on someone to tell you the truth—and they did? When has someone counted on you to tell them the truth—and you did?

> What does all this tell you about the power of truth?

Catholic Faith Words

eternal the term that means "God is" and "has always been," even before the beginning of time, and will be forever

---

i   Teacher Background

Using a Biblical Concordance

A concordance of the Bible is a comprehensive index of the words used in the Bible arranged alphabetically with indications as to the passages where the words occur. Using a biblical concordance helps you delve deeper into Scripture. You can use it:

- to locate passages you vaguely remember by searching for key words.
- to trace the history of words and determine whether the English word was originally translated from Hebrew or Greek, which can affect the meaning.
- to help your students discover the frequency of use of a particular word that connects with your lessons.

God Is Love

Have you ever been hurt and felt like getting back at someone to "punish" that person? This natural reaction is part of what it means to be a human being who is imperfect. But we strive to grow more like God. One of the reasons people stand in awe of God is because he is strong and consistent in showing love for his People. God's love is perfect.

In the Old Testament, we find a God who never stops showing his love to the Israelites in powerful ways. When they were in captivity in Egypt, he led them to freedom. When they grumbled in the desert, he fed them and gave them water. Over and over, the people who belonged to God would fail to act like it, but God's response would always be the same: a forgiving and compassionate love.

The Attributes of God	
○ God is **living**,	in the Heavens and on the Earth.
○ God is **steadfast love**,	always faithful and trustworthy.
○ God is **holy**,	a mystery only vaguely known to us now.
○ God is **eternal**,	without beginning and without end.
○ God is **truth**,	for he is incapable of deception.
○ God is **merciful and gracious**,	always ready to forgive.
○ God is **almighty**,	ruling over and capable of everything.
○ In God **there is only light**;	in him there is no darkness.

1. Highlight the attribute of God that best describes the way you relate to him now.

2. Place a check mark by the attribute you find most comforting.

IN SUMMARY   Catholics Believe

We can come to know God through all that he has created and through human reason.

- Out of nothing, God created the Heavens and the Earth, and made humans in his image and likeness, making it possible to know him and share in his Divine qualities.

- God promised to restore the human race to the harmony and perfection for which he originally created us, and throughout history he has shown himself and his plan in many ways.

- From the Genesis creation accounts and the world around us, we come to know God and get a sense of his attributes—eternal, truth, love, merciful, holy, living.

The Mystery of God   **59**

Optional Activity

Activity Master 1: What Does God Look Like?

Distribute copies of the activity found on teacher page 51G.

- Organize the students in small groups. Provide each group with the supplies listed on the activity master.

- Arrange for the groups to share their creations with the rest of the class.

God Is Love

Invite two volunteers to read aloud the material in this section.

Remind the students that God loves us completely, and his love is perfect.

The Attributes of God

Use the chart to help the class review the attributes of God.

★ Ask the students to highlight the attribute of God that best describes the way they relate to him right now. Then have them put a check mark next to the attribute that they find most comforting.

- Arrange the students in small groups.

- Encourage the groups to discuss their answers.

CLOSE _____

In Summary

Have volunteers read aloud the opening sentence and each of the three summary points.

- Close by asking the students to select an attribute of faith they would like to work on in the coming week.

- Remind them that they do not have to share this information.

DAY 5

Objectives

- Describe adoration and its importance as a prayer form
- Explore the devotion to Our Lady of Fátima
- Offer the Celebration of the Word prayer

OPEN

♥ Invite the students to consider how they know they are loved.

- Allow a minute of silence for their personal prayer and reflection.

BUILD

Our Catholic Life

Ask a volunteer to read aloud the two paragraphs.

- Based on the reading, invite another volunteer to share what he or she understands about prayers of adoration.
- Have the students silently reflect on the two questions at the end of this section.

People of Faith

Explain to the students that Our Lady of Fátima is a title for Mary, the Mother of Jesus.

- Read aloud the People of Faith paragraph.
- Review with the class the People of Faith Background box.
- Invite the students to pray a decade of the Rosary in honor of Our Lady of Fátima.

Our Catholic Life

As we learn more about God, we also learn more about ourselves. We get a sense of who God calls us to be and what he wants for us. We can be sure that he wants to know and love each of us. He speaks to us, calling us to be with him, to respond in some way. This dialogue between God and us takes place in prayer.

We have many forms and expressions of prayer. One is a **prayer of adoration**, which honors our Creator, acknowledges we are his creatures, and holds high his greatness. Adoration is traditionally a prayer of respectful silence in which we adore God who made all things. It humbles us, reminding us that the we are dependent upon God, who is eternally good, loving, merciful. We can trust that he hears our prayers and knows what we need.

> When have you noticed and acknowledged God's greatness? What was it like to do so?

People of Faith

Our Lady of Fátima, 20 B.C.–45 A.D.

Mary, the mother of Jesus, is known by many titles, some of which come from places where she has appeared and given a message of hope and love. In 1917, three children from Fátima, Portugal saw the Blessed Virgin Mary. Mary revealed three "secrets" to the children and encouraged them to tell people to pray the Rosary. Sometimes Mary is called Our Lady of Fátima because of that. The Church celebrates her feast day on **May 13**.

📶 For more, go to aliveinchrist.osv.com

60 Chapter 1

IDENTIFY

List the names of three friends or family who, through their actions, reflect attributes of God.

_____
_____
_____
_____

Choose one and write a concrete example of what he or she has done, or does, to live in God's image.

_____
_____
_____
_____

People of Faith Background

Our Lady of Fátima

Here are some additional details about Our Lady of Fátima to assist you in presenting this section:

- Through a series of apparitions (May 13–October 13, 1971), Mary told three shepherd children that she desired frequent recitation of the Rosary and penance done for sinners.
- Pope Saint John Paul II credited Our Lady of Fátima for his survival of the attempt on his life in 1981.

📶 Encourage the students to go to **aliveinchrist.osv.com** at home to learn more about Our Lady of Fátima.

Celebration of the Word

Leader: Our God is amazing and awesome, beyond our understanding, but here right now—here in our midst. Let us prepare to hear God's Word to us about his creation.

A reading from the Book of Genesis.

Read Genesis 1:1–31.

The word of the Lord.

All: Thanks be to God.

Leader: There is a single and wonderful source of life.
Let us turn in prayer to God the Creator.

Respond to each petition with these words:

Hear us, O Lord.

Reader 1: O God, you have created the Earth and the Heavens, and in your goodness, you created us.
Help us treasure and respect all you have created.

All: Hear us, O Lord.

Reader 2: O God, at times it is hard to imagine that there is a Creator who could envision all the beauty we see around us.
We thank you for all you have given to us.

All: Hear us, O Lord.

Reader 3: O God, with love and generosity you created all we see.
Help us to accept the love you have for us,
And to share that love in the way we live.

All: Hear us, O Lord.

Leader: O God, in your infinite wisdom you have given us life.
In the wonders of nature,
through the seasons of the year
and the seasons of our lives,
we thank you and praise you
with every breath we take.

All: Amen.

▶ *Sing or play "Our God Reigns"*

📶 Go to **aliveinchrist.osv.com** for an interactive review.

A Work with Words **Circle the letter of the choice that best completes the sentence.**

1. Because the depth of who God is cannot be seen or understood by humans, God is ___.
   a. a mystery   c. one
   b. a spirit   d. eternal

2. Because God was, is, and always will be, he is ___.
   a. spirit   c. eternal
   b. love   d. truth

3. Because God is ___, we can believe in his promise to bring salvation to all people.
   a. faithful   c. truth
   b. holy   d. spirit

4. Out of nothing, God created the Heavens and the Earth, and made humans in his ___.
   a. creation   c. image and likeness
   b. care   d. love and affection

5. Our first parents, Adam and Eve, were able to see the reflections of God through his creation because he gave them the gift of ___.
   a. human reason   c. salvation
   b. communion   d. his likeness

B Check Understanding **Complete each sentence with the correct term from the Word Bank. Not all terms will be used.**

compassionate love	Old Testament
God's attributes	salvation
Theological Virtues	communion
Heaven	Divine Revelation
Original Sin	

6. God's relationship with his Chosen People is told in the ___Old Testament___.

7. The exodus of the Israelites from slavery in Egypt foreshadowed the ___salvation___ that Christ would bring.

8. We will only fully know and understand God when we are in ___Heaven___.

9. Even when we disobey him, God shows us ___compassionate love___.

10. The process of God gradually making himself known to us is called ___Divine Revelation___.

C Make Connections **Write a one-paragraph response. Name and describe three attributes of God. Include examples of how you see or experience these attributes in your life today.**

_____
_____
_____
_____
_____
_____

ACTIVITY

Review the directions on page 60.

- Allow time for the students to complete the two sections.
- Invite volunteers to share their responses.

CLOSE

Celebration of the Word

💙 Explain to the students that they will be praying and reflecting on the Word of God.

Choose three readers and allow them to rehearse their parts. You will be the leader.

Gather the students in the prayer space with their books.

Invite them to quiet themselves.

Begin with the Sign of the Cross and follow the order of prayer on the student page.

▶ Conclude by inviting the students to sing or reflect on the song "Our God Reigns," downloaded from **aliveinchrist.osv.com**.

CHAPTER REVIEW

Review the instructions for each section and have the students complete the review.

📶 Go to **aliveinchrist.osv.com** to prepare customized and downloadable assessments, send eAssessments, and assign interactive reviews.

KEY CONCEPT

God speaks to us and tells us about himself and his plan for us.

DOCTRINAL CONTENT

- God is the author and inspiration of the Sacred Scripture that humans have recorded under his guidance and direction. (CCC, 105, 106)

- Scripture can be read and interpreted in a literal sense and a spiritual sense, providing a richness to the living reading of Scripture in the Church. (CCC, 115–117)

- The Gospels, are the center of the Bible because they record the truth of the life and ministry of Jesus. (CCC, 75, 76)

- God continues to speak to us through the Scriptures, as we proclaim them at Mass, reflect on them personally, and study them to learn more about Jesus. (CCC, 81, 1153)

- Moral conscience is present at the heart of every person, but we must assimilate it through the Word of God. (CCC, 1776–1782, 1802)

TASKS OF CATECHESIS

Helping children grow in a faith that is "known, celebrated, lived, and expressed in prayer" (NDC, 20).

This chapter focuses on the following tasks of catechesis:

- Promoting Knowledge of the Faith

- Moral Formation

Teacher Background

> Indeed, the word of God is living and effective, sharper than any two-edged sword, penetrating even between soul and spirit, joints and marrow, and able to discern reflections and thoughts of the heart.   Hebrews 4:12
>
> **> Reflect** Why do we say that the Word of God is living? How does this affect the way you live?

Many Catholics are aware that our Church draws its beliefs from both Sacred Scripture and Sacred Tradition. The New Testament came out of the beliefs of the early Christian Church. Hence, the Church predates the New Testament Scripture; in fact, accounts of the early days of the Church are included there. The leaders of the Church, under the inspiration of the Holy Spirit, eventually determined which books would be included in the New Testament. Their criteria included such things as widespread acceptance and consistency with the whole of Christian doctrine.

The Word of God changes a person who is faithful to its teachings. The Bible teaches, comforts, provokes, challenges, and motivates us in life-changing ways. One cannot seriously delve into Sacred Scripture without being transformed. And because we believe that Jesus Christ is the true Word of God, the nature of the transformation is that the one who takes in the Word becomes more like the Word—that person becomes more Christ-like. Our God, the author of all life, chooses to reveal himself to us through his Word. We bring our lives to that Word with an open heart, and the Church says we enter into a "dialogue" with God. How can we not be changed by that?

> Reflect How has your exposure to Sacred Scripture changed you for the better?

Teacher's Prayer

💜 Loving Father, you promised that you would be with us always. When I feel alone, bless me with awareness of your presence. Through your Word, help me recognize you in others, and give me the grace of appreciation. I ask this in Jesus' most holy name. Amen.

How Seventh Graders Understand Chapter Topics

Seventh graders might think of Scripture as a collection of boring, old stories. When we appreciate that Scripture is the living Word of God, we begin to see our own struggles, joys, and journeys reflected in the stories of God's People.

Teaching Tip: As you help the students understand the various literary forms of Scripture, encourage them to also relate what they find in Scripture to themselves with questions such as, "Have you ever felt like the person in this story?" or "What could this mean for us today?"

Sharing the Message with Seventh Graders

- At this age, young people are beginning to be concerned about establishing friendships that run deeper than those they had with the playmates of their childhood. They want to be able to share their thoughts and feelings with their friends. However, they are not usually comfortable sharing this deeply with the class.

- Having a sense of belonging is important to most people. Because of this, some seventh graders may be enticed to play along with the cruelty of the adolescent pecking order, just so they belong. Help them find other ways to belong.

- Young people sometimes need help making the connection between their lives and the lives of those who have gone before them. Help them understand how the decisions, good and bad, of past generations affect the world we live in today.

ONLINE RESOURCES

 Go to **aliveinchrist.osv.com**

You will find:

- Interactive lesson planning, additional activities, and ideas for the classroom environment

- Step by step lesson instruction from printed Teacher Edition for integrated lesson planning

- Custom-built assessments to download and eAssessment links

- Interactive reviews that provide scores and the option to review answers

- Chapter-specific Lectionary connections and a complete correlation ordered by the Sundays of the year, with suggestions for how to integrate the Scripture readings into chapter lessons

 Go to **osvparish.com** for Ask the Experts Q and A, Community Connections, and Blogs.

Chapter 2 Planner

Objectives	Open

DAY 1—Invite/Preview, Pages 63–65

- Reflect on God's personal invitation through Scripture
- Indicate prior knowledge of chapter concepts and vocabulary

- ♡ Psalm 16:11 Pray the opening prayer.
- 📖 Hebrews 4:12 Proclaim "The Sabbath Rest." Guide the students through the process of Scripture reflection.
- Discuss Have You Ever Thought questions.

DAY 2—Discover, Pages 66–67

- Explain Divine Inspiration as God's direction and guidance of the human writers of Scripture
- Contrast the content of the Old Testament and the New Testament
- Recognize the literary forms contained in the Bible

- ♡ Pray a prayer of blessing.
- Provide a clue to answer the opening question.

DAY 3—Discover, Pages 68–69

- Analyze the literal sense and spiritual sense of Scripture
- Distinguish the different major emphases presented by the four Evangelists in their respective Gospels
- Identify the development of the Gospels from the Person of Jesus to the written Word

- ♡ Pray the **Holy, Holy, Holy, Lord,** page 385.
- Discuss the opening question.

DAY 4—Discover, Pages 70–71

- Recognize that God's "voice" in the proclamation of Scripture and our response comprise a dialogue
- Examine the role of conscience in our lives

- ♡ Pray the **Lord's Prayer,** page 383.
- Share the answer to the opening question.

DAY 5—Live, Pages 72–73

- Demonstrate the capacity to locate a Scripture verse that has personal relevance
- Explore the faith life of Saint Matthew
- Offer the Prayer of Petition

- ♡ Allow time for silence so the students can reflect on their relationship with God.

REVIEW AND ASSESSMENT

Chapter Review, page 74
Chapter Test, page 63F

🛜 **aliveinchrist.osv.com** Customize and Download Assessments, Email Links to eAssessments, Interactive Student Reviews

Build	Close	Materials & Resources
• Present lesson highlights. • Preview **Catholic Faith Words**. ★ The students will share what they know about the Bible.	• Activity Reflect on what God is saying through Scripture.	☐ pencils or pens
• **Catholic Faith Words** Sacred Scripture, Divine Inspiration, canon of Scripture • Discuss what it means to be inspired. • Review literary forms in the Bible.	• Activity Work on a screenplay to explain the story of God and his People. • Conclude with a review of key concepts and objectives.	☐ pencils or pens ☐ board or chart paper
• **Catholic Faith Words** Gospel, Evangelists • Discuss senses in relation to Scripture. • Review the focus and audience of the Gospel writers. 📖 Read and reflect on **John 1:1–14**.	• Activity Read and reflect on the meaning of God's Word in the Gospels. • Conclude with a review of key concepts and objectives. • Optional Activity Symbols of the Evangelists (Activity Master 2)	☐ pencils or pens ☐ Bible ☐ Activity Master 2 (Page 63G)
• Discuss the ways God speaks to us. 📖 Read **Matthew 5:14–16**.	• Review the In Summary statements.	☐ pencils or pens
• Discuss the wisdom in Scripture. • Learn about Saint Matthew. • Activity Reflect on Scripture.	• Assign a reader and a leader. • Follow the order of prayer. ▶ Play the closing song.	☐ pencils or pens ☐ Bibles 📶 "God Has Chosen Me"

FORMING CATHOLIC IDENTITY ACROSS THE CURRICULUM

To integrate the Catholic faith in all aspects of curriculum, this chapter's objectives can be reinforced and applied in the instruction of other disciplines.

Go to **aliveinchrist.osv.com** for cross-curricular activities and projects linked to the doctrinal content discussed in this unit. Activities are available from among the following knowledge categories and content areas:

Language Arts

- Integration of Knowledge
- Literacy
- Speaking and Listening
- Writing Skills

Math

- Algebraic Thinking
- Geometry
- Measurement and Data
- Numbers and Operations

Science

- Earth Science
- Life Science
- Physical Science
- Technology

Social Studies

- Civics
- Economics
- Geography
- History

NCEA IFG: ACRE Edition

Knowledge of the Faith

- **Objective:** To know and understand basic Catholic teaching about the Incarnate Word Jesus Christ as the way, truth, and life

Moral Formation

- **Objective:** To be knowledgeable about the teachings of Jesus and the Church as the basis of Christian morality and to understand Catholic Social Teaching

Catholic Faith Literacy

Bible, conscience, Inspiration, Scripture

Catholic Social Teaching

To integrate Catholic Social Teaching into your lesson, choose one of the following features: Rights and Responsibilities of the Human Person, pages 338–339; or Option for the Poor and Vulnerable, pages 340–341.

- Start the Live step of the process by talking about Saint Matthew on page 72. Then move directly to the Catholic Social Teaching feature.
- Or, to expand the lesson, complete page 72, then move to the Catholic Social Teaching feature.
- Return to Chapter 2 for the prayer on page 73.

Music Option

Use the following song to enhance catechetical learning or for prayer.

- "God Has Chosen Me," Day 5, Page 73

Name _____ Date _____

Circle the letter of the choice that best completes each sentence.

1. ___ is another name for the Bible, the Word of God written by humans acting under the Holy Spirit's inspiration and guidance.

   a. Sacred Tradition

   b. Sacred Scripture

   c. Divine Tradition

   d. Divine Scripture

2. The ___ sense of Scripture refers to the actual words that have been recorded.

   a. analogical

   b. allegorical

   c. literal

   d. spiritual

3. Catholics respond to God and commit themselves to follow God's Word during ___.

   a. Mass

   b. the Gospels

   c. the Epistles

   d. Tradition

4. Divine ___ is the process by which the Holy Spirit assisted the human authors in writing the Bible.

   a. Revelation

   b. Inspiration

   c. Proclamation

   d. Annunciation

Complete each sentence with the correct term.

5. The _____ message is the Good News of God's Kingdom and his saving love.

6. God's Word helps us develop a _____, which helps us judge between right and wrong.

7. In the Bible, the literary form of _____ helps people recall, in a straightforward way, something about God's relationship with the world.

8. The _____ of Scripture explains how to live justly and humbly before God.

Write a response on the lines below.

9. What is the canon of Scripture? _____

   _____

10. Name the four Evangelists and describe their work. _____

   _____

   _____

Name _____ Date _____

Symbols of the Evangelists

Select one of the Evangelists and draw your own version of the symbol associated with him.

When you have completed your drawing, locate other members of the class who drew the same symbol as you and gather together to share your artwork.

Each group will present their drawings to the rest of the class while a group spokesperson reads aloud the text on the Gospel writing of that Evangelist from page 69 of the textbook.

Matthew	Human
Mark	Lion
Luke	Ox
John	Eagle

The Word of God in Sacred Scripture

💙 Let Us Pray

Leader: O Lord, your Word is alive in our hearts. It is our guide, a light on our journey to you.

"You will show me the path to life, abounding joy in your presence." **Psalm 16:11**

All: God, we want to know you better. May your Word light our paths.

📖 Scripture

Indeed, the word of God is living and effective, sharper than any two-edged sword, penetrating even between soul and spirit, joints and marrow, and able to discern reflections and thoughts of the heart."
Hebrews 4:12

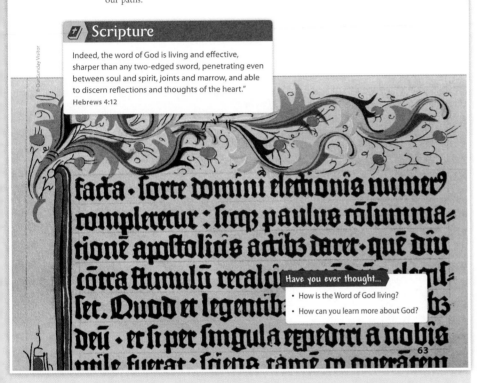

Have you ever thought...
- How is the Word of God living?
- How can you learn more about God?

63

📖 Scripture Background

Scripture Reflection Process

Invite the students to be still, close their eyes, and focus on their breathing. Encourage them to open their minds and hearts to what God is saying to them.

- Proclaim the Scripture and have the students sit in silence.
- *Ask:* What did you hear God say to you today?
- Allow volunteers to share.

 You may play instrumental music to begin the reflection.

Objective
- Reflect on God's personal invitation through Scripture

OPEN _____

💙 Let Us Pray

Invite the students to gather in the prayer space. Have them make the Sign of the Cross. Invite a student to take the role of Leader, praying the first lines as well as the Psalm verse. Lead the rest of the class in the response. Have the students return to their seats.

Say: God's Word is at the heart of our faith. It is alive; it is light on our journey to God; it shows us how to live; it brings us joy. Let's listen as God speaks to us through Sacred Scripture.

📖 Scripture

Guide the students through the process of Scripture reflection (see the Scripture Background box below).

- Remember, this is a spiritual discipline that takes practice. The students will grow in their capacity to sit in silence. Throughout the year, build to four minutes.

Have you ever thought...

Say: God reveals himself to us through Sacred Scripture. His Word "lights our paths" and strengthens us to make better choices.

- Invite the students to respond to the questions.

DAY 1

Objective

- Indicate prior knowledge of chapter concepts and vocabulary

BUILD _____

Use this page to assess the students' knowledge related to the chapter content.

Getting Started

Invite a student to read the first paragraph to the class.

- *Ask:* Why is reading Sacred Scripture such an important part of our faith lives?

- Allow the students to share their thoughts.

Who, Where, and What in the Bible

Have the students work on the chart independently.

★ Invite them to describe some people, places, and events they already know from the Old and New Testaments.

- Provide a couple examples to prompt the students if they need help getting started.

- Allow them to gather in small groups to discuss their answers.

Getting Started

In this chapter, you will learn about how God speaks to us and tells us about himself and his plan for us. God is the author and inspiration of the sacred words of Scripture, and he continues to speak with us today through his Word that we proclaim at Mass, pray with, learn from, and share.

Catholic Faith Words
• Sacred Scripture
• Divine Inspiration
• canon of Scripture
• Gospel
• Evangelists

In the chart below, describe some people, places, and events you already know from both the Old Testament and the New Testament.

Who, Where, and What in the Bible

People	· _____
	· _____
	· _____
Places	· _____
	· _____
	· _____
Events	· _____
	· _____

© Our Sunday Visitor

Reaching All Learners

Helping Shy Students Share

Some students may be shy. It is important to present alternate methods of sharing to give shy students an opportunity to be involved and to tell their own stories. Here are a few suggestions:

- Organize smaller groups for sharing.

- Be aware of who is in the small groups. A boisterous individual can intimidate a shy person into silence.

- Try to distinguish between temperamental shyness (part of a young person's makeup) and environmental shyness (new kid in school).

- Pair a shy person with a friend to possibly help him/her feel more comfortable when sharing.

Let God's Word into Your Heart Look up the following Scripture passages and use these questions to guide your reflection.

Hebrews 4:12 How is God's Word alive in the things I do?

_____

_____

_____

_____

_____

_____

Psalm 118:6 How is this passage meaningful to me now?

_____

_____

_____

_____

_____

_____

Ephesians 5:8 In what ways has God's Word helped me live as a disciple of Jesus?

_____

_____

_____

_____

_____

_____

_____

_____

_____

The Word of God in Sacred Scripture **65**

Work with Words

Point out the Catholic Faith Words box on page 64.

- Invite a volunteer to read aloud the vocabulary words.
- Ask the students to share what they know about Scripture.
- *Say:* When Saint Paul talks about the incredible power of God's Word (on page 63), he uses strong, descriptive action verbs and adjectives to describe it— *living, effective, sharp, penetrating.* There's a sense that, once we let God's Word into our hearts, there is no escaping its impact.
- Tell the class that they will learn more about Sacred Scripture and the other vocabulary words that tie into it as they review this chapter.

CLOSE

ACTIVITY

Introduce the activity as an opportunity for prayerful reflection on the role of God's Word in our lives.

- Have the students look up the suggested Scripture passages.
- Give them time for reflection.
- Encourage the students to journal their thoughts in their books.
- Suggest that they carry the questions about God's Word with them in their hearts as they learn and grow throughout this year.

Teacher Background

Studying Sacred Scripture

The word *theology* means the study of God. Consequently, the *Catechism of the Catholic Church* describes the study of Scripture as the "very soul of sacred theology" (CCC, 132).

- Because the Sacred Scriptures are inspired, they are truly the Word of God.
- The Holy Spirit plays a central role in our interpretation of Scripture. He guides the Church and so our personal revelation from Scripture must always be held inside the public revelation of Scripture.
- The Church "accepts and venerates" both the Old and New Testament books of the Bible (CCC, 138).

DAY 2

Objectives

- Explain Divine Inspiration as God's direction and guidance of the human writers of Scripture
- Contrast the content of the Old Testament and the New Testament
- Recognize the literary forms contained in the Bible

OPEN

♥ Have the class bow their heads as you pray a prayer of blessing.

Invite a student to read aloud the question. Point out that the chapter title provides a clue to the answer.

BUILD

God Speaks in Human Words

Ask a volunteer to read aloud the paragraph.

- Explain that the students will be learning how to build a solid relationship with God.

God Inspires

Direct the students to silently read the text in this section.

- Share that God speaks to us through his inspired Word or Sacred Scripture (the Bible).
- Emphasize that God is working in all of our lives, whether we notice or not, and stress that knowing God's story and how it connects to our lives helps us to better know him and his plan for us.

God Speaks in Human Words

What are some of the ways that God speaks to us?

When we meet someone for the first time, our ideas about the way that person talks or looks can sometimes get in the way of understanding him or her. But once we start to hear that person's story, we have a better understanding of him or her. In a similar way, once we get to know God's story, our friendship with him grows.

God Inspires

God wanted humans to get to know him, so he gradually made himself known to us over time. God chose to speak to his People with human words. Although no word can capture everything about God, these words do tell us what God want us to know about him and his hopes for us. **Sacred Scripture**, also called the Bible, is God's Word to us written by humans acting under the

Holy Spirit's direction and guidance. This direction and guidance is known as **Divine Inspiration**.

Scripture records the story of the relationship between God and his People and the communication that he had with them through history. By the Holy Spirit's action, the authors of Scripture faithfully wrote what God wanted to reveal and taught without error the truth about his plan for us.

Interpreting Scripture

The Church accepts and honors a set number of books as being inspired by God. This body of sacred texts is called the **canon of Scripture**. It includes forty-six books in the Old Testament and twenty-seven books in the New Testament. "The Old Testament prepares for the New and the New Testament fulfills the Old; the two shed light on each other; both are true Word of God" (*Catechism of the Catholic Church*, #140).

The Old Testament tells the story of God's relationship with Abraham and his descendants. It includes the laws, history, and stories of the Israelites.

After Jesus' Resurrection, many different people wrote about his life and ministry.

> **Catholic Faith Words**
>
> **Sacred Scripture** the Word of God written by humans acting under the Holy Spirit's inspiration and guidance; another name for the Bible
>
> **Divine Inspiration** the gift of the Holy Spirit which assisted the human authors in writing the Bible to ensure it contained the truths God wanted us to know
>
> **canon of Scripture** the Church's complete list of inspired books included in Sacred Scripture

66 Chapter 2

Optional Activity

World Religions *Verbal/Linguistic, Interpersonal*

Almost all major religions have sacred writings with guidelines for living good and holy lives. *The Declaration on Religious Freedom*, a document from the Second Vatican Council helps us to understand that there is truth in other religions, while reminding us that the fullness of truth subsists and lives within the Catholic Church.

- Ask the students to name some of the major world religions.
- Direct them to research the names of the sacred writings of those religions and provide a short summary of what they teach.
- Invite the students to compare their results through a class discussion.

The New Testament begins with the Gospels, which tell us about Jesus' ministry and teachings. It includes many Epistles, Letters written by Saint Paul and other disciples so the early Christians could learn about Jesus.

Because God is the author of Scripture, the interpretation of Scripture should help us understand what he wants to tell us in the Biblical text and what he desires for us. The Holy Spirit helps the Church to interpret and apply Scripture.

The Bible contains a variety of literary forms. A literary form is the way something is written. Knowing the form of a written work helps us to understand the meaning of what is being said.

Literary Forms in the Bible

• **Narrative stories** recall in a straightforward way something about God's relationship with the world.	See Matthew 2:1–12
• **Parables** are short stories Jesus told, using examples from everyday life or nature, to illustrate moral or spiritual truths.	See Mark 4:1–20
• **Teaching** enlightens people to understand how to live the Christian life.	See Luke 6:20–36
• **Miracle stories** teach how God's power and healing transform people.	See John 4:46–54
• **Laws** portray the rules of conduct that God has set for us in living in right relationship with him and others.	See Mark 12:28–34 and the Books of Exodus, Leviticus, Numbers, and Deuteronomy
• **Hymns and psalms** show the joy and struggle of being in relationship with God.	See the Book of Psalms
• **Proverbs** are short sentences of wisdom.	See the Book of Proverbs
• **Apocalyptic literature** reflects the expectation of decisive intervention of God in history, especially at the end of the world.	See the Book of Daniel

© Our Sunday Visitor

OUTLINE

Working with a classmate, create an outline for a screenplay or podcast on "The Story of God and His People." The story must span from creation to the present time. Choose what you think are the main points, and outline them here.

_____

_____

_____

The Word of God in Sacred Scripture **67**

ℹ️ Teacher Background

Bible Translations

Let the students know that there are a variety of translations of the Bible in existence. Among those approved by the USCCB and in common use in the U.S. Catholic Church are the New American Bible (the Lectionary is based on this translation); the New Revised Standard Version, Catholic Edition; and Today's English Version (Second Edition).

USCCB approval does not mean that other Bibles' translations are wrong, only that the Catholic Church has found the translations of the above Bibles to be most in concert with Catholic teaching and understanding.

Interpreting Scripture

Summarize the text that begins on page 66 and ends on page 67.

Work with Words

Ask a volunteer to write the three Catholic Faith Words from page 66 on the board or on chart paper.

- Allow the class to discuss what they learned in the text.
- Have the student record the class responses under each respective vocabulary word.
- Invite a volunteer to read aloud the definitions from the book.

Literary Forms in the Bible

Have the students review the different types of literary forms listed in the chart. (They should already be familiar with them.)

- Be sure to point out the various Scriptures that follow these forms.
- Explain to the class that knowing the literary form of a written work helps us understand its meaning.

CLOSE _____

ACTIVITY

Read aloud the directions.

- Allow the students to pair off and complete the activity.

Quick Review Divine Inspiration guided the human authors as they shared the stories of faith between God and his People. The Church honors and accepts specific sacred texts that make up the Old and New Testaments. Knowing the various literary forms that make up these texts helps us better understand and apply Scripture.

DAY 3

Objectives

- Analyze the literal sense and spiritual sense of Scripture
- Distinguish the different major emphases presented by the four Evangelists in their respective Gospels
- Identify the development of the Gospels from the Person of Jesus to the written Word

OPEN

💙 Ask the students to gather in the prayer space to pray the Holy, Holy, Holy Lord, page 385.

Discuss the question at the top of the page as a class.

BUILD

The Importance of the Gospels

Review the text with the class.

- Tell the students that when we use the term *senses* in relation to Scripture, we mean "layers."
- Explain that the senses we use to understand Scripture are the literal sense and the spiritual sense. The spiritual sense can be broken down further into the allegorical sense, moral sense, and anagogical sense.

Christ the Good News

Have the students silently read the text.

- *Ask:* Where in the Bible do we find the main sources of the life, ministry, and teachings of Jesus? in the four Gospels

---

The Importance of the Gospels

How do the senses of Scripture help us understand its message?

Scripture is so rich in expressing Divine truth that there are many senses, or layers, of Scripture. Two layers of meaning that can be seen in Scripture are the *literal sense* and the *spiritual sense*.

The literal sense of Scripture refers to the actual words that have been recorded. Understanding the literal sense involves studying the culture in which the words were written—the meaning of those words to the people of that time and place.

The spiritual sense has three subcategories:

- The allegorical sense shows how certain events pointed to Christ, even before his birth. The crossing of the Red Sea, for example, is a sign of Christ's victory over death.
- The moral sense gives instruction on how to live justly before God.
- The anagogical sense shows how human events and realities are signs of our heavenly future. The word *anagogical* comes from the Greek word *anongoge*, which means "leading." The Church, for example, is understood as leading to the New Jerusalem of Heaven.

Christ the Good News

The word **Gospel** means "good news." The four Gospels according to Matthew, Mark, Luke, and John contain the Good News of God's Kingdom and his saving love. They have the central place in Scripture because they present Jesus' life, ministry, and teaching. We revere the Old Testament, too, because the events recorded in it point to the salvation that God would bring when he sent his only Son to become man.

When the author of the Gospel according to John wrote that the Word was with God and the Word was God, he meant the living Word that is Jesus Christ (see John 1:1). Jesus Christ is the single Word through whom all the other words in Scripture have their meaning. Because Jesus himself is the living Word of God, the Gospels present the ultimate truth of Divine Revelation. Jesus is the fulfillment of God's Word and of God's promise.

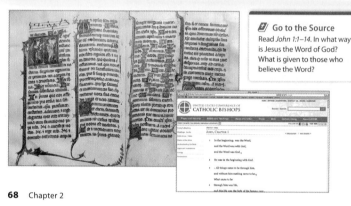

📖 **Go to the Source**
Read *John 1:1–14*. In what way is Jesus the Word of God? What is given to those who believe the Word?

© Our Sunday Visitor

 Teaching Tip

Group Participation

Remember, some students may be uncomfortable reading or sharing aloud. Create an open and accepting classroom to help these students become more comfortable sharing with their classmates.

- Allow time for the students to share both oral and written responses in groups, with partners, and individually.
- Make sure that you and the students avoid criticizing a response. Instead, be sure to encourage further introspection or ask for additional responses.
- Always look for opportunities to help the students succeed and feel good about participating.

A Different Emphasis

Inspired by the Spirit, all four **Evangelists** center their writing on Christ, and emphasize different aspects of his life or mission.

> Think of a time when you heard a single story told by more than one person. Why do you think there can be differences in the way two people tell the same story?

The Gospels and their Authors

 Matthew addresses a Jewish audience and wants to show them that Jesus is the fulfillment of the Old Testament accounts and promises of a Messiah. This Gospel emphasizes Jesus as the new covenant who fulfills the old covenant.

 Mark, in a brief but detailed way, stresses the announcement of God's Kingdom. Mark shows how the disciples did not always understand Jesus, and only gradually came to know who he is. When they did, they were ready to proclaim him to the world.

 Luke focuses on practical and ordinary things so that people will be open to Jesus' message of salvation in their life. Written for Gentiles (Greek Christians), this Gospel emphasizes Jesus as a Savior who helps us overcome the evil of sin, suffering, and death. He often shows Jesus in prayer.

 John focuses on spiritual things, and readers can see they are entering into an intimate relationship of love with God. In this Gospel, Jesus is shown answering questions that people pose to him. When they misunderstand his answers, he tells them more so that they can understand his truth.

© Our Sunday Visitor

Catholic Faith Words

Gospel a word that means "Good News." The Gospel message is the Good News of God's Kingdom and his saving love.

Evangelists the four inspired human authors of the Gospels: Matthew, Mark, Luke, and John

READ AND DISCUSS

In a small group, read a passage from one of the Gospels. Write about what it means to you. Then, as a group, discuss the meanings each member found in the passage.

- What do you learn about God's Word when you see the way different people respond to it?

_____

_____

_____

Go to the Source

Invite some of the students to take turns reading Bible verses from John 1:1–14. Discuss the follow-up questions on page 68 as a class.

A Different Emphasis

Read aloud the introduction.

Point out the Catholic Faith Words box and have a student read aloud the definitions of *Gospel* and *Evangelists*.

The Gospels and Their Authors

If possible, use Activity Master 2 with the class to review this content. If you choose not to use this Optional Activity, then allow time for the students to read about the Gospel authors. Encourage them to pay attention to the different focus of each author.

- Invite the students to discuss the question at the top of the page.

CLOSE _____

ACTIVITY

Have the students break into small groups to complete the activity.

- Discuss the question as a class.

Quick Review There are multiple senses, or layers of meaning, in Scripture that affect what we "take away" from God's Word. The Gospels all center on the work of Christ, but they each offer a different emphasis on his life and mission.

Optional Activity

Activity Master 2: Symbols of the Evangelists

Distribute copies of the activity found on teacher page 63G.

- This activity will help the students identify the symbols connected to each of the Evangelists, and understand the different ways they told the same story.

- As an alternative, you may wish to send the drawing portion of this activity home with the students.

CHAPTER 2 Family Name

Name _____ Date _____

Symbols of the Evangelists

Select one of the Evangelists and draw your own version of the symbol associated with him.

When you have completed your drawing, locate other members of the class who drew the same symbol as you and gather together to share your artwork.

Each group will present their drawings to the rest of the class while a group spokesperson reads aloud the text on the Gospel writing of that Evangelist from page 69 of the textbook.

Matthew	Human
Mark	Lion
Luke	Ox
John	Eagle

63G Alive in Christ, Grade 7 Chapter 2

DAY 4

Objectives

- Recognize that God's "voice" in the proclamation of Scripture and our response comprise a dialogue
- Examine the role of conscience in our lives

OPEN

💗 Have the students pray the Lord's Prayer from page 383.

Read aloud the opening question. Point out that although we don't actually hear God's voice, God speaks to us in the words we hear during Mass, in the Sacred Scriptures we read, and when we take time to pray and reflect on the Word of God.

BUILD

Conversation with God

Have the students silently read the text.

- Ask them to underline the most important sentence.
- Encourage them to share what they underlined.

The Word as Light

Read aloud the text.

- Allow volunteers to share with the class about times when the Word of God was a light for them.

📖 Scripture

Have a student proclaim Matthew 5:14–16.

- Arrange the students in small groups to discuss ways that they can be "a light" to others.

"Your word is a lamp for my feet, a light for my path" (Psalm 119:105).

Conversation With God

How does God speak to us today?

To this very day, God continues to speak to his People. When the Word of God is proclaimed at Mass, it is the voice of God that the assembly hears. This Word proclaimed from the Scriptures is Jesus Christ, a living Word. Even though human readers proclaim this Word, God speaks through them.

The proclamation of the Scriptures at Mass takes place during the Liturgy of the Word. This is just one way in which Catholics today dialogue with God. Through Psalm responses, the homily, and silent reflection, we respond to God and commit ourselves to follow his Word. The worship of the Church relies on God's Word, as do the personal prayer life of Catholics and our growth in virtue, modeled by Jesus.

The Word as Light

When the prophet Isaiah spoke of God's goodness to the Hebrew people, he said that a "people who walked in darkness have seen a great light" (Isaiah 9:1). In a similar way, Jesus explained that people who walk in the darkness will stumble, because people in darkness cannot see where they are going. This is why the Word of God is a light to all people.

📖 Scripture

"You are the light of the world. A city set on a mountain cannot be hidden. Nor do they light a lamp and then put it under a bushel basket; it is set on a lampstand, where it gives light to all in the house. Just so, your light must shine before others, that they may see your good deeds and glorify your heavenly Father."
Matthew 5:14–16

70 Chapter 2

Optional Activity

Voices *Verbal/Linguistic, Intrapersonal, Interpersonal*

This activity gives the students an opportunity to articulate an experience through different voices and to recognize differing points of view.

- Ask the students to recall a brief family story.
- Have them share the story as each family member would do so, using that person's facial expressions, gestures, and mannerisms.
- Invite them to share observations of the story from the various points of view portrayed.

Following the Light

By listening to the Word of God, you develop a conscience—the God-given ability that helps us judge right from wrong—that makes it possible for us to live a right and just life. A conscience formed by God's Word

- challenges us to live a good life and avoid evil.
- helps us judge between choices that are right or wrong, good or bad.
- strengthens us to put God's Word into action and to be signs of his goodness.
- gives us the confidence we need to live with faith. God speaks to followers of Christ through their conscience and the teachings of the Church.

> ### CATHOLICS TODAY
>
> Scripture plays an important role in our lives.
>
> - We proclaim and reflect upon it in communal worship.
> - We discover more about Jesus and his message as we read it by ourselves and in religion class.
> - We discuss its message for us today in Bible study.
> - We pray with it personally and with our families.
> - We turn to it for wisdom and for guidance.

IN SUMMARY   Catholics Believe

God speaks to us and tells us about himself and his plan for us.

- God is the author and inspiration of the sacred words of Scripture that humans have recorded under his guidance and direction.
- The four Gospels, which developed over the course of time after Jesus' Resurrection, are the center of the Bible because they record

the truth of the life, teaching, and saving actions of Jesus.

- God continues to speak to us today through the Scriptures, as we proclaim them at Mass, reflect on them personally, rely on them for making choices, and study them to learn more about the life and teachings of Jesus.

✓ **Teaching Tip**

Recognizing God's Presence

Talk to the students about recognizing God's presence and connecting with him by seeing the truth, beauty, and love in all of creation, especially within the human person. Remind them that God is always present in our lives, including those times when we might feel alone or overwhelmed and when we might not believe that there is truth, beauty, or love around us.

Help the students understand that if they can learn to recognize God's presence in difficult or unloving situations, they will gain strength and support when they need it most.

Following the Light

Have a student read aloud the opening paragraph.

- Assign the reading of each of the bullet points to four different students.

Point out the Catholics Today box. Have the students break into small groups to review it.

- Ask the groups to describe someone they know who, through actions and behavior, appears to have allowed the Bible to shape his or her conscience.
- Invite them to share with one another something they have learned from Scripture.

Urge the students to take note of the moments when they are most aware of connecting to God through his Word. Remind them to consider carefully what God might be saying to them.

CLOSE _____

In Summary

Read aloud the Catholics Believe summary points as a class.

- Allow some time for the students to reflect on ways that they can incorporate God's Word and guidance into their daily lives.

DAY 5

Objectives

- Demonstrate the capacity to locate a Scripture verse that has personal relevance
- Explore the faith life of Saint Matthew
- Offer the Prayer of Petition

OPEN

♥ Invite the students to think about their relationship with God.

- Allow a few minutes of silence for personal reflection.

BUILD

Our Catholic Life

Have a volunteer read aloud the two paragraphs.

- Discuss, as a class, some of the wisdom that can be learned from Scripture.

People of Faith

Explain to the students that Saint Matthew was a Gospel writer and is the source of much of what we know about Jesus Christ.

- Read aloud the People of Faith paragraph, and review with the class the content of the People of Faith Background box.
- *Say:* Knowing this information about Saint Matthew, put yourself in his place and compose a simple three- to four-sentence prayer. The prayer should be something that Matthew would have said to God the Father.

LIVE

Our Catholic Life

Sacred Scripture is a rich source of **wisdom** that can guide you in all aspects of your life. As one of the seven Gifts of the Holy Spirit, wisdom helps us see God's purpose and plan for our lives. Wisdom leads us to see things as God sees so that we might live holy lives. When you have a difficult decision to make, think about how some people you have read about in Scripture may have acted. How were they open to God's direction in their lives?

One easy way to begin to find wisdom and hope in Scripture is to pray one of the Psalms. You may want to use a concordance or index in your Bible to find a Psalm that speaks to what's going on in your life. Read it a few times. Then pray your chosen Psalm and see what help you gain from it.

> What wisdom can you learn from Scripture?

People of Faith

Saint Matthew, first century

As a tax collector, Matthew worked for the Roman governor, the enemy of the Jewish people. Fellow Jews saw Matthew as a traitor, but Jesus called him a close friend. Matthew saw the miracles Jesus performed and witnessed his Resurrection and Ascension. His Gospel was written to convince Jews that Jesus was the promised Messiah. His writings tell how God established a spiritual Kingdom for his Son. Some believe that Matthew died a martyr's death. The Church celebrates his feast day on **September 21.**

📶 For more, go to aliveinchrist.osv.com

RESEARCH

Choose one of your favorite Scripture passages. Write what the Scripture is about, or what it means to you. (Some examples are relating to a new person, choosing values you want to live by, or dealing with conflicts.)

What does it mean?

_____
_____
_____
_____

How does it affect my life?

_____
_____
_____
_____

72 Chapter 2

People of Faith Background

Saint Matthew

Share the following with the class:

- The Gospel according to Matthew was written to proclaim Jesus as the Messiah to the Jewish people. He explained that God had set up a spiritual Kingdom for his Son, rather than the earthly kingdom the Jews expected.
- Matthew spent at least fifteen years preaching and sharing the Good News of God's Kingdom with the Jewish people of Palestine.

📶 Encourage the students to go to **aliveinchrist.osv.com** at home to learn more about Saint Matthew.

Prayer of Petition

Leader: Let us now pray, asking God our Father to help us hear, see, listen, live, and learn from the wisdom of Scripture.

Reader: A reading from the holy Gospel according to Luke.

Read Luke 4:16–22.

The Gospel of the Lord.

All: Praise to you, Lord Jesus Christ.

Side 1: God of love, open our ears to always hear your voice—fill us with your Word.

All: Fill us with your Word.

Side 2: God of light, open our eyes to always see your path—fill us with your Word.

All: Fill us with your Word.

Side 1: God of wisdom, open our hearts to always act as we should—fill us with your Word.

All: Fill us with your Word.

Side 2: God of goodness, open our hands to always reach out and serve—fill us with your Word.

All: Fill us with your Word.

Leader: Loving Father,

You alone have the words of everlasting life.
Send us your Spirit and give us the grace
so that we always welcome your Word,
your wisdom and guidance,
and your love.
May the gifts we have received
be gifts we freely share with others.
We ask this through your Son,
who is Jesus Christ, our friend and brother.

All: Amen.

▶ *Sing or play: "God Has Chosen Me"*

The Word of God in Sacred Scripture **73**

📶 Go to **aliveinchrist.osv.com** for an interactive review.

Ⓐ Work with Words Complete each sentence with the correct term from the Word Bank. Not all terms will be used.

Sacred Scripture	Apostles
Sacred Tradition	Gospels
canon	Divine Inspiration
Evangelists	conscience

1. **Sacred Scripture** records the story of the relationship between God and his People.

2. The complete list of sacred texts accepted by the Church as inspired by God is called the **canon** of Scripture.

3. The authors of the Gospels, called **Evangelists**, wrote about Jesus' life and ministry.

4. It is important for us to know God's laws so our **conscience** can help us make good decisions.

5. The **Gospels** present Jesus' life, ministry, and teachings.

Ⓑ Check Understanding Indicate whether the following statements are true or false. Then rewrite false statements to make them true.

6. Even though the Bible was written by humans, God is the author because he inspired the writers. **True**/False

7. When John writes in his Gospel that the Word was God, he is referring to the Holy Spirit. True/**False**
John was referring to Jesus

8. The primary sense of Scripture refers to the actual words that have been recorded. True/**False**
The literal sense of Scripture refers to the actual words.

9. The spiritual sense of Scripture includes the allegorical sense, showing how certain events pointed to Christ. **True**/False

10. The Letters of Paul are the central books of Scripture because they present Jesus' life, ministry, and teaching. True/**False**
The Gospels are the central books of Scripture.

Ⓒ Make Connections Write a one-paragraph response to the question. Each Gospel presents the life and teaching of Jesus, but each places emphasis on a different aspect of Jesus. Choose one of the four Gospels and explain how it fulfills Jesus' command to spread the Good News.

74 Chapter 2

ACTIVITY

Read aloud the directions for the activity on page 72.

- Allow the students time to find their Scripture passage and reflect on the questions.
- Once everyone has completed their work, allow volunteers to share their passage and their answers with the class.

CLOSE

Prayer of Petition

💜 Appoint one student to serve as the leader and one to be the reader for the prayer celebration.

Divide the remaining students into two groups: Side 1 and Side 2. Tell them to be ready to pray their part of the prayer.

Follow the order of prayer on the student page.

▶ Conclude by playing the song "God Has Chosen Me," downloaded from **aliveinchrist.osv.com**.

CHAPTER REVIEW

Review the instructions for each section and have the students complete the review.

📶 Go to **aliveinchrist.osv.com** to prepare customized and downloadable assessments, send eAssessments, and assign interactive reviews.

KEY CONCEPT

Jesus is the fulfillment of the Law and he perfectly reveals God the Father to us.

DOCTRINAL CONTENT

- Jesus is the fulfillment of the Law; he perfectly reveals God the Father to us. (CCC, 73, 240)

- God showed the depth of his love when he made a new covenant in Jesus Christ. This covenant is made present in the world today through the Eucharist. (CCC, 66, 1113)

- Being baptized in Christ gives us a share in his Divine life as sisters and brothers of Christ. (CCC, 1213, 1271)

- Natural moral law and God's revealed law in the Ten Commandments direct us to live in right relationship with him and with one another. (CCC, 1954–1960)

TASKS OF CATECHESIS

Helping children grow in a faith that is "known, celebrated, lived, and expressed in prayer" (NDC, 20).

This chapter focuses on the following tasks of catechesis:

- Promoting Knowledge of the Faith

- Moral Formation

Teacher Background

> Here is my servant whom I uphold, my chosen one with whom I am pleased. Upon whom I have put my spirit; he shall bring forth justice to the nations. **Isaiah 42:1**
>
> **Reflect** How is Jesus the fulfillment of God's promise, and how does this affect you?

Throughout salvation history, God continued to be with his People as they struggled to be faithful to the covenant. Because of his immense love for them, he chose to give the human race the opportunity for redemption. That opportunity came in the person of his Son, Jesus Christ. Jesus is the true "Word of God," a word of love, hope, and healing spoken to the very heart of the human family. In Jesus, true God and true man, we come to know God intimately, as a friend and brother, and are shown the model of a human life lived as it was meant to be lived: joyfully, generously, and freely.

In his ultimate act of obedience, his Death on the Cross, Jesus restores the union of God and humankind to its original state of harmony, before sin and death entered the human condition. In doing this, he shows us that, while death is still part of the human condition, fear of death does not need to govern our lives. Jesus also knew that resurrected life awaits those who follow him. It was this Good News that gave his first disciples the courage to build the Church and spread Jesus' message throughout the world.

Today we still hear Jesus' Good News whenever and wherever the Gospel is proclaimed. When we gather to celebrate the Eucharist, when we share God's Word, and when we read the Sacred Scriptures, we continue to be nourished by Jesus, the true Word of God.

> **Reflect** What are some ways that you share the Good News?

Teacher's Prayer

 God our Father, I believe that every student in my classroom was sent by you for a special purpose. Help me to honor that purpose. May your Holy Spirit be with me always as I seek to fulfill my ministry as a teacher. I ask this in Jesus' holy name. Amen.

How Seventh Graders Understand Chapter Topics

Adolescents sometimes think of religion and the teachings of Jesus as something uptight or for "old people." They may even have trouble connecting with their faith when, while striving for independence, they are feeling at odds with conventional norms or traditional beliefs.

Teaching Tip: Point out that Jesus made the teaching of God "real" to people in a powerful new way, by revealing the truth of God in human form and showing us how to be truly human. But this was difficult for the religious leaders of the time to understand. Jesus' teachings were radical and down to Earth. He exposed hypocrisy and stood up for the less fortunate. These are aspects of his life that will appeal very much to adolescents today.

Sharing the Message with Seventh Graders

- At this age, adolescent development includes the shift from thinking of themselves based upon their role within their family (child, grandchild, niece) to identifying themselves in more independent ways (student, soccer player, musician).

- Many seventh graders are learning new ways to show love and respect for the adult members of their families. While they still want to know they are loved, they are often more particular about how they choose to respond to that love.

- The first experiences used by young people to understand the relationship of Jesus and the Father is usually their own relationships with their parents. Help them focus on the bonds of love and loyalty in their families without dwelling on the conflicts.

ONLINE RESOURCES

📶 Go to **aliveinchrist.osv.com**

You will find:

- Interactive lesson planning, additional activities, and ideas for the classroom environment

- Step by step lesson instruction from printed Teacher Edition for integrated lesson planning

- Custom-built assessments to download and eAssessment links

- Interactive reviews that provide scores and the option to review answers

- Chapter-specific Lectionary connections and a complete correlation ordered by the Sundays of the year, with suggestions for how to integrate the Scripture readings into chapter lessons

📶 Go to **osvparish.com** for Ask the Experts Q and A, Community Connections, and Blogs.

Chapter 3 Planner

Objectives	Open

DAY 1—Invite/Preview, Pages 75–77

- Reflect on God's personal invitation through Scripture
- Indicate prior knowledge of chapter concepts and vocabulary

♥ **Psalm 66:5** Pray the opening prayer.

📖 **Isaiah 42:1–3, 6–7** Proclaim "The Servant of the Lord." Guide the students through the process of Scripture reflection.

- Discuss Have You Ever Thought questions.

DAY 2—Discover, Pages 78–79

- Explain that Jesus is the perfect Revelation of God the Father
- Understand that God's new covenant is made present in the world through the Eucharist

♥ Pray the **Prayer to the Holy Spirit**, page 384.

- Discuss the opening question.

DAY 3—Discover, Pages 80–81

- Describe how being baptized in Christ gives us a share in his Divine life as sisters and brothers of Christ
- Explore the ways Jesus points us to the coming of God's heavenly Kingdom on Earth

♥ Pray the **Lamb of God**, page 385.

- Discuss the opening question.

DAY 4—Discover, Pages 82–83

- Define natural moral law
- Recognize that God's revealed law in the Ten Commandments directs us to live in right relationship with him and with one another

♥ Pray the **Act of Love**, page 387.

- Point out the topic of discussion.

DAY 5—Live, Pages 84–85

- Explore ways that others reveal God's love to us
- Discover how Saint Maria Goretti lived the law of love
- Offer the Prayer of Adoration

♥ Pray a prayer of thanksgiving.

REVIEW AND ASSESSMENT

Chapter Review, page 86
Chapter Test, page 75F

📶 **aliveinchrist.osv.com** Customize and Download Assessments, Email Links to eAssessments, Interactive Student Reviews

Build	Close	Materials & Resources
• Present lesson highlights. • Preview **Catholic Faith Words**. ★ Give examples of things Jesus said and did to show his love for God the Father.	• *Activity* Reflect on the meaning of love. • *Optional Activity* Show Me the Love (Activity Master 3)	☐ pencils or pens ☐ Activity Master 3 (Page 75G)
• **Catholic Faith Words** covenant • Review the covenant God made with his Chosen People. • Explain that Mass is a renewal of our covenant with Jesus. 📖 Read and reflect on **Matthew 26:26–30**.	• *Activity* Consider the topics of life decisions and sacrifices. • Conclude with a review of key concepts and objectives.	☐ pencils or pens ☐ board or chart paper
• **Catholic Faith Words** abba • Explain that Jesus showed us who God is through his actions. ★ The students will choose the best description of Jesus. 📖 Read and reflect on **Exodus 20:1–17** and **Deuteronomy 5:6–21**.	• *Activity* Consider ways to address God while praying. • Conclude with a review of key concepts and objectives.	☐ pencils or pens ☐ board or chart paper
• **Catholic Faith Words** natural moral law, New Commandment, Ten Commandments • Discuss natural and revealed laws. • Review Jesus' New Commandment.	• Review the In Summary statements.	☐ pencils or pens
• Learn about Saint Maria Goretti. • *Activity* Reflect on ways others have shown love.	• Appoint one leader and four readers and begin the prayer. ▶ Sing with the students the closing song.	☐ pencils or pens 🛜 "We Ever Will Praise You"

Chapter Connections

FORMING CATHOLIC IDENTITY ACROSS THE CURRICULUM

To integrate the Catholic faith in all aspects of curriculum, this chapter's objectives can be reinforced and applied in the instruction of other disciplines.

Go to **aliveinchrist.osv.com** for cross-curricular activities and projects linked to the doctrinal content discussed in this unit. Activities are available from among the following knowledge categories and content areas:

Language Arts

- Integration of Knowledge
- Literacy
- Speaking and Listening
- Writing Skills

Math

- Algebraic Thinking
- Geometry
- Measurement and Data
- Numbers and Operations

Science

- Earth Science
- Life Science
- Physical Science
- Technology

Social Studies

- Civics
- Economics
- Geography
- History

NCEA IFG: ACRE Edition

Knowledge of the Faith

- **Objective:** To know and understand basic Catholic teaching about the Incarnate Word Jesus Christ as the way, truth, and life

Moral Formation

- **Objective:** To be knowledgeable about the teachings of Jesus and the Church as the basis of Christian morality and to understand Catholic Social Teaching

Catholic Faith Literacy

covenant, God the Father, Jesus, Ten Commandments

Catholic Social Teaching

To integrate Catholic Social Teaching into your lesson, choose one of the following features: Life and Dignity of the Human Person, pages 334–335; or Rights and Responsibilities of the Human Person, pages 338–339.

- Start the Live step of the process by talking about Saint Maria Goretti on page 84. Then move directly to the Catholic Social Teaching feature.
- Or, to expand the lesson, complete page 84, then move to the Catholic Social Teaching feature.
- Return to Chapter 3 for the prayer on page 85.

Music Option

Use the following song to enhance catechetical learning or for prayer.

- "We Ever Will Praise You," Day 5, Page 85

Name _____ Date _____

Complete each sentence with the correct term.

1. In the _____, Jesus makes it known that God's Reign and Divine life can be part of our existence.

2. The beginning of the Lord's Prayer refers to God as _____, the English equivalent of "daddy" or "papa."

3. Jesus was God the Father's new _____ with us so that we would be reconciled with him.

4. Precepts about goodness that are written by God in our hearts and accessible through our God-given reason are called _____.

Indicate whether the following statements are true or false. Rewrite the false statements to make them true.

5. A commandment is a sacred promise or agreement between humans or between God and humans. **True/False**

_____

6. When we are baptized, we become adopted children of God. **True/False**

_____

7. The Ten Commandments are the fundamental moral laws given by God to Jesus. **True/False**

_____

8. Christians are called to live holy lives because of the law of love that exists within their hearts. **True/False**

_____

Write a response on the lines below.

9. How does God's revealed law lead us to him? _____

_____

_____

10. What is the New Commandment that Jesus gave us and how does it connect us to God?

_____

_____

_____

Name _____   Date _____

Show Me the Love

Think of your life and your relationship with God. Fill in the blanks to complete the phrases.

I know Jesus loves me because _____

_____

_____

_____

I show Jesus my love by _____

_____

_____

_____

My friends are signs of God's love because _____

_____

_____

_____

My family is a sign of God's love. I know this because _____

_____

_____

_____

I demonstrate my love for my family by _____

_____

_____

_____

If there is one thing I could do to grow as a person of love, it would be to _____

_____

_____

_____

Jesus, Sign of God's Love

💙 Let Us Pray

Leader: Wondrous God, you did not forget your promise to us. You showed us your unconditional love by sending your Son, Jesus. We want to know and love you.

"Come and see the works of God, awesome in deeds before the children of Adam." **Psalm 66:5**

All: Holy God, you sent your Son Jesus to show us the way to you. Be with us through the Holy Spirit as we try to love others unconditionally.

📖 Scripture

"Here is my servant whom I uphold, my chosen one with whom I am pleased.

Upon whom I have put my spirit; he shall bring forth justice to the nations.

He will not cry out, nor shout, nor make his voice heard in the street.

A bruised reed he will not break, and a dimly burning wick he will not quench.

He will faithfully bring forth justice.

I, the LORD, have called you for justice, I have grasped you by the hand;

I formed you, and set you as a covenant for the people, a light for the nations,

To open the eyes of the blind, to bring out prisoners from confinement, and from the dungeon, those who live in darkness." **Isaiah 42:1–3, 6–7**

Have you ever thought...
- What promise did God fulfill in Jesus?
- How would God define love?

75

📖 Scripture Background

Scripture Reflection Process

Invite the students to be still, close their eyes, and focus on their breathing. Encourage them to open their minds and hearts to what God is saying to them.

- Proclaim the Scripture and have the students sit in silence.
- *Ask:* What did you hear God say to you today?
- Allow volunteers to share.

 You may play instrumental music to begin the reflection.

Objective

- Reflect on God's personal invitation through Scripture

OPEN _____

💙 Let Us Pray

Invite the students to gather in the prayer space and make the Sign of the Cross. Have them read the opening prayer to themselves and then quietly reflect on it. Have them move out of the prayer space and back to their seats.

Explain that God reveals himself through the works of Creation, his Word, and his Son, Jesus.

Say: John the Evangelist tells us that "God so loved the world he sent his only Son…" for our salvation. Listen to how God describes his Son in today's Scripture passage.

📖 Scripture

Guide the students through the process of Scripture reflection (see the Scripture Background box below).

- Remember, this is a spiritual discipline that takes practice. The students will grow in their capacity to sit in silence. Throughout the year, build to four minutes.

Have you ever thought…

Say: God made a promise to his People; he fulfilled this promise when he sent his Son, Jesus Christ, to save us from sin and death.

- Invite the students to respond to the questions.

DAY 1

Objective

- Indicate prior knowledge of chapter concepts and vocabulary

BUILD

Use this page to assess the students' knowledge related to the chapter content.

Getting Started

Read aloud the first paragraph.

- Ask the students to think of examples of how they are living as one of God's People.
- Discuss as a class.

Jesus Showed Signs of God's Love

Have a student read aloud the directions that go with the chart.

- List some Scripture passages on the board or on chart paper to assist students who may not have any idea where to find stories that they may recall.
- Have a concordance available so that you can assist those who are looking for a particular story. To review or share how to use a biblical concordance, see the teacher background box on page 58 of the Teacher Edition.
- ★ Invite the students to work independently to list examples of some things Jesus said and did that showed his love for God the Father. Have them put a star next to the example that made the strongest impression on them.
- If time permits, allow volunteers to share their starred response with the class.

Getting Started

In this chapter, you will reflect on how we know God through Jesus Christ and recognize Christ as a sign of the Father's love. When we follow God's laws, we show our love for him and grow in our understanding of his love. His Commandments help us choose what is good so we can live as his People.

Catholic Faith Words

- covenant
- *abba*
- natural moral law
- Ten Commandments
- New Commandment

In the spaces below give examples of some things Jesus said and did that showed his love or the love of God the Father. Draw a star next to the example that has made the strongest impression on you.

Jesus Showed Signs of God's Love

Reaching All Learners

Students and Silence

In a culture that bombards our young people with various forms of information, many students may feel uncomfortable with silence. This will vary from student to student, but research in other sciences has taught us that our brains crave stillness and rest.

- Some students may enjoy moments of silence. Building in occasional opportunities for reflection honors this need.
- For the students who find stillness and silence a challenge, slowly introduce them to the need for quiet over the course of the school year. Give them an opportunity to develop this skill by first asking them to remain quiet, and gradually introduce the idea of reflecting.

Rank It! Rank the following definitions for love by what you think are the most accurate (1) to the least accurate (5). In the space provided below, explain your reason for the ranking.

____ to have an affection for someone

____ to have a strong liking or attraction to someone

____ to care for another with dignity and respect

____ to need or require someone

____ to worship or adore someone

_____

_____

_____

How do you define love? Write your definition below. Then share with a classmate one way you have witnessed or experienced your definition of love.

© Our Sunday Visitor

Jesus, Sign of God's Love **77**

Optional Activity

Activity Master 3: Show Me the Love

Distribute copies of the activity found on teacher page 75G.

- This activity will help the students reflect on the meaning of authentic love, a love that mirrors God's love, and recognize the signs of that love in their human relationships.

- As an alternative, you may wish to send this activity home with the students.

Show Me the Love

Work with Words

Have a student read aloud the five vocabulary words on page 76.

- *Ask:* What are the Ten Commandments and how many of them can you name?

- See how many the students are able to come up with.

- Write their answers on the board or on chart paper.

- Ask the class if they have heard of the New Commandment.

- Encourage them to share what they know.

- Explain that they will learn more about all of these Catholic Faith Words in the following pages of this chapter.

CLOSE

ACTIVITY

Explain the instructions for the activity.

- Invite the students to complete the first part of the activity on their own. Then, tally the rankings from the students to see if the class can reach a consensus-ranking for a definition of "love."

- Give the students several minutes to write their own definitions for love. Suggest that we come to know what love is through our experiences of it.

- Encourage the students to share with a classmate ways they have experienced their own defintions of love.

DAY 2

Objectives

- Explain that Jesus is the perfect Revelation of God the Father
- Understand that God's new covenant is made present in the world through the Eucharist

OPEN

💛 Have the students pray the Prayer to the Holy Spirit from page 384.

Discuss the introductory question with the class. Write their responses on the board or on chart paper.

BUILD

Jesus: God's Own Love

Have a student read aloud the text.

- *Ask:* What is unconditional love?
  steadfast love with no conditions

Jesus: The Way to the Father

Have the students read the text to themselves.

- Discuss as a class whether the students have ever experienced learning something new from reading a book or watching a movie more than once.

Go to the Source

After completing page 79, send the students to the source, Matthew 26:26–30, to find out more about what Jesus gives us to celebrate and commit ourselves to the new covenant with God.

© Our Sunday Visitor

Jesus: God's Own Love

How does God show his love for us?

Being loved is great, but sometimes it can be complicated. Sometimes people will show their love only if we behave in a certain way. At other times, people do love us, but they have a hard time expressing it. Plus, we have to build up trust and friendship with new people in our lives before we get to the point where we love them.

God's love is different, because he loves us without any conditions. God showed how much he loved us by sending his only and much-loved Son into the world.

> **Go to the Source**
> Read *Matthew 26:26–30*. What does Jesus give us to celebrate and commit ourselves to the new covenant with God?

Jesus: The Way to the Father

The relationship between God the Father and God the Son is the most intimate and loving relationship possible. But God the Father did not keep his Son for himself. Instead, he chose to share him with the world: "For God so loved the world that he gave his only Son, so that everyone who believes in him might not perish but might have eternal life" (John 3:16).

In Jesus Christ, God showed us everything he could about himself. What God told us about himself first through creation and history, and then through his Chosen People, the Jews in the Old Testament, he revealed in the most perfect way in Jesus Christ. With the coming of Jesus, there is no further revelation. In Jesus Christ, God has taught us everything there is to be revealed.

Even though God the Father has fully revealed himself in Christ, our understanding of him continues to grow as we discover new things about what God has shared

---

ℹ️ Teacher Background

What's in a Name?

Share with the students that Jesus comes from a long line of ancestors (see Matthew 1:1–17), and his many titles have specific meanings.

- The angel who appeared to Mary at the Annunciation gave Jesus his name. In Hebrew, Jesus' name means "God saves."
- "Christ" is the Greek translation of the Hebrew *messiah*, which means "anointed."
- The genealogy in Matthew points to the reality that Jesus is truly the Messiah and that he has come to save all people.

with us. Our limited human minds cannot understand God the first time we learn about him. It takes years of growing into understanding. New experiences and continually being taught more about God help us come to know him more and more, but we'll never fully understand God because he is a mystery.

> How many times have you heard a story or seen a movie twice, and realized you missed something the first time?

Jesus: Given to Us

As many passages of the Old Testament testify, God made a covenant with his people and said he would never forget his promise. A **covenant** is a binding agreement, in this case, a sacred promise or agreement between God and humans to remain in a relationship of love together.

God showed the depth of his love when he made a new covenant in Jesus Christ, one that would last forever. At the Last Supper, Jesus and the Apostles were celebrating God's original covenant when Jesus explained that now he was going to be the Father's new covenant. God the Father made that covenant present in the world through the gift of Jesus' own Body and Blood. In Luke 22:20 we read, "This cup is the new covenant in my blood." By pouring out his blood, Jesus offered forgiveness for sins so that all people would be reconciled with God. All four Gospels record the Last Supper, and we celebrate this sacrifice in the Eucharist at Mass.

> Imagine that you were asked to give away, or say goodbye to, the person you love the most. How hard would that be for you? Could you do it?

Catholic Faith Words

covenant a sacred promise or agreement between humans or between God and humans

EXPLAIN

What is one of the hardest sacrifices you've made because of your love for a family member, friend, or God? Explain the situation and tell how your decision made a difference in someone's life.

_____
_____
_____
_____
_____
_____
_____

📖 Scripture Background

The Last Supper

The words of the Last Supper that describe the Eucharist appear in the Gospels.

- We hear these words every time we go to Mass, and we are reminded of Jesus' promise to us.
- The part of the Mass when we hear the words of Jesus from the Last Supper is called the Consecration.
- The Eucharistic Prayer, said by the priest, also brings attention to our covenant with Jesus and his continued promise to be with us forever.

Work with Words

Have a volunteer read aloud the definition of *covenant*.

- Ask the students to give an example of two people living in a covenant relationship.

Jesus: Given to Us

Read aloud the text.

- Remind the students that God was faithful to his Chosen People in spite of many reasons to give up on them.
- God made a covenant (a binding agreement or solemn promise) with his Chosen People.
- The depth of God's love is evident in the action, words, and person of Jesus Christ.
- Explain that Mass is a renewal of our covenant with Jesus.
- Facilitate a discussion on the question at the end of this section.

CLOSE _____

ACTIVITY

Allow the students time to review the activity instructions and to respond.

Quick Review What God told us about himself through creation and history, he revealed in the most perfect way in Jesus. God showed the depth of his love when he made a new covenant in Jesus Christ. This covenant is made present today in the Eucharist.

DAY 3

Objectives

- Describe how being baptized in Christ gives us a share in his Divine life as sisters and brothers of Christ

- Explore the ways Jesus points us to the coming of God's heavenly Kingdom on Earth

OPEN

Have the students pray the Lamb of God, page 385.

Ask them what they know about God through what they know about Jesus. You may wish to record their responses on the board or on chart paper.

BUILD

Jesus Shows Us the Father

Have a volunteer read the opening paragraph.

One with the Father

Arrange the students in groups of three or four to read the text together.

- After they have read the text, have them discuss the reflection question.

- Have them brainstorm ideas and record their responses.

Go to the Source

If there is time, have the students read the suggested Bible passages and answer the questions.

Jesus Shows Us the Father

How do we see God through Jesus Christ?

Sometimes we meet people who say all the right things, but we might wonder if they live the way they talk. With Jesus, there is no doubt that everything about his life is true. He not only talked about God the Father, but he also showed us who God is in the way he lived. He did this because he is God. We call Jesus *God*, like we call God the Father, *God*, and God the Holy Spirit, *God*.

One with the Father

We always appreciate it when someone remembers our name when we haven't seen that person for a long time. On the other hand, people are sometimes embarrassed when they can't remember the name of someone they should know. In the Hebrew tradition, knowing a person's name implied a close relationship between the two people.

The Hebrew people thought of themselves as being unworthy to utter God's name. This is why they were shocked when they heard Jesus address God in the most intimate of ways. When he taught the disciples the Lord's Prayer, he began with the Aramaic word **abba** (See Luke 11:2–4). The English equivalent of this word is "Daddy" or "Papa."

Jesus invited his disciples to address God in the same way, as we do today when we pray "Our Father." By being baptized in Christ, Catholics share that close relationship with God. We become adopted children of God, sons and daughters who can count on God's love at all times. (See Galatians 4:6.)

> **What are some ways you call on God?**

Go to the Source
Read *Exodus 20:1–17* and *Deuteronomy 5:6–21*. How are these passages alike? Are there any differences? How does each help you live?

80 Chapter 3

Optional Activity

Interpretations of God *Visual/Spatial, Interpersonal*

Organize the students into small groups. They will need Internet access for this activity.

- Explain to the students that there are many interpretations of what God the Father and God the Son look like in art. Have them research to find examples of artwork of both Divine Persons.

- Ask the students to choose three of their favorite pieces and to prepare to give a report on the artist, the time period, and why they chose those particular art pieces.

What We Learn from Jesus

In every way, Jesus Christ is the fulfillment of God's own revelation. Everything about Jesus points to God and the coming of his heavenly Kingdom on Earth.

- In **prayer**, Jesus shows us how trustworthy God is, how God listens and cares for each of us.
- In **miracles**, Jesus shows us God's desire to heal us physically and spiritually and help us change our lives for the good.
- In **his love for the poor**, for children, and for sinners, Jesus reveals that God cares for every single human being.

- By **accepting death on the Cross**, Jesus shows that following God's plan is the best, even when it involves sacrifice.
- In the **Resurrection**, Jesus makes it known that God's heavenly Reign and Divine life can be a part of our human existence.

> Underline which description gives you your clearest picture of Jesus as God.

Catholic Faith Words

abba the Aramaic word with the English equivalent of "daddy" or "papa"

DESCRIBE

Read the Lord's Prayer (see Luke 11:2–4 and page 383 of the Our Catholic Tradition section of your book). Describe several personal ways that you address God in your own prayers. How do your names for God show how you feel about him?

- _____
- _____
- _____
- _____
- _____

© Our Sunday Visitor

What We Learn from Jesus

Read aloud the opening paragraph. Invite five students to read aloud the bullet points.

★ Have the students underline their preferred "picture" of Jesus as God.

Point out the Catholic Faith Words definition for *abba*.

CLOSE _____

> ACTIVITY

Invite the students to read the directions and work on this task individually.

Quick Review Being baptized in Christ gives us a share in his Divine life. Everything about Jesus points us to the coming of the Kingdom of God on Earth.

✓ Teaching Tip

What to Do about "Father"

The experience and images of "Father" may pose problems for some young people. Be sensitive to those who have no fathers (or loving parents) as a part of their lives by emphasizing God the Father's love for all. As Father, God points to what good fathering can be.

- While some gender discussion of God may arise, take care to keep the emphasis on the mystery of God, who is neither male nor female, and how we are limited in our understanding of who he is by our humanness.

Objectives

- Define natural moral law
- Recognize that God's revealed law in the Ten Commandments directs us to live in right relationship with him and with one another

OPEN

♥ Have the students stand and pray the Act of Love from page 387.

Point out that they will learn in this lesson how laws lead us to God.

BUILD

Laws That Point to God

Have the students silently read the text.

- *Ask:* What are some other positive natural laws?
- Discuss as a class.

God's Revealed Law

Ask a volunteer to read this paragraph to the class.

Jesus, the New Law

Review this content with the class.

- Ask the students what they think was the most surprising thing about Jesus. the way he spoke about the law

---

Jesus Speaking in the Treasury, James Jacques Joseph Tissot

Laws That Point to God

How do laws lead us to God?

When we study the world and the universe, we find a marvelous order to it in the movement of the heavenly bodies, in the cycle of time and seasons, in the fruitfulness of all creation, in the cycle of birth and death, in the relationship of man and woman, and in the laws that are inscribed in our hearts.

This order is created by God. The laws of nature are like building blocks that form the foundation for all life. This **natural moral law** consists of precepts about goodness that are written by God in our hearts and are accessible through our God-given reason. Natural law requires us to do good and avoid evil. Our awareness of natural law can be clouded by the disorder caused by Original Sin.

> What are some other positive natural laws that you can think of?

82 Chapter 3

God's Revealed Law

Besides the natural moral law, God has revealed ways that help us live in covenant relationship with him. God's revealed law was evident when he gave us the **Ten Commandments** through Moses. (See page 373 of the Our Catholic Tradition section of your book.) These laws helped to make clear God's hope for the way all people are to live in relationship with him and one another. God's revealed law continued in the Old Testament and led to the Gospels and the fulfillment of God's revealed law in Christ.

Jesus, the New Law

Jesus not only confused some people by his close relationship with God the Father, but he also surprised people in the way he spoke of the Law. He did not want them to follow God's Law only because they feared punishment. Instead, he wanted them to rely on the love of God that had been planted within their hearts.

Optional Activity

Ways to See God *Interpersonal, Verbal/Linguistic*

Invite the students to survey the adults in their lives to discover how they see God.

- Suggest the topics of prayer, miracles, the marginalized, and Jesus' Death and Resurrection as starters.
- Encourage the young people to listen carefully and to explore other ways of seeing God, should they arise in conversation.
- Having a student write up a report on the findings of their survey would be a great extra credit activity.

He explained it all in the Sermon on the Mount (see Matthew 5:3–10), when he said that those who would be blessed are the poor, those who mourn, the meek, the merciful, and the peacemakers. He showed the positive side of the Law.

Jesus gave his followers a new law, a **New Commandment**—to love one another as he has loved them (see John 13:34). Christ poured out his life for us, and his Holy Spirit dwells within us. God's Spirit within us deepens whenever we gather with fellow Catholics to pray and participate in the Sacraments. We are called to live holy lives,

not primarily because of external laws, but because of the law of love that exists within our hearts.

> **How is it different when you are doing something because you were told to, and when you are doing something because, in your heart, you know it is right?**

Catholic Faith Words

natural moral law precepts about goodness that are written by God in our hearts and accessible through our God-given reason

Ten Commandments the ten fundamental moral laws given by God to Moses, and recorded in the Old Testament, to help his People live by the covenant

New Commandment Jesus' command for his disciples to love one another as he has loved us

WRITE

Write some other signs of God's love, and describe how you can be a sign of that love, too.

_____

_____

_____

_____

_____

_____

_____

_____

_____

_____

_____

IN SUMMARY   Catholics Believe

Jesus is the fulfillment of the Law and he perfectly reveals God the Father to us.

- We know God through Jesus Christ and recognize Christ as a sign of God's love.
- Jesus has a close and intimate relationship with the Father, and he invites us to share in that relationship as God's sons and daughters.

- The natural and revealed laws help us choose what is good and live as God's People; by pouring out the Holy Spirit, Jesus plants within our hearts a New Commandment.

Jesus, Sign of God's Love   **83**

 Teacher Background

Cultural Awareness: The Weak, the Poor, and the Powerless

There are many stories in Scripture that reveal how the weak, the poor, and the powerless are the center of Jesus' attention.

- Jesus shows us that in God's eyes, those in greatest need come first. (See Luke 6:20–26.) The Church calls this the preferential option for the poor.

- In today's culture, learning to place the poor first is not easy. Nevertheless, we are called to give from our own abundance, like the widow who gave her last coins. (See Mark 12:41–44.)

Jesus, the New Law,

continued

Invite the students to consider the Ten Commandments as rooted in love—God's love for them and their love for God—and to discuss the implications.

Read aloud the remaining text to the class.

- Invite three volunteers to explain the Catholic Faith Words in their own words.
- Facilitate a discussion on the summary question.

ACTIVITY

Read aloud the activity instructions.

- Have the students work independently.

CLOSE _____

In Summary

Have the students form small groups to go over the summary points.

- Invite the groups to discuss any new things they learned about God and/or Jesus from this chapter.

DAY 5

Objectives

- Explore ways that others reveal God's love to us
- Discover how Saint Maria Goretti lived the law of love
- Offer the Prayer of Adoration

OPEN

♥ Gather the students in the prayer space. Have them quiet themselves and pray a prayer of thanksgiving for God's love.

BUILD

Our Catholic Life

Have the students silently read the two paragraphs.

- Talk about the importance of working on our friendships.
- Discuss, as a class, ways that we can show friendship with Jesus.

People of Faith

Explain to the students that Saint Maria Goretti is a model of faith and forgiveness.

- Read aloud the People of Faith paragraph.
- Share the content of the People of Faith Background box.
- *Ask:* How can Saint Maria help you see yourself as sacred?
- Invite the students to reflect on forgiveness.

Our Catholic Life

Living in love and friendship with Jesus is in many ways similar to living in love and friendship with those you see every day at home, at school, in church, on teams, in clubs or other extracurricular activities. **Friendship** takes work, but it is some of the best work we can do, and the most fulfilling. Through our friendship, we show our love for people.

There are several ways to get closer to Jesus, all of them important now and later in our lives. They include reading accounts of Jesus in the Gospels and reflecting on how he acts and why it matters, receiving Holy Communion and spending time in prayer with Jesus, seeing Jesus in the faces of those you meet, learning from the example of others, and being grateful for the love that people show you.

> What is one way you can show friendship with Jesus this week?

People of Faith

Saint Maria Goretti, 1890–1902

Maria Goretti's family lived near another family who had a son named Alessandro. One day Alessandro tried to get Maria to commit a sin. When she wouldn't, he stabbed her fourteen times. She died the next day, after forgiving Alessandro. After Alessandro was released from jail, he asked Maria's mother for forgiveness, and eventually became a lay brother in a monastery, where he worked until he died. He and Maria's mother were present at Maria's canonization in 1950. The Church celebrates her feast day on **July 6.**

📶 For more, go to aliveinchrist.osv.com

84 Chapter 3

IDENTIFY

Consider who shows you love, and how, in each of these settings:

At home

_____

_____

At school

_____

_____

In clubs or on teams

_____

_____

In the world

_____

_____

People of Faith Background

Saint Maria Goretti

Share this additional information with the class:

- Even though she was young, Saint Maria Goretti was deeply aware of the connection between her body, mind, and spirit. In those final moments, she wanted her body to be respected as a gift from God.
- Maria understood herself to be sacred because she so intimately knew her Creator.

📶 Encourage the students to go to **aliveinchrist.osv.com** at home to learn more about Saint Maria Goretti.

Prayer of Adoration

Leader: Let us pray.

Reader 1: Father, you gave us
your greatest gift—
your Son, Jesus,
who lived and experienced
the same joys and heartaches that
we experience.

All: We love you and adore you, O God.

Reader 2: You sent Jesus to teach us
how to live,
to grow, to learn,
and to know the happiness
that comes from belonging to you.

All: We love you and adore you, O God.

Reader 3: You had Jesus show us the way
to be a servant;
he washed our feet,
he opened his hands,
and offered his life for us.

All: We love you and adore you, O God.

Reader 4: You raised him up again to
new life,
showing us all that we too can share in
your life,
and become who you want us to be.

All: We love you and adore you, O God.

Leader: Loving Father,
Help us to remember your love always.
We ask this in the name of your Son Jesus,
who is your everlasting love.

All: Amen.

▶ *Sing or play "We Ever Will Praise You"*

📶 Go to **aliveinchrist.osv.com** for an interactive review.

Ⓐ Work with Words Circle the letter of the
choice that best completes the sentence.

1. God's ____ is a promise to remain in a
relationship of love with his People.
- **a.** covenant
- **b.** word
- **c.** law
- **d.** spirit

2. The Aramaic word ____ can be translated as
"Daddy" in English.
- **a.** *Yahweh*
- **b.** *papa*
- **c.** *abba*
- **d.** *padre*

3. The order in the universe created by God is
called ____.
- **a.** creation
- **b.** cycle of time
- **c.** cycle of seasons
- **d.** none of the above

4. ____ requires us to do good and avoid evil.
- **a.** Universal law
- **b.** Original law
- **c.** Laws of nature
- **d.** Natural moral law

5. The ten fundamental moral laws given by God
to Moses, and recorded in the Old Testament,
are the ____.
- **a.** Miracles
- **b.** Nicene Creed
- **c.** Canon of Scripture
- **d.** Ten Commandments

6. Jesus wants people to follow God's Law
out of ____.
- **a.** fear of the Lord
- **b.** conscience
- **c.** trust
- **d.** love

Ⓑ Check Understanding Indicate whether
the following statements are true or false. Then
rewrite false statements to make them true.

7. Through Jesus' miracles we see God's desire to
heal us physically and spiritually. **True**/False

_____
_____
_____

8. Jesus gives us a New Commandment, to love
one another as he loves us. **True**/False

_____
_____
_____

9. God's revealed Law is manifested only in the
Ten Commandments. True/**False**
manifested in other laws and most
especially in Jesus Christ

_____

10. At Jesus' birth, God the Father made the
new covenant through the gift of Jesus'
humanity. True/**False**
At the Last Supper the new covenant
was made through the gift of Jesus'
Body and Blood.

Ⓒ Make Connections On a separate sheet of
paper, write a one-paragraph response to the
questions: How might Jesus' relationship to God
the Father have been surprising to people of the
time? What new law did Jesus give us to help live
out that relationship here on Earth?

Have the students work on their
own to complete the activity on
page 84.

CLOSE _____

Prayer of Adoration

💜 Appoint one student to serve
as the leader and four students to
serve as the readers. The rest of the
class will pray the "All" parts. Give
everyone an opportunity to practice
their parts.

Have the students gather in the
prayer space.

Follow the order of prayer on the
student page.

▶ Conclude by singing with
the students "We Ever Will
Praise You," downloaded from
aliveinchrist.osv.com.

CHAPTER REVIEW

Review the instructions for each
section and have the students
complete the review.

📶 Go to **aliveinchrist.osv.com**
to prepare customized and
downloadable assessments,
send eAssessments, and assign
interactive reviews.

UNIT 1

Use the closing points from Days 2–4 in each chapter to highlight lesson concepts for this unit and prepare for the Unit Review.

Have the students complete the Review pages. Then discuss the answers as a class. Review any concepts with which the students are having difficulty.

 Work with Words

Have the students match the words in the left column with the letter of the correct definitions or descriptions in the right column.

Ⓐ **Work with Words** Match the words on the left with the correct definitions or descriptions on the right.

__e__ 1. New Commandment

__h__ 2. Divine Inspiration

__a__ 3. canon of Scripture

__c__ 4. Evangelist

__g__ 5. covenant

__d__ 6. *abba*

__f__ 7. natural moral law

__b__ 8. image of God

__l__ 9. Gospels

__k__ 10. mystery

__j__ 11. eternal

__i__ 12. Divine Revelation

a. the Church's complete list of inspired books of Sacred Scripture

b. the Divine likeness in all human beings

c. an author of a Gospel

d. Aramaic word that means "daddy"

e. Jesus' command for his disciples to love one another as he has loved us

f. order of the universe created by God

g. God's promise to remain in a loving relationship with his people

h. the gift of the Holy Spirit which assisted the human authors in writing the Bible

i. the process by which God makes himself known

j. a description of God that tells us he was, is, and always will be

k. a truth of faith that cannot be fully understood but that is believed because God has shown it in Scripture, in the life of Jesus, or in the teachings of the Church

l. the central books of Sacred Scripture because Christ is at their center

Revelation **87**

B Check Understanding Complete each sentence with the correct term from the Word Bank. Not all terms will be used.

13. God gave us the gift of _____ **human reason** _____, which allows us to grow in knowledge and search for meaning.

14. The Old Testament tells of God's relationship with the _____ **Chosen People** _____.

15. The freeing of the Israelites from slavery in Egypt that is described in the Book of Exodus foreshadows the _____ **salvation** _____ that Christ would bring us.

16. When John writes in the Gospel that the Word was God, he is referring to _____ **Jesus** _____ as "the Word."

17. As a literary form, _____ **proverbs** _____ contain(s) wisdom in short sentences and sayings.

18. Understanding the _____ **literal sense** _____ of Scripture, which refers to the actual words recorded, requires an understanding of the time in which it was written.

19. The _____ **Gospels** _____ are the central books of Scripture because they present Jesus' life, ministry, and teaching.

20. When God gave Moses the _____ **Ten Commandments** _____, he was giving us evidence of his revealed Law.

21. Natural moral law and revealed Law are part of God's _____ **eternal law** _____.

Word Bank
Ten Commandments
love
literal sense
eternal law
Gospels
human reason
Jesus
salvation
proverbs
Chosen People

C Make Connections Write a short answer to the following questions.

22. Which story about Jesus from the Gospels is your favorite, and why? What does this story reveal to you about God?
    Responses will vary.
    _____
    _____
    _____
    _____
    _____

---

23. What are two ways Catholics today enter into conversation with God?
    Responses will vary; should include two of the following:
    proclamation of the Scriptures at Mass, prayer, silent reflection,
    Psalm responses
    _____
    _____
    _____
    _____

24. How can we connect the way Jesus addressed God with the way we pray the Lord's Prayer?
    Jesus addressed God as *abba,* which is an Aramaic form of "daddy";
    we call on God as Father in the beginning of the Lord's Prayer by
    saying "Our Father ..."
    _____
    _____
    _____
    _____

25. How, in your life today, are you like the Israelites in the desert? In light of how God responded to the Israelites, how do you think God responds to you?
    Responses will vary.
    _____
    _____
    _____
    _____
    _____
    _____
    _____

B Check Understanding
Have the students complete each sentence with the correct term from the Word Bank. Remind the students that not every term will be used.

C Make Connections
Point out that the students will be writing a short answer to the questions. Explain that even though these are short answer responses, they need to be sure that they fully answer the questions.

📶 Go to **aliveinchrist.osv.com** to prepare customized and downloadable assessments, send eAssessments, and assign interactive reviews.

TRINITY

How does Jesus' Incarnation help you to understand the Divine Persons of the Holy Trinity?

CHURCH HISTORY TIMELINE

325 The First Council of Nicaea convenes

387 Conversion of Saint Augustine

1265 Saint Thomas Aquinas begins to write *Summa Theologiae*

1986 First official World Youth Day is held in Rome

Go to page 348 for more

Detail from the *Triptych of the Trinity of Marchiennes*, Jean Bellegambe

Our Catholic Tradition

- Believing in the Holy Trinity is central to our Catholic faith. The Father sent the Son and the Holy Spirit to help us know him and to guide us to him. (CCC, 261)

- The Son of God has existed for all time, and through the Incarnation, became fully man while remaining fully God. Because Jesus is truly Divine and truly human, he saves us and brings us back into relationship with the Father. (CCC, 479, 480)

- The Holy Spirit gives the Church life and unites us as one Body of Christ. The Holy Spirit is our Advocate, comforting and strengthening us to know and live by the truth. (CCC, 729, 747)

Our Catholic Life

- Making the Sign of the Cross reminds us of our Baptism into the life of the Trinity. (CCC, 1235)

- In our worship and personal prayer, we call on Jesus using different titles from Scripture—such as Emmanuel, Christ, Lord, and Messiah. (CCC, 452–455)

- The Holy Spirit guides the Church in her Sacred Tradition and her prayer. The Holy Spirit helps us pray at different times, in different ways, and in different circumstances. (CCC, 2650, 2661)

Introduce Unit Theme

Direct the students' attention to the illustration on the page. Ask them to describe what they see and how this image might relate to the Trinity.

Have the students silently read the timeline information. Allow them to ask questions about these events.

Ask volunteers to read aloud each of the bullet points under the Our Catholic Tradition and Our Catholic Life sections.

After some discussion, explain that the class will learn about the Trinity and related doctrinal concepts in the next three chapters.

Ask the unit's Big Question found on page 90.

Allow time for discussion.

Explain to the students that this is the essential question for the unit. They will be working to fully answer it as they complete the three chapters in the unit.

Go to the Source

As an optional extension, organize the students into three groups, assigning each group one of the main Scripture passages found in this unit.

- Chapter 4: John 17:24–26
- Chapter 5: Philippians 2:9–11
- Chapter 6: Romans 5:1–5

Have each group read its passage and then give a dramatic reading (narrator with silent actors), create a visual representation, or write down one question they would ask God about the passage.

Reading the verses directly from the Bible will familiarize students with the sequence of the canon the of Sacred Scripture.

Explore the Catechism

Ask the students to form three groups, and have each group use the material in the *Catechism of the Catholic Church* to research one Person of the Holy Trinity (see especially CCC 232–267, 422–455, 683–747, and 1830–1832).

- Give each group a poster board or large sheet of paper, and have that group list or visually depict attributes of that Person of the Trinity. If time allows, have each group share their work with the whole class.
- Allow time for any questions the students may have.

Reading the paragraphs directly from the *Catechism* will help the students learn where to find key teachings from the Sacred Tradition of the Church.

CHURCH HISTORY TIMELINE BACKGROUND

Refer the students to the Church History Timeline on pages 348–363 to learn more about important Church events and figures through A.D. 1085.

Summa Theologiae is Written

Saint Thomas Aquinas represents an intellectual movement known as medieval scholasticism, and *Summa Theologiae* is considered his greatest contribution to the faith. One of the most significant classic works of theology and philosophy, *Summa Theologiae* makes arguments for the existence of God and outlines and defines the Gifts of the Holy Spirit as well as other theological doctrines.

First World Youth Day

Begun in 1986 by Pope Saint John Paul II, after more than 300,000 young people crowded Saint Peter's Square for the International Jubilee of Youth in 1984, World Youth Day now takes place every two to three years in various locations around the world. It is attended by millions of young people, who gather to pray and celebrate the faith.

KEY CONCEPT

Believing in the Holy Trinity is central to our Catholic faith.

DOCTRINAL CONTENT

- Trusting in God's presence leads us to look for guidance in his Word. (CCC, 215–216)

- God the Father sent his Son and the Holy Spirit to help us know him and guide us to him. (CCC, 238–248, 261)

- The love among members of the Trinity is a model for human affection and bonds and is the source of God's loving plan. (CCC, 221, 255–260)

- The total union of the Trinity is a mystery that can never be totally understood by the human mind, but can be approached through faith. (CCC, 253–254, 263)

- Grace is a loving gift from God and a sharing in his Divine life. (CCC, 759, 1999)

TASKS OF CATECHESIS

Helping children grow in a faith that is "known, celebrated, lived, and expressed in prayer" (NDC, 20).

This chapter focuses on the following tasks of catechesis:

- Promoting Knowledge of the Faith

- Education for Community Life

Teacher Background

"You loved me before the foundation of the world. . . . I made known to them your name and I will make it known, that the love with which you loved me may be in them and I in them."
John 17:24, 26

> **Reflect** What makes it possible that the love that God has for his Son is also the love that is in each of us?

By belonging to a Church with a highly developed liturgical life, we may discover that sometimes we take our Catholic rituals for granted, especially those that we participate in from memory. Take, for example, the Nicene Creed that we recite every Sunday. The Creed is a magnificent, incredible, and truly radical statement of Trinitarian faith. How would we sound on Sunday if we truly proclaimed the words we were reciting? Professing the core of our Catholic beliefs with passion and meaning can energize our spirits and help remind us to live out what we say we truly believe.

We profess belief in one God in three distinct Persons: God the Father, God the Son, and God the Holy Spirit. All three persons created, redeemed, and continue to sanctify and inspire us. This is a mystery we accept as an article of faith. While we cannot completely understand the Trinity, we must embrace it as truth if we are to appreciate the unique character of Christianity. Like our Jewish and Islamic brothers and sisters, we believe in one God, but what distinguishes us is our understanding of God as an eternal community of Divine Persons. Everything we, as Christians, hold to be true flows from our understanding of the relationship between the Father, Son, and Holy Spirit.

> **Reflect** How do the different relationships in your own life help you to better understand the individual Persons in the Holy Trinity?

Teacher's Prayer

 Dear God, I worship you with my whole being. Help me to always hold you in my heart as I teach. May your love and truth ever be the cornerstone of my catechesis. Amen.

How Seventh Graders Understand Chapter Topics

The doctrine of the Trinity, One God in three Divine Persons, is difficult to grasp for all of us. It is a mystery that we know by faith. Seventh graders are a little more comfortable with this mystery than younger children, but they might still struggle to conceptualize how God can be one and also three at the same time.

Teaching Tip: We can better understand the mystery of the Trinity in terms of the relationships in our own lives. Help the students explore their own relationships with family members, friends, and others. Lead them in a discussion on the joys, challenges, and responsibilities that flow from those relationships.

Sharing the Message with Seventh Graders

- Young people still understand God primarily through the lens of their own lived experience, especially what they experience in their family life, their prayer life, and when interacting with the world around them.
- At this age, the students are expanding their imagery of God. They are beginning to identify with God in different ways as they attempt to understand him more.
- It is essential to teach young adolescents about the Holy Trinity and how the love that God the Father, God the Son, and God the Holy Spirit share is a model for our own relationships.

ONLINE RESOURCES

 Go to **aliveinchrist.osv.com**

You will find:

- Interactive lesson planning, additional activities, and ideas for the classroom environment
- Step by step lesson instruction from printed Teacher Edition for integrated lesson planning
- Custom-built assessments to download and eAssessment links
- Interactive reviews that provide scores and the option to review answers
- Chapter-specific lectionary connections and a complete correlation ordered by the Sundays of the year, with suggestions for how to integrate the Scripture readings into chapter lessons

Go to **osvparish.com** for Ask the Experts Q and A, Community Connections, and Blogs.

Chapter 4 Planner

Objectives	Open

DAY 1—Invite/Preview, Pages 91–93

Objectives
- Reflect on God's personal invitation through Scripture
- Indicate prior knowledge of chapter concepts and vocabulary

Open
- ♥ Psalm 25:5 Pray the opening prayer.
- 📖 John 17:24–26 Proclaim "The Prayer of Jesus." Guide the students through the process of Scripture reflection.
- Discuss Have You Ever Thought questions.

DAY 2—Discover, Pages 94–95

Objectives
- Understand the need to trust in God's presence and look for guidance in his Word
- Recall that God the Father sent his Son and the Holy Spirit to help us find our way to him
- Discover how the Holy Spirit acts as Guide and Counselor for the Catholic Church

Open
- ♥ Pray the **Nicene Creed**, page 367.
- Discuss the opening question.

DAY 3—Discover, Pages 96–97

Objectives
- Describe how the Persons of the Holy Trinity relate to one another and with humanity
- Explain how the love among the members of the Trinity is a model for human affection and bonds
- Explore how the Persons of the Holy Trinity are distinct yet share total union

Open
- ♥ Pray the **Glory Be**, page 383.
- Talk about the opening question.

DAY 4—Discover, Pages 98–99

Objectives
- Discover how the nature of the Holy Trinity is the source of God's loving plan
- Define *grace* as God's free gift and sharing in his Divine life
- Examine how humans journey into deeper truth, wisdom, and love in relationship with God

Open
- ♥ Pray the **Lord's Prayer**, page 383.
- Point out the opening question.

DAY 5—Live, Pages 100–101

Objectives
- Review the Sign of the Cross and what it means
- Explore the faith life of Saint Frances of Rome
- Offer the prayer to Reflect on the Trinity

Open
- ♥ Pray **Psalm 25:5** on page 91.

REVIEW AND ASSESSMENT

Chapter Review, page 102
Chapter Test, page 91F

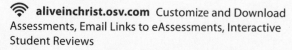 **aliveinchrist.osv.com** Customize and Download Assessments, Email Links to eAssessments, Interactive Student Reviews

Build	Close	Materials & Resources
• Present lesson highlights. • Preview **Catholic Faith Words**. ★ The students will write what they know about each Person of the Holy Trinity.	• *Activity* The students will reflect on the truths of God and write down some things they would like to learn about him.	☐ pencils or pens ☐ board or chart paper
• **Catholic Faith Words** faith • Talk about God's daily guidance. • Share Baptism stories. 📖 Read Matthew 26:16–20. • Explain the ways that the Trinity works in our lives.	• *Activity* Discuss personal relationships with God. • Conclude with a review of key concepts and objectives.	☐ pencils or pens ☐ board or chart paper ☐ Bibles
• **Catholic Faith Words** Holy Trinity • Discuss the mystery of the Trinity. ★ Complete statements about God as Trinity. 📖 Read John 10:31–38.	• *Activity* Consider how faith impacts friendships. • Conclude with a review of key concepts and objectives. • *Optional Activity* Trinity Titles (Activity Master 4)	☐ pencils or pens ☐ Bibles ☐ Activity Master 4 (Page 91G)
• **Catholic Faith Words** grace • Discuss how the Trinity works and how we fit into God's plan. • Explain how faith and grace help our relationship with God.	• *Activity* Review what it means to give our mind and heart to God. • Review the In Summary statements.	☐ pencils or pens
• Discuss the question in the Our Catholic Life section. • Learn about Saint Frances of Rome. • *Activity* Consider how God shows his love and care during life's challenges.	• Ask for four volunteers to serve as leaders and readers. • Follow the order of prayer. ▶ Play instrumental music.	☐ pencils or pens ☐ Bibles 🛜 Instrumental music

Chapter Connections

FORMING CATHOLIC IDENTITY ACROSS THE CURRICULUM

To integrate the Catholic faith in all aspects of curriculum, this chapter's objectives can be reinforced and applied in the instruction of other disciplines.

Go to **aliveinchrist.osv.com** for cross-curricular activities and projects linked to the doctrinal content discussed in this unit. Activities are available from among the following knowledge categories and content areas:

Language Arts

- Integration of Knowledge
- Literacy
- Speaking and Listening
- Writing Skills

Math

- Algebraic Thinking
- Geometry
- Measurement and Data
- Numbers and Operations

Science

- Earth Science
- Life Science
- Physical Science
- Technology

Social Studies

- Civics
- Economics
- Geography
- History

NCEA IFG: ACRE Edition

Knowledge of the Faith

- **Objective:** To know and understand basic Catholic teaching about the Incarnate Word Jesus Christ as the way, truth, and life

Communal Life

- **Objectives:** To know the origin, mission, structure, and communal nature of the Church; to know the rights and responsibilities of the Christian faithful

Catholic Faith Literacy

faith, grace, Holy Trinity

Catholic Social Teaching

To integrate Catholic Social Teaching into your lesson, choose one of the following features: Call to Family, Community, and Participation, pages 336–337; or Solidarity of the Human Family, pages 344–345.

- Start the Live step of the process by talking about Saint Frances of Rome on page 100. Then move directly to the Catholic Social Teaching feature.
- Or, to expand the lesson, complete page 100, then move to the Catholic Social Teaching feature.
- Return to Chapter 4 for the prayer on page 101.

Music Option

Use the following song to enhance catechetical learning or for prayer.

- Instrumental music, Day 5, Page 101

Name _____   Date _____

Circle the letter of the choice that best completes each sentence.

1. God has offered us the free gift of ____ so that we can share in his life.

   a. love

   b. hope

   c. grace

   d. courage

2. When we are baptized, we become members of God's family, the ____.

   a. Holy Trinity

   b. Church

   c. baptized

   d. confirmed

3. Faith is a belief or trust in God and the things he has revealed to us; it is both a gift from God and a ____.

   a. Sacrament

   b. free choice

   c. Mark of the Church

   d. sacrifice

4. Jesus asked the Apostles to go and make ____ of all nations.

   a. brothers and sisters

   b. fathers

   c. disciples

   d. friends

Complete each sentence with the correct term.

5. The _____ is the mystery of one God in three Divine Persons—Father, Son, and Holy Spirit.

6. The _____ between the Father, Son, and Holy Spirit is central to the mystery of the Trinity.

7. The _____ is a counselor for the Church.

8. Christ established the _____ through the Apostles.

Write a response on the lines below.

9. In God's plan for us, how do our best and most loving family and community relationships resemble the relationships of the Holy Trinity?

   _____

   _____

   _____

10. Explain how the gift of faith can be like a compass.

   _____

   _____

Name _____ Date _____

Trinity Titles

Your teacher will assign you to one of three groups. Each group will create a list of titles for one Divine Person of the Trinity. (For example: God the Son is also known as Jesus. The Holy Spirit is also called Counselor.) After the lists have been completed, have a spokesperson from your group present your list to the rest of the class. Ask if anyone has any additional titles to add.

Write some of the titles that you particularly relate to in the shamrock below.

God the Father

God the Son

God the Holy Spirit

God Is Trinity

 Let Us Pray

Leader: O God—Father, Son, and Holy Spirit—always present, always true. Show us the way to you.

"Guide me by your fidelity and teach me, for you are God my savior." Psalm 25:5

All: O God, give us the gift of faith that we may come to know you better.

Scripture

"Father, they are your gift to me. I wish that where I am they also may be with me, that they may see my glory that you gave me, because you loved me before the foundation of the world. Righteous Father, the world also does not know you, but I know you, and they know that you sent me. I made known to them your name and I will make it known, that the love with which you loved me may be in them and I in them." John 17:24–26

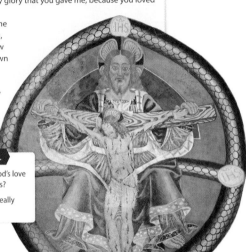

Have you ever thought...

- How is it possible that God's love for his Son is in each of us?
- How much can we ever really understand God?

© Our Sunday Visitor

God Is Trinity **91**

Scripture Background

Scripture Reflection Process

Invite the students to be still, close their eyes, and focus on their breathing. Encourage them to open their minds and hearts to what God is saying to them.

- Proclaim the Scripture and have the students sit in silence.
- *Ask:* What did you hear God say to you today?
- Allow volunteers to share.

 You may play instrumental music to begin the reflection.

Objective

- Reflect on God's personal invitation through Scripture

OPEN _____

 Let Us Pray

Ask the students to gather in the prayer space and make the Sign of the Cross. Pray the leader prayer, including the Psalm. Invite the students to repeat the words from the Psalm verse, then close with the group response. Have the students move out of the prayer space and back to their seats.

Explain that the desire deep inside every human heart is to know the truth about God.

Say: The Holy Trinity—God the Father, God the Son, and God the Holy Spirit—is a perfect communion of love. Because of our Baptism, you and all of the members of the Church, past and present, are a part of this love.

Scripture

Guide the students through the process of Scripture reflection (see the Scripture Background box to the left).

Have you ever thought...

Say: While we can't fully understand the breadth of God's love, it is wondrous to reflect upon the truth that the God who is love, shares his very life and love with us.

- Invite the students to respond to the questions.

God Is Trinity **91**

DAY 1

Objective

- Indicate prior knowledge of chapter concepts and vocabulary

BUILD

Use this page to assess the students' knowledge related to the chapter content.

Getting Started

Invite a volunteer to read aloud the first paragraph.

- *Ask:* In what ways do you see the love of the Holy Trinity modeled in your own life?
- Allow the students to reflect on this.

The Holy Trinity

Point out the boxes for God the Father, God the Son, and God the Holy Spirit.

★ Have the students write in some things they know about each Person of the Holy Trinity.

- After they have had some time to respond, allow them to gather in small groups to share and discuss their answers.

Getting Started

In this chapter, you will explore how our belief in the Holy Trinity is central to our Catholic faith. The Father sent the Son and the Holy Spirit to help us know him and to guide us to him. You will also learn about God's plan of loving goodness and how the love of the Holy Trinity is a model for our own relationships.

 In the web below, record what you know about each Person of the Holy Trinity.

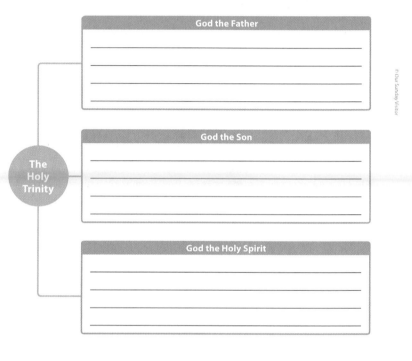

The Holy Trinity

God the Father

_____

_____

_____

_____

God the Son

_____

_____

_____

_____

God the Holy Spirit

_____

_____

_____

_____

✓ Teaching Tip

Guided Reflections

The prayer celebration for this chapter is a guided reflection. This form of prayer invites people to experience God's presence as they imagine a scene.

- Entering into this form of prayer opens the heart to provide a space for God to speak without our egos getting in the way. The process invites students to create mental scenes with direction by a leader.
- These scenes can be based on Scripture or you may sometimes have the students picture places where they feel comfortable and safe.

Catholic Faith Words

- faith
- Holy Trinity
- grace

REFLECT

Step Deeper into Faith Reflect on what you know to be true about God. Write down a few ideas. Then consider what you'd like to learn about God.

What I know to be true about God …

_____
_____
_____
_____
_____
_____

What I want to learn about God …

_____
_____
_____
_____
_____
_____

Name a person you know who you believe has a deep faith. What makes you think that?

_____
_____
_____
_____
_____
_____

93

© Our Sunday Visitor

Work with Words

Point out the Catholic Faith Words box.

- As a class, brainstorm and list, on the board or on chart paper, any information that they know about the words *grace* and *faith*.

- Point out that they will learn more about all three terms later.

CLOSE

ACTIVITY

Have the students read over the activity instructions.

- They should work individually to complete the activity.

- After they complete their work, allow volunteers to share. Remind the students that they do not have to share personal information with the class.

- *Ask:* What is the difference between knowing about God and knowing God more deeply?

Optional Activity

Finding God *Intrapersonal*

Lead the students in a short guided reflection. Have them close their eyes and quiet themselves.

- *Say*: Imagine you are looking for God. You are searching, but you are having a hard time finding him. Now, think about this: To be more certain of finding God, where would you go, what would you do, or whose help would you ask for? Picture it in your minds.

- Afterwards, have the students answer with a show of hands: Who imagined going to a specific place to find God? Who used an action or activity to find God? Who went to a person, or group of persons, for help in finding God?

DAY 2

Objectives

- Understand the need to trust in God's presence and look for guidance in his Word
- Recall that God the Father sent his Son and the Holy Spirit to help us find our way to him
- Discover how the Holy Spirit acts as Guide and Counselor for the Catholic Church

OPEN _____

💙 Have the students stand and pray the Sign of the Cross followed by the Nicene Creed, page 367.

Discuss the ways the students have come to know God so far.

BUILD _____

God Is Always There

Ask: Who do you turn to when you have problems? Possible answers: friends, parents, siblings, other trusted adults

Read aloud the text.

- Add *God* to the list, emphasizing that God is always there for us.

God Takes the First Step

Direct the students to silently read the next three paragraphs.

- Ask volunteers to recap the important points in this section.

📖 Go to the Source

After reviewing Help from Heaven on page 95, have the students look up Matthew 28:16–20 to read about Jesus' commissioning of the Apostles. Discuss the questions.

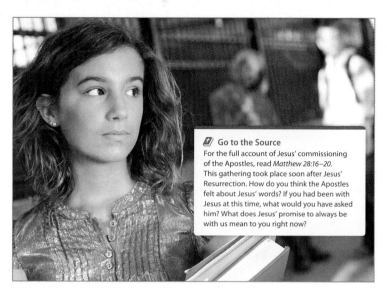

> 📖 **Go to the Source**
> For the full account of Jesus' commissioning of the Apostles, read *Matthew 28:16–20.* This gathering took place soon after Jesus' Resurrection. How do you think the Apostles felt about Jesus' words? If you had been with Jesus at this time, what would you have asked him? What does Jesus' promise to always be with us mean to you right now?

God Is Always There

How do we get to know God?

Have you ever ended up with a problem turning around and around in your head, not sure what to do about it? With so much going on in your life, you might not think of turning to a family member for help. You might wonder how others could even understand what you are feeling, much less help you. Sometimes family and friends can help. Different individuals within a family relate to each other in love—over time and through difficult times.

God is always there, even when you don't think your family and friends can help much. The strongest guide through the ups and downs of life is our faith in his presence and in his words.

God Takes the First Step

God created the universe and keeps it going through Jesus Christ, the Word who has existed forever, and through the Holy Spirit, the giver of all life and goodness. We know God because he chooses to show himself to us. If it were left totally up to us, we could never really know the true God, because he is a mystery beyond our own comprehension. Only with faith can we begin to know God.

Fortunately, God doesn't wait for us to make the first move. He has been there from the beginning of time, and he is with us from the first day of our life. He understands us, even when we don't understand him.

On our own, we would be stuck in misunderstanding and confusion. We would never get close enough to God to

Optional Activity

Biblical Maps *Visual/Spatial, Interpersonal*

Provide the students with biblical maps.

- Organize the students into small groups and ask them to locate the places Peter and Paul traveled (see Acts of the Apostles 13–14; 15:30–18:22; 18:23–21:15; 27–28).
- Display a modern map of the Eastern Mediterranean region using an interactive whiteboard or overhead projector. Then have the students help to plot the locations where Peter and Paul traveled.
- As an extra credit activity, invite the students to research the number of Christian churches present in these areas today.

understand the truth. But he loves us so much he wants us to know the way. God the Father sent us his Son and the Holy Spirit to help us find our way to him. Whenever God sends his Son to us, he also sends his Spirit.

Help from Heaven

The Son of God came down from Heaven to show us the way to God the Father and to bring salvation to all. When his earthly mission was accomplished, Jesus returned to his heavenly Father. Before he ascended, Jesus told his Apostles to continue his work, sharing his message of hope and new life to people everywhere. He instructed them, "Go, therefore, and make disciples of all nations." (Matthew 28:19).

Jesus told his Apostles to baptize new disciples in the name of the Father, and of the Son, and of the Holy Spirit. He promised his friends he would always be with them.

Jesus is always with us, too. In the Sacrament of Baptism, we become members of God's family, the Church, and receive the gift of faith. Through **faith**, we can believe in and rely on God, even though we don't completely understand.

So help from Heaven does not stop with Jesus' time on Earth, his public ministry, and his Ascension. Through the Apostles, Christ established the Church. He sent the Holy Spirit as a guide and counselor to the Church.

Since the time of Jesus and the Apostles, believers have proclaimed God as Father, Son, and Holy Spirit.

> ### Catholic Faith Words
>
> **faith** the Theological Virtue that makes it possible for us to believe in God and the things he has revealed to us. Faith leads us to obey God. It is both a gift from God and a free, human choice.

SHARE

Think about the following questions and share your thoughts with a classmate.

Who or what helps you maintain your relationship with God?

_____
_____
_____
_____

When have you felt closest to God in the last six months?

_____
_____
_____
_____

God Is Trinity **95**

📖 Scripture Background

Matthew 28:16–20

This passage from Matthew is also known as The Great Commission.

- Scholars believe these words were used in Matthew's community, and that they point to the union of the person with the community and with the Father, the Son, and the Holy Spirit through Baptism.
- The passage is also known for its clear expression of the Trinitarian understanding of God and for its emphasis on the teachings of Jesus as the standard for moral conduct.

Help from Heaven

Invite four volunteers to each read aloud one of the paragraphs in this section.

Remind the class that we become members of God's family through Baptism, and through faith, we can believe in and rely on God.

- Ask the students to share what they have been told about their own Baptism.
- Suggest that they talk about things such as when and where they were baptized, who their godparents are, and who attended. Invite them to share whether they still have any mementos from their Baptism.
- Have a volunteer read aloud the definition for *faith*.

Invite a class discussion on the ways each Person of the Trinity works in our lives.

CLOSE _____

ACTIVITY

Invite a volunteer to read aloud the directions and the questions.

- Allow the students time to answer the two questions.
- Encourage them to share their answers with a classmate.

Quick Review We should trust in God's presence and look to his Word for guidance. God the Father sent his Son to save us and the Holy Spirit to be our Guide. Each Person of the Holy Trinity helps us find our way to God.

DAY 3

Objectives

- Describe how the Persons of the Holy Trinity relate to one another and with humanity
- Explain how the love among the members of the Trinity is a model for human affection and bonds
- Explore how the Persons of the Holy Trinity are distinct yet share total union

OPEN

 Have the students gather in the prayer center. Begin with the Sign of the Cross, and pray the Glory Be from page 383.

Talk about ways we can try to understand mysteries.

BUILD

Three Divine Persons in One God

Review this section with the class.

- Reiterate that Catholics are Trinitarian. We believe in one God in three distinct Persons: the Father, the Son, and the Holy Spirit.
- Ask a volunteer to read aloud the definition for *Holy Trinity*.

The Holy Trinity

Instruct the students to silently read this section, including the paragraphs at the top of page 97.

- *Ask:* What is the answer to the mystery of the Trinity? love
- Encourage a volunteer to explain the answer in more detail.

Three Divine Persons in One God

How can we understand a mystery?

At the beginning of every Mass, we make the Sign of the Cross and say, "In the name of the Father, and of the Son, and of the Holy Spirit." Our belief in three Divine Persons in one God is the center of our celebration. When we pray at Mass, we pray in the name of our Trinitarian God. We base our faith on this central belief.

We speak of God as the **Holy Trinity**, which means that there is only one God in three Divine Persons.

- The Father is God, the First Divine Person of the Trinity, who brings everything into existence by the Son through the Holy Spirit.
- Jesus Christ the Son is God, the Second Divine Person of the Trinity, who was sent by the Father and became man.
- The Holy Spirit is also God, the Third Divine Person of the Trinity, who proceeds from the Father and the Son.

> **Catholic Faith Words**
>
> **Holy Trinity** the mystery of one God in three Divine Persons: Father, Son, and Holy Spirit

The three Persons of the Holy Trinity are distinct from one another, so we can talk about them as God the Father, God the Son, and God the Holy Spirit. But they are inseparable in what they do. Each Person of the Trinity is fully God and has the same Divine nature. There is only one God in three Divine Persons.

The Holy Trinity

We are never going to understand this mystery—until we meet God face to face in Heaven. Meanwhile, the gift of faith assures us that what we know about the Holy Trinity is true.

Being human, we still ask questions and search for answers. As people of faith, we are often guided in our relationships not only by our head, but also by our heart. For example, the love someone feels for family members can grow and spread throughout the family. This love makes families stronger than each person could be individually.

Our relationship with God is something like this, too. God's love is always there. Sometimes we just need to become more aware of it. When we sense God's presence and respond to him in our lives, our

> ✏️ **Go to the Source**
> Read *John 10:31–38* to find out how some people could not understand the relationship between Jesus and God the Father. If you had been there, what questions would you have asked Jesus about the mystery of the Trinity?

ℹ️ Teacher Background

The Mystery of God

We use comparisons from our life experience to talk about and describe God. However, our comparisons are limited. They do not capture the true mystery of God. Share the following with the class.

- God is *like* a human parent, a strong father, a loving mother, someone who has our best interests at heart, someone who makes sacrifices for our benefit.
- But God is also different from a parent. Even though we speak of God as "Father," the mystery of God goes beyond any human experience or worldly images we can come up with.

relationship with him and our faith grow stronger. When we place our trust in his love, we feel it in our heart, and we come to believe in it and know it with our mind.

Love is the answer to the mystery of the Trinity. The truth is that the Son loves the Father and the Father loves the Son. The Holy Spirit shares his exact same love with both the Father and the Son.

This love among the Trinity is a model for the connections, affection, and bonds we can make with one another. Families, schools, and groups of friends can mirror the unity of the Trinity.

> When have you felt really loved by God?
> When have you felt out of touch with his love?

We worship one God, the Trinity. Use the following words to fill in the blanks to complete the statements about God as Trinity: universe, creation, communion, distinct, united

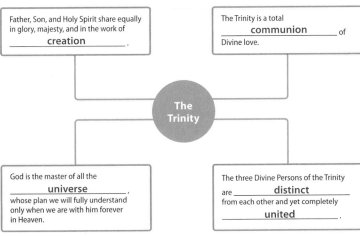

Father, Son, and Holy Spirit share equally in glory, majesty, and in the work of _____ **creation** _____ .

The Trinity is a total _____ **communion** _____ of Divine love.

The Trinity

God is the master of all the _____ **universe** _____ , whose plan we will fully understand only when we are with him forever in Heaven.

The three Divine Persons of the Trinity are _____ **distinct** _____ from each other and yet completely _____ **united** _____ .

REFLECT

Think about your friendships with three different people, including how each friendship differs from the other two. Is your faith a part of any of these friendships? If so, how? If not, how can you share your beliefs with your friends?

God Is Trinity **97**

Optional Activity

Activity Master 4: Trinity Titles

Distribute copies of the activity found on teacher page 91G.

- Organize the students into three groups.
- Have each group come up with titles known for one of the three Persons of the Holy Trinity. Invite the groups to share with the class.

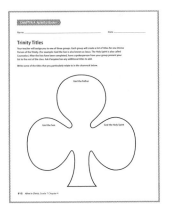

The Holy Trinity, *continued*

Discuss, as a class, the two follow-up questions at the end of this section.

⬛ Go to the Source

Have the students read John 10:31–38 to find out more about the relationship between Jesus and God the Father.

- Instruct the students to work in pairs to answer the question.

The Trinity

Remind the students that we worship one God—the Trinity.

★ Instruct them to use the supplied words to fill in the blanks to complete the statements about God as Trinity.

- Allow them to work with a classmate.
- Review the answers as a class.

CLOSE _____

ACTIVITY

Read aloud the instruction for the activity.

- Have the students work independently to answer the prompts on a separate sheet of paper.
- After they have had time to complete their work and reflect on the questions, discuss these topics as a class.

Quick Review The love among the Persons of the Holy Trinity is a model for human affection and bonds. While the members of the Trinity are distinct, they are also in total union with one another.

DAY 4

Objectives

- Discover how the nature of the Holy Trinity is the source of God's loving plan
- Define *grace* as God's free gift and sharing in his Divine life
- Examine how humans journey into deeper truth, wisdom, and love in relationship with God

OPEN

♥ Have the students stand and pray the Lord's Prayer, page 383, with half of the students praying the beginning of the prayer and the other half praying the ending of the prayer.

Point out the question at the top of the page. Tell the class that this is the main focus of this section.

BUILD

God's Plan for Us

Invite a strong reader to read all three paragraphs in this section.

- Ask the rest of the class to offer examples of God's plan as they understand it.
- Discuss some of the things that can make it difficult to feel God's presence.
- Point out the definition for *grace*.

Home Is Where the Heart Is

Select a volunteer to read the two paragraphs, on pages 98 and 99, to the class.

© Our Sunday Visitor

God's Plan for Us

How does the Trinity work?

The three Divine Persons of the Holy Trinity work together through their relationship with each other something like the way a loving family works together for the same goals. The Father sent the Son on his mission of salvation. The Son acted in obedience to the Father to set humans free from sin. The Holy Spirit came to help us be part of a loving relationship as members of the Church.

The work of the Trinity is all about God's plan of loving goodness. God does have a plan for all his children. He wants us to know and share in his love, to bring his goodness and love to others. He desires us to become like him, and so he cares for us and guides us with his wisdom and love. The Father works through the Son, his Holy Spirit, the Church, and the actions of people to help us. God doesn't give up on us. He continues to show his care and act on our behalf.

The unity, love, and goodness within the Holy Trinity radiate outward toward all. Out of this love and goodness the Trinity shares his own life and special help with us. We call this sharing of Divine life, **grace**. God offers us this free, loving gift of his own life and help so we can become his adopted children and do what he calls us to do. Sometimes we are not aware of God's love, even though it's there. Our own actions and stubbornness may block God out or make it difficult to feel his presence. But God's grace is still available to us if we trust in him and his hopes for us.

Home Is Where the Heart Is

The gift of faith is like a compass that points us in the right direction. When our path is directed by faith, our actions build up God's Kingdom. Our lives show Gospel values such as justice, peace, and love.

> **Catholic** Faith Words
>
> **grace** God's free, loving gift of his own life and help to do what he calls us to do. It is participation in the life of the Holy Trinity.

98 Chapter 4

Optional Activity

Trinitarian Hymns *Musical, Verbal/Linguistic*

Distribute hymnals and have the students look for hymns directly related to the Trinity.

- Ask them to write down the name of the hymns they find. Next to each name, have them identify an important idea about the Trinity that the words of the hymn convey.
- Invite volunteers to share their discoveries.
- Close the activity by singing a familiar hymn. Let the students vote on which hymn they would like to sing.

This is why it is so important to learn and practice what we believe. The teachings of our Catholic Church help us understand and strengthen our relationships with God and others. We are to give our minds, hearts, and lives to God in love and for love. As long as your life is moving in God's direction, you will be journeying into deeper truth, wisdom, and love. You will be on your way home.

> Imagine that your life has been compiled in a book. How has your story followed God's love and the teachings of faith?

> What would you like to change about the way you are living in order to follow the guidance of faith more closely?

WRITE

What does it mean to give your mind and heart to God? Around the illustrations below, write five words or phrases that would describe the mind and the heart of a Catholic. Two examples have been completed for you.

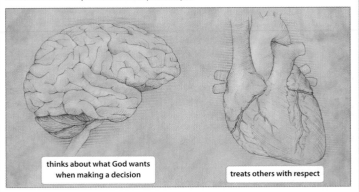

thinks about what God wants when making a decision

treats others with respect

IN SUMMARY   Catholics Believe

Believing in the Holy Trinity is central to our Catholic faith.

- The Holy Trinity is a mystery that can never be totally understood by the human mind, but can be approached through faith. The Father sent the Son and the Holy Spirit to help us know him and to guide us to him.

- The love that the Father, the Son, and the Holy Spirit have for each other shows us what our own relationships should be like.

- God has a plan of loving goodness for all his people and offers the gift of grace so that we can become more like him. This sharing in Divine life helps us trust in God, have faith in him, and work for his Kingdom.

God Is Trinity **99**

Teacher Background

Celtic Spiritual Tradition

Many Celtic prayers highlight Trinitarian belief even in the way they are organized.

- Explore the works of Esther De Waal and J. Philip Newell for examples of Celtic prayer.

- The *Carmina Gadelica*, compiled by Alexander Carmichael, contains the oral prayers and songs from the Highlands and Islands of Scotland, also influenced by the Trinity.

Home Is Where the Heart Is, *continued*

Continue reviewing the content of this section with the class.

Arrange the students in two groups. Assign each group one of the questions at the end of the text.

- Encourage the groups to discuss their question.

- Listen in on each group and provide encouragement and feedback.

- Ask a spokesperson from each group to share their thoughts.

CLOSE

ACTIVITY

Have the students read the instructions and complete the activity individually.

- If time allows, review as a class the words or phrases they came up with.

In Summary

Have three students each read one of the summary bullet points.

- Discuss what the students can learn when they look to the Holy Trinity as a model for their own relationships with others and with God.

DAY 5

Objectives

- Review the Sign of the Cross and what it means
- Explore the faith life of Saint Frances of Rome
- Offer the prayer to Reflect on the Trinity

OPEN _____

♥ Pray Psalm 25:5 and the group response from page 91.

BUILD _____

Our Catholic Life

Invite a volunteer to read aloud this section.

Have the students work in groups of two or three to discuss how they would explain the Sign of the Cross to someone who is not Catholic.

People of Faith

Explain to the students that Saint Frances gave up her time, talent, and treasure to help those in need.

- Invite a volunteer to read aloud the People of Faith paragraph.
- Share with the class the story from the People of Faith Background box.
- Invite the students to join you in a prayer of thanksgiving for the opportunities God has given us to help others.

Our Catholic Life

In the Catholic Church, we use many gestures with our prayers. Every time we make the **Sign of the Cross**, we are reminded of the Holy Trinity. We bless ourselves in the name of the Father, the Son, and the Holy Spirit, as we were baptized in the name of the Trinity. With the Sign of the Cross, we dedicate ourselves to God and call on him to strengthen us. The movements involve your hand, your head, and your heart. In this way you can be reminded that all blessings come from God, and to treat other people with kindness in what you do, what you think, and what you say. This reflects the love, interest, and care God shows you, and remembering these things helps you to show the same love, interest, and care to others.

> How would you explain the Sign of the Cross to someone who is not Catholic?

People of Faith

Saint Frances of Rome, 1384–1440

Frances was born in Rome to a wealthy family and married Lorenzo Ponziani, a nobleman. When flood brought disease and famine to Rome, Frances served in hospitals and sold her jewels and clothes to distribute money to the needy. When civil war came, she turned her home into a hospital and homeless shelter. After her husband's death, Frances entered a second vocation as a consecrated religious sister. Her last words were "The angel has finished his task—he beckons me to follow him." The Church celebrates her feast day on **March 9.**

📶 For more, go to **aliveinchrist.osv.com**

EXPLAIN

Think of a problem you faced recently and how you resolved it. In the space below, explain how you could see God's care for you in the solution to your problem.

_____
_____
_____
_____
_____
_____
_____
_____
_____
_____
_____

People of Faith Background

Saint Frances of Rome

Share the following with the students:

- Saint Frances loved the Roman people so much that she stepped out of the social boundaries of the time to help those in need.
- During a time of disease and famine, Frances and her sister-in-law went out with corn, wine, oil, and clothing from their family's possessions. Her father-in-law tried to stop them, but a miracle happened. The family's empty corn loft and empty wine cask were suddenly full.

📶 Encourage the students to go to **aliveinchrist.osv.com** at home to learn more about Saint Frances of Rome.

Reflect on the Trinity

Leader: We gather here this day in the name of the Father, and of the Son, and of the Holy Spirit, Amen.

Prepare yourselves to be in Jesus' presence.

Close your eyes and focus on opening your mind and heart to God.

Take a deep, relaxing breath, and enter into the reflection:

Read the following, slowly and in reflection:

Reader 1: O God, our Father, Creator, and maker of all creation, we praise you, and we bless you!

(pause)

We thank you for this good Earth, the air we breathe, the rain that cools our nights, the sun that warms our days, and the life you give to each and every one of us.

(pause)

Reader 2: O God the Son, our brother, teacher, and Savior, we praise you, and we bless you!

(pause)

We thank you for showing us the way to live, to trust in the Father and to love one another, to serve our sisters and brothers, and to take care of the poor and those in need.

(pause)

Reader 3: O God the Spirit, Our holy guide, and friend for the journey, we praise you, and we bless you! We thank you for walking with us, in our struggles, our choosing, our playing, and in our praying.

(pause)

Open your eyes and let us pray together the Lord's Prayer.

All: Our Father, who art in heaven, hallowed by thy name; thy kingdom come, thy will be done on earth as it is in heaven. Give us this day our daily bread, and forgive us our trespasses, as we forgive those who trespass against us; and lead us not into temptation, but deliver us from evil. Amen.

Go to aliveinchrist.osv.com for an interactive review.

A **Work with Words** Complete each sentence with the correct term from the Word Bank.

Holy Trinity	counselor
disciples	Father
miracles	Gospel
Holy Spirit	Apostles

1. Jesus gave his Apostles a command to go and make _____**disciples**_____ of all nations.

2. Christ established the Church through the _____**Apostles**_____.

3. God the Father sends his Son to us; he also sends the _____**Holy Spirit**_____.

4. God the Father gave the Holy Spirit as a _____**counselor**_____ for the Church.

5. The love of the _____**Holy Trinity**_____ is a model for the connections and love we can have with others.

B **Check Understanding** Circle the letter of the choice that best completes the sentence.

6. ____ makes it possible for us to believe in God and the things he has revealed to us.
   a. Faith
   b. Life
   c. Prayer
   d. a and b

7. The Divine Persons of the Holy Trinity are ____.
   a. Matthew, Mark, and Luke
   b. Jesus and the Holy Spirit
   c. Father, Son, and Holy Spirit
   d. Paul, Silas, and Timothy

8. ____ is God's free, loving gift of his own life and help to do what he calls us to do.
   a. Faith
   b. Grace
   c. Hope
   d. Baptism

9. ____ is the Second Divine Person of the Trinity.
   a. God, the Father
   b. God, the Son
   c. The Holy Spirit
   d. all of the above

10. Through the Sacrament of ____, we become members of God's Church.
    a. the Eucharist
    b. Confirmation
    c. the Holy Spirit
    d. Baptism

C **Make Connections** On a separate sheet of paper, write a one-paragraph response to the questions. What is God's plan of goodness and love? How does grace fit into God's plan of loving goodness?

Point out the activity on page 100.

- Give the students time to reflect on and respond to the prompt.

CLOSE

Reflect on the Trinity

Ask for four volunteers to serve as leader and readers.

Give the students a few minutes to read over their assigned passages. Remind them to read slowly and reverently.

Set up a prayer table and place on it symbols of the Trinity and a Bible.

Ask the students to gather around the prayer table and begin the prayer. Follow the order of prayer on the student page.

Close by praying together the Lord's Prayer.

▶ Play instrumental music, downloaded from **aliveinchrist.osv.com**, to open and close the celebration.

CHAPTER REVIEW

Review the instructions for each section and have the students complete the review.

Go to **aliveinchrist.osv.com** to prepare customized and downloadable assessments, send eAssessments, and assign interactive reviews.

KEY CONCEPT

Because Jesus is the Son of God, truly Divine and truly human, he saves us and brings us back into relationship with God the Father.

DOCTRINAL CONTENT

- The Son of God has existed for all time, and through the Incarnation, became fully man while remaining fully God. (CCC, 461, 464, 480)

- Through the Incarnation, God the Father speaks directly to us through his Son. (CCC, 51–53, 238–242)

- Through the work of the Holy Spirit, the Son of God was born to Mary; her trust and discipleship serves as a model for our own journey of faith. (CCC, 967, 2030)

- Jesus showed that he was Divine in many ways, particularly through the working of miracles, which also gave us a glimpse into his human nature and emotions. (CCC, 547–550, 1503)

TASKS OF CATECHESIS

Helping children grow in a faith that is "known, celebrated, lived, and expressed in prayer" (NDC, 20).

This chapter focuses on the following tasks of catechesis:

- Promoting Knowledge of the Faith

- Teaching to Pray

Teacher Background

> God greatly exalted him and bestowed on him the name that is above every name, that at the name of Jesus every knee should bend, of those in heaven and on earth and under the earth, and every tongue confess that Jesus Christ is Lord, to the glory of God the Father.   Philippians 2:9–11

> **Reflect** How do we "confess" that Jesus Christ is Lord?

We human beings were created to live in intimacy with our Creator. By choosing to sin, Adam and Eve distanced themselves and their posterity from God. As a consequence, they brought hardship to the human condition. God, always eager to mend broken relationships, was not content to let us suffer or remain apart from him. In his incredible love for us, God chose to become man. In so doing, he restored the intimacy that our first parents lost through their sinfulness. Jesus saves us from the sin, suffering, and death we chose for ourselves and offers us the perfect image of God the Father.

Jesus, true God and true man, also came to offer us the perfect image of a fully human life. In him we have the template for a life lived lovingly and generously, without being bogged down by fear as our lives so often are. Jesus reminds us of the magnificent dignity of the human person, and challenges us to live just as he lived. He also reminds us that, while death is indeed part of the human experience, we do not need to be enslaved by it. Just as Jesus did, we are called to face with courage and faith all the "deaths" in our lives, big and small. For, with death, we have the hope of eternal life with God.

> **Reflect** How has Jesus been an inspiration for you to overcome personal weakness and failure?

Teacher's Prayer

 Jesus, help me to remember your loving presence when I feel alone and to follow your example when I feel weak. May all those I encounter today see your face in mine. I ask this in your holy name. Amen.

How Seventh Graders Understand Chapter Topics

The essential message of the Incarnation is that the Word became flesh. Seventh graders have a low tolerance for hypocrisy in others. They are easily put off when they see someone say one thing and do another. (They are especially sensitive when they see this in the adults in their lives.) God is a God of both Word and deed. This culminates in the person of Jesus Christ, the fullness of God's Revelation. Jesus was a person who perfectly followed his convictions, and perfectly lived what he taught. Sharing this with young people can help you capture their attention and imagination.

Teaching Tip: Compare Jesus' words in the Sermon on the Mount with his deeds among the people. Talk with the students about how Jesus really lived what he preached.

Sharing the Message with Seventh Graders

- Younger adolescents often feel as if they lead multiple lives—they might feel like one person to their families, and another to their friends at school. In the process, they are trying to discover who they are for themselves. Self-definition is a key developmental need for seventh graders.
- Because what others think of them is so important at this age, some young people are often reluctant to share their true feelings with anyone until they feel complete trust in that person.
- Help the students see that living within one core group can lead to a narrow sense of what is important, a poor sense of what is needed, and limited ways of coping with tough times. Encourage them to branch out and connect with multiple groups.

ONLINE RESOURCES

Go to **aliveinchrist.osv.com**

You will find:

- Interactive lesson planning, additional activities, and ideas for the classroom environment
- Step by step lesson instruction from printed Teacher Edition for integrated lesson planning
- Custom-built assessments to download and eAssessment links
- Interactive reviews that provide scores and the option to review answers
- Chapter-specific lectionary connections and a complete correlation ordered by the Sundays of the year, with suggestions for how to integrate the Scripture readings into chapter lessons

Go to **osvparish.com** for Ask the Experts Q and A, Community Connections, and Blogs.

Chapter 5 Planner

Objectives	Open

DAY 1—Invite/Preview, Pages 103–105

- Reflect on God's personal invitation through Scripture
- Indicate prior knowledge of chapter concepts and vocabulary

❤ **Psalm 8:2** Pray the opening prayer.

📖 **Philippians 2:9–11** Proclaim "Plea for Unity and Humility." Guide the students through the process of Scripture reflection.

- Discuss Have You Ever Thought questions.

DAY 2—Discover, Pages 106–107

- Recognize that Jesus was fully human and fully Divine at the same time
- Define the Incarnation as the truth that the Son of God took on a human nature

❤ Pray the **Lord's Prayer**, page 383.

- Read the opening question.

DAY 3—Discover, Pages 108–109

- Understand that through the Incarnation, God the Father speaks directly to us through his Son
- Describe the Holy Spirit's role in the Annunciation
- Identify Mary as the first and most faithful disciple and a model for us

❤ Pray the **Hail Mary**, page 384.

DAY 4—Discover, Pages 110–111

- Recognize that Jesus' miracles revealed God's power, and they were often a response to his compassion, pity, and thirst for justice
- Identify passages in Scripture that reveal the two natures of Jesus

❤ Pray a silent prayer of reflection.

- Discuss the opening question.

DAY 5—Live, Pages 112–113

- Relate to different titles for Jesus
- Explore the faith lives of Saint Maria Zhao-Guo and her daughters Saint Rosa Zhao and Saint Mary Zhao
- Offer the Litany of the Holy Name of Jesus prayer

❤ Pray the **Act of Love**, page 387.

REVIEW AND ASSESSMENT

Chapter Review, page 114
Chapter Test, page 103F

📶 **aliveinchrist.osv.com** Customize and Download Assessments, Email Links to eAssessments, Interactive Student Reviews

Build	Close	Materials & Resources
• Present lesson highlights. • Preview **Catholic Faith Words**. ★ Describe events or signs in Jesus' life that show his divinity and humanity.	• Activity The students will explain their understanding of who Jesus is and what his name conveys.	☐ pencils or pens
• **Catholic Faith Words** Incarnation • Talk about Jesus' two natures. ▱ Read John 1:1–14. ★ Explore the "I Am" statements.	• Activity Consider the many different images of Jesus found in the Gospel according to John. • Conclude with a review of key concepts and objectives.	☐ pencils or pens ☐ board or chart paper ☐ Bibles
• **Catholic Faith Words** Emmanuel, Annunciation • Discuss how Jesus changed our relationship with God. • Talk about the Holy Spirit's role. ▱ Reflect on Matthew 1:18–23.	• Activity Expand on how to be a good disciple of Jesus. • Conclude with a review of key concepts and objectives.	☐ pencils or pens ☐ Bibles ☐ colored pencils or markers
• **Catholic Faith Words** miracle • Discuss what Jesus' miracles signify. ★ Look to Scripture to understand the different natures of Jesus.	• Activity The students will brainstorm solutions Jesus could offer to problems they are facing. • Review the In Summary statements. • Optional Activity God Is with Us (Activity Master 5)	☐ pencils or pens ☐ Bibles ☐ Activity Master 5 (Page 103G)
• Discuss the question in the Our Catholic Life section. • Learn about Saints Maria, Rosa, and Mary Zhao. • Activity The students will describe how they are living a Christian life.	• Assign a leader. • Follow the order of prayer. ▶ Sing or play the closing song.	☐ pencils or pens ☐ board or chart paper 🛜 "Jesus, I Trust in You"

Chapter Connections

FORMING CATHOLIC IDENTITY ACROSS THE CURRICULUM

To integrate the Catholic faith in all aspects of curriculum, this chapter's objectives can be reinforced and applied in the instruction of other disciplines.

Go to **aliveinchrist.osv.com** for cross-curricular activities and projects linked to the doctrinal content discussed in this unit. Activities are available from among the following knowledge categories and content areas:

Language Arts

- Integration of Knowledge
- Literacy
- Speaking and Listening
- Writing Skills

Math

- Algebraic Thinking
- Geometry
- Measurement and Data
- Numbers and Operations

Science

- Earth Science
- Life Science
- Physical Science
- Technology

Social Studies

- Civics
- Economics
- Geography
- History

NCEA IFG: ACRE Edition

Knowledge of the Faith

- **Objective:** To know and understand basic Catholic teaching about the Incarnate Word Jesus Christ as the way, truth, and life

Prayer

- **Objective:** To recognize and learn how to engage in Catholic forms of personal and communal prayer and ways of deepening one's spiritual life

Catholic Faith Literacy

Incarnation, miracle

Catholic Social Teaching

To integrate Catholic Social Teaching into your lesson, choose one of the following features: Life and Dignity of the Human Person, pages 334–335; or Care for God's Creation, pages 346–347.

- Start the Live step of the process by talking about Saints Maria, Rosa, and Mary Zhao on page 112. Then move directly to the Catholic Social Teaching feature.
- Or, to expand the lesson, complete page 112, then move to the Catholic Social Teaching feature.
- Return to Chapter 5 for the prayer on page 113.

Music Option

Use the following song to enhance catechetical learning or for prayer.

- "Jesus, I Trust in You," Day 5, Page 113

Name _____ Date _____

Match each description in Column A with the correct term in Column B.

Column A   Column B

____ **1.** The truth that Jesus Christ is both true God and   **a.** Jesus
true man

____ **2.** An event that can't be explained scientifically   **b.** Annunciation
because it happened through the power of God

____ **3.** The visit of the angel Gabriel to Mary to tell her   **c.** miracle
she would be the Mother of God

____ **4.** The eternal Word of God   **d.** Incarnation

Indicate whether the following statements are true or false. Then rewrite the false statements to make them true.

5. The Holy Spirit was acting in Mary even before she was born so that through her
the Son of God could become man. **True/False**

_____

6. Jesus is like us in all things but sorrow. **True/False**

_____

7. The name Jesus literally means "God lives." **True/False**

_____

8. God the Father speaks directly to us in Christ through the power of the Incarnation. **True/False**

_____

Write a response on the lines below.

9. What is the significance of God the Father's promise to send his Son, who would be

named "Emmanuel," which means "God is with us"? _____

_____

_____

10. In your own words, explain how Jesus is fully God and fully man. _____

_____

_____

_____

Name _____ Date _____

God Is with Us

Think about your own experiences and the experiences of people you know. Complete the diagram below by identifying ways that show God is with us.

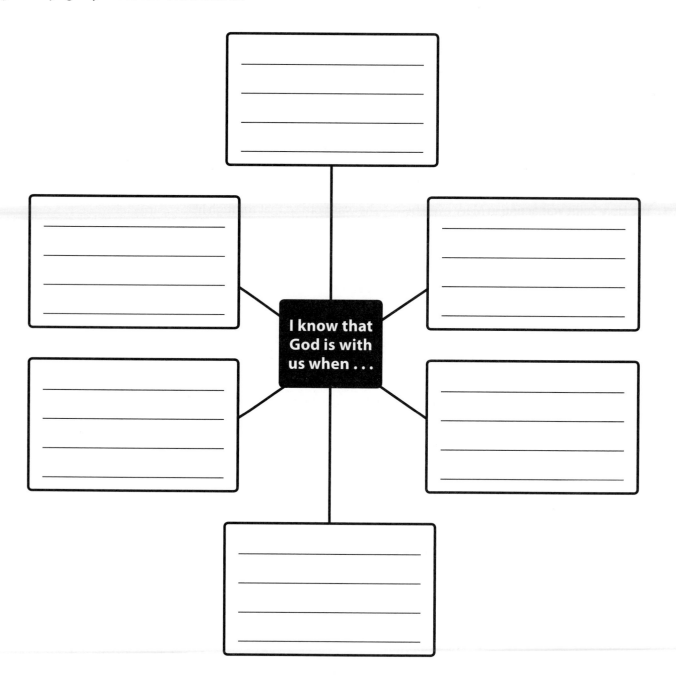

Jesus, Word of God

 Let Us Pray

Leader: O God, from the beginning your Word has brought light and life to our world.

"O LORD, our Lord,
how awesome is your name through all the earth!" Psalm 8:2

All: O God, let your Word be alive in us.

 Scripture

"God greatly exalted him
and bestowed on him the name
that is above every name,
that at the name of Jesus
every knee should bend,
of those in heaven and on earth
and under the earth,
and every tongue confess that
Jesus Christ is Lord, to the glory
of God the Father."
Philippians 2:9–11

Have you ever thought...

- What does it mean to confess that Jesus Christ is Lord?

- How do you really come to have a relationship with Jesus?

Scripture Background

Scripture Reflection Process

Invite the students to be still, close their eyes, and focus on their breathing. Encourage them to open their minds and hearts to what God is saying to them.

- Proclaim the Scripture and have the students sit in silence.

- *Ask:* What did you hear God say to you today?

- Allow volunteers to share.

▶ You may play instrumental music to begin the reflection.

Objective

- Reflect on God's personal invitation through Scripture

OPEN

♡ Let Us Pray

Invite the students to gather in the prayer space and make the Sign of the Cross. Ask a volunteer to pray the leader prayer, including the Psalm verse. Prompt the group's response.

Have the students move out of the prayer space and back to their seats.

Explain that the psalmist's prayer causes us to pause and ask, "What's in a name?" Jesus, the "eternal Word," came among us and changed our relationship with God.

Say: God wants us to be a living sign of his Word to others. Let's listen to what Saint Paul teaches about the name of Jesus.

Scripture

Guide the students through the process of Scripture reflection (see the Scripture Background box to the left).

Have you ever thought...

Say: Jesus Christ is the Son of God, the living Word, and God's greatest gift to us. We should do our best to be a sign to others of God's never-ending love.

- Invite the students to respond to the questions.

DAY 1

Objective

• Indicate prior knowledge of chapter concepts and vocabulary

BUILD

Use this page to assess the students' knowledge related to the chapter content.

Getting Started

Have a volunteer read aloud the opening paragraph for the class.

• *Ask:* Who are some models of the faith that you look up to?

• Encourage a class discussion.

Son of God

Have the students review the chart.

★ Tell them to think about and describe events or signs in each stage of Jesus' life that reveal his divinity and humanity.

• Allow the students to work with a classmate to complete their charts.

• If time allows, invite each pair to share some of their answers with the class.

Getting Started

In this chapter, you will learn what Catholics understand about the "eternal Word" and how the coming of Jesus changed our relationship with God the Father. You will also see how Mary is a model of trust and discipleship for all of us.

In the chart below, describe events or signs in each stage of Jesus' life that reveal to us his divinity and humanity.

His Birth

_____
_____
_____
_____
_____

His Childhood

_____
_____
_____
_____
_____

Son of God

His Adult Life

_____
_____
_____
_____
_____
_____

His Death and Resurrection

_____
_____
_____
_____
_____
_____

© Our Sunday Visitor

✓ Teaching Tip

Internet Use

Throughout the year, there may be times when you will need to allow the students to use the Internet for further research.

• As you know, the Internet can be an excellent teaching tool if the proper parameters are put into place.

• Make sure the students know the difference between someone's opinions and valid facts that are presented by a credible source (e.g., academic and religious institutions).

• Always monitor the students' Internet use to make sure that they are looking at specific information regarding their assignments.

Catholic Faith Words

- Incarnation
- Emmanuel
- Annunciation
- miracle

IDENTIFY

The Name of Jesus Over time, the names of people we know take on deeper meaning as we come to know them better. Think about the name Jesus. On the lines below, describe how your understanding of who Jesus is and what his name conveys has grown as you have gotten older.

105

Work with Words

Have a volunteer read aloud the four Catholic Faith Words.

- Ask the students to circle the words that they are not familiar with.
- Let them know that they should have a full understanding of the meaning of these words after they have completed this chapter.

CLOSE

ACTIVITY

Read aloud the directions.

- Allow the students time to reflect on the prompt and to complete the activity.
- Ask volunteers to share some of their responses with the class.

Optional Activity

The Meaning of a Name *Interpersonal, Verbal/Linguistic*

In biblical times, people would only offer their name or ask for another's name if they wanted to establish a true relationship with that person.

- Ask the students if they know the meanings of their own names. Provide an opportunity for them to do some research, if necessary.
- Give everyone an opportunity to share with the class. Encourage a discussion on how their names fit them.

DAY 2

Objectives

- Recognize that Jesus was fully human and fully Divine at the same time
- Define the Incarnation as the truth that the Son of God took on a human nature

OPEN

Have the students begin with the Sign of the Cross. Offer prayer intentions, and then pray together the Lord's Prayer from page 383.

Read aloud the opening question, and elicit responses.

BUILD

The Eternal Word

Write the word *authentic* on the board or on chart paper and ask the students to explain what it means.

Ask a volunteer to read aloud this section.

- Revisit the word *authentic* to make sure that the students clearly understand its meaning.

The Son of God

Summarize this section for the class.

Go to the Source

After reading the lines from John 1:1–2 on this page, have a student turn to John 1:1–14 in a Bible to read aloud the related Scripture.

Invite the students to describe what is happening in the picture that is shown on this page.

- *Ask:* How does it connect to the reading?

Mary and Joseph look with faith on the child Jesus at his Nativity, Elizabeth Wang

The Eternal Word

What is the "eternal Word"?

As humans, we are called by God to be authentic, which means to be true to who we really are. But our personalities have many different dimensions. We are complex. Sometimes, we are not easy to understand. Other times, we might need to spend some time getting to know ourselves. Because God is our Creator, he knows us best of all. He knows what he made us to be. He even knows us better than we know ourselves! God helps us get in touch with who we really are, and helps us become who we were made to be.

God the Father sent Jesus as our model of being authentic. He was always true to who he was, even when there was a cost. He was fully human and fully Divine at the same time.

Catholic Faith Words

Incarnation the truth that the Second Divine Person of the Holy Trinity, the Son of God, assumed human nature in order to save all people; Jesus Christ is both true God and true man

The Son of God

The Gospel according to John begins differently from the Gospels according to Matthew, Mark, and Luke. Instead of starting with the birth of Jesus or with his ministry on Earth, the author of John goes back to the beginning of time to tell us about Jesus before the world began. That is a side of Jesus we might not think of at first.

Jesus is the Word. He was with God the Father before creation. Then the Son of God became human, like us. What had been invisible, existing above and before all else, became visible. God's loving presence was now in the flesh. Jesus Christ, the only Son of God, is the eternal (everlasting) Word.

Scripture

In the beginning was the Word,
and the Word was with God,
and the Word was God.
He was in the beginning with God.
John 1:1–2

Go to the Source

Read *John 1:1–14.* Why do you think Jesus is called "the Word"? What does belief mean to you?

Scripture Background

The Gospel according to John

This Gospel is very different from the Gospels according to Matthew, Mark, and Luke.

- It is highly symbolic and focuses on emphasizing Jesus as the fully Divine Son of God.
- It highlights relationships, especially Jesus' relationship with the Father and ours with Jesus.
- The Gospel of John contains several passages centered on the Holy Spirit.
- It views Jesus' Death as a glorious return to the Father.

The Wonder of the Incarnation

The **Incarnation** is what we call the truth that the Son of God took on a human nature and became man. This word means "in the flesh," and shows our understanding that Jesus has two different natures—human and Divine—in one Divine Person. Jesus is like us in all things except sin.

Jesus is the only begotten Son of God. Only Jesus has this unique relationship with God the Father. The Son of God not only has the same Divine nature as his heavenly Father, but also shares in our human nature. Jesus is both truly God and truly man.

What's in a Name?

The name *Jesus* literally means "God saves" (see Matthew 1:21). Jesus entered the world to bring salvation to all people. Jesus is not just a wise prophet or miracle worker; he is the only Son of God. That is why we call him "Lord." In the Gospel according to John, we find Jesus using "I am" statements to teach us about who he is and how he relates to his Father and to us.

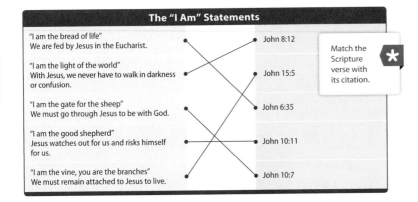

The "I Am" Statements

"I am the bread of life"
We are fed by Jesus in the Eucharist.

"I am the light of the world"
With Jesus, we never have to walk in darkness or confusion.

"I am the gate for the sheep"
We must go through Jesus to be with God.

"I am the good shepherd"
Jesus watches out for us and risks himself for us.

"I am the vine, you are the branches"
We must remain attached to Jesus to live.

John 8:12
John 15:5
John 6:35
John 10:11
John 10:7

Match the Scripture verse with its citation.

© Our Sunday Visitor

CONNECT

Review the "I am" statements above. Which of the images of Jesus do you connect to the most? What other images of Jesus can you think of from Scripture you've heard or read?

_____
_____
_____

Jesus, Word of God **107**

Optional Activity

Poetry and Pictures   *Verbal/Linguistic, Visual/Spatial*

Organize the class into two groups: those who would like to write poetry and those who would prefer to draw. Have the students review the "I am" statements on page 107.

- Ask those in the poetry group to compose a poem based on the statements.
- Ask those who prefer to draw to choose one of the "I am" statements and illustrate it.
- Display the final products from both groups in the prayer space.

The Wonder of the Incarnation

Discuss the important points in this section:

- The Incarnation is a mystery.
- The Son of God took on a human nature and became man.
- Jesus is both human and Divine.
- Jesus is like us in all things except he never sinned.
- Jesus is the only begotten Son of God.

Invite a volunteer to read aloud the Catholic Faith Word definition on page 106.

What's in a Name?

Ask the students if they know what Jesus' name means. God saves

- Give them an opportunity to respond with their thoughts.
- Have a volunteer read the text.

The "I Am" Statements

Call on five different students to read each of the "I am" statements and the lines that explain them.

★ Using a Bible, have the students work alone to match each Scripture verse with its citation.

CLOSE _____

ACTIVITY

Read aloud the directions.

- Allow volunteers to share their images of Jesus with the class.

Quick Review Jesus is the eternal Word. The Incarnation is the truth that the Son of God took on a human nature and became man, while remaining God.

DAY 3

Objectives

- Understand that through the Incarnation, God the Father speaks directly to us through his Son

- Describe the Holy Spirit's role in the Annunciation

- Identify Mary as the first and most faithful disciple and a model for us

OPEN _____

Have the students gather in the prayer space and pray the Hail Mary from page 384.

BUILD _____

God Is with Us

Explain that God's promise of a covenant relationship was fulfilled by the Incarnation of Jesus Christ.

Emphasize the following:

- God the Father speaks directly to us through his Son, Jesus.

- God is close to us in daily life.

- Jesus invites us to follow him.

Give the students an opportunity to share their responses to the question at the end of this section.

Have a volunteer read aloud the text on the Holy Trinity and the Nicene Creed in the Catholics Today box.

- If time allows, have the students turn to page 367 in the Our Catholic Tradition section of their books to read more on the Nicene Creed.

God Is with Us

How did Jesus change our relationship with God?

Long before the birth of Jesus, God used the prophets to speak to his People. Then, in an ancient promise God made to the prophet Isaiah, the Lord said the following: "Behold, the virgin shall be with child and bear a son, and they shall name him 'Emmanuel,' which means, 'God is with us'" (Matthew 1:23).

God fulfilled that promise of closeness to his People through the Incarnation of his Son, Jesus Christ. He is called **Emmanuel**, Prince of Peace, Light of the World, and Son of God.

The Incarnation is amazing news for us. It means that God is not at all distant or removed from our daily lives. In the wonder of the Incarnation, God the Father speaks directly to us in his Son, Jesus. Christ lives among us and invites us to follow him, to make our lives like his own in love.

God the Son became human to lead us back into friendship with the Father and harmony with one another. He comes to bring back all things to himself in love. But how does this great truth of the Incarnation happen?

> When are some times you know that God is with us?

CATHOLICS TODAY

We profess faith in Jesus' divinity and in the Holy Trinity by reciting together the Nicene Creed when we gather for Mass. There are three major sections in the Creed. Each one pertains to a specific Person of the Holy Trinity. The Creed has been translated into almost 1,300 languages all around the world. For more on the Creed, see page 365 of the Our Catholic Tradition section of your book.

The Annunciation,
Anto Carte

---

i   Teacher Background

Christian Solidarity

When we talk about the Incarnation, we are talking about a life-changing event. Jesus came to live among us in order to show us the way to live with and for each other. Again we return to the core truth of love, God's love for us and ours for God.

The principle of solidarity reminds us that we are our brothers' and sisters' keepers and one human family. We must extend our love for God to "loving our neighbor" both locally and globally.

The Holy Spirit Prepares

Jesus is God and shares in the Divine nature. But Jesus came from somewhere—he didn't just show up, already made. He entered the world like any other human being: He was born. However, Jesus' conception is very different from ours. First, Mary was visited by the Angel Gabriel, the messenger from Heaven, who announced to her that she would be the Mother of God and give birth to the Savior.

We call the Angel Gabriel's visit to Mary the **Annunciation**. All of human history hinged on Mary's reply. Because she said "yes" to God's plan, she became the most important woman in history. In conceiving Jesus, Mary helped in God's plan to turn his people back to the life he had always intended for us.

Second, Mary became the Mother of God because God the Holy Spirit made it possible. From before Mary was born, the Holy Spirit was acting in her, so that through her, the Son of God could become man. By the power of the Holy Spirit, not by human means, Mary became pregnant. Jesus Christ was born to Mary and the world, through the power of God.

> Name someone who has a great devotion to Mary the Mother of God.

> How does this devotion seem to be helpful to this person?

Catholic Faith Words

Emmanuel the name given to the Messiah by the prophet Isaiah, meaning "God is with us"

Annunciation the Angel Gabriel's announcement to Mary that she would be the Mother of God and give birth to the Savior

Mary—Mother of God and Our Mother

By cooperating with God's plan, Mary was already helping her Son, Jesus, in his work as Savior. Before he started his ministry of preaching and healing among the people, Mary became her Son's first and foremost disciple. By saying "yes" to God, Mary anticipated and took part in all the things her Son would do for us.

Mary, Mother of God, is our spiritual mother, also. She received the Lord in her heart before he was conceived in her womb. When he was on the Cross, Jesus gave Mary to his beloved disciple John and to all of us. Just like any mother, she shows us the way to live by her example. Her life shows us the way to Jesus.

Go to the Source

The Angel Gabriel did not just appear to Mary. Read *Matthew 1:18–23*. What was God asking Joseph to do? How did Joseph respond to God's call?

IDENTIFY AND DESIGN

What are some ways we, as Catholics, have been asked to be the disciples of Jesus? Design a motto that explains one way you can follow Mary's example and say "yes" to God.

Scripture

To discuss Joseph's response to God's call, have the students read Matthew 1:18–23.

The Holy Spirit Prepares

Remind the students about the divine nature of Jesus.

- Jesus is God. His conception was different from ours.
- Jesus was born to Mary, who is called the Mother of God.

Point out Mary's role in God's plan and the importance of her "yes."

- Discuss the questions on Mary and her devotion.

Mary—Mother of God and Our Mother

Have the students silently read this section.

- Ask them to underline three reasons Mary became the most important woman in history.
- Discuss as a class the content that the students underlined.

CLOSE _____

ACTIVITY

Discuss the opening question.

- Pass out colored pencils or markers.
- Allow the students to spend some time designing their mottos.
- Let volunteers share their mottos.

Quick Review In the wonder of the Incarnation, God the Father speaks directly to us through his Son Jesus. By the power of the Holy Spirit, Mary became the Mother of God and the first and most faithful disciple.

Scripture Background

The Magnificat

From Luke 1:39–56, this is part of Luke's Infancy Narrative describing Jesus' birth and childhood. It is also called The Canticle of Mary and is used in the evening prayer of the Liturgy of the Hours.

The *Magnificat* is Mary's song of praise to God. The themes reflect the focus of the Gospel of Luke: sheer delight in God's greatness, the lowly being lifted up, the reversal of human fortunes, and the fulfillment of Old Testament promises.

DAY 4

Objectives

- Recognize that Jesus' miracles revealed God's power, and they were often a response to his compassion, pity, and thirst for justice

- Identify passages in Scripture that reveal the two natures of Jesus

OPEN

Have the students silently pray and reflect using the TAPP method. (Share the information from the Teacher Background box below.)

Discuss, as a class, how Jesus' actions were signs of God's love.

BUILD

Signs of Divine Power and Love

Have the students silently read this section and circle the topic sentence in each paragraph.

- Ask volunteers to share the topic sentences they chose.

- Review the meaning of the word *miracle*.

Organize the students into six groups.

- Give each group a Bible, and assign them one of the Scripture passages referred to in the reading to look up.

- Have them review and summarize their passages.

- Allow time for the groups to share their summaries.

Encourage a discussion of the questions at the end of the text.

Signs of Divine Power and Love

How were Jesus' actions signs of God's love?

In his public ministry, Jesus worked miracles. A **miracle** is an event for which there is no scientific explanation because it happened by the power of God. When Jesus worked miracles, it was obvious something extraordinary was happening through him. People experienced God's power in amazing ways that changed their lives and led many of them to believe in Jesus and have faith in him as the Son of God.

Jesus healed people of their diseases. He cast out demons. He restored the dead to life. All four Gospels record this miraculous power in Jesus. For example:

Jesus gave sight to a man who had been blind from birth. Because he did so, the man came to believe that Jesus is Lord. He "saw" Jesus for who he truly is and bowed down before him in worship. (See John 9:1–41.)

Jesus restored the ability to walk to a paralyzed man. As he did so, he performed an even greater healing. He forgave the man's sins. To prove that he has this power to forgive sins, the Lord commanded the man to walk—which the man did. The crowd gave glory to God. (See Luke 5:17–26.)

Jesus raised a widow's dead son to life again. The Lord stopped the funeral procession on its way out of the city gates and commanded the young man to rise. The man sat up and began to speak. At first the crowd was fearful; then, they praised God's power, saying "God has visited his people." (Luke 7:11–16)

These miracles, and others like them, show us the divinity of Jesus and the depth of his love. At the same time, they show us the human nature of the Son of God. How? Many of these accounts of Jesus' miracles also tell us about his emotions, like compassion or pity (see Matthew 20:34, Mark 6:34), anger (see John 11:33), and tears (see John 11:35).

> Which do you think was easier: to believe in Jesus after seeing his miracles or after hearing about them from others who saw them?

> Do you agree that seeing is believing? Why or why not?

Catholic Faith Words

miracle an event for which there is no scientific explanation because it happened by the power of God. Jesus worked miracles to help us see the presence of the Kingdom of God.

110 Chapter 5

Teacher Background

Present Skill Steps: How to Pray

Young people need to move beyond the words of memorized prayer and learn to speak to God from the depths of their own spirits and to be open to the Lord's response. Introduce them to the TAPP model: "T" reminds us to *thank* God and praise him for the good things in our life. "A" reminds us to *admit* the things we've done wrong and *acknowledge* the opportunities to help others that we've ignored. "P" calls us to *petition* God for our needs and to intercede for the needs of others. The last "P" calls us to *ponder* what God has to say to us, and reminds us to pause long enough to listen.

1. Look up the Scripture passages and summarize what Jesus did in each one.

2. Then discuss how the images we find of Jesus in these passages symbolize each of his natures.

The Two Natures of Jesus Christ: Divine & Human

Jesus worked miracles
(see Luke 5:1–11)

_____

_____

_____

_____

Jesus fed his disciples
(see John 21:7–13)

_____

_____

_____

_____

BRAINSTORM

Think of a problem that you are facing now. Brainstorm some solutions that Jesus Christ could offer you.

_____

_____

_____

_____

_____

_____

_____

_____

_____

_____

_____

_____

_____

_____

IN SUMMARY Catholics Believe

Because Jesus is the Son of God, truly Divine and truly human, he saves us and brings us back into relationship with God the Father.

- The Son of God has existed for all time, and through the Incarnation, became fully man while remaining fully God.

- Through the work of the Holy Spirit, the Son of God was born to Mary, who is a model

of trust and discipleship for all of us. Her acceptance of God's will brought Jesus into the world.

- Jesus showed that he was Divine in many ways, particularly through the working of miracles, which also gives us a glimpse into his human nature and emotions.

Jesus, Word of God **111**

Optional Activity

Activity Master 5: God Is with Us

Distribute copies of the activity found on teacher page 103G.

- The students will identify ways that they know God is with them.

- As an alternative, you may wish to send this activity home with the students so that their families can help them brainstorm.

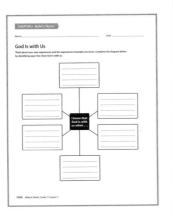

The Two Natures of Jesus Christ: Divine & Human

★ Have the students look up the Scripture passages listed and summarize what Jesus did in each one.

- Then discuss, as a class, how the images we find of Jesus in these passages symbolize each of Jesus' natures.

- Remind the students that Jesus is our model of being authentic.

CLOSE

ACTIVITY

Read aloud the directions.

- Have the students complete the activity on their own.

In Summary

Invite volunteers to read aloud the summary information.

- Encourage the students to spend some time reflecting on one of their spiritual role models, specifically on some of the things they can learn from them.

DAY 5

Objectives

- Relate to different titles for Jesus
- Explore the faith lives of Saint Maria Zhao-Guo and her daughters Saint Rosa Zhao and Saint Mary Zhao
- Offer the Litany of the Holy Name of Jesus prayer

OPEN

Invite the students to reflect on ways that they are a sign of God's love to others.

- Have them close their reflection with the Act of Love prayer from page 387.

BUILD

Our Catholic Life

Ask a volunteer to read aloud this section.

- Discuss the many titles of Jesus.
- Invite the students to share the title for Jesus that they use most often.

People of Faith

Explain to the students that Saints Maria, Rosa, and Mary Zhao gave up their lives for their faith.

- Read aloud the People of Faith paragraph.
- Write some of the interesting points from the People of Faith Background box on the board or on chart paper.
- Invite the students to reflect on the many martyrs of our faith.

Our Catholic Life

Along with Emmanuel, there are many **titles for Jesus** in Scripture. Some of these titles include Christ (which means "the anointed one" in Greek), Jesus (his common Jewish name, which means "God saves"), Lord (used to acknowledge Jesus' divinity), Messiah (the Hebrew word for "the anointed one"), and Rabbi (which means "teacher"). His early followers used these different names to show their understanding of who he was and what his presence meant to their lives. Throughout her history, the Church has used these titles for Jesus, too. Sometimes we address Jesus by different titles in the same prayers. No matter which name we use to call on Jesus, he responds with the same love and grace.

> What title for Jesus do you most often use in prayer, at home or in Church?

© Our Sunday Visitor

People of Faith

Saints Maria, Rosa, and Mary Zhao, d. 1900

In the mid-1800s China was invaded by some of the powerful nations of Europe. At the same time, Jesuit missionaries and others introduced Christianity to China. These missionaries and converts to Christianity were targeted during the Boxer Rebellion. Maria and her daughters, Rosa and Mary, were among them. When the rebels tried to force them to deny their faith, they were defiant. Before they were executed, the family prayed for strength to give up their lives for the faith. The Church celebrates their feast day on **July 9**.

For more, go to aliveinchrist.osv.com

DESCRIBE

Write your name on the line below.

_____

Then write three statements that are unique to you and show ways you are living a Christian life.

I am …

_____

_____

I am …

_____

_____

I am …

_____

_____

112 Chapter 5

People of Faith Background

Saints Maria, Rosa, and Mary Zhao

Share the following points on these Saints:

- When the three women were told to deny their faith or die, Rosa's defiant answer was, "We have already made up our minds that we would rather die than deny our faith."
- The Zhaos, along with more than fifty other Chinese martyrs, were beatified by Pope Pius XII in 1955. Pope Saint John Paul II canonized them on the centennial of their martyrdom in 2000.

Encourage the students to go to **aliveinchrist.osv.com** at home to learn more about Saints Maria, Rosa, and Mary Zhao.

💜 Litany of the Holy Name of Jesus

Leader: We gather here this day in the name of the Father, and of the Son, and of the Holy Spirit.

All: Amen.

Leader: Jesus, Son of the living God . . . have mercy on us.

Jesus, splendor of the Father . . . have mercy on us.

Jesus, brightness of eternal light . . . have mercy on us.

Jesus, King of glory . . . have mercy on us.

Jesus, Son of justice . . . have mercy on us.

Jesus, mighty God . . . have mercy on us.

Jesus, most powerful . . . have mercy on us.

Jesus, most patient . . . have mercy on us.

Jesus, most obedient . . . have mercy on us.

Jesus, author of life . . . have mercy on us.

Jesus, good shepherd . . . have mercy on us.

Jesus, eternal wisdom . . . have mercy on us.

Jesus, our way and our life . . . have mercy on us.

Jesus, Teacher of the Apostles . . . have mercy on us.

Jesus, strength of martyrs . . . have mercy on us.

Let us pray.

Lord Jesus Christ, . . . mercifully listen to our prayers

and grant us the gift of your Divine mercy that we may ever love you with our whole heart

and never cease from praising you and glorifying your holy name.

All: Amen.

▶ *Sing or play "Jesus, I Trust in You"*

🛜 Go to **aliveinchrist.osv.com** for an interactive review.

Ⓐ Work with Words Circle the letter of the choice that best completes the sentence.

1. The ___ is the truth of the Son of God taking on a human nature to save all people.
   - **a.** Incarnation
   - **c.** Holy Trinity
   - **b.** Word
   - **d.** Annunciation

2. The word *Incarnation* literally means ___.
   - **a.** Son of Man
   - **c.** in the beginning
   - **b.** creation
   - **d.** in the flesh

3. At the ___, the Angel Gabriel declared to Mary that she would be the Mother of God.
   - **a.** Incarnation
   - **c.** Resurrection
   - **b.** Annunciation
   - **d.** creation

4. An event for which there is no scientific explanation because it happened by the power of God is called ___.
   - **a.** an Incarnation
   - **c.** a miracle
   - **b.** an act of faith
   - **d.** an Annuciation

5. "Emmanuel" means ___.
   - **a.** God is with us
   - **c.** Lord of all
   - **b.** God who comes
   - **d.** the Risen One

6. In the first chapter of the Gospel according to John, Jesus is called the ___.
   - **a.** Incarnation
   - **c.** Hope of Mankind
   - **b.** Act of Faith
   - **d.** Word

Ⓑ Check Understanding Complete each sentence with the correct term from the Word Bank.

spiritual Mother	Holy Spirit
God	Mary
man	Hope
Jesus	Creed

7. Jesus is both true God and true _____ man _____.

8. The name _____ Jesus _____ literally means "God saves."

9. Mary became pregnant by the power of the _____ Holy Spirit _____.

10. Mary is our _____ spiritual Mother _____ because when Jesus was on the Cross he gave her to us.

Ⓒ Make Connections Write a one-paragraph response to the question: Identify an area in your life where you need to say "yes" to God as Mary did. If you said "yes," how might your life be different?

_____

_____

_____

_____

_____

_____

_____

_____

Have the students work on the activity on their own.

- If time allows, invite volunteers to share one of their "I am" statements.

CLOSE

Litany of the Holy Name of Jesus

💜 Assign a leader and instruct him or her to pause after each petition.

You may want to assign different students to read each line to allow more involvement in the litany.

Follow the order of prayer on the student page.

▶ Conclude by inviting the students to sing or reflect on the song "Jesus, I Trust in You," downloaded from **aliveinchrist.osv.com**.

CHAPTER REVIEW

Review the instructions for each section and have the students complete the review.

🛜 Go to **aliveinchrist.osv.com** to prepare customized and downloadable assessments, send eAssessments, and assign interactive reviews.

KEY CONCEPT

The Holy Spirit is our Advocate, guiding and comforting us, strengthening us to know and live by the truth.

DOCTRINAL CONTENT

- Jesus sent us the Holy Spirit to be our Guide and Comforter and the source of our gifts and talents. (CCC, 243, 1830–1832)

- The members of the Catholic Church are called to be the hands and feet of Jesus; we are the Body of Christ in the world. (CCC, 776–780)

- Just as the Saints often prayed to God for help, we call on the Saints to pray or intercede for us. (CCC, 956, 2683)

- The Holy Spirit guides the Church in her Sacred Tradition and her prayer. The Holy Spirit helps us pray in different ways and in different circumstances. (CCC, 2625–2649, 2661)

TASKS OF CATECHESIS

Helping children grow in a faith that is "known, celebrated, lived, and expressed in prayer" (NDC, 20).

This chapter focuses on the following tasks of catechesis:

- Promoting Knowledge of the Faith
- Teaching to Pray

Teacher Background

> [We] boast of our afflictions, knowing that affliction produces endurance, and endurance, proven character, and proven character, hope, and hope does not disappoint because the love of God has been poured out into our hearts through the holy Spirit that has been given to us.   Romans 5:3–5

> **Reflect** How does God pour love into your heart?

The Holy Spirit is a Christian's greatest asset for living a virtuous life. God the Father and the Son freely and generously share God the Spirit with us to sustain and give us strength as we make our way through the twists and turns of life. Do we take full advantage of the Holy Spirit's power? How might we be different if we gave ourselves the time to be more aware of the activity of the Holy Spirit in our everyday lives? Would this awareness move us to celebrate the feast of Pentecost in a more meaningful way?

Do you remember your Confirmation? In that beautiful liturgy, you received the Gifts of the Holy Spirit: wisdom, understanding, right judgment (counsel), courage (fortitude), knowledge, reverence (piety), and wonder and awe (fear of the Lord). These Gifts of the Holy Spirit are life-changing virtues that give us the ability to live a life of Christian witness and joy.

> **Reflect** Choose one of the Gifts of the Holy Spirit that you see reflected most in your life. How has that gift helped you in your ministry?

Teacher's Prayer

 Holy Spirit, be my inspiration, fill my mind. Holy Spirit, teach me compassion, fill my heart. Oh Holy Spirit, take this poor vessel and, today, make me your own. Amen.

How Seventh Graders Understand Chapter Topics

The Holy Spirit is perhaps the most mysterious of the three Divine Persons in One God. While seventh graders will have some concept of what a "spirit" is, they may not be able to grasp how the Holy Spirit could dwell within each Christian and also be one with God. Because they are beginning to think in more abstract terms, making use of our traditions of symbols and signs may assist seventh graders in understanding more about the Holy Spirit.

Teaching Tip: The Holy Spirit is mysterious and powerful beyond our comprehension, so we use images such as a dove, fire, and wind to help us understand. Have the students come up with some other creative images to symbolize the Spirit. How is each symbol fitting? How is each limited? What does our inability to find a perfect symbol for the Holy Spirit say to us about our inability to fully understand God?

Sharing the Message with Seventh Graders

- Adolescents are often attracted to role models who seem independent or outside of established societal norms and stand apart from traditional authority figures. You may need to help the students discover appropriate role models whom they can relate to.
- Seventh graders often admire those with the capacity to speak out against the status quo and may feel that someone like that would understand them better than others.
- If their respect for counter-cultural role models is appropriately channeled, it can foster in young people an appreciation for Jesus as the ultimate counter-cultural witness.

ONLINE RESOURCES

 Go to **aliveinchrist.osv.com**

You will find:

- Interactive lesson planning, additional activities, and ideas for the classroom environment
- Step by step lesson instruction from printed Teacher Edition for integrated lesson planning
- Custom-built assessments to download and eAssessment links
- Interactive reviews that provide scores and the option to review answers
- Chapter-specific lectionary connections and a complete correlation ordered by the Sundays of the year, with suggestions for how to integrate the Scripture readings into chapter lessons

Go to **osvparish.com** for Ask the Experts Q and A, Community Connections, and Blogs.

Objectives	Open
DAY 1—Invite/Preview, Pages 115–117	
• Reflect on God's personal invitation through Scripture • Indicate prior knowledge of chapter concepts and vocabulary	♥ **Psalm 139:7** Pray the opening prayer. 📖 **Romans 5:1–5** Proclaim "Faith, Hope, and Love." Guide the students through the process of Scripture reflection. • Discuss Have You Ever Thought questions.
DAY 2—Discover, Pages 118–119	
• Explain why Jesus sent the Holy Spirit as an Advocate • Identify the Church as the Body of Christ • Recognize that the members of the Church serve as the hands and feet of Jesus • Examine the Holy Spirit as the source of gifts and talents	♥ Pray the **Prayer to the Holy Spirit**, page 384. • Discuss the opening question.
DAY 3—Discover, Pages 120–121	
• Identify the Holy Spirit as the Comforter • Understand why we call on the Saints to intercede for us	♥ Pray a prayer of intercession.
DAY 4—Discover, Pages 122–123	
• Recognize the relationship between prayer and spiritual growth • Explore how the Holy Spirit guides us through others, Sacred Tradition, and prayer	♥ Pray the last stanza of the **Nicene Creed**, page 367. • Discuss the opening question.
DAY 5—Live, Pages 124–125	
• Reflect on the strength and wisdom of the Holy Spirit • Explore the faith life of Saint Rafqa • Offer the Prayer to the Holy Spirit	♥ Pray **Psalm 139:7**, page 115.

REVIEW AND ASSESSMENT

Chapter Review, page 126
Chapter Test, page 115F

📶 **aliveinchrist.osv.com** Customize and Download Assessments, Email Links to eAssessments, Interactive Student Reviews

Build	Close	Materials & Resources
• Present lesson highlights. • Preview **Catholic Faith Words**. ★ Reflect on symbols of the Holy Spirit.	• *Activity* Write a prayer to the Holy Spirit that can be prayed in times of loneliness. • *Optional Activity* Develop a Plotline (Activity Master 6)	☐ pencils or pens ☐ index cards ☐ Activity Master 6 (Page 115G)
• **Catholic Faith Words** Advocate ▣ Read John 14:15–17. • Share Jesus' promise to send an Advocate to be with his disciples. ★ Point out ways that the Holy Spirit acts through the Church.	• *Activity* Consider ways that the Holy Spirit can be our Advocate. • Conclude with a review of key concepts and objectives.	☐ pencils or pen
• **Catholic Faith Words** Saints, intercession • Explain that the Holy Spirit is there for us when we need comfort. ▣ Read Matthew 26:36–39 as well as Matthew 26:26–29, Mark 14:22–25, and John 13:1–17. ★ Create prayers of intercession.	• *Activity* The students will list things they do in the Church to benefit brothers and sisters in faith. • Conclude with a review of key concepts and objectives.	☐ pencils or pen ☐ board or chart paper ☐ Bibles
• Discuss some of the ways the Holy Spirit guides us. ▣ Read Philippians 2:1. • Examine the five forms of prayer.	• *Activity* Discuss people who exemplify the Gifts of the Holy Spirit. • Review the In Summary statements.	☐ pencils or pen ☐ board or chart paper ☐ Bibles
• Discuss the questions in the Our Catholic Life section. • Learn about Saint Rafqa. • *Activity* Consider how the Holy Spirit changes us for the better.	• Select five students to serve as leaders and readers. • Follow the order of prayer. ▶ Sing or play the closing song.	☐ pencils or pen 🛜 "Spirit, Come Down"

Chapter Connections

FORMING CATHOLIC IDENTITY ACROSS THE CURRICULUM

To integrate the Catholic faith in all aspects of curriculum, this chapter's objectives can be reinforced and applied in the instruction of other disciplines.

Go to **aliveinchrist.osv.com** for cross-curricular activities and projects linked to the doctrinal content discussed in this unit. Activities are available from among the following knowledge categories and content areas:

Language Arts

- Integration of Knowledge
- Literacy
- Speaking and Listening
- Writing Skills

Math

- Algebraic Thinking
- Geometry
- Measurement and Data
- Numbers and Operations

Science

- Earth Science
- Life Science
- Physical Science
- Technology

Social Studies

- Civics
- Economics
- Geography
- History

NCEA IFG: ACRE Edition

Knowledge of the Faith

- **Objective:** To know and understand basic Catholic teaching about the Incarnate Word Jesus Christ as the way, truth, and life

Prayer

- **Objective:** To recognize and learn how to engage in Catholic forms of personal and communal prayer and ways of deepening one's spiritual life

Catholic Faith Literacy

God, the Holy Spirit; prayer; Saint

Catholic Social Teaching

To integrate Catholic Social Teaching into your lesson, choose one of the following features: Call to Family, Community, and Participation, pages 336–337; or Rights and Responsibilities of the Human Person, pages 338–339.

- Start the Live step of the process by talking about Saint Rafqa on page 124. Then move directly to the Catholic Social Teaching feature.
- Or, to expand the lesson, complete page 124, then move to the Catholic Social Teaching feature.
- Return to Chapter 6 for the prayer on page 125.

Music Option

Use the following song to enhance catechetical learning or for prayer.

- "Spirit, Come Down," Day 5, Page 125

Name _____ Date _____

Complete each sentence with the correct term.

1. The Church is the Body of Christ alive in the world; the _____ is the soul.

2. The Holy Spirit is our _____, guiding and comforting us, strengthening us to know and live by the truth.

3. _____ is when we raise our minds and hearts to God.

4. The liturgical feast celebrating the descent of the Holy Spirit upon the Apostles is known as

   _____.

Circle the letter of the choice that best completes each sentence.

5. In a prayer of ____ you pray to God on behalf of another person.
   a. petition
   b. blessing
   c. thanksgiving
   d. intercession

6. The Holy Spirit acts through the ____ of the Church to teach and form us as disciples.
   a. Sacred Scripture
   b. Sacred Tradition
   c. Precepts
   d. Marks

7. When we pray a prayer of ____ we give respect to God by honoring his greatness.
   a. blessing
   b. intercession
   c. thanksgiving
   d. praise

8. A(n) ____ is a person whom the Church declares led a holy life and is enjoying eternal life with God in Heaven.
   a. Advocate
   b. Saint
   c. disciple
   d. member of the Church

Write a response on the lines below.

9. Why do you think we need the Holy Spirit? _____

   _____

   _____

10. Explain this statement: "Neglecting the time and effort for prayer will produce a withered spiritual garden." _____

   _____

   _____

Name _____ Date _____

Develop a Plot Line

Read the prompts below:

Sometimes I struggle.
I feel like no one really understands me.
How can I get through those times?

Work in small groups to outline the key elements of a story that would address the above thoughts and questions.

Characters:

_____

_____

Plot Development:

• What happens?

_____

_____

• Where does it happen?

_____

• When does it happen?

_____

• Why do you think it happens?

_____

• Who is affected?

_____

• How do the characters change or grow?

_____

_____

Holy Spirit, Comforter and Guide

💟 Let Us Pray

Leader: Most gracious God, wherever we go, whatever we do, you are there loving us, guiding us.

"Where can I go from your spirit?
From your presence, where can I flee?"   Psalm 139:7

All: Lord, help us see your presence; help us find you in the moments of our day.

Scripture

"Therefore, since we have been justified by faith, we have peace with God through our Lord Jesus Christ, through whom we have gained access [by faith] to this grace in which we stand, and we boast in hope of the glory of God. Not only that, but we even boast of our afflictions, knowing that affliction produces endurance, and endurance, proven character, and proven character, hope, and hope does not disappoint because the love of God has been poured out into our hearts through the holy Spirit that has been given to us."   Romans 5:1–5

Have you ever thought...
- What keeps you going when things are very difficult?
- What role does the Holy Spirit have in your life?

115

© Our Sunday Visitor

Scripture Background

Scripture Reflection Process

Invite the students to be still, close their eyes, and focus on their breathing. Encourage them to open their minds and hearts to what God is saying to them.

- Proclaim the Scripture and have the students sit in silence.
- *Ask:* What did you hear God say to you today?
- Allow volunteers to share.

▶ You may play instrumental music to begin the reflection.

Objective
- Reflect on God's personal invitation through Scripture

OPEN _____

💟 Let Us Pray

Invite the students to gather in the prayer space and make the Sign of the Cross. Select a few students to read aloud the leader lines and the Psalm verse. Prompt the response from the remainder of the class.

Have the students move out of the prayer space and back to their seats.

Say: God the Father is with us and helps to guide us every day through his gifts to us—God the Son and God the Holy Spirit. Jesus promised to send the Holy Spirit to be with us to help us to live according to his Father's will.

Scripture

Guide the students through the process of Scripture reflection (see the Scripture Background box below).

Have you ever thought…

Say: God the Father sent his Son and the Holy Spirit, as well as his everlasting love to help us on our faith journey and in our daily lives.

Ask: What difference does it make in your life to know that God is always with you to lead you back to him for all eternity?

Invite the students to respond to the questions.

DAY 1

Objective

- Indicate prior knowledge of chapter concepts and vocabulary

BUILD _____

Use this page to assess the students' knowledge related to the chapter content.

Getting Started

Say: No matter what we experience in life, there is an amazing action taking place: the love of God is being poured into our hearts as long as our hearts are open to him. This image describes a God whose love is ever-present, during the good times and the not-so-good.

Read aloud the opening paragraph.

- Discuss the content with the class.
- *Ask:* Have you ever felt the guidance of the Holy Spirit in a decision that you had to make?
- Allow volunteers to respond.

The Holy Spirit

Read aloud the instructions for the graphic organizer.

- ★ Have the students work in small groups to complete the chart.
- Once everyone has completed the assignment, discuss, as a class, how each of the images symbolizes the Holy Spirit.

Getting Started

In this chapter you will learn about God's plan in sending the Holy Spirit. You will also discover the unique and powerful ways the Holy Spirit is present in the Church.

The web below shows three symbols of the Holy Spirit. On the lines below each symbol, explain why it could be associated with the Holy Spirit.

The Holy Spirit

Wind symbolizes the Holy Spirit because:
_____
_____
_____
_____
_____
_____
_____
_____
_____

Oil symbolizes the Holy Spirit because:
_____
_____
_____
_____
_____
_____
_____
_____
_____

Fire symbolizes the Holy Spirit because:
_____
_____
_____
_____
_____
_____
_____
_____
_____

© Our Sunday Visitor

116 Chapter 6

✓ Teaching Tip

Creative Writing

Having students create fictional pieces is a safe way for them to address sensitive or difficult issues in objective, less personal ways. Students will often put their experiences into the writing in indirect ways. This allows them to grapple with life issues on a different level.

An important element in the creative writing process is helping students look at the stories (their own and those of others) in light of the Gospel values they are learning. Would the story be different if faith is taken into consideration?

Catholic Faith Words

- Advocate
- Saints
- intercession

WRITE

Filling the Empty Space Describe an experience when you felt alone. How can the image of the love of God being poured into your heart (see Romans 5:5) fill the empty space of your loneliness?

_____

_____

_____

_____

_____

_____

_____

_____

_____

_____

Write a short prayer to the Holy Spirit that you can pray in times of loneliness.

_____

_____

_____

_____

_____

_____

_____

_____

_____

_____

Holy Spirit, Comforter and Guide **117**

Work with Words

Direct the students' attention to the Catholic Faith Words box.

- Have a volunteer read aloud the three vocabulary words.
- Invite class discussion about the meaning of each word.
- See if the students can share how any of the words connect to the Holy Spirit.

CLOSE _____

ACTIVITY

Remind the students about God's ever-present love for us and the role of the Holy Spirit as our Comforter and Guide.

- Explain the instructions.
- Invite the students to copy their prayers on index cards to keep tucked in their backpack or locker. Encourage them to pray their prayers in times of loneliness.
- Share with the class a common prayer or your own prayer for times of loneliness. Ask a volunteer if he/she would like to share his/her prayer.

Optional Activity

Activity Master 6: Develop a Plot Line

Distribute copies of the activity found on teacher page 115G.

- Have the students work in small groups to write an outline for a short story or play.
- Ask the groups to share their plot lines with the class.

DAY 2

Objectives

- Explain why Jesus sent the Holy Spirit as an Advocate
- Identify the Church as the Body of Christ
- Recognize that the members of the Church serve as the hands and feet of Jesus
- Examine the Holy Spirit as the source of gifts and talents

OPEN _____

♡ Have the students pray the Prayer to the Holy Spirit, page 384.

Allow volunteers to share their answers to the opening question.

BUILD _____

A Promise Kept

Ask: What does it mean to feel alone?

Read the text aloud. Remind the students:

- Jesus said he would be with us always (see Matthew 28:20).
- Jesus counts on us to share his Good News.

Always with Them

Read aloud the text.

📖 Scripture

Proclaim the Scripture.

- *Ask:* What does Jesus mean by "Spirit of truth"? Why do you think Jesus said, "the world cannot accept" the Spirit of truth?
- Discuss the two questions at the end of the section as a class.

A Promise Kept

Why did God send the Holy Spirit to us?

It's hard when you can't be with a close friend anymore. He or she might have moved away, or you might be going to a new school. You miss your friend, and things you do are different because that person isn't there. You might feel lonely, wondering why people don't understand you and what's important to you.

Jesus knew his disciples would miss him when he was no longer with them. His followers were going to feel lost without him. His Death would break their hearts. His Resurrection might certainly confuse them. His return to the Father in Heaven would definitely challenge them.

How could the Apostles continue the work they had done with Jesus when he was no longer with them?

Catholic Faith Words

Advocate literally means "he who is called to one's side." The Holy Spirit is our Advocate, guiding and comforting us, strengthening us to know and live by the truth.

Always with Them

Jesus promised his Apostles he wouldn't stop being with them. In fact, he promised them that he would always be with them through an **Advocate**, the Holy Spirit. An advocate is someone who speaks on your behalf.

📖 Scripture

So Jesus said to his disciples at the Last Supper, "'If you love me, you will keep my commandments. And I will ask the Father, and he will give you another Advocate to be with you always, the Spirit of truth, which the world cannot accept, because it neither sees nor knows it. But you know it, because it remains with you, and will be in you.'" John 14:15–17

> How could the Holy Spirit help the Apostles?
> How could he help you?

Optional Activity

The Descent of the Holy Spirit *Visual/Spatial*

Pentecost, the liturgical feast that closes the Easter season, celebrates the descent of the Holy Spirit upon the Apostles and the enduring legacy of that Spirit in the Church down through the ages. Red vestments are worn to denote the fiery presence of the Spirit.

- Have the students use black and red markers to illustrate their own interpretation of the descent of the Holy Spirit on the Apostles.
- Invite the students to share their artwork with a classmate.
- Consider displaying the drawings outside your classroom door.

The Soul of the Church

The Church is the Body of Christ in the world. We are the hands and feet of Christ, bringing the truth, joy, and love of the Good News to all people. Our own bodies are more than just a collection of flesh and bones. In the same way that your body is given life by your soul, the Body of Christ comes alive through her soul, the Holy Spirit.

The Holy Spirit keeps the Church going, giving her life. He makes the wonderful diversity of people, places, and cultures in the Church one. He brings us together by our belief in Jesus. The Holy Spirit is the source of the many gifts and talents people bring to the Church.

Underline some of the ways the Holy Spirit acts in the Church.

© Our Sunday Visitor

DESCRIBE AND PRAY

Describe two situations in your life when you wished you had someone who could speak for you and look out for your best interests.

_____

_____

_____

_____

Then pray the Prayer to the Holy Spirit (see page 125 in this chapter or 384 in the Our Catholic Tradition section of your book) and consider ways that the Holy Spirit could fill that role of an advocate for you.

119

Teacher Background

The Mass

Mass is a re-presentation of the Paschal Mystery, not a repetition of it. Each celebration brings with it an "outpouring of the Holy Spirit that makes the unique mystery present" (CCC, 1104).

The *Epiclesis* ("invocation upon") is the point during Mass when the priest asks the Father to send the Holy Spirit, so that the offerings "may become the body and blood of Christ" and that we, by receiving Christ, become "a living offering to God" (CCC, 1105).

Ask the students to listen for this prayer during Mass. Encourage them to listen to the prayers that surround the *Epiclesis*. What do they mean to them?

The Soul of the Church

Tell the students that the next two paragraphs are very important to their lives and also to the life of the Church.

✱ As you read aloud the text, ask them to underline ways that the Holy Spirit acts in the Church.

• Provide the students with an opportunity to ask any questions that they have on this material.

Work with Words

Ask a volunteer to read aloud the Catholic Faith Word definition on page 118.

• Invite volunteers to share examples of how they have seen the Holy Spirit work as an Advocate. (You may need to open with some examples to facilitate discussion.)

CLOSE

ACTIVITY

Have the students read the instructions and complete the activity on their own.

• Once everyone has had a chance to finish, have the students stand, make the Sign of the Cross, and pray the Prayer to the Holy Spirit.

Quick Review The Holy Spirit is our Guide and Advocate, the source of our gifts and talents that we bring to the Church. As members of the Church, we are the hands and feet of Jesus. We are the Body of Christ in the world.

DAY 3

Objectives

- Identify the Holy Spirit as the Comforter
- Understand why we call on the Saints to intercede for us

OPEN

💙 Invite the students to bow their heads and silently pray a prayer of intercession for someone close to them.

BUILD

The Holy Spirit, Comforter

Discuss some things that someone might ask of the Holy Spirit.

We May Seem Alone

Have a volunteer read aloud the first two paragraphs.

- Explain that everyone has had to face the dilemma of being alone at some point in life. See if anyone wants to share an experience.

Review the last two paragraphs with the class.

📖 Go to the Source

Ask the students to describe what they know about the events in the Garden of Gethsemane. Have them silently read Matthew 26:36–39.

For more on Jesus' words and actions, send the students to Matthew 26:26–29, Mark 14:22–25, and John 13:1–17 in their Bibles.

© Our Sunday Visitor

the whistles and cheers of fans he has never met. He feels the support of his coach and teammates. At the same time, he will be alone when he reaches for the rings and performs his routine. He will have to remember everything he has learned in practice and previous meets, and apply all his mental and physical strength to the routine. No one else can do it for him.

The Scripture passage below tells of how, as Jesus prepared himself for the Cross, his friends fell asleep. Twice he returned to find them sleeping and unaware of his pain. How must Jesus have felt?

Have you ever had to do something you knew would be difficult—but you also knew that it was important that you do it? Jesus teaches, ". . . how much more will the Father in heaven give the holy Spirit to those who ask him?" (Luke 11:13).

The Holy Spirit, Comforter

How does the Holy Spirit help us in ways that no one else can?

We May Seem Alone

Often, the support and strength of friends helps us through difficult times. There are times, however, when we must face something all on our own. We might be surrounded by our friends, and they might even offer their help and support. But in the end, whatever it is we must face, we need to do it on our own.

Imagine an Olympic gymnast, about to begin his routine on the rings. He has trained for years to get to this point in his athletic career. He knows that his family and friends are in the arena, watching and sending good thoughts his way. He hears

📖 Scripture

"Then Jesus came with them to a place called Gethsemane, and he said to his disciples, 'Sit here while I go over there and pray.'"

He asked his three friends to sit up and wait. He probably wanted them to be there for him, to support him. Then he said to them, 'My soul is sorrowful, even to death.'

Then, he moved farther into the garden where they could not see him. He addressed his heavenly Father in prayer, asking that the Cross be taken from him, if possible. Jesus prayed, 'My Father, if it is possible, let this cup pass from me; yet, not as I will, but as you will.'"
Based on Matthew 26:36–39

📖 Go to the Source

For more on the Last Supper, read *Matthew 26:26–29*, *Mark 14:22–25*, and *John 13:1–17*.

📖 Scripture Background

The Garden of Gethsemane

This is the name used in both Matthew and in Mark to describe the place of Jesus' agony. It is simply called a garden in John 18:1 and is not mentioned at all in Luke, which simply refers to the Mount of Olives.

The Hebrew name, *Gethsemane*, means oil press or oil vat, referring to olive oil.

Today, the Garden of Gethsemane, located in Jerusalem, is filled with olive trees. Some scientists think that some of the olive trees at Gethsemane could be over 2,000 years old.

As you have probably discovered already, none of us can avoid pain and difficulties in life. We will have challenges in our lives that we must face on our own. But we will have the help and special comfort of the Holy Spirit as we face these trials and confront these challenges.

The **Saints** often prayed to God for help, and the prayers they prayed still help people pray effectively today. The Saints poured out their hearts for help from above. We, too, are sure that the Holy Spirit will personally help us. And we call on the Saints to pray for us, asking for their **intercession** on our behalf.

Catholic Faith Words

Saints those whom the Church declares led holy lives and are enjoying eternal life with God in Heaven

intercession a form of prayer that involves praying to God on behalf of another; also called intercessory prayer

We, too, pray a prayer of intercession during the Prayer of the Faithful at Mass.

> When do you turn to God?

> How do you let God know you need him?

Fill in the chart with one prayer of intercession for each of the groups mentioned. ✱

The Prayer of the Faithful	
We pray for the Church	Our prayer: _____ _____
We pray for the world and world leaders	Our prayer: _____ _____
We pray for the sick and for those who have died	Our prayer: _____ _____

LIST

The work of the Holy Spirit benefits the Church by building up the community of faith, helping people to be faithful, and sanctifying the Church (making her holy). List three things that you do in the Church that benefit your brothers and sisters in faith.

1. _____

2. _____

3. _____

Holy Spirit, Comforter and Guide **121**

Teacher Background

Retreats

Retreats are opportunities to take a little time away from the events of our daily lives in order to focus entirely on our relationship with God. There are many retreat centers throughout the country. They offer a variety of methods all designed to help the retreat participant take time away from it all, to listen carefully to God in his or her life.

As teachers, we too need this time away, for the sake of those we serve. Taking the time to go will make room for the Holy Spirit who will help us to grow in holiness. From that sacred place, we give to our students.

We May Seem Alone, continued

Have a volunteer finish reading the text.

- Remind the students that even their teachers face challenges and rely on the help of the Holy Spirit.

- Invite the students to discuss the questions at the end of this section with a classmate.

Work with Words

Have two students read aloud the Catholic Faith Words.

- Ask the rest of the students to give you examples of each of the vocabulary words to ensure their understanding.

The Prayer of the Faithful

✱ Direct the students to fill in the chart with one prayer of intercession for each group.

- The students should complete their prayers individually.

- If there is time, pray as a class one volunteer's prayer from each of the three categories.

CLOSE _____

ACTIVITY

Summarize the directions.

- Have the students work on this activity independently.

- If time allows, let the students share their answers in small groups.

Quick Review We are never alone. The Holy Spirit is our Comforter, and we can always ask for the help of the Saints in prayers of intercession.

Holy Spirit, Comforter and Guide **121**

DAY 4

Objectives

- Recognize the relationship between prayer and spiritual growth
- Explore how the Holy Spirit guides us through others, Sacred Tradition, and prayer

OPEN

 Have the students gather in the prayer space. While focusing on the Holy Spirit, pray together the last stanza of the Nicene Creed on page 367.

Read aloud the opening question and elicit responses from the class.

BUILD

The Holy Spirit, Guide

Ask the students to name examples of important things a gardener must do to help a garden grow.

- *Ask:* How might gardening be like prayer? Possible response: both take nurturing and effort

Summarize the paragraph equating gardening with prayer.

- Discuss how the image on this page relates to the text.
- Allow questions or comments.

Guidance

Invite two volunteers to read aloud the information in this section.

Scripture

Have a student proclaim Philippians 2:1, reading either directly from the student page or from the Bible.

The Holy Spirit, Guide

How does the Holy Spirit help the Church?

A garden grows because someone takes the time and effort to water and weed it. Without weeding, the plants will be choked by unhealthy growth. Without water, the plants in the garden will wither and die.

Similarly, when we raise our minds and hearts to God—which is what prayer is—we cultivate our spiritual garden. Requesting bad things from God will produce in us a spiritual garden full of weeds. Neglecting the time and effort for prayer will produce a withered spiritual garden.

© Our Sunday Visitor

Guidance

We need someone to guide us through life's questions and help us live for God. That guide is the Holy Spirit. He works through the Church and often through the people in our lives.

The Holy Spirit acts through the Church to teach and form us as disciples, guiding the Church in her interpretation of God's Word in Sacred Scripture and Sacred Tradition. This Sacred Tradition is our religious heritage. Sacred Tradition is God's Word to the Church, safeguarded by the Apostles and their successors, the bishops, and handed down verbally—in her Creeds, Sacraments, and other teachings—to future generations. This Sacred Tradition enriches our personal prayer and the prayer life of the Catholic Church, so that we raise our minds and hearts to God in holy and effective ways.

Scripture

"If then there is any encouragement in Christ, any solace in love, any participation in the Spirit, any compassion and mercy, complete my joy by being of the same mind, with the same love, united in heart, thinking one thing."
Philippians 2:1

A Guide to Prayer

Just like you talk to your friends in different ways depending upon what you have to share, you can talk to God in different ways, too. The Holy Spirit is with you when you pray, guiding you in prayer as you grow in faith. Because you have different needs and different experiences during life, the Holy Spirit gives you a variety of ways to pray.

122   Chapter 6

Optional Activity

Forms of Prayer *Verbal/Linguistic, Interpersonal*

Invite the students to practice different forms of prayer: blessing, praise, petition, intercession, and thanksgiving.

- Arrange the students in groups and assign each group one form of prayer.
- Explain each form of prayer and give some examples.
- Ask the groups to write a prayer that fits their form.
- Invite a student from each group to read aloud the group prayer.
- Encourage the students to practice the different ways of praying by using a different form of prayer each day of the week.

The Holy Spirit also teaches you to pray. He does this by helping different generations of Church leaders and Catholics pass on the truth of Jesus through the Church's Seven Sacraments, the Creeds, teachings, and devotional practices such as praying the Rosary or the Liturgy of the Hours.

> When you pray, is it mostly asking God for something, or do you just talk to God as a friend who listens?

The Ways We Pray

Prayers of **blessing and adoration** bless God for being the source of all that is good and show that we need him. We respond to God's gifts and give respect to God by honoring his greatness.

Prayers of **praise** give honor to God for being who he is. We give him glory as his children not for what he does, but simply because he is.

Prayers of **petition** ask God for something we need for ourselves. We might ask for God's mercy, forgiveness, and guidance.

Prayers of **intercession** ask God for something on behalf of another person. We use intercessory prayer on behalf of others as Jesus intercedes for us with God the Father.

Prayers of **thanksgiving** acknowledge and thank God for all he has given us. We express our gratitude to him for the good things in our lives.

EXPLAIN

One of the symbols of the Holy Spirit at Pentecost is wind. Like the Holy Spirit, we cannot see wind, but we can see what wind does. Look at the Fruits of the Holy Spirit named below. Write the name of a person whom you know has been an instrument of the Holy Spirit in bringing two of these fruits to the world, and explain how they did so.

Fruits of the Holy Spirit: Charity, Kindness, Faithfulness, Joy, Goodness, Modesty, Peace, Generosity, Self-control, Patience, Gentleness, Chastity

_____

_____

_____

_____

_____

IN SUMMARY Catholics Believe

The Holy Spirit is our Advocate, guiding and comforting us, strengthening us to know and live by the truth.

• The Holy Spirit, who strengthened the first disciples to spread Jesus' message and understand his truth, keeps the Church going, giving her life and energy and uniting us as one Body of Christ.

• We all experience difficulties and challenges, some that we must face alone. However, we are never truly alone because the Holy Spirit is with us, comforting, strengthening, and supporting us.

• The Holy Spirit guides the Church in her Sacred Tradition and her prayer. The Holy Spirit helps us pray at different times, in different ways, and in different circumstances.

Holy Spirit, Comforter and Guide **123**

✓ Teaching Tip

Brainstorming

Brainstorming is an important part of the learning experience. Make and distribute to your students a list of key factors to keep in mind while brainstorming. The list should include the following:

• Work together in small groups to maximize your brainstorming potential.

• Remember that all answers and ideas need to be considered and affirmed in order to create a welcoming environment.

• Always keep in mind that brainstorming works best when we recognize that every group member's ideas deserve consideration and are important.

A Guide to Prayer

Say: Just as we talk to our friends in different ways, we also talk to God in different ways.

• Inform the students that the Holy Spirit teaches us how to pray and gives us a variety of ways to pray.

Have the students read this section, which begins on page 122.

• Discuss the question at the end of this section.

The Ways We Pray

Invite five volunteers to read aloud the descriptions of the different types of prayers in the chart.

• If you do the Optional Activity on page 122, you could have this information written on chart paper for the groups to refer to.

CLOSE _____

ACTIVITY

Read aloud the instructions.

• Tell the students to work on their own to come up with the name of a person.

• Allow volunteers to share their responses with the class.

In Summary

Go over the summary information as a class.

• Ask the students to identify times when they knew that the Holy Spirit was acting as an Advocate for them.

DAY 5

Objectives

- Reflect on the strength and wisdom of the Holy Spirit
- Explore the faith life of Saint Rafqa
- Offer the Prayer to the Holy Spirit

OPEN

♥ Have the students stand. Begin with the Sign of the Cross and pray together the Invite Psalm from page 115.

BUILD

Our Catholic Life

Read aloud the information in this section.

- Impress upon the students the importance of praying to the Holy Spirit, especially in times of great loneliness or when difficult choices have to be made.
- Have the students reflect on the questions at the end of this text.

People of Faith

Explain that Saint Rafqa felt called by God to the religious life at age fourteen.

- Read aloud the paragraph on Saint Rafqa and review with the class the content of the People of Faith Background box.
- Invite the students to reflect on their relationship with the Holy Spirit.

Our Catholic Life

The Holy Spirit can be a great source of comfort when you feel alone or afraid, as Jesus' followers must have felt after his Death and before the time of Pentecost. Through the strength and wisdom of the Holy Spirit, we are able to lead the life of love Jesus wants us for us. Take the time to **pray to the Holy Spirit** when you need that comfort during a time of difficulty, or when you need guidance in making choices or hard decisions. On the next page you can read the Prayer to the Holy Spirit, but you can address other prayers, either from the Church's liturgy or ones you write or think up yourself, to him. When you pray and listen to what the Holy Spirit is telling you, you allow him to guide you and work in your heart.

> When have you prayed to the Holy Spirit? How did you feel afterward?

© Our Sunday Visitor

People of Faith

Saint Rafqa (Rebecca), 1832–1914

Born in Lebanon as Boutrossieh Ar-Rayes, Rafqa felt a call to religious life at age fourteen and later became a nun. She joined the Order of Saint Anthony of the Maronites (Baladiya Order) in 1871 and took the name of Rafqa (Rebecca).

Blind and near the time of her death, Rafqa asked that her sight be restored for an hour so she could again see the face of her friend Mother Superior Ursula Doumit. The hour of sight was granted. Miracles of healing were later recorded at Rafqa's grave. The Church celebrates her feast day on **March 23.**

📶 For more, go to **aliveinchrist.osv.com**

124 Chapter 6

CONSIDER

Think of one of your favorite movies in which the main character changes considerably during the film. Why did the change take place? Who supported him or her?

_____
_____
_____

How could the Holy Spirit have been involved in this change?

_____
_____
_____
_____

People of Faith Background

Saint Rafqa (Rebecca)

Share this additional information with the class:

- On the Feast of the Holy Rosary in 1885, Rafqa prayed that she might share Christ's sufferings. She became blind and crippled.
- She spent much of her remaining thirty years in prayer and working in the convent, spinning wool and knitting. Despite her frail health, she lived for more than eighty years.

📶 Encourage the students to go to **aliveinchrist.osv.com** at home to learn more about Saint Rafqa.

Prayer to the Holy Spirit

Leader: Come Holy Spirit, fill the hearts of your faithful.

And kindle in them the fire of your love. Send forth your Spirit and they shall be created.

All: And you shall renew the face of the earth.

Reader 1: A reading from the Book of Psalms.

Read Psalm 139:7–12.

Where can I go from your spirit?
From your presence, where can I flee?
If I ascend to the heavens, you are there;
if I lie down in Sheol, there you are.
If I take the wings of dawn
and dwell beyond the sea,
Even there your hand guides me,
your right hand holds me fast.
If I say, "Surely darkness shall hide me,
and night shall be my light"
Darkness is not dark for you,
and night shines in the day.
Darkness and light are but one.
The word of the Lord.

All: Thanks be to God.

Reader 2: Come to us, O Spirit of truth, teach us what we need to know, and remind us of all that Jesus did for us.

Reader 3: Come to us, O Spirit of love, walk with us each and every day, and guide us in all we say and do.

Reader 4: Come to us, O Spirit of compassion, be with us when we are lonely and afraid, when we are confused and don't know how to choose.

All: Come to us, O Spirit of wisdom, help us to know that you are always near, help us to know that you will always guide us, help us to know that you are always for us.

Sing or play "Spirit, Come Down"

Go to aliveinchrist.osv.com for an interactive review.

A **Work with Words** Circle the letter of the choice that best completes the sentence.

1. The Holy Spirit is the Advocate because ___.
   a. he speaks on our behalf
   b. we can't see him
   c. he is the Word
   d. he brings healing

2. ___ is the liturgical feast that celebrates the descent of the Holy Spirit upon the Apostles.
   a. Easter
   b. Christmas
   c. Pentecost
   d. Mass

3. Prayer involves ___.
   a. thoughts about God
   b. raising our hearts and minds to God
   c. guidance by the Holy Spirit
   d. a, b, and c

4. We call on the ___ to pray for us, interceding on our behalf.
   a. clergy
   b. disciples
   c. Saints
   d. shepherds

5. Jesus promised the Apostles he would continue to be present with them after his Death through the ___.
   a. Apostles
   b. Tongues of Fire
   c. Holy Spirit
   d. Creation

B **Check Understanding** Complete each sentence with the correct term from the Word Bank.

ourselves	life and unity
others	intercession
act of faith	Body of Christ
creation	Sacred Tradition
harmony	

6. The Church is the __Body of Christ__ in the world.

7. The Holy Spirit brings __life and unity__ to the Church.

8. A prayer of petition asks God for something needed for __ourselves__.

9. A prayer of __intercession__ asks God for something for another person.

10. __Sacred Tradition__ is God's Word to the Church, safeguarded by the Apostles and their successors, the bishops, and handed down to future generations.

C **Make Connections** Write a one-paragraph response to the questions: How are we connected with God? What do you consider the source of your strongest connection to God?

_____
_____
_____
_____
_____
_____
_____

Discuss the activity instructions with the class.

- Brainstorm some movie ideas with them before they get started.
- Afterwards, have them answer the questions individually.

CLOSE _____

Prayer to the Holy Spirit

Ask five students to serve as the leader and readers.

Invite the students to stand at their places.

Call them to prayer with these words: Holy Spirit, we know you are present among us. Hear us, as we pray.

Have the leader and readers pray their sections; prompt prayer responses by the group, if necessary.

Conclude by singing with the students or playing the song "Spirit, Come Down," downloaded from **aliveinchrist.osv.com**.

CHAPTER REVIEW

Review the instructions for each section and have the students complete the review.

Go to **aliveinchrist.osv.com** to prepare customized and downloadable assessments, send eAssessments, and assign interactive reviews.

UNIT 2

Use the closing points from Days 2–4 in each chapter to highlight lesson concepts for this unit and prepare for the Unit Review.

Have the students complete the Review pages. Then discuss the answers as a class. Review any concepts with which the students are having difficulty.

A **Work with Words**

Have the students match the words in the left column with the letter of the correct definition or description in the right column.

A Work with Words **Match the terms on the left with the correct definitions or descriptions on the right.**

_e_ 1. Pentecost

_h_ 2. Annunciation

_a_ 3. miracle

_c_ 4. Holy Spirit

_g_ 5. grace

_d_ 6. conscience

_f_ 7. Holy Trinity

_b_ 8. Incarnation

_l_ 9. Jesus

_k_ 10. Emmanuel

_j_ 11. bread

_i_ 12. God the Father

a. an event for which there is no scientific explanation because it happened through the power of God

b. the Son of God taking on a human nature to save all people

c. the Third Divine Person of the Trinity

d. the God-given ability that helps us judge right from wrong

e. the outpouring of the Holy Spirit upon the Apostles fifty days after Easter

f. Father, Son, and Holy Spirit

g. the free, loving gift of God's life and help

h. the Angel Gabriel telling Mary that she would be the Mother of God

i. the First Divine Person of the Trinity

j. Jesus described himself in his "I Am" statements as light, a shepherd, a vine, and this

k. A name for Jesus that means "God is with us"

l. the Second Divine Person of the Trinity

© Our Sunday Visitor

Trinity **127**

B Check Understanding Indicate whether the following statements are true or false. If a statement is false, rewrite it to make it true.

13. When God the Father sends his Son to us, he also sends his Spirit.
(True)/False

_____

_____

14. Saint Paul is a guide to the Church. True/(False)
The Holy Spirit is our guide.

_____

15. In the Sacrament of the Eucharist, we become members of God's Church. True/(False)
In the Sacrament of Baptism, we become members of God's Church.

16. Jesus promised his Apostles that he would continue to be present with them after his Death through the Law. True/(False)
He would be present through the Holy Spirit.

17. A prayer of petition is asking God for something we need for ourselves. (True)/False

_____

_____

18. A prayer of blessing and adoration asks God for something for another person. True/(False)
A prayer of intercession asks God for something for another person.

19. Sacred Tradition is God's Word safeguarded by the Apostles and their successors, the bishops, and handed down verbally to future generations. (True)/False

_____

_____

20. In the opening part of the Gospel according to John, John calls Jesus "the Light of the World." True/(False)
He calls Jesus "the Word."

_____

21. The name Jesus literally means "God saves." (True)/False

_____

_____

22. Mary is our spiritual Mother because she shows us the way to Jesus. (True)/False

_____

_____

C Make Connections Write a short answer to these questions.

23. As a young girl, Mary made a decision to follow God. In what ways is Mary an example for your life as a young person today?
Responses may vary, but should include that Mary's "yes" to God's plan for her life is an example of we should respond to God's will in our own lives.

24. The Church is the Body of Christ. What part of the body are you? Use a part of the human body (hand, foot, eye, etc.) to describe your role in the Body of Christ.
Responses will vary.

_____

_____

_____

25. How can the Holy Spirit comfort and guide you in your everyday life at home, at school, or at Church?
Responses will vary.

_____

_____

_____

B Check Understanding

Have the students indicate whether the statements are true or false. If a statement is false, they should correct and rewrite the statement on the lines provided.

C Make Connections

The students should write a short answer for each of the questions. Point out that even though these are short answer responses, they need to be sure that they fully answer the questions.

Go to **aliveinchrist.osv.com** to prepare customized and downloadable assessments, send eAssessments, and assign interactive reviews.

Unit 2 Review **128–129**

JESUS CHRIST

When we accept God's gift of salvation in Jesus, why must our lives be formed by his teaching?

CHURCH HISTORY TIMELINE

431 Council of Ephesus

452 Pope Leo I (the Great) meets Attila the Hun

1565 St. Augustine, Florida, becomes first Catholic presence in America

1978 Pope Saint John Paul II is elected Pope

Go to page 348 for more

Our Catholic Tradition

- Jesus Christ is the Son of God who took on human flesh to redeem us from sin and show us the way to the Father. Because he is true God and true man, Jesus gives us the perfect example of how to live the life the Father planned for us. (CCC, 520)

- The Beatitudes challenge us to live by the values of God's Kingdom and understand that true happiness comes from the hope of eternal life with God. (CCC, 1726, 1728)

- Because God the Father loved human beings, he sent his Son, who freely chose to become human and to offer himself in order to redeem us from the effects of Original Sin and our own sins. (CCC, 620, 621)

Our Catholic Life

- We are called to a life of discipleship: this involves accepting Jesus' invitation to believe in and follow him by studying his ways and putting them into practice. (CCC, 2466)

- Listening to and applying the wisdom of Jesus will help us make choices for the good and turn to him in prayer for guidance when making decisions. (CCC, 459, 1787)

- Through his Paschal Mystery, Jesus conquered death and makes it possible for those who have faith to experience new life through the Seven Sacraments. (CCC, 1076)

Introduce Unit Theme

Open the unit by asking the students to look at and reflect on the photo on page 130. Invite them to share what they see and how they think it relates to the theme of Jesus Christ.

Share some of the highlights from the timeline.

Have a few volunteers read aloud the bullets under the Our Catholic Tradition and Our Catholic Life sections. Ask them to summarize what this information tells them that Unit 3 will be about. Point out that they will learn more about these doctrinal statements as they review the next three chapters.

Ask the unit's Big Question found on page 130.

Allow time for discussion.

Explain to the students that this is the essential question for the unit. They will be working to fully answer it as they complete the three chapters in the unit.

Go to the Source

As an optional extension, organize the students into three groups, assigning each group one of the main Scripture passages found in this unit.

- Chapter 7: Philippians 2:5–8
- Chapter 8: Luke 2:46–52
- Chapter 9: Colossians 1:15, 19–22

Have each group read its passage and then give a dramatic reading (narrator with silent actors), create a visual representation, or write down one question they would ask God about the passage.

Reading the verses directly from the Bible will familiarize students with the sequence of the canon of Sacred Scripture.

Explore the Catechism

Much of modern advertising focuses on the message that people will be happier if they have a particular product.

- Ask the students to read paragraphs 1716–1729 from the *Catechism of the Catholic Church* and design an advertising campaign for how to achieve "true happiness." They may wish to work in groups to develop audio or video commercials, billboards (using poster board and markers), or magazine-style ads.
- Allow time for any questions the students may have.

Reading the paragraphs directly from the *Catechism* will help the students learn where to find key teachings from the Sacred Tradition of the Church.

CHURCH HISTORY TIMELINE BACKGROUND

Refer the students to the Church History Timeline on pages 348–363 to learn more about important Church events and figures through A.D. 1085.

Florida Established as the Site of America's First Catholic Presence

Christianity first entered what was to become the United States by way of Spanish explorers and missionaries. In 1565, Spanish explorers established St. Augustine, a permanent coastal settlement in northeast Florida. Missionaries built the *Nombre de Dios* (Name of God) church there, and it still stands. In 1598, a statue of Our Lady of La Leche, depicting Mary feeding the baby Jesus at her breast, was brought to the mission, and devotion to Our Lady under this title continues there.

Pope Saint John Paul II Elected Pope

In 1978, Karol Józef Wojtyła became the first non-Italian Pope elected in 450 years and the second longest serving Pope after Pope Adrian VI. His pontificate was marked by numerous historical events, including the fall of Communism and an assassination attempt. In the 1980s, he showed his support for a workers' movement in his native Poland called "Solidarity." This led to new freedom in Poland and the end of oppressive governments throughout Eastern Europe. He was declared a Saint by Pope Francis on April 27, 2014.

KEY CONCEPT

Jesus Christ is the only Son of God, who took on human flesh to redeem us from sin and show us the way to the Father.

DOCTRINAL CONTENT

- Jesus, the Son of God, became man to show us how to live and to share his divinity with us. Because he is true God and true man, Jesus Christ is "the way" to the Father. (CCC, 456–460, 480)

- Jesus is the Substantial Image of the Father because he is a visible image of the true nature of God. (CCC, 467, 604, 605)

- When we seek the Lord and live as disciples of Christ, following his example, we will experience the fullness of life. Happiness comes from becoming the people God created us to be. (CCC, 27–30)

TASKS OF CATECHESIS

Helping children grow in a faith that is "known, celebrated, lived, and expressed in prayer" (NDC, 20).

This chapter focuses on the following tasks of catechesis:

- Promoting Knowledge of the Faith

- Moral Formation

Teacher Background

> [He] emptied himself, taking the form of a slave, coming in human likeness; and found human in appearance, he humbled himself, becoming obedient to death, even death on a cross.
> **Philippians 2:7–8**

> **Reflect** How does Jesus being fully human affect the way that you live your life?

Jesus is true God and true man. Saint Paul tells us that Jesus was a human being just like us except for one thing. He did not sin. Did Jesus' lack of sinfulness mean that he was almost—but not quite—fully human? Of course not. Rather, it tells us something profound about what it means to be human.

Jesus didn't sin. He was born without the stain of Original Sin, that pattern of human brokenness that has burdened humankind since the sin of our first parents. Jesus was tempted as all human beings are—in fact, he experienced greater temptations than we can imagine—yet he never gave in to them. And all the while he lived a life of incredible joy, showing his disciples, and us, that the true path to happiness is to do God's will.

Jesus liberated us from sin through his Passion, Death on the Cross, and Resurrection. Through the Sacrament of Baptism, we receive the new life he won for us. In Baptism we are born anew into the life of Christ. It is an initiation that brings with it incredible benefits, but also great responsibilities. Those who are baptized into Christ must be willing, as he was, to pour out their lives in loving service to God and others. The good news is that it is in this very act of offering our lives that we learn how to truly live in joy and abundance.

> **Reflect** How do you use your baptismal gifts in the service of God and others?

Teacher's Prayer

♡ Jesus, my Lord and companion, you know what it is like to be human. Help me to always trust that you are with me to lift me up and give me strength. Thank you for your loving presence. Amen.

How Seventh Graders Understand Chapter Topics

Seventh graders have already begun to dream about the things they think will make them happy and to think about what they will be when they are older. We all search for happiness in the wrong places sometimes, but Jesus shows us a pattern for living that will lead to true and lasting happiness. Young teens often need help understanding that Jesus' life and teachings can be a guide to living today.

Teaching Tip: Teens are often asked what they want to be when they grow up, but they are rarely asked who they think God created them to be. Ask that question in various ways, and ask the students how Jesus shows us what it means to live the lives we were made for.

Sharing the Message with Seventh Graders

- Adolescents observe how they and their peers are developing at different paces. Help them trust the natural process of growth.

- The simpler ambitions of their childhoods are being reevaluated as seventh graders learn about their own gifts and interests. "What do you want to be when you grow up?" is suddenly a more complex question than it once was.

- Encourage the students to look at their future through another lens: "What do you think God imagined for you?"

ONLINE RESOURCES

🛜 Go to **aliveinchrist.osv.com**

You will find:

- Interactive lesson planning, additional activities, and ideas for the classroom environment

- Step by step lesson instruction from printed Teacher Edition for integrated lesson planning

- Custom-built assessments to download and eAssessment links

- Interactive reviews that provide scores and the option to review answers

- Chapter-specific Lectionary connections and a complete correlation ordered by the Sundays of the year, with suggestions for how to integrate the Scripture readings into chapter lessons

🛜 Go to **osvparish.com** for Ask the Experts Q and A, Community Connections, and Blogs.

Chapter 7 Planner

Objectives	Open

DAY 1—Invite/Preview, Pages 131–133

- Reflect on God's personal invitation through Scripture
- Indicate prior knowledge of chapter concepts and vocabulary

- ♥ **Psalm 136:1** Pray the opening prayer.
- 📖 **Philippians 2:5–8** Proclaim "Plea for Unity and Humility." Guide the students through the process of Scripture reflection.
- Discuss Have You Ever Thought questions.

DAY 2—Discover, Pages 134–135

- Explore the understanding of the fullness of human potential
- Explain that the Son of God became man to show us how to live and to share his divinity with us

- ♥ Pray the **Act of Faith**, page 387.
- Discuss the opening question.

DAY 3—Discover, Pages 136–137

- Explain that Jesus is the Substantial Image of the Father because he is a visible image of the true nature of God
- Explore the ways that Jesus' actions demonstrate God's love for us

- ♥ Pray the **Lord's Prayer**, page 383.
- Discuss the opening question.

DAY 4—Discover, Pages 138–139

- Examine the behaviors and dispositions of discipleship that are rooted in the life of Christ
- Identify fullness of life as becoming the people God created us to be

- ♥ Pray a prayer of thanksgiving.

DAY 5—Live, Pages 140–141

- Examine the requirements of discipleship
- Explore the faith life of Saint Maximilian Kolbe
- Offer the Prayer of Thanksgiving

- ♥ Pray a prayer of petition.

REVIEW AND ASSESSMENT

Chapter Review, page 142
Chapter Test, page 131F

📶 **aliveinchrist.osv.com** Customize and Download Assessments, Email Links to eAssessments, Interactive Student Reviews

Build	Close	Materials & Resources
• Present lesson highlights. • Preview **Catholic Faith Words**. ★ Illustrate how Jesus is the Way, the Truth, and the Life.	• Activity Examine how humans can reflect God's glory.	☐ pencils or pens ☐ board or chart paper
• **Catholic Faith Words** Visitation • Talk about Jesus' human and Divine natures. • Reflect on the fullness of life that comes from being a disciple.	• Activity Describe the kinds of things Jesus expects from seventh graders. • Conclude with a review of key concepts and objectives.	☐ pencils or pens ☐ board or chart paper ☐ Bibles
• **Catholic Faith Words** Mediator • Discuss titles for Jesus. 📖 Read John 14:6, Luke 11:9–13, and 1 Timothy 2:5–6. • Review ways Jesus used actions to show God's love for us.	• Activity Complete a word search to find words that describe Jesus. • Conclude with a review of key concepts and objectives.	☐ pencils or pens ☐ highlighters
• **Catholic Faith Words** discipleship • Discuss specific ways that Jesus taught us to be good disciples. ★ The students will indicate ways they already follow Jesus' example. • Consider ways to apply Jesus' teachings on discipleship.	• Activity Reflect on ways that discipleship can be adventurous as well as noble. • Review the In Summary statements. • Optional Activity Do Well (Activity Master 7)	☐ pencils or pens ☐ Activity Master 7 (Page 131G)
• Discuss examples of discipleship. • Learn about Saint Maximilian Kolbe. • Activity Reflect on discipleship and following "the Way."	• Divide the class into two sides. • Follow the order of prayer. ▶ Sing or reflect on the closing song.	☐ pencils or pens 🛜 "Behind and Before Me"

Chapter Connections

FORMING CATHOLIC IDENTITY ACROSS THE CURRICULUM

To integrate the Catholic faith in all aspects of curriculum, this chapter's objectives can be reinforced and applied in the instruction of other disciplines.

Go to **aliveinchrist.osv.com** for cross-curricular activities and projects linked to the doctrinal content discussed in this unit. Activities are available from among the following knowledge categories and content areas:

Language Arts

- Integration of Knowledge
- Literacy
- Speaking and Listening
- Writing Skills

Math

- Algebraic Thinking
- Geometry
- Measurement and Data
- Numbers and Operations

Science

- Earth Science
- Life Science
- Physical Science
- Technology

Social Studies

- Civics
- Economics
- Geography
- History

NCEA IFG: ACRE Edition

Knowledge of the Faith

- **Objective:** To know and understand basic Catholic teaching about the Incarnate Word Jesus Christ as the way, truth, and life

Moral Formation

- **Objective:** To be knowledgeable about the teachings of Jesus and the Church as the basis of Christian morality and to understand Catholic Social Teaching

Catholic Faith Literacy

divine; Elizabeth, cousin of Mary; God, the Son; Rosary

Catholic Social Teaching

To integrate Catholic Social Teaching into your lesson, choose one of the following features: Rights and Responsibilities of the Human Person, pages 338–339; or Solidarity of the Human Family, pages 344–345.

- Start the Live step of the process by talking about Saint Maximilian Kolbe on page 140. Then move directly to the Catholic Social Teaching feature.
- Or, to expand the lesson, complete page 140, then move to the Catholic Social Teaching feature.
- Return to Chapter 7 for the prayer on page 141.

Music Option

Use the following song to enhance catechetical learning or for prayer.

- "Behind and Before Me," Day 5, Page 141

Name _____   Date _____

Match each description in Column A with the correct term in Column B by filling in the appropriate letter.

Column A

____ **1.** Name for disciples of Jesus

____ **2.** Special prayer that focuses on the events
in the lives of Jesus and Mary

____ **3.** Title given to Jesus because he alone is able
to bring us closer to God the Father

____ **4.** The birth of Jesus

Column B

a. Nativity

b. Mediator

c. followers of the Way

d. Rosary

Complete each sentence with the best term or phrase.

5. Jesus is the Second Person of the _____.

6. Becoming the person God calls you to be is reaching your _____.

7. Jesus is known as the _____ of the Father.

8. The _____ is the event in which Mary, who was pregnant with Jesus,
visited her cousin Elizabeth, who was pregnant with John the Baptist.

9. _____ is accepting Jesus' invitation to believe in and follow him
by studying his ways and putting them into practice.

Write a response on the lines below.

10. Jesus is "true God" and "true man." What did Jesus show us by being human?
What did Jesus show us by being Divine?

_____

_____

_____

_____

_____

_____

_____

_____

Name _____   Date _____

Do Well

It is often said:

If you feel good about yourself, you will do well.

Suppose the opposite was true:

If you do well, you will feel good about yourself.

Imagine that you asked Jesus, "What does it mean to do well?" What would he say? Record your thoughts below.

_____

_____

_____

_____

_____

_____

_____

_____

_____

_____

_____

_____

_____

The Way

 Let Us Pray

Leader: Jesus, our brother, you are the Way, the Truth, and the Life. You know our struggles and our joys. Be with us and guide us to know the Father's love.

"Praise the LORD, for he is good; for his mercy endures forever." **Psalm 136:1**

All: God, help us become our best selves.

 Scripture

"Have among yourselves the same attitude that is also yours in Christ Jesus, Who, though he was in the form of God, did not regard equality with God something to be grasped.

Rather, he emptied himself, taking the form of a slave, coming in human likeness; and found human in appearance, he humbled himself, becoming obedient to death, even death on a cross." **Philippians 2:5-8**

Have you ever thought...

• How is Jesus true God and true man?

• What does Jesus being fully human mean for how we live?

The Way **131**

Scripture Background

Scripture Reflection Process

Invite the students to be still, close their eyes, and focus on their breathing. Encourage them to open their minds and hearts to what God is saying to them.

• Proclaim the Scripture and have the students sit in silence.

• *Ask:* What did you hear God say to you today?

• Allow volunteers to share.

 You may play instrumental music to begin the reflection.

Objective

• Reflect on God's personal invitation through Scripture

OPEN _____

 Let Us Pray

Invite the students to gather in the prayer space and make the Sign of the Cross. Pray the leader prayer, including the Psalm verse. Prompt the group's response.

Have the students move out of the prayer space and back to their seats.

Say: We know God more perfectly through Jesus Christ, the Second Person of the Holy Trinity. While Jesus offers us the perfect image of God, he also offers us a way to live fully as human beings.

Scripture

Guide the students through the process of Scripture reflection (see the Scripture Background box below).

Have you ever thought…

Say: God gave us Jesus, his Son, the most wondrous gift. Jesus restores our relationship with the Father and shows us how to live in right relationship with God and our neighbor.

• Invite the students to respond to the questions.

DAY 1

Objective

- Indicate prior knowledge of chapter concepts and vocabulary

BUILD _____

Use this page to assess the students' knowledge related to the chapter content.

Getting Started

Ask a volunteer to read aloud this paragraph.

- *Ask:* What are some specific ways that we can act more like Jesus?

- Have a volunteer list the class responses on the board.

The Way/The Truth/The Life

Read aloud the directions for the chart, including the questions.

- Brainstorm with the class some answers to the questions.

- ★ Have the students work on their own, using words and/or illustrations, to show how Jesus is the Way, the Truth, and the Life.

Getting Started

In this chapter you will learn that Jesus Christ is true God, true man, the Second Divine Person of the Holy Trinity who took on human flesh. He shows us the way God the Father wants us to live to become more like him.

> In the chart below, use words and/or illustrations to show how Jesus is the Way, the Truth, and the Life. How and where does Jesus lead us? What does he teach us? How does he take care of us and give us life?

The Way

The Truth

The Life

© Our Sunday Visitor

i Teacher Background

Food for Thought

Young adolescents will be quite familiar with the concept of "potential." Most will have had adults in their lives who have exhorted them to strive to "reach your potential." It's the "be all you can be" mantra. You can offer additional food for thought with these questions:

- How do you know what your "full potential" is?

- Have you ever tried desperately to do something you really wanted to do only to find you didn't have the gifts or the talent required?

- What are some ways to deal with the disappointment of learning you have personal limits?

Catholic Faith Words

- Visitation
- Mediator
- discipleship

WRITE

Fully Alive Saint Iraneaus said, "The glory of God is a human being fully alive." Write a reflection on what you think Saint Iraneaus means.

_____
_____
_____
_____
_____
_____
_____

Think of someone in your life or in the broader community or larger world who you think is "fully alive" and showing God's glory. Describe that person and his or her impact on others.

_____
_____
_____
_____
_____
_____
_____
_____
_____
_____
_____
_____

Work with Words

Point out the three Catholic Faith Words that will be covered in this chapter.

- Ask volunteers to share with the class any information that they already know about these vocabulary words.

CLOSE

ACTIVITY

Read aloud the instructions.

- Write "The glory of God is a human being fully alive" on the board or on chart paper.
- Invite volunteers to tell about times when they experienced "being fully alive." Tell them about a time when you felt this way.
- Provide several moments of quiet time for the students to write their reflections.

✓ Teaching Tip

Balance

When talking with the students about reaching their full potential, be sure to emphasize the importance of striving for balance in their lives.

- Encourage the students to do their best, keeping in mind that some of them might feel pressured to overachieve while others may lack motivation.
- Remind them that excess in any area of life can cause us to become unbalanced, which can lead to stress.
- Anytime you can put "too much" in front of something you are doing—too much texting, too much time socializing, too much worrying—it's time to refocus and rebalance your life.

DAY 2

Objectives

- Explore the understanding of the fullness of human potential
- Explain that the Son of God became man to show us how to live and to share his divinity with us

OPEN

♥ Have the students pray an Act of Faith, page 387.

Read aloud the opening question and elicit responses from the class.

- Have a volunteer record the responses on the board or on chart paper.

BUILD

True God, True Man

Invite four students to read the opening paragraphs.

- Facilitate a discussion of the question that follows.
- Emphasize that working toward our full potential is a lifelong quest.

The Son of God Became One of Us

Ask: Have you ever imagined Jesus as a child who needed help from his parents, or Jesus as a teenager who felt annoyed with his parents?

- Direct the students to read the text in this section to learn more about Jesus' human life.

True God, True Man

How is Jesus like all of us?

At one time or another, everyone wants to excel—to maximize his or her abilities to the fullest. People often say that it's human nature to want to be the best at something. Is that what it means to be "fully human"? But if you fail, it is okay to just remind yourself, "After all, I'm only human"?

Jesus is "true man and true God," fully human but also fully Divine. He is God. And he is also a human being, a man who walked on Earth, like all of us. He lived the fully human life we are made to live: coming from God and going toward God. So what does that mean for us as his followers?

Sometimes it's hard for us to grasp that Jesus actually lived a human life. Can you picture Jesus as a small child learning to put on his sandals? On sunny days, he might have wanted to go outside and play instead of finishing his chores. Maybe he got tired from too much studying.

134

Yet, these kinds of things probably happened. How do we know? They are the kinds of things that happen to all human beings—and in all families. We all face new challenges, feel tired, and become confused. After all, we're human!

> **What are some examples from Jesus' life that show he was fully human?**

The Son of God Became One of Us

Jesus is true man, like us in all things except sin. He is also true God. Jesus has two natures:

- He has a Divine nature. Jesus is the Son of God, the Second Divine Person of the Holy Trinity.
- He has a human nature. He was born of a human mother, and he had to be fed, kept warm, and loved like all other human babies.

The Son of God chose to become a man in order to bring us back to his Father and show us how to live as God intended. Jesus not only brings us closer to the Father, but he also makes it possible for us to become more like him and the Father. God's Son became human to share his divinity with us. Because of that, we can become united with God the Father. When the Son of God became the Son of Man, we also became God's sons and daughters.

God helps us as his children with the grace to live the full lives he calls us to live. When we fail, we need to accept our disappointments with humility. When our thoughts and actions lead us away from God and living his law, we need to turn to God for forgiveness and strength to do better.

© Our Sunday Visitor

 Teacher Background

Jesus: Human and Divine

Thinking of Jesus as fully God and fully man can be challenging for us.

- Be aware that some people mistakenly believe that Jesus only "seemed" human.
- In Luke 2:52, we read that "Jesus advanced [in] wisdom and in age and favor before God and man." This tells us that Jesus grew and developed as humans grow and develop, and that his understanding of his identity and mission were part of a gradual process as well.
- Jesus was fully human in every way, but unlike us, he never sinned.

The Joyful Mysteries

When praying the Rosary, Catholics remember events from Jesus' and Mary's lives, called the Mysteries of the Rosary. One group of these events is called the Joyful Mysteries. They focus on the great gift of the Incarnation and the joy of the Son of God sharing our human nature.

- The Annunciation—The Angel Gabriel announces to Mary that she has been chosen to be the Mother of Jesus.
- The **Visitation**—Mary, who is pregnant, visits her cousin Elizabeth, who is also pregnant. Elizabeth's son grows up to be John the Baptist.
- The Nativity—Jesus is born.
- The Presentation of the Child Jesus at the Temple—Joseph and Mary present the child Jesus at the Temple in Jerusalem. A man named Simeon had been promised that he would not die before he saw the

Messiah. Simeon recognizes Jesus as the fulfillment of God's promise.
- The Finding of the Child Jesus at the Temple.

Catholic Faith Words

Visitation the event of Mary, who was pregnant with Jesus, visiting her cousin Elizabeth, who was pregnant with Saint John the Baptist

---

> **DESCRIBE**
>
> In your own words, describe the kind of things you think Jesus expects people your age to do in order to live a full life. Describe what things you think Jesus doesn't expect people your age to do.
>
> **What Jesus Expects**
>
> _____
> _____
> _____
>
> **What Jesus Doesn't Expect**
>
> _____
> _____
> _____

© Our Sunday Visitor

Optional Activity

Living Rosary *Interpersonal, Bodily/Kinesthetic*

Help the students organize a living rosary in your school or parish.

- Send them to page 388 in the Our Catholic Tradition section to learn how to pray the Rosary.
- Have the students line up and space themselves like a rosary.
- Each student will represent a bead on the rosary. A student holding a cross will represent the beginning of the rosary.
- Enlist the boys to begin the Rosary and the start of each decade.
- Have the girls say the Hail Marys.

The Joyful Mysteries

Discuss the definition of *Visitation* in the Catholic Faith Words box.

Organize the class into five groups and give each group a Bible.

- Assign each group one of the events from the Joyful Mysteries.
- Allow time for the groups to find their stories in the Bible and work together to summarize the story.
- Invite a spokesperson from each group to share their summary with the class and explain what it tells them about Jesus and his family life.

CLOSE

> **ACTIVITY**

Arrange the students in pairs. Have one of the partners read aloud the instructions.

- Allow the partners to work together to come up with descriptions.
- If time permits, pose specific scenarios and encourage the students to share ways that the issues could be handled, using ideas that reflect the teachings of Jesus.

Quick Review Through Jesus' humanity, we learn what God the Father intended for all human beings. By living as disciples of Christ, we can become all that God created us to be.

DAY 3

Objectives

- Explain that Jesus is the Substantial Image of the Father because he is a visible image of the true nature of God
- Explore the ways that Jesus' actions demonstrate God's love for us

OPEN

 Have the students pray the Lord's Prayer from page 383.

Invite the students to discuss the question with a classmate.

BUILD

Jesus Is the Way to God

Ask the students to describe what they think is happening in the artwork on this page.

Point out that the more closely we follow Jesus' example, the more we fulfill our potential and live the best life possible.

Invite a volunteer to read aloud this section.

Discuss the question at the end of this section.

 Scripture

Proclaim the Scripture.

- You may want to send the students directly to the source, Luke 11:9–13, to find out more about Jesus' teachings on the Father.

Jesus Is the Way to God

How does Jesus show us the way?

Before they were called "Christians," the disciples who followed Jesus were called followers of "The Way." Jesus showed them the way to God. He also showed them a new way to live, a way based on truth and love.

Scripture

"I am the way and the truth and the life."
John 14:6

Go to the Source

Jesus used words to describe the Father. Read *Luke 11:9–13* and find out why Jesus spoke about giving a hungry child a scorpion or a snake, instead of an egg or some fish.

The Apostles and disciples of Jesus learned about God in two ways. Jesus talked about God, letting them know that God is Father, and Jesus showed them God the Father

136 Chapter 7

through his life, the life of the Son. Jesus used words to describe what the Father was like, and Jesus used actions to demonstrate what he was like.

Jesus was able to give us a better picture of God—a picture of a loving, gentle, and affectionate Father—a God who takes care of us and gives us what we need, including expectations and rules to keep us safe and help us grow. He is eternal Father and source of all life. Jesus told us, "For everyone who asks, receives; and the one who seeks, finds . . ." (Luke 11:10) Jesus' words and actions still show us the way today.

> How does "The Way" help you trust in God?

Catholic Faith Words

Mediator the title given to Jesus because, as true God and true man, he alone is able to reconcile all people to God the Father, bringing us closer to God the Father by his words and saving actions

Optional Activity

Titles for Jesus *Verbal/Linguistic, Visual/Spatial*

Organize the students into groups of four. Give each group a Bible and a concordance. Have them look up the titles for Jesus listed on page 137 in the student book, and write down the Scripture passages they find them in.

- Invite each group to make a poster listing titles for Jesus and the Scripture references they uncovered.
- Encourage them to draw images to go with each title listed.
- Hang the posters up in the classroom or throughout the school.

Titles for Jesus

We call Jesus by many titles that describe who he is and what he does. You're probably familiar with Savior, Lord, Christ, and Lamb of God. How about Mediator and Substantial Image?

A mediator brings together those who might normally be separated or apart, reconciling differences between them. Because of his uniqueness as true God and true man, Jesus alone is the mediator between God the Father and humans. As our intermediary or bridge to God the Father, and by his sacrifice that makes reconciliation possible, Jesus is called the **Mediator**. He brings us closer to the Father by his words and his actions.

When Jesus became man, he remained God. So when we look at Jesus, a human being, we get to see God in living color. He is sometimes called the Substantial Image of the Father. An image is a visible likeness. Substantial implies belonging to its nature. When we say Jesus is the Substantial Image of the Father, we mean that he is a visible image of the true nature of God. In the Son of God, you can see what God the Father is like. Here are some ways Jesus used actions to demonstrate God's love for us:

- healing many people who were sick or injured (see Matthew 8:14–17)
- spending time and eating with people who were unpopular (see Luke 5:30–32)
- feeding people who were hungry (see Mark 6:30–44)

> What does knowing Jesus better help you to understand about the Trinity?

Scripture

"For there is one God.
There is also one mediator between God and the human race,
Christ Jesus, himself human,
who gave himself as ransom for all."
1 Timothy 2:5–6

SOLVE AND IDENTIFY

In the puzzle find three words to describe Jesus. Write the words on the lines, then share with a classmate why you think they are an accurate description of Jesus. Discuss people you know who can be described in a similar way.

1. _____
2. _____
3. _____

S	S	E	K	G	W	A	Y
J	H	N	Q	U	P	X	N
M	E	D	I	A	T	O	R
J	P	N	Q	B	R	V	Y
W	H	A	M	D	U	R	A
D	E	N	T	F	T	B	Z
B	R	G	N	R	H	L	P
P	D	E	L	I	G	H	T

The Way **137**

Scripture Background

The Gospel According to Mark

In the Gospel according to Mark, Jesus asks the question: "Who do you say that I am?" (**Mark 8:29**). This is an important question for his disciples and for us today. Our response to Jesus' question affects the way we respond to his call to discipleship.

This Gospel also focuses on what it means to follow Jesus. We see that the Apostles were commissioned early and were present for most of what happened during Jesus' ministry. Yet, just as we struggle with the message of Jesus today, the early followers of Jesus often didn't get the message, either. Fortunately, we can receive reconciliation and renewal through Jesus' Death and Resurrection.

Titles for Jesus

Share the information from the Scripture Background box with the class. Ask the students to respond to the question, "Who do you say that I am?"

- Instruct everyone to privately write a paragraph answering Jesus' question.

Have the students silently read the first two paragraphs.

- Share with them the meaning of the word *Mediator* from the Catholic Faith Words box on page 136.

Scripture

Ask a volunteer to read aloud 1 Timothy 2:5–6.

Review the last paragraph on the page as a class.

- Have the students highlight the meaning of *Substantial Image*.
- Discuss the question that follows this section.

CLOSE _____

ACTIVITY

Have the students read the instructions to themselves and work individually to find the words that describe Jesus.

- Once they've completed the first part of the activity, have them discuss the remaining prompts with a classmate.

Quick Review Jesus is the Substantial Image of the Father because he is a visible image of the true nature of God. Jesus demonstrated God's love for us through his own actions.

Objectives

- Examine the behaviors and dispositions of discipleship that are rooted in the life of Christ
- Identify fullness of life as becoming the people God created us to be

OPEN

♥ Have the students silently pray a prayer thanking Jesus for the guidance he has given us to live the best life possible.

BUILD

The Way to Live

Point out that the more closely we follow Jesus' example, the more we fulfill our God-given potential.

Invite volunteers to read aloud this section.

Jesus' Example

Ask the students to read through the suggestions for following Jesus' example.

★ Direct them to place a check mark beside the ways they have intentionally followed Jesus' example this week.

- Encourage them to reflect on the areas in which they need to grow.

The Way to Live

What did Jesus want to show us?

Jesus gave his followers many examples of how they could become more like him. When you follow his example, you are acting like he did. The more you do so, the more you can discover the person God intends you to be and live the best life possible.

Jesus' Example

○	taking time to pray; see Mark 6:45–46.
○	having a good relationship with his parents; see Luke 2:51–52.
○	relying on his good friends; see Luke 8:1–3.
○	expressing deep feelings; see John 11:32–37.
○	talking about things with those who disagree; see Mark 12:13–17.
○	listening to others and sometimes changing his mind; see Matthew 15:21–28.
○	taking care of others in need; see Matthew 9:27–31.
○	forgiving his enemies; see Luke 23:33–34.
○	saying no to temptation; see Matthew 4:1–11.
○	standing up for others; see Matthew 21:12–13.

Jesus didn't come to show us the way to play perfect chess or piano, swim, paint, or get straight As. Striving to use the gifts and talents God has given us is a good thing. But, Jesus is most concerned with what importance we give God in our lives, how we treat our families and friends, how we pray, how we care for people we don't know, and how we forgive our enemies. Sometimes these things are a lot harder than doing laps in the pool or practicing scales on the keyboard.

Of all the good that God wants for you, he most wants you to live in his love, to know his happiness, and to become like him. You do all of these things when you follow in Jesus' footsteps and become his disciple.

> ★ Place a check mark beside three ways you have intentionally followed Jesus' example this week.

Optional Activity

Activity Master 7: Do Well

Distribute copies of the activity found on teacher page 131G.

- This activity will help the students reflect on what "doing well" might mean to Jesus.

- Have the students compare their reflections to how well-known celebrities seem to define success.

Discipleship is really what living fully, or being fully alive, is all about. It isn't easy. But we don't follow the path of discipleship alone. God gives us the Church and his grace we need to be the people he has called us to be. The Sacraments strengthen us, and our community of faith journeys with us, guiding and supporting us.

Catholic Faith Words

discipleship accepting Jesus' invitation to believe in and follow him by studying his ways and putting them into practice

DISCUSS AND DECIDE

In a famous address to all the young people of the world, Pope Saint John Paul II called on all young people to take on the "noble and authentic adventure" of discipleship.

Why would discipleship be something "noble" and an "adventure"?

_____

_____

_____

What is one thing we can do together to live this noble adventure?

_____

_____

_____

IN SUMMARY   Catholics Believe

Jesus Christ is the only Son of God, who took on human flesh to redeem us from sin and show us the way to the Father.

- Jesus has two natures. He is fully man and fully God. Jesus is the Second Divine Person of the Holy Trinity.

- Because he is true God and true man, Jesus Christ is "the way" to the Father. Through his

words and actions Jesus brings us back to the Father and gives us the perfect example of how to be the people God intended us to be from the beginning.

- Jesus became man to reconcile us to his Father and show us how to live. We need to follow his example and become followers of the Way, disciples who strive to live fully as God's children.

The Way   **139**

Teaching Tip

Brainstorming Ideas

When having the students brainstorm ideas for a noble and authentic adventure, follow these guidelines:

- Invite the students to work in small groups to begin the process.

- Offer positive reinforcement to all who participate.

- Encourage them to consider an adventure that they feel passionate about.

- Acknowledge those ideas you are passionate about, yet let the students' voice be the one that is heard.

The Way to Live, *continued*

Share with the class a video of a person supporting someone else through a challenge or helping someone accomplish their dream.

- Review the definition of *discipleship*.

- *Ask:* If our goal is to be a disciple of Jesus, what kind of support do we need in order to become a committed disciple? the Church, God's grace, the Sacraments, our faith community

- Have each student write his/her thoughts on precut pieces of paper that when assembled will create megaphones (a sign of supporting a team).

CLOSE_____

ACTIVITY

Read aloud the introduction to the activity and the two questions.

- Divide the students into small groups to begin brainstorming.

- After they have answered the questions, ask each group to present their ideas to the class.

- Then decide, as a class, on one thing you can do together.

In Summary

Ask the students to silently read the summary information.

- Have them quietly reflect on how they are living up to their full potential as followers of Jesus.

DAY 5

Objectives

- Examine the requirements of discipleship
- Explore the faith life of Saint Maximilian Kolbe
- Offer the Prayer of Thanksgiving

OPEN _____

♥ Pray a prayer of petition, asking God to help guide your students and strengthen them to reflect Jesus' love to others.

BUILD _____

Our Catholic Life

Ask a volunteer to read aloud the information in the Our Catholic Life section.

- Have the students discuss the question in small groups.

People of Faith

Explain to the students that Saint Maximilian Kolbe followed Jesus' example and offered up his life in love for another.

- Read aloud the People of Faith paragraph.
- Share some of the points from the People of Faith Background box.
- Invite the students to reflect on the great sacrifices that are sometimes asked of the disciples of Jesus.

Our Catholic Life

Jesus tells us that discipleship involves praying to God the Father, studying his teachings, participating in the Eucharist, and living the virtues. **Discipleship** also means bringing the Good News of Christ to others. It requires us to understand and live by what we've learned from Jesus and his Church. It is part of the Church's mission to continue Jesus' work, teaching others about him and helping God in his work of spreading his Kingdom. Being a disciple means living a life of compassion, love, justice, and service, for the glory of God. It includes seeing people as our brothers and sisters, no matter their race, nationality, religious beliefs, social group, or income level. We are all made in God's image, and we can all be disciples.

> What is one way the people in your school or parish are examples of discipleship?

© Our Sunday Visitor

People of Faith

Saint Maximilian Kolbe, 1894–1941

When Raymund Kolbe became a priest, he changed his name to Maximilian Maria in honor of Mary. During World War II, he provided shelter for those fleeing the Nazis, including 2,000 Jews. In 1941, Father Kolbe was arrested by the Nazis and taken to the death camp of Auschwitz. While he was there, the Nazis decided to starve some prisoners to death as a punishment. He offered to take the place of a man who had a wife and children. The man whose life he saved was present at the ceremony of his canonization in 1982. The Church celebrates his feast day on **August 14**.

For more, go to aliveinchrist.osv.com

140 Chapter 7

EXAMINE

Examine your commitment to "the noble adventure of discipleship." How well are you reaching your true potential for discipleship? What is one area that is challenging you right now?

_____
_____
_____
_____

Make some notes as to how you might take some positive steps following "the Way."

_____
_____
_____
_____
_____

People of Faith Background

Saint Maximilian Kolbe

Share this additional information with the students:

- Maximilian's devotion to being a disciple of Christ is seen in his work to defend the Church and her members.
- As a young boy, Maximilian Kolbe had a vision of the Blessed Virgin Mary who offered him a choice of two crowns: one white, which represented purity, and one red, which represented martyrdom. Young Raymund said that he would take them both.

Encourage the students to go to **aliveinchrist.osv.com** at home to learn more about Saint Maximilian Kolbe.

Prayer of Thanksgiving

Leader: God, you are our all-knowing and all-loving Creator. We use the words of King David's psalm to praise and thank you for your goodness.

Side 1: LORD, you have probed me, you know me:
　　you know when I sit and stand;
　　you understand my thoughts from afar.

Side 2: God and Father, you really understand each of us and how we're made. You know how we long to reach our full potential, to be "the best" at something, to make our mark. You see that we are driven and motivated, sometimes in the wrong ways for the wrong reasons.

Side 1: You sift through my travels and
　　my rest; with all my ways you are familiar.

Even before a word is on my tongue,
　　LORD, you know it all.

Side 2: Loving Father, you understand the pain we feel when we fall short and can't meet our goals. You see how disappointed and how broken we often are. Gently, you touch us to comfort, console, and show us how wonderful we are in your eyes.

Side 1: You formed my inmost being;
　　you knit me in my mother's womb.

I praise you, because I am wonderfully made;
　　wonderful are your works!

My very self you know.

My bones are not hidden from you.

When I was being made in secret,
　　fashioned in the depths of the earth.

Side 2: Our Father, you graciously sent your Son Jesus to live and die for us. He shows us what great plans you have for us. You want us to live in your love and share that love with others. You know what will make us happy. You made us!

Side 1: Probe me, God, know my heart;
　　try me, know my thoughts.

See if there is a wicked path in me;
　　lead me along an ancient path.
　　Psalm 139:1–15

Side 2: God, our all-loving Father, you know our strengths and weaknesses as no one else does or can. Deliver us from evil of every sort. Give us the strength to develop the gifts you've given to us. Help us to follow your Son, Jesus.

Leader: Let's conclude our prayer in song.

▶ *Sing or play "Behind and Before Me"*

🛜 Go to **aliveinchrist.osv.com** for an interactive review.

A **Work with Words** Circle the letter of the choice that best completes the sentence.

1. ____ is a special prayer form in honor of the Blessed Virgin Mary.
   a. The Rosary
   b. The Creed
   c. Our Father
   d. all of the above

2. Mary's visit to her cousin Elizabeth is known as the ____.
   a. Annunciation
   b. Nativity
   c. Visitation
   d. Presentation

3. The Nativity refers to ____.
   a. the birth of Jesus
   b. Elizabeth's visit to Mary
   c. the Angel Gabriel's visit to Mary
   d. Jesus at the Temple

4. Jesus is called the Substantial Image of the Father because ____.
   a. he brings us closer to God
   b. he communicates with us
   c. he is human and Divine
   d. in him we can see what God the Father is like.

5. Disciples of Jesus were first called the followers of the ____.
   a. Trinity
   b. Nativity
   c. Way
   d. Creed

B **Check Understanding** Complete each sentence with the correct term from the Word Bank.

Mediator	the Holy Spirit
words and actions	natures
the Gospels	inspiration
discipleship	human

6. The disciples learned about God through the ____**words and actions**____ of Jesus.

7. Jesus is the ____**Mediator**____, the intermediary or bridge between God and humans.

8. Jesus has two ____**natures**____, human and Divine.

9. Being fully ____**human**____ means becoming the person God meant you to be.

10. ____**Discipleship**____ is the process of accepting Jesus' invitation to believe in and follow him by studying his ways and putting them into practice.

C **Make Connections** Write a one-paragraph response to the question: Jesus is both true God and true man. Which aspect of Jesus is harder for you to identify with? Explain why.

_____
_____
_____
_____
_____
_____

Ask the students to read the prompts and complete this activity on their own.

CLOSE _____

Prayer of Thanksgiving

❤ Divide the class down the middle and assign the students to Side 1 or Side 2. You will be the Leader.

Set the prayer table with images of Jesus and a lit candle.

Invite Sides 1 and 2 to stand in the prayer space facing each other.

Call them to prayer with these words: Jesus, bless and strengthen us to live as your disciples.

Follow the order of prayer on the student page.

▶ Conclude by inviting the students to sing or reflect on the song "Behind and Before Me," downloaded from **aliveinchrist.osv.com**.

CHAPTER REVIEW

Review the instructions for each section and have the students complete the review.

🛜 Go to **aliveinchrist.osv.com** to prepare customized and downloadable assessments, send eAssessments, and assign interactive reviews.

KEY CONCEPT

As Catholics, we turn to Jesus as our source of wisdom.

DOCTRINAL CONTENT

- Jesus' wisdom came from being the Son of God; he looked at the world with that perspective and challenged some of the commonly accepted understandings of his time. (CCC, 574–576)

- Jesus taught through his words and actions. He used parables to teach us about the coming of God's Kingdom. (CCC, 546)

- In his Sermon on the Mount, Jesus gave specific directions for living, honoring God, and making our actions reflect our beliefs. (CCC, 1966–1971)

- The Beatitudes challenge us to live by the values of God's Kingdom and to understand that true happiness comes from the hope of eternal life with God. (CCC, 1716–1719)

TASKS OF CATECHESIS

Helping children grow in a faith that is "known, celebrated, lived, and expressed in prayer" (NDC, 20).

This chapter focuses on the following tasks of catechesis:

- Moral Formation
- Teaching to Pray

Teacher Background

📖 He said to them, "Why were you looking for me? Did you not know that I must be in my Father's house?" … his mother kept all these things in her heart. And Jesus advanced [in] wisdom and age and favor before God and man.　Luke 2:49, 51–52

> **Reflect**　How can knowing God's plan for our lives help us to achieve happiness?

Jesus was an excellent teacher. He spoke with passion and clarity about God's Reign, but more than that, he made present all that he taught. Those who heard him believed not only in what he said, but also in him. They were drawn to Jesus and his teachings because they sensed that his authority came from the Father and that his love was generous and forgiving.

What made Jesus' teaching so compelling—and ultimately dangerous—was that he always spoke God's truth. He did not retreat or back down when he was challenged. He didn't change his message when he faced a hostile crowd. He spoke to the injustices that could be found in some of the established religious and social norms.

God's truth transcends time. Jesus satisfied the hunger for God and his truth that dwells in the human spirit, then and now. Those of us who teach in his name are called to do the same.

> **Reflect**　In what ways has the teaching of Jesus been a model for your own catechetical ministry?

Teacher's Prayer

 Lord Jesus, you were the first and greatest teacher of the faith. Bless me as I seek to teach in your name. May I always follow your example and teach fearlessly, honestly, and compassionately. Amen.

How Seventh Graders Understand Chapter Topics

Seventh graders can certainly have a rebellious streak at times. Some of this comes from growing up and feeling more independent, but still being very limited in the choices they can make for themselves. Because of this, they can be attracted to stories of people who buck the system and challenge the establishment.

Teaching Tip: The message Jesus teaches about such things as wealth, power, fame, status, and physical pleasure often have a different meaning than what our culture teaches. Discuss with your students how the teaching of Jesus is a radical challenge to worldly wisdom and popular culture. (Hint: the word "radical" means "getting to the root.")

Sharing the Message with Seventh Graders

- At this age, some young people are beginning to question principles and beliefs they have long held as given truth. This provides a wonderful opportunity to help them review and re-think their childhood understandings.
- Increasingly, seventh graders will see the differences between the values of the Gospel and some of the values reflected in popular culture. At times, they will engage in a serious internal struggle between their desire to endorse the negative or sinful values of some of their peers and their desire to do what is right.
- Help the students see that the message Jesus taught about such things as wealth, power, fame, status, and physical pleasure still applies today.

ONLINE RESOURCES

 Go to **aliveinchrist.osv.com**

You will find:

- Interactive lesson planning, additional activities, and ideas for the classroom environment
- Step by step lesson instruction from printed Teacher Edition for integrated lesson planning
- Custom-built assessments to download and eAssessment links
- Interactive reviews that provide scores and the option to review answers
- Chapter-specific Lectionary connections and a complete correlation ordered by the Sundays of the year, with suggestions for how to integrate the Scripture readings into chapter lessons

 Go to **osvparish.com** for Ask the Experts Q and A, Community Connections, and Blogs.

Chapter 8 Planner

Objectives	Open
DAY 1—Invite/Preview, Pages 143–145	
• Reflect on God's personal invitation through Scripture • Indicate prior knowledge of chapter concepts and vocabulary	♥ **Psalm 90:12** Pray the opening prayer. 📖 **Luke 2:46–52** Proclaim "The Boy Jesus in the Temple." Guide the students through the process of Scripture reflection. • Discuss Have You Ever Thought questions.
DAY 2—Discover, Pages 146–147	
• Illustrate ways that Jesus challenged the commonly accepted understandings of his time • Explain why Jesus used parables to teach • Relate Jesus' use of parables with his proclamation of the coming of God's Kingdom	♥ Pray the **Glory Be**, page 383. • Point out the topic of the lesson.
DAY 3—Discover, Pages 148–149	
• Explore some of the major teachings of the Sermon on the Mount • Describe the attitudes and actions in the world that contradict the teachings of Christ	♥ Pray the **Beatitudes**, page 374. • Ask the opening question.
DAY 4—Discover, Pages 150–151	
• Explain how the Beatitudes offer us the path to a life of happiness and peace • Relate how being obsessed with material things keeps us from living the real values of God's Kingdom	♥ Reflect on Jesus' teachings.
DAY 5—Live, Pages 152–153	
• Identify steps to making a good decision • Explore the faith life of Saint Gerard Majella • Offer the Prayer of Petition	♥ Pray the **Lord's Prayer**, page 383.

REVIEW AND ASSESSMENT

Chapter Review, page 154
Chapter Test, page 143F

📶 **aliveinchrist.osv.com** Customize and Download Assessments, Email Links to eAssessments, Interactive Student Reviews

Build	Close	Materials & Resources
• Present lesson highlights. • Preview **Catholic Faith Words**. ★ Describe Jesus' qualities and his teachings. • *Optional Activity* Once Upon a Time (Activity Master 8)	• *Activity* Expand on the concept of religious wisdom.	☐ pencils or pens ☐ Activity Master 8 (Page 143G)
• **Catholic Faith Words** wisdom, Kingdom of God, parable • Talk about the ways that Jesus taught us to live. 📖 Read John 3:2.	• *Activity* Describe the meaning of a specific parable. • Conclude with a review of key concepts and objectives.	☐ pencils or pens ☐ Bibles
• **Catholic Faith Words** Sermon on the Mount • Discuss how Jesus used actions and words to teach us. 📖 Read and reflect on Matthew 7:24–29. ★ Examine Jesus' teachings from the Sermon on the Mount.	• *Activity* Describe Jesus' wisdom found in the Sermon on the Mount. • Conclude with a review of key concepts and objectives.	☐ pencils or pens
• **Catholic Faith Words** Beatitudes • Discuss the Beatitudes. ★ Fill in missing words to complete the Beatitudes. 📖 Read Matthew 5:3–12 and Luke 6:20–26.	• *Activity* Write two Beatitudes for adolescents today. • Review the In Summary statements.	☐ pencils or pens ☐ Bibles ☐ art supplies ☐ poster board
• Learn about Saint Gerard Majella. • *Activity* Consider incorporating Jesus' wisdom in our daily lives.	• Light a candle. • Follow the order of prayer. ▶ Sing or reflect on the closing song.	☐ pencils or pens ☐ candle 🛜 "You Are the Way"

Chapter Connections

FORMING CATHOLIC IDENTITY ACROSS THE CURRICULUM

To integrate the Catholic faith in all aspects of curriculum, this chapter's objectives can be reinforced and applied in the instruction of other disciplines.

Go to **aliveinchrist.osv.com** for cross-curricular activities and projects linked to the doctrinal content discussed in this unit. Activities are available from among the following knowledge categories and content areas:

Language Arts

- Integration of Knowledge
- Literacy
- Speaking and Listening
- Writing Skills

Math

- Algebraic Thinking
- Geometry
- Measurement and Data
- Numbers and Operations

Science

- Earth Science
- Life Science
- Physical Science
- Technology

Social Studies

- Civics
- Economics
- Geography
- History

NCEA IFG: ACRE Edition

Moral Formation

- **Objective:** To be knowledgeable about the teachings of Jesus and the Church as the basis of Christian morality and to understand Catholic Social Teaching

Prayer

- **Objective:** To recognize and learn how to engage in Catholic forms of personal and communal prayer and ways of deepening one's spiritual life

Catholic Faith Literacy

Beatitudes, Kingdom, parable, Sermon on the Mount

Catholic Social Teaching

To integrate Catholic Social Teaching into your lesson, choose one of the following features: Life and Dignity of the Human Person, pages 334–335; or Option for the Poor and Vulnerable, pages 340–341.

- Start the Live step of the process by talking about Saint Gerard Majella on page 152. Then move directly to the Catholic Social Teaching feature.
- Or, to expand the lesson, complete page 152, then move to the Catholic Social Teaching feature.
- Return to Chapter 8 for the prayer on page 153.

Music Option

Use the following song to enhance catechetical learning or for prayer.

- "You Are the Way," Day 5, Page 153

Name _____ Date _____

Match each description in Column A with the correct term in Column B by filling in the appropriate letter.

Column A

Column B

____ **1.** Summary of key teachings of Jesus found in the Gospel according to Matthew

a. parables

____ **2.** God's rule of peace, justice, and love that exists in Heaven, but is yet to come on Earth

b. Beatitudes

____ **3.** Short stories Jesus told to illustrate moral or spiritual truths

c. Sermon on the Mount

____ **4.** Jesus' eight teachings about the meaning and path to true happiness

d. Kingdom of God

Circle the letter of the choice that best completes each sentence.

5. Jesus used The Parable of the Good Samaritan to illustrate the idea of ____.
   a. discipleship
   b. an eye for an eye
   c. love of neighbor
   d. peace

6. Jesus compared living according to his words to ____.
   a. safe sailing on a stormy sea
   b. preaching from a mountaintop
   c. building a house on solid rock
   d. ignoring stereotypes of others

7. In the Beatitudes, Jesus says we will find true happiness when ____.
   a. we experience much good luck
   b. God's Kingdom becomes real
   c. we read the parables
   d. we change our point of view

8. ____ is the Gift of the Holy spirit that helps us to see God's purpose and plan for our lives.
   a. Fortitude
   b. Apostolic
   c. Piety
   d. Wisdom

Write a response on the lines below.

9. Why do you think Jesus used parables? _____

_____

10. How do accounts of the Beatitudes differ in the Gospels according to Matthew and Luke?

_____

_____

Name _____ Date _____

Once Upon a Time

Wisdom: the spiritual gift that makes it possible for someone to know about the purpose and plan of God.

Reflect on times when you were the source of wisdom for someone else, ignored wisdom, and sought wisdom.

A time when I was a source of wisdom for someone else: _____

The situation: _____

My wisdom message was: _____

I got that wisdom from: _____

A time when I ignored wisdom and made an unwise decision: _____

The situation: _____

The wisdom I ignored: _____

The reason(s) I didn't follow it: _____

The result: _____

The message now: _____

A time when I sought wisdom and found it: _____

The situation: _____

Where I found wisdom: _____

The message was: _____

How I knew it was right: _____

Model of Wisdom

❤ Let Us Pray

Leader: Loving God, we praise and thank you for your presence with us. Teach us and heal us. Fill our hearts with your wisdom that we may always live within your peace.

"Teach us to count our days aright,
that we may gain wisdom of heart." **Psalm 90:12**

All: God, we need your Good News. Give us your wisdom!

✞ Scripture

After three days they found him in the temple, sitting in the midst of the teachers, listening to them and asking them questions, and all who heard him were astounded at his understanding and his answers.

When his parents saw him, they were astonished, and his mother said to him, "Son, why have you done this to us? Your father and I have been looking for you with great anxiety."

And he said to them, "Why were you looking for me? Did you not know that I must be in my Father's house?" But they did not understand what he said to them. He went down with them and came to Nazareth, and was obedient to them; and his mother kept all these things in her heart. And Jesus advanced [in] wisdom and age and favor before God and man." **Luke 2:46–52**

© Our Sunday Visitor

Have you ever thought...

- Did Jesus always know he was God's Son?
- How does knowing God's plan help us to be happy?

143

✞ Scripture Background

Scripture Reflection Process

Invite the students to be still, close their eyes, and focus on their breathing. Encourage them to open their minds and hearts to what God is saying to them.

- Proclaim the Scripture and have the students sit in silence.
- *Ask:* What did you hear God say to you today?
- Allow volunteers to share.

▶ You may play instrumental music to begin the reflection.

Objective

- Reflect on God's personal invitation through Scripture

OPEN _____

❤ Let Us Pray

Invite the students to gather in the prayer space and make the Sign of the Cross. Ask a volunteer to proclaim the opening prayer and Psalm verse and to lead the class in the response.

Explain that this prayer helps us reflect on what wisdom is, particularly God's wisdom.

Have the students return to their seats.

Say: Let's listen to God's Word and see how Jesus seeks wisdom and displays wisdom.

✞ Scripture

Guide the students through the process of Scripture reflection (see the Scripture Background box below).

Have you ever thought...

Say: God is our ultimate source of wisdom and guidance.

- Invite the students to respond to the questions.

DAY 1

Objective

- Indicate prior knowledge of chapter concepts and vocabulary

BUILD

Use this page to assess the students' knowledge related to the chapter content.

Getting Started

Have a volunteer read aloud the introductory paragraph.

- Discuss with the students what they already know about the teachings of Jesus.
- Have a student list the class responses on the board or on chart paper.

Jesus and His Wisdom

Review the instructions with the class.

★ Have the students fill in the chart with words or phrases that describe Jesus and his teachings.

- Remind them that, if they are having trouble, they can use the items listed on the board as a starting point.

Getting Started

In this chapter you will reflect upon the need for wisdom in our daily lives and how Jesus' wisdom answers that need. In the Sermon on the Mount, especially the Beatitudes, we discover the wisdom of Jesus that he calls us to live by.

Catholic Faith Words

- wisdom
- Kingdom of God
- parable
- Sermon on the Mount
- Beatitudes

Fill in the chart with words or phrases that describe Jesus and his teachings. Use the letter at the beginning of the line as the first letter of your word or term. One is done for you.

Jesus and His Wisdom

W	
I	Invited all people to make God the priority in their lives and to trust in the Father's will
S	
D	
O	
M	

© Our Sunday Visitor

144 Chapter 8

✔ Teaching Tip

Fascinating People

Tell the students that even as a young adolescent, Jesus fascinated others with his depth of understanding. Explain that *fascination* means being curious and interested in something or someone.

- Take two or three minutes to share a story about someone with whom you are fascinated.
- *Ask:* Who is someone you find fascinating? Why do you find that person fascinating?
- Expect that many of your students will find popular culture figures fascinating; be sure to listen and be accepting of these ideas, knowing that you will present Jesus as our model within the chapter.

Words to Live By The dictionary defines wisdom as an understanding of what is true, right, or lasting; common sense; or learning. As people of faith, wisdom is more. It involves seeing as God sees.

In your own words, write a definition for wisdom from a Catholic perspective.

_____
_____
_____
_____
_____
_____
_____

Who in your life has been a source of Catholic wisdom?

_____
_____
_____
_____
_____
_____
_____

What are some words of wisdom you live by?

_____
_____
_____
_____
_____
_____
_____

Model of Wisdom **145**

© Our Sunday Visitor

Work with Words

Point out the Catholic Faith Words box on page 144.

- Invite a volunteer to read aloud the five terms.
- Ask the students to circle any of the vocabulary words that they are unsure of.
- Tell them that at the end of this chapter, they can return to this page to see if their understanding of these words has improved.

CLOSE

Read aloud the activity introduction and directions.

- Give the students time to write their own definitions for *wisdom*, and to identify sources of Catholic wisdom and words of wisdom they like to live by.
- Invite volunteers to share their definitions and words of wisdom.
- Tell the class that in this chapter they will explore how Jesus is a model of wisdom, including taking a closer look at some of his words of wisdom.

Optional Activity

Activity Master 8: Once Upon a Time

Distribute copies of the activity found on teacher page 143G.

- This activity will help the students reflect on how they've needed and found wisdom in their lives.
- As an alternative, you may wish to send this activity home with the students.

DAY 2

Objectives

- Illustrate ways that Jesus challenged the commonly accepted understandings of his time
- Explain why Jesus used parables to teach
- Relate Jesus' use of parables with his proclamation of the coming of God's Kingdom

OPEN

 Pray the Glory Be on page 383.

Tell the students that they are going to learn what made Jesus different from other teachers.

BUILD

Jesus, the Wise Teacher

Read aloud the opening paragraph. Point out that Jesus can answer our questions:

- He provides advice and guidance for making life choices.
- He teaches what matters in life and focuses our attention on God's will, not popular culture.
- He shows us what can make us truly happy.

Scripture

Have a student proclaim John 3:2.

A Teacher Like No Other

Direct the students to silently read the text in this section.

- Facilitate a brief discussion of Jesus as a teacher.
- Include discussion of the question at the end of this section.

© Our Sunday Visitor

Jesus, the Wise Teacher

What made Jesus different from other teachers?

When Jesus started teaching, the people listening to him probably had questions: "Who will help us know God's will? Who can make life better?" Jesus gave the answers to these questions, and more!

Scripture

"Rabbi, we know that you are a teacher who has come from God, for no one can do these signs unless God is with him."
John 3:2

A Teacher Like No Other

Once people heard Jesus' words, they realized he was different. He spoke the truth, even when it was difficult to hear. He encouraged people to follow God's ways, even when it wasn't easy. He spoke across social barriers. He astounded the crowds with authority given to him by his Father.

We know that Jesus possessed definitive **wisdom**, the spiritual gift that helps us to know about the purpose and plan of God. Wisdom leads us to see things as God sees so that we might live holy lives. Jesus challenged the commonly accepted understanding of his time. He did not accept stereotypes or judge others by their social or economic status. He spent time with women, children, people who had undesirable jobs, and those who were poor, sick, or in special need. Jesus got to know those most ignored in society. In all of these ways, he showed the dignity of every person he met.

> Think of someone you believe sees things and people as God does. What is this person like?

Ordinary Words, Extraordinary Meaning

Jesus knew things were not perfect in the lives of the people. They needed to turn to God and work on their relationships with one another. They needed forgiveness.

Those who heard Jesus sensed that he was different. He was connected to what was important and truly right. He encouraged people to change how they lived. Jesus wanted his followers to know the true meaning of forgiveness and the way to live by God the Father's will. He spoke often about God's rule in people's lives and hearts, harkening people to the **Kingdom of God**—

---

i Teacher Background

Life at the Time of Jesus

In The Parable of the Good Samaritan (see Luke 10:29–37), the priest and the Levite pass by without helping the injured man.

- Spiritual leaders in Jesus' time would often avoid actions, including helping those in need, if it would make them ceremonially unclean, according to the Law of Moses.
- Part of Jesus' message in this parable is that serving others in need takes precedence over following a set of rules that were created to honor God.

God's rule of peace, justice, and love. Jesus talked about things that were difficult to describe, so he often taught using parables.

A **parable** is a short story Jesus told using examples from everyday life or nature to illustrate moral or spiritual truths. Parables sometimes end with a twist or a surprise, and people didn't always understand the meanings. He used examples from everyday life to give a religious or moral lesson, or to emphasize God's love.

Sometimes Jesus spoke in parables when he was challenged by someone who wanted to trap him in his words. In the Gospel according to Luke a scholar tried to test Jesus. He asked, "Who is my neighbor?" to clarify the law, "love your neighbor as yourself." In response, Jesus told the parable of the Good Samaritan (see Luke 10:30–35). This parable would have surprised Jesus' listeners. The Jewish people and Samaritans of Jesus' time had religious and ethnic differences. They would not have expected the Jewish men to ignore one of their own, or the Samaritan to help a man considered to be the enemy.

There are more than thirty parables in the Gospels, including the well-known parables of the Mustard Seed, the Sower, the Lost Sheep, the Rich Fool, and the Prodigal Son.

© Our Sunday Visitor

Catholic Faith Words

wisdom the spiritual gift that helps us to see God's purpose and plan for our lives. Wisdom is also one of the seven Gifts of the Holy Spirit.

Kingdom of God God's rule of peace, justice, and love that exists in Heaven, but has not yet come in its fullness on Earth

parable a short story Jesus told using examples from everyday life or nature to illustrate moral or spiritual truths

READ AND REFLECT

Choose a parable with which you are not very familiar. Locate, read, and reflect on it. Then use your own words to describe its meaning.

The parable:

_____

_____

Its meaning:

_____

_____

_____

Model of Wisdom **147**

Optional Activity

Modern-Day Parables *Verbal/Linguistic, Visual/Spatial, Bodily/Kinesthetic*

Have the students select one of the parables from the list you provided and reread it several times. Direct them to create their own parable that is set in the present day. It should convey the same message as the parable they read. Tell the students to:

- Select characters and outline the plot.
- Choose specific scenes to focus on, and then write the dialogue between their characters.
- Write and illustrate the parable as a cartoon strip, or act it out.

Ordinary Words, Extraordinary Meaning

Remind the students that people sensed Jesus' uniqueness:

- He connected on their level, even though he spoke about things that were not always easy to understand or accept.
- He taught about God's Kingdom of justice and peace, but people did not always understand him.

Ask the students what a parable is and record their responses.

- After they share their ideas, have volunteers read aloud the text on pages 146 and 147.
- *Ask:* How would you change your description of a parable based upon what you have read?

Have three volunteers each read aloud one of the definitions from the Catholic Faith Words box.

CLOSE

ACTIVITY

Provide a list of parables on the board or on chart paper for the students to choose from.

- Have them find their parable in the Bible and work on the activity.
- Allow volunteers to share what they wrote with the class.

Quick Review What Jesus taught his followers challenged the commonly accepted understanding of his time. But he connected to people with parables, which he used to explain how we ought to live and to proclaim the coming of God's Kingdom.

Objectives

- Explore some of the major teachings of the Sermon on the Mount
- Describe the attitudes and actions in the world that contradict the teachings of Christ

OPEN _____

♥ Have the students pray the Beatitudes from page 374.

Ask: How are Jesus' words surprising and challenging?

BUILD _____

A Unique Message

Point out that Jesus often shared his wisdom in places where people were most comfortable.

- *Ask:* What does this tell us about the kind of teacher Jesus is?
  Possible response: He relates to us where we are; he's like us.

Explain that the author of the Gospel according to Matthew collected many of Jesus' teachings into what we call the Sermon on the Mount.

Have a volunteer read the opening paragraph.

Invite a student to read aloud the definition of *Sermon on the Mount* on page 149.

▨ Go to the Source

Send the students to the Scripture Matthew 7:24–29 to read more on the Sermon on the Mount. Invite them to think about the analogy used in this passage.

A Unique Message

How are Jesus' words surprising and challenging?

Jesus taught everywhere he went. He preached in homes and synagogues, in boats, on the road as he walked, and on the shores. He gathered with his disciples on hilly areas as the crowds followed him, hoping to hear his message or to receive his healing touch. He offered words of wisdom throughout his public ministry, and in the Gospel according to Matthew, many of these teachings are collected into what is known as the **Sermon on the Mount.**

Words and Actions

Have you ever been told that actions speak louder than words? Or that you need to not only say what's right, but also do what's right? Jesus tells us something similar.

Jesus said if you listen to his words, and you pattern your actions on his words, you will have a good foundation. It's like building a house on solid rock. The winds will blow, and the rains will fall, but the house will stand. The strong foundation of Jesus' words will hold up your actions that are based on hearing and believing those words.

▽ WHERE IT HAPPENED

The Gospels do not tell us exactly where Jesus gathered his disciples and the crowds in Galilee. The geography of this part of Galilee contains elevated hills with many associated level places. Some archeologists and people who study the Bible think parts of the Sermon on the Mount took place at Mount Eremos, overlooking the Sea of Galilee. It is often called the Mount of Beatitudes.

▨ **Go to the Source**
Read *Matthew 7:24–29* and think about why the analogy of a house's foundation ended the Sermon on the Mount.

148

ⓘ Teacher Background

Where It Happened: Mount Eremos

Explain to the students that Mount Eremos is where many scholars believe Jesus delivered some of the teachings contained in the Sermon on the Mount.

- Pope Saint John Paul II presided over a Mass to almost 100,000 people on Mount Eremos in March of 2000.
- The photo on this page is of modern-day Mount Eremos, also called the Mount of the Beatitudes.

But if you don't listen to the words of Jesus, it will be like building your house on sand. Your life will have no foundation. The winds and rain will knock it down easily. (See Matthew 7:24–29.)

> **What can you do to become a person who connects your words and your actions?**

Catholic Faith Words

Sermon on the Mount the summary of key teachings of Jesus found in the Gospel according to Matthew

Teachings from the Mount

• You are the salt of the earth.	• When you give to the poor, don't brag about it.
• You are the light of the world.	• Ask and you will receive.
• Our Father is in Heaven; how holy is his name.	• Seek and you will find.
• When you pray, don't use loud and fancy words.	• Knock and the door will open.
• When you fast, don't try to look glum and hungry.	
• Where your treasure is, your heart is, too!	Underline which of these teachings you think people most need to hear and act upon today. Draw a star next to the teachings that are hardest for you to hear or act on.
• Don't judge others harshly, or you will be judged harshly.	

NAME

Name three words or phrases to describe Jesus' wisdom found in the Sermon on the Mount.

1. _____
2. _____
3. _____

What question would you ask Jesus about the points he made in these teachings?

_____
_____

Model of Wisdom **149**

Optional Activity

Judging Others *Intrapersonal/Interpersonal*

In his Sermon on the Mount, Jesus warns about judging others.

- Ask the students to reflect on a time they may have judged others or when others have judged them.
- Allow them some quiet time to think about how they might have made others feel by judging them or how they felt when they were judged by others.
- Invite a few volunteers to share their thoughts with the class.

Words and Actions

Review this section on pages 148 and 149 with the class.

- Discuss the question at the end of the text.

Teachings from the Mount

Divide the students into four groups. Invite the groups to study the teachings listed in the chart.

★ Have each group select and underline one teaching that they think people most need to hear and act upon today. Instruct the groups to mark a star next to the teachings they think are hardest to hear and act on.

- Invite several groups to share which sayings of Jesus they underlined or starred. Elicit additional feedback from the other small groups.

CLOSE _____

ACTIVITY

Have the students read the instructions and complete the activity.

- Invite volunteers to share the questions they would like to ask Jesus.

Quick Review The Sermon on the Mount is a collection of Jesus' major teachings. Jesus showed us, through his words and actions, how to always love God and our neighbor, even when it goes against societal and cultural norms.

DAY 4

Objectives

- Explain how the Beatitudes offer us the path to a life of happiness and peace
- Relate how being obsessed with material things keeps us from living the real values of God's Kingdom

OPEN

💜 Have the students silently reflect on how the teachings of Jesus are evident in their lives.

BUILD

Divine Words for Wise Living

Ask a volunteer to read this section.

Point out that Jesus' wisdom clarified the true meaning of the word *happiness* in his teachings called the Beatitudes.

- When the Beatitudes say that some people are "blessed," they are describing people who are happy because they have the attitudes and behaviors that help promote God's Kingdom.
- True happiness comes from trusting in God and the "things of God."

Invite another volunteer to read the definition of *Beatitudes*.

The Beatitudes

★ Allow the students to work with a classmate to fill in the chart.

Divine Words for Wise Living

What do the Beatitudes teach us about our relationships with God and others?

The part of the Sermon on the Mount that people are perhaps most familiar with is the **Beatitudes**, Jesus' teachings on the meaning of and path to true happiness. The word *beatitude* means "happiness or blessedness." In the Beatitudes, Jesus asks us to align our spirit and our will with God. Only when we rely on God's grace and the guidance of the Spirit, can we find the eternal blessedness, or holiness, to which God calls all of us. In the Beatitudes, Jesus sets forth for us a path of discipleship, with expectations of how to live in relationship with one another. In the Beatitudes we find the values of the Kingdom of God, and the attitudes and behaviors of Christians living in God's Kingdom now and always.

The Beatitudes are recorded in two Gospels: Matthew and Luke. The two accounts are similar, but different.

> **Catholic Faith Words**
>
> **Beatitudes** Jesus' eight teachings about the meaning and path to true happiness; they depict the way to live in God's Kingdom now and always, working toward the eternal holiness or blessedness to which God calls all people

Fill in the missing words based on the passages in both Matthew and Luke.

The Beatitudes

The Words in Matthew 5:3–12	The Words in Luke 6:20–26
Blessed are:	**Blessed are you:**
• the ___poor___ in spirit	• who are poor
• those who mourn and the ___meek___	• who are hungry now
• those who ___hunger___ and thirst for righteousness	• who ___weep___ now
• the merciful and the ___pure___ in heart	• when people ___hate___ you, on account of the Son of Man
• the peacemakers	**Woe to you:**
• those who are persecuted for righteousness	• who are ___rich___
• you when people revile you because of ___Jesus___	• who are full now
	• who are ___laughing___ now

> 📖 **Go to the Source**
> Read both versions of the Beatitudes to find out how each of these groups of people will be blessed.

© Our Sunday Visitor

✝ Scripture Background

Blessedness in the Beatitudes

In the Beatitudes, Jesus reflects some of the words of the prophets and wisdom writers of the Old Testament. Help the students compare the message found in six of the Beatitudes to the Old Testament Scriptures listed below:

First and Second Beatitudes	Isaiah 61:1–3
Third Beatitude	Psalm 37:11
Fourth Beatitude	Psalm 107:4–9
Fifth Beatitude	Proverbs 14:21
Sixth Beatitude	Psalm 24:3–5

The Message

The account in the Gospel according to Matthew focuses on the spiritual and religious virtues of God's Kingdom. Luke's account emphasizes the social and economic inequality of the time. In both, we find Jesus' teaching that happiness comes from trusting in God no matter what is happening now. We will know true happiness when God's Kingdom has come in its fullness. In the meantime, being obsessed with material things or current good fortune will keep us from seeing and living the real values of God's Kingdom.

WRITE

The Beatitudes assure those who are in need of God's help and compassion and our trust that God will make all things good and that we can receive eternal happiness with him in Heaven, regardless of our current circumstances. Write two Beatitudes for adolescents that address their suffering or needs. For example, "Blessed are those whose neighborhoods are filled with violence and fear, trusting that God will bring you peace."

1. _____
   _____
   _____

2. _____
   _____
   _____

IN SUMMARY   Catholics Believe

As Catholics, we turn to Jesus as our source of wisdom.

- Jesus' wisdom came from being the Son of God; he looked at the world with that perspective.

- He taught through his words and actions. In his Sermon on the Mount, he gave advice and specific direction that emphasize just living, honoring God, and making our actions reflect our beliefs.

- Jesus' Beatitudes challenge us to live by the values of God's Kingdom and to understand that true happiness comes from the hope of eternal life with God.

Model of Wisdom   **151**

✓ Teaching Tip

Identifying Consequences

Share with the class some words of wisdom or factors to consider when identifying possible consequences of actions they might take.

- **R**elationships: How will an action affect your relationship with self, God, and others?

- **O**pportunities: Does the action give you opportunities to express what's on your mind and in your heart?

- **C**apabilities: Do you have the capability to accomplish a task?

- **K**nowledge: What do you need to know to accomplish this task?

- **S**tumbling blocks: What problems are you likely to encounter, and how can you deal with them?

 Go to the Source

Have the students read Matthew 5:3–12 and Luke 6:20–26 to check their answers in the Beatitudes chart.

- Invite class discussion.

The Message

Use the image on this page to spark a discussion about happiness and the importance of staying connected to others, but especially to God.

Have the students read the text.

- Ask them to underline the different focuses from the Gospel according to Matthew and the Gospel according to Luke.

- Encourage the students to rephrase, in their own words, the overall message of the Beatitudes.

CLOSE _____

ACTIVITY

Read aloud the instructions.

- Have the students work independently to complete the activity.

In Summary

Have volunteers read aloud each bullet point to summarize the key lesson points.

- Allow time for the students to write one thing about each point that they would share with a friend.

DAY 5

Objectives

- Identify steps to making a good decision
- Explore the faith life of Saint Gerard Majella
- Offer the Prayer of Petition

OPEN

Invite the students to gather in the prayer space. Pray together the Lord's Prayer, page 383.

BUILD

Our Catholic Life

Review with the class the information in the Our Catholic Life section.

- Have the students discuss the closing questions with a classmate.

People of Faith

Explain to the students that Saint Gerard Majella cared for the needs of others.

- Have a volunteer read aloud the People of Faith paragraph.
- Review with the class the content of the People of Faith Background box.
- Invite the students to reflect on times when they received help from someone else.

Our Catholic Life

Jesus is a model of wisdom for us. To gain some of that wisdom and apply it to our own lives, we need to take the time to learn Jesus' teachings, and pray for guidance when making decisions. There are **steps you can take** to find the right answer to hard questions, including: giving yourself plenty of time to think about what you should do, listening to your conscience, considering what the Bible and the Church teach, asking for help and courage in prayer, and being confident in your decision once you've thought and prayed about it. Wisdom helps you make the right choices, and that helps strengthen your relationship with God and others.

> When have you relied on God's wisdom to help you make a decision? How did it feel?

People of Faith

Saint Gerard Majella, 1726–1755

One day, Gerard Majella was visiting a family and dropped his handkerchief. When one of the daughters tried to return it, Gerard told her to keep it because she might need it some day. Years later, after Gerard had died, the girl was pregnant and her baby was in danger of dying. Remembering the handkerchief, she prayed to Gerard to help her. She gave birth to a healthy baby! Many pregnant women began to pray to Gerard and many miracles occurred. To remind himself of what God wants from us, Gerard kept a note that read: "Here the will of God is done, as God wills, and as long as God wills." The Church celebrates his feast day on **October 16.**

For more, go to
aliveinchrist.osv.com

IDENTIFY

Think of an important decision or difficult situation you or someone you know is facing right now. What would the wisdom of the world lead you to do?

_____

_____

What would the wisdom of Jesus found in the Beatitudes or Sermon on the Mount lead you to do?

_____

_____

How could you see things differently, as God does?

_____

_____

152 Chapter 8

People of Faith Background

Saint Gerard Majella

Share the following with the students:

- Saint Gerard's main ambition was to imitate the suffering and humiliation of Jesus.
- When Saint Gerard took his vows, he added an additional one— to do always that which seemed to him more perfect.
- His charitable action earned him the title of Father of the Poor.

Encourage the students to go to **aliveinchrist.osv.com** at home to learn more about Saint Gerard Majella.

Prayer of Petition

All: Lord God, Creator of all things, true source of light and wisdom, graciously let your light give me understanding.

Leader: Lord God, send your wisdom through our parents and families, our teachers, our pastor and church. Help us too, to find that light in the example of your Saints. May we welcome this light and the wisdom it brings.

All: Give me the eyes to see your plan for a good and meaningful life in a world that can be disordered and sinful.

Leader: Lord, sometimes it seems that darkness overwhelms us. We live in a world where there is often violence and disrespect for human life and dignity. Sometimes, we contribute to that darkness. Too often, we're selfish or say mean things that hurt others. Help us to see everyone as you see them. Let your light overcome the darkness.

All: Help me to remember the gift of your truth that I have learned as a child, and help me to understand your will more each day so that I may make choices that reflect your love.

Leader: God, help us to work hard at learning. Learning about your world, the work of your hands will help us draw closer to you. Let us keep in our hearts Saint Thomas Aquinas' insight that all learning begins in realizing that you are the source of all Truth.

All: Grant me the talent of being clear in my explanations and the ability to express myself with kindness and respect for another's point of view.

Leader: God, sometimes we're careless in the way we speak. We brag, we "stretch the truth," or we say something just to be noticed. Guide us in speaking carefully and thoughtfully, as disciples of Jesus, the Way, the Truth, and the Life.

All: Direct my talents and interests, and help me discover your plan for my life. Give me the perseverance to complete the journey to serve you through my work. I ask this through Christ our Lord. Amen.

Leader: God, you know how often we are tempted to quit trying. Remind us to ask for your help. Encourage us in all we do.

All: Amen.

Prayer for Students by Saint Thomas Aquinas

▶ *Sing or play "You Are the Way"*

Model of Wisdom **153**

🔊 Go to **aliveinchrist.osv.com** for an interactive review.

A **Work with Words** Solve the word search to find words that complete the sentences.

H	A	P	P	I	N	E	S	S
J	H	N	Q	U	P	M	N	V
M	L	D	I	A	A	O	R	L
J	I	N	Q	T	R	V	Y	U
W	S	A	T	D	A	R	A	K
D	T	H	T	F	B	B	Z	E
B	E	F	O	L	L	O	W	R
W	N	E	L	I	E	H	T	D

1. The word Beatitude means _____**happiness**_____.

2. In the Sermon on the Mount, Jesus said you need to _____**listen**_____ and _____**follow**_____ his words to have a strong foundation in life.

3. A short story Jesus told using examples from everyday life or nature to illustrate moral or spiritual truths is a _____**parable**_____.

4. The Beatitudes are found in the Gospels according to _____**Luke**_____ and _____**Matthew**_____.

B **Check Understanding** Complete each sentence with the correct term from the Word Bank.

holiness	Kingdom
Good Samaritan	blessedness
truth	Son of God
true happiness	Sermon on the Mount
Prodigal Son	

5. The _____**Sermon on the Mount**_____ is the summary of Jesus' key teachings found in the Gospel according to Matthew.

6. Jesus preached the message of God's _____**Kingdom**_____.

7. In the Beatitudes we learn about the meaning of and path to _____**true happiness**_____.

8. God calls each of us to eternal _____**blessedness or holiness**_____.

9. Jesus taught with authority because he was the _____**Son of God**_____.

10. Jesus' Parable of the _____**Good Samaritan**_____ is a good example of how his wisdom crossed social barriers and cultural norms.

C **Make Connections** Write a brief response to the question: What wisdom does Jesus have to offer us and how can following it make a difference in your life?

_____

_____

_____

Have the students silently read the introduction and the questions.

- Invite them to work on the activity independently.

CLOSE

Prayer of Petition

♥ Place a lit candle on the prayer table.

Call the students to prayer with these words: Jesus, be with us and call on those who embody your Beatitudes to pray with and for us.

Follow the order of prayer on the student page.

Conclude with the following: Jesus, bless us and strengthen us to live as your faithful followers. Amen.

▶ Invite the students to sing or reflect on the song "You Are the Way," downloaded from **aliveinchrist.osv.com**.

CHAPTER REVIEW

Review the instructions for each section and have the students complete the review.

🔊 Go to **aliveinchrist.osv.com** to prepare customized and downloadable assessments, send eAssessments, and assign interactive reviews.

Model of Wisdom **153–154**

KEY CONCEPT

Jesus Christ is our Savior, Redeemer, and Messiah.

DOCTRINAL CONTENT

- Sin and suffering came into the world because of human action, but God sent leaders, prophets, and, ultimately, his Son to guide us back to him. (CCC, 218, 402–406, 410)

- Jesus is sometimes called the new Adam, because his saving action is the only means by which we are saved from the Original Sin of Adam and Eve and our own personal sin. (CCC, 411, 430–431)

- The Paschal Mystery is Christ's work of redemption through his Passion, Death, Resurrection, and Ascension. (CCC, 517, 1708)

- Jesus' saving actions continue through his Church. We can experience new life in Christ in the Seven Sacraments. (CCC, 738–740, 1136–1139)

TASKS OF CATECHESIS

Helping children grow in a faith that is "known, celebrated, lived, and expressed in prayer" (NDC, 20).

This chapter focuses on the following tasks of catechesis:

- Promoting Knowledge of the Faith
- Missionary Initiation

Teacher Background

He is the image of the invisible God, the firstborn of all creation ... making peace by the blood of his cross ... and you who once were alienated and hostile in mind because of evil deeds he has now reconciled ... through his death, to present you holy, without blemish ...   Colossians 1:15, 20, 21, 22

> **Reflect** Why are we in need of reconciliation with God?

The Paschal Mystery is at the very core of our Christian faith. The Passion, Death, Resurrection, and Ascension of Jesus is the central reality around which all of salvation history revolves. Everything that came before was leading up to it; everything that came after was defined by it. In this act of incredible love and self-sacrifice, Jesus repaired the breach of Original Sin and reconciled humanity with God. Is it any wonder, then, that we proclaim this profound mystery of our faith every time we celebrate the Eucharist?

Yet, the Paschal Mystery is not merely a historical event, it is an ongoing part of salvation history and human experience. Part of that which defines us as humans is our awareness that we live and we die. Through our Baptism, we become immersed in the Paschal Mystery, which teaches us that death is not to be feared by those who place their trust in God. When we see how fear of death—and the rampant denial of it—defines so much of our culture, the wisdom of the Paschal Mystery becomes even more crucial. We place our hope in the one who stared death in the eye and did not blink. We are confident that some day, we, like Jesus, will rise to a new and eternal life with God in Heaven.

> **Reflect** How does your faith in the Paschal Mystery influence how you feel about life and death?

Teacher's Prayer

♥ We proclaim your Death, O Lord, and profess your Resurrection until you come again. Lord Jesus, help me to express this belief in everything I do. Amen.

How Seventh Graders Understand Chapter Topics

Seventh graders can understand Jesus' Death within the context of the whole Paschal Mystery, which includes his Resurrection. Stations of the Cross and similar depictions of Jesus' suffering are appropriate for this age group, particularly if we can relate Jesus' own suffering back to our everyday lives. It's important that young people know that doing good sometimes involves sacrifice and suffering. But God is with us and understands suffering because he became a human being who suffered also. The Resurrection teaches us that with God there is an Easter Sunday for every Good Friday.

Teaching Tip: Appreciating Jesus as our Savior requires that we get in touch with our own need for salvation. Help your students recognize and name those things in themselves that bog them down and keep them from living with joy.

Sharing the Message with Seventh Graders

- As they develop physically, intellectually, and emotionally, some adolescents will act out in ways they themselves do not understand. Keep in mind that when they say they don't know why they did something foolish or destructive, they may be telling the truth.
- Seventh graders often navigate between the fear of standing out and the need to be noticed. As is true even for younger children, sometimes negative attention is perceived as better than no attention.
- Appreciating Jesus as our Savior requires that the students get in touch with their own need for salvation. Help them recognize and name the things in themselves that bog them down and keep them from living with joy.

Chapter 9 Planner

Objectives	Open

DAY 1—Invite/Preview, Pages 155–157

- Reflect on God's personal invitation through Scripture
- Indicate prior knowledge of chapter concepts and vocabulary

♥ **Psalm 138:8** Pray the opening prayer.

📖 **Colossians 1:15, 19–22** Proclaim "The Preeminence of Christ." Guide the students through the process of Scripture reflection.

- Discuss Have You Ever Thought questions.

DAY 2—Discover, Pages 158–159

- Examine how sin and suffering came into the world
- Explore God's faithfulness in sending leaders and prophets to guide his People back to him

♥ Pray the **Act of Faith**, page 387.

- Discuss the opening question.

DAY 3—Discover, Pages 160–161

- Identify Jesus' saving action as the only means by which we are saved from Original Sin and personal sin
- Compare and contrast Jesus, the new Adam, with the first Adam

♥ Pray the **Confiteor**.

- Point out the opening question.

DAY 4—Discover, Pages 162–163

- Identify the Paschal Mystery as Christ's work of Redemption
- Describe how the Church continues Jesus' saving actions

♥ Pray the **Lamb of God**, page 385.

- Discuss the opening question.

DAY 5—Live, Pages 164–165

- Explore forgiveness of ourselves and others as an act of faith in God's mercy
- Explore the faith life of Saint Madeleine Sophie Barat
- Offer the Prayer of Praise

♥ Pray the **Hail Mary**, page 384.

REVIEW AND ASSESSMENT

Chapter Review, page 166
Chapter Test, page 155F

🛜 **aliveinchrist.osv.com** Customize and Download Assessments, Email Links to eAssessments, Interactive Student Reviews

Build	Close	Materials & Resources
• Present lesson highlights. • Preview **Catholic Faith Words**. ★ Discuss titles and symbols that represent Jesus. • **Optional Activity** Our Redemption (Activity Master 9)	• **Activity** Consider the meaning of Redemption.	☐ pencils or pens ☐ board or chart paper ☐ Activity Master 9 (Page 155G)
• **Catholic Faith Words** Original Holiness, Original Sin, personal sin • Talk about the cause and consequences of Original Sin. • Discuss God's guidance.	• **Activity** Talk about Original Sin in today's world. • Conclude with a review of key concepts and objectives.	☐ pencils or pens ☐ board or chart paper
• **Catholic Faith Words** salvation • Explain Jesus' saving actions. ★ Discuss the multiple titles for Jesus. 📖 Read 1 John 4:10–11.	• **Activity** Design and display symbols and titles used for Jesus. Conclude with a review of key concepts and objectives.	☐ pencils or pens ☐ Bibles ☐ art supplies ☐ poster board
• **Catholic Faith Words** Paschal Mystery • Discuss the Paschal Mystery. • Explain how Jesus continues his saving actions today.	• Review the In Summary statements.	☐ pencils or pens ☐ board or chart paper ☐ Bibles
• Discuss the questions in the Our Catholic Life section. • Learn about Saint Madeleine Sophie Barat. • **Activity** Consider how good things can come from bad experiences.	• Assign four readers. • Follow the order of prayer. ▶ Sing or play the closing song.	☐ pencils or pens 🛜 "Lord, Your Love Is Everlasting"

FORMING CATHOLIC IDENTITY ACROSS THE CURRICULUM

To integrate the Catholic faith in all aspects of curriculum, this chapter's objectives can be reinforced and applied in the instruction of other disciplines.

Go to **aliveinchrist.osv.com** for cross-curricular activities and projects linked to the doctrinal content discussed in this unit. Activities are available from among the following knowledge categories and content areas:

Language Arts

- Integration of Knowledge
- Literacy
- Speaking and Listening
- Writing Skills

Math

- Algebraic Thinking
- Geometry
- Measurement and Data
- Numbers and Operations

Science

- Earth Science
- Life Science
- Physical Science
- Technology

Social Studies

- Civics
- Economics
- Geography
- History

NCEA IFG: ACRE Edition

Knowledge of the Faith

- **Objective:** To know and understand basic Catholic teaching about the Incarnate Word Jesus Christ as the way, truth, and life

Missionary Spirit

- **Objectives:** To recognize the centrality of evangelization as the Church's mission and identity embodied in vocation and service; to be aware of how cultures are transformed by the Gospel

Catholic Faith Literacy

Original Sin, Paschal Mystery

Catholic Social Teaching

To integrate Catholic Social Teaching into your lesson, choose one of the following features: Call to Family, Community, and Participation, pages 336–337; or Rights and Responsibilities of the Human Person, pages 338–339.

- Start the Live step of the process by talking about Saint Madeliene Sophie Barat on page 164. Then move directly to the Catholic Social Teaching feature.
- Or, to expand the lesson, complete page 164, then move to the Catholic Social Teaching feature.
- Return to Chapter 9 for the prayer on page 165.

Music Option

Use the following song to enhance catechetical learning or for prayer.

- "Lord, Your Love Is Everlasting," Day 5, Page 165

Name _____ Date _____

Circle the letter of the choice that best completes each sentence.

1. Jesus made eternal life with God the Father possible by ____.
   a. the Sacrament of Reconciliation   c. the Paschal Mystery
   b. the practice of fasting   d. Original Sin

2. The Paschal Mystery is Christ's work of ____ through his Passion, Death, Resurrection, and Ascension.
   a. Original Sin   c. suffering
   b. healing   d. Redemption

3. We call ____ the Messiah because he was sent by God the Father to fulfill his promise to redeem his People.
   a. Jesus   c. Peter
   b. John the Baptist   d. Martha

4. The Church has the power to forgive our sins committed after Baptism through ____.
   a. the Old Testament prophecies   c. Mosaic Law
   b. the Sacrament of Reconciliation   d. the Book of Genesis

Write the word or phrase that best completes each sentence.

5. The term "Anointed One" refers to the Greek word _____.

6. _____ is the sin of our first parents that introduced sin, suffering, and death into the world.

7. Because Jesus, in his humanity, remained faithful to God the Father, he is called the

   _____.

8. _____ is the loving action of God's forgiveness of sins and the restoration of friendship with the Father brought by Jesus Christ.

9. A deliberate thought, word, deed, or omission that violates the law of God is called

   _____.

Write a response on the lines below.

10. Describe the Original Holiness of the first humans.

   _____

   _____

Name _____ Date _____

Our Redemption

The reading from Saint Paul's Letter to the Colossians (1:15–22) addresses a central theme of Jesus' mission and ministry: our redemption. We are a people in need of being saved.

Identify "evidence" or examples that indicate we are a people in need of reconciliation. Specifically, focus on ways that we (either as individuals or human beings in general) treat each other and treat God's creation.

_____

_____

_____

_____

_____

What does it mean to be reconciled with God?

_____

_____

_____

_____

_____

_____

How does Jesus help us to be reconciled with God?

_____

_____

_____

_____

_____

_____

Christ Our Savior

 Let Us Pray

Leader: Jesus, you love us and save us. You bless us with infinite love. We thank you and praise you for your mercy toward us.

"LORD, your mercy endures forever.
Never forsake the work of your hands!" Psalm 138:8

All: Jesus, help us to forgive and be forgiven. Help us make things right. Bring us back to the Father's love.

 Scripture

"He is the image of the invisible God,
the firstborn of all creation. ... For in him all the
fullness was pleased to dwell,
and through him to reconcile all things for him,
making peace by the blood of his cross [through him],
whether those on earth or those in heaven.

And you who once were alienated and hostile in mind because of evil deeds he has now reconciled in his fleshly body through his death, to present you holy, without blemish, and irreproachable before him ..."
Colossians 1:15, 19–22

Have you ever thought...

• Why are we in need of reconciliation?
• What weakens our friendship with God?

155

© Our Sunday Visitor

Scripture Background

Scripture Reflection Process

Invite the students to be still, close their eyes, and focus on their breathing. Encourage them to open their minds and hearts to what God is saying to them.

• Proclaim the Scripture and have the students sit in silence.
• *Ask:* What did you hear God say to you today?
• Allow volunteers to share.

 You may play instrumental music to begin the reflection.

Objective

• Reflect on God's personal invitation through Scripture

OPEN _____

 Let Us Pray

Invite the students to gather in the prayer space and make the Sign of the Cross. Pray the leader prayer. Select a few students to read aloud the Psalm verse. Prompt the group response from the remainder of the class.

Have the students return to their seats.

Explain that the opening prayer reminds us of our need for mercy and forgiveness.

Say: Let's listen to God's Word and see how Jesus' sacrifice of love reconciled the world to God the Father.

Scripture

Guide the students through the process of Scripture reflection (see the Scripture Background box below).

Have you ever thought...

Say: The reading from Saint Paul's Letter to the Colossians addresses a central theme of Jesus' mission and ministry: our redemption. Because God so loved the world, he sent his only Son and saved us from sin and death.

• Invite the students to respond to the questions.

DAY 1

Objective

- Indicate prior knowledge of chapter concepts and vocabulary

BUILD _____

Use this page to assess the students' knowledge related to the chapter content.

Getting Started

Point out to the class the topics that will be covered in this chapter.

- *Ask:* Which do you think is harder, forgiving someone else or asking for forgiveness for yourself?
- Invite a class discussion.

Jesus

Review the boxes at the bottom of the page with the students.

★ Instruct them to explain why or how each term is a title or symbol for Jesus.
- Discuss the students' responses as a class.

Getting Started

In this chapter you will learn how sin and suffering entered the world, and about God's never ending love for us. You will explore our need for forgiveness and the ways Jesus makes that forgiveness possible.

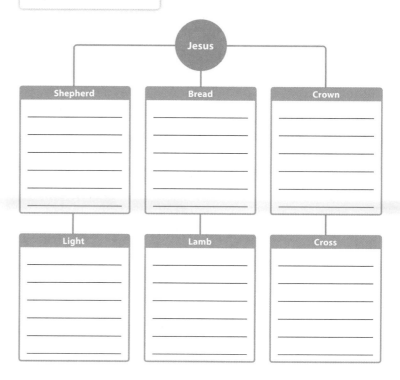

On the lines below each term, explain why it is a title or symbol for Jesus.

Catholic Faith Words

- Original Holiness
- Original Sin
- personal sin
- salvation
- Paschal Mystery

i Teacher Background

Social Sin

Many people focus on personal sin, which individuals commit. The effects of personal sins, committed over a period of time, affect society itself. Hence, "'structures of sin' are the expression and effect of personal sins" (CCC, 1869). By analogy they are called, social sin.

We often don't recognize social sin because it exists in our social, political, and economic systems. Social sin is present when people who have power do not work for the common good of all humankind. We can combat social sin by working to change the attitudes of others, by questioning systems that treat people with an unfair bias, by changing such systems, and by making wise choices as consumers.

Redemption What do you think it means to be redeemed? Use the words below to write a definition. Include an example of how you've experienced one or more of these in your own life.

FORGIVE **SAVE** **RECONCILE**

Definition:

_____

_____

_____

_____

_____

_____

_____

_____

Example:

_____

_____

_____

_____

_____

_____

_____

_____

_____

_____

_____

_____

_____

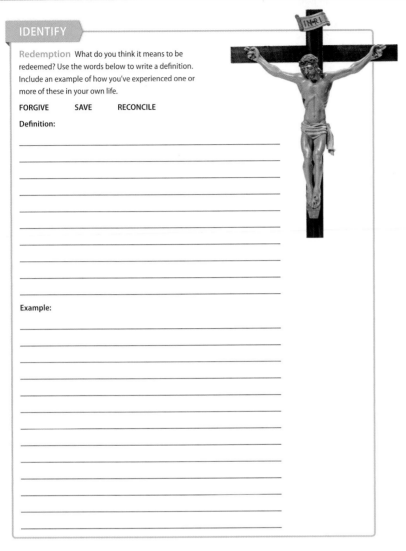

Christ Our Savior **157**

Work with Words

Review the Catholic Faith Words on page 156 with the class.

- Ask the students to choose two of the words that they are familiar with and discuss with a classmate how those words are connected.

CLOSE _____

ACTIVITY

Write the name *Jesus* on the board or on chart paper. Write underneath it these four words: *Forgive*, *Save*, *Redeem*, and *Reconcile*.

- Suggest that *forgiving*, *saving*, *redeeming*, and *reconciling* are actions of Jesus.

- Explain the activity. When the students have completed it, have them share their definitions with a classmate.

Optional Activity

Activity Master 9: Our Redemption

Distribute copies of the activity found on teacher page 155G.

- The students will examine Saint Paul's Letter to the Colossians (1:15–22) to discover why we are a people in need of redemption.

- Allow the students to work in small groups or with a classmate.

CHAPTER 9 Activity Master

Name _____ Date _____

Our Redemption

The reading from Saint Paul's Letter to the Colossians (1:15–22) addresses a central theme of Jesus' mission and ministry: our redemption. We are a people in need of being saved.

Identify "evidence" or examples that indicate we are a people in need of reconciliation. Specifically, focus on ways that we (either as individuals or human beings in general) treat each other and treat God's creation.

_____

What does it mean to be reconciled with God?

_____

How does Jesus help us to be reconciled with God?

_____

155G *Alive in Christ, Grade 7 Chapter 9*

DAY 2

Objectives

- Examine how sin and suffering came into the world
- Explore God's faithfulness in sending leaders and prophets to guide his People back to him

OPEN

💙 Have the students pray the Act of Faith, page 387.

Read aloud the question and elicit responses from the class.

- Have a volunteer record the responses on the board or on chart paper.

BUILD

Original Holiness

Talk with the students about the symbolism in the artwork on this page.

Ask two volunteers to each read aloud one of the opening paragraphs.

- Have the students discuss the question at the end of this section with a classmate.

Work with Words

Come back to this section after reviewing all of the text on pages 158 and 159. Ask a volunteer to write the three Catholic Faith Words on the board.

- Invite the rest of the class to explain the terms based on what was covered in class.
- To check their answers, have three volunteers each read aloud one of the definitions from the Catholic Faith Words box.

Original Holiness

How did suffering and sin enter the world?

You've probably heard the accounts of creation many times. What is God telling us in these accounts? Our first parents, called Adam and Eve, initially experienced only good, because sin had not yet entered the world. God made himself known to them, sharing his love. There was no pain or suffering, no arguments or distrust. The Garden of Eden symbolized true paradise, one in which Adam and Eve lived in **Original Holiness** and justice. They were happy in a way that we cannot imagine. This is what God created all humans for: to be free, to be his friends, and to be close to him.

But that's not how things end. Genesis 3 goes on to describe how Adam and Eve took advantage of their freedom and did not turn to God for answers or trust in his word. Instead, they trusted the serpent. He convinced them that if they ate the fruit of the one tree God said not to eat from, they could have the same knowledge as God. They disobeyed the one command God had given them, and they ate the fruit. By doing this, our first parents introduced shame, sin, and suffering into the world.

> **How do you think God might have felt about Adam and Eve's actions?**

Catholic Faith Words

Original Holiness the state of goodness that humanity enjoyed before our first parents, Adam and Eve, chose to sin against God

Original Sin the sin of our first parents that wounded human nature and introduced sin, suffering, and death into the world; all humans are born with Original Sin and are thus tempted to sin

personal sin a deliberate thought, word, deed, or omission that violates the law of God

The banishment from Paradise, engraving from a Pictorial Bible, German school (19th century)

© Our Sunday Visitor

ℹ Teacher Background

Mortal Sin

A mortal sin (a grave or very serious sin) separates a person from God and causes a break in his or her relationship with God and the community. Mortal sins are signified by three things: the seriousness of the offense, awareness of its seriousness, and it must be committed without coercion and with full consent of will.

- The word *mortal* refers to the dying in the soul caused by mortal sin. In the Sacrament of Reconciliation, we seek healing and receive forgiveness and God's life is restored within us.
- We must be careful not to judge the sins of another person. Our responsibility is to address our own need for forgiveness.

Forever Different

So what happened next? The Book of Genesis tells us that Adam and Eve hid themselves from God, trying to stay away from him because they knew they had sinned. They were afraid. For their disobedience, God expelled them from the Garden.

Everything was different now. The pure happiness and holiness had been lost, not just for Adam and Eve, but for all humans after them. Human nature itself had been harmed. Now, all people suffered because of the choice of our first parents. This disobedience is called **Original Sin**. Original Sin is not something we do; it's something we inherit. Humans can be sad and can suffer because of the sinful actions of others. Humans do not live forever, but die. And all of this is connected to the effects of Original Sin, including the human tendency to commit **personal sin**, to give in to temptation and disobey God. In all of these ways, human nature is affected by Original Sin.

But even though our first parents, and all those who have come after them, disobeyed God, God still loved them. He promised to save them, to bring them back to himself. Throughout history, God sent leaders and prophets to his People, to guide them back to him. Through these people, God promised a Messiah who would bring the people back into the right relationship with God and others, and who would free them from sin.

But why did God allow the physical and moral evil to continue? We do not know the answer to this, but we need to turn to the Son of God whom the Father sent. Jesus Christ died and rose to new life to conquer and defeat evil. In this we must trust.

© Our Sunday Visitor

REFLECT

Think of examples of Original Sin in the world— times when the human tendency to be sinful, imperfect, or flawed was evident. What examples have you heard about in the news reporting on current events or social issues, or seen in movies or on TV?

_____

_____

How would the world be different if those stories were replaced with examples of care, honesty, generosity, and humility?

_____

_____

_____

Christ Our Savior **159**

Optional Activity

A Letter from God *Intrapersonal, Verbal/Linguistic*

Invite the students to consider how God felt when Adam and Eve disobeyed the one command he gave them. Have them imagine what he might say to them in a letter.

- How would God explain to them that they must leave the Garden of Eden?

- What might God wish for them in the future?

- Another option would be to have some of the students write a letter from God to Adam and Eve, and have other students write a letter from Adam and Eve to God.

Forever Different

Remind the students that Original Sin is not something we do; it is something we inherit.

Have the students review this content with a classmate.

- Ask each pair to prepare a summary statement of what they read.

- Invite volunteers to share their summaries with the class.

Offer your own overview of this section by saying:

- The result of Original Sin is that we live with the tendency to give in to temptation, disobey God, and commit sins.

- In spite of our actual sins, God loves us, forgives us, and keeps calling us back to him.

- God sent Jesus to call us back into right relationship with him and one another.

CLOSE _____

ACTIVITY

Read aloud the instructions.

- Arrange the students in small groups to brainstorm and work on this activity together.

- Have each group share their responses with the class.

Quick Review Sin and suffering came into the world because of human action. God sent leaders, prophets, and ultimately sacrificed his Son, in order to guide his People back to him.

DAY 3

Objectives

- Identify Jesus' saving action as the only means by which we are saved from Original Sin and personal sin
- Compare and contrast Jesus, the new Adam, with the first Adam

OPEN

Have the students pray the *Confiteor*, page 385.

Read the focus question and tell the students that the title of today's lesson is a clue to the answer.

BUILD

God So Loved the World

Point out that Jesus saves us because all people need God's saving grace. Like Adam and Eve, we are unfaithful and disobey God, but he sent Jesus to set us free from sin.

Invite two volunteers to read the paragraphs in this section.

 Scripture

Proclaim 1 John 4:10–11.

"The New Adam"

Invite a volunteer to read aloud this section, which continues on page 161.

 Go to the Source

Have the students look up John 1:49, John 11:20–27, Matthew 16:13–20, and John 4:25–29 to read how various people came to recognize Jesus.

God So Loved the World

Why did Jesus save us?

You might have heard "Jesus is our salvation" and wondered why people need "saving." People need to be restored to the friendship Adam and Eve had with God before Original Sin. Because God created our first parents holy and just, only he can save us from the effects of Original Sin and from our sins. That is what we mean by **salvation**.

For many years, the Jewish people—the People God had chosen to show the whole world his plan of salvation—waited for the Messiah to come and set them free, as their prophets had promised. They lived by the laws of the covenant, but often they strayed. Some thought the Messiah was coming to set them free from the Romans, who had captured their land and taken their religious

Catholic Faith Words

salvation the loving action of God's forgiveness of sins and the restoration of friendship with the Father brought by Jesus Christ

freedom. But God wanted to set his People free from the sin that had captured their hearts and all humankind.

"The New Adam"

But how could things be fixed between humans and God? How could the whole human race be redeemed?

Scripture

"In this is love: not that we have loved God, but that he loved us and sent his Son as expiation for our sins. Beloved, if God so loved us, we also must love one another."
1 John 4:10–11

Because God the Father loved human beings, he sent his Son to them. God the Son freely chose to become man and to offer himself in order to redeem us from the effects of Original Sin and from our personal sins. He came into the world as a baby, born from a human mother. Because he did this, no one

Go to the Source
Look up these readings to see how each person came to recognize who Jesus really was.
Nathanael: John 1:49
Martha: John 11:20–27
Peter: Matthew 16:13–20
Woman at the well: John 4:25–29

160 · Chapter 9

© Our Sunday Visitor

Optional Activity

Symbols of God's Love   *Visual/Spatial, Interpersonal, Naturalist*

Take the students outside on the parish or school grounds.

- Give them fifteen minutes to find and collect an item that symbolizes to them God's loving presence in the world.
- Return to the classroom and invite the students to share their item and explain how it is a symbol of God's presence for them.
- Affirm each student for their observations and for sharing.

could ever say that God didn't understand what it was like to be human and to be tempted by sin.

Jesus is called the "New Adam." Adam was unfaithful to God, but Jesus remained faithful to God, even when he was tempted.

Jesus the Messiah

When Jesus became an adult, many people listened to him tell parables and describe God's love. Jesus came to fulfill the Laws of Moses, called the Mosaic Law, which included the Ten Commandments, and give them deeper meaning. Jesus fulfilled the Law.

Some of Jesus' followers came to believe that he was the Messiah, the one who would save them.

Jesus the King

The Jews before and during Jesus' time used precious oil for anointing. Priests anointed new kings by pouring expensive oil on them as a blessing and sign that God would guide them. Anointing with oil was a symbol of power and authority. It meant the person being anointed was chosen in a special way. At his baptism, Jesus was anointed by the Holy Spirit to fulfill the Father's will.

The Jews were waiting for their Messiah, the one anointed by God himself, not with earthly oil. The Son of God was the one who came to save and redeem the human race. We call Jesus the Christ, the Messiah, our Savior and Redeemer.

Use the following terms to complete the definitions for these titles of Christ:
Redeemer   Christ   Savior   Messiah

Titles of Christ

__Messiah__ is a Hebrew word that means "anointed," showing he is chosen and empowered. This word was used by Christians to refer to Jesus as "the Much-Awaited Anointed One from God."

__Christ__ is a Greek word that translates the Hebrew word Messiah. It means "the Anointed One."

In Hebrew, Jesus means "God saves." Jesus is the __Savior__ of the World, the one who saves us from sin and punishment.

Jesus is the __Redeemer__ of the World. God accomplished once and for all his plan of salvation by Jesus' redemptive Death.

LIST AND DESIGN

What titles would you give to Jesus? List titles you think of for Jesus and what they mean. Then design a poster or bulletin board with the headline "His Name Is . . ." Cut out graphic symbols to write each name on, such as a crown with the title "King of Kings" written on it, or a scroll with the title "Messiah" on it to show that Jesus was the one who came to fulfill the Old Testament prophecies.

Christ Our Savior   **161**

Jesus the Messiah

Review this section with the class.

- Point out that Jesus came to fulfill the Law of Moses and to help people understand how to live according to God's law of love.

Jesus the King

Have a volunteer read this section.

- Tell the students that Catholics are anointed in the Sacraments of Baptism, Confirmation, and the Anointing of the Sick.

Titles of Christ

Point out the chart and read aloud the instructions.

★ Direct the students to use the terms provided to complete the definitions for the titles of Christ.

- Review the correct responses with the class.

CLOSE

ACTIVITY

Read aloud the instructions.

- Allow the students to work on this activity individually or with a classmate.

- When the students have had time to complete their projects, invite them to share their posters or bulletin boards with the class.

Quick Review Jesus is called the new Adam. Through his saving action alone we are saved from Original Sin and personal sin.

© Our Sunday Visitor

Teacher Background

Observing Good Friday

Good Friday, the day that Christ died on the Cross (see page 162), is the most somber day in the Church year. It is the second day of the Triduum—the three holiest days of the liturgical calendar. Catholics observe this by:

- participating in the parish Good Friday liturgy.
- venerating the cross by bowing, genuflecting, or touching or kissing it (which symbolizes bending our heart and soul before God).
- taking part in the Stations of the Cross.
- fasting as a sign of the public penance required of the Church on this day.

DAY 4

Objectives

- Identify the Paschal Mystery as Christ's work of Redemption
- Describe how the Church continues Jesus' saving actions

OPEN

 Have the students pray the Lamb of God, page 385.

Direct the students to discuss the opening question with a classmate.

BUILD

Jesus Brings New Life

With the help of several volunteers, read aloud the text on this page.

- Organize the students into small groups and give each group a Bible.
- Direct the groups to look up the different Gospel accounts of Jesus' Passion to see how they are similar and how they are different.
- Ask the groups to record their observations to share with the class.

Remind the students that although Jesus was Divine, he was also human and he truly suffered, died, and was buried.

Discuss what is happening in the painting shown on this page.

If time permits, review some of the Catholic observations of Good Friday with the class from the Teacher Background box on page 161.

This painting of Mary Magdalene at Jesus' tomb by Harold Copping depicts her despair before the Risen Christ appeared to her. (See John 20:11-18.)

Catholic Faith Words

Paschal Mystery Christ's work of redemption through his Passion, Death, Resurrection, and Ascension

Jesus Brings New Life

What happened when Jesus died?

You might be wondering how Jesus actually brought about our salvation from sin. The ultimate result of sin is suffering and death. So another way to ask the question is, how did Jesus conquer suffering and death?

Jesus willingly offered himself on the Cross, which the Church professes in the Nicene Creed every week:

> For our sake he was crucified under Pontius Pilate,
> he suffered death and was buried,
> and rose again on the third day
> in accordance with the Scriptures.

Jesus was free from sin, but he chose to give up his life for the sins of others. He died on the afternoon of what has come to be known as Good Friday. He died for the sins of all people, and we do not hold any one person, or the Jewish people as a whole, responsible for his suffering.

The human and Divine natures are inseparable, and the Son of God suffered, died, and was buried. His redemptive Death won salvation and eternal life in Heaven for all those who had died in God's friendship before him.

His friends saw Jesus die, but no one saw him rise. They found an empty tomb on Sunday morning. However, Mary Magdalene saw the Risen Christ at the tomb. Later, he appeared to many of his disciples. They talked with him and ate with him, before he ascended (went up) into Heaven.

Jesus' redemptive Death was something only God-made-man could do. He was raised to new life, conquering the power of death. His Resurrection was a victory over death. His Death and Resurrection reveal that sin could not keep humans captive forever. Death was not the end, but a passageway to eternal life. This is the salvation that the Son of God won for all who believe in him.

© Our Sunday Visitor

162 Chapter 9

Teacher Background

New Testament Teachings on Forgiveness

You might want to use some of these Scripture passages in your lesson:

- Matthew 6:9–15, The Lord's Prayer
- Luke 5:17–26, The Healing of a Paralytic
- 1 John 1:9, Acknowledging Our Sins
- Colossians 1:9–14, Prayer for Continued Progress
- Matthew 18:21–35, Parable of the Unforgiving Servant
- Mark 1:2–11, Baptism of Repentance for the Forgiveness of Sins

Baptism

Eucharist

Anointing of the Sick

Jesus Continues to Save

The **Paschal Mystery** is the work Christ accomplished principally by his Passion, Death, Resurrection, and Ascension. The Paschal Mystery hinges on the great Easter event of our faith: the Resurrection.

How do Jesus' saving activities continue, since he is no longer with us on Earth? Jesus' saving actions continue through his Church. Jesus makes his Paschal Mystery present in the Eucharist and other Sacraments. In so doing, he continues to offer forgiveness, healing, and new life.

Baptism is the first and primary Sacrament of forgiveness of sins. It unites us to Christ, so we die and rise with him, and gives us the Holy Spirit.

In the name of God, the Church has the power to forgive the sins committed after Baptism. This happens through bishops and priests, normally, in the Sacrament of **Penance and Reconciliation.** We die to sin and rise to renewed life.

The Sacrament of **Eucharist** cleanses us from venial sins and preserves us from future sins. We share in Jesus' suffering and his rising. The Eucharist does not cleanse us from mortal sins. The proper Sacrament for their forgiveness is the Sacrament of Penance and Reconciliation.

The Sacrament of **Anointing of the Sick** also forgives personal sins if the person could not participate in the Sacrament of Penance and Reconciliation.

© Our Sunday Visitor

IN SUMMARY   Catholics Believe

Jesus Christ is our Savior, Redeemer, and Messiah.

- God created human beings with the freedom to live in happiness and harmony with him. By their disobedience, our first parents lost Original Holiness, introduced sin into the world, and became subject to suffering and death.

- God did not abandon his People. He promised them a Messiah who would free them from sin. He sent his own Son to bring that salvation.

- Through his Paschal Mystery, Jesus conquered death and makes it possible for those who have faith to experience new life through the Seven Sacraments.

✓ Teaching Tip

A Sign of God's Love

It is appropriate to promote within your students a deep appreciation for and reverence of the Seven Sacraments. We know that a Sacrament is an outward sign of God's love. As Jesus was a living, breathing Sacrament of God's love, so is the Church called to be a living, breathing sign of God's love in the world today.

Invite the students to consider that they are the Body of Christ and are also called to be a Sacrament to others. We can be a Sacrament to others by living as Jesus did: by loving and forgiving others and by working with and for God to help bring about his Kingdom.

Jesus Continues to Save

Emphasize that Jesus' Paschal Mystery is present today in the forgiveness, healing, and new life offered through the Mass and the Seven Sacraments, especially in the Eucharist.

Have the students silently read this section to themselves.

- Invite volunteers to share summaries of each of the paragraphs on this page.

Write the Scripture passages from the New Testament teachings on forgiveness (see the Teacher Background box on page 162) on the board or on chart paper.

- For an extra credit opportunity, have the students select one of the passages to read and summarize.

- Invite them to bring back their summaries to share with the class at a later date.

CLOSE _____

In Summary

Have volunteers read aloud the summary statements.

Ask: What does the new life that Jesus brings to us really mean? Through Jesus' sacrifice, we can now be forgiven for our sins and look forward to a life of happiness forever with God.

DAY 5

Objectives

- Explore forgiveness of ourselves and others as an act of faith in God's mercy
- Explore the faith life of Saint Madeleine Sophie Barat
- Offer the Prayer of Praise

OPEN

♡ Invite the students to stand at their desks and pray the Hail Mary from page 384.

BUILD

Our Catholic Life

Have the students silently read the content in the Our Catholic Life box.

- Ask them to reflect on the questions at the end of this section.

People of Faith

Explain to the students that Saint Madeleine Sophie Barat helped to open over one hundred schools and convents in her lifetime.

- Read aloud the People of Faith paragraph.
- Review with the class the extra information in the People of Faith Background box.
- Invite the students to pray that God will help them become the person he intends them to be.

Our Catholic Life

We worship a God of second chances, who forgives even when we might not expect him to. During his lifetime, Jesus forgave many people in his Father's name. You can give yourself and someone else a second chance. Ask for **forgiveness** when you make a mistake or hurt someone, and forgive others when they do the same to you. Think of a real-life response you can make to someone from whom you are seeking a second chance, or whom you need to forgive.

God is always ready and waiting to forgive. He will always welcome you back. When you turn away from sin and respond to God's love and forgiveness, you experience conversion, which helps you become the person God intends you to be.

> What second chance do you need right now? Is there someone who needs a second chance from you?

© Our Sunday Visitor

People of Faith

Saint Madeleine Sophie Barat, 1779–1865

Born in France, Sophie was educated by her brother, a priest. She and three companions founded the Society of the Sacred Heart of Jesus in 1800 and started their first convent and school at Amiens. Sister Sophie was appointed Superior General. The Society founded convents and schools in many locations throughout the country. By the time of her death, they had opened 105 schools and convents in twelve countries. The Church celebrates her feast day on **May 25**.

🛜 For more, go to aliveinchrist.osv.com

164 Chapter 9

RECALL AND WRITE

Have you ever learned something "the hard way"? Important lessons can be learned from painful experiences. Recall a time when a good thing came from a "bad" experience. It can be a true report, or a fictional story.

_____
_____
_____
_____
_____
_____
_____
_____

People of Faith Background

Saint Madeleine Sophie Barat

Share these details with the class:

- Saint Madeleine was the Superior General of The Society of the Sacred Heart of Jesus. When a revolution caused the novitiate in Paris to close, Sister Sophie founded a new novitiate in Switzerland.
- From there the Society spread into other European nations and abroad. Among her best-known words of advice were, "Let us attach ourselves to God alone, and turn our eyes and our hopes to Him."

🛜 Encourage the students to go to **aliveinchrist.osv.com** at home to learn more about Saint Madeleine Sophie Barat.

Prayer of Praise

Leader: Blessed be God.

All: Blessed be God forever.

Reader 1: Let us pray.
O Gracious Father,
we praise you, and we thank you for your
endless mercy,
your patience and forgiveness,
your endurance and tolerance,
and the gift of your Son, Jesus,
whom you sent to save us
from all that distracts and keeps us far
from you.

All: We praise you, and we thank you for
your endless mercy.

Reader 2: In you we find a love greater than
any we have ever known.
In you we find hope in the midst of our
darkest act.
In you we find faith in knowing we will
never be alone.

All: We praise you, and we thank you for
your endless mercy.

Reader 3: Be with us in our daily choices.
Guide our hands for service, not for
violence.
Guide our voices for speaking truth, not for
gossip.
Guide our eyes for seeing you in all that we
meet, not for seeking the bad.
Guide our feet to take the "high road," not
for running from responsibility.
Guide our hearts for loving all your people,
not for hating or judging.

All: We praise you, and we thank you for
your endless mercy.

Reader 4: Because we are the young who
search and seek to grow in faith,
remind us always and often that you are on
our side,
that you are for us and never against us,
that you have conquered sin and sadness,
and that through your Son, even in death,
your love is endless.

All: We praise you, and we thank you for
your endless mercy.

 Sing or play "Lord, Your Love Is Everlasting"

Christ Our Savior **165**

Go to **aliveinchrist.osv.com** for an interactive review.

A Work with Words **Circle the letter of the
choice that best completes the sentence.**

1. Our human nature is affected by ____, which
we inherit from Adam and Eve.
   a. Adam's sin
   b. Reconciliation
   c. Original Sin
   d. Paschal Mystery

2. Jesus came to redeem us—to make it possible
for ____.
   a. the Holy Spirit to come
   b. sin to be forgiven
   c. God to become man
   d. man to live a sinless life

3. Jesus is called the "New Adam" because ____.
   a. he was both God and man
   b. he was the son of Adam
   c. he created Adam
   d. he redeemed us from the sin of Adam,
the first man

4. The Paschal Mystery refers to ____.
   a. Jesus' Death
   b. Jesus' Resurrection
   c. Original Sin
   d. both a and b

B Check Understanding **Complete each
sentence with the correct terms.**

5. When Adam and Eve chose to trust the
serpent rather than God, they introduced
_____ sin _____ and
_____ suffering _____ into
the world.

6. Adam and Eve ____ hid themselves
from God after they ate the fruit in the garden.

7. The words *Messiah* and *Christ* both mean
"_____ Anointed _____."

8. Because of _____ Original Sin _____,
people need salvation.

9. By his Death on the Cross and Resurrection,
Jesus made _____ eternal life _____
with God possible.

10. Jesus' _____ saving action _____ is
made present to us today in the Eucharist and
other Sacraments.

C Make Connections **Write a one-paragraph
response to the questions: What is involved in
seeking reconciliation with God? What would
this reconciliation mean for you?**

_____
_____
_____
_____
_____
_____
_____
_____

166 Chapter 9

ACTIVITY

Ask the students to read the
directions; then allow them time
to recall a past experience.

• Invite volunteers to share their
real or fictional stories.

• Remind them that they are not
required to share personal stories.

CLOSE _____

Prayer of Praise

Appoint four readers.

Give them an opportunity to review
their sections.

Set the prayer table by covering it
with a white cloth and a crucifix.

Invite the students to stand.

Call them to prayer with these words:
God, bless us with your grace as we
seek forgiveness and as we seek to
forgive others.

Follow the order of prayer on the
student page.

Conclude by playing the song
or inviting the students to sing
"Lord, Your Love Is Everlasting,"
downloaded from
aliveinchrist.osv.com.

CHAPTER REVIEW

Review the instructions for each
section and have the students
complete the review.

Go to **aliveinchrist.osv.com**
to prepare customized and
downloadable assessments,
send eAssessments, and assign
interactive reviews.

Christ Our Savior **165–166**

Use the closing points from Days 2–4 in each chapter to highlight lesson concepts for this unit and prepare for the Unit Review.

Have the students complete the Review pages. Then discuss the answers as a class. Review any concepts with which the students are having difficulty.

Ⓐ Work with Words

Have the students match each word in the Word Bank with the correct clue to fill in the crossword puzzle.

Ⓐ Work with Words Solve the puzzle using the clues provided.

| Visitation | Nativity | Sermon on the Mount | Rosary |
| Paschal Mystery | Parable | Original Sin | Beatitude |

Across

2. A short story told to illustrate moral or spiritual truths

5. Summary of key teachings of Jesus collected in the Gospel according to Matthew

6. The sin that affected human nature, which we inherit from Adam and Eve

7. A special prayer form in honor of the Blessed Virgin Mary

8. Word that means happiness or blessedness

Down

1. Christ's work of redemption through his Passion, Death, Resurrection, and Ascension

3. The pregnant Mary's time with her cousin Elizabeth, who was pregnant with John the Baptist

4. The birth of Jesus

Jesus Christ **167**

B Check Understanding Circle the letter of the best answer to complete the following statements.

9. The words *Messiah* and *Christ* both mean "___".

   a. King b. Anointed c. Adam d. Prophet

10. The disciples of Jesus were first called followers of ___.

   a. The Spirit b. The Word c. The Way d. The Truth

11. Jesus is called the ___ because he is a visible image of the true nature of God.

   a. Substantial Image of the Father b. Lord c. Messiah d. Savior

12. Jesus is ___.

   a. human b. Divine c. human and Divine d. none of the above

13. The ___ are perhaps the most often quoted part of the Sermon on the Mount.

   a. Beatitudes b. Psalms c. debates d. miracles

14. In the Beatitudes we learn that ___ comes from trusting God and living the values of his Kingdom.

   a. righteousness b. true happiness c. salvation d. faith

15. Jesus taught with ___ because he was the Son of God.

   a. authority b. parables c. the Scriptures d. humor

16. Jesus is called ___ because he redeemed us from the sin of Adam, the first man.

   a. Messiah b. Savior c. the New Adam d. the Lamb of God

17. Sin came into the world when Adam and Eve ___.

   a. left the garden b. chose to disobey God c. were tempted by Satan d. from God

18. Because of Original Sin, people need ___ and salvation.

   a. Beatitudes b. good works c. redemption d. the Bible

19. Jesus made eternal life with God possible through ___.

   a. his Death b. his Resurrection c. his parables d. both a and b

C Make Connections Write a short answer to these questions.

20. How does wisdom make a difference in your life?

   Responses may vary.

21. How are the truths taught by Jesus in the Beatitudes similar to the values found in today's world?

   Responses may vary, but students should be able to identify specific aspects of the Beatitudes and compare and contrast how they see Jesus' teachings reflected in the belief systems of today's world.

22. How are they different?

   As above, responses may vary, but students should be able to identify specific aspects of the Beatitudes and compare and contrast how they see Jesus' teachings reflected in the belief systems of today's world.

23. God helps us as his children with the grace to live the lives he calls us to live. How can you become the person God made you to be?

   Responses may vary, but should reflect an understanding of how we treat our families and friends, how we pray, how we care for people we don't know, how we forgive our enemies, etc.

24. In your own words, describe the elements of Jesus' parables.

   Responses may vary, but should reflect that Jesus used examples from everyday life or nature to illustrate spiritual or moral truths.

25. How do you become a disciple?

   Responses may vary, but should reflect that believing in and following Jesus, learning and applying his teachings, living a life of love and service, and sharing the Good News are all elements of discipleship.

B Check Understanding

Direct the students to circle the letter of the answer that best completes each statement.

C Make Connections

The students should write a short answer for each of the questions or statements. Point out that even though these are short answer responses, they need to be sure that they provide complete answers.

Go to **aliveinchrist.osv.com** to prepare customized and downloadable assessments, send eAssessments, and assign interactive reviews.

THE CHURCH

How does the Holy Spirit form us into the Body of Christ sent to proclaim the Good News of salvation?

CHURCH HISTORY TIMELINE

35	Saint Paul's conversion
596	Saint Augustine of Canterbury evangelizes the English
1649	Maryland colony passes Act of Toleration for religious freedom
1769	Junipero Serra establishes first California missions

Go to page 348 for more

Our Catholic Tradition

- We are disciples of Christ together in his Church, following his example by trusting in the Father, learning, praying, and reaching out to others. (CCC, 520)

- The Church is both visible and spiritual, the Mystical Body of Christ united in and to Christ to continue his mission in the world. (CCC, 779)

- The Church has a mission to bring all people to believe in God and to be baptized. She is both a sign and instrument of the communion between God and his People. (CCC, 780)

Our Catholic Life

- Just as Jesus sent the first disciples out, he wants us to be a sign of the Kingdom of God, and to follow Church teachings. (CCC, 941, 942)

- The Church needs the diverse gifts of all members to be a sign of God's Kingdom. We need one another and Christ to bear fruit in the world. (CCC, 791)

- We must have a personal relationship with God nourished by prayer in order to answer our call to bring his love and truth to others. (CCC, 2614)

Introduce Unit Theme

Have the students examine the photo on the page. Ask them to share what they see and how they believe it relates to the theme of the Church.

Invite six volunteers to each read aloud one of the bullets under the Our Catholic Tradition and Our Catholic Life sections. Encourage the students to share, in their own words, what they think these points mean.

Let them know that they will learn more about all of this information as they work through the next three chapters.

Ask the unit's Big Question found on page 170.

Allow time for discussion.

Explain to the students that this is the essential question for the unit. They will be working to fully answer it as they complete the three chapters in the unit.

Go to the Source

As an optional extension, organize the students into three groups, assigning each group one of the main Scripture passages found in this unit.

- Chapter 10: 1 Timothy 4:6, 12
- Chapter 11: 1 Corinthians 12:12–18
- Chapter 12: Acts 2:1–7

Have each group read its passage and then give a dramatic reading (narrator with silent actors), create a visual representation, or write down one question they would ask God about the passage.

Reading the verses directly from the Bible will familiarize students with the sequence of the canon of Sacred Scripture.

Explore the Encyclical

Use Pope Saint John Paul II's encyclical, *Redemptoris Missio*, to help the students learn about the missionary work of the Church. Ask the following questions:

- Why does the Church engage in missionary activity? (see paragraph 11)
- What is the Kingdom of God, and how is it connected with the Church's mission? (see paragraphs 12–19)
- What is the role of the Holy Spirit in mission work? (see paragraphs 24–29)
- What is the Church's role in spreading the Gospel and appreciating and respecting culture? (see paragraphs 52–54)

CHURCH HISTORY TIMELINE BACKGROUND

Refer the students to the Church History Timeline on pages 348–363 to learn more about important Church events and figures through A.D. 1085.

Religious Freedom Comes to Maryland

Maryland, one of the original thirteen colonies of the United States, was founded by the first Lord Baltimore, a Catholic convert, in 1624. In 1649, Maryland passed the Act of Toleration, which granted freedom of religion, including Catholicism. At the time, it was the only colony to guarantee such freedom.

First California Mission Established

Franciscan missionary Junípero Serra established the first nine of the thirty-one California missions, beginning in 1769 with Mission San Diego de Alcalá. San Juan Capistrano, built in 1782, is famous for the return of the swallows each year on Saint Joseph's Day, March 19. It is believed to be the oldest building in California.

KEY CONCEPT

We are disciples of Christ in his Church, following his example by trusting in the Father, learning, praying, and reaching out to others.

DOCTRINAL CONTENT

- Saint John the Baptist proclaimed the coming of Christ and led people to Jesus. (CCC, 523, 719)

- The Apostles played a critical role in the continuation of Jesus' work and ministry. (CCC, 75–77)

- Just as Jesus sent the first disciples out to spread the Good News, he wants us to be a sign of the Kingdom of God and to follow Church teachings. (CCC, 935, 942)

- We must have a personal relationship with God nourished by prayer in order to answer our call to bring his love and truth to others. (CCC, 3)

TASKS OF CATECHESIS

Helping children grow in a faith that is "known, celebrated, lived, and expressed in prayer" (NDC, 20).

This chapter focuses on the following tasks of catechesis:

- Promoting Knowledge of the Faith

- Teaching to Pray

Teacher Background

If you will give these instructions to the brothers, you will be a good minister of Christ Jesus, nourished on the words of the faith and of the sound teaching you have followed. … Let no one have contempt for your youth, but set an example for those who believe, in speech, conduct, love, faith, and purity. **1 Timothy 4:6, 12**

> **Reflect** How can you help others to know and follow Jesus?

We usually think of discipleship as following the teachings of a spiritual master, and it certainly is that. There is another dimension to discipleship that we don't often reflect upon. The word *disciple* comes from the same root word as "discipline." In Christian terms, discipleship means engaging in the lifelong process of conforming our wills to the will of Jesus Christ.

It seems that conforming our wills to anything other than the pursuit of material happiness runs contrary to the values of contemporary western culture. We have been conditioned to think of personal freedom as the ultimate value, and any belief system that appears to inhibit our freedom is to be avoided at all costs. Christianity values freedom and happiness—in fact, we believe that Jesus sacrificed his life in order for us to be free and happy. Christ's definitions of freedom and happiness are very different from the definitions many of us might have.

Some perceive freedom to be the same as choice. The more choices we have, the freer we feel and the happier we become. Yet, the growing anxiety level in our society would seem to disprove this; today, we have plenty of choices, but we seem to be less happy. For Jesus, freedom and happiness were found in doing the will of his heavenly Father. Jesus lived a completely free life, yet it was a life of total obedience to God. This seeming paradox holds the key to a life of meaning and peace. Following the example of Jesus is the call of each baptized person.

> **Reflect** In what way has your commitment to discipleship made you a freer person?

Teacher's Prayer

💙 Jesus, throughout the ages you have called people of various backgrounds to follow you. You invite everyone to follow you; all that you require is our faith and our willingness to follow your example. Strengthen me to be a model of discipleship for those I teach. Amen.

How Seventh Graders Understand Chapter Topics

Because seventh graders want to fit in and are often insecure, "conformity" and "following the crowd" are a big part of their experience. However, few of them actually want to admit it. In fact, being a "follower" is considered a bad thing in most seventh-grade circles. For this reason, as we discuss discipleship as "following Jesus," it's important to emphasize that Jesus taught us what it means to be fully human. He showed us how to be all God made us to be.

Teaching Tip: Explain to the students that one doesn't have to already "have it together" to be a disciple, as shown by the lives of the Twelve Apostles. God will help us be the people we need to be if we are open to his grace. Peter was, at times, impulsive, stubborn, indecisive, and cowardly, but Jesus chose him to lead his Church. Lead a discussion on Peter and why Jesus chose him. What can we learn about ourselves from Peter's story? (Hint: Compare the impulsive and cowardly Peter in the Gospels with the bold and fearless Peter in the second chapter of Acts.)

Sharing the Message with Seventh Graders

- At this age, students often struggle with the conflicting values of establishing their own unique leadership styles or going along with the crowd.
- Among their peers, seventh graders often perceive leadership as aggressive behavior. Teaching and modeling gentle, virtue-driven leadership shows them that there are other possibilities.
- Young people often learn more by who we are than what we say. Therefore, the joyful living out of our discipleship is one of the most important aspects of catechesis.

ONLINE RESOURCES

 Go to **aliveinchrist.osv.com**

You will find:

- Interactive lesson planning, additional activities, and ideas for the classroom environment
- Step by step lesson instruction from printed Teacher Edition for integrated lesson planning
- Custom-built assessments to download and eAssessment links
- Interactive reviews that provide scores and the option to review answers
- Chapter-specific Lectionary connections and a complete correlation ordered by the Sundays of the year, with suggestions for how to integrate the Scripture readings into chapter lessons

📶 Go to **osvparish.com** for Ask the Experts Q and A, Community Connections, and Blogs.

Chapter 10 Planner

Objectives	Open

DAY 1—Invite/Preview, Pages 171–173

- Reflect on God's personal invitation through Scripture
- Indicate prior knowledge of chapter concepts and vocabulary

♡ **Psalm 23:1, 3** Pray the opening prayer.

📖 **1 Timothy 4:6, 12** Proclaim "Counsel to Timothy." Guide the students through the process of Scripture reflection.

- Discuss Have You Ever Thought questions.

DAY 2—Discover, Pages 174–175

- Recognize that Saint John the Baptist proclaimed the coming of Christ and led people to Jesus
- Analyze why the first disciples followed Jesus

♡ Pray "Jesus, lead me."

DAY 3—Discover, Pages 176–177

- Describe the importance of the Apostles in continuing Jesus' ministry
- Discover sources that contain the official teachings of the Church

♡ Pray the **Apostles' Creed**, page 367.

DAY 4—Discover, Pages 178–179

- Identify the characteristics of a disciple in the world today
- Recall the Church's rich and varied tradition of prayer

♡ Pray the **Beatitudes**, page 374.
- Read aloud the opening question.

DAY 5—Live, Pages 180–181

- Examine contemplative prayer
- Explore the faith life of Saint Théodore (Anne-Thérèse Guérin)
- Offer the Litany of the Saints prayer

♡ Pray **Psalm 23:1, 3** from page 171.

REVIEW AND ASSESSMENT

Chapter Review, page 182
Chapter Test, page 171F

📶 **aliveinchrist.osv.com** Customize and Download Assessments, Email Links to eAssessments, Interactive Student Reviews

Build	Close	Materials & Resources
• Present lesson highlights. • Preview **Catholic Faith Words**. ★ Review common priorities in people's lives.	• Activity Reflect on Jesus' invitations in the past and in the present.	☐ pencils or pens
• **Catholic Faith Words** disciples • Share how John the Baptist prepared the way for the Messiah. 📖 Read and reflect on John 1:43–51, Luke 8:1–3, and Mark 1:16–20.	• Activity Consider Jesus' invitation to follow him and share personal responses. • Conclude with a review of key concepts and objectives.	☐ pencils or pens ☐ Bibles ☐ highlighters
• **Catholic Faith Words** Apostles, Church, apostolic, doctrine 📖 Read and reflect on Matthew 10:1–4, Mark 3:13–19, and Luke 6:12–16. • Discuss the role of the Apostles in spreading the Good News.	• Activity Match Church teachings with their source. • Conclude with a review of key concepts and objectives. • Optional Activity The Chosen Twelve (Activity Master 10)	☐ pencils or pens ☐ Bibles ☐ Church teaching sources ☐ Activity Master 10 (Page 171G)
• Talk about ways to be a disciple. • Discuss different types of prayer. 📖 Read John 8:12. ★ Indicate which of the three "schools" of prayer have been experienced.	• Activity The students will list people who could help them pray one of the three "schools" of prayer. • Review the In Summary statements.	☐ pencils or pens ☐ Bibles ☐ highlighters
• Discuss the question in the Our Catholic Life section. • Learn about Saint Théodore. • Activity Focus on the qualities of a disciple seen in others.	• Appoint a student to serve as the leader. • Follow the order of prayer. ▶ Sing or reflect on the closing song.	☐ pencils or pens 🔊 "Litany"

Chapter Connections

FORMING CATHOLIC IDENTITY ACROSS THE CURRICULUM

To integrate the Catholic faith in all aspects of curriculum, this chapter's objectives can be reinforced and applied in the instruction of other disciplines.

Go to **aliveinchrist.osv.com** for cross-curricular activities and projects linked to the doctrinal content discussed in this unit. Activities are available from among the following knowledge categories and content areas:

Language Arts
- Integration of Knowledge
- Literacy
- Speaking and Listening
- Writing Skills

Math
- Algebraic Thinking
- Geometry
- Measurement and Data
- Numbers and Operations

Science
- Earth Science
- Life Science
- Physical Science
- Technology

Social Studies
- Civics
- Economics
- Geography
- History

NCEA IFG: ACRE Edition

Knowledge of the Faith
- **Objective:** To know and understand basic Catholic teaching about the Incarnate Word Jesus Christ as the way, truth, and life

Prayer
- **Objective:** To recognize and learn how to engage in Catholic forms of personal and communal prayer and ways of deepening one's spiritual life

Catholic Faith Literacy
disciples, Pope, prayer, spirituality

Catholic Social Teaching

To integrate Catholic Social Teaching into your lesson, choose one of the following features: The Dignity of Work and the Rights of Workers, pages 342–343; or Solidarity of the Human Family, pages 344–345.

- Start the Live step of the process by talking about Saint Théodore (Anne-Thérèse Guérin) on page 180. Then move directly to the Catholic Social Teaching feature.
- Or, to expand the lesson, complete page 180, then move to the Catholic Social Teaching feature.
- Return to Chapter 10 for the prayer on page 181.

Music Option

Use the following song to enhance catechetical learning or for prayer.
- "Litany," Day 5, Page 181

Name _____   Date _____

Match each description in Column A with the correct term in Column B.

Column A

    Column B

____ **1.** Official Church teachings on matters of
faith and morals

a. disciples

____ **2.** All the laws of the Church

b. Sacred Scripture

____ **3.** People who learn from and follow the
example of a teacher

c. doctrine

____ **4.** The Old and New Testaments of the Bible

d. Code of Canon Law

Circle the letter of the choice that best completes each sentence.

5. The ____ are the twelve men Jesus chose to be his closest followers and to share in his
work and mission in a special way.

  a. disciples

  b. Apostles

  c. Gospels

  d. followers of John the Baptist

6. Jesus told his disciples to "travel light" because he wanted them to ____.

  a. have total dependence on God the Father to take care of them

  b. get away quickly if there was trouble

  c. find out how hard it is to be poor

  d. go without things

7. The ____ is the community of all baptized people who believe in the Holy Trinity and follow Jesus.

  a. Apostles

  b. Magisterium

  c. Church

  d. Communion of Saints

8. The Church is ____ because her teaching authority comes directly from Jesus and his chosen Apostles.

  a. catholic   **b.** holy   **c.** Papal   **d.** apostolic

Write a response on the lines below.

9. What do you think attracted people to following Jesus? _____

_____

10. How is the Church our guide in all parts of our lives and in everything we do?

_____

_____

Name _____ Date _____

The Chosen Twelve

Refer to the Scripture passages mentioned on pages 174–176 to fill in each blank below. When a line has a number beneath it, transfer that letter to the blank marked with that number at the bottom of the page. When you are finished, the letters that have been transferred to the bottom of the page will spell an important message.

1. __ __ __ __   the   __ __ __ __ __ __ __   was a popular preacher in Jesus' time.
　　　　6　　　　　　　　　　13　　　18

2. Philip invited his friend to meet Jesus by saying   "__ __ __ __   __ __ __   __ __ __."
　　　　　　　　　　　　　　　　　　　　　　　2　11　　　　　　　　　　22

3. Zebedee's sons were also called the   "__ __ __ __   __ __   __ __ __ __ __ __ __."
　　　　　　　　　　　　　　　　　　　24　　　　　　27

4. Thomas was called   __ __ __ __ __ __ __,   which means "the twin."
　　　　　　　　　　20　　　3

5. In the Gospel according to Mark, Matthew is called   __ __ __ __.
　　　　　　　　　　　　　　　　　　8　　21　26

6. Jesus told his disciples not to carry   __ __ __ __ __   or a   __ __ __ __ __ __ __   stick.
　　　　　　　　　　　　　　14　　23　　　　　　10　　7　　　　　19

7. If a town didn't welcome them, they were to shake the dust of that town from their   __ __ __ __ __.
　　　　　　　　　　　　　　　　　　　　　　　　　　　　　　　　　　　4

8. Jesus gave   __ __ __ __ __   the new name,   __ __ __ __ __.
　　　　　　　　　9　　　　　　　　　　　28

9. Don't   __ __ __ __ __ __ __   Jude   __ __ __ __ __ __ __ __   with
　　　　　1　　　5　25　12　　　　　　　　　15

Judas   __ __ __ __ __ __ __ __.
　　16

10. __ __ __ __ __ __ __   called himself "the tax collector."
　　　　17

THE MESSAGE:

__ __ __ __   __ __ __ __ __ __ __ __   __ __ __ __ __ __ __ __
1　2　3　4　　5　6　7　8　9　10　　11　12　　13　14　15　　16　　17　18　7　8

__ __ __ __   __ __ __   __ __ __ __ __.
19　20　21　22　　23　24　25　　7　26　27　28

Disciples in Community

Let Us Pray

Leader: Lord, throughout all ages you have called people to
follow you. May we recognize the work of your Spirit
among us as we strive to follow your example and be
your disciples.

"The Lord is my shepherd;
there is nothing I lack. ...
He guides me along right paths
for the sake of his name." **Psalm 23:1, 3**

All: Jesus, lead us.

Scripture

"If you will give these instructions to the brothers, you will be
a good minister of Christ Jesus, nourished on the words of
the faith and of the sound teaching you have followed. ... Let
no one have contempt for your youth, but set an example for
those who believe, in speech, conduct, love, faith, and purity."
1 Timothy 4:6, 12

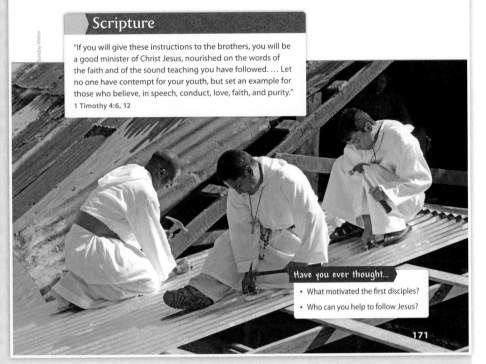

Have you ever thought...
- What motivated the first disciples?
- Who can you help to follow Jesus?

171

Scripture Background

Scripture Reflection Process

Invite the students to be still, close their eyes, and focus on their
breathing. Encourage them to open their minds and hearts to what
God is saying to them.

- Proclaim the Scripture and have the students sit in silence.
- *Ask:* What did you hear God say to you today?
- Allow volunteers to share.

▶ You may play instrumental music to begin the reflection.

Objective
- Reflect on God's personal invitation through Scripture

OPEN _____

♥ Let Us Pray

Invite the students to gather in the prayer space and make the Sign of the Cross. Read aloud the leader prayer. Have the entire class pray the Psalm verses and the group response.

Have the students move out of the prayer space and back to their seats.

Explain that our prayer today challenges us to be a disciple of Jesus.

Say: Jesus, provides the perfect image of what it means to love God and spread the Good News of his love to others. In today's reading, we are called to be an example to others of Jesus' love.

Scripture

Guide the students through the process of Scripture reflection (see the Scripture Background box to the left).

Have you ever thought...

Say: The disciples believed so strongly in Jesus and his message that they responded whole-heartedly to his command to spread the Good News of God's Kingdom to everyone.

- Invite the students to respond to the questions.

DAY 1

Objective

- Indicate prior knowledge of chapter concepts and vocabulary

BUILD

Use this page to assess the students' knowledge related to the chapter content.

Getting Started

Have a volunteer read aloud the opening paragraph.

- *Ask:* What do you know about discipleship?
- Allow the students to respond.

My Priorities

Have the students work alone to complete this activity.

★ Direct them to use this chart as an evaluative tool to uncover areas in their lives that might need more or less of their attention.

- Provide a couple examples from your own experience to prompt the students if they need help getting started.

Getting Started

In this chapter you will reflect on our need for Jesus to lead us and the ways the first disciples responded to him. You will also examine how the Apostles led other disciples, who help us understand what it means to be a disciple today.

The chart below lists different things that take priority in people's lives. In the right hand column, explain how important or unimportant these things are to you.

My Priorities

Physical Appearance	
Family	
Friends	
Faith	
School	
Sports	
Technology	

Optional Activity

Discipleship: A Worthy Challenge *Intrapersonal*

Talk briefly with the group about something you have done in your life that was challenging, but ultimately was very good.

- Tell the students to think about something challenging that they learned to do. Ask a few volunteers to share what they learned and why it was challenging.
- Tell the class that in this chapter they will be reflecting on the worthy challenge of following Jesus in their everyday lives. Suggest that when they accept Jesus' invitation to discipleship, they enter into life's most worthy adventure and challenge!

Invitation to Discipleship Think back to yourself as a second grader having just received an invitation from Jesus. What are you invited to do? Write what Jesus asked of you then, and how you responded.

You're Invited

_____

_____

_____

_____

Today you have received another invitation from Jesus. What is he inviting you to now? What questions do you have for him?

_____

_____

_____

_____

Work with Words

Have the students silently read the list of vocabulary words from the Catholic Faith Words box on page 172.

- *Ask:* What do you know about these words? Which ones have you heard before? How can you connect the words to the chapter title: "Disciples in Community"?
- Invite volunteers to share what they know about the terms with the rest of the class.

CLOSE

ACTIVITY

Explain the activity and give the students time to complete it.

- Brainstorm some ideas as a class, but then have the students work alone to complete the activity.
- Encourage the students to share their questions and comments with a family member.

✓ Teaching Tip

Practicing Empathy

Jesus taught us to love each other in the same way God loves us. This means we must practice empathy. Explain to the students that empathy is the capacity to put ourselves in someone else's shoes—being aware of and sensitive to the thoughts, feelings, needs, and experiences of others. To love one another and work toward the common good, we need to practice empathy.

We are called to proclaim the Good News of God's love to others by what we say and do. We must practice empathy in order to honor our commitment to living as followers of Christ.

DAY 2

Objectives

- Recognize that Saint John the Baptist proclaimed the coming of Christ and led people to Jesus
- Analyze why the first disciples followed Jesus

OPEN

💗 Invite the students to close their eyes and imagine they are with a group of fisherman when Jesus joins the group. Pray "Jesus, lead me." Have the students repeat the prayer three times.

BUILD

A Surprise Invitation

Review this section on John the Baptist with the class.

Tell a Friend

Direct the students to read the text.

- *Ask:* What are some things you could share with others about your faith?
- Point out the Catholic Faith Word and have a volunteer read aloud the definition from page 175.

🔲 Scripture

Ask a volunteer to proclaim John 1:45–46.

- Afterwards, form small groups of four or five and assign each group one of the Scripture passages from the Go to the Source feature.
- Ask each group to discuss the Scripture passage, then share what they learned about whom Jesus called and how he called them.

174 Chapter 10

Jesus blessing children, Carlo De Notaris

A Surprise Invitation

What prompted the first disciples to follow Jesus?

We've probably all known someone who helped us see things differently or to make a commitment. Sometimes that person also leads us to see what matters most in life and to make decisions based on those priorities.

In the time of Jesus, just as today, teachers, politicians, and religious leaders attracted followers. Saint John the Baptist was a preacher whom people followed, but he was preparing the way for the Messiah. When Jesus arrived, John told his followers to follow Jesus. John said, "Now I have seen and testified that he is the Son of God" (John 1:34).

John's followers knew what to expect from him. They must have had to think about leaving the leader they had trusted to follow someone new.

Tell a Friend

Some of John's followers went to see what Jesus was like. After they saw him and heard him speak, they wanted to get to know him better. Many became his **disciples**, and told their friends about Jesus. Jesus asked some to follow him. Other people followed because a friend like Philip told them to come and see Jesus.

> #### 🔲 Scripture
>
> "Philip found Nathanael and told him, 'We have found the one about whom Moses wrote in the law, and also the prophets, Jesus, son of Joseph, from Nazareth.' But Nathanael said to him, 'Can anything good come from Nazareth?' Philip said to him, 'Come and see.'" John 1:45–46
>
> #### 📖 Go to the Source
> Find out more about who Jesus called to follow him and who came to him through the encouragement of a friend, in these passages: John 1:43–51, Luke 8:1–3, Mark 1:16–20.

174 Chapter 10

📖 Scripture Background

Women Disciples

Luke 8:1–3 is included in the Go to the Source text even though Jesus does not explicitly call the women named in this passage. However, we know women accompanied Jesus on his journey to Jerusalem and were witnesses to his Death (see Luke 23:49) and Resurrection (see Luke 24:9–11). We also know that Mary Magdalene was the first proclaimer of the Resurrection in all four Gospels.

The Gospel according to Luke especially emphasizes the importance of women disciples to Jesus. In addition, this Gospel also shows us how much he loved the other members of the marginalized in society during that time—the disabled, sinners, the poor, and children.

Catholic Faith Words

disciples people who learn from and follow the example of a teacher. The disciples of Jesus are those who believe in him, follow his teachings, and put them into practice.

Decisions to Make

Each new disciple already had a family and a job. When Jesus invited them, some people asked if they could have a little time to decide. They wanted to go home and take care of things first. (See Luke 9:61–62.) But Jesus was looking for people who had been looking for his coming and were ready and waiting to go with him. Some people were ready.

Jesus was a vibrant, wise speaker who spoke with authority like only God could do. Some of the things Jesus said confused people. His preaching both challenged and gave hope. Some of the things he did surprised and astounded others. His healing and forgiving of sin brought life and raised questions about his authority. But one thing is certain: people were talking about Jesus in all the towns and villages in the area.

Wouldn't you want to meet a man who was changing people's lives, making things right, and giving people what they desperately needed? Jesus offered the people God's love and compassion, a purpose for living, and hope for renewed life with him and others.

> When have you had to make a choice that meant changing the way you acted or thought about someone or something?

> What are some things about Jesus that surprise or challenge you?

NAME

Imagine you are living in the time of Jesus. Name three reasons why Jesus would choose you to follow him. What would you do if he invited you?

_____
_____
_____
_____
_____
_____
_____
_____

Disciples in Community **175**

Decisions to Make

Read aloud this section.

- As you read, have the students highlight some of the things Jesus was doing that interested people enough to follow him.

- Share a time in your own life when you had to make a choice that required you to change your thinking or actions.

Have the students discuss the closing questions with a classmate.

CLOSE _____

ACTIVITY

Have the students read the instructions to themselves.

- Give them time to list three reasons that Jesus might choose them.

- Invite volunteers to share their responses.

Quick Review Saint John the Baptist prepared the way and led his followers to the Messiah, Jesus Christ. The Apostles chose to follow Jesus because of his exciting and challenging message.

✓ Teaching Tip

Sharing Your Call

Sharing an example from your own life is very appropriate at this point. You have answered a call from Jesus to be a teacher; you were created by God to help children learn.

- Discuss what abilities God blessed you with that helped you to become a teacher.

- Explain how being a teacher is rewarding and how you are able to do God's work in this role.

- The point of telling something about your own life is to offer students a concrete example from someone who might be a role model for them.

DAY 3

Objectives

- Describe the importance of the Apostles in continuing Jesus' ministry

- Discover sources that contain the official teachings of the Church

OPEN

♥ Pray with the students the Apostles' Creed from page 367.

BUILD

A Community of Believers

Invite the students to silently read this section.

- *Ask:* Why did Jesus want his disciples to "travel light"? He wanted them to trust God the Father to take care of them.

We Receive Guidance

Read aloud this section.

- Explain that Jesus trusted his Apostles to teach everyone what he taught them, and to spread the Good News of his love that restored our relationship with God the Father.

📘 Go to the Source

Organize the students into three groups and assign each group one of the Gospel references.

- Ask each group to list the names of the Apostles in their Gospel.

- Invite the students to share their findings and to note the differences between the Gospels as they arise.

A Community of Believers

How did the Apostles and their successors lead?

After the disciples had been with him awhile, Jesus gave the Twelve a mission, sending them out two by two. We read in Mark 6:7–13 that they were to announce the coming of the Kingdom of God and were even given the authority to cure some of the sick people they met as they traveled. We also read in Mark 6:7–13 that the Twelve disciples had some important instructions from Jesus. He told them:

- bring no money or food
- do not pack a bag or bring extra clothes
- find a home to stay where the people welcome you
- leave a town that does not welcome you, and shake the dust of that town from your shoes

Jesus wanted his disciples to have total dependence upon God the Father to take care of them. He wanted them to travel light.

> What do you think this message means for us today?

We Receive Guidance

We know Jesus had many followers. But Jesus chose twelve men to be his **Apostles** and to share in his work and mission in a special way. The Twelve were Jesus' closest followers. The Apostles continued Jesus' ministry after his Ascension to Heaven.

The night before he died, Jesus said to the Apostles at the Last Supper: "The Advocate, the holy Spirit that the Father will send in my name—he will teach you everything and remind you of all that [I] told you" (John 14:26).

Since then and to this day the **Church** has been built on the faith and foundation of the Apostles. This is what we mean when

📘 **Go to the Source**
You can find the names of the Twelve Apostles in Matthew 10:1–4, Mark 3:13–19, and Luke 6:12–16. For more information, see page 364 in your book.

Optional Activity

Activity Master 10: The Chosen Twelve

Distribute copies of the activity found on teacher page 171G.

- This activity will help the students recall the chapter and its message.

- Direct the students to use the information from the Scripture passages and text on pages 174–176 to help them fill in the blanks in this puzzle.

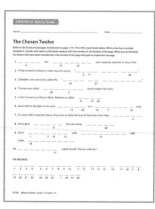

we say the Church is apostolic. One of the four Marks of the Church—the essential characteristics that distinguish Christ's Church and her mission—is that she is **apostolic**.

The work the Apostles began has been continued down through the ages. The teachings they received from Jesus and his Holy Spirit have been handed on through them to us in the Church today.

How do we know what the Church teaches? How does she hand down the teachings of Christ to everyone? Here is a list of places where Church teaching is found, including **doctrine**, encyclicals and other documents of the Church.

Catholic Faith Words

Apostles the twelve men Jesus chose to be his closest followers and to share in his work and mission in a special way

Church the community of all baptized people who believe in the Holy Trinity and follow Jesus. The word is often used for the Catholic Church because we trace our origins back to the Apostles.

apostolic a Mark of the Church. The Church is apostolic because her teaching authority comes directly from Jesus and his chosen Apostles, handed down through the bishops of the Church, who are direct successors of the Apostles.

doctrine official Church teachings on matters of faith and morals. Catholics are obliged to believe these truths.

MATCH

Match the source of Church teachings with its description.

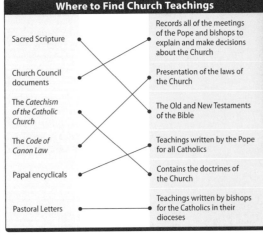

Where to Find Church Teachings

Sacred Scripture	Records all of the meetings of the Pope and bishops to explain and make decisions about the Church
Church Council documents	Presentation of the laws of the Church
The *Catechism of the Catholic Church*	The Old and New Testaments of the Bible
The *Code of Canon Law*	Teachings written by the Pope for all Catholics
Papal encyclicals	Contains the doctrines of the Church
Pastoral Letters	Teachings written by bishops for the Catholics in their dioceses

Archbishop Timothy Dolan speaks at a remembrance ceremony for policemen killed in the attacks of September 11, 2001.

Disciples in Community **177**

✓ Teaching Tip

The Church Teachings and Young People

Giving young people the opportunity to discover and familiarize themselves with the Church's teachings will provide them with a resource they can use for life.

- Bring in copies of some or all of the sources of Church teachings listed in the graphic organizer on page 177.

- Allow the students to look through these materials.

📶 Give the students an opportunity to look through the Vatican website at **www.vatican.va** to locate some of the sources.

We Receive Guidance,

continued

Finish reading this section.

- Discuss the photo on this page.

- *Ask:* How does this image connect to the reading?

Work with Words

Invite the students to circle all four vocabulary terms in the text on pages 176 and 177.

- See if they can define or explain the words by the way they are used on these pages.

- As the students share what they believe each word means, ask a volunteer to follow each description with the definition from the Catholic Faith Words box.

CLOSE _____

ACTIVITY

Have the students work on their own to match each source of Church teachings with its description.

- Review the correct answers as a class.

Quick Review Jesus taught the Twelve Apostles what he wanted the Church to know so they would pass it on. The teachings of the Catholic Church today are still the teachings that Jesus first gave to his Apostles. We can use Church teachings to guide our lives.

DAY 4

Objectives

- Identify the characteristics of a disciple in the world today
- Recall the Church's rich and varied tradition of prayer

OPEN _____

💗 Have the students stand and pray the Beatitudes from page 374. Explain that the Beatitudes guide us in being good disciples.

Read aloud the opening question. Tell the students they will learn the answer in today's lesson.

BUILD _____

Disciples in the Church Today

Have a volunteer read aloud this section.

- Emphasize the last sentence of the second paragraph.
- Direct the students to underline the things in the paragraph that we can do together.
- Ask them to offer more examples of their own.

📖 Scripture

Proclaim John 8:12.

A Praying Community

Direct the students to scan the first paragraph of this section to find and highlight the list of the five types of prayers Christians pray (blessing, petition, intercession, thanksgiving, or praise) and to circle the entire second paragraph because it is so important.

Disciples in the Church Today

What does it mean to be a disciple in the Church right here and now?

We have the Church to guide us in all parts of our lives and in everything we do. The Church shows us how to live as Jesus lived. His life and his teachings are light showing us the way to Heaven.

📖 Scripture

Jesus spoke to them again, saying, "I am the light of the world. Whoever follows me will not walk in darkness, but will have the light of life." John 8:12

We never have to find our way through life alone. In the Church, we belong to a family of faith, a community of disciples who are following Jesus together. We turn to other Church members for support, guidance, and encouragement. We ask God's forgiveness through the Church. We join with others to help people who are in need. Together we can feed the hungry, shelter the homeless, clothe the naked, visit the sick, and try to change laws and policies that do not protect life and promote human dignity. No one could do as much alone as we can all do together.

A Praying Community

The Holy Spirit also teaches us to pray as disciples of Jesus. We pray alone, and we pray together with the Church in communal prayer and worship. Whether we are praying prayers of blessing, petition, intercession, thanksgiving, or praise and adoration, it is the Holy Spirit who inspires us and calls us to pray.

The most important way we pray together is the celebration of the Eucharist. We are worshipping God together and we are receiving the Body and Blood of Christ.

As we grow in our faith, we learn new ways of prayer. Different ways of praying and living as a disciple, known as spiritualities, have developed over the centuries. In our two thousand years as a Church, many great Saints have guided others in ways of prayer.

There are several "schools" of prayer and Christian spirituality. They are all part of the Church's living Tradition of prayer, and although they are very different, they all come from the Holy Spirit.

When we come together for Mass, we are praying the Church's central and most important prayer.

© Our Sunday Visitor

ℹ️ Teacher Background

Help with Prayer

In prayer we raise our minds and hearts to God. There are many forms of prayer, including blessing and adoration, petition for our own needs, intercession for the needs of others, and praise and thanksgiving. By experiencing and practicing various forms of prayer, we can learn new things about ourselves and discover other forms of spirituality that deepen our intimacy with God. Prayer can become a greater source of comfort, hope, guidance, and growth as we learn to overcome distractions.

What helps you pray? Music? Pictures or images? Nature? Pass these ideas on to your students.

Schools of Prayer

○ **Spiritual direction:** learning alone from a guide

○ **Prayer groups:** learning to pray with others; Church ministers leading and teaching liturgical prayer

○ **Catechesis:** learning about prayer through classes and ministry involvement; consecrated religious teaching contemplative (wordless) prayer

 Place a check mark next to the "schools" of prayer you have already experienced. Name someone who taught you to pray in this way.

IDENTIFY

Look at the "schools" of prayer listed. Choose one of the schools you have not yet experienced, then identify some people you think would be able to teach you how to pray in these ways, and how they could do so.

_____

_____

_____

_____

_____

_____

_____

_____

IN SUMMARY   Catholics Believe

We are disciples of Christ in his Church, following his example by trusting in the Father, learning, praying, and reaching out to others.

- Each follower of Christ receives a personal call from him and must choose whether or not to follow Christ.

- Just as Jesus sent the first disciples out, he wants us to be a sign of the Kingdom of God, and to follow Church teachings.

- The Holy Spirit uses many different spiritualties and "schools" of prayer to teach us how to pray.

Disciples in Community   **179**

Liturgy Link

Prayer of the Faithful

The Prayer of the Faithful is recited at every Mass and follows the homily and the recitation of the Creed by the entire community. The sequence of the Prayer of the Faithful may include praying for the Church, for the leadership of the Church, for civil authorities, for the needs of others (often mentioning current events), for the sick and the deceased of a parish community, and for the salvation of the world.

Invite young people to listen carefully to the Prayer of the Faithful at Mass on Sunday. Ask them to take note of the pattern of prayers at their parish.

A Praying Community,
continued

Have the students silently read the rest of this section on page 178.

Schools of Prayer

Review the content of the chart with the class.

★ Direct the students to place a checkmark next to the "schools" of prayer they have already experienced.

- Invite them to share the name of someone who taught them how to pray in one of these ways.

CLOSE_____

ACTIVITY

Ask the students to read the instructions and brainstorm some responses.

- Discuss their responses as class.

In Summary

Read aloud the opening sentence.

- Have the students read over the three bullet points as if they were teachers.

- Direct them to make up one test question for each bullet point.

- Have the students exchange their questions with a classmate.

- See if they can answer the other student's question.

DAY 5

Objectives

- Examine contemplative prayer
- Explore the faith life of Saint Théodore (Anne-Thérèse Guérin)
- Offer the Litany of the Saints prayer

OPEN

❤️ Have the students stand and pray together the Invite Psalm from page 171.

BUILD

Our Catholic Life

Ask the students to silently read the Our Catholic Life content.

- Have them write their response to the question about contemplative prayer versus other types of prayer.
- Allow volunteers to share their thoughts.

People of Faith

Explain to the students that Saint Théodore had a strong faith that did not waiver due to hardships.

- Have a student read aloud the People of Faith paragraph.
- Review with the class the content found in the People of Faith Background box.
- Invite the students to discuss hardships they have seen others rise above.
- Encourage the students who choose to research Saint Théodore from home to bring back the information they find and share it with the class.

Our Catholic Life

Prayer connects us with God's love and his plan for us. You may already know about finding a place to pray so you can better speak to and listen to God, but have you thought about finding a quiet prayer space inside yourself? In this chapter, you read about **schools of prayer** and considered ones you have and have not experienced. Contemplative prayer is a special form that establishes a deep connection with God. It is intense and silent, and grows through love and adoration of God's goodness. Choose a time to explore this form of prayer and listen for what God has to tell you.

> How is the experience of contemplative prayer different from other types of prayer?

People of Faith

Saint Théodore (Anne-Thérèse Guérin), 1798–1856

After Anne-Thérèse Guérin took her final vows to become a nun, she and other sisters established the Academy of St. Mary-of-the-Woods at Terre Haute, Indiana, the first Catholic women's liberal arts college in the United States. During her nearly sixteen years of ministry in Indiana, Mother Théodore encountered countless hardships, but her faith did not waver. She told the sisters, "With Jesus, what shall we have to fear?" Mother Théodore was canonized by Pope Benedict XVI in 2006. The Church celebrates her feast day on **October 3**.

📶 For more, go to **aliveinchrist.osv.com**

LIST

Write down the name of someone you personally know who is a true follower of Jesus. Why did you think of this person? List the qualities of a disciple that you see in this person.

Name

_____

_____

Qualities

_____

_____

_____

_____

_____

_____

180 Chapter 10

People of Faith Background

Saint Théodore

Share the following with the class:

- Mother Théodore committed her life to teaching, healing, and caring for the needy. She is an excellent example of someone who, despite many challenges, answered God's call and accepted her mission.
- In addition to founding the first Catholic liberal arts college for women in the United States, Théodore also founded eleven other schools, two orphanages, and gave free medicine to those in need.

📶 Encourage the students to go to **aliveinchrist.osv.com** at home to learn more about Saint Théodore.

🩷 Litany of the Saints

Leader: Let us take time to pray to the Saints for their guidance.
Begin with the Sign of the Cross.
Saint Thérèse of Lisieux, you relied on God, not possessions, and knew the comforting embrace of God.

All: Saint Thérèse, pray for us.

Leader: Saint Elizabeth Ann Seton, you suffered many losses and felt the comforting embrace of God.

All: Saint Elizabeth Ann, pray for us.

Leader: Saint Francis de Sales, you treated yourself and others with patience and gentleness.

All: Saint Francis, pray for us.

Leader: Saint Thomas of Villanova, you showed freedom to many slaves and care for many orphans.

All: Saint Thomas, pray for us.

Leader: Saint Genevieve, you showed mercy to prisoners and others in need.

All: Saint Genevieve, pray for us.

Leader: Saint Clare of Assisi, you lived a simple and humble life.

All: Saint Clare, pray for us.

Leader: Saint Francis of Assisi, you sought peace during the Crusades.

All: Saint Francis, pray for us.

Leader: Saint Paul Miki, you preached the Word of God and died on a cross.

All: Saint Paul, pray for us.

Leader: In this great community of the Saints, we find strength and inspiration to seek and to do God's will.

All: Amen.

▶ *Sing or play "Litany"*

🛜 Go to **aliveinchrist.osv.com** for an interactive review.

Ⓐ Work with Words Circle the letter of the choice that best completes the sentence.

1. The ___ continued Jesus' ministry after his Ascension to Heaven.
　a. Apostles
　b. Samaritans
　c. Jews
　d. Pharisees

2. ___ is the official teaching of the Church that all Catholics are obliged to believe.
　a. Papal Encyclicals
　b. Catechism
　c. Scriptures
　d. Doctrine

3. Ways of praying and living as a disciple are called ___.
　a. spiritualities
　b. church teachings
　c. doctrines
　d. Papal law

4. The ___ are the essential characteristics that distinguish Christ's Church and her mission.
　a. Prayers of the Church
　b. Precepts of the Church
　c. Marks of the Church
　d. Laws of the Church

Ⓑ Check Understanding Complete each sentence with the correct terms from the Word Bank.

Apostles	Pentecost
Old Testament	Last Supper
Church	disciples
Saint John the Baptist	sacramental seal
	apostolic

5. ___Saint John the Baptist___ prepared for the coming of the Messiah.

6. The ___Church___ is the community of the baptized who believe in the Holy Trinity and follow Jesus.

7. Jesus called twelve men to be his ___Apostles___ and to share in his mission and work in a special way.

8. The Church is ___apostolic___ because her teaching authority comes directly from Jesus and his chosen Apostles and is handed down through the bishops of the Church, who are direct successors of the Apostles.

9. Jesus promised the Holy Spirit to the Apostles at the ___Last Supper___.

10. The ___disciples___ of Jesus are those who believe in him, follow his teachings, and put them into practice.

Ⓒ Make Connections On a separate sheet of paper, write a one-paragraph response to the question. How is celebrating the Eucharist the most important way we pray?

Have the students read the directions and work on the activity independently.

CLOSE

Litany of the Saints

🩷 Appoint one student to serve as the leader and have the rest of the students respond as a group.

Give the students a few minutes to read over the passages.

Call the class to prayer by reading the first leader line yourself.

Have the student leader begin with the section on Saint Thérèse of Lisieux.

Follow the order of prayer on the student page.

▶ Conclude by inviting the students to sing or reflect on the song "Litany," downloaded from **aliveinchrist.osv.com**.

CHAPTER REVIEW

Review the instructions for each section and have the students complete the review.

🛜 Go to **aliveinchrist.osv.com** to prepare customized and downloadable assessments, send eAssessments, and assign interactive reviews.

Christ Present Among Us

KEY CONCEPT

The Church is both visible and spiritual, made up of people with many gifts and talents who are united by Christ in the Holy Spirit to continue Christ's mission in the world.

DOCTRINAL CONTENT

- The Church is both visible and spiritual. We call the spiritual part the Mystical Body of Christ. (CCC, 771, 779)

- The Church is the Body of Christ; she is one because she acknowledges one Lord, confesses one faith, and is born of one Baptism. (CCC, 813–816, 866)

- Each individual member is united with all members as part of Christ's Body. When members of the Church live in communion with the Holy Spirit and with one another, harmony results. (CCC, 341, 752)

- The Church needs the diverse gifts of all members to be a sign of God's Kingdom here on Earth. (CCC, 791, 814)

TASKS OF CATECHESIS

Helping children grow in a faith that is "known, celebrated, lived, and expressed in prayer" (NDC, 20).

This chapter focuses on the following tasks of catechesis:

- Education for Community Life
- Missionary Initiation

Teacher Background

> 📖 As a body is one though it has many parts, and all the parts of the body, though many, are one body, so also Christ. For in one Spirit we were all baptized into one body … as it is, God placed the parts, each one of them, in the body as he intended.
> 1 Corinthians 12:12–13, 18
>
> **> Reflect** What does being a member of the Body of Christ require of you?

Belonging to a group—any group—is both a blessing and a challenge. The blessing part comes in the support and companionship of the community, the value of shared wisdom, and the strength in facing adversity together. The challenge comes with differences of opinion and in not always being able to do what you would like to do as an individual. Whether the group in question is your family, your nation, or your church, this has always been a reality.

The Church is the Mystical Body of Christ to which we belong. We discover our true selves as individuals within our communities. Each of us is created for union with God, our one true source of happiness. The Church is the path Jesus has given us in order to fulfill that sacred destiny.

For Catholics, community is central to our understanding of who God is and who we are in relationship to him. In a sense, there is no such thing as a solitary Catholic because even when we are alone, we are still in solidarity with the Church. Catholicism has a communal core to it: the Holy Trinity, our sacramental theology, and our understanding of salvation. To be Catholic is to experience God through the Christian community and for the community to experience God through each individual.

> **> Reflect** How has your membership in the Church been both a challenge and a source of blessing?

Teacher's Prayer

 God our Father, you have blessed me with wonderful traveling companions by calling me to be a member of your Church. Help me to be a faithful companion for those I serve in the Christian community. I ask this in Jesus' name. Amen.

How Seventh Graders Understand Chapter Topics

Belonging to groups is usually very important for students this age. The groups to which they belong help them form their identities. Feeling like one doesn't belong can be devastating for seventh graders. They need to see that there is a place for everyone, including them, in God's Church.

Teaching Tip: Lead a discussion on the communities in the lives of your students. Have them list some of these communities, such as family, church, school, sports teams, social groups, and so on. For each group, reflect on these questions: What are the benefits of this group? What are the sacrifices that you make in order to belong? How would your life be different if you didn't belong to the group?

Sharing the Message with Seventh Graders

- Belonging to a peer group is very important, but some young people may see their membership as a matter of conformity rather than a matter of contributing something new and distinct.
- Most people want friends and groups that will accept them without condition and will be there for them in tough times. Seventh graders are no exception.
- The Church is the beginning of the Kingdom of God here on Earth. It is important that we utilize the ministry of catechesis to instill in young people a deep appreciation of the Christian community to which they belong.

Chapter 11 Planner

Objectives	Open

DAY 1—Invite/Preview, Pages 183–185

- Reflect on God's personal invitation through Scripture
- Indicate prior knowledge of chapter concepts and vocabulary

○ **Psalm 133:1** Pray the opening prayer.

▨ **1 Corinthians 12:12–18** Proclaim "One Body, Many Parts." Guide the students through the process of Scripture reflection.
- Discuss Have You Ever Thought questions.

DAY 2—Discover, Pages 186–187

- Explore the visible and spiritual aspects of the Church
- Examine how the Church is the Body of Christ

○ Pray the **New Commandment**, page 373.
- Point out the lesson focus.

DAY 3—Discover, Pages 188–189

- Recognize that the Church is one because she acknowledges one Lord, confesses one faith, and is born of one Baptism
- Discover the harmony that results as members of the Church live in communion with the Holy Spirit and one another

○ Pray the **Prayer to the Holy Spirit**, page 384.
- Discuss the opening question.

DAY 4—Discover, Pages 190–191

- Compare the diversity of gifts that allow the Church to help God manifest his Kingdom

○ Pray a prayer of thanksgiving.

DAY 5—Live, Pages 192–193

- Learn ways we can use our personal gifts to serve others and the Church
- Explore the faith life of Saint John Bosco
- Offer the prayer celebrating the Word of God

○ Pray the **Act of Hope**, page 387.

REVIEW AND ASSESSMENT

Chapter Review, page 194
Chapter Test, page 183F

📶 **aliveinchrist.osv.com** Customize and Download Assessments, Email Links to eAssessments, Interactive Student Reviews

Build	Close	Materials & Resources
• Present lesson highlights. • Preview **Catholic Faith Words**. ★ List gifts and talents that can be used to serve the Church.	• *Activity* Write about gifts and talents that can be used to meet the needs of others. • *Optional Activity* Group Analysis (Activity Master 11)	☐ pencils or pens ☐ Activity Master 11 (Page 183G)
• **Catholic Faith Words** Mystical Body of Christ, hierarchy • Examine how the Church is both visible and spiritual. 📖 Read and reflect on Acts 9:1–5 and 1 Corinthians 12:12–31.	• *Activity* Discuss the visible and spiritual aspects of the Church. • Conclude with a review of key concepts and objectives.	☐ pencils or pens ☐ Bibles ☐ board or chart paper
• **Catholic Faith Words** one • Explain that the Church is made up of many unique members, united as one Body of Christ. 📖 Read John 15:4–5.	• *Activity* List differences and similarities in Catholics from different cultures and countries. • Conclude with a review of key concepts and objectives.	☐ pencils or pens
• Discuss how we can use our unique gifts to serve the Church. • Explain that we need to reach out to help those in need. 📖 Read Matthew 25:35–36.	• *Activity* List ways that Church members use their gifts to be a sign of God's Kingdom. • Review the In Summary statements.	☐ pencils or pens ☐ parish bulletins
• Discuss the question in the Our Catholic Life section. • Learn about Saint John Bosco. • *Activity* Make a list of hymns that mention the Body of Christ.	• Divide the class into three groups. • Follow the order of prayer. ▶ Sing or reflect on the closing song.	☐ pencils or pens ☐ hymnbooks 🛜 "Alive in One Spirit"

Chapter Connections

FORMING CATHOLIC IDENTITY ACROSS THE CURRICULUM

To integrate the Catholic faith in all aspects of curriculum, this chapter's objectives can be reinforced and applied in the instruction of other disciplines.

Go to **aliveinchrist.osv.com** for cross-curricular activities and projects linked to the doctrinal content discussed in this unit. Activities are available from among the following knowledge categories and content areas:

Language Arts

- Integration of Knowledge
- Literacy
- Speaking and Listening
- Writing Skills

Math

- Algebraic Thinking
- Geometry
- Measurement and Data
- Numbers and Operations

Science

- Earth Science
- Life Science
- Physical Science
- Technology

Social Studies

- Civics
- Economics
- Geography
- History

NCEA IFG: ACRE Edition

Communal Life

- **Objectives:** To know the origin, mission, structure, and communal nature of the Church; to know the rights and responsibilities of the Christian faithful

Missionary Spirit

- **Objectives:** To recognize the centrality of evangelization as the Church's mission and identity embodied in vocation and service; to be aware of how cultures are transformed by the Gospel

Catholic Faith Literacy

Catholic Social Teaching, Church, hierarchy

Catholic Social Teaching

To integrate Catholic Social Teaching into your lesson, choose one of the following features: Call to Family, Community, and Participation, pages 336–337; or Solidarity of the Human Family, pages 344–345.

- Start the Live step of the process by talking about Saint John Bosco on page 192. Then move directly to the Catholic Social Teaching feature.
- Or, to expand the lesson, complete page 192, then move to the Catholic Social Teaching feature.
- Return to Chapter 11 for the prayer on page 193.

Music Option

Use the following song to enhance catechetical learning or for prayer.

- "Alive in One Spirit," Day 5, Page 193

Name _____   Date _____

Circle the letter of the choice that best completes each sentence.

1. The Church is ____ because the power of the Holy Spirit unites all her members through one faith and one Baptism.

   a. apostolic

   b. communal

   c. one

   d. catholic

2. The organization of the Church into different levels of leadership and membership is the ____.

   a. hierarchy

   b. vine and the branches

   c. Mystical Body of Christ

   d. Communion of Saints

3. In the Beatitudes, Jesus asks us to recognize his presence in ____.

   a. our parish priest

   b. the Church hierarchy

   c. people who are poor or persecuted

   d. the prayer of great Saints

4. Saul (Paul) became a believer and wrote that the Church is ____.

   a. always going to be persecuted

   b. the Body of Christ

   c. people in a building

   d. sad that Jesus died

Complete each sentence with the correct terms.

5. Because of the different _____ of her members, the Church is able to help build God's Kingdom in many ways and places.

6. The _____ is the Church, united to Christ and one another through the Holy Spirit, forming one holy people with Christ as her head.

7. Acts that meet people's physical needs are the _____.

8. A word that means a "gathering" or an "assembly" is _____.

Write a response on the lines below.

9. Why do we need both the physical and spiritual parts of the Church?

   _____

   _____

   _____

10. How do you think you can make a difference in the Church? Why is each member important?

   _____

   _____

Name _____   Date _____

Group Analysis

Name of Group: _____

_____

_____

_____

Purpose of Group: _____

_____

_____

_____

Why I Belong: _____

_____

_____

_____

What I Get from the Group: _____

_____

_____

_____

What I Give to the Group: _____

_____

_____

_____

Christ Present Among Us

💙 Let Us Pray

Leader: O God of every good gift, help us to love your people by sharing our gifts with each other.

> "How good and how pleasant it is,
>   when brothers dwell together as one!" Psalm 133:1

All: Lord, you are the God of all unity.

📖 Scripture

"As a body is one though it has many parts, and all the parts of the body, though many, are one body, so also Christ. For in one Spirit we were all baptized into one body, whether Jews or Greeks, slaves or free persons, and we were all given to drink of one Spirit.

Now the body is not a single part, but many. If a foot should say, 'Because I am not a hand I do not belong to the body,' it does not for this reason belong any less to the body. Or if an ear should say, 'Because I am not an eye I do not belong to the body,' it does not for this reason belong any less to the body. If the whole body were an eye, where would the hearing be? If the whole body were hearing, where would the sense of smell be? But as it is, God placed the parts, each one of them, in the body as he intended."

1 Corinthians 12:12–18

© Our Sunday Visitor

Have you ever thought...

- What does being part of the Body of Christ require?
- How do people's individual gifts and talents contribute to the Church?

183

📖 Scripture Background

Scripture Reflection Process

Invite the students to be still, close their eyes, and focus on their breathing. Encourage them to open their minds and hearts to what God is saying to them.

- Proclaim the Scripture and have the students sit in silence.
- *Ask:* What did you hear God say to you today?
- Allow volunteers to share.

▶ You may play instrumental music to begin the reflection.

Objective

- Reflect on God's personal invitation through Scripture

OPEN _____

💙 Let Us Pray

Choose one of the students to be the Leader. Have the class gather in the prayer space and make the Sign of the Cross. Ask the Leader to proclaim the opening prayer and Psalm verse, and lead the class in the response.

Have the students move out of the prayer space and back to their seats.

Remind them that the Church has many members, but we are one Body in Christ.

Say: Let's listen to God's Word and see how our individual gifts and talents contribute to the Body of Christ.

📖 Scripture

Guide the students through the process of Scripture reflection (see the Scripture Background box below).

Have you ever thought…

Say: Every individual of the Church has unique gifts and talents given by the Holy Spirit that help them to work together united as the Body of Christ to love others in his name.

- Invite the students to respond to the questions.

Christ Present Among Us   **183**

DAY 1

Objective

• Indicate prior knowledge of chapter concepts and vocabulary

BUILD _____

Use this page to assess the students' knowledge related to the chapter content.

Getting Started

Read aloud the paragraph.

• *Say:* Think of someone in your parish who shares his or her gifts and talents.

• *Ask:* Why do you think this person shares his or her gifts with the Church?

• Allow the students to respond.

Gifts and Talents

★ Invite the students to name different gifts and talents needed in the Church to help us continue Jesus' work.

• After they've had time to come up with some ideas, encourage them to share their responses with the class.

Getting Started

In this chapter you will gain a deeper understanding of the Church as the Body of Christ, made up of a diversity of members united by the Holy Spirit. You will also consider how individuals' gifts and talents contribute to the whole Church.

Catholic Faith Words

• Mystical Body of Christ
• hierarchy
• one, as a Mark of the Church

In the web below, name different gifts and talents our Church needs in order to continue Jesus' work.

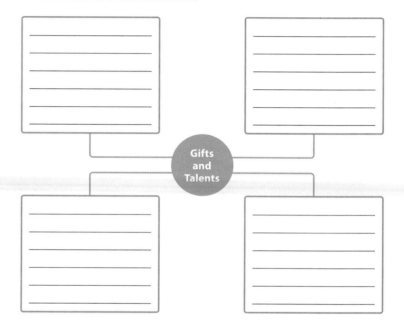

Gifts and Talents

184   Chapter 11

Optional Activity

Activity Master 11: Group Analysis

Distribute copies of the activity found on teacher page 183G.

• Instruct the students to think of three groups to which they belong.

• Have them complete the chart to "analyze" those groups and their participation in them.

• Provide an opportunity for group discussion on what the charts reveal.

DESCRIBE

Needs and Gifts What are three gifts or talents you have? Write about them on the lines below. Then describe how you can use one of your gifts to help meet the needs of another person—such as a family member, friend, classmate, or neighbor—or to help your parish or school.

· _____
   _____
   _____
   _____

· _____
   _____
   _____
   _____

· _____
   _____
   _____
   _____

Christ Present Among Us **185**

Work with Words

Point out the Catholic Faith Words box at the top of page 184.

- Have a volunteer read aloud the words.

- *Ask:* Have you heard any of these words before? Where? What do they mean to you?

- Allow the students to respond.

CLOSE

ACTIVITY

Read the activity instructions to the class. Provide an example of how gifts we have can match the needs of others.

- Give the students time to complete the activity.

- Invite volunteers to share how they can use their gifts in the parish or school.

Teaching Tip

The Need to Belong

In this chapter, your students will be learning about how they belong to the Church, the Body of Christ. Studies of early adolescents tell us that group membership is a high priority with them.

God can use the teen's need to belong to help bring him or her into relationship with the Christian community. Even though they are required to be in class, creating an environment of real hospitality that is welcoming and affirming allows young people to become comfortable. As trust develops through mutual respect and the perception that they are truly being listened to, the students will experience an authentic communal life.

DAY 2

Objectives

- Explore the visible and spiritual aspects of the Church
- Examine how the Church is the Body of Christ

OPEN

Ask the students to stand and reflect on the unity of the Body of Christ. Pray together the New Commandment from page 373.

Tell the students that unity in the Church is the focus of this lesson.

BUILD

The Church Is the Body of Christ

Read aloud the text.

- Ask the students to reflect on why they chose the groups to which they belong.
- This would be a good time to review their answers on Activity Master 11 (see page 184).

Visible and Spiritual

Have the students silently read the text and underline the topic sentence in each paragraph.

- *Ask:* What is the main thing that you learned from this section?
- Emphasize the importance of both the visible and spiritual aspects of the Church.
- Discuss the questions at the end of this section.

© Our Sunday Visitor

The Church Is the Body of Christ

How are all the different members of the Church united in one Body?

People gather into groups for many other reasons, but friendship is often the result. It could be that a group forms because there is a job that needs to be done. Sometimes a group forms because of common interests or problems. Some groups become known and visible to others.

Visible and Spiritual

Like Jesus, the Church he founded—our Catholic Church—is both human and divine. The Church is both visible and spiritual. For Jesus told us, "For where two or three are gathered together in my name, there I am in the midst of them" (Matthew 18:20).

Visible The word *church* means a "gathering" or an "assembly." Jesus has gathered all who believe in him into a visible group with leaders and members. In our visible gathering as the Church we are the People of God.

Spiritual In Christ we become more than just a visible assembly of people. In the Eucharist Jesus feeds us his own Body, and we become his Body. As a spiritual group, the Church is called the **Mystical Body of Christ**, for Christ is present among us, and through the Church, people come in contact with Christ.

The Church brings us in touch with the sacred, but she is made up of human beings, with all our imperfections and potential.

It is easier to understand the visible part of the Church. You can see how people gather in buildings for worship, for education, and for service. And you can see how the Church is organized into a **hierarchy**, with levels of leadership and membership.

However, the visible part of the Church is not enough. Without the spiritual part, the Church would be like any other organization. Our spiritual part is Christ's presence among us through the power of the Holy Spirit.

> When are some times people gather together in Jesus' name?

> How do you think Jesus makes his presence known among them?

Catholic Faith Words

Mystical Body of Christ a name for the Church, whose baptized members are all united to Christ and one another through the Holy Spirit, forming one holy people with Christ as her head

hierarchy the organization of the Church into different levels of leadership and membership

186 Chapter 11

Scripture Background

Proclaiming the Word of God

Repeating and/or displaying short passages from the Bible allows God's Word to take root in the hearts of your students. Matthew 18:20 is a powerful promise from Jesus. Just prior to this passage, Jesus is talking about the need to bring an accused brother before the whole assembly of the Temple where God would hear the prayers of the large group. Jesus goes on to say that even the smallest group—two people—gathered in the name of Jesus, is equally important. Saying, "As we gather for prayer let us remember that Jesus promised, 'Whenever two or three are gathered…'" is a powerful example of rooting the Word in the students' hearts.

One in Christ

Jesus died, but he rose again to new life. Now, through the Holy Spirit, and through his actions in the Eucharist and the other Sacraments, Jesus establishes the Church as his own Body. Christ is the Head of this Body. The Church lives from him, in him, and for him; Christ lives with and in the Church. Here is how Saint Paul, who was also called "Saul," found out that Jesus considers the Church his Body.

Scripture

"Now Saul, still breathing murderous threats against the disciples of the Lord . . . on his journey . . . a light from the sky suddenly flashed around him. He fell to the ground and heard a voice saying to him, 'Saul, Saul, why are you persecuting me?' He asked, 'Who are you, sir?' The reply came, 'I am Jesus, whom you are persecuting.'"
Acts 9:1–5

Go to the Source
Read 1 Corinthians 12:12–31. What is most comforting to you in this passage? Most challenging?

Paul realized that he was persecuting Jesus himself by persecuting the Church. In letters he wrote to various groups of early Christians in Ephesus, Rome, Corinth, and Colossae, Saint Paul mentions often that we (the Church) are "One in Christ," or that we are "His Body": "For as in one body we have many parts, and all the parts do not have the same function, so we, though many, are one body in Christ" (Romans 12:4–5).

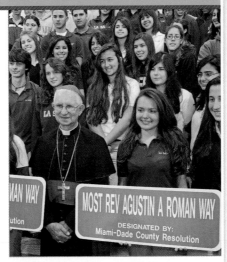

Students from LaSalle Catholic High School in Miami celebrate with the late Archbishop Agustin Roman at his street naming ceremony in 2011.

EXPLAIN

Give some examples of how the Church is both visible and spiritual. Then in small groups make a list of how the Church is visible and spiritual in your school.

_____

_____

_____

_____

_____

_____

_____

_____

_____

Christ Present Among Us **187**

Optional Activity

Helping to Build God's Kingdom *Verbal/Linguistic, Visual/Spatial*

Arrange the students in pairs. Have them gather images of people or cultures who are in need of help. These could range from a picture of someone fighting cancer to a group of children in Haiti in need of drinking water.

- Have the students make paper hands to glue beneath the images.
- On the hands should be written the gifts and talents of others that are needed to help serve the needs of these people (e.g., for the image of a sick person, the words on the hands could be about the gift of compassion that a nurse might show or the gift of intelligence evident in those searching for a cure).

One in Christ

Direct the students to quietly read the first paragraph.

Point out the photo on this page.

- Invite a volunteer to read aloud the caption.
- *Ask:* What are the students doing as the Body of Christ? They are gathering in Jesus' name and showing their support for the Archbishop.

Scripture

Have the students read Acts 9:1–5 to themselves.

- Ask a volunteer to read aloud 1 Corinthians 12:12–31.
- Discuss the questions as a class.

Read aloud the last paragraph.

Ask a student to read aloud the definitions of *Mystical Body of Christ* and *hierarchy* from the Catholic Faith Words box on page 186.

CLOSE _____

ACTIVITY

Read aloud the activity instructions.

- Have the students work in small groups to complete the activity.
- Allow time for each group to share their responses with the class.

Quick Review The Church is both visible and spiritual and all of her members are united as the Body of Christ.

DAY 3

Objectives

- Recognize that the Church is one because she acknowledges one Lord, confesses one faith, and is born of one Baptism
- Discover the harmony that results as members of the Church live in communion with the Holy Spirit and one another

OPEN

 Have the students stand at their desks or move to the prayer space. Invite them to make the Sign of the Cross and pray the Prayer to the Holy Spirit from page 384.

Read aloud the opening question and allow volunteers to respond.

Say: Let's read this first section for an answer to the question.

BUILD

One Body, Many Members

Invite a volunteer to read the opening paragraph to the class.

- Emphasize that each person in the Church does not get "lost" as part of the one Body of Christ.

📖 Scripture

Ask the students if they have heard Jesus' story about the vine and the branches before.

- Allow volunteers to share what they know.
- Read John 15:4–5 to the class.

One Body, Many Members

What are some signs of our unity as the Body of Christ?

The Church is a body of many members, and each individual is important to the working of the whole Body. Each of us is needed, and we don't lose our individuality as part of the whole. And each member also needs to remain part of the Church and faithful to her mission. We are one Church united in Jesus. Being **one** is another Mark of the Church. The Gospel according to John tells us that Jesus explained it this way at the Last Supper.

> ### 📖 Scripture
>
> [Jesus] said, "Just as a branch cannot bear fruit on its own unless it remains on the vine, so neither can you unless you remain in me. I am the vine, you are the branches. Whoever remains in me and I in him will bear much fruit, because without me you can do nothing."
> John 15:4–5

All Parts of the Body of Christ Work Together

There is no use being part of a group if we do not work together with the other members of the group. When even one member of the Church does not participate with the rest of the Church, we are all affected. And when even one member remains faithful and bears the fruit of good works, the whole Church is also affected. All over the world today, the Church is bearing good fruit. The many parts are all connected in Christ. The reception of Holy Communion strengthens the union we have with Christ and others in the Church—locally, nationally, and worldwide. The Eucharist therefore is a sign and a source of our unity.

> How do you participate in the Church right now? What can you do to improve the role you have?

> **Catholic Faith Words**
>
> **one** a Mark of the Church. The Church is one because the power of the Holy Spirit unites all the members through one faith and one Baptism.

188 Chapter 11

ℹ️ Teacher Background

Church Community

When people think about the Church, they often only think about the building they attend every Sunday and the people they know within those walls. Point out to the students that the Church refers to all Christians who live throughout the world as the Body of Christ.

- Discuss some of the similarities and differences that might be found in different Church communities throughout the world.
- Explain how different Church communities can work together.
- Invite the students to consider how they can become more actively involved in their Church community by joining one of the ministries at their Church.

COMPARE AND CONTRAST

Catholics represent many cultures and countries. Still, all Catholics are one. Look at the pictures. List the types of differences and similarities you see.

Differences

1. _____
2. _____
3. _____
4. _____

Similarities

1. _____
2. _____
3. _____
4. _____

Imagine speaking with a member of one of the Catholic Churches in the pictures about what you have in common, and what things about you are different. What would you want to tell this person? Write a few ideas on the lines below.

_____
_____
_____
_____
_____
_____
_____
_____
_____
_____
_____

Ontario, Canada

Réunion Island

Kerala, India

Christ Present Among Us **189**

Optional Activity

Different Churches, Same Beliefs *Verbal/Linguistic*

Some students have likely been members of different Church communities at some point in their lives. Perhaps some of them have even been members of a church in a different country.

- Invite the students to describe the church they currently attend.
- Ask those who have been members of different Church communities to share some of the differences they have observed.
- Emphasize that even though some Catholic churches may be different in some ways, we all share the same beliefs, Creeds, and Sacraments.

All Parts of the Body of Christ Work Together

Read aloud this section and the questions that follow on page 188.

- Give the students time to reflect on the questions. (If your class prefers to discuss the questions, give them time to do so.)

Work with Words

Point out the Catholic Faith Words box on page 188.

- *Ask:* What does the word *one* mean in reference to the Catholic Church?
- Have a volunteer read the definition aloud to the class.

Point out the various photos of churches on page 189. Share that Catholic church buildings can look different but we all share the same desire to help build God's Kingdom.

CLOSE _____

ACTIVITY

Have a volunteer read aloud the instructions.

- Allow the students to complete this activity with a classmate.
- Ask volunteers to share their ideas with the class.

Quick Review The Church is one because she acknowledges one Lord, confesses one faith, and is born of one Baptism. When members of the Church live in communion with the Holy Spirit and each other, we live in harmony.

© Our Sunday Visitor

DAY 4

Objective

- Compare the diversity of gifts that allow the Church to help God manifest his Kingdom

OPEN

💗 Invite the students to think about their own gifts and talents from God and pray a prayer of thanksgiving for them.

BUILD

Many Gifts for the Good of All

Summarize the material in these paragraphs, perhaps by showing the main points in a PowerPoint presentation. Share an experience you have had of working with someone on a project:

- Describe the different gifts each of you brought to the work.
- Emphasize how the use of different gifts benefited the project.
- Mention differences that surfaced as you worked on the project and how they were resolved.

Discuss the question as a class, giving the students an opportunity to share their own observations.

For Those Who Are in Need

Read aloud this section, including the paragraphs on page 191.

- If you want to share the list of the Corporal Works of Mercy, turn to page 374.

Many Gifts for the Good of All

How are each person's gifts and talents important to the whole Church?

God gave each individual person different gifts. If we were all good at the same things, we would probably all be bad at the same things, too. Some things would not be done well, or at all.

Often people use their gifts to compete with each other. But God did not give us gifts just for competition. As the Church, he wants us to share our gifts to bring Christ to others and to share the message of his Good News with the world.

Because of this diversity, the Church is able to help God build his Kingdom in many ways. The gifts of every member are needed.

In his letter to the Ephesians, Saint Paul tells us that the gifts God gave to his People were "some as apostles, others as prophets, others as evangelists, others as pastors and teachers" (Ephesians 4:11). God still gives those gifts in the Church today.

> What would your parish or the whole Church be like without the gifts of all her different people?

For Those Who Are in Need

Jesus tells a story about the Last Judgment to teach us that we will be judged by how we show our love in the ways we help him. In his story, the people are surprised to hear Jesus say that they are going to be rewarded for helping him on Earth. They wondered when they had helped him. ". . . whatever you did for one of these least brothers of mine, you did for me" (Matthew 25:40). He goes into more detail:

📖 Scripture

I was hungry and you gave me food.
I was thirsty and you gave me drink.
I was a stranger and you welcomed me.
I was naked and you clothed me.
I was in prison and you visited me.
I was ill and you cared for me.
Based on Matthew 25:35–36

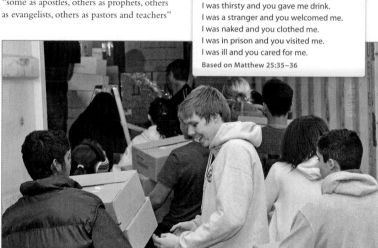

© Our Sunday Visitor

📖 Scripture Background

Matthew 25:31–46

The passage containing what we call the Corporal Works of Mercy, is entitled "The Judgment of the Nations." Here, we learn:

- the nations will be judged by what they have done for the least among them.
- the least are those who have suffered from hunger, thirst, illness, imprisonment, nakedness, and alienation.
- that Matthew was probably addressing the Christian missionaries of his time.
- that whoever rejects one of these least also rejects Jesus.

WHERE IT HAPPENED

Maybe it was because there were so many different kinds of people and occupations in Ephesus that Saint Paul wrote to the Church there about different gifts. Ephesus was a big, important seaport of ancient Greece, in an area that is now western Turkey. Travelers to Turkey today can see the ruins of the ancient city, including those of the Basilica of St. John, which was built over the alleged burial site of Saint John the Apostle. Travelers can also visit a museum, and a Church shrine to honor Mary.

For more, go to **aliveinchrist.osv.com**

Because we are members of the Body of Christ, everyone in the Church is linked to everyone else, especially to people who are suffering, poor, and persecuted. In these people we can most closely see Jesus, who suffered and died for us. When we reach out to help others who are in need, we are doing what Jesus did and what he told us to do.

You might recognize Jesus' words as the Church's Corporal Works of Mercy, actions that care for the physical needs of people. The complete list adds another work, burying the dead.

LIST

Find a copy of your parish bulletin and identify some of the ways that Church members are using their gifts to be a sign of God's Kingdom and to care for those who are in great need. List some of the ways below, and place a check mark beside two ways you can contribute your own gifts to these efforts.

_____

_____

_____

IN SUMMARY   Catholics Believe

The Church is both visible and spiritual, made up of people with many gifts and talents who are united by Christ in the Holy Spirit to continue Christ's mission in the world.

- We call the spiritual part of the Church the Mystical Body of Christ. Jesus is the Head of his Body, the Church.

- Each individual member is united with all members as part of Christ's Body; we need one another and Christ to bear fruit in the world.

- The Church needs the diverse gifts of all members to be a sign of God's Kingdom.

Christ Present Among Us   **191**

© Our Sunday Visitor

Teacher Background

Where It Happened: A Brief History of Ephesus

Saint Paul traveled to Ephesus during his missionary journeys, sharing the Gospel of Christ throughout the Mediterranean region.

- At the time Paul traveled to Ephesus, many idolaters who worshipped the goddess Artemis converted to Christianity.

- The Church at Ephesus is one of the seven Churches mentioned in the book of Revelation. It is credited as having endured in its faith but is admonished for being in need of repentance for its loss of love (see Revelation 2:2–5).

- The 3rd Ecumenical Council, presided over by St. Cyril of Alexandria, took place in Ephesus in A.D. 431.

 Scripture

Have a volunteer read aloud Matthew 25:35–36 from page 190.

Where It Happened

Review the information in the Where It Happened box.

- If time permits, allow the students to go online to **aliveinchrist.osv.com** to find out more about Ephesus, or modern-day Turkey.

ACTIVITY

Invite a volunteer to read aloud the activity instructions as you pass out parish bulletins to each student.

- Have the students work independently on the activity.

- After they have had time to assign where their gifts are most needed, allow volunteers to share their responses with the class.

CLOSE

In Summary

Have the students silently read the summary information.

- *Ask:* Which part of this lesson did you find most interesting.

- Allow volunteers to respond. Use this conversation as a way to review the material.

DAY 5

Objectives

- Learn ways we can use our personal gifts to serve others and the Church
- Explore the faith life of Saint John Bosco
- Offer the prayer celebrating the Word of God

OPEN

Ask the students to move to the prayer space. Pray the Act of Hope, page 387, together as a class.

BUILD

Our Catholic Life

Have the students silently read the Our Catholic Life feature.

- Ask them to reflect on the gifts they have that they can share with their communities.
- Allow volunteers to share their responses to the question with the class.

People of Faith

Explain to the students that Saint John Bosco devoted his life to helping troubled children come to know Christ.

- Share important points from the People of Faith paragraph.
- Provide additional information to the class from the People of Faith Background box.
- *Say:* God revealed Saint John's calling to him through his dreams.
- *Ask:* How has God reached out to you?

Our Catholic Life

Sharing your gifts and talents is one of the easiest ways to feel part of your parish and school community. As a young person, you can use your **personal gifts** to form friendships, help or mentor younger children, assist in the liturgy by reading, singing, or being an altar server at Mass, or performing some of the Corporal or Spiritual Works of Mercy. But you may wonder about what gifts you have to share. Ask your friends and an adult at your parish or in your school about what they see as some of your gifts, and then think about how you could share them in your community. If you're still not sure about your own gifts or what use they could be, pray to God for guidance. The Church needs the gifts of all her members—including you—to continue Christ's work in the world.

> What is one gift you can share in your community this week?

© Our Sunday Visitor

People of Faith

Saint John Bosco, 1815–1888

At the age of nine, John Bosco of Turin, Italy, began having dreams that would reveal God's plan for his life. John knew that his life's work would be to help troubled children to become more Christ-like. As a priest, he ministered to poor and neglected boys, taking them to Mass, and founded the Salesian Society, which opened homes for young boys to be educated and train for the priesthood. The Church celebrates his feast day on **January 31**.

 For more, go to **aliveinchrist.osv.com**

192 Chapter 11

IDENTIFY

Explore the hymnbook your parish uses to celebrate liturgies. Make a list of hymns that mention the Body of Christ, our oneness in Christ, our giving of our personal gifts, or our outreach to those in need.

_____
_____
_____
_____
_____
_____
_____
_____
_____

People of Faith Background

Saint John Bosco

Share this information about Saint John Bosco:

- Saint John gave the children in his orphanage a safe place to live and receive daily love and care, ministered to them, made sure they attended Mass, and showed them how to follow Jesus' example.
- He left a lasting legacy of helping those who were less fortunate. Saint John Bosco is an excellent example of someone who took the teachings of Jesus to heart and daily lived out those teachings.

Encourage the students to go to **aliveinchrist.osv.com** at home to learn more about Saint John Bosco.

Celebration of the Word

Leader: Let us pray.
O God, of every good gift,
we praise you and we thank you for this time of prayer,
this time of quiet, this time to ask ourselves the question,
"What are the gifts you have given me?"

Reader 1: A reading from the Letter of Paul to the Corinthians.

Read 1 Corinthians 12:4–11.

The word of the Lord.

All: Thanks be to God.

Reader 2: Open our hearts to receive and understand.
Open our minds to trust in your plan.
Open our hands to take hold of all you give us.
Open our lives to share what you offer.

Reader 3: Let us pray to the God who gives us what we need.
Pray aloud your intercessions, one by one.

After each, respond:

All: Lord, hear our prayer.

Leader: Help us see how we all fit together, how each of us offers a different piece, a different gift to strengthen the whole.
Teach us to know the Holy Spirit is with us, guiding us and giving us courage and wisdom.
Help us recognize our gifts and use them with care.

All: Amen.

▶ *Sing or play "Alive in One Spirit"*

📶 Go to **aliveinchrist.osv.com** for an interactive review.

A Work with Words **Complete each sentence.**

1. The word _____ Church _____ means a gathering or assembly.

2. As we gather as the Church, we are the _____ People of God _____.

3. As a spiritual group, the Church is called the _____ Mystical Body of Christ _____.

4. The Church is organized into a(n) _____ hierarchy _____ with different levels of leadership and membership.

5. The Church is _____ one _____ because the power of the Holy Spirit unites all the members through one faith and one Baptism.

B Check Understanding **Indicate whether the following statements are true or false. Then rewrite false statements to make them true.**

6. Through the Holy Spirit, Baptism, and the Eucharist, Jesus forms the Church as his Body. (True)/False

_____

7. Jesus taught his disciples that they were the roots and he was the branches. True/(False)
Jesus is the vine, we are the branches

8. The Church is both invisible and spiritual. True/(False)
The Church is both a visible reality and a spiritual one.

9. Everyone in the Church is responsible to care for those in need. (True)/False

_____

10. Jesus taught that people would be rewarded at the Assumption for the ways they helped him on Earth. True/(False)
People would be rewarded at the Last Judgment.

C Make Connections **Write a one-paragraph response to the question below. What do we need to do so that our efforts "bear fruit" as Jesus instructed?**

_____
_____
_____
_____
_____
_____
_____
_____
_____
_____
_____
_____
_____
_____
_____
_____

Explain the activity to the students.

- Pass out hymn books.
- Have the students work in small groups to find the specific types of hymns asked for in the activity.

CLOSE

Celebration of the Word

♥ Ask each student to make a simple drawing of something that symbolizes one of their gifts. Add their drawings to the prayer space.

Divide the class into three groups; designate each group to say the part of Reader 1, Reader 2, or Reader 3.

Take the role of Leader yourself and read the invitation to prayer.

Follow the order of prayer on the student page.

▶ Conclude by inviting the students to sing or reflect on "Alive in One Spirit," downloaded from **aliveinchrist.osv.com**.

CHAPTER REVIEW

Review the instructions for each section and have the students complete the review.

📶 Go to **aliveinchrist.osv.com** to prepare customized and downloadable assessments, send eAssessments, and assign interactive reviews.

KEY CONCEPT

The Church has a mission to bring all people to believe in God and to be baptized.

DOCTRINAL CONTENT

- God created us with free will. He helps us learn to use it to choose that which is good. (CCC, 302, 1730)

- We receive new life in the gift of salvation that Jesus, the Mediator, offers us in Baptism. (CCC, 771, 1257)

- The Church is catholic—for all people at all times and in all places, and, through the actions of her members, people come to know God and share in his life. (CCC, 831)

- Purgatory is the process of purification we experience after death, before we enter complete communion with the Holy Trinity. (CCC, 1030, 1031)

- Prayer is an important means of communion with God, and an important part of the call to live a life of love and truth. (CCC, 3, 2559)

TASKS OF CATECHESIS

Helping children grow in a faith that is "known, celebrated, lived, and expressed in prayer" (NDC, 20).

This chapter focuses on the following tasks of catechesis:

- Teaching to Pray
- Missionary Initiation

Teacher Background

> 📖 When the time for Pentecost was fulfilled … there came from the sky a noise like a strong driving wind … there appeared to [the Apostles] tongues as of fire, which parted and came to rest on each one of them. And they were filled with the holy Spirit … Acts 2:1–4
>
> > **Reflect** In what ways does the Holy Spirit strengthen you to evangelize and help God build his Kingdom?

The Nicene Creed that we proclaim every Sunday states that our Church is "one, holy, catholic and apostolic." The word *catholic* is spelled with a small "c." The Creed is using that word in its broader sense, meaning that the Church is universal. Our mission from Jesus is one of reaching out to the ends of the Earth. It is a daunting mission, and one that must be embraced anew by every generation of believers.

The Creed acknowledges the Church as one and holy. The Church is one in that she professes one Lord, one faith, one Baptism, and one Body in Christ. Holiness is central to the life of the Church because Jesus, acting with the Holy Spirit and sent by the Father, gave his life to make her holy—unique and pure; so that she is set apart for God and his purposes. The lives of the Saints and of the Blessed Mother are the holiness to which we are called, for the sake of the unity of the Body of Christ.

Finally, the Creed states that the Church is apostolic. This means the Church is founded on the Apostles. We inherit our identity from the Twelve Apostles. Their authority is passed on to the Pope and bishops of the Church. The role of the bishop is the same as it was two thousand years ago: to faithfully guard the truth of the Gospel and to make it known in every generation by leading, governing, and providing for the sacramental life of the Church. Those who work in catechesis are privileged to share in that ministry.

> **Reflect** How do you see your catechetical ministry as a sharing in the Church's role of handing on the faith?

Teacher's Prayer

 Lord Jesus, when I drift from you I fail. Help me always remember that you are the source of all that is good in my ministry and that apart from you, I can accomplish nothing. Amen.

How Seventh Graders Understand Chapter Topics

Seventh graders may not have the sense that they could hand on their faith to others. They are still learning what Catholics believe, and may lack the confidence to feel they could spread the faith in any systematic way. They need to see how what they say and do in everyday life sends a message to others about who they are and what they believe.

Teaching Tip: Lead a discussion about the nature of missionary work in the world today. What is the difference between being a missionary and proselytizing (persuading a person to conversion)? When is it important to connect our acts of service with preaching, and when should we just let the service itself be the preaching? (Hint: You might share the statement attributed to Saint Francis of Assisi: "Proclaim the Gospel always, and if necessary use words.")

Sharing the Message with Seventh Graders

- Younger adolescents may need help seeing the connection between their local world (their main reality) and the global reality.
- Young people are often torn between cynicism and idealism. Providing healthy, practical avenues for them to serve in response to local needs can help nurture the virtue of hope.
- Help seventh graders see that they must build and maintain a personal relationship with God, nourished by prayer, in order to answer his call to bring God's love and truth to others.

ONLINE RESOURCES

 Go to **aliveinchrist.osv.com**

You will find:

- Interactive lesson planning, additional activities, and ideas for the classroom environment
- Step by step lesson instruction from printed Teacher Edition for integrated lesson planning
- Custom-built assessments to download and eAssessment links
- Interactive reviews that provide scores and the option to review answers
- Chapter-specific Lectionary connections and a complete correlation ordered by the Sundays of the year, with suggestions for how to integrate the Scripture readings into chapter lessons

Go to **osvparish.com** for Ask the Experts Q and A, Community Connections, and Blogs.

Chapter 12 Planner

Objectives	Open
DAY 1—Invite/Preview, Pages 195–197	
• Reflect on God's personal invitation through Scripture • Indicate prior knowledge of chapter concepts and vocabulary	♡ **Psalm 84:5** Pray the opening prayer. 📖 **Acts 2:1–7** Proclaim "The Coming of the Spirit." Guide the students through the process of Scripture reflection. • Discuss Have You Ever Thought questions.
DAY 2—Discover, Pages 198–199	
• Explain that God helps us learn to use our free will to choose what is good • Recognize that Jesus is the Mediator who brings us to salvation • Express that faith and Baptism are necessary for salvation	♡ Pray the **Gloria**, page 385. • Discuss student reactions to the photo.
DAY 3—Discover, Pages 200–201	
• Describe how the Church is catholic, or universal • Identify the process of purification we must go through before we can enter Heaven	♡ Pray a prayer of petition. • Discuss the opening question.
DAY 4—Discover, Pages 202–203	
• Discuss prayer as a means of communion with God • Explore the relationship between a deep prayer life and the call to live a life of love and truth	♡ Pray the **Lord's Prayer**, page 383. • Discuss the opening question.
DAY 5—Live, Pages 204–205	
• Explore ways the Church can use social media to share the Good News • Explore the faith life of Saint Lorenzo Ruiz • Offer a Prayer for Peace	♡ Pray **Psalm 84:5**, page 195.

REVIEW AND ASSESSMENT

Chapter Review, page 206
Chapter Test, page 195F

🛜 **aliveinchrist.osv.com** Customize and Download Assessments, Email Links to eAssessments, Interactive Student Reviews

Build	Close	Materials & Resources
• Present lesson highlights. • Preview **Catholic Faith Words**. ★ Name ways that the Church works in today's world.	• Activity List things the school does to continue Jesus' work.	☐ pencils or pens
• **Catholic Faith Words** free will, Baptism • Talk about God's gift of free will. • Explain that we can only be saved through Jesus.	• Activity Name significant aspects of the Catholic Church. • Conclude with a review of key concepts and objectives.	☐ pencils or pens
• **Catholic Faith Words** eternal life, catholic • Explain that the Church is an integral part of our relationship with God. • Discuss why the Church is catholic. 📖 Read Matthew 28:19–20.	• Activity Reflect on ways we are close to God, and think of ways to help others become closer to him. • Conclude with a review of key concepts and objectives.	☐ pencils or pens ☐ highlighters
• Discuss prayer as a way to communicate with God. ★ Write examples of the five forms of prayer. 📖 Reflect on Matthew 6:9–13. • Optional Activity Prayer in My Life (Activity Master 12)	• Activity Discuss questions on prayer. • Review the In Summary statements.	☐ pencils or pens ☐ Bibles ☐ Activity Master 12 (Page 195G)
• Discuss the question in the Our Catholic Life section. • Learn about Saint Lorenzo Ruiz. • Activity Construct text messages about the work of the Church.	• Select students for the leader parts. • Follow the order of prayer. ▶ Sing or reflect on the closing song.	☐ pencils or pens 🛜 "Make Me a Channel"

FORMING CATHOLIC IDENTITY ACROSS THE CURRICULUM

To integrate the Catholic faith in all aspects of curriculum, this chapter's objectives can be reinforced and applied in the instruction of other disciplines.

Go to **aliveinchrist.osv.com** for cross-curricular activities and projects linked to the doctrinal content discussed in this unit. Activities are available from among the following knowledge categories and content areas:

Language Arts

- Integration of Knowledge
- Literacy
- Speaking and Listening
- Writing Skills

Math

- Algebraic Thinking
- Geometry
- Measurement and Data
- Numbers and Operations

Science

- Earth Science
- Life Science
- Physical Science
- Technology

Social Studies

- Civics
- Economics
- Geography
- History

NCEA IFG: ACRE Edition

Prayer

- **Objective:** To recognize and learn how to engage in Catholic forms of personal and communal prayer and ways of deepening one's spiritual life

Missionary Spirit

- **Objectives:** To recognize the centrality of evangelization as the Church's mission and identity embodied in vocation and service; to be aware of how cultures are transformed by the Gospel

Catholic Faith Literacy

catholic, mission, missionary, Our Father

Catholic Social Teaching

To integrate Catholic Social Teaching into your lesson, choose one of the following features: Call to Family, Community, and Participation, pages 336–337; or Option for the Poor and Vulnerable, pages 340–341.

- Start the Live step of the process by talking about Saint Lorenzo Ruiz on page 204. Then move directly to the Catholic Social Teaching feature.
- Or, to expand the lesson, complete page 204, then move to the Catholic Social Teaching feature.
- Return to Chapter 12 for the prayer on page 205.

Music Option

Use the following song to enhance catechetical learning or for prayer.

- "Make Me a Channel," Day 5, Page 205

Name _____   Date _____

Match each description in Column A with the correct term in Column B.

Column A	Column B
___ **1.** Purification, on Earth or in Purgatory, frees us from this consequence of sin	**a.** temporal punishment
___ **2.** The Church is universal, for all people in all times	**b.** Baptism
___ **3.** The God-given freedom and ability to make choices	**c.** catholic
___ **4.** Takes away Original Sin and all personal sin	**d.** free will

Circle the letter of the choice that best completes each sentence.

5. Along with faith in God, we need to be ___ into new life in Christ and experience the gift of salvation.
  a. baptized   **b.** saved   **c.** signed up   **d.** forced

6. The ___ explains that "all salvation comes from Christ the Head through the Church which is his Body."
  a. First Vatican Council   **c.** Second Vatican Council
  b. parish bulletins   **d.** Liturgy of the Eucharist

7. The ___ builds the Church, brings her to life, and makes her holy.
  a. Lord's Prayer   **b.** Eucharist   **c.** Pope   **d.** Holy Spirit

8. The Church's treasury is ___.
  a. a collection of money
  b. all the holiness and goodness from Jesus, Mary, and the Saints
  c. the many people who are members of the Church
  d. jewels and works of art

Write a response on the lines below.

9. Provide some examples of the universal nature of the Church.

_____

_____

_____

10. What is eternal life?

_____

_____

Name _____   Date _____

Prayer in My Life

Answer the survey below honestly. Spend some quiet time really thinking about your answers and what they say about prayer in your life. Talk with a friend and compare your answers and ideas.

My best times of day for prayer: _____

_____

Things that make it hard for me to pray: _____

_____

My favorite prayers or kinds of prayer: _____

_____

I like to pray alone when: _____

_____

I like to pray with other people when: _____

_____

Some things I often ask God for: _____

_____

I know God answered my prayer when: _____

_____

I am thankful to God for: _____

_____

I most need God's help with: _____

_____

I have heard God tell me in my heart: _____

_____

Source of Life

 Let Us Pray

Leader: God of peace and justice, you call us to be your holy people. May the Holy Spirit open our hearts and minds to you today and throughout our lives. May we be your witnesses to the ends of the Earth!

"Blessed are those who dwell in your house!
    They never cease to praise you." **Psalm 84:5**

All: Help us continue your saving work, O Lord. Hear our prayer.

Scripture

When the time for Pentecost was fulfilled, they were all in one place together. And suddenly there came from the sky a noise like a strong driving wind, and it filled the entire house in which they were. Then there appeared to them tongues as of fire, which parted and came to rest on each one of them. And they were filled with the holy Spirit and began to speak in different tongues, as the Spirit enabled them to proclaim.

Now there were devout Jews from every nation under heaven staying in Jerusalem. At this sound, they gathered in a large crowd, but they were confused because each one heard them speaking in his own language. They were astounded, and in amazement they asked, "Are not all these people who are speaking Galileans?" Acts 2:1–7

Have you ever thought...

- How does the Holy Spirit strengthen the Church to spread the Good News of salvation?

- How much does faith have to do with everyday life?

195

Scripture Background

Scripture Reflection Process

Invite the students to be still, close their eyes, and focus on their breathing. Encourage them to open their minds and hearts to what God is saying to them.

- Proclaim the Scripture and have the students sit in silence.

- *Ask:* What did you hear God say to you today?

- Allow volunteers to share.

 You may play instrumental music to begin the reflection.

Objective

- Reflect on God's personal invitation through Scripture

OPEN _____

 **Let Us Pray**

Invite the students to gather in the prayer space and make the Sign of the Cross. Pray the leader lines. Select a few students to read aloud the Psalm verse. Prompt the response from the remainder of the group.

Have the students move out of the prayer space and back to their seats.

Say: Let's listen to the Scripture reading and recall that God sent the Holy Spirit to the Apostles at Pentecost so that they could proclaim the Good News to the ends of the Earth!

Scripture

Guide the students through the process of Scripture reflection (see the Scripture Background box below).

Have you ever thought...

Say: We are all called to continue this mission and invite others to know and love Jesus. The Holy Spirit continues to help guide us on our faith journey.

- Invite the students to respond to the questions.

DAY 1

Objective

- Indicate prior knowledge of chapter concepts and vocabulary

BUILD _____

Use this page to assess the students' knowledge related to the chapter content.

Getting Started

Read aloud the opening paragraph.

- Ask the class what faith has to do with a person's daily life.
- Challenge the students to give examples of how faith is lived, either from their own lives or from lives of people they know.

The Church

Remind the class that it is the Holy Spirit that energizes and breathes life into the Church.

★ Have the students name ways that the Church brings people close to God, and how she is a sign of God's grace to the world.

- *Ask:* How does the Church continue Jesus' mission?
- Have the students work on their own to complete the chart.
- Allow time for volunteers to share their responses with the class.

Getting Started

In this chapter you will learn about the need for faith and Baptism, and the ways the Church helps us restore our friendship with God. The Church keeps us close to God, showing us how to pray and helping us open our minds and hearts to God.

Catholic Faith Words
• free will
• Baptism
• eternal life
• catholic, as a Mark of the Church

In the web below, name ways that the Church brings people close to God, and how she is a sign of God's grace to the world.

The Church ...

brings people closer to God by:
_____
_____
_____

is a sign of God's grace to the world when:
_____
_____
_____

continues Jesus' mission by:
_____
_____
_____

© Our Sunday Visitor

Optional Activity

Play "Four Corners" *Bodily/Kinesthetic, Verbal/Linguistic*

Four Corners will help the students clarify their thinking.

- Attach labels to the four corners of the room: "Agree," "Strongly Agree," "Disagree," and "Strongly Disagree."
- Gather the students in the center of the room. Offer an opinion statement and ask the students to stand in the corner that best describes their opinion.
- Ask some students to share why they chose their position. After the discussion, ask if anyone wants to move to a different corner.

LIST

Live the Good News List five things that your school does to continue Jesus' work. It could be things within the school or for others in the community.

1. _____

2. _____

3. _____

4. _____

5. _____

Then describe how you are or can be involved in one or more.

_____

_____

_____

_____

_____

_____

_____

_____

_____

_____

Source of Life   **197**

Work with Words

Point out the Catholic Faith Words box at the top of page 196.

- Have a volunteer read aloud each of the vocabulary words.
- Invite volunteers to share what they know about the term *free will*.
- Explain that this is an important concept that they will learn about as they study this chapter.

CLOSE _____

ACTIVITY

Read aloud the directions for the class.

- Allow the students to brainstorm, in small groups, ways that the school continues Jesus' work.
- For the second part of the activity, have the students reflect on what they do or how they can help to further the work of Jesus.

✓ Teaching Tip

Communicate Respectfully

Most students enjoy and learn from activities where they can take a stand, have a chance to explain themselves, and listen to other people's views. It is important to communicate with respect. Good communication skills involve refraining from talking over one another, arguing without listening, or name-calling.

As a teacher, you have the opportunity to be a role model for students and demonstrate effective techniques for communicating. Be sure to explain that listening to others is an important part of communication. This helps us to understand one another—even if we disagree.

DAY 2

Objectives

- Explain that God helps us learn to use our free will to choose what is good
- Recognize that Jesus is the Mediator who brings us to salvation
- Express that faith and Baptism are necessary for salvation

OPEN

💗 Have the students pray the *Gloria* from page 385.

Ask: What is happening in the image on this page? What might this photo tell us about the chapter?

BUILD

That All May Have Life

Ask a volunteer to read this section.

- Use the two questions at the end to further discuss free will.

Faith and Baptism

Read aloud each paragraph, across pages 198 and 199, and have the students underline the most important information. Here are some key statements:

- Jesus is the only one who can save us from our sins.
- We need to be baptized into new life in Christ.
- The Church is needed for salvation.
- Living a good life can still save a person who, through no fault of their own, has not heard of Jesus and the Church. (See the Teacher Background box on page 199.)

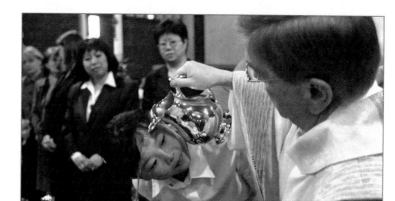

© Our Sunday Visitor

That All May Have Life

Why does the Church continue Jesus' saving work?

We are made in God's image. And God created us to be with him—completely happy and whole. But, he wanted us to choose to be in relationship with him. So he also created us with **free will**, the ability to act freely in making choices. Because humans are free to choose, and because each person is born with Original Sin, they sometimes choose hurtful, sinful actions. But God can help us learn to use free will to choose what is good. Free will is one of God's greatest gifts to us, but it is very easy to misuse it.

After Jesus died, Saint Paul wrote to the Corinthians about the salvation God offered us through Jesus: "God was reconciling the world to himself in Christ" (2 Corinthians 5:19). If we accept Jesus Christ as our Savior, and

have faith in him, we will be reconciled, or restored, in our relationship with God. But it is our free will to choose. And not everyone accepts Jesus as his or her Lord, not even those who believe in God. Until they do, the world will not be in full communion with God.

> When have you used your free will to decide to do something good?

> When has it been hard for you to choose good instead of evil?

Faith and Baptism

Jesus is the only one who can save us from our sins. When he returned to be with his Father in glory, he left on Earth his Body, the Church, to continue bringing people hope, new life, and salvation. The Second Vatican Council explains that, "all salvation comes from Christ the Head through the Church which is his Body." The Council based this statement on Sacred Scripture and

---

 Teaching Tip

Free Will

Remind the students that through the Sacrament of Baptism they are welcomed into God's family. Discuss that although their parents may have made the decision for them to be baptized, God has given each of them the gift of free will. Point out that they can use this gift to make good choices that bring them closer to God or make bad choices that can lead them away from God.

- Ask the students to reflect on some of the choices they have made with the free will they have been given.
- Encourage them to think about what choices and actions will bring them closer to God.

Sacred Tradition. Christ is the one Mediator who can bring us to salvation. He is present in the world now in his Body, the Church.

We cannot be restored to the right relationship with God without faith. Jesus said, "Whoever believes and is baptized will be saved; whoever does not believe will be condemned" (Mark 16:16). We can see that faith is not enough. We need to be baptized into new life in Christ. We receive **Baptism** in and through the Church, so again we see that the Church is needed for salvation.

But what about those who have never heard of Christ and his Church? Living a good life and following his or her conscience can still save a person who, through no fault of their own, has not heard of Jesus and the Church. And Jesus is still bringing such a person new life. The same is true for those preparing to become Catholic, but who for some reason are not baptized before they die. Some

people die for the faith even though they are not baptized, and they, too, can be saved.

We might also wonder about children who have died without Baptism. It is best for babies to be baptized, but if they die before they are baptized, we can trust our loving God to have mercy on them and save them. That is what we pray for all unbaptized infants and children.

> **What else do we need besides our faith?**

Catholic Faith Words

free will the God-given freedom and ability to make choices. God created us with free will so we can have the freedom to choose good.

Baptism the Sacrament in which a person is immersed in water or has water poured on him or her. Baptism takes away Original Sin and all personal sin, and makes a person a child of God and member of the Church.

NAME

Imagine you have just been asked by an exchange student at your school who is a Hindu to explain what Catholics believe. Name the five most important things you would say about your faith.

_____

_____

_____

_____

_____

_____

Faith and Baptism,

continued

Say: All salvation comes through Jesus, even for those who don't know enough to realize it!

Ask the students the question at the end of this section and allow volunteers to respond.

- Use this time to help the students brainstorm ideas for the activity at the bottom of the page.
- If they haven't mentioned it, add that free will is a gift from God and an important part of our faith.
- Have a volunteer read aloud the Catholic Faith Word definitions.

CLOSE _____

ACTIVITY

Read aloud the directions.

- Tell the students that they should use your discussion of the last section's question as a starting point for completing the activity.
- Have them work independently.
- Once everyone is finished, allow volunteers to share their responses with the class.

Quick Review Free will is a gift from God that allows us to make our own choices. Jesus' gift of salvation is offered to each person. We respond to this gift in faith and are joined to Christ through Baptism.

ⓘ Teacher Background

Believe It or Not

All salvation comes from Christ through the Church (see CCC, 846). We remember that Jesus died for everyone, whether or not they know it or believe it. And since the Church is the Body of Christ here on Earth, it is only through the Church that anyone is saved. There is only one Baptism, so those baptized into other Christian faiths can also be saved. "Those who through no fault of their own, do not know the Gospel of Christ or his church, but who nevertheless seek God with a sincere heart, and, moved by grace, try in their actions to do his will as they know it through the dictates of their conscience—those too may achieve eternal salvation" (CCC, 847).

Objectives

- Describe how the Church is catholic, or universal
- Identify the process of purification we must go through before we can enter Heaven

OPEN

💙 Pray a prayer of petition that all people will find salvation through Jesus Christ.

Discuss, as a class, ways that the Church helps people have a close relationship with God.

BUILD

Communion with God

Tell the students to look for the answer to the opening question as they silently read the first three paragraphs.

The Church's Treasury

Invite the students to review this section and highlight any information that is completely new to them.

- *Ask:* How confident do you feel in your understanding of the new material?
- If the students need further clarification, spend more time on the material to help them understand the concepts presented in this section.

Communion with God

How does the Catholic Church help people be close to God?

The Church is the Sacrament, or sign, of our salvation. She is also the way of getting to know God, or having communion with him. We are in communion with God when we are members of the Church. Only through the Church do we receive the Eucharist, which deepens our union with Christ. The Eucharist is Christ's sacrifice on the Cross. The Eucharistic sacrifice is offered to make reparation for people's sins and to gain both material and spiritual gifts from God.

We celebrate the Holy Trinity, the mystery of one God in three Divine Persons: Father, Son, and Holy Spirit. We celebrate that mystery through, with, and in Christ. We are drawn to God the Father through the Son's sacrifice and the Holy Spirit's action.

On our own we could never even imagine being this close to God. The Holy Spirit

brings about this communion between God and all of us in the Church. Jesus has poured out his Holy Spirit on all the members of the Church. This Spirit builds the Church, brings her to life, and makes her holy.

The Church's Treasury

We have a "treasury" in the Church—not a collection of money, but a spiritual treasury of all the holiness and goodness from Jesus, and from the prayers and good works of Mary and all the Saints. There is "an abundant exchange of all good things" among the Saints in Heaven, the souls in Purgatory, and all of us on Earth (CCC, 1475).[1] Jesus gave the Church the authority over this spiritual treasury.

The forgiveness of sins removes eternal punishment, but it is still necessary to be purified, either on Earth or in Purgatory, of the unhealthy attachment of sin. This purification frees us from the temporal punishment of sin. The Church has the power to grant indulgences based on this spiritual treasury. Indulgences, such as particular prayers or actions, allow faithful Catholics who have met certain requirements to avoid some of the temporal punishment that is the consequence of our sin. We can obtain indulgences for ourselves and for souls waiting in Purgatory. This helps us work toward the salvation and **eternal life** that God offers all who respond to his grace.

> **Catholic Faith Words**
>
> **eternal life** life forever with God for all who die in his friendship
>
> **catholic** a Mark of the Church. The Church is catholic because she is universal, meant for all people in all times and in all places.

© Our Sunday Visitor

200 Chapter 12

Optional Activity

Missionary Research *Verbal/Linguistic, Visual/Spatial*

Divide the students into pairs or triads.

- Assign each group or have each group choose a country anywhere in the world.
- Provide materials from mission magazines and diocesan newspapers.
- Have the groups research what missionary activity is carried out in their assigned country.
- Encourage the groups to put together a presentation on the country they researched and to share it with the rest of the class.

Young missionaries celebrate before a visit from Pope Francis to Rio de Janeiro, Brazil

© Our Sunday Visitor

Missionary Church

Another Mark of the Church is that she is **catholic**, or universal. Jesus did not found his Church to exist in only one time or place. He sent her out to all nations to preach the Gospel to everyone. She is the universal Sacrament of salvation.

 Scripture

"Go, therefore, and make disciples of all nations, baptizing them in the name of the Father, and of the Son, and of the holy Spirit, teaching them to observe all that I have commanded you. And behold, I am with you always, until the end of the age."
Matthew 28:19–20

Salvation is not meant for just a select few people. God wants everyone to come to him because he loves all human beings. The Church believes in God's universal plan of goodness, salvation, and redemption, so she has to be a missionary Church.

Salvation is found in the truth. Even before people know about Jesus and his Church, or come to faith in God, they are drawn to seek the truth. They have begun to move toward salvation without even knowing it. They are following the promptings of the Holy Spirit.

God has entrusted the truth about himself to the Church. While people are searching, she goes out to bring them the truth.

> Where do missionaries work in the Church today?

> What are some things they do to help bring the truth and Good News about Jesus to people?

IDENTIFY

List some ways that you are close to God. Then think of who or what helps you to be close to him. How can you help others realize that God wants to be close to them?

1. _____
2. _____

Source of Life **201**

---

i | **Teacher Background**

Indulgences

The *Catechism of the Catholic Church* defines indulgence as "the remission before God of the temporal punishment due to sin whose guilt has already been forgiven" (CCC, Glossary).

- Our sins are forgiven in the Sacrament of Penance and Reconciliation.

- Temporal punishment is the grace of purification that prepares us for the holy presence of God.

- Indulgences are the Church's way of moving our lives toward the works of devotion, penance, and charity. They reconcile us to God and connect us to the Communion of Saints and the Body of Christ.

Missionary Church

Read aloud this section.

- Divide the students into small groups. Assign one of the questions at the end of the section to each of the groups.

- Have the students brainstorm responses.

- Invite each group to share their answers with the class.

 **Scripture**

Proclaim the Scripture.

Ask: What does this Scripture passage mean to you?

- You may want to allow the students to write their responses.

Work with Words

Point out the Catholic Faith Words box on page 200.

- Have two volunteers read aloud the definitions.

- Be sure to emphasize the difference between "Catholic" and "catholic."

CLOSE _____

ACTIVITY

Discuss the first two prompts of the activity as a class.

- Have the students work independently or with a classmate to answer the question.

Quick Review The Church continues through the presence of the Holy Spirit to help her members know and understand more deeply the person of Jesus and his message. Because the Church is catholic, she is also a missionary Church, always seeking to spread God's Word.

DAY 4

Objectives

- Discuss prayer as a means of communion with God
- Explore the relationship between a deep prayer life and the call to live a life of love and truth

OPEN

💗 Have the students pray the Lord's Prayer from page 383.

Shift the students' focus to the opening question. Discuss the question as a class.

BUILD

The Church Prays

Divide the students into six small groups.

- Assign each group one of the paragraphs in this section.
- Ask each group to summarize their paragraph and share their information with the class.
- Be ready to supplement any material that the group left out of their summary.

Invite the students to write responses to the two questions at the end of this section.

📕 Go to the Source

You may wish to send the students directly to Matthew 6:9–13 to read and reflect on the words of the Lord's Prayer.

- Discuss the question as a class.

The Church Prays

Why is prayer an important part of the Church's life?

We cannot give ourselves a share in God's life. Salvation is a gift from God, not something we can either cause or earn. God uses the Church to give us the hope of life forever with him.

But we do not have to wait until we are in Heaven to be united with God. We can already be in communion with him while on Earth. In the Lord's Prayer, Jesus taught us to say: "your kingdom come, your will be done, on earth as in heaven" (Matthew 6:10).

The Lord's Prayer brings us into communion with God the Father, and his Son, Jesus. When we pray it, it is a bit like holding up a mirror—the Lord's Prayer shows us who we are as children of God and members of his Church.

God tirelessly calls each of us individually to meet him and live in his love. He never stops loving individuals and wanting each one to be in communion with him. Salvation history also tells how God has repeatedly called out to individual human beings and how they have answered his call in the quiet of their own hearts.

It is not always easy to pray, so people might be tempted to stop or even to skip praying. We can get distracted while we are praying, but God wants us to stay in prayer even when we are distracted. With practice, we can send distractions out of our minds and pay more attention to God.

Sometimes good feelings come to us in prayer, but not always. Sometimes people feel nothing while they pray, unsure if they are really praying. We don't need to have special feelings when we pray. All we need to have is faith. God will speak to us and listen to us if we remain faithful to have a time of prayer.

> When do you like to pray alone?
> How can you find a certain time of day or a certain place that is best for you?

© Our Sunday Visitor

📕 **Go to the Source**
Read *Matthew 6:9–13*. What do you think the world would be like if all humans truly desired what we ask for in this prayer?

202 Chapter 12

📖 Scripture Background

The Lord's Prayer

Jesus taught his disciples to pray in Matthew 6:9–13 and in Luke 11:1–4. A comparison of the two versions shows that neither one is exactly the prayer we pray today. The formula we know as the Lord's Prayer grew from the early liturgical prayer of the Church and continues to this day at every Eucharistic Liturgy. At our liturgy, we also pray the doxology, "For the kingdom, the power and the glory are yours …" as an additional line of praise during worship.

Protestant Christians usually add the doxology immediately after the Lord's Prayer no matter when it is prayed.

The Church's Forms of Prayer

In a prayer of **blessing and adoration**, we acknowledge our dependence upon God and respond to his goodness with joy and gratitude.

_____

_____

Prayers of **petition** ask God for something specific, turning to him for help with things we need, such as forgiveness or guidance.

_____

_____

Prayers of **intercession** are requests made on behalf of someone else. For example, you might ask God to bring healing to someone who is ill.

_____

_____

In prayers of **thanksgiving**, we acknowledge God as our Creator and thank him for his goodness. We can also offer prayers of thanksgiving for specific gifts God has given us.

_____

_____

Prayers of **praise** give God honor and glory not for what he does, but simply for who he is.

_____

_____

Write examples of each kind of prayer on the lines below.

DISCUSS

Think about the following questions and discuss your answers with a partner. When do you pray best? What are some things that make it hard for you to pray? What forms of prayer do you find yourself praying most often? How do you feel after you have prayed?

IN SUMMARY — Catholics Believe

The Church has a mission to bring all people to believe in God and to be baptized.

- Faith and Baptism are necessary for the freedom and new life that come from salvation.
- The Church is both a sign and instrument of the communion between God and his

People; it is through her actions that people can come to know God and share in his life.

- We must have a personal relationship with God nourished by prayer in order to answer our call to bring his love and truth to others.

Source of Life **203**

Optional Activity

Activity Master 12: Prayer in My Life

Distribute copies of the activity found on teacher page 195G.

- This activity will help the students focus on their prayer experiences.
- Give them time to complete the page alone. Then invite them to share their ideas with a classmate.

The Church's Forms of Prayer

Have the students select a classmate to work with.

Tell them to read the instructions next to the chart first, then read over the kinds of prayers.

✱ Instruct the pairs to write examples of each kind of prayer on the lines provided.

- Invite volunteers to share some of their examples.

CLOSE _____

ACTIVITY

Have the students remain with their partners for this activity.

- Allow them to discuss the questions with their partner.
- Afterwards, invite volunteers to share some of their responses with the class.

In Summary

Move the students' attention to the summary bullets at the bottom of the page.

- Ask them to read over the summary content.
- Make sure that they don't have any further questions on these topics before moving on.

DAY 5

Objectives

- Explore ways the Church can use social media to share the Good News
- Explore the faith life of Saint Lorenzo Ruiz
- Offer a Prayer for Peace

OPEN _____

❤ Invite the students to stand and pray the Invite Psalm from page 195.

BUILD _____

Our Catholic Life

Have the students silently read the Our Catholic Life section.

- *Ask:* How would you present the Church's message through social media?
- Brainstorm as a class possible answers to the question.

People of Faith

Explain to the students that Saint Lorenzo Ruiz held fast to his faith, even in the face of persecution, torture, and death.

- Read aloud the People of Faith paragraph.
- Review with the class the additional content in the People of Faith Background box.
- Invite the students to reflect on and write about ways they can strengthen their faith life and better serve the Church.

Our Catholic Life

The Catholic Church encourages bishops, priests, and others to share her message in many ways. In the United States, most parishes and dioceses have websites that share information with God's People. Blogs, podcasts, and other **forms of social media** can play a positive role in teaching and informing Catholics. In 2013, millions around the world waited for news of the Papal Conclave that elected Pope Francis, and social networks were quick to share his first messages to the faithful. Pope Francis soon counted millions among his followers on social media sites. No matter how the message of the Church is sent out to the world, it is important to present it faithfully.

> How would you present the Church's message through social media?

People of Faith

Saint Lorenzo Ruiz, c. 1600–1637

Saint Lorenzo Ruiz of the Philippines served as an altar boy and later was a helper and clerk-sacristan in his parish Church. In 1636, he was accused of a serious crime. While proclaiming his innocence, he fled to Okinawa, Japan. The Japanese rulers didn't like the Christians. Lorenzo and his companions were taken to Nagasaki and given the choice of renouncing their faith or being executed. All six were tortured, but they refused to deny Christ. In 1981, Pope Saint John Paul II beatified Lorenzo Ruiz along with other Philippine and Japanese martyrs. All were canonized six years later. The Church celebrates Saint Lorenzo's feast day on **September 28.**

📶 For more, go to aliveinchrist.osv.com

TEXT

You have just been appointed the person in charge for sending out text messages from your parish Church this week. These messages need to tell people about the work that the Church is doing to serve others. Research seven different things you could text for seven days. Remember each message can only be 140 characters!

_____
_____
_____
_____
_____
_____
_____
_____
_____
_____
_____

People of Faith Background

Saint Lorenzo Ruiz

Share the following with the class:

- Saint Lorenzo was involved in the Church throughout his life. When he was younger, he served as both an altar boy and a clerk-sacristan in his parish.
- As an adult, Saint Lorenzo was a member of the Confraternity of the Rosary. At the cost of his life, he held onto his love for the Church and for his faith.

📶 Encourage the students to go to **aliveinchrist.osv.com** at home to learn more about Saint Lorenzo Ruiz.

A Prayer for Peace

Leader: Lord Jesus, Saint Francis of Assisi was just a young man when he responded to a call to become your great instrument. Although we are young, help us to see how we too can be instruments of your peace. Let us pray:

Lord, make me an instrument of your peace.

Where there is hatred, let me sow love;

All: God, help me to sow the seeds of love by…

Leader: where there is injury, pardon;

All: God, help me to sow the seeds of pardon by…

Leader: where there is doubt, faith;

All: Jesus, you understood that even good people have doubts about you. Help me to encourage the growth of faith by…

Leader: where there is despair, hope;

All: God and Father, I am growing up in a world where many people have lost hope. Help me to be instrumental in planting seeds of hope by…

Leader: where there is darkness, light;

All: Jesus, you are "the Light of the World." Give me the courage to reflect your light by…

Leader: and where there is sadness, joy.

All: Jesus, you knew all the joys of life and wanted to share them. Show me how to be your joyful witness by…

All: O Divine Master, grant that I may not so much seek to be consoled as to console; to be understood as to understand; to be loved as to love.

For it is in giving that we receive; it is in pardoning that we are pardoned; and it is in dying that we are born to eternal life. Amen.

Leader: Let's sing the Prayer of Saint Francis together.

▶ *Sing or play "Make Me A Channel"*

🛜 Go to **aliveinchrist.osv.com** for an interactive review.

Ⓐ **Work with Words** Circle the letter of the choice that best completes the sentence.

1. God created human beings with ___, the freedom and ability to make choices.
 (a.) free will   c. good will
 b. open will   d. free choice

2. Along with faith, ___ is necessary for salvation.
 a. Free will   c. Reason
 (b.) Baptism   d. Penance

3. The Church is ___ because she is universal, meant for all people in all times and places.
 a. holy   c. apostolic
 b. temporal   (d.) catholic

4. The Church has a spiritual ___ of all the holiness and goodness from Jesus, and from the prayers and good works of Mary and all the Saints.
 a. inheritance   c. library
 (b.) treasury   d. account

5. When waiting in the state of Purgatory, the soul suffers ___ punishment for sin.
 a. final   c. eternal
 b. earthly   (d.) temporal

Ⓑ **Check Understanding** Indicate whether the following statements are true or false. Then rewrite false statements to make them true.

6. The Church is a sign or Sacrament of John. True/(False)
 She is a Sacrament of Christ.
 _____

7. For the world to be in communion with God, all people must have received Communion. True/(False)
 All people must have faith and
 sorrow for their sins.

8. The Lord's Prayer brings us into communion with God the Father and his Son, Jesus. (True)/False
 _____
 _____

9. The Eucharist makes present on the altar Christ's sacrifice on the Cross offered to make reparation for people's sins. (True)/False
 _____
 _____

10. Prayers of petition are prayers that thank God for specific gifts. True/(False)
 Prayers of thanksgiving thank God
 for specific gifts.

Ⓒ **Make Connections** On a separate sheet of paper, write a one-paragraph response to the questions. How does the missionary Church bring people into communion with God? How does the prayerful Church do so?

Ask a volunteer to read aloud the activity instructions.

- Allow the students to work with a classmate to research important work that the Church is doing.
- Have them write down their text messages.
- Ask each pair to share their favorite text with the class.

CLOSE

A Prayer for Peace

🤍 Select students to take the parts of the Leader in this prayer. Choose seven people to each read one section.

Have the student leaders stand up near the prayer table.

Direct the first leader to begin. After each section, all will respond.

Follow the order of prayer on the student page.

▶ Conclude by inviting the students to sing or reflect on the song "Make Me a Channel," downloaded from **aliveinchrist.osv.com**.

CHAPTER REVIEW

Review the instructions for each section and have the students complete the review.

🛜 Go to **aliveinchrist.osv.com** to prepare customized and downloadable assessments, send eAssessments, and assign interactive reviews.

Use the closing points from Days 2–4 in each chapter to highlight lesson concepts for this unit and prepare for the Unit Review.

Have the students complete the Review pages. Then discuss the answers as a class. Review any concepts with which the students are having difficulty.

 Work with Words

Have the students fill in the letter to match the words in the left column with the correct definitions or descriptions in the right column.

 Work with Words **Match the words on the left with the correct definitions or descriptions on the right.**

_e_ **1.** doctrine

_h_ **2.** indulgences

_a_ **3.** spiritualities

_c_ **4.** temporal punishment

_g_ **5.** Apostles

_d_ **6.** hierarchy

_f_ **7.** spiritual treasury

_b_ **8.** People of God

_l_ **9.** encyclicals

_k_ **10.** schools

_j_ **11.** Church

_i_ **12.** Mystical Body of Christ

a. ways of praying and living as a disciple

b. image for the Church; first used to refer to God's Chosen People in the Old Testament

c. the purification of a sinner, here on Earth or in Purgatory due because of forgiven sins or the attachment to sin

d. levels of leadership and membership in the Church

e. official Church teachings we are obliged to believe

f. the holiness of Jesus and the good works of Mary and the Saints accounted to the Church

g. the twelve men Jesus chose to be his closest followers and to share in his work and mission in a special way

h. release from some of the punishment for sin

i. a name for the Church, whose baptized members are all united to Christ and one another through the Holy Spirit, forming one holy people with Christ as her head

j. word meaning a gathering or assembly

k. different ways to pray

l. letters written by the Pope to the Church community

B Check Understanding Circle the letter of the best answer to complete the following statements.

13. Church laws are contained in the ___.

    a. Bible   **b.** Church Council   **(c.)** Code of   **d.** Old Testament
                     Documents   Canon Law

14. Jesus sent the Twelve out two by two to announce the coming of the ___.

    (a.) Kingdom of God   **b.** Messiah   **c.** Church   **d.** Ascension

15. The ___ teaches us as disciples to pray.

    a. Canon Law   **b.** Rosary   **c.** Roman Missal   **(d.)** Holy Spirit

16. The ___ reality of the Church includes Christ's presence among us through the power of the Holy Spirit.

    (a.) spiritual   **b.** invisible   **c.** literal   **d.** allegorical

17. Through the Holy Spirit, Baptism, and the ___, Jesus forms the Church as his Body.

    a. Word   **b.** Resurrection   **(c.)** Eucharist   **d.** Apostles

18. Jesus taught his disciples that he was the ___ and they were the branches.

    a. roots   **(b.)** vine   **c.** fruit   **d.** both a and b

19. ___ is one of the Marks of the Church.

    a. Legalisic   **b.** Eucharistic   **c.** Canonical   **(d.)** Apostolic

20. ___ is silent, reflective prayer.

    (a.) Contemplative   **b.** Eucharistic   **c.** Meditative   **d.** Choral prayer
       prayer   prayer   prayer

B Check Understanding

Have the students circle the letter of the answer that best completes each statement.

C Make Connections

Point out that the students will be writing a short answer to the questions. Explain that even though these are short answer responses, they need to be sure that they fully answer the questions.

📶 Go to **aliveinchrist.osv.com** to prepare customized and downloadable assessments, send eAssessments, and assign interactive reviews.

C Make Connections Write a short answer to these questions.

21. Why do we need both faith and Baptism for salvation?

Even if we have faith, we must be baptized into new life in Christ to receive salvation. Baptism takes away Original Sin and makes a person a child of God.

22. How is our celebration of the Eucharist unique in terms of prayer?

When we celebrate the Eucharist, we are praying the Church's most important prayer. We are worshipping God together and receiving the Body and Blood of Christ.

23. Describe how the Church is both visible and spiritual.

In our visible gathering as the Church, we are the People of God. As a spiritual group, we are the Mystical Body of Christ, for Christ is present among us.

24. Jesus said that we are like branches. He also used other comparisons in the Gospels to describe the Kingdom of God. Now create your own comparison. What is your relationship with Jesus "like"?

Responses will vary.

25. Imagine that you are standing before Jesus at the Last Judgment. What would you say to him about how you have treated him? What would he say to you?

Responses will vary.

MORALITY

Why are practicing the virtues and developing a well-formed conscience necessary?

CHURCH HISTORY TIMELINE

34 Death of Stephen, first Christian martyr

81 Domitian persecution begins

1870 First Ecumenical Vatican council clarifies papal infallibility

1962 Second Ecumenical Vatican council convenes

Go to page 348 for more

Our Catholic Tradition

- God made us with a free will, an intellect, and a soul, and we are responsible for our choices. A well-formed conscience—and the help of Christ's teachings, the Church, the Holy Spirit, prayer, and wise people—will guide us to do what is right and good. (CCC, 1711, 1783)

- All human life is sacred and a gift from God. All people possess the human dignity that comes from being made in God's image. We have a responsibility to honor and protect life at all stages, from conception to old age. (CCC, 2319)

- Virtues are good spiritual habits that strengthen us and help us make good moral decisions and guide our conduct. The Theological Virtues make the moral (human) virtues possible. (CCC, 1803)

Our Catholic Life

- Morally good actions require that their object, intention, and circumstance be good; the end does not justify the means. (CCC, 1750–1756)

- We respect the dignity of the human person by respecting the rights of others, taking care of ourselves physically and emotionally, not abusing ourselves or others, and by not leading others into sin. (CCC, 2288–2290)

- The Cardinal Virtues of prudence, justice, fortitude, and temperance can help us respect ourselves and others and act with integrity. Learning about and practicing the virtues can help us live truthful, faith-filled lives. (CCC, 1804–1809)

Introduce Unit Theme

Start the lesson by taking a look at the Church History timeline events. Then move the students' focus to the image on the page. Invite volunteers to share the words they see and how they think these tie in to the theme of Morality.

Have the students review the bullets under the Our Catholic Tradition and Our Catholic Life sections. Invite volunteers to share what this information tells them they will be focusing on in Unit 5.

Let them know that they will learn more about the subject of morality as they review the next three chapters.

Ask the unit's Big Question found on page 210.

Allow time for discussion.

Explain to the students that this is the essential question for the unit. They will be working to fully answer it as they complete the three chapters in the unit.

Go to the Source

As an optional extension, organize the students into three groups, assigning each group one of the main Scripture passages found in this unit.

- Chapter 13: The Wisdom of Ben Sira 15:14–17
- Chapter 14: Deuteronomy 30:19–20
- Chapter 15: Colossians 3:12–15

Have each group read its passage and then give a dramatic reading (narrator with silent actors), create a visual representation, or write down one question they would ask God about the passage.

Reading the verses directly from the Bible will familiarize students with the sequence of the canon of Sacred Scripture.

Explore the Catechism

Assign students or groups of students to read individual articles in the *Catechism of the Catholic Church* chapter on The Dignity of the Human Person (paragraphs 1700–1877).

- Ask them to prepare several bullet points on the teachings in that chapter. For example, what does the *Catechism* say about people being created in God's image? What is meant by "vocation to Beatitude"? What does the *Catechism* teach about freedom?
- Allow time for any questions the students may have.

Reading the paragraphs directly from the *Catechism* will help the students learn where to find key teachings from the Sacred Tradition of the Church.

CHURCH HISTORY TIMELINE BACKGROUND

Refer the students to the Church History Timeline on pages 348–363 to learn more about important Church events and figures through A.D. 1085.

First Ecumenical Vatican Council Defines Papal Infallibility

Pope Pius IX convened Vatican Council I on June 29, 1868. Among its major accomplishments was the clarification of the doctrine of papal infallibility in 1870, which states that the Pope is protected from error, "when, as supreme pastor and teacher of all the faithful—who confirms his brethren in the faith—he proclaims by a definitive act a doctrine pertaining to faith or morals."

Second Ecumenical Vatican Council Convenes

On October 11, 1962, Pope Saint John XXIII opened Vatican II, the 21st ecumenical council of the Catholic Church. The Council enacted many changes, including the use of native languages instead of Latin in the Mass. It also condemned all forms of social and cultural discrimination as incompatible with God's design, stating that each person is created in the image of God and is gifted with dignity equal to all other humans.

KEY CONCEPT

We are free to choose, responsible for our choices, and guided in our moral decision-making.

DOCTRINAL CONTENT

- God made us with a free will, an intellect, and a soul; our conscience works with these gifts to help us choose good and avoid sin. (CCC, 1705, 1706, 1711)

- The distinction between mortal and venial sin is part of the tradition of the Church. Mortal sin and venial sin both affect a sinner's relationship with God, but in different ways. (CCC, 1854–1863)

- Morally good actions require that their object, intention, and circumstance be good; the end does not justify the means. (CCC, 1750–1754)

- A well-formed conscience— and the help of Christ's teachings, the Church, the Holy Spirit, prayer, and wise people— will guide us to do what is right and good. (CCC, 1783–1785)

TASKS OF CATECHESIS

Helping children grow in a faith that is "known, celebrated, lived, and expressed in prayer" (NDC, 20).

This chapter focuses on the following tasks of catechesis:

- Promoting Knowledge of the Faith

- Moral Formation

Teacher Background

> God in the beginning created human beings and made them subject to their own free choice. If you choose, you can keep the commandments; loyalty is doing the will of God. … Before everyone are life and death, whichever they choose shall be given them.
> **The Wisdom of Ben Sira (Sirach) 15:14–15, 17**
>
> **> Reflect** How does God's gift of freedom affect our responsibilities?

The Church teaches that a person's first obligation in making moral decisions is to form one's conscience. Saint Thomas Aquinas teaches us that conscience is our ability to reason so as to discern the will of God. Conscience then is a gift that we are given by God, a gift that begins with the presumption that what we seek is to do God's will.

Each of us has the obligation to work to keep our consciences informed. When we have important choices to make, we need to pray, learn the Church's teachings, and seek counsel from a committed disciple, someone who can help us understand God's revelation through Sacred Scripture and Sacred Tradition.

In this way, the law written in our hearts is uncovered and becomes the guide for our attitudes, words, and actions. We have a treasure of incredible value in our moral teaching, formed by the revelation of God in Sacred Scripture and illuminated through the centuries by the Magisterium. From generation to generation, the Church hands down the "language of faith" so as to open our hearts to the "understanding and the life of faith." The Church keeps central the Paschal Mystery of Jesus Christ for the sake of salvation and unity of all people.

> Reflect What do you do to try to maintain a healthy, well-formed conscience?

Teacher's Prayer

 God, the Father of life, help me to set a good example for my students. Help me to keep my actions and my words consistent with one another and with the teachings of the Church. I ask these things in Jesus' name. Amen.

How Seventh Graders Understand Chapter Topics

Seventh graders have many competing voices in their lives when it comes to moral decision making. Often popular culture gives one message (especially through television, music, movies, and video games), while the Church (and perhaps the family) gives quite another. It's important for seventh graders to understand that only God knows what is best for us, because God made us.

Teaching Tip: Research has shown that when making decisions about risky behaviors, it helps seventh graders to think about their bigger life goals and how a particular decision might either get them closer to that goal or make the goal less possible. Discussing some decisions this way in a group setting can help seventh graders be more prudent in their daily decision making.

Sharing the Message with Seventh Graders

- Younger adolescents are still prone to making impulsive decisions, particularly when pressured by peers.
- Seventh graders need to be taught to think through the various consequences of their choices.
- At this age, the students are still focused on themselves, but they are also beginning to grow into a deeper awareness of the rights and feelings of others. It's important to encourage and nurture this growth.

ONLINE RESOURCES

 Go to **aliveinchrist.osv.com**

You will find:

- Interactive lesson planning, additional activities, and ideas for the classroom environment
- Step by step lesson instruction from printed Teacher Edition for integrated lesson planning
- Custom-built assessments to download and eAssessment links
- Interactive reviews that provide scores and the option to review answers
- Chapter-specific Lectionary connections and a complete correlation ordered by the Sundays of the year, with suggestions for how to integrate the Scripture readings into chapter lessons

 Go to **osvparish.com** for Ask the Experts Q and A, Community Connections, and Blogs.

Chapter 13 Planner

Objectives	Open

DAY 1—Invite/Preview, Pages 211–213

- Reflect on God's personal invitation through Scripture
- Indicate prior knowledge of chapter concepts and vocabulary

- ♡ **Psalm 8:5–6** Pray the opening prayer.
- 📖 **The Wisdom of Ben Sira (Sirach) 15:14–17** Proclaim "Free Will." Guide the students through the process of Scripture reflection.
- Discuss Have You Ever Thought questions.

DAY 2—Discover, Pages 214–215

- Discuss the interrelationship of the soul, intellect, and conscience in following the moral law
- Contrast mortal and venial sin and their effect on the sinner's relationship with God

- ♡ Pray a prayer of petition, page 214.

DAY 3—Discover, Pages 216–217

- List and explain the elements that determine the morality of an action
- Explain how the circumstances of an action can increase or decrease its moral goodness

- ♡ Pray the **Act of Contrition**, page 387.
- Focus on the opening question.

DAY 4—Discover, Pages 218–219

- Relate the formation of a good conscience to the need to learn and practice new skills
- Explore the steps needed to make a good moral decision

- ♡ Pray the **Evening Prayer**, page 386.
- Discuss the photo.

DAY 5—Live, Pages 220–221

- Identify resources that will aid a person in making a moral decision
- Explore the faith life of Blessed Aloysius Stepinac
- Participate in an examination of conscience

- ♡ Pray the **Morning Prayer**, page 386.

REVIEW AND ASSESSMENT

Chapter Review, page 222
Chapter Test, page 211F

🛜 **aliveinchrist.osv.com** Customize and Download Assessments, Email Links to eAssessments, Interactive Student Reviews

Build	Close	Materials & Resources
• Present lesson highlights. • Preview **Catholic Faith Words**. ★ Consider the relationship between freedom and responsibility.	• Activity Discuss how peer pressure affects decision making.	☐ pencils or pens ☐ board or chart paper
• **Catholic Faith Words** soul, intellect, conscience, mortal sin, venial sin • Talk about soul, intellect, and conscience. 📖 Read Matthew 7:12. • Discuss different levels of sin.	• Activity Reflect on being aware of and having a well-formed conscience. • Conclude with a review of key concepts and objectives.	☐ pencils or pens ☐ board or chart paper ☐ highlighters
• Explain the three elements of the decision-making process. • Discuss the teaching that the end result determines the morality of an action. 📖 Reflect on Matthew 6:2–4.	• Activity Write about a moral issue. • Conclude with a review of key concepts and objectives. • Optional Activity What's Your Decision? (Activity Master 13)	☐ pencils or pens ☐ board or chart paper ☐ Bibles ☐ Activity Master 13 (Page 211G)
• Talk about practice in relation to conscience formation. ★ Review the five steps in moral decision-making based on personal application.	• Review the In Summary statements.	☐ pencils or pens ☐ board or chart paper
• Discuss the question in the Our Catholic Life section. • Learn about Saint Aloysius Stepinac. • Activity Review some decision-making resources.	• Select three readers. • Follow the order of prayer. ▶ Sing or play the closing song.	☐ pencils or pens 🔊 "Be Merciful, O Lord"

FORMING CATHOLIC IDENTITY ACROSS THE CURRICULUM

To integrate the Catholic faith in all aspects of curriculum, this chapter's objectives can be reinforced and applied in the instruction of other disciplines.

Go to **aliveinchrist.osv.com** for cross-curricular activities and projects linked to the doctrinal content discussed in this unit. Activities are available from among the following knowledge categories and content areas:

Language Arts

- Integration of Knowledge
- Literacy
- Speaking and Listening
- Writing Skills

Math

- Algebraic Thinking
- Geometry
- Measurement and Data
- Numbers and Operations

Science

- Earth Science
- Life Science
- Physical Science
- Technology

Social Studies

- Civics
- Economics
- Geography
- History

NCEA IFG: ACRE Edition

Knowledge of the Faith

- **Objective:** To know and understand basic Catholic teaching about the Incarnate Word Jesus Christ as the way, truth, and life

Moral Formation

- **Objective:** To be knowledgeable about the teachings of Jesus and the Church as the basis of Christian morality and to understand Catholic Social Teaching

Catholic Faith Literacy

conscience, mortal sin, venial sin

Catholic Social Teaching

To integrate Catholic Social Teaching into your lesson, choose one of the following features: Rights and Responsibilities of the Human Person, pages 338–339; or Solidarity of the Human Family, pages 344–345.

- Start the Live step of the process by talking about Blessed Aloysius Stepinac on page 220. Then move directly to the Catholic Social Teaching feature.
- Or, to expand the lesson, complete page 220, then move to the Catholic Social Teaching feature.
- Return to Chapter 13 for the prayer on page 221.

Music Option

Use the following song to enhance catechetical learning or for prayer.

- "Be Merciful, O Lord," Day 5, Page 221

Name _____ Date _____

Match each description in Column A with the correct term in Column B by filling in the appropriate letter.

Column A

Column B

____ **1.** A sin that weakens a person's relationship with God

a. mortal sin

____ **2.** The God-given ability that makes it possible to think, reason, and judge

b. venial sin

____ **3.** The spiritual principle of humans that is individual, created by God, and exists forever

c. soul

____ **4.** A grave sin by which someone turns completely away from God

d. intellect

Indicate whether the following statements are true or false. Then rewrite false statements to make them true.

5. It is all right to do evil if a good result will come from it. **True/False**

_____

6. Conscience is the God-given ability that helps individuals judge whether actions are right or wrong. **True/False**

_____

7. We do not need to do anything to form our conscience. **True/False**

_____

8. Follow these steps to make a good moral decision: **1)** Think about possible consequences, **2)** Compare your options to the Commandments and Beatitudes, **3)** Talk with someone who can advise you, **4)** Pray to the Holy Spirit, and **5)** Act with confidence that you have made the right decision. **True/False**

_____

Write a response on the lines below.

9. Why is it important to have a well-formed conscience?

_____

_____

10. Explain the three elements that determine the morality of a human action.

_____

_____

Name _____ Date _____

What's Your Decision?

For each moral dilemma described below, identify the object, the intention, and the circumstances of each situation. Use these elements to decide what you would do.

MORAL DILEMMA #1 You were directed to read six books over the summer. For most of the summer you did not do the reading and spent time with your best friend. It is now August, your best friend is on a trip, and so you begin the work. You realize that you probably won't have time to finish the book list. So, you find someone who has done the work and use his/her notes.

What is the object? _____

What is the intention? _____

What are the circumstances? _____

What is your decision? _____

MORAL DILEMMA #2 You want to give your mom a nice birthday present, but you don't have enough money. You would never steal anything from a store in the small town where you live because you know how that would hurt the store owners. But today you are in the mall. Many of the stores at the mall are owned by big corporations that get their merchandise at a discount and charge too much. The gift would really make your mom happy and she has had a really difficult year.

What is the object? _____

What is the intention? _____

What are the circumstances? _____

What is your decision? _____

MORAL DILEMMA #3 There is a group of students at your school who have singled out one person in the class. They constantly make fun of that person and now you hear that they are harassing this person online. You and your friends do not participate in the bullying but you also haven't taken any action to stop what is happening.

What is the object? _____

What is the intention? _____

What are the circumstances? _____

What is your decision? _____

Freedom and Responsibility

 Let Us Pray

Leader: Wondrous God, you have given us the awesome gift of freedom. With that gift comes the responsibility to make choices that show our love for you, each other, and ourselves.

"What is man that you are mindful of him,
and a son of man that you care for him?
Yet you have made him little less than a god,
crowned him with glory and honor." **Psalm 8:5–6**

All: Jesus, we want to do what is right. Show us. Teach us. Be with us as we discover how to love you well.

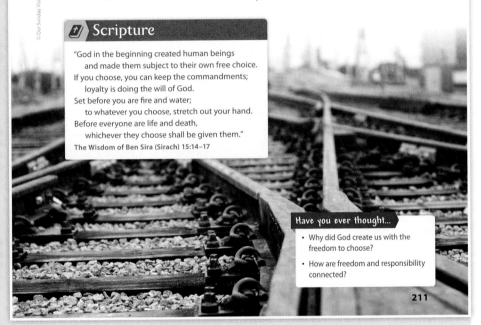

 Scripture

"God in the beginning created human beings
and made them subject to their own free choice.
If you choose, you can keep the commandments;
loyalty is doing the will of God.
Set before you are fire and water;
to whatever you choose, stretch out your hand.
Before everyone are life and death,
whichever they choose shall be given them."
The Wisdom of Ben Sira (Sirach) 15:14–17

Have you ever thought...
- Why did God create us with the freedom to choose?
- How are freedom and responsibility connected?

211

© Our Sunday Visitor

 Scripture Background

Scripture Reflection Process

Invite the students to be still, close their eyes, and focus on their breathing. Encourage them to open their minds and hearts to what God is saying to them.

- Proclaim the Scripture and have the students sit in silence.
- *Ask:* What did you hear God say to you today?
- Allow volunteers to share.

▶ You may play instrumental music to begin the reflection.

Objective
- Reflect on God's personal invitation through Scripture

OPEN _____

 Let Us Pray

Invite the students to gather in the prayer space and make the Sign of the Cross. Have a volunteer pray the Psalm verses aloud for the class. Prompt the group response.

Have the students move out of the prayer space and back to their seats.

Say: Because of free will, we have the ability to choose to follow God's will or to act against it. In today's reading, we'll learn about the responsibility that comes with the freedom to choose.

 Scripture

Guide the students through the process of Scripture reflection (see the Scripture Background box below).

Have you ever thought...
Say: God the Father gave us the gift of free will, and with that comes the great responsibility to live a moral life by following Jesus' teaching and actions.

- Invite the students to respond to the questions.

DAY 1

Objective

- Indicate prior knowledge of chapter concepts and vocabulary

BUILD _____

Use this page to assess the students' knowledge related to the chapter content.

Getting Started

Have a volunteer read aloud the opening paragraph.

- *Say:* This chapter will ask us to think about *freedom*.

- *Ask:* When you hear that word, what are some things that come to your mind?

- Allow the students to share their thoughts.

Freedom and Responsibility

Point out the chart at the bottom of the page.

- ✱ Direct the students to work independently on recording synonyms for *freedom* and *responsibility*.

- Have volunteers share their responses with the class.

- Discuss, as a class, whether these two words are opposites.

Getting Started

In this chapter you will gain a deeper understanding of human free will and responsibility for choices and actions, and explore how you can make morally good decisions. You will also learn about forming and informing your conscience.

Catholic Faith Words

- soul
- intellect
- conscience
- mortal sin
- venial sin

 In the chart below, record synonyms for "freedom" and "responsibility." With the class, discuss the connection between the two words.

Freedom and Responsibility

Synonyms for Freedom	_____
	_____
Synonyms for Responsibility	_____
	_____

© Our Sunday Visitor

---

i Teacher Background

Moral Development

Several psychologists have attempted to identify stages of moral development in children. They have found that there is no one identifiable stage where we will find all our students. Some will be in the pre-conventional stages—acting morally out of fear of punishment or in order to get some reward. Others will have moved into the conventional stage—seeking approval from those in authority. This presents challenges in teaching moral decision making to seventh graders. Careful teaching of this material is necessary for helping your students understand the need to form and inform their conscience according to Sacred Scripture and Tradition.

WRITE

Everyone's Doing It! Imagine a situation where someone your age is feeling pressured to do something wrong that the group they are hanging out with is about to do. On the lines below, describe that situation.

_____

_____

_____

_____

_____

_____

_____

_____

_____

_____

What might be going through the person's head as he or she decides whether or not to participate?

_____

_____

_____

_____

_____

_____

_____

_____

_____

_____

_____

Optional Activity

Topic Warm-Up _Verbal/Linguistic, Bodily/Kinesthetic_

Use this activity as a warm-up activity at the beginning of the chapter.

- Toss a foam ball around the room with these instructions: The person holding the ball is to name a choice he or she had to make today. It can be as simple a choice as "what to eat for breakfast."

- Continue until the ball has been tossed to all of the students.

- Next, repeat with these instructions: The person holding the ball is to name a responsibility he or she has. It can be as simple as "unloading the dishwasher in the morning."

- After a minute or two, connect the activity to the topic of the chapter: Freedom and Responsibility.

Work with Words

Point out the Catholic Faith Words box on page 212.

- Read aloud the five vocabulary terms.

- Encourage the class to define each of the vocabulary terms in their own words.

- Call on several students to share their ideas.

- Have a volunteer record their answers on the board or on chart paper.

- As you move through the chapter and review the words in context, invite the students to come back to this list and compare the definitions with what they originally thought.

CLOSE

ACTIVITY

Read aloud the activity instructions.

- Have the students work on this assignment with a classmate.

- Allow each pair of students to share their scenarios with the class.

- Encourage the class to offer comments on how they would make a decision for the situations presented.

DAY 2

Objectives

- Discuss the interrelationship of the soul, intellect, and conscience in following the moral law
- Contrast mortal and venial sin and their effect on the sinner's relationship with God

OPEN

💗 Have the students pray the prayer of petition from the Teacher Background box.

BUILD

Living Is Thinking and Doing

Direct the students to read the first paragraph.

📘 Scripture

Proclaim Matthew 7:12.

- *Ask:* How do you think this Scripture ties in to making decisions?

Your Decisions

Review these paragraphs with the class.

- Have the students underline or highlight what they think are the most important ideas.

Made to Choose

Tell the students to silently read this section.

- *Ask:* What are three things humans have that make us unique from other creatures?
  a soul, intellect, and a conscience

Living is Thinking and Doing

How can you make good choices?

Every day, you are faced with choices that require decisions. Some decisions seem more important than others, and you might not know how to make the more difficult ones. Just remember, you've been given some important tools to help you.

📘 Scripture

"Do to others whatever you would have them do to you. This is the law and the prophets." Matthew 7:12

Your Decisions

Sometimes other people make decisions for you because they have authority over you. But all those decisions that you make freely are your own responsibility. Something that you decide to do (or not to do) is a decision that belongs to you alone and no one else.

Why is this important? You are not morally responsible for decisions that you have not voluntarily made. Your intentional thoughts, decisions, and actions are yours. Morally, you are responsible for your freely-made decisions, and the action or inaction that comes from them.

Made to Choose

You have the ability to choose to act in a variety of ways. Why? Because God made humans unique from all other creatures.

You have a **soul**—the spiritual part of you that lives forever; **intellect**—that which makes it possible for you to think, reason, and judge; and free will—the God-given freedom and ability to make choices on your own without being forced to choose or act in a certain way. This unique combination makes you an image of God. You are created with the tremendous ability to seek what is good and true, and therefore reach happiness with God in Heaven.

God gives you another important gift to help you make decisions: your **conscience**. Your conscience is like an inner voice, part of your ability to reason, that helps you to judge whether actions are right or wrong.

Conscience is what moves you to know and follow the moral law, to do good and avoid what is evil. It is important for us to know God's laws so our conscience can help us make good decisions. You are called by God to develop an informed conscience.

214 Chapter 13

© Our Sunday Visitor

ℹ Teacher Background

Prayer of Petition

Write the following prayer on the board or on chart paper, or, if you prefer, create a printout of the prayer for the students. Pray the petitions below and follow each with: "I want to do what's right."

- When I'm with my family, Lord . . .
- When I'm with my friends, Lord . . .
- When I'm at school, Lord . . .
- Every day of my life, Lord . . .

Before closing the prayer, invite the students to add any petitions of their own, following this same pattern.

Choices That Lead You from God

Listening to your conscience leads you along the path that keeps you in the right relationship with God and away from sin—any deliberate thought, word, or action that goes against moral law and offends God. Sin is a deliberate choice to disobey God. It's not a mistake or an accident.

Catholic Faith Words

soul the spiritual principle of a human person that is individual, created by God, and will exist forever

intellect the God-given ability which makes it possible for humans to think, reason, and judge

conscience the God-given ability that helps individuals judge whether actions are right or wrong

mortal sin a grave (very serious) sin by which someone turns completely away from God and breaks his or her relationship with God

venial sin a sin that weakens, but does not destroy, a person's relationship with God

There are two types of personal sins for which someone is responsible. **Mortal sin** breaks a person's relationship with God. The effect of mortal sin, without repenting and being forgiven, is total separation from God forever. For a sin to be mortal, three conditions must be met:

- the matter involved must be very serious;
- the person must know the action is serious and sinful (called sufficient reflection); and
- the person freely chooses or agrees to commit the wrong anyway (full consent of the will to do what is wrong).

The Commandments specify gravely serious matter. But not all sins are gravely damaging or mortal. Less serious sin, called **venial sin**, weakens a person's relationship with God, but does not destroy it. Venial sins lessen the love of God in your heart and make it more difficult for you to resist sin. Venial sins arise from not using moderation or acting without full knowledge, and can sometimes lead to mortal sin.

NAME AND DISCUSS

Name three things someone might do to become more aware of his or her conscience.

1. _____
2. _____
3. _____

How would someone know if his/her conscience has been well formed? Discuss your answers with a classmate.

_____
_____

Optional Activity

Differences in Meanings *Verbal/Linguistic*

Divide the students into small groups. Tell them to look up the words *conscience*, *mortal*, and *venial* in a dictionary that includes the sources of words. Then have them answer the questions below.

- What are the secular meanings of these words?
- What are the religious meanings of these words?
- What is the danger in equating conscience with opinion?
- Discuss, as a class, what the groups come up with.

Choices That Lead You from God

Challenge the students to find the two definitions of *sin* in the first paragraph. Sin is "any deliberate thought, word, or action that goes against moral law and offends God," and "a deliberate choice to disobey God."

Point out the three conditions for a sin to be mortal:

- The matter involved must be very serious.
- The person must know the action is serious and sinful.
- The person must freely choose to commit the wrong anyway.

Be sure that everyone understands these points before moving on.

Work with Words

Help the students study the Catholic Faith Words and their definitions.

- Ask them to shut their books for a quick review of the vocabulary.
- Write the Catholic Faith Words on the board and read aloud each definition, letting volunteers match it to the correct word.

CLOSE

ACTIVITY

Have the students complete the activity with a classmate.

Quick Review Because we are made in God's image, we have a soul, our intellect, and a conscience that help us as we make choices. This leaves open the possibility for personal sin, which can hurt our relationship with God.

DAY 3

Objectives

- List and explain the elements that determine the morality of an action
- Explain how the circumstances of an action can increase or decrease its moral goodness

OPEN

💗 Have the students stand at their seats and make the Sign of the Cross before praying the Act of Contrition, page 387.

Ask a volunteer to read aloud the opening question. Invite ideas and comments from the group.

BUILD

The Sources of Action

Point out the three things that determine the morality of a human action by reading aloud the bullet points. Share the quote from the *Catechism of the Catholic Church*.

- Write *object, intention,* and *circumstances* on the board or on chart paper.

Ask volunteers to read aloud the paragraphs in the case study.

- Pause after each paragraph to make sure everyone understands.
- Discuss the question on page 217.
- Give the students an opportunity to ask any additional questions about the example.

The Sources of Action

What determines whether an action is good?

How do you know if what you are doing is morally right? Three things determine the morality of a human action:

- the object, which characterizes the action in and of itself.
- the intention, which is the immediate end or purpose the person intends to achieve through the action.
- the circumstances, which surround the action.

"A morally good act requires the goodness of the object, of the end, and of the circumstances together . . . One may not do evil so that good may result from it" (see the *Catechism*, 1755–1756).

Consider this situation: Your older brother is driving Grandma to the doctor using Dad's car with his permission. The *object* of this action is to drive his grandmother to the doctor.

A bike rider loses control and swerves in front of the car. Your brother makes a snap decision and turns the steering wheel, causing the car to jump the curb. There are no pedestrians at the curbside. The object of his action and his intention are to avoid hitting the biker. Your brother's *intention* is not to break the rules of the road or to put pedestrians in danger, but to avoid hitting and hurting the bike rider.

The *circumstances* are that no pedestrians are at or near the curb and that your brother only drove on the curb long enough to avoid the biker. In this case, the immediate object of the brother's action was to avoid the biker. This too was his intention.

The circumstances permitted him to do this without hurting anyone else. Even though he technically violated the law by going off the road, the immediate object of his action was to avoid hitting the biker. The object, intention, and circumstances were good. His was a morally good act.

216 · Chapter 13

Optional Activity

Activity Master 13: What's Your Decision?

Distribute copies of the activity found on teacher page 211G.

- The students will make decisions based on the three things that help to determine the morality of a human action.
- Have them work on the activity alone. After they've completed their work, allow them to share their ideas with a classmate.

🖉 Go to the Source
Read Matthew 6:2–4 to find out more of what Jesus had to say about good deeds.

When making a choice, you have to consider all three elements: what is the action or object itself; why are you doing it, or not doing it; and what are the pressures, environment, or issues surrounding it that might be affecting your judgment.

> Why is the brother's action described earlier a morally good act?

Consider This

A good intention—such as wanting to help your sister—does not make an object or behavior that is morally wrong—such as lying to your parents—good. A bad intention—such as the desire to boast—can make an object or behavior that is good—such as donating money or time to a worthy cause—morally bad. As Jesus said, "[But] take care not to perform righteous deeds in order that people might see them" (Matthew 6:1).

Saint Thomas Aquinas argued that whether an act is good or evil depends on the end result of that action. Human acts are good if they promote the purpose and honor of God. Aquinas taught that by repeating a good action, people develop a moral habit, which allows them to do good easily. He wrote, "An evil action cannot be justified by reference to a good intention." Today we say, "The end does not justify the means." In an extreme example of this belief, if asked what to do in a situation where killing one person would save one hundred other lives, a Catholic person's answer is that murder is wrong no matter how many lives it saves.

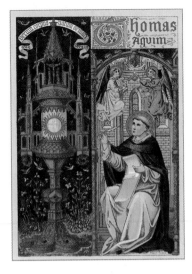

The circumstances of an action can increase or decrease the moral goodness of the action. Factors such as fear, ignorance, and pressure are some examples. But circumstances cannot change whether an act is morally good or not, only the degree of its goodness or evilness. Some acts, such as murder, are always wrong no matter the intention or the circumstances because choosing them entails so great an evil that they are against the natural moral law.

THINK AND WRITE

Think about a moral decision you are currently dealing with, or have dealt with recently. Write about the act, the intention, the circumstances, and what your conscience tells you.

📖 Scripture Background

What's in Matthew?

Matthew 6:2–8 is the source for considering one's intention in determining the morality of an action. Doing good for selfish reasons diminishes the rightness of the action. Interestingly, this section is followed by the Lord's Prayer, which keeps us focused on what is really important in God's eyes.

Tertullian is known to have said that the Lord's Prayer is "the summary of the whole Gospel." The words of the Lord's Prayer are Jesus' words.

🖉 Go to the Source
Have the students read Matthew 6:2–4 to find Jesus' teaching on the need for the appropriate intention when doing good deeds.

Consider This
Tell the students to silently read this section.

- Explain how the circumstances of an action can increase or decrease its moral goodness.

- Discuss how the philosophies of Saint Thomas Aquinas still apply today.

CLOSE _____

ACTIVITY

Have the students read the instructions for themselves.

- Give them time to reflect on a personal moral decision.

- Have them complete this activity on their own.

Quick Review There are three elements that determine the morality of an action: the object, the intention, and the circumstances. Saint Thomas Aquinas taught that whether an act was good or evil depended on the end results of that action, and that the circumstances of an action can increase or decrease its moral goodness.

DAY 4

Objectives

- Relate the formation of a good conscience to the need to learn and practice new skills
- Explore the steps needed to make a good moral decision

OPEN

💙 Have the students pray the Evening Prayer from page 386.

Invite them to share what they think this photo has to do with conscience formation.

BUILD

Formation for Doing Right

Give the students time to read through the first three paragraphs.

Conscience Formation

Read aloud the first paragraph.

- Tell the students that this concept is very similar to practicing to get better at a sport or a subject in school.
- Let them know that teachers are often required to learn or deepen a new skill as well.
- Explain that this same principle holds true for developing our conscience.

Ask a volunteer to read aloud the three bullet points.

- Have the students underline the last sentence in this section. rely on the wisdom found in Sacred Scripture and the teachings of the Church in Sacred Tradition

"Listen to counsel and receive instruction, that you may eventually become wise" (Proverbs 19:20).

© Our Sunday Visitor

Formation for Doing Right

How can a well-formed conscience help you?

Athletes know that if a person wants to build up his or her body, he or she has to work at it. He or she has to establish a routine involving exercise and the right food.

Building and shaping a conscience is similar. If you want to make good decisions through life and do the right things, then forming a conscience is critical. If a conscience has been formed well, it will lead you to what is truthful and just. It will help you make sound, rational judgments and follow what is good.

When you have a moral decision to make, your conscience will move you to make a right (morally good) judgment that follows reason and God's law. Or it can lead you to make an incorrect (morally bad) judgment that does not follow reason and God's law.

218 Chapter 13

Conscience Formation

Someone who wants to become a better pianist will seek out a teacher who can introduce skills and guide the student to feel the music as they play. The person will spend a lot of time practicing, and accepting the fact that their development will be ongoing; if you don't use the skills, you'll lose them. The same holds true with building up your conscience. There are a few important ways to do this:

- **Scripture:** What does the Bible tell you?
- **Church teaching:** What does the Church say about it?
- **Getting advice:** Ask for input from family members or trusted adults, study the facts of the situation, and look at the standards of society (e.g., is the action legal?).

> How can taking one or more of these steps help you?

ℹ️ Teacher Background

Forming a Conscience

We have the freedom to make our own choices, but we also have the responsibility to make good decisions. Tell the students that forming and educating their conscience and making the right choices is one way for them to respond to God's love. We don't do this only to grow closer to God and others; we do this to make our lives better.

Remind the students that not everyone has the opportunity or takes advantage of the opportunity to inform his or her conscience. There is also a difference in a conscience formed as a result of passive indoctrination by society, culture, and media versus the conscience formed by actively seeking wisdom.

When you use these resources to inform your conscience and find that there is a conflict between some of these sources, rely on the wisdom found in Sacred Scripture and the teachings of the Church in Sacred Tradition.

Vices and Virtues

You've probably heard that practice makes perfect, but have you ever thought of it in the reverse? What happens when you keep repeating the same negative, sinful behavior over and over? You create in yourself a vice, a habit or tendency to be more sinful. The Church uses the term *vices* to refer to the seven capital sins that tend to produce other sinful behavior. Vices incline us to actions that are harmful to ourselves and to others. Traditionally, the Church has identified seven capital sins or vices: pride, covetousness, envy, anger, gluttony, lust, and sloth or laziness.

Fortunately the Cardinal Virtues of prudence, justice, fortitude, and temperance are good habits within us that, when strengthened and practiced, help us counter these vices in our daily lives. Virtues help us respond consistently to the situations we face, guiding us to make morally good decisions. The more we intentionally practice the virtues, the more we can rely on them to guide us.

Underline which step you tend to rely on most when making a moral decision. Circle one that you could do more often.

Steps in Making a Moral Decision	
Think	Take time to consider your options and the possible consequences to yourself, others, and your relationship with God. Take time to hear what your conscience might be saying.
Compare	How do your options compare to Jesus' Beatitudes, his New Commandment, the Ten Commandments, and Church teachings? If an option contradicts any of these, then it's not really an option anymore.
Talk	Find someone who can understand the situation you are in. Tell him or her what you are thinking and why. Ask for advice.
Pray	Turn to the Holy Spirit in prayer, asking for guidance to make the right decision.
Act	Make your choice and be confident that you have made the right one based upon your conscience.

IN SUMMARY Catholics Believe

We are free to choose, responsible for our choices, and guided in our moral decision-making.

- God made us with a free will, an intellect, and a soul. Our conscience works with these gifts so that we can choose to do good and avoid sin.

- Morally good actions require that their object, intention, and circumstance be good; the end does not justify the means.

- A well-formed conscience will guide us to do what is right and good, and with the help of Christ's teachings, the Church, the Holy Spirit, prayer, and wise people, we can make good decisions.

Freedom and Responsibility   **219**

✓ Teaching Tip

Moral Decision Making

It is likely that there are Catholics who do not know the three bulleted points in the Catholics Believe text.

- As you read over them with your students, stress that many people of other faiths share these beliefs about conscience and free will.
- Catholics have the gift of the *Catechism of the Catholic Church*, which is a collection of the teachings of our faith.
- In order to be faithful Catholics, we need to use the Church's teachings to help us develop well-formed consciences.

Vices and Virtues

Introduce the students to the seven capital sins, or vices, and the Cardinal Virtues that help us counter them.

Steps in Making a Moral Decision

Invite five students to read the five steps in the chart.

- Review each step with the group, clarifying as needed.
- ★ Have the students underline the step they depend on most and circle the one they could do more often.

Write the five steps for making a moral decision on the board or on chart paper: *Think, Compare, Talk, Pray, Act*.

- Arrange the students in small groups. Assign each group a situation and invite them to use the steps to make a recommendation on how someone could respond.
- Sample situations: telling the truth, even if it gets you into trouble; cheating on tests; drinking, using drugs or tobacco; gossiping.

Invite the groups to share their results with the class.

CLOSE _____

In Summary

Read aloud the opening statement. Invite three volunteers to read the bullet points.

- *Ask*: Are these beliefs only for Catholics? Do you think other people follow them, too? Do you think all Catholics follow them?

Freedom and Responsibility   **219**

DAY 5

Objectives

- Identify resources that will aid a person in making a moral decision
- Explore the faith life of Blessed Aloysius Stepinac
- Participate in an examination of conscience

OPEN

Ask the students to stand at their seats and pray the Morning Prayer, from page 386, as a class.

BUILD

Our Catholic Life

Have a volunteer read aloud this section.

- Allow the students to privately write their responses to the Our Catholic Life question.

People of Faith

Explain to the students that Blessed Aloysius Stepinac believed very strongly in the freedom of all people.

- Read aloud the People of Faith paragraph.
- Review with the class the additional details in the People of Faith Background box.
- Invite the students to silently pray the Act of Hope from page 387.

Our Catholic Life

Your conscience is meant to be maintained and used to guide you in doing what is right and good. You can **inform and strengthen your conscience** by listening with your heart and mind to the Word of God, the teachings of the Church, and the prompting of the Holy Spirit. You can also seek guidance from parents, teachers, and mentors when making big and small choices. You can practice informing your conscience by ending each day with a prayer and an examination of conscience like the one on the next page to think about how you might have helped or hurt others that day, and how you might do more or better the next day.

> What is on your mind that an examination of conscience might help or make clear?

People of Faith

Blessed Aloysius Stepinac, 1898–1960

Aloysius Stepinac was ordained as a priest after World War I, and eventually was appointed Archbishop of Zagreb. During World War II, he raised his voice against the Nazi tyranny. After that war, during the pro-communist regime of Marshal Tito, Stepinac was imprisoned. He was released after five years on the orders of Tito, who wished to meet him. At their meeting, Stepinac told Tito, "I am for the freedom of the people and accordingly I will raise my voice against you every time you should encroach on this freedom." The Church celebrates his feast day on **September 7**.

For more, go to aliveinchrist.osv.com

PRACTICE

Choose a tough issue you are dealing with in your life and practice informing your conscience by consulting these four resources.

What does God tell you in the Bible?

What does the Church teach?

What do respected and wise figures in your life say?

What are your community's laws and values?

_____
_____
_____
_____
_____
_____
_____

220 Chapter 13

People of Faith Background

Blessed Aloysius Stepinac

Here are some additional details to share:

- Blessed Aloysius Stepinac didn't just raise his voice against the Nazi regime, he also helped to hide many Jewish people in order for them to avoid persecution.
- Even though it was very dangerous, Blessed Aloysius Stepinac spoke out against the persecution of gypsies and the Serbs in addition to his protesting of the treatment of those who were Jewish.

Encourage the students to go to **aliveinchrist.osv.com** at home to learn more about Blessed Aloysius Stepinac.

Examination of Conscience

Leader: Jesus, we know that you came into the world to cast out the darkness of sin, ignorance, and death. You are the Light of the World. As your followers, show us how to reflect your light. Let us take a moment to reflect on the times we have not been a sign of your light in the world, and ask the Lord for his mercy and his forgiveness.

Reader 1: Did I take God's name in vain? Did I curse or use bad language?

Reader 2: Did I miss Mass on a Sunday or Holy Day of Obligation without any serious reason?

Reader 3: Did I obey my parents, teachers, or trusted adults?

Reader 1: Was I selfish in how I treated others?

Reader 2: When have I forgiven others? When have I refused to forgive?

Reader 3: Did I look at indecent pictures or videos?

Reader 1: Did I steal or damage another's property?

Reader 2: Did I tell lies?

Reader 3: When have I stopped people from gossip? Did I gossip or make fun of someone through my words, texts, or social media?

Leader: Let us now pray the Act of Contrition as a way to show that we are truly sorry for our failings.

All: My God,
I am sorry for my sins with all my heart.
In choosing to do wrong
and failing to do good,
I have sinned against you
whom I should love above all things.
I firmly intend, with your help,
to do penance,
to sin no more,
and to avoid whatever leads me to sin.
Our Savior Jesus Christ
suffered and died for us.
In his name, my God, have mercy.
Amen.
Rite of Penance

Leader: Lord, teach us to be persistent, to be strong, and to be courageous. Nourish in us a practical desire to build up rather than tear down; to reconcile instead of polarize. Send your Holy Spirit to enlighten us and show us the way.

All: Amen.

▶ *Sing or play "Be Merciful, O Lord"*

Freedom and Responsibility **221**

🛜 Go to **aliveinchrist.osv.com** for an interactive review.

Ⓐ Work with Words Complete each sentence with the correct term from the Word Bank.

soul	free will
moral law	intention
conscience	circumstances
sin	intellect

1. _____**Conscience**_____ is a God-given ability that helps you judge whether something is right or wrong.

2. Conscience moves you to know and follow the _____**moral law**_____, which directs us to do good and avoid evil.

3. _____**Sin**_____ is any deliberate thought, word, action, or omission that goes against moral law and offends God.

4. Every human action is composed of three elements—the object, the _____**intention**_____, and the circumstances.

5. The _____**circumstances**_____ of an action can increase or decrease the moral goodness of the action.

Ⓑ Check Understanding Circle the letter of the choice that best completes the sentence.

6. Your ___ is the spiritual principle in humans that is created by God and exists forever.
   a. intellect   (c.) soul
   b. free will   d. conscience

7. Your ___ is the God-given ability to think, reason, and judge.
   (a.) intellect   c. soul
   b. free will   d. conscience

8. The effect of ___, without repenting and being forgiven, is separation from God forever.
   a. venial sin   c. free will
   (b.) mortal sin   d. moral law

9. ___ weakens, but does not destroy, a person's relationship with God.
   (a.) Venial sin   c. Free will
   b. Mortal sin   d. Moral law

10. If a(n) ___ has been formed well, it will lead you to what is truthful and just.
   a. intellect   c. free will
   (b.) conscience   d. soul

Ⓒ Make Connections Write a one-paragraph response to the question. What types of decisions are people your age currently facing? Write about the process of making a moral decision using the steps *think, compare, talk, pray,* and *act.*

_____
_____
_____
_____
_____
_____
_____
_____
_____
_____

Have the students read the instructions and complete the activity independently.

- As an alternative activity, you may wish to work through a hypothetical issue as a class.

CLOSE

Examination of Conscience

♡ Ask three volunteers to each be one of the readers.

Gather the students in the prayer space with their textbooks opened and ready to read the responses in the prayer.

Follow the order of prayer on the student page.

▶ Conclude by playing or singing with the students "Be Merciful, O Lord," downloaded from **aliveinchrist.osv.com**.

CHAPTER REVIEW

Review the instructions for each section and have the students complete the review.

🛜 Go to **aliveinchrist.osv.com** to prepare customized and downloadable assessments, send eAssessments, and assign interactive reviews.

Freedom and Responsibility **221–222**

KEY CONCEPT

All human life is sacred and a gift from God.

DOCTRINAL CONTENT

- All human life is sacred and a gift from God. All people possess the human dignity that comes from being made in God's image. (CCC, 2258)

- The Fifth Commandment forbids direct and intentional killing as gravely sinful. If anger reaches the point of a deliberate desire to kill or seriously wound a neighbor, it is a mortal sin. (CCC, 2268, 2302)

- The Church teaches about and advocates the right to life of every person. We have a responsibility to honor and protect life at all stages, from conception to old age. (CCC, 2270, 2319)

- We respect the dignity of the human person by respecting the rights of others, taking care of ourselves physically and emotionally, not abusing ourselves or others, and by not leading others into sin. (CCC, 2288–2290)

TASKS OF CATECHESIS

Helping children grow in a faith that is "known, celebrated, lived, and expressed in prayer" (NDC, 20).

This chapter focuses on the following tasks of catechesis:

- Promoting Knowledge of the Faith

- Moral Formation

Teacher Background

📖 I call heaven and earth today to witness against you: I have set before you life and death, the blessing and the curse. Choose life, then that you and your descendants may live, by loving the LORD, your God, obeying his voice, and holding fast to him.
Deuteronomy 30:19–20

> **Reflect** What does *always* choosing life mean to you?

Being a Christian in any age isn't easy, but today we face moral challenges that our parents and grandparents never dreamed of. It seems that every scientific advance brings with it new moral and ethical dilemmas. Issues such as reproductive technologies, stem-cell research, cloning, and artificial life-support (just to name a few) force us to make new and complex moral choices, and this is often done without proper formation and prayerful reflection. For some, the prevailing ethic seems to be if you can do something, you should do it, but the wisdom of our Catholic Tradition says otherwise. Our decisions are based upon the essence of who we are as humans: created in God's own image and likeness and bestowed with inherent dignity, possessors of the sacred gifts of life from the Giver of life.

Today, perhaps more than ever before, the stability of the Catholic Church is a priceless gift. In a world in which change comes rapidly, and in which the poor and the weak are in greater danger of being neglected or mistreated, the Church provides a powerful voice of timeless, unwavering moral truth. One fundamental principle from which this truth flows is our belief in the life and dignity of every human person, taught to us by Jesus Christ and modeled in his life and ministry. If the Son of God became human, there must be something intrinsically good about humanity. For two thousand years, the Church has affirmed that goodness. All have the right to life, no matter their age or capabilities, and that life starts from the moment of conception and lasts until death.

> **Reflect** In what ways do you purposefully attempt to affirm human life and dignity?

Teacher's Prayer

♥ Loving God, help me to set a good example for my students. May I see your face in every person's face, and may I affirm each person's dignity. Amen.

How Seventh Graders Understand Chapter Topics

Seventh graders are aware of individual rights, at least so far as it concerns their own rights. They might need help in stepping outside themselves and understanding that every person has dignity by virtue of being created in God's image. This is a message that is increasingly countercultural, so it might be important to emphasize that although they might get the message that some lives are worth less than others, this is simply not true.

Teaching Tip: Ask the students how and why some people seem to be valued more or less than others. They probably have some personal experience with this in their own school. Have the students reflect on the following questions, but remind them not to mention aloud any specific names: Who are the popular people at school, and why? Who are the people being treated as if they matter less? What can we do to show and promote equal value among all?

Sharing the Message with Seventh Graders

- At this age, younger adolescents are more inclined to notice others for their differences rather than their commonalities.
- Some seventh graders tend to form judgments based on appearance, talents, or personality traits. It's important to clearly communicate to them what the Church believes about human life and dignity.
- Students at this age can be cruel to each other, especially online or by gossiping. This negative behavior is often used to keep them in good graces with others. Help them see how their words and/or actions affect others.

ONLINE RESOURCES

🛜 Go to **aliveinchrist.osv.com**

You will find:

- Interactive lesson planning, additional activities, and ideas for the classroom environment
- Step by step lesson instruction from printed Teacher Edition for integrated lesson planning
- Custom-built assessments to download and eAssessment links
- Interactive reviews that provide scores and the option to review answers
- Chapter-specific Lectionary connections and a complete correlation ordered by the Sundays of the year, with suggestions for how to integrate the Scripture readings into chapter lessons

🛜 Go to **osvparish.com** for Ask the Experts Q and A, Community Connections, and Blogs.

Chapter 14 Planner

Objectives	Open

DAY 1—Invite/Preview, Pages 223–225

- Reflect on God's personal invitation through Scripture
- Indicate prior knowledge of chapter concepts and vocabulary

- ♥ **Psalm 34:13** Pray the opening prayer.
- 📖 **Deuteronomy 30:19–20** Proclaim "The Choice Before Israel." Guide the students through the process of Scripture reflection.
- Discuss Have You Ever Thought questions.

DAY 2—Discover, Pages 226–227

- Explain that each human life has value because we are made in God's image
- Identify murder as an action that violates the sacredness of human life

- ♥ Pray **Psalm 139:13–14**, page 226.
- Point out the title and opening question.

DAY 3—Discover, Pages 228–229

- Explore the aspects of the Fifth Commandment that deal with anger and vengeance
- Examine why the Church advocates for the rights of others on life issues

- ♥ Pray the *Memorare*, page 384.
- Discuss the opening question.

DAY 4—Discover, Pages 230–231

- Examine the ways in which we do not show respect for our own lives or the lives of others
- Explain why scandal harms individuals and society
- Identify the basic rights people need to grow and mature

- ♥ Pray the last lines of the **Litany of Saint Joseph**, page 390.
- Ask the opening question.

DAY 5—Live, Pages 232–233

- Discuss how the Church protects the right to life of all human beings
- Explore the faith life of Saint Martin de Tours
- Offer the Prayer for Life

- ♥ Pray a prayer of thanksgiving.

REVIEW AND ASSESSMENT

Chapter Review, page 234
Chapter Test, page 223F

📶 **aliveinchrist.osv.com** Customize and Download Assessments, Email Links to eAssessments, Interactive Student Reviews

Build	Close	Materials & Resources
• Present lesson highlights. • Preview **Catholic Faith Words**. ★ Consider actions and attitudes that do and do not honor the dignity of human life.	• Activity Work on empathizing with the situations of others. • Optional Activity Worst and Best Case Scenarios (Activity Master 14)	☐ pencils or pens ☐ Activity Master 14 (Page 223G)
• **Catholic Faith Words** human dignity, murder • Talk about the sacredness of life. 📖 Read and reflect on Psalm 139:13–20. • Discuss the concept of a throwaway culture in relation to human dignity.	• Activity Compare and contrast humans and the rest of creation. • Conclude with a review of key concepts and objectives.	☐ pencils or pens ☐ Bibles
• **Catholic Faith Words** abortion, euthanasia • Explain Jesus stance on the value of human life. 📖 Reflect on Matthew 5:38–48.	• Activity Identify ways that we can value and honor life at various stages. • Conclude with a review of key concepts and objectives.	☐ pencils or pens ☐ board or chart paper ☐ Bibles
• **Catholic Faith Words** scandal • Discuss the importance of respecting ourselves. ★ Review ways that we can damage God's artistry in us. • Explain scandal and its effects.	• Activity Discuss using respectful language. • Review the In Summary statements.	☐ pencils or pens
• Discuss the question in the Our Catholic Life section. • Learn about Saint Martin de Tours. • Activity Discuss modern media sources that encourage respect for life.	• Have the students bring images to the prayer service representing those who need prayer. • Follow the order of prayer. ▶ Sing or reflect on the closing song.	☐ pencils or pens 📶 "Lover of Life"

Chapter Connections

FORMING CATHOLIC IDENTITY ACROSS THE CURRICULUM

To integrate the Catholic faith in all aspects of curriculum, this chapter's objectives can be reinforced and applied in the instruction of other disciplines.

Go to **aliveinchrist.osv.com** for cross-curricular activities and projects linked to the doctrinal content discussed in this unit. Activities are available from among the following knowledge categories and content areas:

Language Arts

- Integration of Knowledge
- Literacy
- Speaking and Listening
- Writing Skills

Math

- Algebraic Thinking
- Geometry
- Measurement and Data
- Numbers and Operations

Science

- Earth Science
- Life Science
- Physical Science
- Technology

Social Studies

- Civics
- Economics
- Geography
- History

NCEA IFG: ACRE Edition

Knowledge of the Faith

- **Objective:** To know and understand basic Catholic teaching about the Incarnate Word Jesus Christ as the way, truth, and life

Moral Formation

- **Objective:** To be knowledgeable about the teachings of Jesus and the Church as the basis of Christian morality and to understand Catholic Social Teaching

Catholic Faith Literacy

abortion, euthanasia, sin

Catholic Social Teaching

To integrate Catholic Social Teaching into your lesson, choose one of the following features: Life and Dignity of the Human Person, pages 334–335; or Rights and Responsibilities of the Human Person, pages 338–339.

- Start the Live step of the process by talking about Saint Martin de Tours on page 232. Then move directly to the Catholic Social Teaching feature.
- Or, to expand the lesson, complete page 232, then move to the Catholic Social Teaching feature.
- Return to Chapter 14 for the prayer on page 233.

Music Options

Use one or more of the following songs to enhance catechetical learning or for prayer.

- "Lover of Life," Day 5, Page 233
- "Apple of My Eye," Day 5, Page 233
- "Mother to Another," Day 5, Page 233

Name _____ Date _____

Complete each sentence with the correct term.

1. _____ is the destructive behavior by which a person leads another person, either through action or inaction, to sin.

2. _____ is the deliberate termination of a pregnancy by killing an unborn child.

3. To deliberately cause the death of someone who is sick, dying, or suffering either through action or inaction is called _____.

4. The Fifth Commandment says that _____, the deliberate killing of another person when the killing is not in self-defense, is always a grave sin.

Circle the letter of the choice that best completes each sentence.

5. The sacredness of all human life comes directly from ____.
   a. how people think
   b. the kind of work they do
   c. their heredity
   d. being created by God

6. Of all the creatures made by God, humans are the only ones who have the capacity to ____.
   a. recognize God's presence
   b. help others
   c. learn
   d. communicate

7. When Jesus taught about the Fifth Commandment, he widened the understanding of "You shall not kill" to include ____.
   a. anger and vengeance
   b. accidental killing
   c. suicide
   d. lying

8. When Jesus was arrested, he ____.
   a. ordered his Apostles to fight to defend him
   b. upheld and honored every human life, including those who were harming him
   c. expressed his anger at those arresting him
   d. practiced passive resistance

Write a response on the lines below.

9. Explain your understanding of the "consistent ethic of life." _____

   _____

10. What is human dignity? _____

    _____

Name _____   Date _____

Worst and Best Case Scenarios

As much as we'd like to deny it, we've all experienced times when we acted at our worst. We've also made some pretty good choices and been at our best. Choose one of the situations listed below and describe both the worst and the best ways people could act in these circumstances. You may also make up a different situation.

Join the small group to which you have been assigned. Compare ideas, and select one of the situations to role-play. Present both worst and best case scenes in a way that shows you understand how people can get drawn into acting at their worst. Use the scenarios to illustrate how we can overcome the temptation to act contrary to Jesus' teachings and how we can behave in ways that show respect for all life.

SITUATION #1 The smartest person in your class, whom everyone expected to win the school spelling bee, just lost in the fourth round.

The worst you and your friends could do: _____

The best you and your friends could do: _____

SITUATION #2 A new student registered in your school this morning and will be in your homeroom. The student is blind and has a seeing-eye dog as a constant companion.

The worst you and your friends could do: _____

The best you and your friends could do: _____

SITUATION #3 On a class field trip, everyone wanted to make an extra stop to buy lunch at a fast-food restaurant. Pat, however, did not get off the bus with everyone else to buy lunch. You wonder if this is from lack of appetite or lack of money.

The worst you and your friends could do: _____

The best you and your friends could do: _____

SITUATION #4 _____

_____

_____

_____

The worst you and your friends could do: _____

The best you and your friends could do: _____

Respecting Life

Let Us Pray

Leader: God of all life, we thank and praise you for the many gifts you have given us. Your care and love for us goes deeper than the human mind can comprehend. Even before we came to be you have loved us. May we choose life!

"Who is the man who delights in life, who loves to see the good days?" Psalm 34:13

All: Lord, thank you for your blessings and the abundance you share with us.

Scripture

"I call heaven and earth today to witness against you: I have set before you life and death, the blessing and the curse. Choose life, then that you and your descendants may live, by loving the LORD, your God, obeying his voice, and holding fast to him. For that will mean life for you, a long life for you to live on the land which the LORD swore to your ancestors, to Abraham, Isaac, and Jacob, to give to them."
Deuteronomy 30:19–20

Have you ever thought...
- What does it mean to *always* choose life?
- What does it mean to respect and value *all* human life?

Respecting Life **223**

Scripture Background

Scripture Reflection Process

Invite the students to be still, close their eyes, and focus on their breathing. Encourage them to open their minds and hearts to what God is saying to them.

- Proclaim the Scripture and have the students sit in silence.
- *Ask:* What did you hear God say to you today?
- Allow volunteers to share.

▶ You may play instrumental music to begin the reflection.

DAY 1

Objective
- Reflect on God's personal invitation through Scripture

OPEN _____

Let Us Pray

Choose one of the students to be the Leader. Invite the students to gather in the prayer space and make the Sign of the Cross. Ask the Leader to proclaim the opening prayer and Psalm verse, and lead the class in the group response. Have the students return to their seats.

Explain that all life is a gift—that we each are works of art, and God's desire is that we treat all life the way he does, with great dignity and respect.

Say: Every human life is precious to God. We are called to respect and care for our own lives and the lives of others, just as Jesus did. Let's listen to God's Word and hear how we should choose life.

Scripture

Guide the students through the process of Scripture reflection (see the Scripture Background box to the left).

Have you ever thought...

Say: Because we are made in God's image, we must respect and care for every human life.

- Invite the students to respond to the questions.

DAY 1

Objective

- Indicate prior knowledge of chapter concepts and vocabulary

BUILD

Use this page to assess the students' knowledge related to the chapter content.

Getting Started

Say: We heard in the Scripture reading that we choose life by loving the Lord our God, obeying him, and holding fast to him. The Catholic Church teaches that we are to honor life at all of its stages.

Discuss the information in the opening paragraph with the students.

- Invite volunteers to share about a time when they cared for someone else or when someone helped to care for them.

Dignity and Worth

Ask a volunteer to read aloud the instructions.

- Discuss, as a class, what having dignity and worth as a human being really means.
- Allow the students to work with a classmate to brainstorm actions and attitudes that do and do not show respect for life.
- ★ Direct the partners to add the actions and attitudes that they come up with to the chart.
- Once everyone has had time to complete the activity, allow volunteers to share their responses with the class.

Getting Started

In this chapter, you will learn how the Fifth Commandment requires us to value and respect all life, which is sacred because all people have human dignity and worth. You will also explore the Church's teachings about protecting and honoring life at all stages.

Use the chart below to show what you already know about the dignity and value of human life. First, in your own words describe what it means for all people to have human dignity and worth. Then list actions and attitudes that acknowledge, respect, and honor the dignity of others, and actions and attitudes that do not.

Dignity and Worth
What it Means
What Honors Life and Dignity?
What Does Not Honor Life and Dignity?

Optional Activity

Activity Master 14: Worst and Best Case Scenarios

Distribute copies of the activity found on teacher page 223G. Arrange the students in small groups.

- This activity will allow the students to practice treating others as Jesus would treat them.
- It will also allow them to see how easily we can lead or follow others down a wrong path.

Stand in Another Person's Shoes Think about a person you know who, because of his or her life situation, faces challenges that are different from yours. Maybe this person is a neighbor who is elderly and homebound, or a classmate who has a learning disability. Perhaps this person is physically impaired or has a medical condition. Stand in the shoes of this person. List the challenges you might face.

_____

_____

_____

_____

_____

_____

_____

_____

How can you "choose life" (Deuteronomy 30:19) by the way you treat others?

_____

_____

_____

_____

_____

_____

_____

_____

_____

_____

Work with Words

Point out the Catholic Faith Words box on page 224.

- Explain that the vocabulary words in this chapter describe several issues that are very important to the Catholic Church and her teachings.

- Point out that all of the words are related to the term *human dignity* in some way.

- Invite the students to share their understanding of human dignity.

CLOSE _____

ACTIVITY

Explain this activity by illustrating an example from your own life of trying to stand in the shoes of another person. This is an important habit for a young adolescent to develop—to be able to seek to understand where another person is coming from.

- Allow the students to brainstorm ideas with a classmate.

- Once they've had ample time to discuss some ideas and list some challenges, have them answer the question on their own.

✔ Teaching Tip

Another Approach

The fifth habit listed in *The 7 Habits of Highly Effective Teens* by Sean Covey and Debra Harris is to "Seek First to Understand, Then to Be Understood." This habit helps us see the needs and the basic human dignity of others. In *The 7 Habits Journal for Teens*, young people are given the following journaling instructions, which can be used as an alternative to the Invite activity on page 225: "'You never really understand a person until you consider things from his point of view—until you climb into his skin and walk around in it.' (Harper Lee) Imagine yourself inside someone else's skin, someone very different from you. Write about how it feels to think from a different perspective."

DAY 2

Objectives

- Explain that each human life has value because we are made in God's image
- Identify murder as an action that violates the sacredness of human life

OPEN

💜 Ask a volunteer to read Psalm 139:13–14 as the opening prayer.

Point out that the title of this lesson answers the opening question.

BUILD

A Sacred Gift from God

Read aloud the first two paragraphs.

📖 **Go to the Source**

Have a volunteer read Psalm 139:13–20 from a Bible.

- *Ask:* What does this song of praise tell you about your relationship to God? What good can come from praising God for creating you and knowing you?
- Facilitate a class discussion.

Review the rest of the text on the page.

Ask a volunteer to read the caption that goes with the artwork.

- *Ask:* How do you think this image ties in to today's lesson?

Invite a student to read aloud the definition of *human dignity* on page 227.

A Sacred Gift from God

Why does human life have value?

If we could choose how we look and what abilities we have, we might change some things. But it's not up to us to choose our challenges. We do not enter this world on our own. Each of us owes his or her life to God. So one life is not more valuable than another. We are all equally valuable because we are each made in God's image.

Human beings are so unique and beautifully made because God designed us. For this reason, the author of the psalm praises God:

📖 **Scripture**

"You formed my inmost being;
  you knit me in my mother's womb.
I praise you, because I am wonderfully made."
Psalm 139:13–14

📖 **Go to the Source**
Read *Psalm 139:13–20*. What does this song of praise tell you about your relationship to God—past, present, and future? What good can come from praising God for creating and knowing you?

Now, we really don't know what the man who wrote that psalm looked like or what his limitations were. But he praised God for the way he was made. He believed God had a plan for his life that he was made to fulfill.

Not only are we made by God, but of all the creatures, humans alone have the capacity for "self-awareness"—we know we are individuals, separate from the world around us. We are able to recognize God's presence and to freely choose to know, love, and serve him.

For these reasons, each human life has a sacred value from conception to death. This **human dignity** cannot be taken away or lessened by any condition or situation.

The Creation of Adam in stone, based on Michelangelo

226

📖 **Scripture Background**

God Is with Us

Asking your students to speculate about the writer of Psalm 139 will provide you with many insights about their understanding of a person's heart. The psalm is referred to as a psalm of David, which means it might have been composed by King David or by someone from his court. No matter who wrote it, it is one of the most endearingly human psalms in the Psalter. When we are sitting, standing, in light or darkness, running away, or lying in bed at night, God is always with us. This psalm is a beautiful hymn praising God's care for us. A famous musical version of Psalm 139 is the hymn "You Are Near" by Dan Schutte. Consider playing this for your students.

Usefulness

We tend to get rid of things when they're not useful anymore. Usefulness determines their value to us. Human beings, however, are different. Our value is not determined by our usefulness. It comes from God, who made us and for whom we exist. We have that value when we are healthy or sick, young or old. Even when dying, our life has worth. When we die, our existence continues. We continue to fulfill our purpose with our Creator.

We who are sacred should not be discarded, judged useless, or killed. Those decisions are not ours to make. The Fifth Commandment instructs us not to kill another person. **Murder** is the deliberate killing of another person. It is always gravely sinful. It shows the contempt the murderer has for human dignity as well as for the holiness and goodness of God.

Sometimes life is so difficult that people don't feel valued or respected; they may feel helpless, and forget that life is a gift from God, who wants us to stick with this gift. Suicide is never an option because it goes against God's love and our hope, and it's forbidden by the Fifth Commandment. The *Catechism* tells us that suicide "unjustly breaks the ties of solidarity" with humanity (see *CCC*, 2281). But praying and asking for help is an option.

> Why do you think some people have so little respect for human life?

Catholic Faith Words

human dignity the worth each person has because he or she is made in the image of God

murder the deliberate killing of another person when the killing is not in self-defense. It is always gravely sinful.

LIST

Imagine God has asked you to take notes on the creation of human beings. Make a list of how we are different from the rest of creation.

Humans:

_____
_____
_____
_____

The Rest of Creation:

_____
_____
_____
_____

Optional Activity

In God's Hands *Visual/Spatial, Verbal/Linguistic, Interpersonal*

Have the students silently read Isaiah 49:14–16.

- Ask them to reflect on this Scripture and think about the images they see as they read the words.
- Provide the students with art supplies and invite them to draw what they saw.
- Allow volunteers to share and explain their artwork with the class.
- Discuss how this Scripture passage describes God's love for his People and how deeply committed he is to us.

Usefulness

Ask two volunteers to read aloud the first two paragraphs.

Check for understanding by asking:

- Where does our value as human beings come from? from God
- What happens to our value after we die? We continue to fulfill our purpose in eternal life.
- Why is it wrong to kill another human being? God decides who should die, not us.
- Why is murder always a grave sin? Because the murderer has shown contempt for human life (or dignity) and for God's goodness.

Ask a volunteer to read the definition of *murder* to the class.

Read aloud the last paragraph on suicide, pausing for comments and questions. Be attentive to questions that signal the need for further (private) attention.

Discuss the question at the end of the reading.

CLOSE _____

ACTIVITY

Have the students work in pairs to complete this activity.

- If time allows, let volunteers share some of their responses.

Quick Review Because we are all made in God's image and because our life is a gift from him, every human life is sacred and every human being has dignity. Committing murder is a grave sin because it violates the sacredness of human life.

DAY 3

Objectives

- Explore the aspects of the Fifth Commandment that deal with anger and vengeance
- Examine why the Church advocates for the rights of others on life issues

OPEN

💜 Have the students pray the *Memorare* from page 384.

Read aloud the opening question and elicit responses from the class.

BUILD

Honoring Life

Tell the students to silently read this first section.

- Ask for comments or questions.

📘 Go to the Source

Direct the students to read the Sermon on the Mount from Matthew 5:38–48.

- *Ask*: What does Jesus teach us in this passage about retaliation and loving your enemies? turn the other cheek, don't retaliate, love your enemies
- Explain that Jesus lived what he taught.

The Church Follows Her Master

Read aloud this section.

- *Ask*: In what ways does the Church show that she values life?
- Write student responses on the board or on chart paper.

> 📘 **Go to the Source**
> Read more of the Sermon on the Mount from Matthew 5:38–48. What does Jesus teach about retaliation and loving your enemies?

© Our Sunday Visitor

Honoring Life

What does the Church teach about protecting life at all stages?

In the Sermon on the Mount, Jesus refers to the Fifth Commandment, which bans murder. He then widens the understanding to include anger and vengeance: "But I say to you, whoever is angry with his brother will be liable to judgment . . ." (**Matthew 5:22**).

Jesus understands human nature and speaks against destructive emotions that can lead to worse things. Anger, hatred, and vengeance tear peoples' lives apart. Jesus didn't preach one message and live another. His actions and behavior show that he lived in a way that valued life. He told the disciples, "But I say to you, offer no resistance to one who is evil. When someone strikes you on (your) right cheek, turn the other one to him as well" (**Matthew 5:39**).

When Jesus is arrested, he allows his enemies to lead him to an unjust trial and execution. He upholds and honors every human life to the point of not raising a hand against his oppressors or allowing his disciples to take up the sword against them.

The Church Follows Her Master

The Church has taken a stand on life issues, advocating for the rights of others. Over the centuries the Church has established hospitals; outreach organizations; and programs for the poor, immigrants, children, victims of domestic abuse, and others in need.

The Church also confronts today's culture. She gets the message out—through preaching, outreach, papal encyclicals, bishops' letters, media campaigns, and more—that each human life, from conception to natural death, is innately valuable and deserves respect.

228 Chapter 14

📘 Scripture Background

Turn the Other Cheek

The message in Matthew 5:38–48 makes it clear that Jesus expects his followers to value human life at a level beyond that demanded in the Law of Moses. The Book of Leviticus directed "an eye for an eye," not to encourage vengeance, but to moderate it. Unlike the tribes around them who took lives in retaliation for even small offenses, Jewish law sought to control the amount of vengeance taken for an offense. This was a radical idea for its time. Jesus came with a far more radical challenge—"turn the other cheek"—to offer an enemy more than what was taken and to love those who have harmed you. This is exactly what Jesus did at the end of his life. It is what he calls us to do.

Safeguarding Life

A human life still in the womb or a life that is no longer as strong as it once was is to be protected from direct harm.

Because of this teaching, **abortion**, the deliberate termination of a pregnancy by killing an unborn child, is a grave sin. The Church does not believe that human life begins at some arbitrary point later in a pregnancy. An embryo requires the same efforts of care as any human. Life is bestowed by God at conception. We are called to protect the life of the most vulnerable.

In the same way, our lives cannot be considered less valuable because we are older or sick. For this reason, **euthanasia**—the deliberate action or inaction that causes the death of someone who is sick, or dying, or has disabilities—is also a grave sin. We owe tender care to those who, at the end of their lives, are most fragile.

It follows from this principle that sometimes we must defend ourselves, or others, from a person or group of people causing harm. It is legitimate and necessary to defend the lives of others, and this is a serious duty for those who have responsibility for the lives of others.

The late Joseph Cardinal Bernardin, Archbishop of Chicago, described our Catholic beliefs and teachings as a "consistent ethic of life." Catholics should honor, respect, and defend all life. Bernardin taught that Catholics must be consistent in opposing abortion, the death penalty, war, the nuclear arms race, and anything that threatens life. Being consistent in our approach to the sacredness of human life makes the human family, and the Church, stronger.

> Who helps you to respect the dignity and sacredness of life?

IDENTIFY

Think about the different organizations or people that protect the right to life of people at different stages of life. On the lines below, name one way you can value and honor life at each stage. Then discuss with classmates two ways you can value and honor life, no matter the age.

Seniors _____

Infants _____

Adults _____

Adolescents _____

All ages _____

Catholic Faith Words

abortion the deliberate termination of a pregnancy by killing an unborn child. It is a grave sin.

euthanasia the deliberate action or inaction which causes the death of someone who is sick, dying, or suffering because of disabilities or a debilitating condition. It is a grave sin.

Respecting Life **229**

© Our Sunday Visitor

Safeguarding Life

Read aloud the introductory paragraph. Ask the students to silently read the rest of the text.

- Assign half of the class the topic of *abortion* and the other half the topic of *euthanasia*.
- Encourage the students to make a list of some key points on their topic.
- Invite volunteers to share why these two actions are considered grave sins.
- Allow the students to ask any questions that they have about these two words.
- Ask the class to consider the question at the end of this section.
- Offer an opportunity, for those who are willing, to share responses.

CLOSE _____

ACTIVITY

Have the students read the instructions. Ensure that they understand the activity.

- Give them time to write the ways they can value and honor life.
- Allow the students to discuss their responses with a classmate.

Quick Review Jesus both preached and lived in a way that valued all life. The Church advocates for the rights of others on life issues because it is our responsibility as human beings, made by God in his image, to do so.

DAY 4

Objectives

- Examine the ways in which we do not show respect for our own lives or the lives of others
- Explain why scandal harms individuals and society
- Identify the basic rights people need to grow and mature

OPEN

Invite the students to stand and pray the last part of the Litany of Saint Joseph, page 390.

Ask: Why is it important to take care of ourselves and others?

BUILD

Respecting the Human Person

Invite volunteers to read aloud this section.

- Revisit the opening question to ensure student understanding in relation to this text.

Raising Ourselves Up

Summarize, in your own words, the two paragraphs referring to respecting the human person.

Things That Damage God's Artistry in You

Review the examples listed in the chart to ensure the students understand how each is something that damages human beings.

✱ Have the students add to the list further examples of ways we can damage ourselves.

Respecting the Human Person

Why is it important to take care of ourselves and others?

Unkind words are hurtful. They can affect how people think and feel about themselves, and they don't have a positive purpose.

If words can be demeaning and cause damage, think about how much worse it is to allow harmful conditions to continue. Harmful conditions that deny people their rights exist all around us: people living in poverty with no means to change the situation, trapped in unsafe housing, or people who don't have access to an education, health care, or a job.

People need to be able to meet these basic rights in order to grow and mature. Without them, they are constantly using all of their energy merely to survive. They cannot flourish as God would want.

© Our Sunday Visitor

> **Catholic Faith Words**
>
> **scandal** the destructive behavior by which a person deliberately leads, through his or her own action or inaction, another person to sin

Raising Ourselves Up

A great piece of artwork is meant to be put on display so that everyone can appreciate it and be made better by it. We are God's work of art. The human person is the pinnacle of creation.

We honor the human person, so that all might appreciate and be made better by the creative work of God among us. We avoid all the things that damage the artistry of God at work in the human person, such as overindulgence, extremism, or physical and mental intimidation.

Things that Damage God's Artistry in You
abusing food, alcohol, tobacco, and drugs
sacrificing everything else for the sake of physical perfection
promoting success in school, popularity, and sports without considering those involved
bullying
sexual exploitation or manipulation of another person
pornography
kidnapping, hostage-taking, terrorism, and torture

Add two more examples to the list. ✱

Optional Activity

Role-Playing Rights *Verbal/Linguistic, Bodily/Kinesthetic*

Assign one of the following scenarios to three small groups:

- A school district tells parents they must home school their child because the school will not make accommodations for a wheel chair.
- A man who is fired is told someone younger was hired so the company could pay the new person less money.
- A man is put in jail for stealing food because his family was starving.

Have the students defend the person whose rights have been violated. Tell them to use one Scripture passage and one passage from the *Catechism of the Catholic Church* in arguing for basic human rights.

Care for Others

Harsh words are not the only way people harm others. Another way is to encourage others to do sinful things. Jesus warns his disciples against leading others into sin. He says, "Whoever causes one of these little ones who believe in me to sin, it would be better for him to have a great millstone hung around his neck and to be drowned in the depths of the sea" (Matthew 18:6).

Scandal is the name given to the destructive behavior by which we deliberately lead others to sin through our own action or inaction. For example, the sin of scandal is committed when a radio talk show host rallies his listeners to engage in racism.

Those in authority have a greater responsibility to guard against scandal. Teachers and government and business leaders must exercise care for others by not misleading and manipulating them. The *Catechism* teaches that anyone who uses his or her power to lead others to scandal is "responsible for the evil that he has directly or indirectly encouraged" (*CCC*, 2287). This special responsibility also includes those who influence public opinion because these are areas of life that can promote or hinder how we perceive and care for one another.

> **THINK**
>
> Think of some phrases you have heard or maybe even said that are either respectful or disrespectful. Which would you use more or less based on the things you have learned in this chapter?

IN SUMMARY Catholics Believe

All human life is sacred and a gift from God.

- All people possess the human dignity that comes from being made in God's image, and we do not have the right to take that life away from others or ourselves.

- We have a responsibility to honor and protect life at all stages, from conception to old age to death.

- We respect the dignity of the human person by respecting the rights of others, taking care of ourselves physically and emotionally, not abusing ourselves or others, and by not leading others into sin.

Respecting Life **231**

Care for Others

Read the quote from Matthew 18:6 from this page, and discuss why Jesus would make this statement.

- Point out the Catholic Faith Word and read aloud the definition on page 230.

- Ask volunteers to give examples of scandal based on this definition.

Review the rest of the text with the class.

CLOSE

> **ACTIVITY**

Have the students read the directions and work in pairs to complete this activity.

In Summary

Share the summary points with the class.

- Invite and discuss any questions that the students have regarding this content.

✓ **Teaching Tip**

Respect

There are words that respect life and there are words that are disrespectful of life.

- Identify words the students use that may belittle or dismiss others.

- Guard against a tendency to dismiss some words as "not that bad," or "everybody says it—it really doesn't mean anything."

- Help the students to be very honest about the hurtful, destructive nature of words that label, belittle, or set some people apart from the rest of a group.

DAY 5

Objectives

- Discuss how the Church protects the right to life of all human beings
- Explore the faith life of Saint Martin de Tours
- Offer the Prayer for Life

OPEN

Pray a prayer of thanksgiving, focusing on the sacredness of all human life. Allow the students to add their own relevant prayers.

BUILD

Our Catholic Life

Ask a volunteer to read aloud this section.

- Invite the students to discuss the Our Catholic Life question with a classmate.
- If there is enough time, ask a few volunteers to share their responses with the class.

People of Faith

Explain to the students that Saint Martin de Tours recognized that all life was sacred.

- Have a volunteer read aloud the People of Faith paragraph.
- Share the bullet points from the People of Faith Background box.
- Invite a group discussion on what young people can do to promote the sacredness of life.

Our Catholic Life

The Fifth Commandment tells us "you shall not kill." The Catholic Church has always been clear about protecting human life from the moment of conception to natural death. The Church also calls us to provide special protection to the unborn, who are among the most vulnerable and innocent. Through prayer and action, the Church calls governments to protect the **right to life** of all human beings, the unborn as well as the terminally ill and aged. She provides prayer, guidance, and many types of support to people facing challenges in these areas. The Church also protects those who are sick or have serious disabilities. Because God made each of us, the value and human dignity of every human life is an important teaching of the Catholic Church.

> How do you show respect for human dignity in your life right now?

People of Faith

Saint Martin de Tours, 316–397

Saint Martin joined the Roman army at age fifteen. One day while stationed in Gaul (now France), he gave half his cloak to a beggar. That night, Martin dreamed that he saw Jesus wearing half of his cloak. He heard Jesus say, "Here is Martin, the Roman soldier who is not baptized; he has clad me." Martin was baptized when he was 18. He traveled and preached throughout the country and was eventually named bishop of Tours. Saint Martin helped people understand true Christianity and not believe errors, called heresies. The Church celebrates his feast day on **November 11**.

📶 For more, go to **aliveinchrist.osv.com**

LIST

Make a list of movies, television shows, books, or songs that encourage respecting life.

_____
_____
_____
_____
_____
_____
_____

As a class, discuss the items you have listed in common, and think about watching or reading some of your classmates' suggestions.

232 Chapter 14

People of Faith Background

Saint Martin de Tours

Use the following information in your class discussion.

- When Saint Martin de Tours was twenty, he studied under Hilary of Poitiers, who also helped to defend the Church from heresies.
- Saint Martin lived as a hermit during the time that Hilary of Poitiers was in exile. Afterwards, both men helped to build the first Benedictine Abbey in Gaul.

📶 Encourage the students to go to **aliveinchrist.osv.com** at home to learn more about Saint Martin de Tours.

Prayer for Life

Leader: Father and Creator, you are the source of all life. You gave your son Jesus to redeem our fallen world and offer us new life on Earth and in Heaven. When your angel Gabriel asked Mary of Nazareth to become the Mother of your Son, she graciously accepted. Not knowing what would come with this "Yes" to life, she trusted in you.

Thank you, Mary, the Blessed Mother of the world's Redeemer. Jesus told the world, "I came so that they might have life and have it more abundantly" (**John 10:10b**). Please guide us in honoring the gift of life. Give us courage, the courage of Pope Saint John Paul II, to defend the right to life for all.

All: [recite together slowly]: O Mary, bright dawn of the new world, Mother of the living, to you do we entrust the cause of life. Look down, O Mother, upon the vast numbers of babies not allowed to be born, of the poor whose lives are made difficult, of men and women who are victims of brutal violence, of the elderly and the sick killed by indifference or out of misguided mercy.

Grant that all who believe in Your Son may proclaim the Gospel of life with honesty and love to the people of our time. Obtain for them the grace to accept that Gospel as a gift ever new, the joy of celebrating it with gratitude throughout their lives and the courage to bear witness to it resolutely, in order to build, together with all people of good will, the civilization of truth and love, to the praise and glory of God, the Creator and lover of life.

Prayer of the Gospel of Life, by Pope Saint John Paul II

▶ *Sing or play "Lover of Life"*

🛜 Go to **aliveinchrist.osv.com** for an interactive review.

A Work with Words Circle the letter of the choice that best completes the sentence.

1. Murder is always gravely sinful because it shows contempt for the ___ of human life as well as for the holiness and goodness of God, the Creator.
- **a.** dignity ⟵
- **b.** happiness
- **c.** love
- **d.** wonder

2. ___ is deliberately ending a pregnancy on purpose by killing an unborn child.
- **a.** Euthanasia
- **b.** Genocide
- **c.** Suicide
- **d.** Abortion ⟵

3. Deliberate action or inaction that causes the death of someone who is sick, or dying, or suffering because of disabilities is called ___.
- **a.** euthanasia ⟵
- **b.** genocide
- **c.** suicide
- **d.** abortion

4. Behavior or attitudes that leads others to sin are known as ___.
- **a.** disobedience
- **b.** scandal ⟵
- **c.** free will
- **d.** suicide

5. Because humans are made in the ___ and likeness of God, each human life is sacred.
- **a.** shadow
- **b.** mirror
- **c.** image ⟵
- **d.** awareness

6. The human person is the ___ of creation.
- **a.** zenith
- **b.** pinnacle ⟵
- **c.** image
- **d.** purpose

B Check Understanding Complete each sentence with the correct term from the Word Bank.

abortion	kill
overindulgence	sin
life	self-awareness
love	action
breath	covet

7. The Fifth Commandment instructs us not to ___**kill**___ another person.

8. We avoid ___**overindulgence**___ and extremism because these actions can damage the artistry of God at work in the human person.

9. Jesus warns his disciples that it would be better to drown in the sea than to lead others into ___**sin**___.

10. Not only are we made by God, but we humans alone, of all creatures, also have the capacity for ___**self-awareness**___.

C Make Connections On a separate sheet of paper, write a one-paragraph response to the following questions. Choose a current issue (local, national, or worldwide) in which human life is being valued, respected, or protected. Who are the people involved, and what impact are their actions having on others? How can this be an example of living out the Fifth Commandment?

Have the students complete the first part of the activity independently.

- Invite them to share some of their ideas with the class.
- Encourage the students to think about watching or reading some of their classmates' suggestions.

CLOSE _____

Prayer for Life

💙 Have the students locate and bring to the prayer service a photo of an individual, group, or country that needs "prayer for life."

Follow the order of prayer on the student page.

Have the students take turns holding up the photos of a person, group, or event for which they want to offer prayer.

▶ Conclude by inviting the students to sing or reflect on the song "Lover of Life," downloaded from **aliveinchrist.osv.com**.

Additional Music Options: "Apple of My Eye" or "Mother to Another"

CHAPTER REVIEW

Review the instructions for each section and have the students complete the review.

🛜 Go to **aliveinchrist.osv.com** to prepare customized and downloadable assessments, send eAssessments, and assign interactive reviews.

KEY CONCEPT

We are called to strive for what is right, just, holy, and gracious.

DOCTRINAL CONTENT

- Virtues are strong habits of doing good that help us make moral decisions and contribute to how we become the people God created us to be. (CCC, 1803–1804)

- The Theological Virtues are gifts from God that help us believe in him, trust in his plan for us, and love him as he loves us. (CCC, 1812–1813)

- The Cardinal Virtues of prudence, justice, fortitude, and temperance can help us respect ourselves and others and act with integrity. (CCC, 1805–1809)

- The Eighth Commandment forbids misrepresenting the truth in our relationships with others. This sin damages our integrity and character, but by practicing the virtues and avoiding sin, we can live truthful and faith-filled lives. (CCC, 2464, 2468)

TASKS OF CATECHESIS

Helping children grow in a faith that is "known, celebrated, lived, and expressed in prayer" (NDC, 20).

This chapter focuses on the following tasks of catechesis:

- Promoting Knowledge of the Faith

- Moral Formation

Teacher Background

> Put on then, as God's chosen ones, holy and beloved, heartfelt compassion, kindness, humility, gentleness, and patience, bearing with one another and forgiving one another, if one has a grievance against another; as the Lord has forgiven you, so must you also do.
> **Colossians 3:12–13**
>
> **> Reflect** How can practicing the virtues shape you into the person that God created you to be?

Everybody wants to be happy. There is nothing wrong with that. Indeed, God wants us to be happy as well. The problem is that we often confuse happiness with momentary pleasure. True happiness comes in doing the will of God. Jesus and the Scriptures teach us that true happiness is the same as blessedness, and blessedness is the result of living in right relationship with God. If we really want to be happy, there is no other path than that which leads to eternal life with God, for God is our one, true source of happiness.

It stands to reason that since the path to God leads to happiness, the path that leads away from God leads to unhappiness. We walk this path when we believe that pleasure is the only goal worth achieving. Indulging in inappropriate television shows, magazines, or websites can be a very popular and seductive notion these days. The good news is that we have a wonderful traveling companion in Christ and the guidance of the Holy Spirit to help us stay on the right road.

> **> Reflect** How have you experienced in a personal way the happiness that comes from having a right relationship with God?

Teacher's Prayer

♥ Lord Jesus, you are the first and finest teacher of virtue. May your Holy Spirit be with me, that I may reflect your virtue in all I do, and may my life serve as an inspiration for those I teach. Amen.

How Seventh Graders Understand Chapter Topics

Seventh graders often live in the "here and now." They are still learning to control their impulses and can often fall into the trap of putting momentary pleasure over lasting happiness. They need guidance to think about larger goals for the future—who they are called to be and how they will get there.

Teaching Tip: Talk about the difference between happiness and pleasure. Pleasure is only momentary, but happiness continues. *Ask:* What things will make you happy in the future? What pleasures are worth sacrificing in the present so that you can be truly happy? Encourage discussion, especially pointing out the difference between what the Church teaches about how to achieve happiness and what popular culture teaches.

Sharing the Message with Seventh Graders

- Seventh graders' bodies are changing rapidly during this period and so are their emotions. Show them how the virtues can help guide their emotions and conduct.

- At this age, learning how to understand and control their budding sexual interests is critical. According to Church teaching, parents should take the lead in guiding their children in these issues.

- As adolescents discover themselves and others as sexual beings, it is important that they be taught, and see modeled, respect for the gift of sexuality. Discuss with them the importance of both modesty and chastity.

Chapter 15 Planner

Objectives	Open
DAY 1—Invite/Preview, Pages 235–237	
• Reflect on God's personal invitation through Scripture • Indicate prior knowledge of chapter concepts and vocabulary	♡ **Psalm 11:7** Pray the opening prayer. 📖 **Colossians 3:12–15** Proclaim "Renunciation of Vice." Guide the students through the process of Scripture reflection. • Discuss Have You Ever Thought questions.
DAY 2—Discover, Pages 238–239	
• Examine how virtues can help us make good moral decisions • Identify the Theological Virtues as gifts from God that help us believe in him, trust in his plan for us, and love him as he loves us	♡ Pray the **Lamb of God**, page 385.
DAY 3—Discover, Pages 240–241	
• Explain the relationship between the Cardinal Virtues and other moral virtues • Explore the roles of modesty and chastity in our lives	♡ Pray a prayer of petition.
DAY 4—Discover, Pages 242–243	
• Examine how sins against the Eighth Commandment damage our integrity and character as they oppose the virtue of truth	♡ Pray the **Hail Mary**, page 384. • Ask the opening question.
DAY 5—Live, Pages 244–245	
• Discuss ways to strengthen virtuous living • Explore the faith life of Saint Margaret Ward • Offer the Act of Hope and Love prayer	♡ Pray **Hail, Holy Queen**, page 384.

REVIEW AND ASSESSMENT

Chapter Review, page 246
Chapter Test, page 235F

📶 **aliveinchrist.osv.com** Customize and Download Assessments, Email Links to eAssessments, Interactive Student Reviews

Build	Close	Materials & Resources
• Present lesson highlights. • Preview **Catholic Faith Words**. ★ Connect symbols to the Theological Virtues, and share something about the Cardinal Virtues.	• *Activity* The students will consider how their good habits affect their faith life.	☐ pencils or pens ☐ board or chart paper
• **Catholic Faith Words** virtue, Theological Virtues • Explain the Theological Virtues and how they can help us be our best. 📖 Read and reflect on Philippians 4:8 and 4:13.	• *Activity* Define *virtuous,* and describe a virtuous person. • Conclude with a review of key concepts and objectives. • *Optional Activity* My Truest and Best Self (Activity Master 15)	☐ pencils or pens ☐ Bibles ☐ Activity Master 15 (Page 235G)
• **Catholic Faith Words** Cardinal Virtues • Discuss how modesty and chastity help us respect others and ourselves. ★ The students will indicate the Cardinal Virtues most affecting their lives.	• *Activity* Discuss people who exemplify the Cardinal Virtues. • Conclude with a review of key concepts and objectives.	☐ pencils or pens ☐ index cards ☐ highlighters
• Discuss behaviors that can damage our character and integrity. • Explain that Jesus is the perfect model for how we should live.	• *Activity* Discuss behaviors that do not build up excellence. • Review the In Summary statements.	☐ pencils or pens
• Discuss the question in the Our Catholic Life section. • Learn about Saint Margaret Ward. • *Activity* The students will rate themselves on how well they are living the virtues.	• Ask a student to read the Scripture. • Follow the order of prayer. ▶ Play the closing song.	☐ pencils or pens 🛜 "I Love You, Lord"

Chapter Connections

FORMING CATHOLIC IDENTITY ACROSS THE CURRICULUM

To integrate the Catholic faith in all aspects of curriculum, this chapter's objectives can be reinforced and applied in the instruction of other disciplines.

Go to **aliveinchrist.osv.com** for cross-curricular activities and projects linked to the doctrinal content discussed in this unit. Activities are available from among the following knowledge categories and content areas:

Language Arts

- Integration of Knowledge
- Literacy
- Speaking and Listening
- Writing Skills

Math

- Algebraic Thinking
- Geometry
- Measurement and Data
- Numbers and Operations

Science

- Earth Science
- Life Science
- Physical Science
- Technology

Social Studies

- Civics
- Economics
- Geography
- History

NCEA IFG: ACRE Edition

Knowledge of the Faith

- **Objective:** To know and understand basic Catholic teaching about the Incarnate Word Jesus Christ as the way, truth, and life

Moral Formation

- **Objective:** To be knowledgeable about the teachings of Jesus and the Church as the basis of Christian morality and to understand Catholic Social Teaching

Catholic Faith Literacy

faith, hope, love, virtue

Catholic Social Teaching

To integrate Catholic Social Teaching into your lesson, choose one of the following features: Life and Dignity of the Human Person, pages 334–335; or Solidarity of the Human Family, pages 344–345.

- Start the Live step of the process by talking about Saint Margaret Ward on page 244. Then move directly to the Catholic Social Teaching feature.
- Or, to expand the lesson, complete page 244, then move to the Catholic Social Teaching feature.
- Return to Chapter 15 for the prayer on page 245.

Music Options

Use one or more of the following songs to enhance catechetical learning or for prayer.

- "I Love You, Lord," Day 5, Page 245
- "My Hope," Day 5, Page 245

Name _____ Date _____

Match each description in Column A with the correct term in Column B by filling in the appropriate letter.

Column A

Column B

_____ 1. Good spiritual habit that strengthens and enables you to do what is right and good

a. Cardinal Virtues

b. virtue

_____ 2. Faith, hope, and charity (love)

_____ 3. Prudence, temperance, justice, and fortitude

c. fortitude

_____ 4. Courage to do what is right, even if others disagree

d. Theological Virtues

Complete each sentence with the correct term.

5. Giving God and others what is due to them is the virtue of _____.

6. The virtue of _____ helps us keep our desires from ruling our lives.

7. _____ helps us maintain the right balance of body and spirit in human sexuality.

8. When we are discreet in the way we dress and speak, we are practicing the virtue of _____.

Write a response on the lines below.

9. List two of the four behaviors that can damage our integrity and keep us from living a life of excellence. Why are these behaviors sinful?

_____

_____

_____

_____

10. Why is it not always easy to live a virtuous life? What can we do to get help?

_____

_____

_____

_____

Name _____   Date _____

My Truest and Best Self

"Whatever is true, whatever is honorable, whatever is just, whatever is pure, whatever is lovely, whatever is gracious, if there is any excellence and if there is anything worthy of praise, think about these things" (Philippians 4:8).

It's time to be honest and "think about these things."

1. Describe your true self.

_____

_____

2. Describe what is honorable about you.

_____

_____

3. When have you been a just person?

_____

_____

4. What about you is pure?

_____

_____

5. What about you is lovely?

_____

_____

6. When have you been gracious to somebody?

_____

_____

7. What about you is worthy of praise?

_____

_____

Being Virtuous

 Let Us Pray

Leader: Holy God, you are the source of all faith, hope, and love. These are three gifts you give us so that we can be happy and holy. May your Spirit be our strength and our guide as we strive to love you completely in all we do and say.

"The LORD is just and loves just deeds;
the upright will see his face." **Psalm 11:7**

All: Lord, we belong to you.

Scripture

"Put on then, as God's chosen ones, holy and beloved, heartfelt compassion, kindness, humility, gentleness, and patience, bearing with one another and forgiving one another, if one has a grievance against another; as the Lord has forgiven you, so must you also do. And over all these put on love, that is, the bond of perfection. And let the peace of Christ control your hearts, the peace into which you were also called in one body. And be thankful."
Colossians 3:12–15

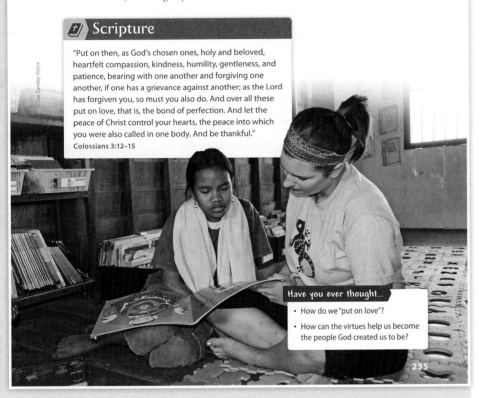

© Our Sunday Visitor

Have you ever thought...
- How do we "put on love"?
- How can the virtues help us become the people God created us to be?

235

Scripture Background

Scripture Reflection Process

Invite the students to be still, close their eyes, and focus on their breathing. Encourage them to open their minds and hearts to what God is saying to them.

- Proclaim the Scripture and have the students sit in silence.
- *Ask:* What did you hear God say to you today?
- Allow volunteers to share.

▶ You may play instrumental music to begin the reflection.

Objective
- Reflect on God's personal invitation through Scripture

OPEN

 Let Us Pray

Invite the students to gather in the prayer space and make the Sign of the Cross. Pray the entire prayer together as a group.

Have the students move out of the prayer space and back to their seats.

Explain that virtues are the foundation for living a holy life.

Say: God is the source of our faith, hope, and love. Let's listen to today's Scripture reading for what God's Word has to say about living a virtuous life.

Scripture

Guide the students through the process of Scripture reflection (see the Scripture Background box below).

Have you ever thought…
Say: God gave us many gifts that enable us to act as his faithful disciples.

- Invite the students to respond to the questions.

DAY 1

Objective

- Indicate prior knowledge of chapter concepts and vocabulary

BUILD _____

Use this page to assess the students' knowledge related to the chapter content.

Getting Started

Tell the students that this chapter is about virtues.

Say: In the Scripture reading, Saint Paul names compassion, kindness, humility, gentleness, patience, and forgiveness as necessary attitudes and virtues for those who are God's chosen ones. Over all these, he says, put on love, the bond of perfection.

- Suggest that the students describe people they know who have "put on love," and people they know who practice the virtues.

- Invite them to consider how they can "put on love" in their daily lives.

The Theological Virtues/The Cardinal Virtues

Explain the instructions to the class.

★ Give the students enough time to explain the symbols for the Theological Virtues, and to share what they know about each of the Cardinal Virtues.

Getting Started

In this chapter, you will study and identify virtues and understand the importance of becoming the person God has created you to be, by living the virtues in your daily life.

Catholic Faith Words

- virtue
- Theological Virtues
- Cardinal Virtues

In the space next to each symbol, explain why that symbol is used to represent that virtue. In the second chart, share something you know about each of the Cardinal Virtues. ★

The Theological Virtues

Virtue	Symbol	Explanation
Faith		_____ _____
Hope		_____ _____
Charity		_____ _____

The Cardinal Virtues

Virtue	Description
Prudence	_____ _____
Justice	_____ _____
Temperance	_____ _____
Fortitude	_____ _____

236 Chapter 15

Optional Activity

The Definition of Virtuous *Verbal/Linguistic, Interpersonal*

Write the word *virtuous* on newsprint (a large sheet of paper). Brainstorm words and phrases that describe it. Write the words and phrases on the newsprint. Have each student, without looking at a dictionary, write his or her own definition for *virtuous*.

- Form groups of five to six participants. The groups' task is to reach an agreement about the best definition for *virtuous*.

- Have each group write its final definition on newsprint and post it on the wall.

- The students can return to these definitions and further refine them for the activity on page 239.

Holy Habits Good habits are keys to excellence. For example, good study habits are keys to excellence in school and learning. Good eating and exercise habits are keys to excellence for our health.

What are your best habits? How do they help you be a better person?

_____

_____

_____

_____

_____

_____

_____

_____

_____

Good habits are also keys to excellence in our spiritual lives. How do the habits you've identified help you be the person God made you to be?

_____

_____

_____

_____

_____

_____

_____

_____

Being Virtuous **237**

© Our Sunday Visitor

Work with Words

Point out the Catholic Faith Words box at the top of page 236.

- Read aloud the three Catholic Faith Words.
- Ask the students what they already know about these words.
- Tell the class that they will be learning more about virtues as the chapter progresses.

CLOSE

ACTIVITY

Have a volunteer read the introductory text.

- Brainstorm as a class two lists: *Good Habits* and *Bad Habits*. Have the students explain why the good habits they have named are "good" and the bad habits are "bad."
- Ask a volunteer to read the questions.
- Give the students time to complete the activity.

✓ Teaching Tip

Sacred Conversations

While seventh graders are often exposed to graphic sexual content in the media, many of them will still be uncomfortable when discussing this issue in class. Preface this conversation with a reminder that sexuality is a sacred gift from God that is important.

Using a symbol that "marks" your sacred conversations may help set the tone. Lighting a trust candle, ringing a bell at the beginning and end of the conversation, or having the students place faith-themed rubber bracelets on their wrists are some suggestions you may want to consider.

DAY 2

Objectives

- Examine how the virtues can help us make good moral decisions
- Identify the Theological Virtues as gifts from God that help us believe in him, trust in his plan for us, and love him as he loves us

OPEN

Have the students pray the Lamb of God prayer from page 385.

BUILD

Good and Holy

Ask: Is living a good life easy?

- Invite discussion.

Our Truest and Best Selves

Tell the students to silently read this section.

Scripture

Ask a volunteer to read aloud Philippians 4:8 as well as 4:13.

- Invite the students to think about some of the ways God gives us the strength that we need.

Discuss the closing question.

Helping Habits

Ask: What do you think is most challenging from Saint Paul's list?

- Refer back to Philippians 4:8, whatever is true, honorable, just, pure, lovely, gracious, excellent, and worthy of praise.

Good and Holy

How do you grow to be the person God made you to be?

The freedom God gives us is meant to be used for doing good. Living a good life requires practice and self-discipline. The truth is, it's not always easy.

Our Truest and Best Selves

God shares his love completely with you. Your response should be just as strong and focused. By responding to his love, you can discover and strengthen your truest, best self.

Many things contribute to who you are and who you can become, such as your individual talents, gifts, and uniqueness;

the way you typically relate to others; and how you learn from life experiences and from others.

These things together can be a powerful force to reach your ultimate goal: to be good and holy, to be loving and welcoming, to become more like God, and to one day be with him forever.

But what does being good and holy look like? Saint Paul tells us that we are to help one another strive for those things that are most worthwhile in life.

Scripture

"Finally, brothers, whatever is true, whatever is honorable, whatever is just, whatever is pure, whatever is lovely, whatever is gracious, if there is any excellence and if there is anything worthy of praise, think about these things."
Philippians 4:8

Go to the Source

Read *Philippians 4:13* and think about the ways God gives you the strength that you need, just as he gave it to Paul.

> If Saint Paul were writing to you and your friends, how do you think he might word his message differently?

Helping Habits

Saint Paul's list is pretty challenging. In specific situations, it is sometimes difficult to determine exactly what is true, honorable, and just. All kinds of positive and negative pressures and assumptions can be at play. Some situations require us to really think through how the final outcome will impact everyone.

238 Chapter 15

Optional Activity

Activity Master 15: My Truest and Best Self

Distribute copies of the activity found on teacher page 235G.

- This activity will help the students think about the virtues in Philippians 4:8 and connect them with their lives.
- Have the students work in pairs; this will allow them to identify gifts they may see in each other.

The virtues help us do this. A **virtue** is a good spiritual habit that strengthens you and enables you to do what is right and good. Virtues develop over time with our practice and openness to God's grace. Virtues guide our conduct and emotions. Faith, hope, and charity (love) are the **Theological Virtues**. They are gifts from God that help us believe in him, trust in his plan for us, and love him as he loves us. We have to respond to God's gift and live out the virtues for them to be strong in our lives.

- **Faith** means believing in God and all that he has revealed to us and believing in all that the Church proposes for our belief.
- **Hope** is a desire, strengthened by trust in Jesus' promises, to do God's will, and achieve eternal life and the graces to make this desire come true.
- **Charity** means we love God above all else, and our neighbors as ourselves.

The Theological Virtues make the human, or moral, virtues possible. These virtues guide the way we act and feel. They help us live according to our conscience, control our passions, and deal with how we respect others and ourselves in light of our faith.

Moral virtues don't automatically appear within us. They grow when we learn about them and are intentional about practicing them, even in the face of struggles. God's grace helps us cultivate virtue. In this way, the virtues that we are growing get strong inside us.

> ### Catholic Faith Words
>
> **virtue** a good spiritual habit that strengthens you and enables you to do what is right and good
>
> **Theological Virtues** gifts from God that help us believe in him, trust in his plan for us, and love him as he loves us; they are faith, hope, and charity

DEFINE AND DESCRIBE

Imagine you are writing a dictionary entry for the term virtuous. Write your entry here.

virtuous (adj.)

_____
_____
_____
_____

Now describe how a virtuous person would act. A virtuous person...

_____
_____
_____
_____

Being Virtuous **239**

![Scripture Background icon] **Scripture Background**

Greek Influence

Saint Paul wrote his letter to the citizens of Phillipi while he was in prison. It may have been when he was under house arrest in Rome, but it was more likely when he was in prison in Ephesus, a city with great Greek influence. The philosophy of the Greek Stoics may have been on his mind when he wrote Philippians 4:8. The terms he uses, "Whatever is honorable, just, pure, lovely, gracious," were terms from Stoic philosophy. Clearly, Paul is taking his friends at Phillipi far past the philosophy of the Stoics. In spite of his imprisonment, he is happy. In fact, he uses the words *rejoice* and *joy* fifteen times. Paul tells us that the way to be happy, even in times of trouble, is to imitate Jesus Christ.

Helping Habits, *continued*

Ask volunteers to help read this section, starting on page 238.

Work with Words

Explore the meaning of *virtue* and *Theological Virtues* as used in the text.

- Invite two volunteers to read aloud the definitions from the Catholic Faith Words box.

- Discuss any questions or comments the students may have about these words and the text on this page.

CLOSE _____

ACTIVITY

Have the students read the instructions and complete this activity independently.

- If you carried out the Optional Activity on page 236, refer the students back to the original brainstorming session.

- If time allows, ask volunteers to share their descriptions of a virtuous person.

Quick Review God created us and gave us many gifts, called virtues, to help us make good moral decisions and become our best selves. The Theological Virtues help us believe in God, trust in his plan for us, and love him as he loves us.

DAY 3

Objectives

- Explain the relationship between the Cardinal Virtues and other moral virtues
- Explore the roles of modesty and chastity in our lives

OPEN

♥ Have the students write and pray a prayer of petition, asking God for help to lead a more moral life.

Tell them to write their specific petitions on an index card, starting each one with, "Lord, help me to be . . ." and ending with the response, "Lord, I belong to you."

Invite the students to carry the index card with them and read it every day.

BUILD

Moral Virtues

Explain that today's lesson describes the four most important moral virtues: the Cardinal Virtues.

Have the students silently read this section.

- Direct their attention to the Catholic Faith Words box and have a volunteer read aloud the definition.
- Tell them that the root word of "Cardinal" is *cardo*, meaning hinge. Cardinal Virtues are virtues on which other virtues hinge.

Moral Virtues

What are the Cardinal Virtues?

If someone asked you what the word *cardinal* meant, how would you answer? You might say it's a bird, or a name for a bishop in the Church, or maybe even a shade of red.

The Church uses *cardinal* to describe the four most important moral virtues: prudence, justice, fortitude, and temperance. They are called the **Cardinal Virtues**. All the other moral virtues can be grouped under them. The word *cardinal* comes from the Latin *cardo*, which means "hinge," or "that which something turns on, its principal point." So other moral virtues—such as patience, piety, gratitude, abstinence, and truth—flow from one of the four Cardinal Virtues.

We develop the moral virtues by responding to God's help in our lives and through our own efforts. As we learn more about life and how we should respond to different situations and as we practice the virtues in our daily lives, these moral virtues can grow inside us.

Modesty and Chastity

God created both males and females in his image and likeness. Both share in equal dignity, and are unique to each other. The gift of human sexuality comes from God, and it is part of his plan for humans to share in his creative abilities.

Your sexuality is more than whether you are biologically a male or female. It includes the way you think and feel, the way you pray, the way you are inclined to act, and the interests you have. The virtue of chastity helps you express your sexuality and show love in the right way for your state of life. Jesus is our model of chastity, and we are called to be chaste and to respect our own sexuality and the sexuality of others.

> **Catholic Faith Words**
>
> **Cardinal Virtues** the four principal moral virtues—prudence, temperance, justice, and fortitude—that help us live as children of God and from which the other moral virtues flow. We strengthen these good habits through God's grace and our own efforts.

240

© Our Sunday Visitor

Optional Activity

The Cardinal Virtues *Visual/Spatial*

Tell the students that Cardinal Virtues are virtues on which other virtues hinge. Have them make a virtues mobile whose core is a real metal hinge with holes.

- From the holes, have them hang the four Cardinal Virtues.
- The students will then consider other virtues that connect to each of the Cardinal Virtues. These additional virtues should each be hung from the Cardinal Virtue they relate to best.
- Display the finished work of each student around the classroom.
- If possible, invite other classes to come and view the display.

Chastity is not a lack or a denial. Rather, it is through chastity that we include our sexuality in a beautiful and meaningful way with all the other elements of who we are. Everyone who is baptized is called to chastity, even though Catholics have different states in life—married, single, ordained and consecrated religious. For women and men religious, this means living a celibate life.

Chastity requires discipline. It won't happen overnight. It involves a long process of growth and maturity. Inner peace and wholeness are the fruits of this process.

The virtue of modesty also helps you respect your sexuality. It helps us to dress, talk, and move in appropriate ways. Modesty is about decency. It's about being discreet in the way you dress, the things you say (or choose not to say), and the way you handle curiosity about sexual matters. It also means that we treat our bodies and the bodies of every other person with great respect.

Extreme tattooing and body piercing are forms of disrespect toward one's body. Self-mutilation and disfigurement for the purpose of shocking others would be sinful. When the human body is so intentionally deformed, it shows disrespect for God's creation.

Place a check mark by which of the Cardinal Virtues would help you the most. Draw a star next to the one you find easiest to live by, and an X by the one that is hardest.

The Cardinal Virtues

○ **Prudence:** being wise, careful, and sensible and making correct decisions on what is right and good helps you
  - to be aware of what's really going on in a situation
  - see ahead to the consequences of actions

○ **Justice:** giving God and others what is due to them as children of God helps you
  - act fairly and respect the rights of others
  - promote equality and harmony among groups of people

○ **Fortitude:** showing courage, having strength to get through difficult times, and not giving up helps you
  - resist temptation and be consistent in your choices and attitudes
  - overcome obstacles to doing good

○ **Temperance:** balancing your thoughts, actions, and feelings so that your desires don't rule your life helps you
  - enjoy all good things in moderation
  - practice self-control

NAME AND EXPLAIN

For two of the Cardinal Virtues, name a person who you believe exemplifies that virtue and why.

Virtue	Person	How They Exemplify the Virtue
_____	_____	_____
_____	_____	_____

Being Virtuous **241**

Modesty and Chastity

Review the text on page 240 with the students. Explain that a lot of desires could rule our lives if there were not virtues to control them. One type of desire is sexual desire, which, at its core, is a gift from God for it calls us into loving relationship with others.

Ask the students to quietly read the text on this page and highlight the points they want to remember.

- Facilitate a discussion on both chastity and modesty as they are explained here.

The Cardinal Virtues

Have the students review the chart.

★ Instruct them to place a check mark by the Cardinal Virtues they believe would help them the most at this point in their life. Have them draw a star next to the one they find easiest to live by, and an *X* by the one that is the hardest.

CLOSE

ACTIVITY

The students should complete this activity on their own.

- Invite volunteers to share their responses with the class.

Quick Review The Cardinal Virtues are the four most important moral virtues. The virtues of modesty and chastity, both stemming from the Cardinal Virtue of temperance, help us to respect our bodies and to have appropriate relationships with others.

---

i Teacher Background

Modesty and Chastity

The idea of modesty and chastity may seem old fashioned in today's world but these virtues are, in fact, of vital importance, especially for students of this age. The teaching on chastity in the *Catechism of the Catholic Church* can be found in the section written about the Sixth Commandment, while the teachings on modesty are in the section about the Ninth Commandment. These two virtues are closely linked and both stem from temperance.

It would be very helpful to familiarize yourself with paragraphs 2337–2359 and 2520–2527 in the *Catechism* for this lesson. You can find this information online at **www.usccb.org**.

Objective

- Examine how sins against the Eighth Commandment damage our integrity and character as they oppose the virtue of truth

OPEN

💙 Have the students pray the Hail Mary from page 384.

Ask: Why should you try to live a life of virtue?

- Point out that this is what the students will be learning about during today's lesson.

BUILD

A Life of Virtue

Read aloud the opening paragraph.

- Allow volunteers to share their own dreams about their future occupation or activities.

Keys to Excellence

Read or use your own words to share the information on the importance of virtues in the first paragraph, emphasizing that virtues are the keys to excellence.

- Explain that actions against the Eighth Commandment damage our integrity and character. Share the examples in the text.
- Ask the students if they have questions on this material or if they'd like to share additional examples of behaviors against this Commandment.
- Have two volunteers read the last two paragraphs on this page to the class.

A Life of Virtue

Why should you try to live a life of virtue?

People have dreams for themselves and where they want their lives to go. Some people want to be explorers and travel to distant lands. Some people want to be great teachers, influencing others. Dreams are important. They fuel our lives. They provide the motivation for what we learn and how we grow.

Keys to Excellence

In a similar way, striving for excellence is fueled by virtues. They are powerful keys that help to open the doorway into a faithful, reasonable life of excellence. In that sense, they help us to follow the Ten Commandments, Jesus' Beatitudes, and his New Commandment to love one another as he has loved us.

There are some behaviors that do not build up excellence in our life. The Eighth Commandment has identified some that damage our character and integrity:

- **lying**: deliberately saying false things by which we intend to deceive others
- **slander or calumny**: false words or even attitudes that maliciously injure others
- **revenge**: words or actions that return injury to another whom we perceive as having harmed ourselves
- **not living up to our promises**: behavior that shows that we are not worthy of another's trust

These behaviors are sinful. They hurt the person doing them and others. They are signs that a person is not interested in pursuing what is good and beautiful in life.

These behaviors are opposite of the virtue of truth, by which a person shows that he or she is true and honest in words and actions. Truth helps people avoid being deceitful, hypocritical (saying one thing but doing another), or disguising their true intentions.

Optional Activity

Virtuous Behavior Skits *Verbal/Linguistic, Bodily/Kinesthetic, Interpersonal*

Organize the students into small groups.

- Ask each small group to create and present a skit illustrating one concrete example of striving for good and virtuous behavior.
- Make sure every group member is involved in some way.
- After each group has shown their skit to the class, facilitate a discussion on the skits and what they accomplished.

© Our Sunday Visitor

The Blessing of Children in the Church of the Saviour of Spilled Blood, St. Petersburg, Russia

A Challenge

Pursuing the good life by striving for excellence within ourselves and in our behavior does not necessarily mean that we will have it easy or that life will be comfortable. Just the opposite!

Because society does not always believe as Catholics do, you may end up frustrated that people don't get it. You may be tempted to "sit down and go with the flow." You may have to stand up for things or act in ways that your friends or acquaintances don't understand or agree with. Sometimes this will cost you. You may be laughed at or ignored because of it.

Does this sound like the life of someone you know and have learned about? Jesus faced all of these things, but we know that he was happy in the truest sense of the word. He is our model for living a life of excellence. Living a life of virtues brings true inner peace.

> **DISCUSS**
>
> Talk with a classmate about two of the four behaviors that do not build up excellence, listed above. Think of concrete examples of those behaviors and discuss how someone your age could stand up to or address this behavior.

IN SUMMARY Catholics Believe

We are called to strive for what is right, just, holy, and gracious.

- The virtues are good spiritual habits that strengthen us and help us make good moral decisions and guide our emotions and conduct. The Theological Virtues make the moral, or human, virtues possible.

- The Cardinal Virtues of prudence, justice, fortitude, and temperance can help us respect ourselves and others and act with integrity.

- Learning about and practicing the virtues can help us live truthful, faith-filled lives.

Being Virtuous **243**

Teacher Background

Virtue and the Good Life

All too often, the phrase "the good life" refers to a life of material comfort and has little if anything to do with virtue. The good life for a virtuous Christian is a life that is directed outward toward other people and inward toward God. For a Christian, life cannot truly be "good" if our good fortune has come about at the expense of someone else. The sinful behaviors listed in this section not only harm the individuals involved, but actually weaken the whole fabric of our society. Our relationship to one another has to be based on God's truth.

A Challenge

Organize the students into small groups and have them read the three paragraphs on this page with their groups.

- Allow the groups to discuss the content, then facilitate a class discussion.

- Ask the students if they have ever had to stand up for things that others didn't understand or agree with.

- Allow volunteers to share.

CLOSE

ACTIVITY

Read aloud the instructions for the activity, then arrange the students in pairs.

- Have each pair choose two of the four sinful behaviors mentioned on page 242.

- Direct the pairs to think of concrete examples for their chosen behaviors and to discuss how someone could stand up to or address these bad behaviors.

- Invite volunteers to share their thoughts with the class.

In Summary

Review the summary information with the class.

- Make sure the students have no further questions about the virtues discussed in this chapter.

DAY 5

Objectives

- Discuss ways to strengthen virtuous living
- Explore the faith life of Saint Margaret Ward
- Offer the Act of Hope and Love prayer

OPEN

💜 Invite the students to gather in the prayer space and make the Sign of the Cross. Pray together Hail, Holy Queen from page 384.

BUILD

Our Catholic Life

Have the students silently read this content.

- Invite them to reflect on and write their responses to the Our Catholic Life question.

People of Faith

Explain to the class that Saint Margaret Ward stood strong for her faith.

- Share her interesting story in the People of Faith paragraph.
- Review with the class the extra content from the People of Faith Background box on the time in which Saint Margaret lived.
- Invite the students to share with a classmate or write about a hard decision that they had to make.

LIVE

Our Catholic Life

The virtues are important habits that give us strength and make it easier for us to do the right things. You can learn more about **virtuous living** by studying Catholic teachings, Scriptures, and the lives of the Saints, and from the good examples of family members, leaders, mentors, and friends who exemplify virtuous living. Charity, or love—the Theological Virtue that directs us to love God above all things and our neighbor as ourselves—may be easiest to see in other people from day to day, but the virtues of faith and hope can be seen, too, sometimes when we least expect it. Make a commitment to practice more of the Virtues in a disciplined way for a period of time to help develop the "muscles" to make this virtue part of your life.

> How can you show the Theological Virtues to yourself and others this week?

People of Faith

Saint Margaret Ward, d. 1588

Father Watson was a priest imprisoned during a time when Catholics in England were persecuted. Margaret Ward, a Catholic, helped him escape by smuggling a rope into the prison, but she was arrested when authorities traced the rope back to her. Even under torture, she refused to tell where Watson was hidden. At her trial, she was told that if she asked for forgiveness and joined the Church of England, she would be pardoned. She refused, saying she had done nothing wrong and that it was against her conscience to join a Protestant church. The Church celebrates Saint Margaret's feast day on **August 30.**

📶 For more, go to aliveinchrist.osv.com

244 Chapter 15

IDENTIFY

Examine the list of virtues and practices below. How well would you rate yourself (on a scale of 1 to 10) in practicing each virtue? Think about things you could do to become more virtuous.

Gratitude

Prudence

Fortitude

Truth

Abstinence

People of Faith Background

Saint Margaret Ward

Share the following on the time period Saint Margaret lived in:

- In 1588, King Philip II of Spain sent a fleet of warships to England, hoping to conquer the island and bring it back to the Catholic Church, but the effort failed.
- Because of this conflict, Catholics in England were persecuted to the point of death—there were even six new gallows built in various parts of London to accommodate the increase.

📶 Encourage the students to go to **aliveinchrist.osv.com** at home to learn more about Saint Margaret Ward.

Act of Hope and Love

Leader: God, come to my assistance.

All: Lord, make haste to help me.

Leader: Glory be to the Father and to the Son, and to the Holy Spirit,

All: as it was in the beginning is now, and ever shall be world without end. Amen.

Leader: A reading from the Letter to the Ephesians.

Read Ephesians 6:10–20.

Leader: The word of the Lord.

All: Thanks be to God.

Leader: God, source of our faith, hope, and love, give us the strength to be the people you call us to be, a witness and light for all to see.

All: O God, relying on your almighty power and your endless mercy and promises, we hope to gain pardon for our sins, the help of your grace, and life everlasting, through the saving actions of Jesus Christ, our Lord and Redeemer.

O God, we love you above all things, with our whole heart and soul, because you are all good and worthy of all love. We love our neighbor as ourselves for the love of you. We forgive all who have injured us and ask pardon of all whom we have injured.

O God, we love you because you are supremely good and worth loving; and because we love you, We are sorry with all our hearts for offending you. Lord, have mercy on us sinners, Amen.

▶ *Sing or play "I Love You, Lord"*

Being Virtuous **245**

📶 Go to **aliveinchrist.osv.com** for an interactive review.

A Work with Words Circle the letter of the choice that best completes the sentence.

1. A ___ is a good spiritual habit that strengthens you and enables you to do what is right and good.
   - **a.** virtue
   - **b.** discipline
   - **c.** Sacrament
   - **d.** reparation

2. When we attempt to indirectly correct the damage done by sin, we are making amends or ___.
   - **a.** forgiveness
   - **b.** virtue
   - **c.** reparation
   - **d.** justice

3. The ___ Virtues are the four most important moral virtues.
   - **a.** Theological
   - **b.** Divine
   - **c.** Lost
   - **d.** Cardinal

4. The virtue of ___ helps us to dress, talk, and move in appropriate ways.
   - **a.** modesty
   - **b.** chastity
   - **c.** prudence
   - **d.** both a and c

5. The virtue of ___ helps us express sexuality in the right way for our state in life.
   - **a.** modesty
   - **b.** fortitude
   - **c.** chastity
   - **d.** prudence

B Check Understanding Indicate whether the following statements are true or false. Then rewrite false statements to make them true.

6. Theological Virtues help us live as children of God and gain life everlasting with God. **True**/False

   _____

7. Prudence, justice, fortitude, and charity are four of the most important moral virtues. True/**False**
   Prudence, justice, fortitude, and temperance

8. Temperance is showing courage, having strength to get through difficult times, and not giving up. True/**False**
   Fortitude

9. Your sexuality affects the way you think and feel about things and the way you are inclined to act. **True**/False

   _____

10. The Tenth Commandment identifies lying, slander, and revenge as sins that damage our character and integrity. True/**False**
    The Eighth Commandment

C Make Connections On a separate sheet of paper, write a one-paragraph response to the question: We should think about things that are true, honorable, just, and pure. Think about some movies, music, and magazines. How do they encourage virtue?

246 Chapter 15

ACTIVITY

Have the students read the instructions and complete the activity on their own.

- Ask them to be honest with themselves. Assure them that this exercise is completely private and is meant to help them gauge which virtues they need to work on.

CLOSE

Act of Hope and Love

💙 Take the part of the Leader and remind the class to respond as a group.

Invite the students to gather in the prayer space with their books.

Select a student to read the Scripture passage.

Follow the order of prayer on the student page.

▶ Conclude by playing the song "I Love You, Lord," downloaded from **aliveinchrist.osv.com** while the students reflect on God's love and mercy.

Additional Music Option: "My Hope"

CHAPTER REVIEW

Review the instructions for each section and have the students complete the review.

📶 Go to **aliveinchrist.osv.com** to prepare customized and downloadable assessments, send eAssessments, and assign interactive reviews.

Being Virtuous **245–246**

UNIT 5

Use the closing points from Days 2–4 in each chapter to highlight lesson concepts for this unit and prepare for the Unit Review.

Have the students complete the Review pages. Then discuss the answers as a class. Review any concepts with which the students are having difficulty.

 Work with Words

Tell the students to use the clues to identify the correct words and complete the crossword puzzle.

A Work with Words Use the clues below to complete the crossword puzzle.

Word list:
Reparation
Intention
Sin
Circumstances
Scandal
Soul
Euthanasia
Virtue
Chastity

Crossword answers:
2 Across: SCANDAL
4 Across: EUTHANASIA
5 Across: CHASTITY
6 Across: CIRCUMSTANCES
7 Across: INTENTION
1 Down: REPARATA (REPARATION)
2 Down: SOUL
3 Down: VIRTUE
8 Down: SIN

Across

2. Destructive behavior by which we deliberately lead others to sin

4. Deliberate action or inaction that causes the death of someone who is sick, dying, or suffering

5. Virtue that helps you express sexuality and show love in the right way for your state of life

6. The aspect of human action that can increase or decrease its moral goodness

7. The object, the circumstances, and ____ are the elements included in human action.

Down

1. An attempt to indirectly correct the damage done by sin

2. Your unique combination of intellect, free will, and ____ make you an image of God.

3. A good spiritual habit that strengthens you and enables you to do what is right and good

8. Any deliberate thought, word, action, or omission that goes against moral law and offends God.

Morality **247**

B Check Understanding Fill in the correct term from the Word Bank to complete the sentences.

Word Bank:
- faith
- prudence
- human dignity
- life
- Cardinal
- temperance
- modesty
- thought
- Theological
- fortitude

9. The _____Cardinal_____ Virtues are the most important moral virtues.

10. The virtue of _____modesty_____ is being discreet in the way you dress and the things you say.

11. Prudence, justice, fortitude, and _____temperance_____ are four of the most important moral virtues.

12. _____Fortitude_____ is showing courage, having strength to get through difficult times, and not giving up.

13. Each human _____life_____ is sacred because humans are made in the image and likeness of God.

14. _____Faith_____ is believing in God and all that he has revealed to us, and in all that the Church proposes for our belief.

15. The worth each person has because he or she is made in the image of God is called _____human dignity_____.

Indicate whether the following statements are true or false. Then rewrite false statements to make them true.

16. Your free will is the spiritual principle of a human person that is individual, created by God, and will exist forever. True/**False**
Your soul is this principle… _____.

17. The effect of venial sin, without repenting and being forgiven, is total separation from God forever. True/**False**
This is the effect of mortal sin _____.

18. If a conscience has been formed well, it will lead you to what is truthful and just. **True**/False
_____

19. We humans, alone of all creatures, have the capacity for self-awareness. **True**/False
_____

20. Mortal sin breaks a person's relationship with God **True**/False
_____

C Make Connections Write a short answer to these questions.

21. Choose a television show or book whose characters struggle with Eighth Commandment issues. What are the issues, how do the characters choose to act, and what is the impact of their actions?
Responses will vary. _____

22. How do self-indulgence and extremism damage the artistry of God at work in the human person?
Responses will vary. _____

23. Describe the five steps to making good moral decisions.
Think (take time to consider options), Compare (compare options to Jesus' teachings), Talk (get advice from people you trust who understand the situation), Pray (ask the Holy Spirit for help), and Act (make a choice and be confident in that choice)

24. All human life is sacred. What implications does this statement have for your relationships with others—friends, family, neighbors, and strangers?
Responses will vary. _____

25. How is Jesus your model for living a life of excellence?
Responses will vary. _____

B Check Understanding

For problems 9–15, have the students fill in the blanks with the correct terms from the Word Bank to complete each sentence. For 16–20, they will need to indicate if the statements are true or false. Direct the students to rewrite false statements to make them true.

C Make Connections

Have the students write a short answer to the questions and statements on this page. Explain that even though these are short answer responses, they need to be sure that they fully answer the questions.

🛜 Go to **aliveinchrist.osv.com** to prepare customized and downloadable assessments, send eAssessments, and assign interactive reviews.

SACRAMENTS

How do the Sacraments help us to encounter God's presence so to receive the grace to live as Christ's disciples?

CHURCH HISTORY TIMELINE

33 Holy Spirit empowers Apostles to baptize and preach at Pentecost

313 Edict of Milan establishes religious freedom for Christians

1215 Fourth Ecumenical Lateran Council ends

1992 Publication of the new *Catechism of the Catholic Church*

Go to page 348 for more

Our Catholic Tradition

- Christ is a Sacrament because he makes God known to us and makes it possible for us to share in God's life. The Church is a Sacrament because in her we come to know God and share in his life through the Sacraments, which Christ instituted and in which he is always present. (CCC, 775–776)

- As Christ first welcomed and fed his followers, we are welcomed and belong to the Church though the Sacraments of Initiation. (CCC, 1212)

- Jesus shows us that God is compassionate, always willing to forgive and care for those who turn to him and believe. God heals us spiritually, emotionally, and sometimes physically in the Sacraments of Healing. (CCC, 1421)

Our Catholic Life

- Christ instituted the Sacraments so that we would always know and experience his welcoming, forgiving, healing, and nourishing power. (CCC, 1114, 1210)

- In the Eucharist, the Sacrament that we celebrate regularly, we are fed with the Body and Blood of Christ and are brought closer to Christ and one another. (CCC, 1382, 1416)

- In the Sacrament of Penance and Reconciliation, those who are truly sorry for their sins receive God's forgiveness and are reconciled with him and the Church. (CCC, 1424)

Introduce Unit Theme

Invite the class to share what they see in the image on this page and what they think it has to do with the Sacraments.

Point out the events on the timeline.

Ask six volunteers to each read aloud one of the bullet points under Our Catholic Tradition and Our Catholic Life. Discuss, as a class, what this information tells them about Unit 6.

Share that they will learn more about these doctrinal statements and the Sacraments as the class works through the next three chapters.

Ask the unit's Big Question found on page 250.

Allow time for discussion.

Explain to the students that this is the essential question for the unit. They will be working to fully answer it as they complete the three chapters in the unit.

📖 Go to the Source

As an optional extension, organize the students into three groups, assigning each group one of the main Scripture passages found in this unit.

- Chapter 16: Ephesians 3:14–21
- Chapter 17: Romans 6:1–4, 8
- Chapter 18: 2 Corinthians 5:17–21

Have each group read its passage and then give a dramatic reading (narrator with silent actors), create a visual representation, or write down one question they would ask God about the passage.

Reading the verses directly from the Bible will familiarize students with the sequence of the canon of Sacred Scripture.

Explore the Catechism

Divide the students into groups (either seven groups, one group for each of the Sacraments; or three groups, one for each division of Sacraments: Initiation, Healing, and Service). Have the groups read the portion from the *Catechism of the Catholic Church* that applies to their Sacrament(s) (paragraphs 1213 through 1666).

- Ask each group to list the visible signs of the Sacrament (the matter and actions) and the invisible realities, or effects, of the Sacrament.
- Allow time for any questions the students may have.

Reading the paragraphs directly from the *Catechism* will help the students learn where to find key teachings from the Sacred Tradition of the Church.

CHURCH HISTORY TIMELINE BACKGROUND

Refer the students to the Church History Timeline on pages 348–363 to learn more about important Church events and figures through A.D. 1085.

Fourth Ecumenical Lateran Council Ends
This important council issued a number of proclamations, including the first definition of transubstantiation, the teaching that, at Mass, the bread and wine truly become the Body and Blood, Soul and Divinity of Jesus Christ. This doctrine was later expanded at the Council of Trent. The Fourth Ecumenical Lateran Council is considered to be the most important council of the Middle Ages; it marked a high point in ecclesiastical life and papal power.

New *Catechism of the Catholic Church* Published
The new *Catechism of the Catholic Church* was first published in Latin and French in 1992, followed by many other languages, including English in 1994. A definitive explanation of the teachings of the Catholic Church, it is the preeminent source for understanding the Catholic faith. The decision to publish this new *Catechism* was made at the Extraordinary Assembly of the Synod of Bishops convened by Pope Saint John Paul II in 1985, and a commission of bishops and experts in theology and catechesis took on the task.

KEY CONCEPT

We know that Christ continues to be with us and take care of us in the Seven Sacraments.

DOCTRINAL CONTENT

- Every sacramental celebration is a meeting between God's children and their Father, a dialogue in the form of actions and words, a celebration woven from signs and symbols. (CCC, 1145, 1153)

- Jesus himself is a Sacrament because he makes God known to us; he is a visible sign of the mystery of the Holy Trinity. (CCC, 1114–1115, 2812)

- The Holy Spirit works with the Church in making Jesus' saving work present in the Sacraments. (CCC, 1116–1118)

- The Catholic teaching that Jesus is really and truly with us in the Eucharist—Body, Blood, Soul, and Divinity—is called Real Presence. (CCC, 1380, 1381)

TASKS OF CATECHESIS

Helping children grow in a faith that is "known, celebrated, lived, and expressed in prayer" (NDC, 20).

This chapter focuses on the following tasks of catechesis:

- Promoting Knowledge of the Faith

- Liturgical Education

Teacher Background

> … I kneel before the Father, from whom every family in heaven and on earth is named, that he may grant you in accord with the riches of his glory to be strengthened with power through his Spirit in the inner self, and that Christ may dwell in your hearts through faith; that you, rooted and grounded in love … may be filled with all the fullness of God.   **Ephesians 3:14–17, 19**

> **Reflect** What are your favorite Church traditions? Why are they so meaningful for you?

The Seven Sacraments are gifts from a wise and loving God. They make visible the saving action of Christ. In the Sacraments, some of the earthly elements of life—like water, bread, and oil—are transformed through the Holy Spirit's action in the Church, into signs of God's intimate presence and life with, and within, us. The Sacraments are also reminders that God journeys with us through the great and small moments of our lives. He is present at times that have great, life-changing consequences, and he is equally present in our daily ups and downs. He is there in moments of great success and joy, and equally there in times of sorrow and fear. The Sacraments deepen our relationship with God the Father, Son, and Holy Spirit and open us to live in deeper relationship with others.

More than anything else, the Sacraments give us a share in divine life and bring us into a deeper, more intimate relationship with Jesus Christ. Jesus is the one from whom the Sacraments originally came, and it is he who gives them their fullness of meaning. Jesus, in a sense, is the original Sacrament, for he was the full and complete visible sign of God's presence. The Seven Sacraments continue Christ's saving action in the Church today. They are liturgical celebrations in which God is made known to us in ways that go beyond rational explanation, transforming us as his children and the Body of Christ.

> **Reflect** Consider a particularly moving experience of the Sacraments in your life. What made that experience so memorable for you?

Teacher's Prayer

Lord Jesus, you make yourself known to us in your Sacraments. Help me to remain faithful to my sacramental heritage, and through the Sacraments, may I grow in grace so as to better serve my sisters and brothers. Amen.

How Seventh Graders Understand Chapter Topics

Seventh graders are more capable than they were before of abstract thought, including understanding the meaning behind signs and symbols. Until now, their understanding of the Sacraments might have been limited to the visible, concrete aspects of the celebration. Now they are ready to dive deeper, to learn more about the theological meaning and invisible realities behind the signs.

Teaching Tip: Emphasize that every sacramental celebration has visible signs and invisible realities. Be sure to talk about each of the Seven Sacraments in terms of these two aspects.

Sharing the Message with Seventh Graders

- Adolescents are growing into a deeper awareness of how their past is connected to their present.
- Students this age are very open to being taught about the power of rituals and traditions.
- Help seventh graders find the balance between continuing to participate in comfortable family traditions and expressing themselves in new and independent ways.

ONLINE RESOURCES

Go to **aliveinchrist.osv.com**

You will find:

- Interactive lesson planning, additional activities, and ideas for the classroom environment
- Step by step lesson instruction from printed Teacher Edition for integrated lesson planning
- Custom-built assessments to download and eAssessment links
- Interactive reviews that provide scores and the option to review answers
- Chapter-specific Lectionary connections and a complete correlation ordered by the Sundays of the year, with suggestions for how to integrate the Scripture readings into chapter lessons

Go to **osvparish.com** for Ask the Experts Q and A, Community Connections, and Blogs.

Chapter 16 Planner

Objectives	Open

DAY 1—Invite/Preview, Pages 251–253

- Reflect on God's personal invitation through Scripture
- Indicate prior knowledge of chapter concepts and vocabulary

- ♡ **Psalm 30:12–13** Pray the opening prayer.
- 📖 **Ephesians 3:14–21** Proclaim "Prayer for the Readers." Guide the students through the process of Scripture reflection.
- Discuss Have You Ever Thought questions.

DAY 2—Discover, Pages 254–255

- Discover that the Sacraments begin with God's invitation given in signs and symbols and require our faith-filled response
- Explain why we call Jesus the first Sacrament
- Explore how the Holy Spirit works with the Church to make Jesus' saving work present in the Sacraments

- ♡ Pray the **Prayer to the Holy Spirit**, page 384.

DAY 3—Discover, Pages 256–257

- Recognize that all of the Sacraments draw us into the Paschal Mystery
- Explain how the Edict of Milan changed the lives of Christians

- ♡ Pray the **Sacraments Prayer**, page 256.
- Discuss the opening question.

DAY 4—Discover, Pages 258–259

- Explore how the physical elements used in the Seven Sacraments help us experience God's presence
- Identify what Real Presence means in Catholic teaching

- ♡ Pray the **Litany of Saint Joseph**, page 390.
- Read the opening question.

DAY 5—Live, Pages 260–261

- Review different types of grace and how they touch our lives
- Explore the faith life of Saint Ludmilla
- Offer the Prayer to Saint Joseph

- ♡ Pray **Psalm 30:12–13**, page 251.

REVIEW AND ASSESSMENT

Chapter Review, page 262
Chapter Test, page 251F

🛜 **aliveinchrist.osv.com** Customize and Download Assessments, Email Links to eAssessments, Interactive Student Reviews

Build	Close	Materials & Resources
• Present lesson highlights. • Preview **Catholic Faith Words**. ★ Categorize and discuss each of the Seven Sacraments.	• Activity Describe favorite traditions, both inside and outside of the Church.	☐ pencils or pens
• **Catholic Faith Words** Seven Sacraments • Talk about how the Sacraments are a part of Church Tradition. 📖 Read John 14:1–10. ★ Point out the Holy Spirit's role in the Sacraments.	• Activity Unscramble words to discover how the Seven Sacraments connect us to God through Jesus. • Conclude with a review of key concepts and objectives. • Optional Activity Masterworks of God (Activity Master 16)	☐ pencils or pens ☐ Bibles ☐ Activity Master 16 (Page 251G)
• **Catholic Faith Words** Sacraments of Initiation, Sacraments of Healing, Sacraments at the Service of Communion • Discuss how the Sacraments draw us into the Paschal Mystery.	• Activity Connect Jesus' actions and attitudes from Scripture to specific Sacraments. • Conclude with a review of key concepts and objectives.	☐ pencils or pens ☐ board or chart paper ☐ Bibles
• **Catholic Faith Words** Real Presence • Reflect on the influence that Jewish traditions had on Christian traditions.	• Activity Discuss and carry out ways to be a Eucharistic person. • Review the In Summary statements.	☐ pencils or pens ☐ board or chart paper ☐ highlighter
• Discuss the questions in the Our Catholic Life section. • Learn about Saint Ludmilla. • Activity Write ways to be mindful of God's presence in daily life.	• Recruit a leader and four readers. • Follow the order of prayer. ▶ Sing the closing song.	☐ pencils or pens 🛜 "Let It Be Done"

Chapter Connections

FORMING CATHOLIC IDENTITY ACROSS THE CURRICULUM

To integrate the Catholic faith in all aspects of curriculum, this chapter's objectives can be reinforced and applied in the instruction of other disciplines.

Go to **aliveinchrist.osv.com** for cross-curricular activities and projects linked to the doctrinal content discussed in this unit. Activities are available from among the following knowledge categories and content areas:

Language Arts

- Integration of Knowledge
- Literacy
- Speaking and Listening
- Writing Skills

Math

- Algebraic Thinking
- Geometry
- Measurement and Data
- Numbers and Operations

Science

- Earth Science
- Life Science
- Physical Science
- Technology

Social Studies

- Civics
- Economics
- Geography
- History

NCEA IFG: ACRE Edition

Knowledge of the Faith

- **Objective:** To know and understand basic Catholic teaching about the Incarnate Word Jesus Christ as the way, truth, and life

Liturgical Life

- **Objective:** To know the Paschal Mystery of Jesus: in the Church's liturgical life—feasts, seasons, symbols, and practices—and in the Sacraments as signs and instruments of grace

Catholic Faith Literacy

anointing, Eucharist, Liturgy of the Word, Sacrament

Catholic Social Teaching

To integrate Catholic Social Teaching into your lesson, choose one of the following features: Life and Dignity of the Human Person, pages 334–335; or Solidarity of the Human Family, pages 344–345.

- Start the Live step of the process by talking about Saint Ludmilla on page 260. Then move directly to the Catholic Social Teaching feature.
- Or, to expand the lesson, complete page 260, then move to the Catholic Social Teaching feature.
- Return to Chapter 16 for the prayer on page 261.

Music Option

Use the following song to enhance catechetical learning or for prayer.

- "Let It Be Done," Day 5, Page 261

Name _____   Date _____

Circle the letter of the choice that best completes each sentence.

1. The ___ are effective signs of God's grace instituted by Christ and given to his Church.

   a. Saints

   b. Seven Sacraments

   c. Precepts

   d. Real Presence

2. Jesus is the perfect ___ between God the Father and humanity because he is fully God and fully man.

   a. Mediator

   b. Sacrament

   c. image

   d. Messiah

3. The Sacraments of Healing bring God's ___ to those who are physically and spiritually sick.

   a. justice and healing

   b. forgiveness and sacrifice

   c. forgiveness and healing

   d. sacrifice and healing

4. Jesus followed the ___ customs of prayer and worship.

   a. Jewish

   b. Christian

   c. Roman

   d. European

Indicate whether the following statements are true or false. Then rewrite false statements to make them true.

5. God gives us grace when we do something to earn it. **True/False**

   _____

6. The three Sacraments of Initiation celebrate membership into the Church. **True/False**

   _____

7. Jesus Christ is called the first Sacrament. **True/False**

   _____

8. Pentecost describes that Jesus is really and truly with us in the Eucharist. **True/False**

   _____

Write a response on the lines below.

9. What are the two Sacraments at the Service of Communion and what do they celebrate?

   _____

   _____

10. Where is Jesus when we celebrate the Sacraments?

   _____

Name _____ Date _____

Masterworks of God

In Europe during the Middle Ages, many people could not read. Those who built churches designed artwork to teach about Christ and the Church. Pretend you are a designer; your assignment is to create a window in a new church to teach about one of the Seven Sacraments. The plan is to have seven stained-glass windows—one for each of the Seven Sacraments, so you will need to work in a group with six others. Discuss with your group who will work on each Sacrament. Sketch in your designs.

SACRAMENT OF _____

God's Masterworks

💙 **Let Us Pray**

Leader: Father of life, you sent your Son, Jesus, to us so that we could come to know you completely. Jesus' actions have the power to save us and bring us to you.

"You changed my mourning into dancing;
you took off my sackcloth
and clothed me with gladness
O Lᴏʀᴅ, my God,
forever will I give you thanks." **Psalm 30:12–13**

All: Open our hearts to your grace.

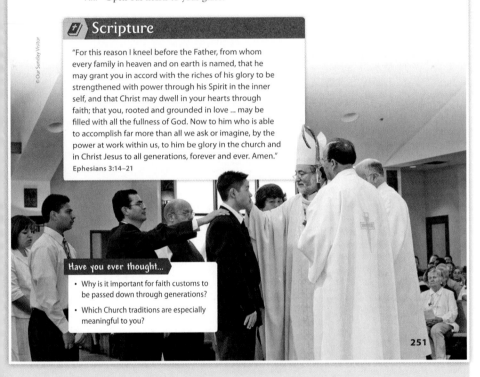

📖 Scripture

"For this reason I kneel before the Father, from whom every family in heaven and on earth is named, that he may grant you in accord with the riches of his glory to be strengthened with power through his Spirit in the inner self, and that Christ may dwell in your hearts through faith; that you, rooted and grounded in love ... may be filled with all the fullness of God. Now to him who is able to accomplish far more than all we ask or imagine, by the power at work within us, to him be glory in the church and in Christ Jesus to all generations, forever and ever. Amen."
Ephesians 3:14–21

Have you ever thought...

- Why is it important for faith customs to be passed down through generations?
- Which Church traditions are especially meaningful to you?

251

© Our Sunday Visitor

📖 Scripture Background

Scripture Reflection Process

Invite the students to be still, close their eyes, and focus on their breathing. Encourage them to open their minds and hearts to what God is saying to them.

- Proclaim the Scripture and have the students sit in silence.
- *Ask:* What did you hear God say to you today?
- Allow volunteers to share.

▶ You may play instrumental music to begin the reflection.

Objective

- Reflect on God's personal invitation through Scripture

OPEN _____

💙 **Let Us Pray**

Invite the students to gather in the prayer space and make the Sign of the Cross. Read aloud the Psalm verses. Prompt the response from the group.

Have the students move out of the prayer space and back to their seats.

Explain that Jesus is always with us, loving us. His greatest desire is to bring us to his Father.

Say: God's greatest gift to us is his Son, Jesus Christ. Let's listen to God's Word and remember that we are rooted and grounded in the love of Christ.

📖 Scripture

Guide the students through the process of Scripture reflection (see the Scripture Background box below).

Have you ever thought...

Say: The Sacraments are Jesus' gift to us as a way for us to always experience his welcoming, forgiving, healing, and nourishing power in our lives.

- Invite the students to respond to the questions.

DAY 1

Objective

- Indicate prior knowledge of chapter concepts and vocabulary

BUILD

Use this page to assess the students' knowledge related to the chapter content.

Getting Started

Read the introductory paragraph to the students.

The Seven Sacraments

Ask a volunteer to read aloud the instructions that go with the chart.

- Explain to the class that the category titles can also be found in the Catholic Faith Words box.

★ Have the students indicate which category each of the Seven Sacraments belong in and explain how each relates to that category title.

- Allow the students to ask any questions that they may have regarding the chart.

Getting Started

In this chapter, you will gain an understanding of how the Holy Trinity is the source of the Sacraments, how Christ instituted each of the Sacraments, and how he is present today in their celebration.

> **Catholic Faith Words**
> - Seven Sacraments
> - Sacraments of Initiation
> - Sacraments of Healing
> - Sacraments at the Service of Communion
> - Real Presence

1. For each Sacrament identify the category (Sacraments of Initiation, Sacraments of Healing, or Sacraments at the Service of Communion) to which it belongs.
2. Then explain how each relates to its category title.

The Seven Sacraments

Sacrament	Category	How It Relates
Baptism		
Confirmation		
Eucharist		
Penance and Reconciliation		
Anointing of the Sick		
Holy Orders		
Matrimony		

© Our Sunday Visitor

> ✓ **Teaching Tip**
>
> ### Signs and Symbols
>
> In the Sacraments, ordinary things become signs of God's extraordinary love. Use this as a starting point for teaching about the power of signs and symbols.
>
> - Encourage the students to bring common items from their homes and their lives into the classroom to share.
> - Ask the students to share their symbols along with an explanation of how these things point to deeper truths or meanings. (Examples could be something like a special mug or a family plate, an athletic uniform, a ticket stub from a memorable event, and so on.)
> - Share a personal symbol or sign of your own.

DESCRIBE

Meaningful Traditions How do you mark time, remember important events, celebrate special milestones? Of your traditions, which is your favorite? In the spaces provided, describe in words or symbols one or more of your favorite personal and/or family traditions and favorite Church traditions.

_____

_____

_____

_____

_____

Using two of the traditions you've identified (one personal and/or family tradition, and one Church tradition), explain what these traditions mean to you.

_____

_____

_____

_____

_____

_____

God's Masterworks **253**

Work with Words

Again, refer to the Catholic Faith Words box at the top of page 252.

- Have a volunteer read aloud all of the vocabulary terms.
- To talk about the first four words, review the chart that the students just completed on page 252.
- Point out the vocabulary term not used in the chart, _Real Presence_.
- Encourage the students to share what they know about Real Presence.

CLOSE _____

ACTIVITY

Read aloud the instructions.

- Make it clear that the students need to identify at least one Church tradition and one personal and/or family tradition.
- Allow them time to brainstorm and work on their symbols or statements.
- Encourage a few volunteers to share their favorite traditions with the class.

Teacher Background

The Roots of Church Traditions

When you speak of Church traditions, you will probably be speaking of liturgical practices within your own parish.

- Some Church traditions are universal and some are of local origin.
- The _Catechism of the Catholic Church_ explains that diverse liturgical traditions have arisen because of the Church's mission to the whole world. "Through the liturgical life of a local church, Christ, the light and salvation of all peoples, is made manifest to the particular people and culture to which that Church is sent and in which she is rooted" (1202).

© Our Sunday Visitor

DAY 2

Objectives

- Discover that the Sacraments begin with God's invitation given in signs and symbols and require our faith-filled response
- Explain why we call Jesus the first Sacrament
- Explore how the Holy Spirit works with the Church to make Jesus' saving work present in the Sacraments

OPEN

 Gather the students in the prayer space to pray the Prayer to the Holy Spirit from page 384.

BUILD

It All Starts with Jesus

Tell the students to silently read this section.

The Seven Sacraments

Invite a volunteer to read the first paragraph.

- *Ask:* What is another name for the Seven Sacraments?
  the masterworks of God

Read aloud the second paragraph.

- Point out how the People of God perform the rituals (read, process, sing), provide the materials (wheat, grapes, vestments), and participate in the celebration of each Sacrament.
- Challenge the students to name some additional examples.

Finish reading this section, including the paragraphs on page 255.

It All Starts with Jesus

How is Jesus the source of the Seven Sacraments?

The best traditions are always about the people who keep the traditions alive with us. If you ever made a card or present for your parents when you were a child, someone else probably provided the materials, cleaned up, and helped you wrap. This is similar to Christ's presence in his Church and our experience of grace, which is God's free, loving gift of his own life and help. We receive this gift of grace directly from God.

254 Chapter 16

The Seven Sacraments

The Church celebrates seven "masterworks of God" (CCC, 1116): the **Seven Sacraments**. The Seven Sacraments are effective signs of God's grace instituted by Christ and given to his Church. In the celebration of each Sacrament, there are visible signs and Divine actions that give grace and allow us to share in God's work.

Every sacramental celebration is a meeting between God's children and their Father, a dialogue in the form of actions and words. We, the People of God, perform the rituals (read, process, sing, anoint) provide the materials (plant wheat and grapes, sew priestly vestments, order hosts and candles) and participate in the celebration (choir practice, seminary training, lector workshops).

We do these things to give God our praise and thanks, as well as offer ourselves to him. Yet God took the initiative in sending his Son. We are totally dependent upon God's Divine action in the celebration of each of the Sacraments.

So how do we begin to understand the Seven Sacraments? We start with Jesus Christ. Jesus himself is a Sacrament because he is a visible sign of the mystery of the Holy Trinity. He makes God known to us perfectly because he is God. Jesus said, "Whoever has seen me has seen the Father" (John 14:9). Jesus is the Mediator between God and humanity, because he is fully God and fully man.

> **Go to the Source**
> Read *John 14:1–10*. What does Jesus say about God's works?

© Our Sunday Visitor

📖 Scripture Background

One with the Father

John 14:1–10 is in the middle of the collection of discourses that John places at the Last Supper. It is here that John most clearly states what is mentioned in other places in his Gospel: Jesus is the way to the Father. If we know Jesus, we know God the Father.

Many teachers can probably relate to Jesus' frustration with his followers. They don't seem to know what he has tried to teach them. The questions from Thomas and Philip can be a comfort and an inspiration to us.

Jesus' claim that he is one with God the Father can be difficult to comprehend. We can know this only through faith.

So his actions have the power to save—whether it is by healing a lame man or carrying his Cross. His whole life, from his Incarnation to the sending of his Spirit, is sacramental: it shows us God, shares God's life with us, and is the source of our salvation and new life.

Through Jesus, we have access to God the Father and God the Holy Spirit; from him, we receive Divine help in becoming God's children.

The Church Is the Sign and Source of God's Life

Every Sacrament always starts with remembering the works of God the Father, and being thankful, and celebrating Christ's presence. God the Holy Spirit helps us remember all that Christ said and did, and everything he taught about God the Father. In fact, the Holy Spirit, working with the Church, makes Jesus' saving work present in the Sacraments. Through the power of the Holy Spirit working in us and in the Church, we not only remember what brings us new life, but that new life is made available to us. The Holy Spirit unites us to the Son of God, drawing us into relationship with the Father as his adopted children.

In this way, the Church herself is "the sacrament of Christ's action at work in her through the mission of the Holy Spirit" (CCC, 1118). The Church is a sign of God's love and action in the world.

> Underline what the Holy Spirit does for us in the Sacraments.

Catholic Faith Words

Seven Sacraments effective signs of God's grace instituted by Christ and given to his Church. In the celebration of each Sacrament, there are visible signs and Divine actions that give grace and allow us to share in God's work.

SOLVE

Unscramble the words to discover how what we do in two of the Seven Sacraments connects us to God through Jesus Christ.

Humans plant and grow the **HETWA** ___wheat___ and grapes for use in the Sacrament of **TRISUECAH** ___Eucharist___. We also sew the **RMNGTEAS** ___garments___ for the Sacraments of Baptism and Holy **DRORES** ___Orders___.

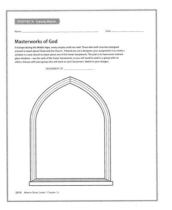

© Our Sunday Visitor

Have the students open their Bibles to read John 14:1–10. Identify that Jesus says the works he has done have been God's works.

The Church Is the Sign and Source of God's Life

Instruct the class to silently read this section.

★ Tell them to underline what the Holy Spirit does for us in the Sacraments.

- *Ask:* Why do we say that the Church is a Sacrament? because God works through the Church How is the Church a Sacrament? She is a sign of God's love; she puts us in direct contact with God; she is our passage into God's Kingdom.

CLOSE

ACTIVITY

Have the students read the instructions and complete this activity on their own.

- Facilitate a class discussion to make sure everyone recorded the correct information.

Quick Review The Sacraments, given to us by Jesus, begin with God's invitation given in signs and symbols and require our faith-filled response. The Church is a sign of God's love and action in the world; the Holy Spirit works within her to show us Jesus' saving work, which is present in the Sacraments.

Optional Activity

Activity Master 16: Masterworks of God

Distribute copies of the activity found on teacher page 251G.

- Arrange the class into groups of seven so that each group member will cover one of the Seven Sacraments.

- This activity will use the creative arts to reinforce what the students know about the Seven Sacraments.

Objectives

- Recognize that all of the Sacraments draw us into the Paschal Mystery

- Explain how the Edict of Milan changed the lives of Christians

OPEN

♥ Have the students stand and pray the Sacraments Prayer from the Teacher Background box on this page.

Ask the opening question and list responses on the board or on chart paper.

- Come back to the question after the class has completed pages 256 and 257 to see if they can add more to the list.

BUILD

The Foundation of the Seven Sacraments

Summarize the first three paragraphs, stressing the following:

- All of the Sacraments are rooted in the life of Jesus.

- Jesus did not dictate the words, gestures, and symbols to be used in each Sacrament. However, we find the source of each Sacrament in the attitudes and actions of Jesus that we read about in Scripture.

Review the three categories of Sacraments with the class.

The Foundation of the Seven Sacraments

How did Jesus institute the Sacraments?

At Pentecost, the Apostles became certain that they had to share the Good News of Jesus. They knew they now had the strength from the Holy Spirit to carry out Jesus' command to:

- teach and baptize,
- remember him in the breaking of the bread, and
- continue his work of forgiving and healing.

All the Sacraments are rooted in the life of Jesus and show us something about him and eternal life. They draw us into Christ's Paschal Mystery, connecting us to his suffering and rising to new life. Through the work of the Holy Spirit we are made more like Jesus.

256

Peter Baptizing the Centurion Cornelius, by Francesco Trevisani

We share in the divine life so that we can have the hope of life forever with God. Jesus wanted future believers to know him as his first followers did. This is why he told the Apostles to baptize, break bread, forgive, heal, and bless in his name. Jesus did not leave manuals with his Apostles, or dictate the words and symbols to be used in each Sacrament. In the Bible, we find the attitudes and actions of Jesus that are still those of the Church today, expressed in the Seven Sacraments.

The **Sacraments of Initiation**—Baptism, Confirmation, and Eucharist—make individuals full members of the Catholic Church. The **Sacraments of Healing**, received when a member is in need of God's healing, forgiveness, or strength, are Penance and Reconciliation, and the Anointing of the Sick. The **Sacraments at the Service of Communion**, celebrated in commitment to the Church and her members, are Matrimony and Holy Orders.

Following Jesus' Command

On Pentecost the Apostles baptized nearly three thousand new believers. From Jerusalem they went out to share the message of Jesus. Everywhere they went, the Holy Spirit worked through them to establish the Church. They gathered to celebrate the Eucharist in the evening after their day of work. They would gather for a meal followed by *eucharistia*, "giving thanks" with bread and wine in memory of Jesus. They still followed the Law of Moses and worshipped in the synagogues on the Sabbath. They were like other Jews, but they believed in the Risen Lord.

Teacher Background

Sacraments Prayer

Write this prayer response on the board: "God, open our hearts to experience grace through the Seven Sacraments." Explain to the students that this will be their prayer response today. Pray the following prayers and have the students respond after each one:

- Lord, thank you for Baptism, which has made us all members of your Church . . .

- Lord, help us to receive you worthily each time we receive the Eucharist . . .

- Lord, may the grace of Confirmation fill us with the gifts of your Holy Spirit . . .

As people spread the Good News, they settled in other areas like Antioch, where "the disciples were first called Christians" (Acts 11:26). The Gentiles—people of non-Jewish cultures—who became believers there wanted to be baptized as well. Eventually Christianity became a separate religion.

Constantine issued the Edict of Milan in A.D. 313, ordering tolerance toward Christians in the Roman Empire after many years of persecution. Sunday became a day of rest, and Christians celebrated the Eucharist on Sunday mornings. More importantly, Christians began to shape the Lord's Day. Their traditions changed to respond to their desire to be a serious part of their Church community.

Catholic Faith Words

Sacraments of Initiation the three Sacraments that celebrate membership into the Catholic Church: Baptism, Confirmation, and Eucharist

Sacraments of Healing Penance and Reconciliation and the Anointing of the Sick. In these Sacraments, God's forgiveness and healing are given to those suffering physical and spiritual sickness.

Sacraments at the Service of Communion Holy Orders and Matrimony. They celebrate people's commitment to serve God and the community and help build up the People of God.

IDENTIFY

Read the following Scripture passages:

- John 2:1–11
- Matthew 8:1–4
- Matthew 16:19
- Luke 22:4–20
- John 21:15–17
- Acts 1:2–4
- Matthew 28:15–20

Identify the Scripture passage that goes with the corresponding action or attitude of Jesus and Sacrament to complete the chart below.

Jesus and the Sacraments		
Jesus' Action or Attitude	Sacrament that Reflects Jesus	Scripture Passage
Jesus told Apostles to make disciples of all nations.	Baptism	_____
The Holy Spirit filled Jesus' Apostles with his Gifts so they could continue Jesus' work.	Confirmation	_____
Jesus ate the Passover meal as a Last Supper with his disciples.	Eucharist	_____
Jesus gave Peter the keys to the Kingdom.	Reconciliation	_____
Jesus healed a leper.	Anointing of the Sick	_____
Jesus turned water to wine at a wedding feast.	Matrimony	_____
Jesus asked Peter to tend his sheep.	Holy Orders	_____

God's Masterworks **257**

© Our Sunday Visitor

Liturgy Link

Prayer to Saint Joseph

This chapter emphasizes the sacramental presence of Jesus in the Church. The prayer celebration for this chapter focuses on Saint Joseph, the foster father of Jesus and the Patron and Protector of the Church.

In 1870, Pope Pius IX named Saint Joseph as "the Patron and Protector of the Universal Church." Because this prayer experience is a reconnection with the real-life story of Jesus and his family, it may be easier for the students to see that the Church founded by Jesus is a family of faith on many levels.

Following Jesus' Command

Have the students silently read this section that begins on page 256.

- Discuss any questions that they may have on how Christianity became a separate religion.
- Be sure to point out the importance of the Edict of Milan.

Work with Words

Point out the Catholic Faith Words box on this page.

- Have three volunteers each read aloud one of the definitions.

CLOSE

ACTIVITY

Explain the instructions to the students.

- Have them work with a classmate to read the Scripture passages and complete the chart.
- After the class has had time to complete the assignment, review the chart to ensure that everyone has the correct answers. Baptism, Matthew 28:15–20; Confirmation, Acts 2:1–4; Eucharist, Luke 22:4–20; Reconciliation, Matthew 16:19; Anointing of the Sick, Matthew 8:1–4; Matrimony, John 2:1–11; Holy Orders, John 21:15–17

Quick Review Jesus instituted the Sacraments to help us stay connected to him and to draw us into the Paschal Mystery. The Edict of Milan changed the lives of Christians because it allowed them to practice their religion without persecution.

DAY 4

Objectives

- Explore how the physical elements used in the Seven Sacraments help us experience God's presence

- Identify what Real Presence means in Catholic teaching

OPEN

♥ Gather in the prayer space and pray the Litany of Saint Joseph from page 390.

BUILD

Christ Acts in the Church

Read aloud the three paragraphs.

- As you read, have the students highlight the most important sentence in each paragraph.

- Review as a class to see what the students chose to highlight.

- Emphasize that Christ is present in the Sacraments.

Christ's Presence in the Liturgy

Tell the students to silently read this section.

- Invite volunteers to explain why they think the words *assembly*, *priest*, and *Word* are bold-faced.

Point out the Catholic Faith Words box at the bottom of this page.

- Go over the definition and answer any questions that the students may have.

- Point out that Real Presence is a very important teaching in the Catholic faith.

Christ Acts in the Church

How is Christ present today when we worship?

God created us to be human, so he knew that we really needed things to touch and smell and taste and count and hear. The Seven Sacraments involve symbols and rituals that we can see, touch, hear, taste, and smell. They help us grasp an invisible God.

We taste the Body of Christ, smell the fragrance of incense, feel the touch of the Sacred Chrism, hear the words spoken and sung, and see the light of a candle's flame and the faces of the assembly gathered to pray. Through our senses, we know the presence of Christ. To receive a Sacrament is to meet Christ.

Because Christ is present, he is acting in the celebration of the Seven Sacraments. When the Church baptizes, Christ baptizes. When the Church witnesses a marriage, Christ is there. When the Church forgives sins, the power of God's forgiveness is right there. When the Church anoints the sick, it is the healing touch of Jesus upon those in need.

Christ's Presence in the Liturgy

Day after day the main place where we meet Christ is in the **assembly**, the baptized members of the community. Next Sunday, look around at the assembled congregation to see the face of Christ. The **priest** gathers our prayers and leads our sacrifice of praise. Next Sunday, when the priest says, "Let us pray," think of your needs.

When the Gospel is read, it is Christ who speaks to his People. Next Sunday, let the Responsorial Psalm and Gospel Acclamation show your belief that Christ is present in his **Word**. Christ is uniquely present in the Eucharist itself, his Body and Blood received in Holy Communion and adored as the Blessed Sacrament. The phrase **Real Presence** is used to describe the Catholic teaching that Jesus is really and truly with us in the Eucharist—Body, Blood, Soul, and Divinity.

> **Catholic** Faith Words
>
> **Real Presence** a phrase used to describe the Catholic teaching that Jesus is really and truly with us in the Eucharist—Body, Blood, Soul, and Divinity

258

© Our Sunday Visitor

♥ **Liturgy Link**

Blessings

At every Eucharistic liturgy, we hear two examples of the Jewish *berakoth* prayer. Those blessings are probably very like the ones Jesus prayed at the Last Supper.

As he offers bread, the priest says, "Blessed are you, Lord God of all creation, for through your goodness we have received the bread we offer you: fruit of the earth and work of human hands . . ." As he offers wine, the priest says, "Blessed are you, Lord God of all creation, for through your goodness we have received the wine we offer you: fruit of the vine and work of human hands . . ." To both we respond, "Blessed be God for ever" (The Order of Mass, Preparation of the Gifts).

Looking Back

Jesus was Jewish, and followed the Jewish traditions of prayer and worship. He celebrated great feasts like Passover. The Apostles were also Jewish, and so were many of the first people who believed in Jesus. It's not surprising that the rituals that they would use to remember the presence of the Risen Lord would sound and look like the traditions of their Jewish culture. There are still connections between the Jewish liturgy and our Christian liturgy.

At the Jewish synagogue service, the Torah is read and reflected upon. As the early Christians gathered, it was only natural to read Scripture. Maybe they even read a letter they just received from Peter or Paul! The structure of proclaiming and responding to the Word of God is now part of the Mass called the Liturgy of the Word.

As part of their Jewish background, the Apostles and early Christians would have been accustomed to celebrating the weekly feast of the Sabbath from sundown Friday to sundown Saturday. Christians shifted to celebrating the weekly feast on Sundays—the day of the Resurrection, and thus the Lord's Day—by breaking bread, discussing Scriptures, and honoring the Lord.

© Our Sunday Visitor

WRITE

To be a Eucharistic person, show gratitude to God and others. Add thanks to your daily prayer. Also express your thankfulness this week in a card, email, or spoken word to persons who have helped you.

IN SUMMARY — Catholics Believe

We know that Christ continues to be with us and take care of us in the Seven Sacraments.

- Christ is a Sacrament because he makes God known to us and makes it possible for us to share in God's life. The Church is a Sacrament because in her we come to know God and share in his life through the Seven Sacraments.

- Christ instituted the Sacraments so that we would always know and experience his welcoming, forgiving, healing, and nourishing power.

- Christ is present in the Sacraments, through the assembly gathered, the priest presiding, the Scripture proclaiming, and most especially in the Eucharist, his Body and Blood.

God's Masterworks **259**

ℹ Teacher Background

Jews and Catholics

The U.S. Conference of Catholic Bishops has addressed the relationship of Catholics and Jews many times since Vatican Council II:

- how Christians should read and interpret Scripture, especially narratives about the Crucifixion, with reference to the Jews

- the Church's opposition to anti-Semitism

- the unique place Jewish people and the Jewish religion hold in the unfolding of salvation

Teachers are to take care that their use of words and their attitudes reflect respect for the Jewish people and the Jewish religion.

Looking Back

Direct the students to silently read this section. Tell them to make sure that they pay close attention as they read.

- Ask the students if they know what is happening in the photo on this page. Invite a volunteer to explain.

- Write two column headings on the board: "Jewish Tradition" and "Christian Tradition."

- Invite volunteers to come to the board and list points in each column from what they have just read.

CLOSE

ACTIVITY

Read the activity instructions to the class and encourage them to work on being a Eucharistic person over the next few weeks.

In Summary

Have four volunteers read the summary statement and the three bullet points.

- Ask the students to reflect on their most memorable experience during one of the Sacraments that they have celebrated.

- Invite them to share.

DAY 5

Objectives

- Review different types of grace and how they touch our lives
- Explore the faith life of Saint Ludmilla
- Offer the Prayer to Saint Joseph

OPEN _____

♥ Gather the students in the prayer space. Divide the class into two sides and have one side start the prayer and the other side repeat each line. Pray Psalm 30:12–13 from page 251.

BUILD _____

Our Catholic Life

Ask the students to silently read over the information.

- Have three volunteers summarize the meanings of the bold-faced words for the class.
- Invite the students to discuss the questions with a classmate.

People of Faith

Read aloud the People of Faith paragraph on Saint Ludmilla.

- Share the content of the People of Faith Background box.
- Invite the students to share what they know about other important people who helped spread Christianity.

Our Catholic Life

Grace is participation in the life of the Holy Trinity, and helps us to do what God calls us to do. **Actual grace** is the gift God gives us to make the right decisions and think and act according to God's will for you in a particular situation. **Sanctifying grace** allows you to share in God's own life. It is a permanent gift that builds your friendship with God and assures you of eternal life. The grace we receive in the Sacraments is called **sacramental grace**, and each Sacrament provides us with its own particular grace. Sometimes it's hard to recognize grace in our lives, but it is there. Give thanks for the moments of grace God sends you.

> What kind of grace do you most need in your life right now? How will you ask for it?

© Our Sunday Visitor

People of Faith

Saint Ludmilla, c. 860–921

Saint Ludmilla was a duchess in Bohemia, part of the Czech Republic today. She and her husband built the first Catholic Church in Prague. Ludmilla helped her grandson Wenceslaus rule Bohemia when he was still a child. Wenceslaus's mother didn't want him to learn about Jesus, so she had Ludmilla killed. However, Wenceslaus never forgot what his grandmother taught him about God and Jesus. As an adult, he spread Christianity throughout Bohemia. Today Saint Ludmilla is venerated as a patron Saint of Bohemia. The Church celebrates her feast day on **September 18**.

📶 For more, go to aliveinchrist.osv.com

260 Chapter 16

CONSIDER

In the space below, write some ways you can be more mindful of God's presence in your daily life.

at school:
_____
_____
_____

at home:
_____
_____
_____

in your community:
_____
_____
_____

People of Faith Background

Saint Ludmilla

Explain to the students that Saint Ludmilla helped to bring Christianity to Bohemia, which was part of the Holy Roman Empire.

- Although Christianity first appeared in Bohemia in the early 9th century, it didn't become dominant until the 10th or 11th century. It is still a major religion in Bohemia today.
- Ludmilla's grandson, Wenceslaus, later became a Saint himself and is celebrated in the Christmas song "Good King Wenceslaus."

📶 Encourage the students to go to **aliveinchrist.osv.com** at home to learn more about Saint Ludmilla.

Prayer to Saint Joseph

Leader: Saint Joseph, the foster father of Jesus, you were always present for Jesus and his Mother, Mary. You were always nearby, loving, encouraging, and protecting him from all harm.

Reader 1: When we see images of Saint Joseph, we see in each a loving, protective father. Saint Joseph is also the Patron and Protector of the Universal Church. We can pray for his help and intercession.

Reader 2: A reading from the holy Gospel according to Matthew 1:18–24.

Read Matthew 1:18–24.

The Gospel of the Lord.

All: Praise to you, Lord Jesus Christ. O glorious Saint Joseph, you were chosen by God to be the foster father of Jesus, the most pure spouse of Mary ever Virgin, and the head of the Holy Family. You have been chosen by the Pope as the heavenly patron and protector of the Church founded by Christ. It is with great confidence that we ask for your powerful assistance for the whole Church on Earth. Protect in a special manner, with true fatherly love, the Pope and all bishops and priests in communion with him. Protect all who labor for souls amid the trials and tribulations of this life, and grant that all peoples of the world may follow Christ and the Church he founded.

Reader 3: A reading from the holy Gospel according to Matthew 2:13–15.

Read Matthew 2:13–15.

The Gospel of the Lord.

All: Praise to you, Lord Jesus Christ. Dear Saint Joseph, accept the offering of myself which I now make to you. I dedicate myself to your service, that you may ever be my father, my protector, and my guide in the way of salvation. Obtain for me great purity of heart and a fervent love for the spiritual life. May all my actions, after your example, be directed to the greater glory of God, in union with the divine Heart of Jesus, the Immaculate heart of Mary, and your own paternal heart. Finally, pray for me that I may share in the peace and joy of your holy death.

Reader 4: A reading from the holy Gospel according to Matthew 3:19–23.

Read Matthew 3:19–23.

The Gospel of the Lord.

All: Praise to you, Lord Jesus Christ. Saint Joseph, patron of the universal Church, watch over the Church as carefully as you watched over Jesus. Help protect and guide her, just as you did with Jesus. Saint Joseph, pray for us. Amen.

▶ *Sing or play "Let It Be Done"*

God's Masterworks **261**

📶 Go to **aliveinchrist.osv.com** for an interactive review.

A **Work with Words** Complete each sentence with the correct term from the Word Bank.

Mediator	Sacraments
counselor	Ascension
salvation	miracles
grace	Pentecost
Baptism	the Gospel

1. Through _____ **grace** _____ we freely receive God's help in coming to know and love him.

2. _____ **Sacraments** _____ are effective signs of God's grace, instituted by Christ and given to his Church.

3. Jesus is the perfect _____ **Mediator** _____ between God and humanity, because he is fully God and fully man.

4. The Church, a means to _____ **salvation** _____, is a visible community in the world.

5. On _____ **Pentecost** _____, the Holy Spirit descended unto the Apostles and filled them with his Gifts.

B **Check Understanding** Circle the letter of the choice that best completes the sentence.

6. Jesus' whole life is _____ because it is the source of our salvation and new life.
   - (a.) sacramental
   - b. tradition
   - c. holy
   - d. mysterious

7. The Church is like a _____ because she is a sign of God's love and action in the world.
   - a. Spirit
   - b. Rosary
   - c. Memorial
   - (d.) Sacrament

8. The term _____ is used to describe the Catholic teaching that Jesus is really and truly with us in the Eucharist—Body, Blood, Soul, and Divinity.
   - a. Holy Sign
   - b. Real Symbol
   - (c.) Real Presence
   - d. Holy Word

9. The Seven Sacraments use _____ that we can see, touch, hear, taste, and smell.
   - a. symbols
   - b. rituals
   - c. prayers
   - (d.) a, b, and c

10. Christian liturgy is rooted in the _____ traditions of prayer and worship.
   - a. disciples'
   - (b.) Jewish
   - c. Gentile
   - d. Church

C **Make Connections** On a separate sheet of paper, write a one-paragraph response to the question: Name the seven "masterworks of God." What role have these celebrations had in your family?

Have the students read the instructions and complete the activity independently.

CLOSE _____

Prayer to Saint Joseph

💗 Recruit one student as prayer leader and four others to be readers.

Invite several other students to collaborate in preparing the prayer space. Suggest that they include a lit candle, an image of Saint Joseph, and an open Bible.

Follow the order of prayer on the student page.

▶ Conclude by singing with the students the song "Let It Be Done," downloaded from **aliveinchrist.osv.com**.

CHAPTER REVIEW

Review the instructions for each section and have the students complete the review.

📶 Go to **aliveinchrist.osv.com** to prepare customized and downloadable assessments, send eAssessments, and assign interactive reviews.

God's Masterworks **261–262**

KEY CONCEPT

As Christ first welcomed and fed his followers, we are welcomed and belong to the Church through the three Sacraments of Christian Initiation.

DOCTRINAL CONTENT

- We are welcomed to the Church though the Sacraments of Initiation. (CCC, 1275)

- Confirmation is the Sacrament of Initiation through which the spiritual life, received in Baptism, is strengthened and the person is sealed with the Gifts of the Holy Spirit. (CCC, 1121, 1285)

- Transubstantiation is the process by which, through the power of the Holy Spirit and the words and actions of the priest, the bread and wine are transformed into the Body and Blood of Christ. (CCC, 1376, 1377)

- In the Eucharist, we are fed with the Body and Blood of Christ and are brought closer to Christ and one another. (CCC, 1382, 1416)

TASKS OF CATECHESIS

Helping children grow in a faith that is "known, celebrated, lived, and expressed in prayer" (NDC, 20).

This chapter focuses on the following tasks of catechesis:

- Promoting Knowledge of the Faith

- Liturgical Education

Teacher Background

📖 We were indeed buried with him through baptism into death, so that, just as Christ was raised from the dead by the glory of the Father, we too might live in newness of life. … If, then, we have died with Christ, we believe that we shall also live with him. Romans 6:4, 8

> **Reflect** What helps you feel at home with your family, with your friends, with God?

Through our membership in the Church, we are privileged to become God's children, to have the support of the Christian community in good times and in bad. Most importantly, we are privileged to receive Jesus himself in the Sacrament of Eucharist.

But being part of God's family also brings with it responsibilities. Baptism empowers us with the Holy Spirit to make us ministers or stewards of the Gospel. The role of the lay members of the Church is different from that of our ordained priests. Our mission is to serve in the world—the home, the marketplace, the ballot box—and our call is to live the values of the Gospel in all of these places.

Our reception of Jesus in the Eucharist is not for our own sakes alone, but so that we can serve as Christ in the world. We come together to celebrate the Eucharist, to be nourished by Christ and sent out again into a wounded world. We are Jesus' hands and feet and eyes and ears in that world, and it is our role to bring him to others through acts of service and through the virtue of our lives. When we take on membership in the Christian community, we accept Jesus' mission.

> **Reflect** How do you continue to draw upon the graces of the Sacraments in your life and ministry?

Teacher's Prayer

♥ Loving God, you brought me into the community of your People. May I strive to live in a manner worthy of the privilege of membership in your Church with the opportunity to touch the lives of the young people you have placed in my care. I praise your most holy name. Amen.

How Seventh Graders Understand Chapter Topics

Many young people this age will have only a distant memory of experiencing the Sacraments of Initiation. Several were baptized as infants, and will not remember their Baptism, except from photos. Many more will remember their first Eucharist, but the most prominent memories will be of the clothing they wore, the gifts they received, or the reception afterwards. Seventh graders will need some help appreciating the significance of becoming members of Christ's Body. Many Saints who came before us risked everything, even death, for the privilege of being part of this Church.

Teaching Tip: Talk about some Saints who risked persecution or death to become Christians and share the message of salvation. Some examples from Scripture are Nicodemus, Saint Stephen, and Saint Paul. There are also many brave women in Church history, such as Saints Felicity and Perpetua and Saint Lucy.

Sharing the Message with Seventh Graders

- Students this age are beginning to want to understand why they are here on Earth and what their purpose is.
- As they develop intellectually and spiritually, adolescents will begin to question their roles in life in a more serious way.
- Seventh graders are drawn to groups that give them personal support while also affirming their desire to be a part of something bigger than themselves.

Chapter 17 Planner

Objectives	Open

DAY 1—Invite/Preview, Pages 263–265

- Reflect on God's personal invitation through Scripture
- Indicate prior knowledge of chapter concepts and vocabulary

♡ **Psalm 138:2** Pray the opening prayer.

📖 **Romans 6:1–4, 8** Proclaim "Freedom from Sin; Life in God." Guide the students through the process of Scripture reflection.

- Discuss Have You Ever Thought questions.

DAY 2—Discover, Pages 266–267

- Explain how the Sacraments of Initiation bring us into a relationship with Christ and the Church
- Identify the effects of Baptism

♡ Pray the **Apostles' Creed**, page 367.

DAY 3—Discover, Pages 268–269

- Describe Confirmation as the Sacrament of Initiation through which the spiritual life received in Baptism is strengthened
- Give examples of ways to use the Gifts of the Holy Spirit in life situations

♡ Pray a Confirmation prayer, page 268.

- Ask the opening question.

DAY 4—Discover, Pages 270–271

- Relate the strength that we gain from receiving the Eucharist to each person's call to participate in the mission of the Church
- Examine how we experience the presence of Christ in the two parts of the Mass, but most fully in the Eucharist
- Define transubstantiation

♡ Pray the *Pater Noster*, page 383.

DAY 5—Live, Pages 272–273

- Discuss feeling in awe of God
- Explore the faith life of Saint Catherine of Genoa
- Offer a Renewal of Baptismal Promises

♡ Pray the **Act of Faith**, page 387.

REVIEW AND ASSESSMENT

Chapter Review, page 274
Chapter Test, page 263F

📶 **aliveinchrist.osv.com** Customize and Download Assessments, Email Links to eAssessments, Interactive Student Reviews

Build	Close	Materials & Resources
• Present lesson highlights. • Preview **Catholic Faith Words**. ★ The students will list what they know about each of the Sacraments of Initiation.	• Activity Reflect on belonging to the Church or being Catholic.	☐ pencils or pens ☐ chart paper
• Talk about the Sacrament of Baptism and its effects. 📖 Read and reflect on **Galatians 3:26–28**. • Review the RCIA process.	• Activity Describe the symbols in the Sacrament of Baptism. • Conclude with a review of key concepts and objectives.	☐ pencils or pens ☐ Bibles
• **Catholic Faith Words** Confirmation, Gifts of the Holy Spirit • Discuss the effects of the Sacrament of Confirmation. • Optional Activity The Gifts of the Holy Spirit (Activity Master 17)	• Activity Explain the Gifts of the Holy Spirit. • Conclude with a review of key concepts and objectives.	☐ pencils or pens ☐ board ☐ Activity Master 17 (Page 263G)
• **Catholic Faith Words** Eucharist, transubstantiation • Discuss how the Sacrament of Eucharist connects us to mission. 📖 Read **Luke 15:1–2, 19:1–10,** and **22: 21–23,** and **Matthew 9:9–13.**	• Activity Consider ways to help feed others' spiritual and physical hunger. • Review the In Summary statements.	☐ pencils or pens ☐ board or chart paper ☐ Bibles
• Discuss the questions in the Our Catholic Life section. • Learn about Saint Catherine of Genoa. • Activity Consider how to emulate the characteristics of Jesus.	• Invite the students to the prayer space with their books. • Follow the order of prayer. ▶ Sing or play the closing song.	☐ pencils or pens 📶 "I Will Choose Christ"

FORMING CATHOLIC IDENTITY ACROSS THE CURRICULUM

To integrate the Catholic faith in all aspects of curriculum, this chapter's objectives can be reinforced and applied in the instruction of other disciplines.

Go to **aliveinchrist.osv.com** for cross-curricular activities and projects linked to the doctrinal content discussed in this unit. Activities are available from among the following knowledge categories and content areas:

Language Arts

- Integration of Knowledge
- Literacy
- Speaking and Listening
- Writing Skills

Math

- Algebraic Thinking
- Geometry
- Measurement and Data
- Numbers and Operations

Science

- Earth Science
- Life Science
- Physical Science
- Technology

Social Studies

- Civics
- Economics
- Geography
- History

NCEA IFG: ACRE Edition

Knowledge of the Faith

- **Objective:** To know and understand basic Catholic teaching about the Incarnate Word Jesus Christ as the way, truth, and life

Liturgical Life

- **Objective:** To know the Paschal Mystery of Jesus: in the Church's liturgical life—feasts, seasons, symbols, and practices—and in the Sacraments as signs and instruments of grace

Catholic Faith Literacy

Baptism, Confirmation, Eucharist(ic), Gifts of the Holy Spirit, Initiation

Catholic Social Teaching

To integrate Catholic Social Teaching into your lesson, choose one of the following features: Call to Family, Community, and Participation, pages 336–337; or Care for God's Creation, pages 346–347.

- Start the Live step of the process by talking about Saint Catherine of Genoa on page 272. Then move directly to the Catholic Social Teaching feature.
- Or, to expand the lesson, complete page 272, then move to the Catholic Social Teaching feature.
- Return to Chapter 17 for the prayer on page 273.

Music Option

Use the following song to enhance catechetical learning or for prayer.

- "I Will Choose Christ," Day 5, Page 273

Name _____ Date _____

Match each description in Column A with the correct term in Column B.

Column A

_____ **1.** We are brought closer to Jesus through his Body and Blood

_____ **2.** Adults receive Baptism, Confirmation, and Eucharist in the same celebration

_____ **3.** The Sacrament that is always celebrated first

_____ **4.** Seals a person with the Gifts of the Holy Spirit

Column B

a. Baptism

b. Confirmation

c. Eucharist

d. Rite of Christian Initiation

Circle the letter of the choice that best completes each sentence.

5. _____ is the Sacrament of new life in Christ through the forgiveness of sins and incorporation into the Church.

a. Confirmation

b. Eucharist

c. Baptism

d. Initiation

6. In Confirmation the bishop anoints candidates with the oil of _____.

a. catechumens

b. Sacred Chrism

c. Initiation

d. transubstantiation

7. When the bread and wine are transformed into the Body and Blood of Christ in the Eucharist, this change is called _____.

a. transubstantiation

b. reconciliation

c. a Mystery of the Faith

d. transfiguration

8. After we are fed at the Lord's table, we must go out and _____.

a. clean up

b. feed others

c. sing a hymn

d. meet people

Write a response on the lines below.

9. What do the Gifts of the Holy Spirit do for us? _____

_____

10. Why can we only receive Baptism and Confirmation once? _____

_____

Name _____   Date _____

The Gifts of the Holy Spirit

The Holy Spirit gives us many different gifts to help us on our faith journey:

WISDOM: Helps us see things more like God sees them. We can make decisions with clear thinking.

UNDERSTANDING: Helps us know why people say and do things. We can "stand with them" even if we don't agree with them.

KNOWLEDGE: Helps us learn the teachings of our faith and of our world. We gain facts and information we need.

REVERENCE (PIETY): Helps us show respect for God and all of God's creation.

RIGHT JUDGMENT (COUNSEL): Helps us seek good advice and give good advice before decisions are made.

COURAGE (FORTITUDE): Helps us stand up for what we believe in and live our faith without fear of what others think.

WONDER AND AWE (FEAR OF THE LORD): Helps us know our place before God. We see God's power and his great love for us.

In the chart below, write about a time or situation when you need each gift. List one person you have seen use each gift and tell how they used it. Write on a separate sheet of paper if necessary.

	I need this gift when:	Who I saw use this gift:	How the person used this gift:
WISDOM			
UNDERSTANDING			
KNOWLEDGE			
REVERENCE (PIETY)			
RIGHT JUDGMENT (COUNSEL)			
COURAGE (FORTITUDE)			
WONDER AND AWE (FEAR OF THE LORD)			

Sacraments of Initiation

 Let Us Pray

Leader: We pray in the name of the Father, and of the Son, and of the Holy Spirit. By water and the Spirit, O Lord, we have received the gifts of faith and new life.

"I bow low toward your holy temple;
    I praise your name for your mercy and faithfulness.
For you have exalted over all
    your name and your promise." **Psalm 138:2**

All: God, help us find our place in your Church.

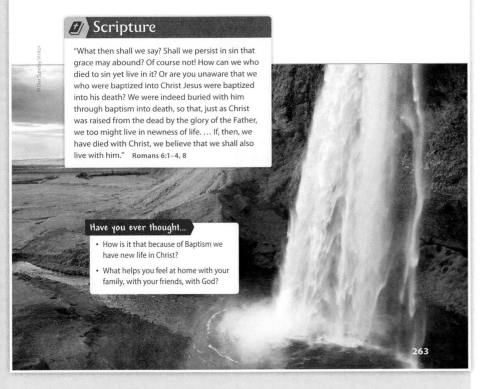

Scripture

"What then shall we say? Shall we persist in sin that grace may abound? Of course not! How can we who died to sin yet live in it? Or are you unaware that we who were baptized into Christ Jesus were baptized into his death? We were indeed buried with him through baptism into death, so that, just as Christ was raised from the dead by the glory of the Father, we too might live in newness of life. … If, then, we have died with Christ, we believe that we shall also live with him." **Romans 6:1–4, 8**

Have you ever thought...

- How is it that because of Baptism we have new life in Christ?
- What helps you feel at home with your family, with your friends, with God?

263

Scripture Background

Scripture Reflection Process

Invite the students to be still, close their eyes, and focus on their breathing. Encourage them to open their minds and hearts to what God is saying to them.

- Proclaim the Scripture and have the students sit in silence.
- *Ask:* What did you hear God say to you today?
- Allow volunteers to share.

 You may play instrumental music to begin the reflection.

Objective

- Reflect on God's personal invitation through Scripture

OPEN _____

 Let Us Pray

Choose one of the students to be the Leader. Invite the students to gather in the prayer space and make the Sign of the Cross. Ask the Leader to proclaim the opening prayer and Psalm verse, and lead the class in the response.

Have the students move out of the prayer space and back to their seats.

Say: We are baptized into Christ and through our Baptism, we each have a special place in the Church.

Scripture

Guide the students through the process of Scripture reflection (see the Scripture Background box below).

Have you ever thought...

Say: We receive the gifts of faith and new life through our Baptism, our initiation into the Church.

- Invite the students to respond to the questions.

DAY 1

Objective

- Indicate prior knowledge of chapter concepts and vocabulary

BUILD _____

Use this page to assess the students' knowledge related to the chapter content.

Getting Started

Summarize this information for the students.

Sacraments of Initiation

Ask a volunteer to read aloud the instructions.

★ Have the students fill in the chart with information that they know about each Sacrament.

- Remind them that this will be a great study tool and that they can fill in more information as they work through the chapter.

Getting Started

In this chapter, you will gain a deeper understanding of the purpose and effects of the Sacraments of Baptism and Confirmation and study the parts of the Mass and the effects of the Eucharist.

Catholic Faith Words

- Confirmation
- Gifts of the Holy Spirit
- Eucharist
- transubstantiation

In the web below, list what you know about each of the Sacraments. Include information about the outward signs and ritual actions of each Sacrament and the meaning or effects of the Sacrament.

Sacraments of Initiation

Baptism	Confirmation	Eucharist

264 Chapter 17

✔ Teaching Tip

Categorizing Questions

As the students start to ask questions about the Sacraments, try to discern whether the current section of the chapter that you are working in is the best place to address these questions. For each question that is asked, you may be covering that exact topic in another section of this chapter or in one of the other chapters in this unit.

If this happens, acknowledge that each question is important.

Write each question on the board or on a sticky note and make sure to come back to them once you've arrived at the appropriate section or chapter.

ILLUSTRATE

We Belong to Christ Illustrate within the frames below some different times when you experienced a strong sense of belonging to the Church or being Catholic.

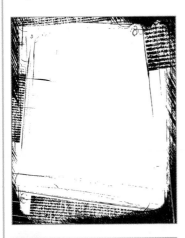

Sacraments of Initiation **265**

Work with Words

Point out the Catholic Faith Words box on page 264.

- Have four volunteers each read aloud one of the terms listed.
- Ask the students if they can name any of the Gifts of the Holy Spirit.
- Have a volunteer record their answers on chart paper.
- Save the list so that you can come back to it when you cover this information later in the chapter.

CLOSE

ACTIVITY

Remind the students that the Sign of the Cross is a sign of our Baptism into Christ, and of our belonging to the Church.

- Read the instructions for the activity and give the class time to complete it.
- Have the students work independently.
- Allow volunteers to show and explain their illustrations to the class.

Teacher Background

Belonging

The students are learning about the process of becoming a full member in the Catholic Church and what it means to belong to Christ.

For young adolescents, belonging is important. Studies have shown that the most important influence and concern for children this age is their family. As children mature, they gradually and naturally pull away from family—but not without some fear and confusion.

We need to be sensitive to the pull younger adolescents are beginning to feel, both away from and toward their families, as they find their own place in the Catholic Church.

DAY 2

Objectives

- Explain how the Sacraments of Initiation bring us into a relationship with Christ and the Church
- Identify the effects of Baptism

OPEN _____

💗 Have the students pray the Apostles' Creed from page 367.

BUILD _____

Baptism

Point out the description of the Sacraments of Initiation in the second paragraph.

- Ask the students to name the three Sacraments that make up this category.

✝ Go to the Source

Have the students read Galatians 3:26–28, to find out what Saint Paul says about Baptism.

What Happens

Tell the students to silently read this section.

- Invite a volunteer to summarize what he or she has read.

Rite of Christian Initiation of Adults

Connect this section, on page 267, with the Rite as it is celebrated in your parish.

- Give the students an opportunity to share what they know about RCIA in their own parishes.

Baptism

What does Baptism do?

We all want to find a place where we feel at "home." Spiritually, your faith finds home in the Church. It is that place where your soul can find what it has been longing for.

The Church welcomes new members through the Sacraments of Initiation. These Sacraments are about beginnings and belonging. Through them, you are initiated into a relationship with Christ and the Church. Baptism begins your new life in Christ, Confirmation strengthens it, and Eucharist feeds Christ's life within you so that you can follow him. These Sacraments can be received all at once, over a few years, or over a period of time. But no matter when they are celebrated, Baptism is always first.

Pope Francis celebrates a Baptism during the Easter Vigil in St. Peter's Basilica at the Vatican in 2013

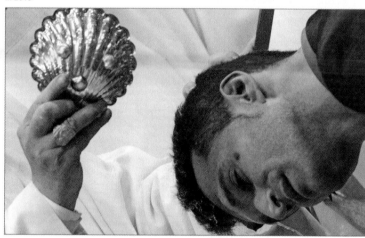

✝ Go to the Source

Read *Galatians 3:26–28* to find out what Saint Paul says about Baptism. How did Baptism begin the process of bringing you "home"?

What Happens

In the Sacrament of Baptism, the person baptized is immersed in water three times—or has water poured over his or her head three times—while the priest or deacon says, "I baptize you in the name of the Father, and of the Son, and of the Holy Spirit. Amen" (Rite of Baptism, no. 60).

Baptism is God's gift to us. Its grace does not require any action on our part. So, Baptism is open to anyone: infant, young child, teen, or adult. In fact, since the earliest times, infants have been baptized in the faith of the Church. In the Baptism of an infant or young child, the parents and godparents agree to bring up the child in the faith.

© Our Sunday Visitor

Optional Activity

Baptismal Symbols *Visual/Spatial, Interpersonal*

Have the students work together in small groups to create a poster or display explaining each symbol of Baptism: water, chrism, candle and light, and white clothing. If possible, have the students:

- display photos and/or videos of their own Baptisms.
- bring in baptismal garments if anyone still has them.
- include their baptismal candles if they can bring them in.

Rite of Christian Initiation of Adults

In the early years of the Church, there were many adults who chose to become members of the Church. Often they, and their families, would celebrate all three Sacraments of Initiation at one time. Today non-baptized men, women, older children, and those who are baptized from non-Catholic faiths are initiated in a process lasting several months to two years called the Rite of Christian Initiation of Adults (RCIA). They prepare to receive all three Sacraments at the same celebration, usually during the Easter Vigil.

RCIA has several stages, including a time of inquiry in which the person can get to know the Church and see if they want to learn more, then a time for formation and information involving weekly classes. Non-baptized candidates are called catechumens (learners). The catechumens are then called "the elect" to show that they are preparing for the Easter when they will celebrate the Sacraments of Initiation. After that comes mystagogy, a period of fifty days during

which the newly baptized, called neophytes, reflect on the mysteries of the Sacraments, what the celebrations meant to them, and how they can live out their faith.

The Effects of Baptism

- A participation in the Paschal Mystery—dying to sin and rising to new life—and new identity as belonging to Christ: "For all of you who were baptized into Christ have clothed yourselves with Christ" (Galatians 3:27)

- Forgiveness of Original Sin and any personal (actual) sins that may have been committed

- A new relationship with Christ as his sister or brother and a new connection to God the Father as his adopted child

- The gift of the Holy Spirit that incorporates the person into the Body of Christ, the Church

- A share in the mission of Jesus as priest, prophet, and royalty in God's Kingdom

- A special seal or character that blesses the person to worship. This character is permanent and, because of it, the Sacrament cannot be repeated.

FILL IN THE BLANKS

Fill in the blanks to describe the symbols involved in the Sacrament of Baptism.

- _____Water_____ is a sign of cleansing and birth, like the waters God first created.
- Sacred _____Chrism_____, the anointing oil, is a reminder that God has chosen and called each person to be his own.
- The _____candle_____ and its light are a sign that Christ is the Light of the World and that all who are baptized are called to be the light of Christ to others.
- The white clothing is a sign of being _____purified_____ and being clothed in Christ to imitate him and put on his ways.

Sacraments of Initiation **267**

Scripture Background

Galatians 3:26–28

Here, Paul describes God's complete impartiality. How wonderful the world, or for that matter, our classrooms, would be if we could see as God sees: no slave or free person, male or female, Jew or Gentile. Since God sees us all as children in the same family, isn't that something we should do as well?

Paul tells us we have to "put on" Christ. These verses were probably part of the liturgy of Baptism in the early Church. Paul uses the imagery of "putting on" Christ, putting on his light, and putting on the armor of God in several places. (See Romans 13:12, 14, Galatians 3:27, and Ephesians 6:11.)

Consider inviting a parishioner who is involved in RCIA to speak with the class. Note: It is possible that some of your students were baptized as older children or saw a parent go through the RCIA process. Allow them to share what they remember.

Review the content of this section with the class.

The Effects of Baptism

Say: We know Baptism begins our new life in Christ. Let's read about some of the other effects of Baptism.

- Go over the information in the chart with the class. Begin each bullet with "Baptism gives us …"
- Invite the students to put a star beside the effect that they identify with the most.

CLOSE _____

ACTIVITY

Allow the students to work with a classmate to complete the activity.

- Go over the answers as a class to make sure that everyone has the correct information.

Quick Review We are initiated into a relationship with Christ and the Church through the Sacraments of Initiation: Baptism, Confirmation, and Eucharist. Adults who wish to join as members of the Church prepare to receive the Sacraments of Initiation through the Rite of Christian Initiation of Adults.

DAY 3

Objectives

- Describe Confirmation as the Sacrament of Initiation through which the spiritual life received in Baptism is strengthened

- Give examples of ways to use the Gifts of the Holy Spirit in life situations

OPEN

Have the students pray a prayer for Confirmation from the Teacher Background box below.

Ask: What happens during Confirmation?

BUILD

Confirmation

Explain that Confirmation is our way of confirming our commitment to discipleship.

- Invite a volunteer to read aloud these two paragraphs.

- Give the students time to reflect on the question at the end of the section.

- Allow volunteers to share their responses with the class.

The Effects of Confirmation

Point out the bullet points that were used in the opening prayer.

- Ask the students if they have any questions regarding this information.

An Ongoing Journey

Tell the students that our faith journey is never over—it will last a lifetime.

Confirmation

What happens during Confirmation?

In Baptism, persons are "christened," meaning they receive Christ, the Anointed One. In **Confirmation**, there is a similar anointing, in which we are strengthened in the grace we received at Baptism, and grow in our relationship with the Anointed One and his Spirit. Blessed and scented oil, called Sacred Chrism, is used in both Sacraments.

At Confirmation, the bishop (or priest) extends his hands over the candidates and prays that the Holy Spirit will come upon them as a Helper and a Guide. Then he anoints each candidate on the forehead, which is done by the laying on of the hands, saying, "[Candidate's name], be sealed with the Gift of the Holy Spirit" (The Rite of Confirmation, no. 27). Like Baptism, Confirmation leaves a spiritual character on the soul. This means that the Sacrament can be received only once.

> What role does the Spirit play in your journey of faith?

The Effects of Confirmation

- A deepening and perfection of the life of God in us, which we first received in Baptism

- An outpouring of the Holy Spirit, which increases the Gifts already working in us

- A strengthening of our relationship with God and our unity with Christ

- A perfection of our connection with the Church, a special strengthening by the Holy Spirit, to take part in the mission of the Church, to show others by our words and actions that we are Catholics, and to tell others about the Good News of Jesus

An Ongoing Journey

Every week, we meet situations that demand more sacrifice, less anger, greater patience, or outreach. The Sacraments give us help along the way.

268   Chapter 17

© Our Sunday Visitor

 Teacher Background

Confirmation Prayer

Write the following prayer response on the board: "God, help us find our place in your Church."

- Ask four volunteers to each read aloud one of the bullet points in the Effects of Confirmation chart, making it a prayer by adding the following to the beginning of each point: "God, please send us . . ."

- Instruct the rest of the class to use the response you have written on the board.

- Begin the prayer with the Sign of the Cross. Then signal the first reader to begin. Lead the group in the response.

The Sacraments are not "things" we deserve or earn. During the celebration of Confirmation, we are sealed in a special way with the **Gifts of the Holy Spirit**. These gifts help us follow the Spirit's guidance and live the Christian life.

Catholic Faith Words

Confirmation the Sacrament of Initiation through which the spiritual life received in Baptism is strengthened and the person is sealed with the Gifts of the Holy Spirit

Gifts of the Holy Spirit seven powerful gifts God gives us to follow guidance of the Holy Spirit and live the Christian life. We are sealed with the Gifts of the Holy Spirit at Confirmation.

CATHOLICS TODAY

In the United States, different people celebrate the Sacrament of Confirmation at different ages. It varies by diocese. Some people are confirmed between the ages of seven and ten; others receive Confirmation when they are twelve or thirteen; others when they are fifteen, sixteen, or seventeen; and still others anytime in between!

The Church teaches us that the person being confirmed should be old enough to reason (which is often considered the age of seven), have been baptized and be free of serious sin, and be prepared to take on greater discipleship.

IDENTIFY

In the space provided, write what you think each Gift of the Holy Spirit describes or means. Then check your ideas against the descriptions on page 375 in the Our Catholic Tradition section of your book.

The Gifts of the Holy Spirit

Wisdom _____

Understanding _____

Right Judgment (Counsel) _____

Courage (Fortitude) _____

Knowledge _____

Reverence (Piety) _____

Wonder and Awe (Fear of the Lord) _____

Select one Gift of the Holy Spirit that you would like to grow in, and briefly explain how it can help you.

_____

_____

Optional Activity

Activity Master 17: The Gifts of the Holy Spirit

Distribute copies of the activity from teacher page 263G.

- This activity will help the students gain a better understanding of the Gifts of the Holy Spirit.
- Becoming more aware of these Gifts and opening themselves to the deepening of these Gifts will change their lives and the lives of others.

An Ongoing Journey,

continued

Say: Luckily, we have the guidance of the Holy Spirit to help us live a Christian life.

Review the definitions of the two Catholic Faith Words with the class.

Invite two students to each read a paragraph from the Catholics Today box.

- Ask if anyone in the class has already been confirmed and how old they were at Confirmation.
- Discuss the reasons why the age of Confirmation may vary.

CLOSE _____

ACTIVITY

Tell the students to silently read the instructions.

- Direct them to write what they think each Gift of the Holy Spirit describes or means.
- Have them work on the activity independently, then check their answers against the descriptions on page 375 in the Our Catholic Tradition reference section at the back of their books.

Quick Review At Confirmation, the spiritual life that we received in Baptism is strengthened and we are sealed with the Gifts of the Holy Spirit. We should utilize these Gifts in our daily lives.

DAY 4

Objectives

- Relate the strength that we gain from receiving the Eucharist to each person's call to participate in the mission of the Church

- Examine how we experience the presence of Christ in the two parts of the Mass, but most fully in the Eucharist

- Define transubstantiation

OPEN

 Invite the students to pray the lines of the *Pater Noster*, page 383, after you. Remind them that Latin is the official language of the Church.

BUILD

Eucharist

Say: Some people are surprised to learn that the Eucharist, which we can receive every day, is a Sacrament of Initiation like the one-time-only Sacraments of Baptism and Confirmation.

- Tell the class to silently read the opening section to find out why the Eucharist is so important.

- Direct the students to read the definition of *Eucharist* in the Catholic Faith Words box.

The Parts of the Mass

Read aloud the first four paragraphs of this section, which continues on page 271.

- After each paragraph, ask a volunteer to summarize what you've just read to ensure their understanding.

Eucharist

What does it mean to eat at the Lord's Table?

Baptism and Confirmation are once-in-a-lifetime Sacraments, but we are offered the benefits of the **Eucharist**, the Sacrament in which the bread and wine become the Body and Blood of Christ, over and over again throughout our lives.

We need food for the journey, nourishment for the soul through listening to the Scripture and through receiving Holy Communion. This is so important that we are welcomed to take part in daily Mass along with our obligation to attend Sunday Mass.

You've probably heard the saying "You are what you eat." That's why it's important to care about a healthful diet. The food you eat today is becoming you in a true physical way. In Holy Communion, we receive the Body and Blood of Christ and become what we eat—the Body of Christ, the Church.

The Parts of the Mass

We begin with the **Introductory Rites**, prayers and songs of thanksgiving to God the Father for all of his gifts, most especially his Son. This part of the Mass gathers us together and prepares us to listen to God's Word.

The first main part of the Mass is the **Liturgy of the Word**. This includes readings from the Scripture, usually from both the Old Testament and New Testament, and always from the Gospels. We also profess the Nicene or Apostles' Creed and offer prayers in the Prayer of the Faithful.

The second main part of the Mass is the **Liturgy of the Eucharist**—the recalling of what Jesus said and did at the Last Supper: "This is my Body, which will be given up for you . . . This is the chalice of my Blood . . ." and the words of the priest and blessing of the Holy Spirit so that the wheat bread and grape wine are consecrated and become the Body and Blood of Christ. To receive

> **Catholic Faith Words**
>
> **Eucharist** the Sacrament of Initiation during which the bread and wine become the Body and Blood of Christ and all who receive him in Holy Communion are brought closer to him and one another
>
> **transubstantiation** the process by which, through the power of the Holy Spirit and the words and actions of the priest, the bread and wine are transformed into the Body and Blood of Christ

270 Chapter 17

Scripture Background

To Eat with Sinners

The four Scripture passages that the students will read today are stories of Jesus' desire to be with sinners and to call them to conversion.

Sharing a meal was a way for Jesus to spend time with sinners, and a way for him to offer them a spiritual food that would help them to change their lives and turn their hearts to his Father. That spiritual food was his very life.

Jesus' primary concern was to share God's love with the repentant sinner, a love that changes one's life, a love we can experience each time we participate in the Church's Eucharistic liturgy.

the invitation to the Table of the Lord and reception of Holy Communion, you must be free from serious sin, so it might be necessary to receive the Sacrament of Penance and Reconciliation before Mass.

In the **Concluding Rites**, we are sent out in peace to announce the Gospel by our words and actions.

The most important aspect of the Mass is Jesus' Real Presence in the Eucharist. During the consecration, in the Liturgy of the Eucharist, through the words and actions of the priest and by the power of the Holy Spirit, the bread and wine become the Body and Blood of Christ. This change is called **transubstantiation**. Jesus is truly present under the appearances of bread and wine. This is not just a memorial of what Jesus offered to us. Jesus' sacrifice is made present and we are given the gift of his life.

Jesus taught us that all are welcome at his table—especially those who are neglected,

the outcasts, and those in need of healing. The table that Jesus creates is a model for our Church. The connection between Eucharist and justice is real. After we are fed at the Supper of the Lamb, we must go out and feed others with our generosity, talent, service, and resources.

The Effects of the Eucharist
• Increases our union with the Lord
• Forgives venial sins and help to avoid serious sin
• Strengthens our connection with others and supports the unity of all the members of the Church
• Inspires us to self-sacrifice and commits us to caring for the needs of others

CONSIDER

What are some ways that you "feed" people by sharing your time and gifts and satisfying their hunger for love and attention? What are some ways that you could feed people by helping to take care of their physical needs for food, shelter, or clothing?

Go to the Source
Divide the following Scripture texts among your classmates. See how Jesus accepted everyone at his table in Luke 15:1–2; Luke 19:1–10; Luke 22:21–23; and Matthew 9:9–13.

IN SUMMARY — Catholics Believe

As Christ first welcomed and fed his followers, we are welcomed and belong to the Church through the three Sacraments of Initiation.

• In Baptism, the first Sacrament, we celebrate new life in Christ through the forgiveness of sins and incorporation into the Church.

• In Confirmation, the spiritual life received in Baptism is strengthened and we are sealed with the Gift of the Holy Spirit so that we can live out our journey of faith.

• In the Eucharist, the Sacrament that we celebrate regularly, we are fed with the Body and Blood of Christ and are brought closer to Christ and one another.

Sacraments of Initiation **271**

Teacher Background

Eucharistic Grace

The Church echoes Jesus' command to welcome strangers and feed those in need. In a world where people are often primarily focused on their own needs, this teaching of Jesus can be a challenge. That is why we so desperately need the Eucharist. In receiving the love of God poured out for us in his Body and Blood with open hearts, we receive the grace to love others as God loves us.

True and complete faith in the Eucharist leads to open-hearted outreach to others, to compassion, and to genuine love.

The Parts of the Mass,
continued

Have a student read aloud the last two paragraphs of this section.

• *Ask:* What is transubstantiation?

• Invite a volunteer to read the definition from page 270.

Go to the Source
Arrange the class in groups of four and assign each member of each group one of the following readings: Luke 15:1–2, Luke 19:1–10, Luke 22:21–23, or Matthew 9:9–13.

• Direct each group to create a poster. Divide the poster into two parts—one part to illustrate the physical feeding and the other to represent the spiritual feeding that happened in the passages they read.

• *Ask:* How can we "feed" others? by being generous with our time, talents (gifts), and resources

The Effects of the Eucharist
Direct the students to study the bullet points and to circle the effect of the Eucharist that they feel they need the most.

CLOSE

ACTIVITY

Read aloud the prompt and discuss actual ways to help feed the spiritual and physical hunger of others.

In Summary
Read the summary statement to the class. Ask the students to silently read the bullets.

DAY 5

Objectives

- Discuss feeling in awe of God
- Explore the faith life of Saint Catherine of Genoa
- Offer a Renewal of Baptismal Promises

OPEN _____

💗 Have the students stand and pray the Act of Faith from page 387.

BUILD _____

Our Catholic Life

Invite a volunteer to read this section to the class.

- Have the students discuss the questions with a classmate.

People of Faith

Ask a volunteer to read aloud the paragraph on Saint Catherine of Genoa.

- Share the information from the People of Faith Background box.
- Allow the students a few quiet moments to reflect on their own faith journeys.
- Encourage them to think about obstacles they have faced during their faith journeys and how facing these obstacles has brought them closer to God.
- *Ask:* Have you encountered unexpected outcomes or some surprising opportunities along the way?

Our Catholic Life

Catholics are sealed with the Gifts of the Holy Spirit at Confirmation. We receive the gifts of wisdom, understanding, counsel, fortitude, knowledge, piety, and fear of the Lord, and we are meant to put them to good use in our lives. Some of the Gifts are easy to understand and apply to everyday life, but others are harder. You may wonder how fear of the Lord could help you! But **fear of the Lord** also means *awe*, and remaining in awe of God and all that he has done and his plan for you is important. To be in awe of him means to know that God is greater and more wonderful than any created thing in the world, and to be open to his surprising and powerful goodness. His plan for you is the right one.

> When have you felt in awe of God? How would you explain the feeling to someone else?

People of Faith

Saint Catherine of Genoa, 1447–1510

At the age of thirteen, Catherine said she wanted to become a nun. However, she was considered too young at the time and was told to wait. As she knelt in devotion in a convent in Genoa, she was overcome by a blinding ray of Divine light. She fell into a trance and then lost consciousness. When she regained her senses, she was filled with the Holy Spirit. She began writing about her feelings and experiences. She described life as a process of continual purification that would allow the soul to receive Christ, pure in heart and mind. The Church celebrates her feast day on **September 15**.

📶 For more, go to **aliveinchrist.osv.com**

EXPLAIN

If "you are what you eat," then by receiving Jesus in the Eucharist you can develop some of his characteristics, such as the ones below. In the space below, explain how you have or will take on two of these characteristics.

Compassionate · Just · Loving · Accepting · Strong in Faith · Prayerful

_____
_____
_____
_____
_____
_____
_____
_____
_____

272 Chapter 17

People of Faith Background

Saint Catherine of Genoa

Add the following points to your class review:

- Saint Catherine's most famous writings are *Dialogues of the Soul and Body* and *Treatise on Purgatory*.
- After her husband's death, Saint Catherine devoted herself to the sick at the hospital of Genoa, where she eventually became the director and treasurer.

📶 Encourage the students to go to **aliveinchrist.osv.com** at home to learn more about Saint Catherine of Genoa.

♥ Renewal of Baptismal Promises

Leader: On the day of your Baptism, your family and the Church claimed you for Christ. By water and the Holy Spirit you received the gifts of faith and new life. On that day your family and the members of the parish remembered their baptismal promises and professed their faith. Let us now do the same.

Do you renounce Satan?

All: I do.

Leader: And all his works?

All: I do.

Leader: And all his empty show?

All: I do.

Leader: Do you believe in God the Father almighty, Creator of heaven and earth?

All: I do.

Leader: Do you believe in Jesus Christ, his only Son, our Lord, who was born of the Virgin Mary, suffered death and was buried, rose again from the dead and is seated at the right hand of the Father?

All: I do.

Leader: Do you believe in the Holy Spirit, the holy Catholic Church, the communion of saints, the forgiveness of sins, the resurrection of the body, and life everlasting?

All: I do.

Leader: This is our faith. This is the faith of the Church. We are proud to profess it, in Christ Jesus our Lord.

All: Amen.

▶ *Sing or play "I Will Choose Christ"*

Sacraments of Initiation **273**

🛜 Go to **aliveinchrist.osv.com** for an interactive review.

A **Work with Words** Circle the letter of the choice that best completes the sentence.

1. In ___, a person experiences a rising to new life and new identity as belonging to Christ, through the forgiveness of sins and incorporation into the Church.
   - **(a.)** Baptism
   - **b.** Eucharist
   - **c.** Confirmation
   - **d.** Church

2. We receive the Body and Blood of Christ during the Sacrament of ___.
   - **a.** Baptism
   - **(b.)** Eucharist
   - **c.** Confirmation
   - **d.** Initiation

3. ___ is the process by which, through the power of the Holy Spirit and the words and actions of the priest, the bread and wine are transformed into the Body and Blood of Christ.
   - **a.** Confirmation
   - **b.** Salvation
   - **(c.)** Transubstantiation
   - **d.** Transfiguration

4. One of the effects of the Sacrament of ___ is that we are sealed with the Gifts of the Holy Spirit, which increases the Gifts already working in us.
   - **a.** Baptism
   - **b.** Eucharist
   - **(c.)** Confirmation
   - **d.** Pentecost

B **Check Understanding** Complete each sentence with the correct terms from the Word Bank.

Initiation	Baptism
venial sins	spiritual character
Invitation	Last Supper
Sacred Chrism	Candle
mystagogy	

5. The Church welcomes new members through the celebration of the Sacraments of ___**Initiation**___.

6. In Baptism, the ___**Sacred Chrism**___ is a reminder that God has chosen and called each one to be his own.

7. The Rite of Christian Initiation of Adults ends with ___**mystagogy**___, a period of fifty days during which the newly baptized reflect on the mysteries of the Sacraments.

8. As in Baptism, a person who celebrates the Sacrament of Confirmation receives a ___**spiritual character**___ on one's soul.

9. During the Liturgy of the Eucharist, we remember what Jesus said and did at the ___**Last Supper**___.

10. The Eucharist forgives ___**venial sins**___ and helps us avoid serious sin.

C **Make Connections** On a separate sheet of paper, write a one-paragraph response to the question: Which part of the Celebration of the Eucharist is most meaningful for you? Explain your answer.

274 Chapter 17

KEY CONCEPT

We know that God heals us spiritually, emotionally, and sometimes physically in the Sacraments of Healing.

DOCTRINAL CONTENT

- Jesus shows us that God is compassionate, always willing to forgive and care for those who turn to him and believe. God heals us spiritually, emotionally, and sometimes physically in the Sacraments of Healing. (CCC, 1421, 1503–1508)

- Conversion happens when we desire to change and are open to God's help. (CCC, 1989)

- In the Sacrament of Penance and Reconciliation, those who are truly sorry for their sins receive God's forgiveness and are reconciled with him and the Church. (CCC, 1424, 1440–1445)

- In the Sacrament of the Anointing of the Sick, those who are seriously ill or suffering from old age receive God's grace to be strong, courageous, and hopeful in their trials. (CCC, 1520–1522)

TASKS OF CATECHESIS

Helping children grow in a faith that is "known, celebrated, lived, and expressed in prayer" (NDC, 20).

This chapter focuses on the following tasks of catechesis:

- Liturgical Education
- Moral Formation

Teacher Background

And all this is from God, who has reconciled us to himself through Christ and given us the ministry of reconciliation, namely, God was reconciling the world to himself in Christ, not counting their trespasses against them and entrusting to us the message of reconciliation. For our sake he made him to be sin who did not know sin, so that we might become the righteousness of God in him. **2 Corinthians 5:18–19, 21**

> **Reflect** What effect does Jesus' teaching on forgiveness have on your life?

Anyone who lives long enough comes to terms with the fact that human life has its share of pain and suffering. Some pain is brought about by our own choices, while other pain and suffering is simply the consequence of living in a broken and imperfect world. Sometimes we suffer through no fault of our own. Sometimes the faults are all too apparent.

Jesus, in his Incarnation, fully embraced the human experience. He experienced all that it meant to be human except for sin. He knows what it means to grieve and to suffer physical and emotional pain. In Jesus, we do not have a distant and aloof God, but one who stands with us in the darkest and most distressing places experienced by the human spirit.

Because Jesus, the Son of God, entered into such intimate solidarity with our suffering, he is the perfect agent of healing and forgiveness. Jesus has the authority to forgive because he is God. Jesus is the one who brings healing and hope to the human spirit, and he is the one who shows us that death is not the final destination for those who place their trust in his mercy and grace.

> **Reflect** How has the Sacrament of Reconciliation been a source of strength and growth for you?

Teacher's Prayer

 God of healing and compassion, I know my failures. But I know that your grace is more than enough to make up for all my inadequacies. May I always rely on that grace, and may it always sustain me. Amen.

How Seventh Graders Understand Chapter Topics

It is difficult for children and teens, who have a strong sense of justice, to understand why there is so much suffering in the world. There are no easy answers to this, but one thing we do know, as Pope Saint John Paul II stated, "God is always on the side of the suffering."

Teaching Tip: In catechizing for the Sacraments of Healing, we must be honest and clear in teaching about the nature of sin, its relationship to suffering, and the generous, healing compassion of our God. Help your seventh graders make the connection between the Sacraments of Healing and God's compassion and desire to bring healing to a suffering world.

Sharing the Message with Seventh Graders

- As younger adolescents' social relationships develop, they may be influenced by sexual values they see reflected in popular culture.
- Seventh graders need help in filtering all they see and hear in the culture through the lens of our Catholic faith.
- Students this age need to be encouraged to look to the Church as a source of teaching and wisdom and as a place where they belong.

ONLINE RESOURCES

 Go to **aliveinchrist.osv.com**

You will find:

- Interactive lesson planning, additional activities, and ideas for the classroom environment
- Step by step lesson instruction from printed Teacher Edition for integrated lesson planning
- Custom-built assessments to download and eAssessment links
- Interactive reviews that provide scores and the option to review answers
- Chapter-specific Lectionary connections and a complete correlation ordered by the Sundays of the year, with suggestions for how to integrate the Scripture readings into chapter lessons

Go to **osvparish.com** for Ask the Experts Q and A, Community Connections, and Blogs.

Chapter 18 Planner

Objectives	Open

DAY 1—Invite/Preview, Pages 275–277

- Reflect on God's personal invitation through Scripture
- Indicate prior knowledge of chapter concepts and vocabulary

💛 **Psalm 25:18** Pray the opening prayer.

📖 **2 Corinthians 5:17–21** Proclaim "The Ministry of Reconciliation." Guide the students through the process of Scripture reflection.
- Discuss Have You Ever Thought questions.

DAY 2—Discover, Pages 278–279

- Explain why Jesus healed people
- Discuss the process of conversion
- Recognize the need for the Sacrament of Penance and Reconciliation

💛 Pray the **Act of Contrition**, page 387.
- Point out the opening question.

DAY 3—Discover, Pages 280–281

- Describe the four elements of the Sacrament of Penance and Reconciliation
- Review the steps in the Rite of the Sacrament of Reconciliation
- Identify the benefits of receiving the Sacrament of Penance

💛 Pray a prayer of petition.
- Discuss the photo.

DAY 4—Discover, Pages 282–283

- Explore the need for and the effects of the Sacrament of the Anointing of the Sick

💛 Pray a prayer for the sick.

DAY 5—Live, Pages 284–285

- Examine the giving and receiving of forgiveness
- Explore the faith life of Blessed Carlos Manuel Cecilio Rodriguez Santiago
- Pray the Psalm of Lament

💛 Pray **Psalm 25:18**, page 275.

REVIEW AND ASSESSMENT

Chapter Review, page 286
Chapter Test, page 275F

📶 **aliveinchrist.osv.com** Customize and Download Assessments, Email Links to eAssessments, Interactive Student Reviews

Build	Close	Materials & Resources

- Present lesson highlights.
- Preview **Catholic Faith Words**.
- ★ List outward signs and ritual actions of the two Sacraments of Healing.

- *Activity* The students will design a symbol of forgiveness.

☐ pencils or pens

- **Catholic Faith Words** contrition, Penance and Reconciliation
- Talk about the impact of Jesus' healing actions.
- 📖 Read Matthew 9:35–36.
- Discuss conversion and contrition.

- *Activity* Describe moments of personal conversion.
- Conclude with a review of key concepts and objectives.
- *Optional Activity* Conversion: To Walk with Jesus (Activity Master 18)

☐ pencils or pens
☐ highlighters
☐ Activity Master 18 (Page 275G)

- **Catholic Faith Words** penance, absolution
- Review the four elements of Penance and Reconciliation.
- ★ Match the parts of the Sacrament of Penance with their effects.
- 📖 Reflect on Matthew 18:21–35.

- *Activity* Create an examination of conscience.
- Conclude with a review of key concepts and objectives.

☐ pencils or pens
☐ board or chart paper
☐ Bibles

- **Catholic Faith Words** Anointing of the Sick
- Talk about the Sacrament of the Anointing of the Sick and its effects.
- 📖 Read James 5:13–15.

- *Activity* Think of ways to reach out to those who are sick.
- Review the In Summary statements.

☐ pencils or pens
☐ highlighters
☐ paper and art supplies

- Discuss the question in the Our Catholic Life section.
- Learn about Blessed Carlos Santiago.
- *Activity* Complete Scripture quotations relating to forgiveness.

- Divide the class into two sides.
- Follow the order of prayer.
- ▶ Sing or reflect on the closing song.

☐ pencils or pens
☐ board or chart paper
☐ Bibles
🛜 "The Lord Is My Light and My Salvation"

Chapter Connections

FORMING CATHOLIC IDENTITY ACROSS THE CURRICULUM

To integrate the Catholic faith in all aspects of curriculum, this chapter's objectives can be reinforced and applied in the instruction of other disciplines.

Go to **aliveinchrist.osv.com** for cross-curricular activities and projects linked to the doctrinal content discussed in this unit. Activities are available from among the following knowledge categories and content areas:

Language Arts
- Integration of Knowledge
- Literacy
- Speaking and Listening
- Writing Skills

Math
- Algebraic Thinking
- Geometry
- Measurement and Data
- Numbers and Operations

Science
- Earth Science
- Life Science
- Physical Science
- Technology

Social Studies
- Civics
- Economics
- Geography
- History

NCEA IFG: ACRE Edition

Liturgical Life
- **Objective:** To know the Paschal Mystery of Jesus: in the Church's liturgical life—feasts, seasons, symbols, and practices—and in the Sacraments as signs and instruments of grace

Moral Formation
- **Objective:** To be knowledgeable about the teachings of Jesus and the Church as the basis of Christian morality and to understand Catholic Social Teaching

Catholic Faith Literacy
anointing, confess, confession, contrition, forgiveness, reconciliation, Sacrament of Penance

Catholic Social Teaching

To integrate Catholic Social Teaching into your lesson, choose one of the following features: Rights and Responsibilities of the Human Person, pages 338–339; or Solidarity of the Human Family, pages 344–345.

- Start the Live step of the process by talking about Blessed Carlos Manuel Cecilio Rodriguez Santiago on page 284. Then move directly to the Catholic Social Teaching feature.
- Or, to expand the lesson, complete page 284, then move to the Catholic Social Teaching feature.
- Return to Chapter 18 for the prayer on page 285.

Music Option

Use the following song to enhance catechetical learning or for prayer.

- "The Lord Is My Light and My Salvation," Day 5, Page 285

Name _____ Date _____

Circle the letter of the choice that best completes each sentence.

1. A turning away from sin and back to God is ___.

   a. sorrow   **c.** Eucharist

   b. confession   **d.** conversion

2. The Church celebrates Jesus' forgiveness and healing in the two Sacraments of ___.

   a. Initiation   **c.** Service

   b. Healing   **d.** children

3. True sorrow for disobeying God and committing to try to avoid sin in the future is called ___.

   a. reparation   **c.** contrition

   b. conversion   **d.** regret

4. The Anointing of the Sick unites those who are seriously ill or dying with Christ's ___.

   a. suffering   **c.** birth

   b. teachings   **d.** Mother

Indicate whether the following statements are true or false. Then rewrite false statements to make them true.

5. The Sacrament of the Eucharist celebrates a sinner's reconciliation with God and the Church. **True/False**

_____

6. When we confess our sins to a priest, we are actually talking to Christ. **True/False**

_____

7. Contrition is the prayer, offering, or good work given by the priest in Reconciliation. **True/False**

_____

8. Jesus taught us that God's compassion will end if we don't turn back to him. **True/False**

_____

Write a response on the lines below.

9. What is absolution? _____

_____

10. Why do you think it is important for people who are ill or in danger of death to receive the Anointing of the Sick? _____

_____

Name _____   Date _____

Conversion: To Walk with Jesus

When we recognize our faults and desire to make changes for the better, turning our life toward God, we are participating in the process of conversion. Fill in the left side of the page with types of thoughts, feelings, and actions that separate us from God. Fill in the right side of the page with thoughts, feelings, and actions that can bring us closer to God.

Things That Separate Us from God   **Things That Bring Us Closer to God**

Thoughts	→	Thoughts

Feelings	→	Feelings

Actions	→	Actions

Sacraments of Healing

 Let Us Pray

Leader: God, you reach out to us in loving forgiveness. Your love heals all of our hurts. Be with us as we turn to you for healing and forgiveness.

> "Look upon my affliction and suffering; take away all my sins." **Psalm 25:18**

All: God, please heal us and help us to forgive.

 Scripture

"So whoever is in Christ is a new creation: the old things have passed away; behold, new things have come. And all this is from God, who has reconciled us to himself through Christ and given us the ministry of reconciliation, namely, God was reconciling the world to himself in Christ, not counting their trespasses against them and entrusting to us the message of reconciliation. So we are ambassadors for Christ, as if God were appealing through us. We implore you on behalf of Christ, be reconciled to God. For our sake he made him to be sin who did not know sin, so that we might become the righteousness of God in him."
2 Corinthians 5:17–21

© Our Sunday Visitor

Have you ever thought...
- What does it mean to be a new creation in Christ?
- How is forgiveness the key?

275

Scripture Background

Scripture Reflection Process

Invite the students to be still, close their eyes, and focus on their breathing. Encourage them to open their minds and hearts to what God is saying to them.

- Proclaim the Scripture and have the students sit in silence.
- *Ask:* What did you hear God say to you today?
- Allow volunteers to share.

▶ You may play instrumental music to begin the reflection.

DAY 1

Objective
- Reflect on God's personal invitation through Scripture

OPEN _____

 Let Us Pray

Invite the students to gather in the prayer space and make the Sign of the Cross. Select a few students to read aloud the Psalm verse. Prompt the response from the remainder of the group.

Have the students move out of the prayer space and back to their seats.

Explain that God reaches out to us constantly with loving forgiveness when we fall short of loving him, ourselves, and others as we should.

Say: Let's listen to God's Word and discover how we are a new creation in Christ.

Scripture

Guide the students through the process of Scripture reflection (see the Scripture Background box below).

Have you ever thought...

Say: Jesus sacrificed his life so that we could become part of a new creation, one that strives to share God's love and righteousness with the world.

- Invite the students to respond to the questions.

DAY 1

Objective

- Indicate prior knowledge of chapter concepts and vocabulary

BUILD _____

Use this page to assess the students' knowledge related to the chapter content.

Getting Started

Ask a volunteer to read aloud the opening paragraph.

Sacraments of Healing

Read aloud the directions for completing the web.

★ Have the students work independently to fill in what they know about each Sacrament of Healing.

- Remind them to come back to this chart and add information as they read through the chapter. This will be a great study tool for them later.

Getting Started

In this chapter, you will discover the relationship between healing and forgiveness, understand that we can count on God's forgiveness and healing, and learn the form and effects of the Sacrament of Penance and Reconciliation.

Catholic Faith Words

- contrition
- Penance and Reconciliation
- penance
- absolution
- Anointing of the Sick

In the web below, list what you know about these two Sacraments. Include information about the outward signs and ritual actions of each Sacrament and the meaning or effects of the Sacrament.

Sacraments of Healing

Penance and Reconciliation

Anointing of the Sick

✓ Teaching Tip

Share Your Experience

Your students may not have much experience with the Sacrament of the Anointing of the Sick.

- Discuss an experience that you have had with this Sacrament or invite a priest to come and share some of his experiences. Share only what you are comfortable with.

- Be sure to tell the students how the effects of this Sacrament helped you, or someone you know, to heal and to connect with the suffering of Jesus.

- Allow them to ask you questions about your experience.

Forgiveness is Key We don't have to travel far and wide to be ambassadors for Christ (see 2 Corinthians 5:20). We can practice forgiveness and reconciliation every day, where we are. What do you believe about forgiveness? Design a "forgiveness key" that symbolizes what you believe about forgiveness, and that you can symbolically carry with you as an ambassador for Christ.

© Our Sunday Visitor

What "doors" in your life can be opened by this key?

_____
_____
_____
_____
_____
_____
_____
_____
_____
_____
_____

Work with Words

Point out the five Catholic Faith Words on page 276.

- Have a volunteer read aloud the vocabulary words.
- *Say:* Four of these terms are connected to the Sacrament of Reconciliation.
- Invite the students to circle these terms.
- *Ask:* What is left? Anointing of the Sick
- Use the Teaching Tip box from page 276 to discuss this term with the class.

CLOSE _____

ACTIVITY

Remind the students that Saint Paul says that we are ambassadors for Christ.

Discuss what ambassadors do, then paraphrase the activity instructions by suggesting that we don't have to travel to the far ends of the Earth to be ambassadors for Christ. We can practice forgiveness and reconciliation every day, wherever we are. We can be Christ's ambassadors in our homes, schools, churches, and neighborhoods.

- Explain how the students can design a "forgiveness key" and how it symbolizes what they know to be true about forgiveness.
- Talk about some of the "doors" that forgiveness can open.
- Invite the students to share their designs with one another.

Teacher Background

Growing in Self-Understanding

Remember that early adolescents can be uncomfortable talking about times of hurt and the need for healing. By this time in the year, however, the students may have developed a sense of trust with one another. While recognizing there may still be some nervousness that shows itself in giggles or jokes, create ways to continue to invite seventh graders into self-reflection.

For example, give each student a paper bag and have them place inside words or pictures that describe feelings of hurt. Have them write their name on the outside of the bag and staple it shut. Place the bags on the prayer table for the prayer celebration at the end of the chapter.

DAY 2

Objectives

- Explain why Jesus healed people
- Discuss the process of conversion
- Recognize the need for the Sacrament of Penance and Reconciliation

OPEN

💛 Invite the students to think about God's forgiveness and pray the Act of Contrition from page 387.

Ask the question at the top of the page. Point out that the answer can be found in the lesson title.

BUILD

A Merciful God

Summarize the information in the first two paragraphs.

📘 Scripture

Have a volunteer read aloud Matthew 9:35–36.

- Point out that Jesus did not intend for God's compassion to stop with him.
- Ask the students to offer definitions for the word *compassionate*. Possible responses: sympathy, feeling concern for others

Always There

Direct the class to silently read this section.

- Give the students an opportunity to discuss the question with a classmate.

A Merciful God

Why can we count on God's forgiveness and healing?

At some point or another, each of us realizes that we've done something we regret, or that we have been blaming a friend or parent for something that really isn't his or her fault. We might be confused and worried about someone who is in pain, needing help to get through a really difficult time, or facing an illness. At times like these, we need to give or receive compassion, hope, and possibly forgiveness. And God can give us all of these. Jesus shows us that God's compassion does not end.

📘 Scripture

"Jesus went around to all the towns and villages, teaching in their synagogues, proclaiming the gospel of the kingdom, and curing every disease and illness. At the sight of the crowds, his heart was moved with pity for them because they were troubled and abandoned, like sheep without a shepherd." Matthew 9:35–36

The Gospels are filled with accounts of Jesus healing those who were sick, and forgiving the sins of those who truly believed. Whether they were emotional, spiritual, or physical healings, these life-changing events had a tremendous impact. Most people believed, changed their lifestyles, and went out to tell others about Jesus and his message.

Always There

God is always there to heal us spiritually (when we feel separated from God), emotionally (when we're in psychological pain), and physically (when we are sick or injured). Because Jesus forgave sinners and healed the sick, we know that's just the way God is—forgiving and eager to heal. The Church celebrates Jesus' forgiveness and healing in two Sacraments of Healing: the Sacrament of Reconciliation and the Sacrament of the Anointing of the Sick.

> How could your day be different if you remembered God's compassion for you and his desire to heal and forgive?

© Our Sunday Visitor

📘 Scripture Background

Jesus, Our Help

Matthew 9:35–36 tells of the great needs Jesus found among the people and the compassion he felt for them. In Matthew 9:37–38, he tells his disciples that the harvest is great, but that there are not many workers. Then he asks the disciples to pray that God will send someone to help.

Matthew 10:1 tells us that Jesus "summoned his twelve disciples and gave them authority over unclean spirits to drive them out and to cure every disease and every illness." Here, we see Jesus giving his healing power to his disciples, a power he has continued to give to his Church, down through the ages.

Holding Ourselves Up to the Light

Did you ever put on a "clean" T-shirt only to discover spots in the light? When we hold ourselves up to the light of Christ, we all have "spots": bad attitudes, grudges, prejudices, emotional wounds, bad memories, and sins. With God's help we recognize and admit our need for and desire to change. We are open to conversion.

Conversion can mean many things:

- a return to God, sorrow for sin, trust in God's mercy, commitment to do better in the future, rooting out bad habits, and more.
- making ourselves more and more like Christ.
- ongoing, always possible, always needed.
- goes together with repentance.

Repentance, also called **contrition**, is being truly sorry for disobeying God and committing to try not to sin again. If contrition comes out of love for God above all things, it is called "perfect"; if someone is sorry for sins because they feel guilty or are afraid of the punishment, it is called "imperfect contrition." Both are promptings of the Holy Spirit in us, moving us to seek forgiveness. We sometimes stray from the path by venial sin, which weakens our relationship with God.

© Our Sunday Visitor

Catholic Faith Words

contrition true sorrow for disobeying God and the commitment to try to avoid sin in the future

Penance and Reconciliation the Sacrament of Healing that celebrates God's mercy and forgiveness and a sinner's reconciliation with God and the Church through absolution from a priest

Some people may walk away from God (through a grave, or mortal sin). The Sacrament of **Penance and Reconciliation**—also called the Sacrament of conversion, confession, or penance—is the Sacrament of forgiveness for sins committed after Baptism. Required for the forgiveness of mortal sin and recommended for the forgiveness of venial sin, it is a sure way to get back on the path of conversion.

DESCRIBE

In what ways have you been (or could be) open to conversion? Describe one or two conversions you have been through that improved the way you walk with God. Try finishing this phrase:

I used to (think/feel/believe/try to)

_____

_____

_____

_____

but now I

_____

_____

_____

and it has helped my relationship with God because

_____

_____

_____

_____

Sacraments of Healing **279**

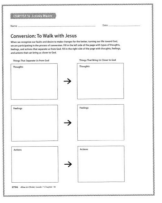
Holding Ourselves Up to the Light

Direct the students to read this section and to underline or highlight the definitions of *conversion* and *contrition* within the text.

- Point out that conversion involves a change of heart, and contrition is true sorrow for our sins. The two always go together in the lives of Christians seeking to get closer to God.
- Explain that we are required to confess all unabsolved mortal sins and encouraged to confess venial sins in the Sacrament of Penance and Reconciliation, where we can receive forgiveness.
- Gauge their understanding of the material by encouraging the students to ask questions.

CLOSE

ACTIVITY

Allow time for the students to read the instructions and complete this activity on their own.

Quick Review Jesus' healing actions inspired others to spread his message and helped show us that God's compassion never ends. We can show that we are open to conversion and God's forgiveness by participating in the Sacrament of Penance and Reconciliation.

Objectives

- Describe the four elements of the Sacrament of Penance and Reconciliation
- Review the steps in the Rite of the Sacrament of Reconciliation
- Identify the benefits of receiving the Sacrament of Penance

OPEN

Invite the students to quietly pray a personal prayer of petition, asking for God's help, mercy, guidance, and forgiveness.

Point out the photo. Ask the students to describe what they believe is happening.

BUILD

Reconciliation

Divide this part of the chapter, including the Catholic Faith Words and the left column on page 281, into sections. Assign a group to read and determine the important points for each section.

- Allow a spokesperson from each group to teach their section to the rest of the class.
- Discuss any questions that the students may have about the definitions or the content thus far.

The Sacrament of Penance and Reconciliation

★ Have the students match the parts of the Sacrament with the effects.

- Share the correct answers with the class.

Reconciliation

What are the rites and effects of this Sacrament?

Today the Church celebrates the Sacrament of Penance and Reconciliation in three ways, with one form for the Rite for Reconciliation of Individual Penitents, and two for Several Penitents.

No matter which Rite (see page 371 in the Our Catholic Tradition section of your book) is used in the celebration of the Sacrament of Penance and Reconciliation, it always contains four important elements: contrition, confession, **penance**, and **absolution**.

Catholic Faith Words

penance the name for the prayer, offering, or good work the priest gives you in the Sacrament of Reconciliation

absolution words spoken by the priest during the Sacrament of Penance and Reconciliation to grant forgiveness of sins in God's name

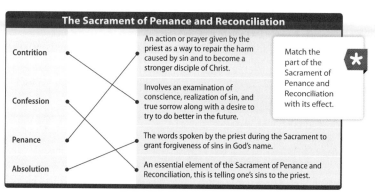

The Sacrament of Penance and Reconciliation

Contrition	An action or prayer given by the priest as a way to repair the harm caused by sin and to become a stronger disciple of Christ.
Confession	Involves an examination of conscience, realization of sin, and true sorrow along with a desire to try to do better in the future.
Penance	The words spoken by the priest during the Sacrament to grant forgiveness of sins in God's name.
Absolution	An essential element of the Sacrament of Penance and Reconciliation, this is telling one's sins to the priest.

★ Match the part of the Sacrament of Penance and Reconciliation with its effect.

✔ Teaching Tip

Student Teachers

Having students teach part of a lesson can be very effective or very ineffective, depending on how you prepare them.

- Form groups small enough (no more than four) so that everyone can get involved. If your class is large, you can always assign a section to more than one group and have them work and present separately.
- Give each group something very specific to teach.
- Invite the groups to use graphics to teach their part of the lesson—something drawn on the board or a poster.

Whether the Sacrament takes place with an individual meeting with the priest for the entire celebration, or with a group of penitents gathering together for prayers and reflection, with individual confession and absolution, there is a similar structure to the celebration.

- gathering
- reading Scripture
- expressing contrition
- confessing sin individually and privately to a priest who can forgive sins in Christ's name by the authority of the Church. Priests cannot tell anyone what you have told them; this is called the Sacramental Seal of Confession.
- receiving a penance and having sins absolved by a priest
- praising God

You might be thinking you don't want to tell someone all the things you've done. But you need to remember that you are actually talking to Christ when you talk to the priest. And there are so many spiritual benefits from receiving the Sacrament: reconciliation with God and the Church, freedom from eternal separation from God, a peaceful conscience, spiritual help and guidance, and strength to live as a disciple of Christ.

Let Go

Sometimes we hold a grudge as bitter revenge for our hurt feelings even if the person who hurt us is unaware. The same might be true of prejudices, bad memories, emotional wounds, and psychological scars. We become like Peter, who wondered how many times he absolutely had to forgive. Or we're like the Unforgiving Servant who was excused a huge debt, but wouldn't let go of a small debt someone owed him. (See Matthew 18:21–35.)

📕 Go to the Source
Read the Parable of the Unforgiving Servant found in Matthew 18:21–35. Do you feel more like Peter, the Unforgiving Servant, or the person who owes? What is your favorite line in the parable? Why?

Consider these ways to become freed from emotional pain.

- When angry or vengeful thoughts pop into your mind, redirect your thoughts and adrenaline through activity or prayer.
- Talk with your parents or a mentor, a trusted friend, or an older sibling.
- Talk to your parents and ask if they think you could talk to a counselor if other things aren't working.

CREATE

Turn to page 373 to review the Ten Commandments. Using the Commandments as a guide, create an examination of conscience. On the lines below, write a reflection question that corresponds to two different Commandments.

_____

_____

Sacraments of Healing **281**

Optional Activity

Scripture Readings *Interpersonal, Visual/Spatial, Bodily/Kinesthetic*

Explore different ways to "read" Scripture. For today's Scripture passage, Matthew 18:21–35, choose one or more of the following methods of presentation:

- Invite a group of students to prepare the reading by assigning the parts of narrator and characters in the passage.
- Have the students illustrate and present the passage to the group.
- Provide props and costumes for a dramatic presentation of the passage.

Let Go
Read aloud the first paragraph.

📕 Go to the Source

Have a volunteer read the passage from Matthew 18:21–35. (See the Optional Activity below for different ways to approach this.)

- Allow the students to discuss the questions with a classmate.

Ask three volunteers to read aloud the suggestions for becoming freed from emotional pain.

- Facilitate a class discussion on other ways to deal with emotional pain.
- Write the students' suggestions on the board or on chart paper.

CLOSE

ACTIVITY

Read the directions for the activity to the class.

- Note: It might be helpful to brainstorm a few examples with the students.
- Then have them work on their own reflection questions.

Quick Review The Sacrament of Penance and Reconciliation has four important elements: contrition, confession, penance, and absolution. The benefits of receiving this Sacrament are a peaceful conscience, spiritual guidance, and strength to live as a disciple of Christ.

DAY 4

Objective

- Explore the need for and the effects of the Sacrament of the Anointing of the Sick

OPEN _____

♥ Gather the students in the prayer space to pray for those who are sick. Invite volunteers to pray for someone who is ill, ending each specific prayer with, "we pray to the Lord," and responding, "Lord, hear our prayer."

BUILD _____

Anointing of the Sick

Ask the students to silently read the first paragraph on the page.

- Direct them to underline or highlight the last sentence.

Have the students silently read the remainder of this section and locate the following information in the last paragraph:

- Who can be anointed?
- Who can administer this Sacrament?
- What is used for this Sacrament?
- What does the ritual consist of?

Direct the class to the Catholic Faith Words box on page 283.

- Read aloud the definition.

✝ Scripture

Proclaim James 5:13–15.

- *Ask:* How does this passage connect to the Sacrament of the Anointing of the Sick?

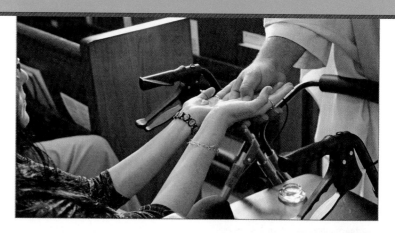

Anointing of the Sick

What are the rituals and effects of this Sacrament?

In the District of the Decapolis, people brought a man with a hearing loss and a speech impediment to Jesus. At Bethsaida people brought a man who was blind. When the people of Gennesaret saw Jesus, they scurried about to bring the sick on mats. Wherever Jesus went, people counted on his power to heal. Fortunately, Jesus left his power to heal in his Church.

Healing the sick was so much a part of the life of Jesus that the first thing the seventy-two disciples were told to do was "Cure the sick" in each town, "and say to them, 'The kingdom of God is at hand for you'" (Luke 10:9). They had the simple faith to follow his example.

The early Church continued the practice of curing the sick. The letter of James tells us about praying over sick people and anointing them. We learn that the faith of the community is essential for healing to take place.

> ### ✝ Scripture
>
> "Is anyone among you suffering? He should pray. Is anyone is good spirits? He should sing praise. Is anyone among you sick? He should summon the presbyters of the church and they should pray over him and anoint [him] with oil in the name of the Lord, and the prayer of faith will save the sick person, and the Lord will raise him up. If he has committed any sins, he will be forgiven."
> **James 5:13–15**

The Church does the same today in the **Anointing of the Sick**. When someone falls seriously ill or the illness worsens, or when someone is in danger of death, they are invited to seek the prayers and anointing of the Church. Only priests can administer the Sacrament, using oil consecrated by the bishop during Holy Week. The ritual consists of laying on of hands and anointing the forehead and hands while praying for the grace of the Sacrament to strengthen the person to be able to handle the difficulties of serious illness or old age.

282 Chapter 18

Optional Activity

In Rhythm with the Sacrament *Interpersonal, Musical*

Have the students work in groups to create rhymes for each of the Sacraments. The rhymes can be read as a poem or they can be lyrics to a song.

- Allow each group to choose a different Sacrament.
- Instruct the students to write at least four stanzas that teach about the importance of the Sacrament and its effect on those who receive it.
- Invite the students to sing or read their lyrics or poem to the class.

Why It's Important

What do you think of when you hear words like courage, health, peace, grace, and suffering? Probably a whole range of things. These words can be used to describe the effects of the Anointing of the Sick.

This Sacrament has a tremendous impact on those who receive it, and that's why the Church wants to make sure that everyone knows that this Sacrament is for anyone who is seriously sick, no matter the age or reason.

As in all the Sacraments, the Anointing of the Sick gives a special grace to the person who receives it. In this Sacrament, the person who is sick is united to Christ's suffering and receives spiritual healing. That's pretty amazing when you think about it. The Son of God actually suffered, and so God understands our suffering. And, because new life comes from Jesus' suffering, people are connected to his new life in this Sacrament.

The Sacrament gives courage, peace, and spiritual healing to endure suffering or old age, and sometimes health is restored. For those who are near death, the Sacrament helps prepare them and their sins are forgiven if they are unable to receive Penance.

© Our Sunday Visitor

CONSIDER

We sometimes want to help someone who is sick, but don't know how to do it. One way is to simply say, "I will keep you in my prayers, okay?" or "I'll say a prayer for you." Think of some other ways you can reach out to those who are sick.

Catholic Faith Words

Anointing of the Sick one of the Sacraments of Healing for people who are seriously ill or in danger of dying. In the Sacrament, the person's forehead and hands are anointed with the blessed oil of the sick.

IN SUMMARY Catholics Believe

We know that God heals us spiritually, emotionally, and sometimes physically in the Sacraments of Healing.

- Jesus' words and actions show us that God is compassionate, always willing to forgive and care for those who are willing to turn to him and believe.

- In the Sacrament of Penance and Reconciliation, those who are truly sorry for their sins receive God's forgiveness and are reconciled with him and the Church.

- In the Sacrament of the Anointing of the Sick, those who are seriously ill or are suffering from old age receive God's grace to be strong, courageous, and hopeful in their trials.

Sacraments of Healing **283**

✓ Teaching Tip

Spiritual and Emotional Healing

Be sensitive to the potential for personal loss and suffering in the lives of your students. Chemical abuse, broken relationships, harmful sexual encounters, and personal histories of abuse may well be part of the unspoken dynamic in the classroom. Be sure to temper any discussion of these issues with the awareness that they are likely to be more than hypothetical for some of your students. Seek out guest speakers who have faced and overcome some of the challenges your students might be facing. If your Church has a youth ministry, there may be some children who are a part of this group that can speak about how God has helped them to overcome the obstacles they have faced.

Why It's Important

Have the students read aloud these paragraphs and discuss the points that they determine are important.

- *Ask:* What are the effects of the Anointing of the Sick? courage, health, peace, grace, relieving and understanding of suffering

CLOSE

ACTIVITY

Invite a student to read the instructions to the class.

- Have a list of parishioners who are sick, shut-in, or in nursing homes ready to share with the class.

- Invite the students to select one of the parishioners and make a card of encouragement for them.

- Note: Be sure to include all the parishes that your students attend.

- Provide paper and art materials so that the students can send a card with good wishes and promises of prayer.

In Summary

Read aloud the summary statement and ask three volunteers to each read one of the bullet points.

- Make sure to answer any questions that the students may still have about the material in this chapter.

DAY 5

Objectives

- Examine the giving and receiving of forgiveness
- Explore the faith life of Blessed Carlos Manuel Cecilio Rodriguez Santiago
- Pray the Psalm of Lament

OPEN

Ask the students to stand and pray Psalm 25:18 from page 275. Close the prayer with the group response.

BUILD

Our Catholic Life

Review the information in the Our Catholic Life feature.

- Discuss, as a class, some ways to approach inviting someone to confession who might be nervous about confessing their sins.
- List the students' ideas on the board or on chart paper.

People of Faith

Explain to the students that Blessed Carlos Santiago didn't let his illness keep him from spreading the Good News.

- Read aloud the People of Faith paragraph.
- Share the information in the People of Faith Background box.
- *Ask*: Do you know anyone who does Jesus' work, even through their suffering?

Our Catholic Life

Giving and receiving **forgiveness** is an important way we can show the work and grace of God in our lives. Remember how you have felt when you've been forgiven for something or chosen to forgive someone else for hurting you. When you are in emotional or physical pain, or need to be forgiven, you can always turn to God in prayer. If you need to forgive someone, ask God to help you do that, too. It is one of the Precepts of the Church to receive the Sacrament of Penance and Reconciliation at least once a year to have your personal sins forgiven and your relationships with God and the Church healed. Parishes often have Reconciliation services during the seasons of Advent and Lent.

> How would you describe Reconciliation to someone who is nervous about confessing their sins?

© Our Sunday Visitor

People of Faith

Blessed Carlos Manuel Cecilio Rodriguez Santiago, 1918–1963

As a child in Puerto Rico, Carlos Santiago began experiencing symptoms of an illness from which he would suffer for the rest of his life. However, it never undermined his commitment to Christ and his Church. Carlos used his modest salary as a translator to publish two Christian magazines. He also worked at a university, where he evangelized students and teachers. He encouraged liturgical renewal, and many of his reforms were adopted by the Church at the Second Vatican Council in the 1960s. The Church celebrates his feast day on **July 13**.

For more, go to aliveinchrist.osv.com

IDENTIFY

You can keep in mind the benefits of forgiveness by turning back to your Bible when you are struggling. Use your Bible to match the beginnings of these scriptural quotes to the correct endings.

1. Forgiving one another . . . __C__
2. I have brushed away your offenses like a cloud . . . __A__
3. You are a forgiving God, gracious and merciful . . . __B__

   A. your sins like a mist. (Isaiah 44:22)
   B. slow to anger and rich in mercy. (Nehemiah 9:17)
   C. as God has forgiven you in Christ. (Ephesians 4:32)

284 Chapter 18

People of Faith Background

Blessed Carlos Manuel Cecilio Rodriguez Santiago

Share the following:

- Blessed Carlos was born with a severe digestive disorder that caused him much suffering and inconvenience, but he didn't let this keep him from his commitment to Christ and the Church.
- He encouraged liturgical renewal among clergy and laity, the use of vernacular language, and devotion to the Paschal Vigil. Many of his proposed reforms were adopted by the Church during Vatican II.

Encourage the students to go to **aliveinchrist.osv.com** at home to learn more about Blessed Carlos Santiago.

Psalm of Lament

Leader: Be with us, O God,
As we sit here in quiet,
as we look deep inside at the ways
we have turned away from you.

Side 1: The Lord is my light and my salvation;
whom should I fear?
The Lord is the stronghold of my life:
of whom should I be afraid?

Side 2: One thing I asked of the Lord,
that will I seek after:
to live in the house of the Lord
all the days of my life,
to behold the beauty of the Lord,
and to inquire in his Temple.

Side 1: For he will hide me in his shelter
in the day of trouble;
he will conceal me under the cover of his tent;
he will set me high on a rock.

Side 2: Hear, O Lord, when I cry aloud,
Be gracious to me and answer me!
"Come," my heart says, "seek his face!"
Your face, Lord, do I seek.
Do not hide your face from me.
You are my salvation; do not cast me off!
Do not forsake me, God my savior!
Based on Psalm 27:1, 4, 5, 7, 9

Leader: O God of all goodness,
Your love heals all.
Come now and be with us, as we turn
toward you.
Help us to be patient when we stumble
and fall,
help us to be forgiving of ourselves and
each other.
Strengthen our determination to be more
and more like Jesus.

All: Amen.

▶ *Sing or play "The Lord Is My Light and My Salvation"*

Sacraments of Healing   **285**

🛜 Go to **aliveinchrist.osv.com** for an interactive review.

A Work with Words **Complete each sentence with the correct term from the Word Bank.**

Word Bank	
Baptism	contrition
Penance and Reconciliation	forgiveness
	conversion
Anointing of the Sick	Eucharist
suffering	

1. The Sacrament of __Anointing of the Sick__ consists of laying on of hands and anointing a person's forehead and hands with oil while praying for the grace of the Sacrament to strengthen the person.

2. __Contrition__ is being truly sorry for disobeying God and committing oneself to avoid sin in the future.

3. The Sacrament of __Penance and Reconciliation__ is the Sacrament of forgiveness for sins committed after Baptism. It celebrates God's mercy and forgiveness and reconciles a sinner with God and the Church.

4. In the Sacrament of Anointing of the Sick, the sick person is united to Christ's __suffering__.

5. __Conversion__ can mean many things: a return to God, sorrow for sin, trust in God's mercy, commitment to do better in the future, and more.

B Check Understanding **Indicate whether the following statements are true or false. Then rewrite false statements to make them true.**

6. Perfect conversion comes out of love for God above all things. **True**/(**False**)
__Perfect contrition__

7. The Sacrament of Penance and Reconciliation is required for forgiveness of mortal sin committed after Baptism and recommended for forgiveness of venial sin. (**True**)/**False**

8. The Sacrament of Penance and Reconciliation always includes contrition, confession, anointing, and absolution. **True**/(**False**)
__contrition, confession, penance,__
__and absolution__

9. Priests in confession cannot tell anyone what you have told them; this is called the Sacramental Seal of Confession. (**True**)/**False**

10. Only priests can give the Sacrament of Reconciliation using the oil consecrated by the bishop during Holy Week. **True**/(**False**)
__Sacrament of the Anointing of__
__the Sick__

C Make Connections **On a separate sheet of paper, write a one-paragraph response to the question: Write about a time when someone forgave you or a time when you forgave someone. What was the experience of forgiveness like, and how did it affect your relationship with that person?**

286   Chapter 18

Instruct the students to use their Bibles to complete the activity.

CLOSE _____

Psalm of Lament

💗 Invite a volunteer to prepare to be the leader.

Divide the remainder of the class into two sides.

Direct the students to gather in the prayer space.

Have the leader stand in front of the group and begin the prayer when all are in place.

Follow the order of prayer on the student page.

▶ Conclude by inviting the students to sing or reflect on the song "The Lord Is My Light and My Salvation," downloaded from **aliveinchrist.osv.com**.

CHAPTER REVIEW

Review the instructions for each section and have the students complete the review.

🛜 Go to **aliveinchrist.osv.com** to prepare customized and downloadable assessments, send eAssessments, and assign interactive reviews.

Sacraments of Healing   **285–286**

UNIT 6

Use the closing points from Days 2–4 in each chapter to highlight lesson concepts for this unit and prepare for the Unit Review.

Have the students complete the Review pages. Then discuss the answers as a class. Review any concepts with which the students are having difficulty.

A **Work with Words**

Have the students use the clues to complete the crossword puzzle.

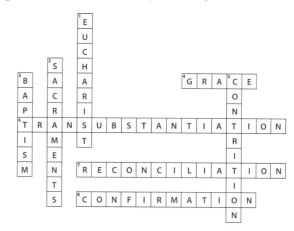

A Work with Words Use the clues below to complete the crossword puzzle.

Across

4. God's free, loving gift of his own life and help to do what he calls us to do
6. the process by which, through the power of the Holy Spirit and the words and actions of the priest, the bread and wine become the Body and Blood of Christ
7. the Sacrament of Penance and ____ celebrates God's mercy and forgiveness
8. One of the Sacraments of Initiation

Down

1. the Sacrament during which the bread and wine become the Body and Blood of Christ
2. Seven effective signs of God's grace instituted by Christ and given to his Church
3. Sacrament through which a person experiences new life in Christ and forgiveness of sins and incorporation into the Church
5. Being truly sorry for disobeying God and committing to try to avoid sin in the future

Sacraments **287**

B Check Understanding Circle the letter of the choice that best completes the sentence.

9. Jesus is the perfect ___ between God and man, because he is fully God and fully man.

   (a.) Mediator   b. Symbol   c. Division   d. Conversion

10. The Church, a means to ___, is a visible community in the world.

    (a.) salvation   b. grace   c. divinity   d. power

11. The Sacrament of Reconciliation reflects Jesus' giving ___ the power to forgive sins.

    a. us   **(b.) the Church**   c. John   d. one person

12. All Seven Sacraments involve ___ and ___ that we can see, touch, hear, taste, and smell.

    (a.) symbols, rituals   b. oil, blessings   c. attitudes, gifts   d. signs, words

13. The Church welcomes new members through the Sacraments of ___

    a. Contrition   **(b.) Initiation**   c. Conviction   d. Invitation

14. In Baptism, the ___ is a reminder that God has chosen and called each one to be his own.

    a. water   b. candle   **(c.) Sacred Chrism**   d. prayer

15. Like Baptism, Confirmation imparts a(n) ___ character on one's soul.

    a. acceptable   b. invisible   c. conversion   **(d.) spiritual**

16. ___ can mean many things: a return to God, sorrow for sin, trust in God's mercy, a commitment to do better in the future, and more.

    a. Contrition   b. Sacraments   **(c.) Conversion**   d. Reconciliation

17. The Sacrament of Anointing of ___ consists of the priest's laying on of hands and putting oil on the forehead and hands.

    (a.) the Sick   b. Reconciliation   c. the Dying   d. Baptism

18. The Sacrament of Penance and Reconciliation always includes contrition, ___, penance, and absolution.

    a. conversion   **(b.) confession**   c. penance   d. consideration

19. In Confirmation, a person is sealed with the ___ of the Holy Spirit.

    a. Sacraments   **(b.) Gifts**   c. Chrism   d. Confession

20. ___ refers to the words spoken by the priest during the Sacrament of Penance and Reconciliation to grant forgiveness of sins in God's name.

    (a.) Absolution   b. Penance   c. Confession   d. Contrition

---

C Make Connections Write a short answer to these questions.

21. How do you experience God through the customs and practices of the Church? Give a specific example.

    Responses may vary. _____
    _____
    _____
    _____

22. What does it mean to live out the Eucharist? How are you living out the Eucharist in your family, at school, and in the world?

    Responses may vary. _____
    _____
    _____
    _____

23. What are the benefits of the Sacrament of Penance and Reconciliation?

    The benefits include reconciliation with God and the Church, freedom
    from eternal separation from God, a peaceful conscience, and strength
    to live as a disciple of Christ. _____
    _____

24. Choose one Sacrament and describe how Jesus instituted it.

    Responses may vary. _____
    _____
    _____
    _____

25. How does the Sacrament of Confirmation strengthen our connection with the Church?

    Confirmation strengthens our connection with the Church through
    being sealed with the Gifts of the Holy Spirit, which gives us strength
    to share in the mission of the Church. _____
    _____

B Check Understanding

Instruct the students to circle the letter of the choice that best completes each sentence.

C Make Connections

Point out that the students will be writing a short answer response to the questions. Explain that even though these are short answer responses, they need to be sure that they fully answer the questions.

🛜 Go to **aliveinchrist.osv.com** to prepare customized and downloadable assessments, send eAssessments, and assign interactive reviews.

KINGDOM OF GOD

How does listening for and responding to God's invitation help you to be happy in this world and the next?

CHURCH HISTORY TIMELINE

528 Benedict begins monastery at Monte Cassino

910 Monastery at Cluny founded

1205 Saint Francis of Assisi establishes what becomes the Franciscan Order

2013 Jorge Bergoglio elected as Pope Francis

Go to page 348 for more

Our Catholic Tradition

- We share a call to know, love, and serve the Lord, and share our time, talent, and treasure. God's Word, the Church, family, and prayer help us discern and respond to our vocation. (CCC, 2030)

- God's Kingdom is fully present in Heaven but not complete on Earth. We work toward the Kingdom through prayer, sharing the Good News, action, and advocacy for those in need. (CCC, 2820)

- By his Death and Resurrection, Jesus makes it possible for believers to have eternal life. We will be judged at the time of our death based on how we have accepted and acted on God's grace in our lives. (CCC, 934, 1019)

Our Catholic Life

- We are called to faith. Each of us must live our particular vocation, whether married, single, ordained, or consecrated. (CCC, 871–873)

- We will be judged at our death based upon the ways we have accepted and acted on God's grace in our lives. God desires all of us to make the right choices in life, so we can be with him forever in the happiness of Heaven. (CCC, 1051)

- The Works of Mercy are ways to respond to Jesus when we see him in those who are poor or in need. (CCC, 2447)

Introduce Unit Theme

Ask volunteers to read aloud the bullets under the Our Catholic Tradition and Our Catholic Life sections. Discuss what these statements tell them Unit 7 will be about.

Review the events listed on the timeline. Point out that the students can turn to the Church History Timeline at the back of their books for more information on the first two dates.

Assure the students that they will learn more about the Kingdom of God as they review the next three chapters.

Ask the unit's Big Question found on page 290.

Allow time for discussion.

Explain to the students that this is the essential question for the unit. They will be working to fully answer it as they complete the three chapters in the unit.

📖 Go to the Source

As an optional extension, organize the students into three groups, assigning each group one of the main Scripture passages found in this unit.

- Chapter 19: 1 Samuel 3:4–10
- Chapter 20: Psalm 9:8–11, 10:14, 18
- Chapter 21: Romans 8:22–25, 28

Have each group read its passage and then give a dramatic reading (narrator with silent actors), create a visual representation, or write down one question they would ask God about the passage.

Reading the verses directly from the Bible will familiarize students with the sequence of the canon of Sacred Scripture.

Explore Papal Statements

Encourage the students to research a message of one of the recent Popes on World Youth Day.

- Provide them with Internet access or hard copies of various research material in the classroom, or assign this research as something to be done from home.
- *Ask:* What does the message say to you about finding your calling and working for justice in the world?
- Allow time for any questions the students may have.
- Invite them to share their findings with the rest of the class.

Reading directly from the papal statements will help the students learn where to find key teachings from the Sacred Tradition of the Church.

CHURCH HISTORY TIMELINE BACKGROUND

Refer the students to the Church History Timeline on pages 348–363 to learn more about important Church events and figures through A.D. 1085.

Saint Francis of Assisi Founds the Franciscan Order

A native of Assisi, Saint Francis renounced his family's fortune and founded what would later become the Franciscan Order. One of the most popular Saints in the world, he is known for his poverty, love of nature, and reforms of the Church.

Resignation of Pope Benedict XVI and Election of Pope Francis

On February 28, 2013, Pope Benedict XVI became the first Pope in 598 years to step down from office. Citing declining health due to old age, he took the title of Pope Emeritus and continued to live at the Vatican. Cardinal Jorge Mario Bergoglio, Archbishop of Buenos Aires, Argentina, became his successor, taking the name Pope Francis. Pope Francis is the first Pope from the Americas and the first Pope from the Society of Jesus, commonly known as the Jesuits.

KEY CONCEPT

We share a common call to know, love, and serve the Lord. The Church helps us respond to our unique call.

DOCTRINAL CONTENT

- The Catholic family is a domestic Church—a holy community of love, grace, and prayer. Our families help teach us to hear God's call and respond to him in faith and love. (CCC, 1656–1657, 2685)

- Whether married, single, ordained, or consecrated, we are called to share our time, talent, and treasure through our vocation in order to serve the Church. (CCC, 871–873)

- Discernment is the process by which we reflect, discuss, pray, and are ultimately drawn toward our vocation. (CCC, 2226, 2232)

- Whether we choose to be ordained, enter consecrated religious life, or remain a member of the laity, we are all called to faith and to continue the mission of Jesus. (CCC 1, 542–543)

TASKS OF CATECHESIS

Helping children grow in a faith that is "known, celebrated, lived, and expressed in prayer" (NDC, 20).

This chapter focuses on the following tasks of catechesis:

- Education for Community Life
- Missionary Initiation

Teacher Background

The LORD called Samuel again . . . Then Eli understood that the LORD was calling the youth. So he said to Samuel, "Go to sleep, and if you are called, reply, 'Speak, LORD, for your servant is listening.'" When Samuel went to sleep in his place, the LORD came and stood there, calling out as before: Samuel, Samuel! Samuel answered, "Speak, for your servant is listening." **1 Samuel 3:8–10**

> **Reflect** How do you use the gifts that God has given you to better serve him and to make a difference in the lives of those around you?

Some of us have been conditioned to think of a vocation as something reserved only for the ordained. But, in fact, quite the opposite is true. A vocation is every Christian's invitation to listen to Jesus' call and to follow him, to use our personal gifts to serve him and his Church. This is a challenging and exciting way to live, for it is a response to God's call. In the Beatitudes, Jesus teaches that happiness is of the utmost importance to our loving Creator. In fact, the word "beatitude" means "happiness." Reaching our fullest potential generates happiness.

Since being human means living in relationship with others, there is another aspect to vocation as well. Each of us is called to use our gifts and abilities for the glory of God rather than ourselves. After all, they are called gifts because we have done nothing to merit them. We are responsible for nurturing them and learning how they can benefit others. And when we seriously evaluate how we can best live out the Gospel in our lives, we are led to the fact that our gifts are meant to be shared with others around us no matter what might be happening in our daily lives.

> **Reflect** Think about the relationship between lifestyle and vocation. How are they similar? How does vocation go beyond lifestyle?

Teacher's Prayer

Lord of all, I thank you for calling me to be a teacher. I ask that you empower me with all that I need to fulfill my vocation. I honor you and teach in your name. Amen.

How Seventh Graders Understand Chapter Topics

Seventh graders are often asked, "What do you want to be when you grow up?" They might be less familiar with the idea that God has a plan for their lives or that they can experience this plan as a calling, or vocation, from God. With guidance, they might see signs of God's call through the talents they are given, the opportunities they have, or the things they hear about themselves from others.

Teaching Tip: Instead of asking your students what they want to do when they grow up, practice using the language of vocation, asking instead who they feel God is calling them to be.

Sharing the Message with Seventh Graders

- For better or worse (and probably both), young people at this age tend to identify themselves by the qualities others see and name in them.
- For some seventh graders, their personal abilities and gifts may just be beginning to blossom.
- Remember that young adults need affirmation by those in positions of authority to help reinforce their positive abilities and qualities.

ONLINE RESOURCES

Go to **aliveinchrist.osv.com**

You will find:

- Interactive lesson planning, additional activities, and ideas for the classroom environment
- Step by step lesson instruction from printed Teacher Edition for integrated lesson planning
- Custom-built assessments to download and eAssessment links
- Interactive reviews that provide scores and the option to review answers
- Chapter-specific Lectionary connections and a complete correlation ordered by the Sundays of the year, with suggestions for how to integrate the Scripture readings into chapter lessons

Go to **osvparish.com** for Ask the Experts Q and A, Community Connections, and Blogs.

Objectives	Open
DAY 1—Invite/Preview, Pages 291–293	
• Reflect on God's personal invitation through Scripture • Indicate prior knowledge of chapter concepts and vocabulary	♥ **Psalm 4:4** Pray the opening prayer. 📖 **1 Samuel 3:4–10** Proclaim "The Call of Samuel." Guide the students through the process of Scripture reflection. • Discuss Have You Ever Thought questions.
DAY 2—Discover, Pages 294–295	
• Discuss the role of family in teaching us to hear God's call, and respond to him in faith and love • Examine how a Catholic family is a domestic Church—a holy community of love, grace, and prayer • Identify the laity's role in being witnesses to Christ	♥ Pray the **Act of Faith**, page 387. • Discuss the opening question.
DAY 3—Discover, Pages 296–297	
• Explain the process of discerning a vocation • Identify people who can help someone discern his or her vocation • Name ways we can share in Jesus' mission	♥ Pray the Prayer for Vocation Assistance, page 296. • Discuss the opening question.
DAY 4—Discover, Pages 298–299	
• Compare and contrast the parish priesthood and a priest in consecrated religious life • Explore the vows taken by those in consecrated religious life	♥ Pray the **Hail Mary**, page 384.
DAY 5—Live, Pages 300–301	
• Discover how the laity serve the Church • Explore the faith life of Saint Anthony of Padua • Offer the Vocation Prayer	♥ Reflect on vocations and pray the **Lord's Prayer**, page 383.

REVIEW AND ASSESSMENT

Chapter Review, page 302
Chapter Test, page 291F

📶 **aliveinchrist.osv.com** Customize and Download Assessments, Email Links to eAssessments, Interactive Student Reviews

Build	Close	Materials & Resources
• Present lesson highlights. • Preview **Catholic Faith Words**. ★ Discuss vocation, discernment, and service and how they affect our daily lives.	• Activity The students will reflect on those who have been God's voice in their lives.	☐ pencils or pens ☐ highlighter
• **Catholic Faith Words** domestic Church, laity • Talk about nurturing our gifts. 📖 Read and reflect on Luke 2:41–52. • Explain the importance of the domestic Church and the laity.	• Activity The students will consider ways to add prayer into their daily routine. • Conclude with a review of key concepts and objectives.	☐ pencils or pens ☐ Bibles
• **Catholic Faith Words** vocation, discernment • Discuss the process of discernment. ★ The students will consider how they have shared in Jesus' mission. • Optional Activity How Can I Serve? (Activity Master 19)	• Activity Discuss ways that specific talents can be used to help others. • Conclude with a review of key concepts and objectives.	☐ pencils or pens ☐ board or chart paper ☐ Activity Master 19 (Page 291G)
• **Catholic Faith Words** consecrated religious life • Discuss listening for God's call and obstacles to hearing it.	• Activity Brainstorm a list of parish ministries and vocations. • Review the In Summary statements.	☐ pencils or pens ☐ board or chart paper ☐ parish publications
• Discuss the questions in the Our Catholic Life section. • Learn about Saint Anthony of Padua. • Activity Reflect on responding to God's call.	• Select four readers. • Follow the order of prayer. ▶ Sing or play the closing song.	☐ pencils or pens 🛜 "Find Us Ready"

Chapter Connections

FORMING CATHOLIC IDENTITY ACROSS THE CURRICULUM

To integrate the Catholic faith in all aspects of curriculum, this chapter's objectives can be reinforced and applied in the instruction of other disciplines.

Go to **aliveinchrist.osv.com** for cross-curricular activities and projects linked to the doctrinal content discussed in this unit. Activities are available from among the following knowledge categories and content areas:

Language Arts

- Integration of Knowledge
- Literacy
- Speaking and Listening
- Writing Skills

Math

- Algebraic Thinking
- Geometry
- Measurement and Data
- Numbers and Operations

Science

- Earth Science
- Life Science
- Physical Science
- Technology

Social Studies

- Civics
- Economics
- Geography
- History

NCEA IFG: ACRE Edition

Communal Life

- **Objectives:** To know the origin, mission, structure, and communal nature of the Church; to know the rights and responsibilities of the Christian faithful

Missionary Spirit

- **Objectives:** To recognize the centrality of evangelization as the Church's mission and identity embodied in vocation and service; to be aware of how cultures are transformed by the Gospel

Catholic Faith Literacy

laity, priest, religious life, vocation

Catholic Social Teaching

To integrate Catholic Social Teaching into your lesson, choose one of the following features: Call to Family, Community, and Participation, pages 336–337; or The Dignity of Work and the Rights of Workers, pages 342–343.

- Start the Live step of the process by talking about Saint Anthony of Padua on page 300. Then move directly to the Catholic Social Teaching feature.
- Or, to expand the lesson, complete page 300, then move to the Catholic Social Teaching feature.
- Return to Chapter 19 for the prayer on page 301.

Music Option

Use the following song to enhance catechetical learning or for prayer.

- "Find Us Ready," Day 5, Page 301

Name _____ Date _____

Match each description in Column A with the correct term in Column B.

Column A

Column B

____ **1.** A sweet-smelling oil used at Baptism

a. laity

____ **2.** A process by which one reflects, discusses, and prays about how God might be calling him/her

b. domestic Church

____ **3.** All baptized members of the Church who share in Jesus' mission but are not priests or consecrated brothers or sisters

c. vocation

____ **4.** The Catholic family; a community of Christians in the home

d. Sacred Chrism

____ **5.** Our purpose; the way we answer and live out God's call

e. discernment

Circle the letter of the choice that best completes each sentence.

6. A man who has received Holy Orders is known as a ____.

a. lay person

c. lector

b. religious brother

d. priest

7. At a Baptism, parents and godparents are called to bring the baptized up in ____.

a. a vocation

c. the practice of the faith

b. communion

d. consecrated religious life

8. Consecrated religious life is a communal life characterized by the vows of poverty, chastity, and ____.

a. obedience

c. fear of the Lord

b. fortitude

d. right counsel

9. Children should first learn about God from their ____.

a. family members

c. school teachers

b. parish priest

d. friends

Write a response on the lines below.

10. Why do you think vocations to the religious life are important? _____

_____

11. Describe the role of lay people as priests, prophets, and kings. _____

_____

Name _____   Date _____

How Can I Serve?

In the left column, write three or four talents you have. In the right column, match your talents with a possible need in the Church. In the space below, make a plan for a way that you will begin to use one of your talents to fill a need in the Church.

My Talents:

1. _____

_____

2. _____

_____

3. _____

_____

4. _____

_____

Needs in the Church:

1. _____

_____

2. _____

_____

3. _____

_____

4. _____

_____

My plan for using my talent now:

_____

_____

_____

_____

_____

_____

_____

_____

_____

_____

_____

Called by God

💙 Let Us Pray

Leader: Lord, you call us by name. Help us to know your voice when you call; help us to say "Yes, Lord."

"Know that the LORD works wonders for his faithful one; the LORD hears when I call out to him." Psalm 4:4

All: O God, help us know your will for our lives. Help us hear you when you call.

Scripture

The LORD called to Samuel, who answered, "Here I am." He ran to Eli and said, "Here I am. You called me." "I did not call you," Eli answered. "Go back to sleep." So he went back to sleep.

Samuel did not yet recognize the LORD, since the word of the LORD had not yet been revealed to him. The LORD called Samuel again ... Then Eli understood that the LORD was calling the youth. So he said to Samuel, "Go to sleep, and if you are called, reply, 'Speak, LORD, for your servant is listening.'"

When Samuel went to sleep in his place, the LORD came and stood there, calling out as before: Samuel, Samuel! Samuel answered, "Speak, for your servant is listening." 1 Samuel 3:4–10

Have you ever thought...

- What does it mean to be called by God?
- How can your gifts serve God and make a difference for others?

Called by God **291**

© Our Sunday Visitor

Scripture Background

Scripture Reflection Process

Invite the students to be still, close their eyes, and focus on their breathing. Encourage them to open their minds and hearts to what God is saying to them.

- Proclaim the Scripture and have the students sit in silence.
- *Ask*: What did you hear God say to you today?
- Allow volunteers to share.

 You may play instrumental music to begin the reflection.

Objective

- Reflect on God's personal invitation through Scripture

OPEN

💙 Let Us Pray

Invite the students to gather in the prayer space and make the Sign of the Cross. Pray the leader prayer and the Psalm verse together. Prompt the group's response.

Have the students move out of the prayer space and back to their seats.

Remind them that God calls us, and that God hears us when we call on him.

Say: Let's listen to God's Word and recognize the ways God calls us— because he does indeed call each of us to use our gifts to bring his life and love to the world.

Scripture

Guide the students through the process of Scripture reflection (see the Scripture Background box below).

Have you ever thought...

Say: Each of us is called by God to share our time, talent, and treasure with the Church in our unique way.

- Invite the students to respond to the questions.

DAY 1

Objective

- Indicate prior knowledge of chapter concepts and vocabulary

BUILD _____

Use this page to assess the students' knowledge related to the chapter content.

Getting Started

Summarize the opening paragraph for the students.

In Your Own Words

★ Instruct the students to describe the terms *vocation, discernment,* and *service* and what role they play in our daily lives.

- Allow volunteers to share some of their ideas with the class.

Getting Started

In this chapter, you will learn about the role of the family in faith and the meaning of vocation. You will also explore how God calls each of us to use the gifts he has given us.

In the chart below, describe what each term means to you and how it is important in our lives as individuals, families, school communities, and the Church.

Catholic Faith Words
• domestic Church
• laity
• vocation
• discernment
• consecrated religious life

In Your Own Words		
Vocation	**Discernment**	**Service**

© Our Sunday Visitor

 Teaching Tip

Vocations

Have the students create a Venn diagram that includes "things they enjoy" and "things they are good at." In the part of the Venn diagram that overlaps, students should list things they both enjoy and are good at. They should think about what their vocation might be by focusing on this section of the diagram. You may also want to encourage the students to identify careers or different types of volunteer work that require the skills they possess (visit a library or search the Internet to identify required skills associated with different career paths or different types of volunteer work).

Do You Hear God's Call? Think of a time when someone who cared about you encouraged you to be a better friend, brother or sister, son or daughter. God's voice comes to us in many ways. Write the names of the people who have been God's voice in your life.

_____

_____

_____

_____

_____

_____

Choose one of the people you listed above and describe how he or she helped you hear and respond to God's voice in your life.

_____

_____

_____

_____

_____

_____

_____

_____

_____

_____

_____

_____

Called by God **293**

Work with Words

Point out the Catholic Faith Words box on page 292.

- Ask a volunteer to read aloud the five vocabulary words.

- Remind the students that they described two of the terms in the chart on page 292. Have them circle the two words.

- Encourage them to share what they know about the other three vocabulary terms.

- Tell them that they will learn more about all of these words and how they connect to the chapter title by the time they complete this chapter.

CLOSE

ACTIVITY

Share with the class a person who has been God's voice in your life.

- Explain the activity instructions to the students and give them time to complete it.

- Remind them to thank God often for the people in their lives who help them hear God's call.

Optional Activity

Gift Giving _Interpersonal, Verbal/Linguistic_

Form small groups of seven or eight and give each student a large piece of Christmas wrapping paper.

- Have each student write his or her name on the decorative side of the paper.

- Instruct them to pass the wrapping papers around the small group.

- As each group member receives wrapping paper belonging to someone else, that member should write (on the plain side) a gift they see in that person.

- Make sure each student gets his/her wrapping paper back.

DAY 2

Objectives

- Discuss the role of family in teaching us to hear God's call, and respond to him in faith and love

- Examine how a Catholic family is a domestic Church—a holy community of love, grace, and prayer

- Identify the laity's role in being witnesses to Christ

OPEN _____

💗 Direct the students to begin with the Sign of the Cross. Then pray the Act of Faith from page 387.

Ask the opening question and allow time for the students to consider the relationship between family and faith before discussing it.

BUILD _____

The Importance of Family

Have the students silently read the text.

- Invite them to consider ways their parents helped them to grow in faith as well as ways they might one day help their own children.

- Discuss the question at the end of the section.

📖 Go to the Source

Have the students read Luke 2:41–52 and then discuss the questions.

Faith Begins at Home

Introduce the idea of the family as a model of the Church.

Jesus in the Temple, among the teachers

A mother found herself praying one day. She and her husband had lost track of their son, who was around twelve years old. The parents' names were Mary and Joseph, and they finally found their son, Jesus, in the Temple, teaching the teachers. They had looked for him for three days, probably worrying and praying all the while. But, even though the Bible tells us they were upset with Jesus, they were also amazed by him (see Luke 2:51).

> 📖 **Go to the Source**
> Read *Luke 2:41–52*. Imagine that you were a friend of Jesus when he was growing up. What might you have seen him doing in daily life? What do you think it would be like to have Jesus as a friend or classmate today?

The Importance of Family

What role does the family have in faith?

Each of us has potential gifts and talents. Some of us are artistic, some are athletic, some are thinkers, and some are speakers. And many have more than one of these gifts. We might discover our talents early in life, or we might stumble across them by accident. Our families often point out gifts and talents they see in us, and our teachers, coaches, and friends can help us figure them out, too. When we use our talents to work together, we can bring about good in the world.

Despite our different talents, we all share the same calling to know and love God. We are first called to this mission in our Baptism, and our parents and guardians play a pivotal role in our responding to that call.

The Gospel according to Luke also tells us that Mary "kept all these things in her heart" (Luke 2:51). She and Joseph recognized Jesus' great gifts, nurtured him with love, prayed with him, and helped him fulfill God's will.

Prayer begins in our family. Parents and guardians put roofs over our heads, clothes on our backs, and food on our plates, and provide for our spiritual needs. If you become a parent, you will be responsible for helping your children grow in faith.

> What different roles do the people in your family have?

Faith Begins at Home

Before you were baptized, your parents and godparents were given an important task. They were told: "You must make it your constant care to bring him/her up in the practice of the faith" (Rite of Baptism).

📖 Scripture Background

The Finding in the Temple

This story is the only Gospel story about Jesus' youth. It comes between Simeon and Anna's words about the infant Jesus at the Presentation in the Temple and John the Baptist's proclamations about the Messiah.

- The story highlights the devout practices of the Holy Family.

- In this story, we see a family that is being asked to recognize and support their child's call. Jesus is drawn to the teachers of God's law and to the sacred space of the Temple. He is "at home" in his Father's house.

Constant means all the time; every day. This kind of care includes things like teaching you to pray, telling you to "turn the other cheek" instead of getting even, or getting you to Mass on Sunday.

The home is the first place where children learn about God and the Catholic faith. It is here that they should first appreciate what a community of love is. They should experience solid Catholic virtues and values. In that sense, a family is a unique dimension of the Church. A Catholic home and family is a **domestic Church**—a holy community of grace and prayer where children first learn about God through the love, teaching, and good examples of parents and family. For example, when such a family gathers around a table for a meal or in the car on the way to school, they can thank God for the gifts they received that day.

No family is perfect. All families face challenges and have growing pains. Sometimes a home seems more like a domestic Church than at other times. The important thing for families to do, even in hard times, is to keep trying and to ask God for help.

Witnesses to Christ

Lay people are called to be witnesses to Christ at all times and places, as parents or single persons, at work, in home, and in the community. **Laity** is the name for all the baptized members of the Church who share in Jesus' mission but are not ordained. Lay people witness to Jesus' message in their families, workplaces, and civic communities.

We are witnesses when our words and actions reflect the teachings of Jesus and the Church. At home, in school, on the bus, or at work we can show others what it means to follow Christ. And we don't do this alone. God gives us the love and strength to make it happen.

Catholic Faith Words

domestic Church a name for the Catholic family, because it is the community of Christians in the home. God made the family to be the first place we learn about loving others and following Christ.

laity all baptized members of the Church who share in Jesus' mission and witness to him and his message but are not priests or consecrated sisters or brothers; sometimes called lay people

CONSIDER

Think about how you can add prayer to your daily routine. Be creative. Keep it simple. Think about how you can pray at different times and in different places: before bed, at breakfast, after a ball game or practice. Get ideas from the people in your family on other ways to build your domestic Church.

_____

_____

_____

_____

Called by God **295**

© Our Sunday Visitor

---

i Teacher Background

Supporting Families

The Catholic Church supports economic and political policies that help maintain the family, society's central social institution. The family, in turn, nurtures individuals so they can become productive members of society.

- Families are considered the "sanctuary of life" (*Centesimus Annus*) because children are born into and brought up in the care of a family.

- It is important to remember that families are the gift God gives to us in order that the love that binds us is turned outward to transform the world.

Faith Begins at Home, *continued*

Point out that family and Church members have obligations to one another.

- Review the Catholic Faith Word definition of *domestic Church*.

- Explain that as a domestic Church, the main goal of a family is to create a sacred place where all members can grow in faith and holiness.

Invite the students to silently read this section.

Witnesses to Christ

Summarize the text. Explain that most Catholics are lay people who have an important role in being witnesses.

- Have a volunteer read the definition of *laity*.

- Brainstorm ways that lay people can be witnesses for Christ.

CLOSE _____

ACTIVITY

Organize the class into groups. Have each group write their suggestions on small slips of paper that are to be collected and read aloud.

- Encourage the students to discuss this activity and brainstorm more ideas with their families.

Quick Review Our families, the domestic Church, are a holy community of love, grace, and prayer that help to teach us about God, his love and teachings, and our calling in the Church. Every member of the Church is important.

DAY 3

Objectives

- Explain the process of discerning a vocation
- Identify people who can help someone discern his or her vocation
- Name ways we can share in Jesus' mission

OPEN

❤ Hand out copies of the Prayer for Vocation Assistance from the Teacher Background box below. Pray this prayer together.

Ask: What does it mean to have a vocation?

- List the students' responses on the board or on chart paper.

BUILD

A Common Mission

Summarize this information for the class.

Living It Out

Choose a volunteer to read aloud the text.

- *Ask*: Who has a vocation? We all have a vocation as baptized members of the Church.
- Point out the definition for *vocation* on page 297.
- Discuss the question at the end of this section.

What About You?

Read through the paragraphs.

- *Ask*: How do prayer and advice from trusted adults help you with discernment?

A Common Mission

What does it mean to have a vocation?

In Baptism and Confirmation, we are called to be holy in every aspect of our lives—when we're alone, with our family and friends, and as part of our Church. At Baptism, we are anointed with consecrated, sweet-smelling oil called Sacred Chrism as the priest or deacon tells us that Christ unites us to his People and his Body, and we share in Christ's ministry as Priest, Prophet, and King.

Living It Out

You can't apply for a job as a king. It's not as simple as our deciding alone to become an ordained priest, or a religious sister or brother. Those vocations begin with a call from God and require years of prayer and study. **Vocation** is the purpose for which God made us, and the particular way to answer and live out that call to love and serve God and others.

We all have a vocation as baptized members of the Church. Some have a vocation to priesthood or religious life. Others live out their vocation as part of a married couple or through single life. God may give married Catholics the gift of children, while sisters and

brothers in religious communities dedicate their lives to the faith in many different ministries and lifestyles. Whatever path you follow is a sacred one when you take Christ's love with you and share it with others.

> Who do you turn to for help when you are making a big decision? Why?

What About You?

Do you get tired of being asked, "What do you want to be when you grow up?" It's normal for the answer to change many times as you get older. Maybe you wanted to be a star athlete, but didn't have the physical skills. Dreams and plans change for many reasons.

The process by which you reflect, discuss, and pray about how God might be calling you to a particular vocation is called **discernment**. Think about what you enjoy doing, and what you are good at. Talk with your parents, family, friends, Church leaders, and others who know you best. They should respect and encourage your choices of a vocation. This is more likely if they understand what you are thinking.

Pray with them, like Jesus surely did with his parents. Parents can encourage their children to see that they are called to follow Jesus, whatever they do.

296 Chapter 19

© Our Sunday Visitor

ℹ️ Teacher Background

Prayer for Vocation Assistance

Make copies of this prayer to share with the students:

God, my loving Father, you created me with the ability to live in relationship with you. Help me to grow in understanding your great love for me. Help me to know that it is in loving you and serving you that I will find my greatest happiness. Send your Holy Spirit to show me how you want me to serve you. Give me the courage to listen for your voice even though there are so many other messages that come from other places. Jesus, give me the desire to do what you ask. Help me to find and fulfill my vocation. Amen.

Lay People Share in Jesus' Mission

○ Priest	Like Jesus, we offer our lives to God and bring his love to the world. We pray for those in need, we offer what we do at school and at home as a gift to God, and we participate in the Mass.
○ Prophet	Like Jesus and the Apostles, as prophets we speak God's powerful truth to people by the way we act and the things we say. We show them what it means to follow Christ.
○ King	Christ is King, and all of the baptized are part of the Body of Christ. We are co-heirs, with Christ, to the Kingdom of God.
What I Did This Week	_____ _____ _____ _____

Place a check mark by one way you have shared in Jesus' mission this week. In the space provided, explain what happened.

Catholic Faith Words

vocation the purpose for which God made us and the particular way to answer and live out his call, whether as a lay person (married or single), a member of a religious community, or a member of the ordained ministry

discernment the process by which a person reflects, discusses, and prays about how God might be calling him or her to live out a particular vocation

LIST

List some things you enjoy doing and those things you take seriously. How can you use these talents to make a difference in the lives of people around you?

Things I Enjoy Doing

1. _____
2. _____

Things I Take Seriously

1. _____
2. _____

Called by God **297**

© Our Sunday Visitor

Optional Activity

Activity Master 19: How Can I Serve?

Distribute copies of the activity found on teacher page 291G.

- This activity will help the students reflect on their talents and how they can be used by Christ.

- Use this activity to encourage them to understand service as a way of life for a disciple, not as an occasional project.

Lay People Share in Jesus' Mission

Have the students read the text in the chart to review some of the ways we can share in Jesus' mission.

★ Direct them to place a check mark next to one way they have shared in Jesus' mission this week. Encourage them to write about what happened.

- Allow volunteers to share their response with a classmate.

Ask: How are you a priest, prophet, and king? Possible responses: We bring God's love to the world; we speak God's truth and show others what it means to follow Christ; we are co-heirs to God's Kingdom.

CLOSE _____

ACTIVITY

Tell the students to read the instructions and complete the activity individually.

- Afterwards, have them work with another student to generate ideas for how to use their talents to better the world.

Quick Review As baptized members of the Church, we all have a vocation—our way of helping to carry out God's plan. Through reflection, discussion with others, and prayer, we can discern which vocation God is calling us to.

Objectives

- Compare and contrast the parish priesthood and a priest in consecrated religious life
- Explore the vows taken by those in consecrated religious life

OPEN

💗 Invite the students to stand and pray the Hail Mary, page 384.

Explain that priests and religious sisters and brothers have had to discover their vocations, just as the students will be discovering their own vocations in the years to come.

BUILD

Listening for God's Call

Have the students silently read the text.

- *Ask:* What are some obstacles that may get in the way of people hearing or responding to God's call? What slows us down?
- Discuss these questions as a class.

Emphasize the following:

- It is our job to respond to needs in the Church and the world.
- We must respond with our time, talent, and treasure.

Sacred Vows

Invite a volunteer to read the first paragraph.

- Have the students underline the vows that those in consecrated religious life take.

Listening for God's Call

What gifts does the Church call on you to share?

We can be inspired by the words and witness of priests, religious women and men, lay leaders, and good Catholic parents. There are many needs in our Church, and we're called to listen and respond.

Sometimes we respond with our treasure, like when disaster strikes a poor country. The collection basket is passed, and we give what we can.

As we grow older, and our gifts develop, we also share our talent and time. We might be altar servers, work at a soup kitchen, or help at Vacation Bible School. We might read at Mass, teach a class, or make an even bigger commitment to participate in parish life.

When a man becomes a parish priest, he will promise to respect and obey his bishop, live a simple lifestyle, and be celibate. Celibacy means to not get married and to not have sexual relations. These promises require great sacrifices, but they're made out of love for God and the Church community.

Sacred Vows

Other people may choose to serve God by entering **consecrated religious life.** This includes members of religious orders, who are known as brothers or sisters, as well as priests in religious orders. The men and women called to live a consecrated life live in a community and take vows of poverty, chastity, and obedience.

> **Catholic** Faith Words
>
> **consecrated religious life** a state of life lived by religious sisters, brothers, and priests in community and characterized by the vows of poverty, chastity, and obedience

© Our Sunday Visitor

A religious brother works in the library of San Salvador de Leyre monastery in Navarra, Spain

> ℹ️ **Teacher Background**
>
> ## Priests, Brothers, and Sisters
>
> Members of religious orders fall into three main groups: priests, brothers, and sisters. Members take solemn, or irrevocable, vows that typically include poverty, chastity, and obedience.
>
> - Priests have been ordained to the priesthood by a bishop. They can be part of a religious order or be diocesan priests.
> - Brothers are men who have taken solemn vows and live in community. Sisters are women who have taken solemn vows and live in community.
> - Many religious orders serve the needs of others by creating schools, hospitals, orphanages, nursing homes, and homeless shelters.

The Vows

In **poverty**, a consecrated person owns nothing in his or her own name. His or her few possessions are given to him or her and often shared with others. This helps the person to better understand and serve those who are poor.

Obedience shows that the common good is more important than our personal desires and helps a person to more fully serve the Church.

For men and women in consecrated life, **chastity** means living a celibate life. It shows that their love for God is the most important thing.

Although these vows, also called evangelical counsels, are required for people in consecrated religious life, Christ calls all of his disciples to live by them. Everyone should strive to live simply, love God above all things, and care deeply for others. A married couple needs to treat their relationship as a sacred partnership and mutual vocation. Through their communion, they are meant to grow closer together and nearer to the Lord.

> In what ways do you feel called to serve the Church community and all God's people?

REPORT

Brainstorm a list of all the different ministries and vocations that keep your parish running. Go beyond the immediately familiar groups or people and think about others working behind the scenes as well. Share a brief report on these ministries or vocations with your class or ask one person in your parish if he or she will speak to the class about his or her vocation.

IN SUMMARY Catholics Believe

We share a common call to know, love, and serve the Lord. The Church helps us respond to our unique call.

- We are called to relationship. We discern our vocation with the help of God's Word, family, the Church, and prayer.

- We are called to work. The Church asks us to share our time, talent, and treasure.

- We are called to faith. Each of us must live our particular vocation, whether married, single, ordained, or consecrated.

Called by God **299**

Optional Activity

The Peace Prayer *Musical*

"The Peace Prayer," or Prayer of Saint Francis, has been set to music a number of times.

- Ask your music teacher or parish music minister to help you find a version to teach to your students. Your parish hymnal will probably have at least one version. A recorded version may be available to aid your efforts.

- If you have any musically gifted students, challenge them to write music to fit the prayer, then teach it to the class.

Sacred Vows, *continued*

Ask the students to differentiate between the terms *priesthood*, *consecrated life,* and *vocation*.

Have them read the rest of the text on vows and silently reflect on the question at the end of the text.

The Vows

Point out that vows are also called evangelical counsels. Read aloud each of the descriptions of the vows from the chart.

CLOSE _____

ACTIVITY

Divide the class into smaller groups of three to five students. Consider having parish publications available to show some of the different types of ministries.

- After the groups are finished brainstorming, have them compile a report and share it with the class.

In Summary

Invite four volunteers to read aloud the summary statement and bullet points.

- After each bullet is read, ask how we can help others answer these particular calls.

DAY 5

Objectives

- Discover how the laity serve the Church
- Explore the faith life of Saint Anthony of Padua
- Offer the Vocation Prayer

OPEN

Invite the students to silently reflect on how God might be calling them toward a certain vocation. Close with the Lord's Prayer from page 383.

BUILD

Our Catholic Life

Read the information on the role of the laity.

- Have the students work with a classmate or in a small group to discuss the questions.

People of Faith

Explain to the students that certain events in Saint Anthony of Padua's life helped him to discern his vocation.

- Have the students silently read the People of Faith paragraph.
- Discuss, with the class, the content of the People of Faith Background box.
- Encourage the students to conduct more research on Saint Anthony at home and bring their findings back to share with the rest of the class.

Our Catholic Life

Jesus and the Jewish people knew that being active in their religion, community, and local government was essential to their faith. With Jesus as their model, many saintly men and women of the Church started out and remained members of the **laity**. We can learn from their example by sharing in the work of the laity in our parishes and schools. As laity, we speak up for what is right and teach others to share in the mission of Christ through our words and actions. Baptized lay people participate in Christ's mission when we speak the truth, work for what is right and just, and help those in need, especially in our works of service.

> How do you continue Christ's mission on Earth? What makes your work easy or hard?

People of Faith

Saint Anthony of Padua, 1195–1231

Fernando Martins de Bulhões was an Augustinian priest, and later a Franciscan friar, taking the name Anthony. One day, when no one was prepared to give a sermon at the hospital where he worked, Anthony was asked to preach what the Spirit told him to say. His homily impressed Saint Francis so much that he had Anthony train young men to become Franciscan priests. Pope Gregory IX called him "a jewel case of the Bible." He was named a Doctor of the Church in 1946 and today is especially remembered as the patron Saint of finding lost objects. The Church celebrates his feast day on **June 13**.

For more, go to aliveinchrist.osv.com

IDENTIFY

You're called to many things. Take some time to evaluate how you're responding by thinking about and answering the questions below.

How are you responding to the call of faith at this time in your life?

_____
_____
_____

How are you responding to your call in the subjects you are studying, the skills you are developing, and your after-school commitments?

_____
_____
_____
_____

300 Chapter 19

© Our Sunday Visitor

People of Faith Background

Saint Anthony of Padua

Share more on Saint Anthony:

- Anthony met five Franciscan friars who were going to Morocco to preach to the Muslims. A year later, he learned they had been martyred. He was so impressed with their faith and bravery that he decided to become a Franciscan himself.

- His sermons were collected into a book called *Sermons for Feast Days*.

Encourage the students to go to **aliveinchrist.osv.com** at home to learn more about Saint Anthony of Padua.

Vocation Prayer

Reader 1: God, our Father and Creator, you have called each one of us to a vocation. Every vocation is a holy calling. Every vocation asks us to love and serve you and others. The Church, the Holy Spirit, and our families will guide us in finding the vocation you have planned for us. Help us to be patient and generous. Help us also to find the best way to use our gifts.

Reader 2: O God, you have given to the Church the gift of priesthood and religious vocations. Those whom you call to these vocations serve your Church and the People of God with a special and constant devotion. For all those called to the priesthood and to religious vocations:

All: We ask your abundant blessings, O God.

Reader 3: God and Father, you are the heavenly Father of all, the Creator of family. You have called many to the holy vocation of marriage and parenthood. The family, we know, is the domestic Church, the first community to share the faith with children. For all those whom you will call to marriage and to lives as mothers and fathers:

All: We ask your abundant blessings, O God.

Reader 4: God, some of your sons and daughters are also called to be holy in the committed single life. Dedicated single people can serve you, the Church, and the community. For all those called to live holy and fruitful lives as single men and women:

All: We ask your abundant blessings, O God.

Reader 1: Jesus, Son of God, and our Savior, you called Saint Ignatius of Loyola in a new way when he was wounded and disillusioned as a soldier. Together, we pray his prayer, a Prayer for a Generous Spirit, knowing that you will also call us to serve God in different life vocations and in different jobs and professions.

All: Lord, teach me to be generous.
Teach me to serve you as you deserve;
to give and not to count the cost,
to fight and not to heed the wounds,
to toil and not to seek for rest,
to labor and not ask for reward,
save that of knowing that I do your will.
Amen.

▶ *Sing or play "Find Us Ready"*

🛜 Go to **aliveinchrist.osv.com** for an interactive review.

A Work with Words **Complete each sentence with the correct term from the Word Bank.**

Sacred Chrism	domestic School
laity	domestic Church
witness	vocation
family	community

1. A member of the _____**laity**_____ is a baptized member of the Church who shares in Jesus' mission and witnesses to him, especially in his or her families, workplaces, and the civic community.

2. The purpose for which God made us and the particular way to answer his call is a _____**vocation**_____.

3. The _____**family**_____ is the first place to learn about the good within people and discover Christ's love.

4. A home and family can be a _____**domestic Church**_____—the community of the home where children learn about God through the love, teaching, and example of parents and other family members.

5. Those who live in consecrated religious life live in _____**community**_____.

B Check Understanding **Indicate whether the following statements are true or false. Then rewrite false statements to make them true.**

6. Parents and godparents promise to make it their "constant care to bring him (her) up in the practice of the faith" before a child is confirmed. True/**False**
   This happens before a child is baptized.

7. Men and women called to live a consecrated religious life take vows of poverty, modesty, and obedience. True/**False**
   poverty, chastity, and obedience

8. Lay people share in Jesus' priesthood by praying and offering what we do as a gift to God. **True**/False

9. In Baptism and Confirmation, we are called to be holy in all parts of our lives. **True**/False

10. When you use discernment, you pray silently and wait for God's sign. True/**False**
    You weigh your choices and pray for guidance.

C Make Connections **On a separate sheet of paper, write a one-paragraph response to the question: What vocation do you think you will be called to, and how will your gifts from God help you follow that path?**

Read aloud the introduction to the activity.

- Have the students work on their own to answer the questions.

CLOSE _____

Vocation Prayer

💙 Prepare the prayer space with lit candles and a Bible.

Invite four students to serve as the readers. Allow time for them to familiarize themselves with their respective parts.

Say: Prayer for vocational guidance in both state of life and work is extremely important for Christians who wish to follow Jesus.

Follow the order of prayer on the student page.

▶ Conclude by playing or singing with the students "Find Us Ready," downloaded from **aliveinchrist.osv.com**.

CHAPTER REVIEW

Review the instructions for each section and have the students complete the review.

🛜 Go to **aliveinchrist.osv.com** to prepare customized and downloadable assessments, send eAssessments, and assign interactive reviews.

KEY CONCEPT

Jesus made justice a priority. It was central to his teaching on God's Kingdom toward which we all long.

DOCTRINAL CONTENT

- We can work together with God as he builds his Kingdom by choosing to believe, having faith, and making the necessary changes in our lives to work toward what is just, peaceful, and loving. (CCC, 2819–2820)

- Justice is giving what is due to God and what is due to others as children of God made in his image and possessing equal human dignity. (CCC, 1929–1931)

- The Tenth Commandment focuses on the intentions of our heart. To live right, we must rely on God, trust in his care, and have the right attitude toward money and things. (CCC 2534–2536, 2548)

- Society does not always support the values of God's Kingdom, so we must stand together in solidarit y with those who need our help. (CCC 1939–1942)

TASKS OF CATECHESIS

Helping children grow in a faith that is "known, celebrated, lived, and expressed in prayer" (NDC, 20).

This chapter focuses on the following tasks of catechesis:

- Promoting Knowledge of the Faith

- Moral Formation

Teacher Background

The Lord rules forever . . . It is he who judges the world with justice, who judges the peoples with fairness. The Lord is a stronghold for the oppressed, a stronghold in times of trouble. Those who know your name trust in you; you never forsake those who seek you, Lord. . . . To you the helpless can entrust their cause . . .   **Psalm 9:8–11, 10:14**

> **Reflect** According to Jesus' teachings, what do we "owe" to those who are in need, physically and spiritually?

The Gospel that we hear during Mass can bring us comfort and spiritual healing. But hearing God's Word should also challenge us. Jesus calls us to a life of discipleship. This means we should dedicate ourselves to live for Christ. We are called upon to live by the Word of God, to take his message out into the world, and to love and care for one another. This requires individual effort and personal commitment. Jesus led the way, but it is up to us to choose to follow and continue his work in this world.

This sense of mission is part of the identity of the Catholic Church: salvation is not just a God-and-me prospect. As with other aspects of Catholic life, community plays an important part in our understanding of being reconciled with God and experiencing his transforming life and love. We are given new life through our faith in Jesus Christ, but that faith comes to us through others, is supported in the Church community, and is expressed and witnessed through our actions. We serve Christ as we serve others.

> **Reflect** How do your actions reflect your recognition of the presence of Christ in those who are poor and vulnerable?

Teacher's Prayer

 Loving Jesus, in your public ministry you had a strong passion for justice. May I too be passionate about justice, may I not be content to ignore suffering, and may I be an agent of your hope and healing for all I meet. Amen.

How Seventh Graders Understand Chapter Topics

Seventh graders have a strong sense of justice and fairness, but they may miss the practical ways in which they can work with God to help him build his Kingdom in their everyday lives. They sometimes miss injustices around them (unless they are involved in them), or they feel they are too young or too small to make changes.

Teaching Tip: Point out that we cooperate with God as he builds his Kingdom when we stand up for what is right and fair in the smallest moments of our everyday lives. This can include defending or befriending those who are lonely, unpopular, teased, or bullied.

Sharing the Message with Seventh Graders

- A characteristic of younger adolescents is that they can sometimes bounce back and forth between great self-absorption and concern for others.
- Children this age may or may not recognize their own giftedness. They should be encouraged to engage in discernment experiences to help surface those gifts.
- Affirming the virtuous qualities of seventh graders often encourages them to act more generously.

Objectives	Open

DAY 1—Invite/Preview, Pages 303–305

- Reflect on God's personal invitation through Scripture
- Indicate prior knowledge of chapter concepts and vocabulary

○ **Psalm 89:15** Pray the opening prayer.

▨ **Psalm 9:8–11, 10:14, 18** Proclaim "Thanksgiving for Victory and Prayer for Justice." Guide the students through the process of Scripture reflection.

- Discuss Have You Ever Thought questions.

DAY 2—Discover, Pages 306–307

- Define justice as giving what is due to God and what is due to others as children of God made in his image and possessing equal human dignity
- Discover that to live in God's Kingdom, people must choose to believe, to have faith, and to make the necessary changes in their lives

○ Pray the **Morning Prayer**, page 386.

- Connect the images on pages 306 and 307 with the text.

DAY 3—Discover, Pages 308–309

- Identify people of the Kingdom of God by the actions that work toward what is just, peaceful, and loving

○ Pray the **Lord's Prayer**, page 383.

- Respond to the opening question.

DAY 4—Discover, Pages 310–311

- Explain why solidarity is a Christian virtue
- Describe how being poor in spirit can be connected to the Tenth Commandment

○ Pray the **Beatitudes**, page 374.

- Point out the opening question.

DAY 5—Live, Pages 312–313

- Connect social media with sharing the Church's message
- Explore the faith life of Pope Leo XIII
- Offer the Prayer of Petition

○ Pray a prayer of thanksgiving.

REVIEW AND ASSESSMENT

Chapter Review, page 314
Chapter Test, page 303F

📶 **aliveinchrist.osv.com** Customize and Download Assessments, Email Links to eAssessments, Interactive Student Reviews

Build	Close	Materials & Resources
• Present lesson highlights. • Preview **Catholic Faith Words**. ★ Describe the meaning of justice. • Optional Activity Encouraging Changes (Activity Master 20)	• Activity Consider the differences between fairness and justice.	☐ pencils or pens ☐ Activity Master 20 (Page 303G)
• **Catholic Faith Words** justice • Talk about why the Church is responsible for seeking justice. ▣ Reflect on Luke 4:14–22. ★ Consider what Jesus came to do and what we need to do to live for the Kingdom.	• Activity List ways to help others who assist God in building up his Kingdom. • Conclude with a review of key concepts and objectives.	☐ pencils or pens ☐ Bibles ☐ board or chart paper
• **Catholic Faith Words** peace • Relate the Parable of the Mustard Seed to the Kingdom of God. ▣ Read Matthew 13:31–32. • Share why the Lord's Prayer is called the perfect prayer.	• Activity Design a collage of signs of God's Kingdom. • Conclude with a review of key concepts and objectives.	☐ pencils or pens ☐ magazines or newspapers ☐ scissors, glue ☐ poster board or chart paper
• **Catholic Faith Words** solidarity • Discuss the practice of solidarity. ▣ Reflect on Luke 18:18–30.	• Review the In Summary statements.	☐ pencils or pens ☐ board or chart paper ☐ highlighters
• Discuss the question in the Our Catholic Life section. • Learn about Pope Leo XIII. • Activity Practice the decision-making steps: see, judge, and act.	• Divide the class into two sides. • Follow the order of prayer. ▶ Sing or reflect on the closing song.	☐ pencils or pens 📶 "We Will Follow"

Chapter Connections

FORMING CATHOLIC IDENTITY ACROSS THE CURRICULUM

To integrate the Catholic faith in all aspects of curriculum, this chapter's objectives can be reinforced and applied in the instruction of other disciplines.

Go to **aliveinchrist.osv.com** for cross-curricular activities and projects linked to the doctrinal content discussed in this unit. Activities are available from among the following knowledge categories and content areas:

Language Arts
- Integration of Knowledge
- Literacy
- Speaking and Listening
- Writing Skills

Math
- Algebraic Thinking
- Geometry
- Measurement and Data
- Numbers and Operations

Science
- Earth Science
- Life Science
- Physical Science
- Technology

Social Studies
- Civics
- Economics
- Geography
- History

NCEA IFG: ACRE Edition

Knowledge of the Faith
- **Objective:** To know and understand basic Catholic teaching about the Incarnate Word Jesus Christ as the way, truth, and life

Moral Formation
- **Objective:** To be knowledgeable about the teachings of Jesus and the Church as the basis of Christian morality and to understand Catholic Social Teaching

Catholic Faith Literacy
conscience, discrimination, stewardship

Catholic Social Teaching

To integrate Catholic Social Teaching into your lesson, choose one of the following features: Life and Dignity of the Human Person, pages 334–335; or Option for the Poor and Vulnerable, pages 340–341.

- Start the Live step of the process by talking about Pope Leo XIII on page 312. Then move directly to the Catholic Social Teaching feature.
- Or, to expand the lesson, complete page 312, then move to the Catholic Social Teaching feature.
- Return to Chapter 20 for the prayer on page 313.

Music Option

Use the following song to enhance catechetical learning or for prayer.

- "We Will Follow," Day 5, Page 313

Name _____   Date _____

Match each description in Column A with the correct term in Column B.

Column A

____ **1.** The sin that the Tenth Commandment warns us about

____ **2.** The desire to give what is due to God and and what is due to others as children of God

____ **3.** A state of calm and harmony when things are in order and people settle problems with kindness

____ **4.** Christian virtue that motivates believers to share their spiritual and material gifts

Column B

a. justice

b. peace

c. solidarity

d. envy

Circle the letter of the choice that best completes each sentence.

5. The Kingdom of God will be complete when ____.

a. Jesus comes again

b. we recite the Lord's Prayer

c. everyone has enough food

d. the Bible is finished

6. By supporting workers in Poland, Pope Saint John Paul II showed ____.

a. hope

b. pride

c. solidarity

d. charity

7. ____ is called the perfect prayer because it sums up the message of the Gospels.

a. The Mass

b. The Lord's Prayer

c. The Hail Mary

d. The Glory Be

8. Jesus compares the Kingdom of God to a mustard seed that ____.

a. withers in the sun

b. becomes food for everyone

c. grows and spreads

d. falls on poor soil

Write a response on the lines below.

9. What opportunities to further justice do you see in your everyday life?

_____

_____

10. Why is it important for everyone to work for the Kingdom of God?

_____

_____

Name _____   Date _____

Encouraging Changes

Identify a couple of situations in your school that take away from the dignity of others.

Situation: _____

How it robs people of dignity: _____

Why people would act this way: _____

Situation: _____

How it robs people of dignity: _____

Why people would act this way: _____

Select one of the situations. Complete the rest of the sheet with this situation in mind.

Define the situation: _____

_____

Tell specific reasons why what is happening is wrong: _____

_____

List possible ways of resolving this situation directly (for example, go to the people involved and
ask them to stop). _____

_____

_____

List ways of resolving the situation indirectly (for example, distract people from the situation by
scheduling another activity). _____

_____

_____

Would it be better to resolve this situation directly or indirectly? Why? _____

_____

_____

Now make a plan of action to stop the harmful situation. _____

_____

_____

Act with Justice

💙 Let Us Pray

Leader: Jesus, give us the wisdom to learn about our faith and the courage to live our faith. Help us bring your message of hope to the world.

"Justice and judgment are the foundation of your throne; mercy and faithfulness march before you." **Psalm 89:15**

All: Jesus, guide us to hear your voice and to act with justice.

📖 Scripture

The LORD rules forever,
  has set up his throne for judgment.

It is he who judges the world with justice,
  who judges the peoples with fairness.

The LORD is a stronghold for the oppressed,
  a stronghold in times of trouble.

Those who know your name trust in you; you
  never forsake those who seek you, LORD. ...

To you the helpless can entrust their cause; you
  are the defender of orphans. ...

You win justice for the orphaned and oppressed;
  no one on earth will cause terror again.
  Psalm 9:8–11, 10:14, 18

Have you ever thought...

- What would a just world be like?
- What do we owe to other people who are in need?

303

© Our Sunday Visitor

📖 Scripture Background

Scripture Reflection Process

Invite the students to be still, close their eyes, and focus on their breathing. Encourage them to open their minds and hearts to what God is saying to them.

- Proclaim the Scripture and have the students sit in silence.
- *Ask:* What did you hear God say to you today?
- Allow volunteers to share.

▶ You may play instrumental music to begin the reflection.

Objective

- Reflect on God's personal invitation through Scripture

OPEN _____

💙 Let Us Pray

Invite the students to gather in the prayer space and make the Sign of the Cross. Proclaim the opening prayer and Psalm verse, and lead the class in the response.

Have the students move out of the prayer space and back to their seats.

Explain that it is not enough to believe; we need to act on what we believe. Our Lord is a just Lord, and he loves just deeds.

Say: Justice is at the heart of a disciple. Jesus calls his disciples to see as he sees so that injustice can be named and challenged through words and actions. Let's take a glimpse into what God's Kingdom is like.

📖 Scripture

Guide the students through the process of Scripture reflection (see the Scripture Background box to the left).

Have you ever thought...

Say: The Bible makes it very clear that we are not only to recognize Jesus in those who are in need, but also to help them. This helps to build up the Kingdom of God.

- Invite the students to respond to the questions.

DAY 1

Objective

- Indicate prior knowledge of chapter concepts and vocabulary

BUILD _____

Use this page to assess the students' knowledge related to the chapter content.

Getting Started

Ask a volunteer to read aloud the introductory paragraph.

- Allow students to share some of what they already know about the Kingdom of God.

What Is Justice?

★ Have the students fill in the chart by using words, terms, or phrases that describe justice.

- Explain that each phrase or word they add should begin with a letter from the word *justice*.

- Point out the example that has already been filled in.

- Invite volunteers to share a word or phrase with the class.

Getting Started

In this chapter, you will learn about what it means to live in the Kingdom of God. You will also learn ways that you can serve and attitudes you need in order to be part of God's Kingdom.

Catholic Faith Words
• justice
• peace
• solidarity

Fill in the chart with words or phrases that describe justice. Use the letter at the beginning of the line as the first letter of your words, terms or phrases. One has been done for you.

	What Is Justice?
J	_____
U	_____
S	_____
T	_____
I	_____
C	ompassion: show kindness and care for others.
E	_____

✔ Teaching Tip

Faith through Action

To illustrate how we should aid people who are in need, or our responsibility to them, share a story about someone you know who lives his or her faith through action. This is an example of someone who embodies the value of justice or the promotion of human dignity.

Provide the students with stories of people who have lived a life of justice. Let them summarize, in groups, some of the things they can learn from these examples and report back to the rest of the class.

WRITE

Fair or Just? Recall a situation in which you or someone you know was treated unfairly. Record the story in the space below. Then tell why you think it was unfair.

_____

_____

_____

_____

_____

_____

_____

_____

Record three situations or issues in the world that you know have changed because people have cried out for justice.

1. _____

2. _____

3. _____

Explain what you think the differences are between what is fair and what is just.

_____

_____

_____

_____

_____

_____

_____

_____

_____

_____

Act with Justice **305**

Work with Words

Point out the Catholic Faith Words box on page 304.

- Ask the students to review the three Catholic Faith Words.
- As a class, discuss how these three words relate to one another and see if the students can relate them to our mission to help God build his Kingdom.
- Remind them that this chapter will provide them with more information on these terms.

CLOSE _____

ACTIVITY

Read aloud the activity instructions.

- Have the students work independently to respond to the prompts.
- Allow a few volunteers to share their stories or other answers with the class.

Optional Activity

Activity Master 20: Encouraging Changes

Distribute copies of the activity found on teacher page 303G.

- This activity will help the students reflect on how they can actually be a part of accomplishing changes.
- Give them incentive to be thoughtful in their responses by asking if you can share appropriate suggestions with the school administration or with another school.

DAY 2

Objectives

- Define justice as giving what is due to God and what is due to others as children of God made in his image and possessing equal human dignity
- Discover that to live in God's Kingdom, people must choose to believe, to have faith, and to make the necessary changes in their lives

OPEN _____

❤ Invite the students to pray the Morning Prayer from page 386.

Direct them to look at the images on pages 306 and 307.

Ask: How do you think these images connect with the chapter?

BUILD _____

All Are Invited

Review the text with the students.

- Facilitate a discussion around these questions: What does the word *justice* mean to you? What feelings do you get when you hear or see the word?
- Read the definition in the Catholic Faith Words box.
- Point out that justice is not necessarily related to legal issues, but to everyday situations involving equality.

📖 Go to the Source

Have a student locate and read aloud Luke 4:14–22 to discover where Jesus announced his mission and how his followers responded.

> 📖 **Go to the Source**
> Read *Luke 4:14–22* to discover where Jesus announced his mission and how those who heard him responded.

© Our Sunday Visitor

All Are Invited

What does Jesus offer us?

We all deserve to be treated fairly and to be given the same respect. Jesus told us to "do to others whatever you would have them do to you" (Matthew 7:12). His words and actions remind us that we are equal in God's eyes. We need to show the world by our actions that all people are equal, deserving of what is their due, and worthy of fair treatment.

We all also have the responsibility to make sure that groups of people, society, and its organizations promote human dignity and don't undermine it. Sometimes we have to work to change the way things are so that people can get what they deserve and need. This is the **justice** Jesus taught us: giving God and others what is due to them as children of God made in his image, and possessing equal human dignity.

306   Chapter 20

On a Mission

It is the Father's will that Jesus bring the Kingdom of Heaven to life right here on Earth. "The kingdom of God is at hand," Jesus said as he began his ministry. "Repent, and believe in the gospel" (Mark 1:15).

But what is God's Kingdom? It's not a physical location, or a fairy tale. The Kingdom of God, sometimes called the Kingdom of Heaven, or the Reign of God, is God's rule of peace, justice, and love that exists in Heaven, but has not yet come in its fullness on Earth. Jesus invited everyone to the Kingdom. All that's required is that people choose to believe, to

> **Catholic Faith Words**
>
> **justice** the constant and firm desire to give God and other people what is their due as children of God made in his image and possessing equal human dignity

---

📖 Scripture Background

Jesus Begins His Ministry

This passage from Luke (4:14–22) begins Christ's public life in Nazareth. The quotations from Isaiah show that he views his role as bringing justice to those who cannot achieve it on their own.

- The "year acceptable to the Lord" mentioned in verse 19 is the jubilee year. A jubilee year occurred every 50 years; the custom was to forgive debts and free slaves.
- The people of Nazareth are somewhat incredulous that Jesus is preaching. Their reactions prompt Jesus to remark that prophets are often unappreciated by those who know them best.

have faith, and to make a change in their lives and the way they look at the world and others.

Jesus came to teach us about the Kingdom of God. At the beginning of his ministry, he made it clear that he had fulfilled the words of the prophet Isaiah: that he had come to bring the Good News to the poor, to proclaim liberty to captives, recovery of sight to the blind, and to free the oppressed. (See Luke 4:14–22.)

> In what ways did Jesus do the things he said he had come to do?

Making It Real

Jesus reached out to people whom most leaders in his time would have pushed away: women, children, lepers, and especially those who were poor and in need. He challenged society and those in authority to act justly themselves, and to change the attitudes and structures that kept people from having what they needed to live.

An important attitude of the Kingdom is that we prefer God to all else. We put God first in our lives, and working for the Kingdom seems second nature. Through his parables and other teachings, Jesus tells us that words are not enough to enter the Kingdom. Our actions need to show that we believe and are working toward what is just, peaceful, and loving. The Kingdom and justice are so closely tied that you can't have one without the other. That's something Jesus showed us.

Underline the things Jesus came to do, and what our actions need to be in order to live for the Kingdom.

Think of someone in your community who has made it his or her life's work to help others. How does this person's work help solve poverty, end hunger, or fight injustice? How does he or she put God first in life? List two things you could do to help this person.

I could help

_____

by:

_____
_____
_____
_____
_____
_____
_____
_____
_____
_____

Optional Activity

Goats and Sheep *Verbal/Linguistic, Interpersonal*

Arrange the students in groups of three. Have each group read Matthew 25:31–36.

- Instruct the groups to look online for six headlines that would be "sheep-worthy" and six that would be "goat-worthy."
- Gather all of the groups' headlines and compile one complete list for the goats and one for the sheep.
- Ask another student to find sound effects of a goat and a sheep online. Record it. Then give each student one of the headlines and after he or she reads it, play the appropriate sound effect.
- *Ask:* What does it take to change from a goat to a sheep?

On a Mission

Create a word web with *Kingdom of God* in the center. After the class silently reads the text, which starts on page 306, have them add phrases about the Kingdom to the web.

- Discuss the question at the end of this section.
- ★ As you read this section and the next, have the students underline what Jesus came to do and what we must do to live for the Kingdom of God.

Making It Real

Remind the students that words are easy to say but sometimes it's hard to follow up with actions.

- *Ask:* Why are the Kingdom of God and justice so closely related? Possible response: Justice begins with love and leads to peace, all signs of God's Kingdom.

CLOSE _____

ACTIVITY

Have the students work with a classmate to complete the activity.

- Compile the students' responses on the board or on chart paper, then determine whether the class can do any of the suggestions.

Quick Review We must work to change the world so that everyone has what they need and have a right to as a person created in God's image; we must work for justice. By working for justice, we are working for God's Kingdom. We must choose to believe, have faith, and treat others in loving, peaceful, and just ways in order to help build up God's Kingdom.

DAY 3

Objective

- Identify people of the Kingdom of God by the actions that work toward what is just, peaceful, and loving

OPEN

 Invite the students to form a circle in the prayer space. Have them pray the Lord's Prayer from page 383, then offer a sign of peace.

Read aloud the opening question and elicit responses from the class.

BUILD

Not Yet Complete

Challenge the students by reading the first two sentences in the text and discussing possible answers before returning to the rest of the text for answers. Continue reading.

- Point out the definition of *peace* in the Catholic Faith Words box on page 309.

- *Ask*: How can we help bring about peace? Possible response: by living as God intended

📖 Scripture

Invite a student to read aloud Matthew 13:31–32.

The Kingdom Grows

Say: Jesus lived in a remote area long ago, yet his words and actions continue to influence people today.

Have a student read the paragraph.

- Discuss the two questions as a class.

Red and blue and yellow macaws rest on a branch in a rainforest

Not Yet Complete

How can we work with God as he builds his Kingdom?

If Jesus came to proclaim and witness to God's Kingdom, why isn't the world a place of perfect **peace**, love, and justice? Why does so much injustice still exist? It's because the Kingdom is here, but it's not yet complete. Jesus gave us the Church to continue his mission and work. At the Second Coming, when Christ comes again in his glory at the end of time to judge the living and the dead, then the Kingdom will be complete and all creation will be fulfilled.

The Kingdom Grows

The amazing thing about the Kingdom of God is that it's meant to grow and expand. Jesus once told this parable to help his followers understand the Kingdom.

📖 Scripture

"The kingdom of heaven is like a mustard seed that a person took and sowed in a field. It is the smallest of all the seeds, yet when full-grown it is the largest of plants. It becomes a large bush, and the 'birds of the sky come and dwell in its branches.'"
Matthew 13:31–32

But how does the Kingdom grow? It grows by God's presence and work and the ways we work with him to spread the Gospel message. What an amazing idea: Jesus sends us on a mission to bring his life and love to others, just like he sent the first disciples.

> How do you think the Kingdom has grown since Jesus' time?

> How can you continue to be a sign of God's Kingdom?

308 Chapter 20

Optional Activity

Globalization of Christianity *Visual/Spatial, Interpersonal*

Organize the students into small groups. Give each group a world map, and assign a part of the world to each group. Tell the students to use library resources to find out how and when Christianity came to that part of the world.

- Have the groups record their findings on the maps.

- Invite them to share their information with the rest of the class.

- As a class, discuss the global spread of Christianity.

Catholic Faith Words

peace a state of calm and harmony when things are in their proper order and people settle problems with kindness and justice

So What Should We Do?

We need to say and do things that reflect God's love, peace, and justice. We can start with our family and friends. How do we respond to their needs? Are we trustworthy? Do we tell them the truth even when it might be difficult? Do we consider how our choices will affect them? When we make the wrong decisions, we affect others, perhaps even taking away from their dignity. We can avoid saying hurtful things during tense conversations as a way to prevent conflicts.

There's a lot we can do in our immediate circle, but then we need to take it a step further. We realize that social justice comes about by people working together.

Our parishes make choices to do good, to participate in activities that treat people fairly, and to take a stand for what is right regarding local, national, and global issues. The Church has many nonprofit agencies and organizations that look out for others and seek to change what harms others and keeps them from following Jesus. In all of these activities, the Church trusts that the Holy Spirit leads us where we need to be.

CATHOLICS TODAY

We can cooperate with God as he builds his Kingdom, including praying for it to come. We do this when we pray the Lord's Prayer: "Thy kingdom come, thy will be done on earth as it is in heaven." This prayer is made up of praise, hope, petition, and a desire for goodness.

- We begin by giving glory to God, our Father. We praise the goodness of his name. We ask the Father to build up his Kingdom and that he join our will to his to fulfill his plan of salvation for all.

- We follow this by asking God for what we need to help make his Kingdom spread. We need "daily bread"—not just food to eat, but also the love and joy that keep us going. We ask God not only to forgive our sins, but also to help us forgive those who have hurt us.

The Lord's Prayer is often called the perfect prayer because it captures the message of the Gospels. Praying to our Father should make our hearts more trusting and humble, and at the same time inspire a desire to be more like God. For the full text of the Lord's Prayer, see page 383 in the Our Catholic Tradition section of your book.

DESIGN

Work in small groups to design a collage of signs of the Kingdom in your local community. Use photos cut from magazines or newspapers, or create your own drawings. Write captions to describe how the images are signs of God's love, peace, and justice.

Act with Justice **309**

Liturgy Link

The Lord's Prayer

The Lord's Prayer, the central prayer of Christians, was given to us by Jesus. The prayer itself is in the form of seven petitions; the first three honor God, and the remainder ask for blessings from him. It is repeated at the beginning of the Communion Rite of the Mass, literally asking for the bread of life that we will soon receive. The use of "Our Father" at the beginning of the prayer is especially symbolic when we pray it within the context of the Mass and as we are gathered with our family of faith.

So What Should We Do?

Have a few volunteers read this section to the class.

- *Ask:* What are some ways that you and those you know are working for the Kingdom of God?

Emphasize the power of prayer as you lead the students into a review of the Catholics Today feature.

- Ask a strong reader to read aloud the entire section.

- Invite volunteers to share two or three important points from this text.

CLOSE

ACTIVITY

Divide the students into small groups to complete their Kingdom collages.

- Provide them with magazines or newspapers, scissors, glue, and poster board or chart paper.

- Be sure to allow enough time for each group to present their collage to the class.

Quick Review Members of the Kingdom of God must continue to nurture and work toward positive changes in the world. When we work toward what is just, peaceful, and loving, we help to build up the Kingdom of God.

DAY 4

Objectives

- Explain why solidarity is a Christian virtue
- Describe how being poor in spirit can be connected to the Tenth Commandment

OPEN

Invite the students to gather in the prayer space. Pray together the Beatitudes from page 374.

Point out the question at the start of the text.

BUILD

Living for the Kingdom

Summarize the text:

- Competing and consuming often overshadow what is truly important in our lives.
- We can appreciate God's power and Jesus' role as our teacher and our leader in the Resurrection.

Go to the Source

Ask a student to read Luke 18:18–30, which tells what Jesus said about detaching ourselves from our riches.

- Have the class brainstorm a list of riches and discuss whether these things are hard or easy to give up.
- Record the list on the board or on chart paper.

Our Brothers' and Sisters' Keepers

Write the word *solidarity* on the board.

- Ask the students what the word means and what feelings surface when they hear it.

> **Go to the Source**
> Read *Luke 18:18–30.* Jesus teaches that we must detach ourselves from our riches if we want to enter the Kingdom of God. Discuss what your riches are, how difficult or easy it is to give them up, and where you might start simplifying your lifestyle.

Living for the Kingdom

What attitudes reflect God's Kingdom?

You can't fight City Hall. . .Whoever gets the most toys, wins. . . Bigger is better. . . If you can't beat 'em, join 'em.

We hear messages like these a lot, whether it's on social media sites or in real life. Sometimes the lines blur, and our lives become too much like a video game or a reality show. Often, competing and consuming become more important than cooperating. In the struggle for money, popularity, and power, many good people get chewed up and spit out. Maybe you've heard this message: *Nice guys finish last.* Is that what happened to Jesus?

We know better than that. Through his Death on the Cross and his Resurrection, Jesus accomplished the coming of his Kingdom. Some people might see a crucifix and think that Jesus failed. We know that Jesus won the ultimate battle when he defeated death itself by rising to new life.

Our Brothers' and Sisters' Keepers

Our Church teaches that government and business leaders must respect people's fundamental rights and also the conditions that let them use their rights. Everyone has a right to life and to the necessities of life such as food, clothing, shelter, medicine, and education. People have the right to vote, speak freely, own property, and run their own businesses. If governments or businesses don't let people have these rights, the Church speaks out. Ultimately, "We must obey God rather than men" (Acts 5:29).

Solidarity is a word our Church uses to describe unity with all of our brothers and sisters throughout the world. In solidarity, we practice the sharing of spiritual and material goods. It encourages us to be generous and to live simply, so that others might be blessed with our generosity. Solidarity is a Christian principle that motivates us to share our spiritual gifts, even more so than our material ones.

Objects and people, even the ones you love or who love you the most, are no substitute for God. Life is freer and simpler when you

Catholic Faith Words

solidarity a Christian principle that motivates believers to share their spiritual gifts as well as their material ones

Scripture Background

Luke 18:18–30

In this passage, a wealthy man asks how he can enter Heaven. After hearing that the man has observed the Commandments governing relationships with others, Jesus challenges the man to sell his worldly goods and follow him. The man reacts with sadness, and Jesus says that it is harder for a rich man to enter Heaven than for a camel to pass through the eye of a needle. As the crowd wonders whether a rich person can ever enter Heaven, Jesus affirms God's willingness to save everyone who has lost earthly goods for the sake of the Kingdom. The lesson here is that by giving away worldly goods, we are making ourselves more dependent upon God and less dependent on things.

The Catholic Church calls for acts of justice around the world. A brave example of this happened in the 1980s when Pope Saint John Paul II showed his support for a workers' movement called "Solidarity" in his native Poland. He encouraged workers to rise up for their rights. This led to new freedom in Poland and eventually contributed to the end of oppressive governments throughout Eastern Europe, including Russia. Even today, Pope Francis continues this mission of the Church by speaking out against injustice.

Pope John Paul II with President Lech Walesa, leader of the Polish Solidarity movement

make God's love your true goal. Believing in God makes it possible for you to put him, not things or accomplishments, first in your life.

In the Beatitudes found in the Gospel according to Matthew, Jesus teaches us: "Blessed are the poor in spirit, for theirs is the kingdom of heaven" (Matthew 5:3). Poor in spirit doesn't mean not having money. Even rich people can be poor in spirit. It means that we humans cannot make money or riches into a god, but we need to depend on the one true God for strength and guidance.

The Tenth Commandment teaches us:

- to be glad for others' good fortune and not envious of them
- not to be jealous of the things others have
- not to be greedy or overly concerned about power or being in charge (See Exodus 20:17.)

It's sometimes difficult not to want what others have. But we can keep things in perspective. Prayer, goodwill toward others, and trusting in God's care of us help us resist envy.

IN SUMMARY   Catholics Believe

Jesus made justice a priority. It was central to his teaching on God's Kingdom for which we all long.

- Jesus welcomes all people to God's Kingdom of love, peace, and justice. As his followers, we have to show others we are called to give God and others their due, respecting the dignity of all, and work to end hunger, poverty, and injustice.

- God's Kingdom is present but not yet complete. We prepare for and work toward the Kingdom through worship and prayer, sharing Jesus' Good News, just action, and advocacy for those in need.
- We need to rely on God, trust in his care, and have the right attitude toward money and things. Doing so helps us concentrate on what's important and work for the rights of others.

Act with Justice   **311**

Optional Activity

Solidarity   *Verbal/Linguistic, Interpersonal*

The rise of the Solidarity Union in Poland in the last quarter of the twentieth century was one of the greatest examples in history of victory over oppression.

- Encourage the students to use library resources and/or the Internet to research Lech Walesa's leadership of this union.
- Other students may wish to investigate the support Pope Saint John Paul II gave to the union in his native land.
- Ask them to share their findings with the rest of the class.

Our Brothers' and Sisters' Keepers, *continued*

Read aloud the first two paragraphs on page 310.

- Direct the students' attention to the definition of *solidarity* in the Catholic Faith Words box.

Review the rest of this text, pointing out how "being poor in spirit" ties in to the Tenth Commandment.

- Invite the students to highlight the sentence that tells what helps us resist envy.

Ask: What are some examples of solidarity in your everyday lives? Possible responses: working in a study group, helping with parish activities, assisting younger siblings with homework

Call attention to the Where It Happened feature and discuss the text with the class.

Point out the photo of Pope Saint John Paul II and invite the students to share some extra facts they know about this Pope.

CLOSE _____

In Summary

Go over the summary statements with the class.

- Ask if anyone has any further questions on these important points.

DAY 5

Objectives

- Connect social media with sharing the Church's message
- Explore the faith life of Pope Leo XIII
- Offer the Prayer of Petition

OPEN _____

♥ Ask the students to quietly reflect on the good people and organizations that are helping to build up God's Kingdom and to say a private prayer of thanksgiving for them.

BUILD _____

Our Catholic Life

Share the information in this feature.

- Brainstorm, as a class, some answers to the question.

People of Faith

Explain that Pope Leo XIII did much to help keep the Church alive and to help build God's Kingdom.

- Ask a volunteer to read aloud the People of Faith paragraph.
- Share the content in the People of Faith Background box with the class.
- *Say*: Following the example of Jesus in his pursuit of justice and peace, Leo used his diplomatic skills to help settle troubles between nations and within nations.

Our Catholic Life

With all the ways we have to share our reactions to what people are doing and thinking, as well as our opinions on local and worldwide events, with people around the world on **social media** sites, it can be hard to know when to hold back on those reactions or even sometimes exactly what to say. The Catholic Church has an important role in sharing her messages and views on events in a way that makes clear she is Christ's Church, and that her members are able to act as good examples, both online and off. Pope Francis shares the Church's message regularly online, and offers a role model for how to communicate it. The next time you post a status, think about the message you are sending. Does it reflect well on you as a member of the Church?

> What is one thing you could share online this week about the Catholic Church?

People of Faith

Pope Leo XIII, 1878–1903

Gioacchino Vincenzo Raffaele Luigi Pecci witnessed political and social upheavals and helped define the role of the modern Church. His papacy, as Leo XIII, helped the Church survive a stormy period in history. Following the example of Jesus in his pursuit of justice and peace, Leo helped settle troubles between nations and within nations, including helping end the persecution of Catholics in Germany. By the time of Leo's death, he was already regarded as one of the greatest Popes of all time.

📶 For more, go to **aliveinchrist.osv.com**

IDENTIFY

Think about an issue that concerns you. Write your response to these decision-making steps.

See an issue that gets me thinking

_____

Judge what I've learned from the news

_____

What Jesus and the Church say

_____

Act on things I can do

_____
_____
_____

312

People of Faith Background

Pope Leo XIII

Here are some additional details on Pope Leo XIII:

- Drawing upon his diplomatic experience as a papal legate to Belgium, Pope Leo XIII helped guide the government of that nation and others down the path of justice and religious tolerance.

- As Germany unified under Otto von Bismarck, Pope Leo XIII helped Bismarck win the much-needed support of the nation's Catholics in exchange for ending Kulturkampf (the persecution of Catholics).

📶 Encourage the students to go to **aliveinchrist.osv.com** at home to learn more about Pope Leo XIII.

❤ A Prayer of Petition

Leader: Lord Jesus, we know that you came to establish the Kingdom of God here on Earth. You wanted God's rule of peace and justice to take root among us. You wanted everyone to welcome and live in this Kingdom, which you also called the Kingdom of Heaven. You came to bring Good News to the poor, proclaim liberty to the captives, and to heal people. You have called us, and all of your followers, to continue your Kingdom work. But, as Blessed Mother Teresa of Calcutta said in her prayer, this Kingdom work is hard. It is often rejected or unappreciated. Give us the strength—as you gave Mother Teresa—to "do it anyway." Let's pray Mother Teresa's prayer:

Side 1: People are often unreasonable, irrational, and self-centered. Forgive them anyway.

Side 2: If you are kind, people may accuse you of selfish, ulterior motives. Be kind anyway.

Side 1: If you are successful, you will win some unfaithful friends and some genuine enemies. Succeed anyway.

Side 2: If you are honest and sincere, people may deceive you. Be honest and sincere anyway.

Side 1: What you spend years creating, others could destroy overnight. Create anyway.

Side 2: If you find serenity and happiness, some may be jealous. Be happy anyway.

Side 1: The good you do today will often be forgotten. Do good anyway.

Side 2: Give the best you have, and it will never be enough. Give your best anyway.

Leader: "In the final analysis," Mother Teresa wrote, "it is between you and God. It was never between you and them anyway." We know, Jesus, that your Kingdom is not fully established among us. As young Catholics, we too have the responsibility to work for justice. When each of us tries to live, speak, and share with charity and respect, we help people see God's Kingdom in our midst.

Take turns praying for the works of justice that each of you can do, for example: "Lord, give me the courage to confront those who bully and speak up for those who are victims of bullying."

All: Lord, even if this is hard, help us to do it anyway. Amen.

▶ *Sing or play "We Will Follow"*

Act with Justice **313**

🛜 Go to **aliveinchrist.osv.com** for an interactive review.

A Work with Words **Circle the letter of the choice that best completes the sentence.**

1. ___ gives God and other people what is due to them as children of God made in his image and possessing equal human dignity.
   a. Tolerance   c. Patience
   (b.) Justice   d. Kindness

2. Solidarity is a Christian ___ that motivates believers to share their spiritual gifts as well as their material ones.
   a. prayer   (c.) principle
   b. tradition   d. law

3. To ___ means to be sorry for our sins and change our ways.
   a. anoint   (c.) repent
   b. pray   d. rehabilitate

4. The Kingdom of God is God's rule of love, ___, and justice in our hearts, lives, and the world. This Kingdom exists in Heaven, but has not yet come in its fullness on Earth.
   (a.) peace   c. holiness
   b. repentance   d. mission

B Check Understanding **Complete each sentence with the correct term from the Word Bank.**

Rosary	Kingdom
sin	Lord's Prayer
salvation	envious
justice	mustard seed

5. The Tenth Commandment teaches us not to be ____**envious**____ of what others have and accomplish.

6. Hunger, poverty, and injustice all come from ____**sin**____.

7. When Christ comes again, the ____**Kingdom**____ of God will be complete.

8. In a parable, Jesus tells us that the Kingdom of Heaven is like a ____**mustard seed**____.

9. Jesus showed us that you cannot have the Kingdom without ____**justice**____.

10. The ____**Lord's Prayer**____ is often called the perfect prayer because it sums up the message of the Gospels.

C Make Connections **On a separate sheet of paper, write a one-paragraph response to the question: How does the Lord's Prayer connect with your life? Write the prayer one line at a time. Below each line, write what it means for you right now.**

Have the students read the instructions and work through the activity on their own.

CLOSE_____

A Prayer of Petition

❤ Appoint a strong reader to serve as the leader; divide the rest of the class into two sections: Side 1 and Side 2. Let everyone review their parts.

Tell the students to bring their textbooks as you invite them to process into the prayer space.

Say: Dear God, you instilled in us the vision of your Kingdom. Help us work for its presence on Earth.

Follow the order of prayer on the student page.

▶ Conclude by inviting the students to sing or reflect on the song "We Will Follow," downloaded from **aliveinchrist.osv.com**.

CHAPTER REVIEW

Review the instructions for each section and have the students complete the review.

🛜 Go to **aliveinchrist.osv.com** to prepare customized and downloadable assessments, send eAssessments, and assign interactive reviews.

KEY CONCEPT

By his Death and Resurrection, Jesus makes it possible for believers to have eternal life—life with God forever.

DOCTRINAL CONTENT

- The raising of Lazarus showed that Jesus had power over death. Jesus' Resurrection makes it possible for us to have a life with God forever and gives us hope for our future. (CCC, 988–991, 1021)

- We will be judged at our death based upon the ways we have accepted and acted on God's grace in our lives. (CCC, 1051)

- At the end of time, Jesus will come to judge both the living and the dead and to bring the Kingdom of God in its full glory. (CCC 1036, 1038–1042)

- The Corporal and Spiritual Works of Mercy are actions that are expected of us as members of the Church and disciples of Christ. (CCC 1473, 2447)

TASKS OF CATECHESIS

Helping children grow in a faith that is "known, celebrated, lived, and expressed in prayer" (NDC, 20).

This chapter focuses on the following tasks of catechesis:

- Promoting Knowledge of the Faith

- Moral Formation

Teacher Background

In hope we were saved. Now hope that sees for itself is not hope. For who hopes for what one sees? But if we hope for what we do not see, we wait with endurance … We know that all things work for good for those who love God, who are called according to his purpose. Romans 8:24–25, 28

> **Reflect** In what ways do you wait with hope for God's Kingdom?

Many of us would prefer not to think of Jesus as a judge. It doesn't seem to fit the image of him that so many of us have formed—mild, gentle, merciful. But it is important to remember that Jesus was also passionate about justice, and when that passion was aroused, he was more than capable of expressing righteous anger. The one thing that appeared to anger him more than anything else was when people in power used their advantage to oppress the poor and the weak. Jesus promised that he will return to Earth as judge at the end of time, and when he does, justice will reign for all.

In the Parable of the Last Judgment in Matthew 25, Jesus equates how we treat others with how we treat him. More importantly, he connects eternal salvation with that recognition: those who served others in need (the sheep) are saved, while those who ignored the needs of their fellow human beings (the goats) are condemned. This story teaches a profound truth about salvation, that our task as disciples is not only to be Christ for others but also to see Christ in others.

> **Reflect** How is the desire for justice reflected in your life and ministry?

Teacher's Prayer

♡ Father, Son, and Holy Spirit, you have guided me to be a teacher, and I thank you. May all I do reflect your glory, and may my strongest desire be to serve you. Thank you for the hope and the promise that I will live with you forever. Amen.

How Seventh Graders Understand Chapter Topics

Many seventh graders have a works-based idea of salvation (i.e., "If I'm good enough, I'll go to Heaven" or "Evil people go to Hell."). A more complex and more accurate concept is that those who have a relationship with Jesus will naturally do loving things. This gives hope to students who feel like they can't be "good enough," and it challenges those who might become prideful or judgmental.

Teaching Tip: Emphasize that in the story of Christ separating the sheep and the goats, he says to the goats, "I never knew you." Ask the students how we are influenced by those we know well. How would this translate to a relationship with Jesus?

Sharing the Message with Seventh Graders

- Seventh graders are becoming aware, in a personal way, of their own mortality. This can be frightening, but it can also provide an avenue for teaching about eternal life.
- Young people at this age are likely to experience the deaths of family members (in particular grandparents and other older relatives) in ways they have not before.
- Students this age need caring adults to help them process these losses and look at them through the lens of faith.

ONLINE RESOURCES

🛜 Go to **aliveinchrist.osv.com**

You will find:

- Interactive lesson planning, additional activities, and ideas for the classroom environment
- Step by step lesson instruction from printed Teacher Edition for integrated lesson planning
- Custom-built assessments to download and eAssessment links
- Interactive reviews that provide scores and the option to review answers
- Chapter-specific Lectionary connections and a complete correlation ordered by the Sundays of the year, with suggestions for how to integrate the Scripture readings into chapter lessons

🛜 Go to **osvparish.com** for Ask the Experts Q and A, Community Connections, and Blogs.

Chapter 21 Planner

Objectives	Open
DAY 1—Invite/Preview, Pages 315–317	
• Reflect on God's personal invitation through Scripture • Indicate prior knowledge of chapter concepts and vocabulary	♡ **Psalm 13:6** Pray the opening prayer. 📖 **Romans 8:22–25, 28** Proclaim "Destiny of Glory." Guide the students through the process of Scripture reflection. • Discuss Have You Ever Thought questions.
DAY 2—Discover, Pages 318–319	
• Explore how the raising of Lazarus showed that Jesus had power over humanity's greatest fear—death • Discuss why Jesus' Resurrection gives us hope for our future	♡ Pray the **Act of Hope**, page 387. • Point out the lesson title.
DAY 3—Discover, Pages 320–321	
• Express the Church's teaching on Heaven, Hell, and Purgatory • Explain how our life on Earth affects our destiny for eternity	♡ Pray the last stanza of the **Nicene Creed**, page 367. • Discuss the opening question.
DAY 4—Discover, Pages 322–323	
• Describe the Last Judgment • Explain the significance of the Works of Mercy in relationship to eternal life	♡ Pray the **Glory Be**, page 383. • Discuss the opening question.
DAY 5—Live, Pages 324–325	
• Discuss All Souls Day • Explore the faith life of Saint Francis de Sales • Offer the prayer using Psalm 23	♡ Pray the **Act of Faith**, page 387.

REVIEW AND ASSESSMENT

Chapter Review, page 326
Chapter Test, page 315F

📶 **aliveinchrist.osv.com** Customize and Download Assessments, Email Links to eAssessments, Interactive Student Reviews

Build	Close	Materials & Resources
• Present lesson highlights. • Preview **Catholic Faith Words**. ★ The students will share what they know about Heaven, Hell, and Purgatory.	• Activity The students will consider what kind of person they want to be. • Optional Activity Remembering the Departed (Activity Master 21)	☐ pencils or pens ☐ Activity Master 21 (Page 315G)
• Share the story of Jesus and Lazarus. ▱ Read and reflect on John 11:1–44. • Explain that Jesus' Resurrection allows us to be hopeful for our own eternal life.	• Activity Brainstorm why the Saints give us hope for eternal life. • Conclude with a review of key concepts and objectives.	☐ pencils or pens ☐ Bibles
• **Catholic Faith Words** Heaven, Hell, Particular Judgment, Purgatory ▱ Read Luke 23:42–43. • Discuss what will happen during Particular Judgment.	• Activity List behaviors that lead to disobeying God and those that help strengthen our relationship with him. • Conclude with a review of key concepts and objectives.	☐ pencils or pens ☐ board or chart paper
• **Catholic Faith Words** Last Judgment, Works of Mercy ▱ Read Matthew 25:31–46. • Talk about the Works of Mercy and how they please Jesus. ★ List examples of ways to live the Works of Mercy.	• Review the In Summary statements.	☐ pencils or pens ☐ board or chart paper
• Discuss the question in the Our Catholic Life section. • Learn about Saint Francis de Sales. • Activity Name ways to become a more hope-filled person.	• Separate the class into two sides. • Follow the order of prayer. ▶ Sing or reflect on the closing song.	☐ pencils or pens 🛜 "My Sheep"

Chapter Connections

FORMING CATHOLIC IDENTITY ACROSS THE CURRICULUM

To integrate the Catholic faith in all aspects of curriculum, this chapter's objectives can be reinforced and applied in the instruction of other disciplines.

Go to **aliveinchrist.osv.com** for cross-curricular activities and projects linked to the doctrinal content discussed in this unit. Activities are available from among the following knowledge categories and content areas:

Language Arts

- Integration of Knowledge
- Literacy
- Speaking and Listening
- Writing Skills

Math

- Algebraic Thinking
- Geometry
- Measurement and Data
- Numbers and Operations

Science

- Earth Science
- Life Science
- Physical Science
- Technology

Social Studies

- Civics
- Economics
- Geography
- History

NCEA IFG: ACRE Edition

Knowledge of the Faith

- **Objective:** To know and understand basic Catholic teaching about the Incarnate Word Jesus Christ as the way, truth, and life

Moral Formation

- **Objective:** To be knowledgeable about the teachings of Jesus and the Church as the basis of Christian morality and to understand Catholic Social Teaching

Catholic Faith Literacy

final judgment, Heaven, Hell, Purgatory, redemption, Resurrection, salvation

Catholic Social Teaching

To integrate Catholic Social Teaching into your lesson, choose one of the following features: Life and Dignity of the Human Person, pages 334–335; or Care for God's Creation, pages 346–347.

- Start the Live step of the process by talking about Saint Francis de Sales on page 324. Then move directly to the Catholic Social Teaching feature.
- Or, to expand the lesson, complete page 324, then move to the Catholic Social Teaching feature.
- Return to Chapter 21 for the prayer on page 325.

Music Option

Use the following song to enhance catechetical learning or for prayer.

- "My Sheep," Day 5, Page 325

315E Chapter 21

Name _____ Date _____

Complete each sentence with the correct term.

1. The Theological Virtue that helps us look forward to the future is _____.

2. _____ is eternal separation from God because of a choice to turn away from him and not seek forgiveness.

3. _____ is a state of final cleansing after death and before Heaven.

4. The _____ is God's final triumph over evil when Christ will return to judge all of the living and the dead.

Circle the letter of the choice that best completes the sentence or answers the question.

5. The full joy of living eternally in God's presence is ___.

   a. Heaven   c. Hell

   b. Purgatory   d. Earth

6. The ___ are actions that show care for the physical and spiritual needs of others.

   a. Sacraments   c. Works of Mercy

   b. Sacred Chrism   d. Cardinal Virtues

7. Which will NOT happen at the Second Coming of Jesus?

   a. the dead will rise   c. bodies and souls will be united

   b. all humanity will be judged   d. God will recreate the world

8. Which person was raised from the dead by Jesus?

   a. Mary   c. Martha

   b. Lazarus   d. Paul

Write a response on the lines below.

9. Why should knowing about Heaven make us hopeful?

   _____

   _____

   _____

10. What happens during Particular Judgment?

   _____

   _____

Name _____ Date _____

Remembering the Departed

This activity will help you design a memorial prayer card to honor someone who is special to you that has died.

Write the name of the person you wish to remember and to honor with your prayer card:

_____

Write three things that were special about this person:

1. _____

_____

2. _____

_____

3. _____

_____

Write what you will remember most about this person: _____

_____

_____

_____

Explain how you think this person helped to make you a better person (or helped to make the world a better place): _____

_____

_____

_____

Make a prayer card by following the instructions below.

On the front of the card, be sure to include:

• Name of the person you are making the prayer card for

• A picture of this person

On the back of the card, be sure to include:

• His or her date of birth and date of death

• Information about the person's life (use the information you wrote above)

Be prepared to share your prayer card with the class.

Our Reason for Hope

♡ Let Us Pray

Leader: Jesus, by your Death and Resurrection you transformed death into new life. Give us the hope that comes with the Resurrection and the grace to live life as you taught.

"But I trust in your mercy.
    Grant my heart joy in your salvation,
I will sing to the LORD,
    for he has dealt bountifully with me!" **Psalm 13:6**

All: O God, teach us to watch and pray. Teach us to trust in your goodness, and in your plan for us to be with you forever.

 Scripture

"We know that all creation is groaning in labor pains even until now; and not only that, but we ourselves, who have the firstfruits of the Spirit, we also groan within ourselves as we wait for adoption, the redemption of our bodies. For in hope we were saved. Now hope that sees for itself is not hope. For who hopes for what one sees? But if we hope for what we do not see, we wait with endurance …. We know that all things work for good for those who love God, who are called according to his purpose."

Romans 8:22–25, 28

Have you ever thought...
- What does it mean to wait with hope?
- What does it take to get to Heaven?

315

📖 Scripture Background

Scripture Reflection Process

Invite the students to be still, close their eyes, and focus on their breathing. Encourage them to open their minds and hearts to what God is saying to them.

- Proclaim the Scripture and have the students sit in silence.
- *Ask:* What did you hear God say to you today?
- Allow volunteers to share.

▶ You may play instrumental music to begin the reflection.

Objective
- Reflect on God's personal invitation through Scripture

OPEN _____

♡ Let Us Pray

Invite the students to gather in the prayer space and make the Sign of the Cross. Pray the opening of the prayer. Select a few students to read aloud the Psalm verse. Prompt the response from the remainder of the group.

Have the students move out of the prayer space and back to their seats.

Explain that hope comes with the Resurrection of Jesus, the hope of eternal life that Jesus' Death and Resurrection made possible.

Say: Let's listen to God's Word as we are reminded that in hope we are saved, and that there is life beyond death.

📖 Scripture

Guide the students through the process of Scripture reflection (see the Scripture Background box to the left).

Have you ever thought...

Say: We look forward, hope-filled, to the coming of God's Kingdom and to living in eternal happiness with him.

- Invite the students to respond to the questions.

DAY 1

Objective

- Indicate prior knowledge of chapter concepts and vocabulary

BUILD

Use this page to assess the students' knowledge related to the chapter content.

Getting Started

Read this information to your students.

- *Say:* We may wonder where people go when they die, or if we will ever see them again. We may also wonder what it takes to get to Heaven. But Jesus promises us eternal life, and that he will come again.

- Ask the students if they are familiar with the Church's teachings about life after death.

- Encourage them to share what they know.

The Last Things

Invite a volunteer to read the instructions to the class.

★ Give the students time to record what they know about Heaven, Hell, and Purgatory in the chart at the bottom of the page.

- Let volunteers share some of what they know with the class.

- Remind the students that they can add to the chart as they learn more in the chapter. This will be a great study tool for them later.

Getting Started

In this chapter, you will learn about Jesus' promises of eternal life and the meaning of the Second Coming. You will also study the Church's teachings about life after death, and how her members act through the Works of Mercy to show God's Kingdom to the world.

Catholic Faith Words

- Heaven
- Hell
- Particular Judgment
- Purgatory
- Last Judgment
- Works of Mercy

In the web below, record what you know about Heaven, Hell, and Purgatory. Share your ideas with the class. You may add to the web as you study the chapter.

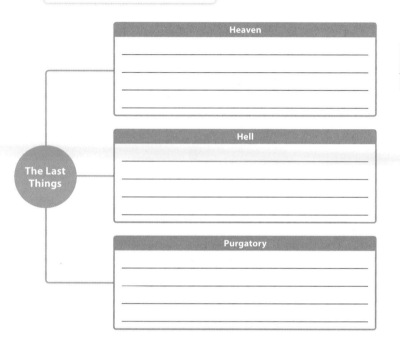

The Last Things

Heaven

Hell

Purgatory

Teaching Tip

Sensitive Issues

This chapter deals with death and the afterlife. For students who have suffered a loss, these topics may be particularly difficult to address.

- Try to be aware of any such losses in the lives of your students. If students show evidence of needing help, find ways of connecting them with trained counselors.

- Learning about the afterlife and Church rituals can comfort the bereaved. Some students may find solace in studying this chapter, while others may struggle with this topic. Your sensitivity and understanding are critical in this discussion.

WRITE

The Person You Want to Be On a gravestone, we often see the years a person was born and died, with a hyphen in between (July 25, 1945– October 30, 1995). Someone once said, "Life is all about what you do in the hyphen." When you think about your life and that it had a beginning and will have an end, what do you hope to do with your hyphen? What kind of person do you want to be?

_____

_____

_____

_____

_____

_____

_____

_____

_____

_____

_____

_____

_____

_____

_____

_____

Work with Words

Point out the vocabulary words on page 316.

- Have a volunteer read aloud all six terms.
- *Ask:* How are all of these words related? They all have to do with Church teachings on life after death.
- Remind the students of the chapter title: "Our Reason for Hope."
- Ask them why Church teachings give us hope.
- Point out that the students will learn more about these terms in the following pages of this chapter.

CLOSE

ACTIVITY

Explain the activity and give the students time to complete it.

- Invite volunteers to share their responses with the class, but only if they feel comfortable doing so.

Optional Activity

Activity Master 21: Remembering the Departed

Distribute copies of the activity found on teacher page 315G.

- This activity will help the students honor special people who have died.
- Allow the students share their memorial cards with the class if they wish to do so.

DAY 2

Objectives

- Explore how the raising of Lazarus showed that Jesus had power over humanity's greatest fear—death

- Discuss why Jesus' Resurrection gives us hope for our future

OPEN

 Have the students bring their books and gather in the prayer space. Begin with the Sign of the Cross, then pray the Act of Hope from page 387. Have the students move back to their seats.

Point out the title of today's lesson.

BUILD

Jesus Gives Us Hope

Invite a volunteer to read aloud the first paragraph.

Scripture

Ask another volunteer to proclaim the reading based on John 11:1–44.

- If time permits, have the students open their Bibles to read the entire story on Lazarus.

Read aloud the rest of the text in this section.

- Allow time for personal reflection on the question beneath the second paragraph.

- Invite volunteers to share.
  Possible responses: immortality, a life of peace, a life of hope

---

Jesus Gives Us Hope

What does Jesus promise about eternal life?

We always worry about death when someone is seriously ill. But it's also natural to wonder about what will come after. We might think about how things will be different when someone we love is no longer with us. Our concern for a relative or friend who is very sick might send us running to be with that person and help however we could.

Martha told Jesus that she believed he is the Messiah. Because of her belief, and because Jesus wants people to believe in him and give glory to his Father who sent him, Jesus called Lazarus out of the tomb. Lazarus did not rise under his own power, but under the power of God. Jesus showed that he had power over humanity's greatest fear, death.

> **What kind of life is Jesus offering us?**

Scripture

One day while traveling with his disciples, Jesus heard that his friend Lazarus was ill. Then Lazarus died. When Jesus arrived at their home, Lazarus's sister Martha said, "Lord, if you had been here, my brother would not have died. But even now I know that whatever you ask of God, God will give you."

Jesus told her:

"I am the resurrection and the life; whoever believes in me, even if he dies, will live, and everyone who lives and believes in me will never die. Do you believe this?"

She said to him, "Yes, Lord, I have come to believe that you are the Messiah, the Son of God." Based on John 11:1–44

Go to the Source

Read *John 11:1–44* and think about Jesus' love for his friends.

The Raising of Lazarus, Maurice Denis

© Our Sunday Visitor

i Teacher Background

The Raising of Lazarus

This passage comes at the end of Jesus' public life in the Gospel of John. Jesus' demonstration of power over life and death in the Lazarus story leads to his condemnation to death by Jewish authorities.

- Although Jesus had raised others who were dead, the miracles had taken place soon after death. In Lazarus's case, he had been dead several days and was already buried.

- Lazarus's illness, which provides an opportunity for Jesus' power to be manifested, parallels the place of the Cross in Jesus' Death: it is the instrument that leads to revealing Jesus' divinity.

Christian Hope

Lazarus and his sisters were great friends with Jesus. Because of this, Jesus came for Lazarus. Because of Martha's belief, he raised Lazarus. Because of their hope and belief, Jesus gave them even more reason to hope.

Lazarus's return to earthly life is very different from Jesus' Resurrection. Jesus rose to new life, a glorified life in which he returned to the Father. Jesus' Resurrection gives those who believe hope.

As you know, hope is one of the three Theological Virtues. The other two are faith and charity (love). The Theological Virtues are gifts from God that help you live your life in ways that strengthen your relationship with the Holy Trinity.

Christian hope puts things into this perspective: that happiness comes from life with God. It helps you put your trust in Jesus' promises and the strength of the Holy Spirit. This hope keeps you motivated and going even during difficult times. It helps you put the right emphasis on the things that really matter, the things that relate to loving God and others.

Saint Paul wrote to the Colossians that Jesus is "the beginning, the firstborn from the dead" (Colossians 1:18). There will be more to come. Because of Jesus' Resurrection to new life, we, too, hope to rise again.

Saint Paul wrote to the Romans that if the Spirit of God is in us, it will give life to our bodies, even though they are dead. (See Romans 8:11.) Our Baptism joins us with Christ; we die with him to sin, and we live a full and new life in God.

A tapestry in the Cathedral of Los Angeles depicts Saints and holy people such as Bridget of Sweden, Justin de Jacobis, Boniface, Martin de Porres, John Vianney, and the children of Fátima.

BRAINSTORM

In groups of three, brainstorm reason(s) why the Saints help give us hope in eternal life. Also talk about what makes it hard to have such hope.

_____
_____
_____
_____
_____
_____
_____
_____
_____

Our Reason for Hope **319**

Christian Hope

Expand on the theme of the Scripture story by inviting several volunteers to read aloud the text.

- *Ask*: Why should the raising of Lazarus and Jesus' Resurrection give us hope? They show us that we, too, can have life after death.

CLOSE

ACTIVITY

Divide the class into groups of three. Have the groups read the instructions and complete the activity together.

- Make sure that they record their answers to both of the prompts.
- Have each group share some of their responses with the class.
- Discuss the connection between the activity and the illustration on this page.

Quick Review The raising of Lazarus showed that Jesus had power over humanity's greatest fear—death. Jesus' Resurrection and new life give us hope for our future.

Teaching Tip

Life and Dignity of the Human Person

The Catholic belief in the sanctity of human life and dignity of the human person are manifested in many issues relating to the end of life. The condemnation of the death penalty and euthanasia, for example, reflect reverence for all life.

- Explain to the students that the rituals surrounding death, including care for the body after death and religious services, show reverence for the person who died.
- Tell the students that they can act on their belief in life after death by praying for the dead and comforting those who are mourning.

DAY 3

Objectives

- Express the Church's teaching on Heaven, Hell, and Purgatory
- Explain how our life on Earth affects our destiny for eternity

OPEN

💙 Have the students pray the last stanza of the Nicene Creed from page 367.

Read aloud the opening question and elicit responses from the class.

BUILD

Life after Death

Point out that most of what we think about life after death is based on Jesus' teachings.

Summarize the text. Be sure to include these points:

- Heaven is the state, or experience, of the full joy of living eternally in God's presence.
- Hell is the state, or experience, of eternal separation from God because of a choice to turn away from him and not seek forgiveness.

Elicit responses to the question at the end of this section. Possible responses: repent of sins, try to be a better person

How Late Is Too Late?

Explain that we have choices while we are alive, but those choices end when we die. At the time of death, each soul is judged according to his or her faith and works. This is called Particular Judgment.

Review the text in this section.

Life after Death

How will we be judged by God?

No one can be sure what **Heaven** will be like, but Sacred Tradition tells us that Heaven is the state, or experience, of being happy with God forever for all who die in his friendship. The souls of the just experience the full joy of living in God's presence forevermore.

Jesus warns us about judgment at our death in a parable he tells about a rich man who ignored a beggar. They both eventually die, but the beggar is carried away by angels, while the rich man winds up in the netherworld, which we know as Hell. There he suffers in flames.

Jesus also describes a great chasm—a gap that would probably make the Grand Canyon look like a gopher hole—between the rich man and Heaven. (See Luke 16:19–31.) **Hell** is the state, or experience, of eternal separation from God because of a choice to turn away from him and not seek

forgiveness. God is the source of our life and happiness. Imagine being apart from him forever, without life or happiness.

> If you knew your life would end tomorrow, what would you do?

How Late Is Too Late?

When we die, we'll be out of time to accept or to reject the love and grace Jesus offers us. We can take it or leave it today, but at the moment we die, our destiny for eternity will be based on whether we have accepted God's love. After a person's death, God decides where that person will spend eternity according to his or her faith and works. Each person's soul is rewarded with the blessings of Heaven, given a time of purification called Purgatory, or condemned to eternal separation from God in Hell. We call this individual judgment the **Particular Judgment**.

God's willingness to accept our repentance, forgive us, and bring us to eternal happiness is available to us as long as we live. Jesus proves this on the Cross.

320 Chapter 21

Optional Activity

Iconography Symbols *Visual/Spatial*

Christian iconography has many symbols that relate to death, immortality, and salvation; many of these symbolize Christ's Resurrection and our own. They include: the anchor, an arch, balances, a banner, bees, butterflies, a candle, a door, eggs, evergreens, an hourglass, ivy, a lamb, a lily, an owl, a palm, a phoenix, a raven, a rooster, a trumpet, and water.

- Research ahead of time the meanings of each of the symbols or make it a part of the activity for the students to research.
- Distribute drawing materials and a list of these symbols. Have the students design a sympathy card using one or more symbols.

Scripture

One of the criminals crucified with Jesus admits that he has sinned and asks, "Jesus, remember me when you come into your kingdom." Jesus tells him ". . . today you will be with me in Paradise." Luke 23:42–43

But we can never know for sure when we will die. And think about this: Isn't it much more satisfying to go through life with the inner peace that comes with knowing that you are living as God asks?

God's way is not just about happiness later in Heaven; living in his love and guidance is the surest way to peace and joy in this lifetime, too.

So what is **Purgatory**? We receive God's grace through Baptism and accept his loving friendship. If we accept God's grace and have repented of our sins, die in God's friendship, and are perfectly purified, we are welcomed into Heaven. However, if we have remained in God's friendship but are in need of satisfaction for temporal punishment for sins already forgiven, we will enter a condition called Purgatory. Purgatory is not a place, but a state of purification between death

Catholic Faith Words

Heaven the state, or experience, of the full joy of living eternally in God's presence

Hell the state, or experience, of eternal separation from God because of a choice to turn away from him and not seek forgiveness

Particular Judgment the individual judgment by God at the time of a person's death; when God decides, after a person's death, where that person will spend eternity according to his or her faith and works

Purgatory a state of final cleansing after death and before entering into Heaven that removes any remaining personal obstacles to eternal union with God. Purgatory frees the person from temporal punishment (being deprived of the entrance into Heaven for a time) due to sin.

and Heaven that removes any remaining personal obstacles to eternal union with God. This cleansing needs to happen before we experience the joy of eternal happiness with God.

Purgatory purifies us, but it's very different from the punishment of Hell. Our prayers for the dead help provide the grace that the souls in Purgatory need to be welcomed into God's heavenly Kingdom.

IDENTIFY AND LIST

Think about some actions and behaviors that would be disobeying or turning away from God. Then list three positive behaviors or actions that can counter these and help you strengthen your relationship with God.

1. _____
2. _____
3. _____

Our Reason for Hope **321**

Teacher Background

Heaven, Hell, and Purgatory

Heaven is being in the presence of God. Hell is reserved for those who die in the state of serious sin, who have rejected God and his mercy. Purgatory is final purification, an oft-misunderstood concept. The *Catechism of the Catholic Church* states: "All who die in God's grace and friendship, but still imperfectly purified, are indeed assured of their eternal salvation; but after death they undergo purification, so as to achieve the holiness necessary to enter the joy of heaven" (1030).

Although we often think that the poor souls in Purgatory are beyond our help, that is far from true. Our prayers and sacrifices for them are a true act of charity that can hasten their purification.

How Late Is Too Late?,

continued

Share that living in God's love and guidance is the surest way to peace and joy in this lifetime and eternally.

- Explain *Purgatory* more thoroughly by reading the definition from the Catholic Faith Words box.
- Point out that souls in Purgatory have hope of seeing God when they are purified, while souls in Hell have no hope of ever being in God's presence.

 Scripture

Invite a volunteer to read aloud the Scripture from Luke 23:42–43.

CLOSE _____

ACTIVITY

Tell the students to read the directions and complete the exercise alone and in a thoughtful manner.

- Encourage them to act on the positive behaviors they have listed.

Quick Review Heaven is the state of being happy with God for all eternity, while Hell is the state of eternal separation from God. The way we live our lives on Earth affects our destiny for eternity.

DAY 4

Objectives

- Describe the Last Judgment
- Explain the significance of the Works of Mercy in relationship to eternal life

OPEN

💜 Have the students make the Sign of the Cross, then pray the Glory Be from page 383.

Ask the opening question and list student responses on the board.

BUILD

The Second Coming

Read aloud the first paragraph.

- *Ask*: What do you think the end of the world will be like?

📖 Go to the Source

Send the students to Matthew 25:31–46 to learn more about Jesus' Judgment at the end of time.

Who Will Inherit the Kingdom?

Recall that at each person's death, the soul will first go through the Particular Judgment.

Have the students read the text to find out what the Last Judgment is. God's final judgment that will occur at the end of time

Tell them to continue reading to find out what will happen to our bodies at the Last Judgment. Our bodies will reunite with our souls.

- Allow time for quiet reflection after reading the questions at the end of this section.

The Second Coming

How can we be with Jesus on the last day?

Someday, at God's word, our world will end. Nobody knows for sure when or why, or exactly what it will look or be like. We just know that life as we know it will end and creation will be transformed. And as we pray in the Nicene Creed at Mass, Jesus "will come again in glory to judge the living and the dead."

Who Will Inherit the Kingdom?

Jesus described pretty simply what will happen when he comes again.

> **Go to the Source**
> Read *Matthew 25:31–46* to find out how Jesus, the King of Glory, will judge all people at the end of time.

The Resurrection of Jesus, from the Church of St. Ann, in Emmaus, Pennsylvania

At the Second Coming, the **Last Judgment** will take place, during which all the living and dead will be judged. The Last Judgment is God's final triumph over evil that will occur at the end of time when Christ returns and judges all the living and the dead. Then, all will fully see and understand God's plan for creation.

Those who have died will appear in their own bodies before Christ. In the description of this judgment in the Gospel according to Matthew, the glorified Christ will sit on a throne, putting the righteous people on his right side and the others on his left.

The faithful people will have life forever in Heaven with God because they had a relationship with Jesus and showed this by living good lives and reaching out to people in need. This includes feeding someone who was hungry, welcoming a stranger, or taking care of a sick person. At the end of the world, Jesus will reveal the secrets of our hearts and judge each of us in light of our works and the degree that we accepted his grace or refused it and sinned. Jesus knows what each one of us does, just as he knows when we turn to him or turn away from him in our lives.

The Kingdom that Jesus talked so much about will come into fullness at the Last Judgment. As Christ has risen, so will we. Our bodies will be transformed by reuniting

> ### Catholic Faith Words
>
> **Last Judgment** God's final triumph over evil that will occur at the end of time when Christ returns and judges all the living and the dead. Then, all will fully see and understand God's plan for creation.
>
> **Works of Mercy** actions that show care for the physical and spiritual needs of others

---

📖 Scripture Background

The Judgment of the Nations

This passage appears only in the Gospel of Matthew and portrays the Son of Man as dividing the just and the unjust at the Second Coming. His judgment is based on the Works of Mercy that were done for the "least brothers" of Jesus. The just will enter the Kingdom, while the unjust will be doomed to "eternal fire."

The passage gets its name from verse 32 and shows Jesus' concern with preparing for Heaven by serving others on Earth. It presents realistic ways of ministering to others and is meant to show that good works are a sign of devotion to God.

with our souls. The righteous will be with Jesus forever and the world will be transformed.

> What do you think about being judged?
> What can you do to prepare yourself?

The Works of Mercy

The **Works of Mercy** are ways to respond to Jesus when we see him in the poor and needy. The Corporal Works of Mercy are actions that provide for people's physical needs, and the Spiritual Works of Mercy are actions that address the needs of the heart, mind, and soul.

Often several Works of Mercy are done together. For instance, if a friend's grandmother dies, you're more likely to comfort your friend and pray for her grandma, while somebody else will deliver flowers and other people will assist with the funeral. Jesus is pleased with whatever we do for people in need.

 Fill in the right column of the chart with ideas on how you can perform the Works of Mercy listed in the left column. Some have been done for you.

The Works of Mercy	
Corporal	**One Thing You Can Do**
Feed the hungry.	Donate to a food drive.
Give drink to the thirsty.	
Clothe the naked.	Donate your old clothing.
Shelter the homeless.	
Visit the sick.	
Visit those in prison.	Support parish outreach.
Bury the dead.	
Spiritual	**One Thing You Can Do**
Counsel the doubtful.	
Instruct the ignorant.	Help teach kids at church.
Admonish the sinner.	
Comfort the sorrowful.	Help a friend who's sad.
Bear wrongs patiently.	
Pray for the living and the dead.	Pray for a loved one.

IN SUMMARY Catholics Believe

By his Death and Resurrection, Jesus makes it possible for believers to have eternal life—life with God forever.

- Christian hope is based upon putting our trust in God and having hope that we will rise one day as Jesus did.
- We will be judged at our death based upon the ways we have accepted and acted on

God's grace in our lives. God desires all of us to make the right choices in life, so we can be with him forever in the happiness of Heaven.

- Jesus will come at the end of time to judge the living and the dead, and the Kingdom of God will be complete and full in its glory.

Our Reason for Hope **323**

The Works of Mercy

Read aloud the text in this section. Point out the Corporal and Spiritual Works of Mercy listed in the chart on the side of the page.

- Emphasize that the Corporal Works of Mercy provide for people's physical needs, while the Spiritual Works of Mercy address the needs of the heart, mind, and soul.

★ Have the students fill in the right column of the chart with examples of how they can perform each of the Works of Mercy.

- Allow volunteers to share some of their responses with the class.

CLOSE

In Summary

Invite four volunteers to read the summary statement and the three bullets to summarize what Catholics believe about eternal life.

- Provide time for questions or comments.

Optional Activity

Catholic Hymns *Musical*

The Catholic Church has many beautiful hymns designed to comfort the sorrowful and depict the joys of Heaven.

- Select several such hymns from your parish hymnal, or invite the students to review the hymnal and select their favorites or those they would like to learn.
- Select a CD featuring some of the hymns and play a few of them for the class.

DAY 5

Objectives

- Discuss All Souls Day
- Explore the faith life of Saint Francis de Sales
- Offer the prayer using Psalm 23

OPEN

💜 Invite the students to pray the Act of Faith on page 387.

BUILD

Our Catholic Life

Discuss All Souls day using the information in the Our Catholic Life section.

- *Ask*: What special prayers can we use to remember those we know who have died?
- Invite the students to respond.
- Remind them about the prayers listed in the back of their books on pages 382–390.

People of Faith

Tell the students that Saint Francis de Sales devoted himself to making God's love known to others.

- Invite a volunteer to read aloud the People of Faith paragraph.
- Share the extra information in the People of Faith Background box.
- Invite the students to do further research on Saint Francis de Sales and his teachings.
- Encourage them to bring their findings back to share with the rest of the class.

Our Catholic Life

Two special days celebrated during the liturgical year are All Saints Day, which occurs on November 1, and **All Souls Day**, which is celebrated on November 2. All Saints Day is a Holy Day of Obligation for Catholics in the United States, but All Souls Day is important, too. On All Souls Day, the Catholic Church prays for those who have died in friendship with God but are undergoing final purification before enjoying eternal happiness with him in Heaven. During All Souls Day celebrations, Catholics attend Mass, sometimes visit gravesites, and sometimes participate in processions through towns and cities. While Catholics are always encouraged to pray for the dead as well as the living, All Souls Day is a special occasion in which to do so.

> What special prayers can you use to remember those you know who have died?

© Our Sunday Visitor

People of Faith

Saint Francis de Sales, 1567–1622

Saint Francis de Sales was born into a noble French family and was extremely well educated. He devoted his life to teaching other people about God's love. His way of teaching is sometimes called the Way of Divine Love. In 1877 Blessed Pope Pius IX named him a Doctor of the Church. In one of his most famous books, *Introduction to the Devout Life,* he explains how an ordinary person can lead a holy life. People still follow his advice today. The Church celebrates his feast day on **January 24.**

 For more, go to aliveinchrist.osv.com

CONSIDER

You can take the meaning of Christian hope to heart to change your outlook on troubling issues. Consider what it really means to trust in God, and apply it to your relationships. Using what you have learned this year, you can offer hope-filled advice to friends and family. On the lines below, name something you can do to become a more hope-filled person.

_____
_____
_____
_____
_____
_____
_____
_____

324 Chapter 21

People of Faith Background

Saint Francis de Sales

Share the following with the students:

- As a young man, Saint Francis de Sales worried that he might not get to Heaven, but once he was convinced that God is love, his worries left him. He devoted his life to teaching others about God's love.
- He lived at a time when the Church faced many problems because of the Protestant Reformation, but he always urged people to treat one another with kindness, even if they disagreed with one another.

📶 Encourage the students to go to **aliveinchrist.osv.com** at home to learn more about Saint Francis de Sales.

Praying Psalm 23

Leader: Psalm 23 reminds us that we have good reason to be hopeful.

Side 1: The LORD is my shepherd; there is nothing I lack.

Side 2: God, I know that you love me and know what I need. I don't need an endless pile of things and piles of spending money. My needs are deeper. Help me to understand and accept the way you are leading me through my parents, teachers, and the Church. Help me to trust.

Side 1: to still waters he leads me; he restores my soul.

He guides me along right paths for the sake of his name.

Side 2: Jesus, my Good Shepherd, you know how stressed I get sometimes. You are calling me to find my peace in the things that really matter. Help me to follow your lead, and to grow in virtue, especially love.

Side 1: Even though I walk through the valley of the shadow of death,

I will fear no evil, for you are with me; your rod and your staff comfort me.

Side 2: Lord and Savior, I know that even though I'm young, I will someday face the end of my life. Even before that day, I will face many frightening situations. I draw comfort in knowing you are always nearby, even when nobody else is.

Side 1: You set a table before me in front of my enemies;

You anoint my head with oil; my cup overflows.

Side 2: Jesus, you know that there are many things that try to block the person I'm trying to be. Some of my "enemies" are my own faults and weaknesses. No worries. You will feed and provide for me even in the face of those things. You will treat me as if I were royalty, anointing my head with oil.

Side 1: Indeed, goodness and mercy will pursue me all the days of my life;

I will dwell in the house of the LORD for endless days.

Side 2: God, although I often forget, I know I can place my trust and hope in you. I know that you will love and protect forever. What more could anyone want from a shepherd? Lead me, Lord.

Leader: Let's sing together.

▶ *Sing or play "My Sheep"*

📶 Go to **aliveinchrist.osv.com** for an interactive review.

A Work with Words Circle the letter of the choice that best completes the sentence.

1. Faith, hope, and charity are ____.
   a. Moral Virtues   **c.** Theological Virtues
   b. Canon Laws   d. Sacraments

2. In Jesus' parable of the rich man and the beggar, the rich man is sent to ____.
   a. the netherworld   c. Heaven
   b. Purgatory   d. both a and c

3. ____ Judgment is the individual judgment by God at the time of a person's death when God decides where that person will spend eternity.
   a. Divine   c. Eternal
   b. Particular   d. Honest

4. Purgatory is a process of being ____ before entering Heaven.
   a. purified   c. condemned
   b. judged   d. rewarded

5. In the Gospel according to John, when Jesus goes to raise Lazarus from the dead, Jesus says he is the ____ and the ____.
   a. source, life   c. hope, peace
   b. Resurrection, life   d. mercy, grace

B Check Understanding Indicate whether the following statements are true or false. Then rewrite false statements to make them true.

6. Sacred Tradition defines Heaven as the state, or experience, of the full joy of living eternally in God's presence. **True**/False

   _____

7. Hell is defined as a state where people are separated from God for a short time. True/**False**
   It is a state where people are
   separated from God forever.

8. Prayers for the dead help provide the grace needed by souls in Hell in order to be welcomed into Heaven. True/**False**
   These prayers help provide grace
   needed by souls in Purgatory.

9. At the Second Coming of Jesus, the Last Judgment will take place. **True**/False

   _____

10. At the Last Judgment, those who have died in God's good graces will become spirits. True/**False**
    They will appear before God in
    their own bodies.

C Make Connections On a separate sheet of paper, write a one-paragraph response to the question: Think about the Corporal and Spiritual Works of Mercy. What would happen in your life and in the lives of others if you responded to people's needs with God's love? Give a specific example.

Read aloud the instructions for the activity.

- Have the students work on this assignment independently.
- Encourage them to reflect on it further at home.

CLOSE

Praying Psalm 23

💙 Divide the class into two sides: Side 1 and Side 2.

Gather in the prayer space and remind the students to bring their books.

Say: Jesus, we want to be with you on the last day. Teach us how to show love to others.

Begin the prayer as the leader. Follow the order of prayer on the student page.

▶ Conclude by inviting the students to sing or reflect on the song "My Sheep," downloaded from **aliveinchrist.osv.com**.

CHAPTER REVIEW

Review the instructions for each section and have the students complete the review.

📶 Go to **aliveinchrist.osv.com** to prepare customized and downloadable assessments, send eAssessments, and assign interactive reviews.

UNIT 7

Use the closing points from Days 2–4 in each chapter to highlight lesson concepts for this unit and prepare for the Unit Review.

Have the students complete the Review pages. Then discuss the answers as a class. Review any concepts with which the students are having difficulty.

 Work with Words

Direct the students to match the terms in the left column with the correct definitions or descriptions in the right column.

A **Work with Words** Match the terms on the left with the correct definitions or descriptions on the right.

g **1.** laity

d **2.** domestic Church

i **3.** vocation

a **4.** justice

j **5.** repent

c **6.** Kingdom of God

b **7.** solidarity

e **8.** Theological Virtues

f **9.** Particular Judgment

h **10.** Purgatory

k **11.** evangelical counsels

a. the constant and firm desire to give God and other people what is due to them

b. unity of all people around the world

c. God's rule of love, peace, and justice that exists in Heaven but has not yet come in its fullness on Earth

d. the family as a community of grace and prayer

e. faith, hope, and charity

f. time when souls are rewarded with Heaven, given a time of purification called Purgatory, or condemned to Hell

g. baptized members of the Church who share in Jesus' mission and witness to him, especially in their families, workplaces, and civic communities

h. the state of being cleansed, or purified, before being able to enter Heaven

i. the purpose for which God made us and the particular way to answer his call

j. to be sorry for sin and change behavior

k. poverty, obedience, and chastity

© Our Sunday Visitor

Kingdom of God **327**

B Check Understanding Indicate whether the following statements are true or false. Then rewrite false statements to make them true.

12. The family is the first place to learn about the good within people and discover Christ's love. (True)/False

_____
_____

13. Lay people share in Jesus' priesthood by teaching in parables as he did. True/(False)

They do so by sharing the love of
Christ with all people.

14. When you use discernment, you weigh your choices and pray for guidance. (True)/False

_____
_____

15. Jesus taught us that we cannot have the Kingdom without justice. (True)/False

_____
_____

16. The Lord's Prayer is often called the perfect prayer because it sums up the message of the Gospels. (True)/False

_____
_____

17. Hell is defined as being apart from the people you love forever. True/(False)

Hell is defined as being apart
from God.

18. In the Gospel according to John, when Jesus goes to raise Lazarus from the dead, he says he is the sacrifice and the life. True/(False)

He is the Resurrection and the life.

_____

19. At the Last Judgment, those who have died in God's friendship will be glorified in body and soul. (True)/False

_____
_____

C Make Connections Write a short answer to the questions below.

20. How can your school community actively work toward the Kingdom of God—God's love, peace, and justice—on campus?

Responses will vary. _____
_____
_____
_____

21. Imagine you are a reporter at the Last Judgment. What do you see happening? How are people responding? What are your reactions?

Responses will vary. _____
_____
_____
_____
_____

22. Name two Corporal Works of Mercy and describe how you could perform them in your everyday life.

Responses will vary. _____
_____
_____
_____

23. Name two Spiritual Works of Mercy you have performed in your everyday life and what effect they had.

Responses will vary. _____
_____
_____
_____

24. Of the three vows taken in consecrated religious life—poverty, celibacy, and obedience—which do you think is the hardest? Why?

Responses will vary. _____
_____
_____
_____

25. How does the Church describe Heaven?

The Church describes Heaven as a state, or experience, of being happy
with God forever, or eternal life with God.
_____
_____

B Check Understanding

Have the students indicate whether each statement is true or false. If the answer is false, instruct them to rewrite the statement in order to make it true.

C Make Connections

Point out that the students will be writing a short answer to the questions. Explain that even though these are short answer responses, they need to be sure that they fully answer the questions.

📶 Go to **aliveinchrist.osv.com** to prepare customized and downloadable assessments, send eAssessments, and assign interactive reviews.

Have the students complete the Post-Test. Then discuss the answers as a class. Review any concepts with which the students are having difficulty.

On pages 330–331, instruct the students to circle the letter of the response that best completes each statement.

Circle the letter of the response that correctly completes the statement.

1. The ___ is the term for the mystery of the Son of God taking on human nature.
   a. Annunciation
   b. Nativity
   c. Miracle
   d. Incarnation

2. Jesus instructed the Apostles to travel in such a way that they ___.
   a. would meet with important people
   b. could gather monetary treasures for the Church
   c. would trust in God to provide for them
   d. could leave a place quickly if they were persecuted

3. Jesus' ___ teach us about the meaning and path to true happiness and the ways to live in the Kingdom of God.
   a. Ten Commandments
   b. miracles
   c. Beatitudes
   d. first books of the Bible

4. The process by which, through the power of the Holy Spirit and the words and actions of the priest, the bread and wine are transformed into the Body and Blood of Christ is known as ___.
   a. discernment
   b. conversion
   c. transubstantiation
   d. transfiguration

5. The deliberate ending of a pregnancy by killing the unborn child is known as ___.
   a. suicide
   b. scandal
   c. abortion
   d. euthanasia

6. Much of Catholic liturgy has its roots in the ___ traditions that Jesus took part in as he grew up.
   a. Jewish
   b. Roman
   c. Apostolic
   d. Gentile

7. A ___ is a the purpose for which God made us and the particular way to answer and live out his call.
   a. spirituality
   b. vocation
   c. reparation
   d. covenant

8. A soul that is in Purgatory is in the process of being ___.
   a. judged
   b. punished
   c. rewarded
   d. cleansed

9. Contemplative prayer is ___.
   a. based on songs
   b. group prayer
   c. part of the Mass
   d. wordless prayer

© Our Sunday Visitor

10. ___ is the God-given ability that helps individuals judge whether actions are right or wrong.

a. Free will

b. Conscience

c. Reason

d. Judgment

11. When we attempt to indirectly correct the damage caused by sin, we are making ___.

a. reparation

b. contrition

c. conscience formation

d. reconciliation

12. The ___ Commandment identifies lying as a sin that damages our character and integrity.

a. Tenth

b. Eighth

c. Fourth

d. Sixth

13. Jesus told the Beatitudes during the ___.

a. Last Supper

b. journey to Jerusalem

c. Sermon on the Mount

d. wedding at Cana

14. Letters from the Pope to the Church community are known as ___.

a. spiritual treasury

b. encyclicals

c. evangelical counsels

d. spiritualities

15. God is ___, which means he always was, is now, and always will be.

a. faithful

b. eternal

c. holy

d. love

16. A prayer that acclaims God for his nature is a prayer of ___.

a. intercession

b. thanksgiving

c. blessing

d. praise

17. Through ___, God promised to remain in a relationship with his People.

a. his law

b. his grace

c. the covenant

d. the spiritualities

18. The Church's complete list of inspired books included in Sacred Scripture is called ___.

a. the canon of Scripture

b. Sacred Tradition

c. Church doctrine

d. natural law

19. ___ is the free, loving gift of God's life and help.

a. Solidarity

b. Inspiration

c. Grace

d. Conscience

For questions 20–27, instruct the students to circle the letter of the response that best completes each statement. For questions 28–40, have the students write short responses. Explain that even though these are short answer responses, they need to be sure that they fully answer the questions.

20. The Church is organized into ___ that has different levels of leadership and membership.
   (a.) a hierarchy
   b. the Magisterium
   c. a canon
   d. an encyclical

21. The Cardinal Virtues include all of the following **except** ___.
   a. prudence
   b. justice
   (c.) charity
   d. fortitude

22. We show our ___ when we are sorry for our sins and pledge to try to not sin again.
   (a.) contrition
   b. forgiveness
   c. suffering
   d. confession

23. ___ is the courage to do what is right even if others disagree with or challenge you.
   a. Justice
   b. Temperance
   (c.) Fortitude
   d. Prudence

24. When we act with ___, we give God and our neighbor what is due to them.
   a. prudence
   b. hope
   (c.) justice
   d. temperance

25. The ___ is the event of the Angel Gabriel telling Mary she would be the Mother of God.
   a. Assumption
   (b.) Annunciation
   c. Ascension
   d. Attribution

26. The ___ Commandment instructs us not to kill another person.
   a. First
   b. Tenth
   c. Third
   (d.) Fifth

27. Jesus told ___, or stories that taught moral or spiritual truths.
   a. passages
   (b.) parables
   c. poems
   d. pastiches

Write a short answer to the questions or statements below.

Name the Marks of the Church, and describe what each means, in your own words.

28. **One: The Church is united by the Spirit through one faith and one Baptism**

29. **Holy: The Church is holy, because she comes from God.**

30. **Catholic: The Church is universal, meant for everyone in every time.**

31. **Apostolic: The Church's teaching authority comes from Jesus and the Apostles and handed down to the bishops, Apostles' successors.**

32. Describe the Kingdom of God in your own words.

Responses will vary, but should include that the Kingdom is God's rule of peace, justice, and love that exists in Heaven but has not yet come in its fullness on Earth.

33. What is the Paschal Mystery?

Responses will vary, but should include that the Paschal Mystery is Christ's work of redemption through his suffering, Death, Resurrection, and Ascension.

34. What is the mission of the Catholic Church?

The mission of the Church is to share the message of God's love and announce the Good News of his Kingdom to the world.

35. Define *Sacrament* and list the Seven Sacraments.

Effective signs of God's grace, instituted by Christ and given to his Church; Baptism, Confirmation, Eucharist, Penance and Reconciliation, Anointing of the Sick, Holy Orders, Matrimony

36. How does your conscience help you make good decisions?

Responses will vary, but may include thinking about possible options, comparing options to Jesus' teachings, talking to someone you can trust, praying for guidance, and acting on your choice.

How are the three Divine Persons of the Trinity related to one another?

37. God the Father, our Creator who gave us his Son, Jesus Christ

38. God the Son, Jesus Christ, shows us the way and reconciles us to the Father.

39. God the Holy Spirit, our Advocate, guides the Church in her work.

40. Who are the Saints and why are they important to us?

Saints are models of faith who led holy lives, are in Heaven, intercede for us, and help us know how to live as disciples.

Live Your Faith/Our Catholic Tradition at a Glance

Live Your Faith

" Let us keep a place for Christ in our lives, let us care for one another and let us be loving custodians of creation. "

—Pope Francis via Twitter, March 19, 2013

The Seven Themes of Catholic Social Teaching

The Catholic Church's Social Teaching helps build a just society and shows us how to live lives of holiness amidst the challenges of modern society. The wisdom of this tradition can be understood best through a direct reading of Church documents, but here is a synopsis of each of the seven key themes that are part of our Catholic Social Tradition.

Life and Dignity of the Human Person

Each person is created in God's image and all people have rights that flow from their human dignity. The equal dignity of all people means we must work to eliminate social and economic inequalities. We strive to value all people over our personal wealth or possessions.

Call to Family, Community, and Participation

In order for our society to be healthy, we must all make positive contributions to it, bringing to it the light of the Gospels. We can do this by finding practical ways to participate more fully in our own families, in our parishes, and in our communities.

Rights and Responsibilities of the Human Person

Every person has a right to life and the rights needed to live in dignity. The fundamental rights of all people are freedom, justice, and the basic necessities of everyday life. As individuals and as a society, we must work to protect these rights for all people.

Option for the Poor and Vulnerable

God loves all people, and he calls us to love one another as he loves us. In a world where many people live in great poverty while others enjoy great wealth, we must pay special attention to the needs of the poor and reach out to them in Christian charity.

The Dignity of Work and the Rights of Workers

Through labor all people participate in the work of creation and all workers have the following rights that must be protected: the right to productive work, to fair wages, and to pursue economic opportunity. Catholics believe that our work can be a valuable way to serve God and others.

Solidarity of the Human Family

All people—rich and poor, young and old, weak and strong—have equal dignity and rights that flow from that dignity. As part of one human family, we are all dependent on one another and responsible for one another, and must work to reduce social inequalities and provide for one another's needs.

Care for God's Creation

God is the Creator of all people and all that exists in nature. He has given us the bounty of the Earth and its resources and has entrusted us with its care. We are called to respond by protecting and caring for all God's creation for generations to come.

 Go to **aliveinchrist.osv.com** for a complete listing of chapters and Church year lessons correlated to the themes of Catholic Social Teaching.

About This Principle This section presents an overview of the theological foundation of the theme so that teachers have background information at point of use.

Wrap Instruction An easy-to-follow side column provides teachers with directions and activities for presenting the Catholic Social Teaching in developmentally appropriate ways.

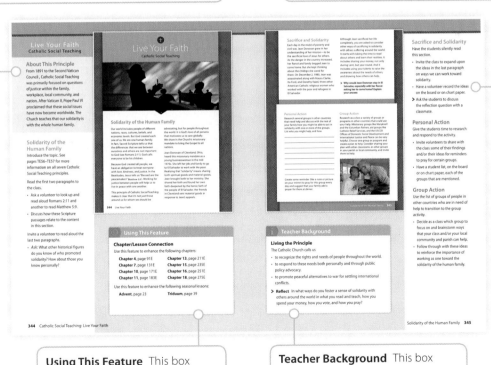

Using This Feature This box identifies core chapters and seasonal lessons to which the Live Your Faith feature is connected.

Teacher Background This box identifies ways the Church calls us to practice the principle and includes a question for teacher reflection.

About This Principle

The dignity of the human person flows from the fact that all persons are created in the image and likeness of God. And because God is love, loving God and loving others is the Great Commandment. This is a very important teaching that members of the Catholic Church not only recognize, but are encouraged to live by.

Life and Dignity of the Human Person

Introduce the topic. See pages TE56–TE57 for more information on all seven Catholic Social Teaching principles.

Proclaim the Scripture and summarize the first paragraph.

Invite the students to read through the remaining three paragraphs.

- Ask them to highlight or underline the main point in each paragraph.
- Have volunteers share their answers with the class.

Ask: What are some ways that you can help share God's love with others?

- Select a volunteer to write responses on the board or on chart paper.

Live Your Faith
Catholic Social Teaching

Life and Dignity of the Human Person

In Scripture God tells us, "Before I formed you in the womb I knew you" (Jeremiah 1:5). God created each one of us. Every person is unique and unrepeatable. He has a special plan for each of our lives. He knows what he made us to be.

Because God made each person, we are called to treat each person with human dignity. Every life is valuable to God. We should take care of the bodies and minds God gave us and use them to do good things. We are meant to be kind toward others, and solve problems peacefully instead of fighting. If we see someone else being bullied, teased, or disrespected, we are called to speak up and defend that person, and get help if necessary. It is our responsibility to help to protect others, because every single life is important to God.

Each one of us, every person on Earth, is created in the image and likeness of God and is equally precious in the eyes of God. That's the basis of our dignity as human persons. Because God is love and loves all persons, we too are called to love everyone, even those who may seem difficult to love.

It almost seems easy to tease certain kids, to make fun of strange-looking adults, or to hang out only with people like ourselves. Everybody does it, right? There are some wonderful movies about kids who are "different," whether in size or ability. These show us the beauty and dignity of people we don't usually respect. What about your own experiences of being disrespected? Most kids have been teased, picked on, or talked about at some point. You know how it feels.

334 Live Your Faith

 Using This Feature

Chapter/Lesson Connection

Use this feature to enhance the following chapters:

Use this feature to enhance the following seasonal lesson:

Stand Up for Dignity

One of the most basic aspects of respect is a person's reputation. We all want others to think highly of us. Sometimes the meanest thing we can do to people is to tell half-truths about them. Sometimes we do this to look good in the eyes of others. Sometimes we do it because we want to get even with someone or maybe because we're hurting, too. No matter what the reason, the Church is clear that this is sinful.

You might sometimes hear other kids teasing or telling lies about someone. That's when you are called to stand up for the person being talked about. The Holy Spirit is there to give all of us the courage to challenge friends, classmates, or others who are not respecting human dignity. God and the Church call us to speak up and show the love of Christ every day.

> Why is it often easier to disrespect people than to stand up for them?

Personal Action

Identify and write down at least one time you remember disrespecting someone else or watching it happen and doing nothing.

_____

_____

_____

_____

Write down at least one time when you stood up for someone who was being disrespected.

_____

_____

_____

_____

Group Action

In small groups, select one of the following groups of people who are often excluded or are among the least respected: people who have physical challenges, people with mental illness, people who have less common interests, and people who dress differently or have distinctive head wear.

Draw a tree. On the trunk, write the name of the excluded group. On the branches, write the actions some people take that are disrespectful. On the roots of the tree, write the reasons or things that might motivate people to act disrespectfully to this group.

Stand Up for Dignity

Read aloud this section.

- Invite volunteers to share about times when they have felt the Holy Spirit give them courage during a challenging situation.

> Discuss the reflection question as a class.

Personal Action

Have the students read the instructions.

- Allow time for them to write some of the things they remember.

Group Action

Invite a volunteer to read aloud the instructions.

- Discuss certain groups that are often disrespected in our culture.

Arrange the students into small groups. Assign each group one of the marginalized groups mentioned and have them work together to create the "tree" for that group.

- Remind the students to be respectful of others as they write words on their "trees" or speak about different groups of people.

- Have each group share their project with the class.

- Discuss with the class ways they might be able to use these projects to help bring awareness to a disrespected group.

---

i Teacher Background

Living the Principle

The Catholic Church calls us

- to realize that all persons, as children of God, are equal in dignity and deserving of love.

- to recognize that God created each of us to be unique. The natural differences between us are good and do not mean that we are of greater or less value than anyone else.

- to respect and protect the dignity of others and their reputations.

> **Reflect** As a teacher, how do you affirm the dignity of your students and others you encounter in the course of your day?

Live Your Faith
Catholic Social Teaching

About This Principle

The very meaning of the word *catholic* is universal; our Church is a community that is meant for all. As we are created in the image of God who is a communion of three co-equal Persons, we have a responsibility to build a sense of community in our families, in our school and parish, and in our local community and nation. In Catholic Social Teaching, justice is understood as the right and responsibility of every person to participate in these communities.

Call to Family, Community, and Participation

Introduce the topic. See pages TE56–TE57 for more information on all seven Catholic Social Teaching principles.

Proclaim the Scripture.

Ask: How might the photo on this page connect with the Scripture? God made people to be in relationship with one another.

Have volunteers read aloud the remaining three paragraphs.

Emphasize that:

- God gave us the gift of community and our families, the domestic Church.

- As we were welcomed and nourished at Baptism, we need to welcome and nourish others.

- We each bring different gifts to the Body of Christ.

Live Your Faith
Catholic Social Teaching

Call to Family, Community, and Participation

From the very beginning, God made people to be in relationship with one another. Scripture tells us, "The LORD God said: It is not good for the man to be alone. I will make a helper suited to him" (Genesis 2:18). God gave us communities of persons so that we could take care of one another.

The family is a very special type of community. The Catholic Church teaches that the family is the "school of holiness" and the "domestic Church." These names reflect the Catholic teaching that the family is where we first learn who God is and how to live a Christian life. It is in our families that we learn what it means to live in a community and how to love and respect others. This love and respect extends to other communities.

In the Sacrament of Baptism, we are welcomed to and included in the Church. Now who needs us to be more welcoming or inclusive to them? Exactly how can you do so? In the Eucharist, we are nourished. Now who needs us to nourish them? Exactly how can we be more nourishing to this person? In the Sacrament of Confirmation, we affirm our call to discipleship. Now what do we need to work on to improve the way we live as disciples?

We are the Church, the Body of Christ. With our different gifts, we form one Body in Christ, made of many parts. Created in the image of God who is a Communion of three Divine Persons, we are all created to develop and participate in community.

336 Live Your Faith

 ### Using This Feature

Chapter/Lesson Connection

Use this feature to enhance the following chapters:

Use this feature to enhance the following seasonal lessons:

You and Your Community

Today, so many people seem to spend more time at work or in front of the TV or computers, while fewer people seem to care or participate at school or in their parish. In most elections, the percentage of people who vote is going down rather than up. Are people giving up? Are they finding other things to give their time to? It's a huge challenge. But people called, confirmed, and sent forth by God's Spirit of courage and love have a responsibility to say "yes, we truly are Christ's disciples in our world."

You are sent to school to help build a community of learners who care about others, including your classmates. At home, you are called to help create a family community. Your parish needs your talents and your ideas. And your country needs you to care about others and your ideals enough that you will speak out when something's wrong. The Church is clear—political authority must be consistent with morality and promote the common good.

> Why do you think so many people don't participate in their community?

Personal Action

List some things you can do to help build a greater sense of community in the following areas.

At home:

_____

_____

_____

At school:

_____

_____

_____

In my neighborhood:

_____

_____

_____

Group Action

With your classmates make a list of reasons why people do not get involved at school, in your neighborhood, and in the broader community. Then create a response to each of the reasons. Put a star next to the more significant reasons and discuss which would need a change of perspective or priority.

Teacher Background

Living the Principle

The Catholic Church calls us

- to recognize and promote the family as the foundation of society.
- to promote a sense of community (the common good) in every level of society.
- to participate actively in the groups we are part of, starting with our own families.

> **Reflect** How often do you participate in your parish? In local and national political issues? How often do you encourage your students to do so?

You and Your Community

Have the students silently read this section.

- *Ask:* Who do you know who has spoken out about an important issue or taken action in order to improve the lives of the people in their community or country?
- > Read aloud the reflection question.
- Discuss responses to this question as a class.

Personal Action

Tell the students to think back on the previous discussion and some of the ways that people helped their communities.

- Challenge them to reflect on and respond to the personal prompts.
- Invite volunteers to share their responses with the class.

Group Action

Go over the instructions and brainstorm some ideas as a class.

- Arrange the students in small groups and assign one of the reasons listed to each group. They will need to work together to construct their response(s).
- Encourage each group to share their responses with the class.

About This Principle

The rights and responsibilities of the human person are clearly defined through Sacred Scripture and Sacred Tradition and are affirmed by Catholic Social Teaching. Many of these rights and responsibilities are also reflected in secular documents, such as the Declaration of Independence and the Universal Declaration of Human Rights. The rights or freedoms we have as individuals always go hand in hand with our responsibility to promote the common good.

Rights and Responsibilities of the Human Person

Introduce the topic. See pages TE56–TE57 for more information on all seven Catholic Social Teaching principles.

Read aloud the first paragraph.

Invite a volunteer to read aloud the second paragraph, emphasizing the information from the *Catechism of the Catholic Church*.

• Reiterate the basic rights that are listed here.

Discuss the information provided on the Declaration of Independence.

• *Ask:* How does the Church take this basic principle a step further? The Church teaches that we are to use our freedom for the common good of all.

Summarize the last paragraph.

Live Your Faith
Catholic Social Teaching

Rights and Responsibilities of the Human Person

Because God made every person, each of us has rights and responsibilities. Rights are the freedoms or things every person needs and should have. Responsibilities are our duties, or the things we must do.

Jesus tells us to "love your neighbor as yourself" (Mark 12:31). The *Catechism* teaches that when we respect the dignity of another person, we treat them as "another self." We respect the rights that come from their dignity as a human being (CCC, 1943–44). Everyone has a basic human right to food, shelter, clothing, rest, and the right to see a doctor if they need one. While we work for individual rights, we also have a responsibility to treat others well and work together for the good of everyone.

"All men [and women] are created equal and endowed with certain inalienable rights. . . ." This basic principle of the United States Declaration of Independence is found first in Church teaching. But the Church goes a step further. Yes, we are all endowed with rights and freedom, but we are also called to use this freedom constructively, for the common good.

Governments, too, are meant to respect the fundamental rights of the human person, promote freedom, and defend the common good. Public authority is part of God's plan for promoting positive values in society and the well-being of all. The Church, too, gets involved in political affairs whenever economic and social issues affect peoples' fundamental human rights.

338 Live Your Faith

Using This Feature

Chapter/Lesson Connection

Use this feature to enhance the following chapters:

Chapter 1, page 51E   **Chapter 9**, page 155E

Chapter 2, page 63E   **Chapter 13**, page 211E

Chapter 3, page 75E   **Chapter 14**, page 223E

Chapter 6, page 115E   **Chapter 18**, page 275E

Chapter 7, page 131E

Use this feature to enhance the following seasonal lessons:

Ordinary Time, page 19   **Lent,** page 35

Our Human Rights

What are these fundamental human rights? They start with the right to life and the basic necessities of life—food, shelter, clothing, health care, education, and work.

Second, all people have the right to their own dignity and religious and cultural expression. This means being respected and appreciated for how unique each one of is. It also means developing relationships with people—learning from them as well as helping them.

Third, all have a right to participate in decisions that affect their lives. With rights go responsibilities. We all have the responsibility to exercise our own rights and to work with others to gain, support, and expand their human rights. Too often the voices of people who need our support are silenced, and we are called to help them make their voices heard. Disciples of Jesus are called to bring the light of the Gospel to unjust situations, and help make them right.

> **How does the Church support human rights in the world?**

Personal Action

As you read about current events, listen to the news, or observe how different people live or are treated in your community or in other parts of the world, who are the people that are treated unfairly?

_____

_____

_____

_____

_____

Which of these people do you want to stand up for and help?

_____

_____

_____

_____

_____

Group Action

Work in groups to identify human rights issues that interest you, and learn how organizations are working on behalf of these issues. Then, consider making some kind of slogan, button, or badge members of your class can use or wear to express your concern and invite others to join you in action.

Our Human Rights

Review the information on fundamental human rights with the class.

- After each paragraph, have a volunteer summarize the right(s) discussed.

> *Ask:* How does the Church support human rights in the world?

- Invite the students to respond.

- Note: You might want to consider having specific concrete examples prepared for the class.

Personal Action

Invite the students to respond to the questions in this section.

Group Action

Ask a student to read aloud the instructions to the class.

- Have the students arrange themselves in small groups to work on their slogans, buttons, or badges.

- Invite each group to present their slogan, button, or badge to the class and explain what/who it represents and why they chose it.

Teacher Background

Living the Principle

The Catholic Church calls us

- to recognize and respect the basic human rights of all people, especially the poor.

- to exercise the responsibilities that accompany our basic human rights.

- to work for public policies that protect and promote our basic human rights.

> **Reflect** In what ways do you promote the common good of all in your classroom, at home, and in your community?

About This Principle

This principle of a "preferential option for the poor" is a Church teaching based on Jesus' special love for "the least" of God's People. The poor come first, not last. Those who have more than they need are obligated to share with those in need. In deciding what to do with our time and talents or how to vote in an election, the well-being of the poor and most vulnerable (including the elderly and unborn) should be the most important factor.

Option for the Poor and Vulnerable

Introduce the topic. See pages TE56–TE57 for more information on all seven Catholic Social Teaching principles.

Summarize the first paragraph.

- Invite a volunteer to find and read aloud the Scripture passage from Matthew 25:40–45.

Review the last three paragraphs with the class.

- Emphasize the teachings/quotes from Pope Francis, the *Catechism of the Catholic Church,* and Saint Rose of Lima.
- Invite volunteers to explain how the photo at the top of the page connects with the text they just covered.

✝ Live Your Faith
Catholic Social Teaching

Option for the Poor and Vulnerable

In Scripture, Jesus says that whatever we have done for people who are poor or needy, we have also done for him and what we have not done for them, we haven't done for Jesus (see Matthew 25:40–45). This means we should treat people in need the same way we would treat Jesus himself. We should give special priority to people who are hungry, thirsty, homeless or alone.

Pope Francis has said, "Among our tasks as witnesses to the love of Christ is that of giving a voice to the cry of the poor." Our Church teaches that we should put the needs of those who are poor first. This is called the preferential option for the poor. The *Catechism* teaches that "God blesses those who come to the aid of the poor" (CCC, 2443).

We can clearly see in the life of Jesus his love for the poor and others considered outcasts by society. In fact, the Church says that Jesus had a "preferential love" for these people.

Saint Rose of Lima also put it this way: "When we serve the poor and the sick, we serve Jesus. We must not fail to help our neighbors, because in them we serve Jesus, (P. Hansen, *Vita mirablis* [Louvain, 1668])." No wonder the Church tells us that among the options we face when we decide what to do with our time, with our talents, and with our possessions and money, our first option, perhaps after our own family, should be the poor. We should prefer (show "preferential love" for) them more than we do others.

340 Live Your Faith

 ## Using This Feature

Chapter/Lesson Connection

Use this feature to enhance the following chapters:

Chapter 2, page 63E   **Chapter 12**, page 195E

Chapter 8, page 143E   **Chapter 20**, page 303E

Use this feature to enhance the following seasonal lessons:

Advent, page 23   **Easter,** page 43

Lent, page 35

Sacrificial Love

This may be easy to say, but it is certainly difficult to do. Everyone wants to hang out with his or her friends and take care of their own needs. Spending time with those who don't have lots of friends or things, sharing with them, or helping them in some way—that's sacrificial love. But that's our mission: to be the sacrificial love of Jesus for others.

An American soldier during World War II was marching with his unit across an Italian hillside. When they stopped for a break, he wandered into some tall bushes, where he discovered a statue of Jesus, but the hands were missing. He stared at that statue for a long time. Then he took out a piece of paper and wrote these words: "I have no hands but yours." Jesus tells each of us the same thing. He has no hands but ours, and we are called to use them to show his love in the world.

> How can you show Jesus' preferential love for the poor in your own life and community?

Personal Action

Figure out how much "free time" you have each month and how you could choose to spend at least one or two hours a month with those around you who have no home, are sick, or are lonely.

_____

_____

_____

Figure out how much "spending money" you have each month (or week) and what ten percent of that would be. Then decide how best to use that ten percent on behalf of others who are in need.

_____

_____

_____

_____

Group Action

As a class identify organizations in your community that serve people struggling to meet their needs. Which groups might be able to use students' artwork for their facilities? Assign a person or team to contact each group and report their findings. Choose which groups you want to work with and then create a plan for providing the artwork.

Sacrificial Love

Have the students silently read this section.

- *Ask:* Who do you know that has served as "the hands" of Jesus? In what way?
- Allow volunteers to respond.
> Read aloud the reflection question to get the students thinking as you transition to the activity portion of the lesson.

Personal Action

Read aloud the instructions.

- Give the students time to respond to both prompts.
- Invite volunteers to share their ideas with the class.

Group Action

Ask a volunteer to read aloud the instructions for the group activity.

- Have the students brainstorm possible facilities that could use artwork. They should also consider what images they would like to show in the artwork.
- If any students seem especially interested in the project, invite them to follow up with some of the organizations and to report back to the class.

---

i Teacher Background

Living the Principle

The Catholic Church calls us

- to put our time, talents, possessions, and money at the service of the poor and vulnerable.
- to show the poor the same love that Jesus did.
- to advocate for public policies that benefit the poor and vulnerable.

> **Reflect** In what ways do you make the poor a priority when you make decisions about your time, talents, possessions, and money?

About This Principle

The rebirth of Catholic Social Teaching in 1891 began with Pope Leo XIII's defense of the dignity of work and the rights of workers. Because the exploitation of workers has not ended, the Church continues to speak out on this issue. In instances where the power of corporations has increased as the power of workers has decreased, this issue is very relevant and very important.

The Dignity of Work and the Rights of Workers

Introduce the topic. See pages TE56–TE57 for more information on all seven Catholic Social Teaching principles.

Divide the class into groups and assign each group one of the paragraphs in this section.

- Instruct each group to summarize their paragraph and share their summary with the class.

- Be sure to bring up anything important that the groups might have missed.

Ask: What examples of "social sin" are you aware of? Do you know of anyone or any groups who are trying to correct these unjust situations or practices?

- Encourage class discussion.

Live Your Faith
Catholic Social Teaching

Dignity of Work and the Rights of Workers

All adults have a right and responsibility to work. Work helps people earn money to buy food and other necessities. It also helps to give their lives meaning as they cooperate with God's creation. Everyone should have access to meaningful work, whether that work is within the home or outside the home.

Sacred Scripture and Sacred Tradition teach that workers deserve to be treated with justice by their employers (see Deuteronomy 24:14). Employees also have a right to a fair wage for their work (see Leviticus 19:13 and Deuteronomy 24:15). When there is a conflict between workers and employers, workers have a right to get together and express their opinion.

Workers and their employers should treat one another with respect and solve those conflicts peacefully.

Part of spreading God's love is working for justice for those who are treated unfairly. Workers in our own country as well as the rest of the world are sometimes treated unfairly. Because of our oneness in God's family, such unfair treatment is a sin against human solidarity.

The equal dignity of all people, no matter what kind of work they do or whether they are able to work at all, calls Catholics to work to eliminate these sinful inequalities, and promote the dignity and respect of all workers.

342 Live Your Faith

 Using This Feature

Chapter/Lesson Connection

Use this feature to enhance the following chapters:

Chapter 10, page 171E   **Chapter 19**, page 291E

Use this feature to enhance the following seasonal lessons:

Ordinary Time, page 19   **Ascension,** page 47

Easter, page 43

Supporting the Workers

We can support the right of workers to form unions to protect their rights. When unions go on strike, we can refuse to cross their picket lines, even when that is inconvenient. Many people and some dioceses joined boycotts to support farm workers in receiving a living wage. Some have boycotted companies who use sweatshop labor or refuse to pay their workers fairly.

Some people support workers by buying directly from farmers at markets, rather than buying produce in giant supermarkets. Others choose to patronize locally owned restaurants and stores rather than large chains, even if they have to pay more. Communities have challenged superstores because they put some local stores out of business and pay nonunion-level wages. There are many ways to help. For example, buying "Fair Trade Coffee" supports coffee cooperatives that pay their workers a fair wage.

> **Which of these ways to help appeals to you the most?**

Personal Action

Make a list of all the places you shop or eat. Put an "L" next to those that are locally owned. Put a "C" next to those that are out-of-town chains. For each chain store you list, identify at least one locally owned alternative that is not too inconvenient for you.

_____

_____

_____

_____

_____

_____

_____

Make a decision to change one of your shopping habits in order to support workers in your community. Share this decision with others you trust, and invite them to join you.

Group Action

Research with your classmates any consumer boycotts going on in your area. Share your findings, choose one of these boycotts to participate in, and create a plan for doing so.

Teacher Background

Living the Principle

The Catholic Church calls us

- to recognize and respect the dignity of work.
- to support the rights of workers, including their right to form unions.
- to work for public policies that protect small producers and promote employment and a living wage.

> **Reflect** How conscious are you of workers who are treated unfairly, small producers, and locally owned businesses when you make your shopping decisions?

Supporting the Workers

Ask two volunteers to each read aloud one of these paragraphs.

- Emphasize that there are many effective ways that people can unite to protect the rights of workers.
- Review those highlighted in the reading and ask volunteers to share any other effective ways that we can help to protect the rights of workers.
- Invite a volunteer to list the ideas presented by the class on the board or on chart paper.
- > *Ask:* Which of these ways to help appeals to you the most?
- Encourage silent reflection.

Personal Action

Explain the activity.

- Give the students time to reflect on and answer the prompts.

Group Action

Read aloud the instructions.

- The students will need access to the Internet and/or the library to complete their research.
- Allow them to work in pairs to research and create their participation plan.
- Invite each pair to share their findings and their plans with the class.

About This Principle

From 1891 to the Second Vatican Council , Catholic Social Teaching was primarily focused on questions of justice within the family, workplace, local community, and nation. After Vatican II, Pope Paul VI proclaimed that these social issues have now become worldwide. The Church teaches that our solidarity is with the whole human family.

Solidarity of the Human Family

Introduce the topic. See pages TE56–TE57 for more information on all seven Catholic Social Teaching principles.

Read the first two paragraphs to the class.

- Ask a volunteer to look up and read aloud Romans 2:11 and another to read Matthew 5:9.
- Discuss how these Scripture passages relate to the content in this section.

Invite a volunteer to read aloud the last two paragraphs.

- *Ask:* What other historical figures do you know of who promoted solidarity? How about those you know personally?

 Live Your Faith
Catholic Social Teaching

Solidarity of the Human Family

Our world includes people of different nations, races, cultures, beliefs, and economic levels. But God created each one of us. We are one human family. In fact, Sacred Scripture tells us that the differences that we see between ourselves and others are not important to God (see Romans 2:11). God calls everyone to be his children.

Because God created all people, we have an obligation to treat everyone with love, kindness, and justice. In the Beatitudes, Jesus tells us "Blessed are the peacemakers" (Matthew 5:9). Working for justice between people will help us to live in peace with one another.

This principle of Catholic Social Teaching makes it clear that it's not just those around us for whom we should be advocating, but for people throughout the world. It is God's love of all persons that motivates us to care globally. We share in the Church's missionary mandate to bring the Gospel to all nations.

Jean Donovan of Cleveland, Ohio, heard this missionary mandate as a young businesswoman in the mid-1970s. She left her job and family to go to El Salvador to work with the poor. Realizing that "solidarity" means sharing both spiritual goods and material goods, Jean brought both to her ministry. She shared her faith and found her own faith deepened by the heroic faith of the people of El Salvador. Her friends in Cleveland sent material goods in response to Jean's appeals.

344 Live Your Faith

Using This Feature

Chapter/Lesson Connection

Use this feature to enhance the following chapters:

Use this feature to enhance the following seasonal lessons:

Sacrifice and Solidarity

Each day in the midst of poverty and civil war, Jean Donovan grew in her understanding of her mission—to be the sacrificial love of Jesus for others. As the danger in the country increased, her fiancé and family begged Jean to come home. But she kept thinking about the children she cared for there. On December 2, 1980, Jean was assassinated along with Maura Clarke, Ita Ford, and Dorothy Kazel, three other American Catholic religious women who worked with the poor and refugees in El Salvador.

Although Jean sacrificed her life completely, you are asked to consider other ways of sacrificing in solidarity with others suffering around the world. It starts with taking the time to read about others and learn their realities. It includes sharing your money, not only during Lent, but year-round. And it includes using your talents to raise the awareness about the needs of others, and showing how others can help.

> Why would Jean Donovan stay in El Salvador, especially with her fiancé asking her to come home? Explain your answer.

Personal Action

Research several groups in other countries that need help and discuss with the rest of your family how you might be able to act in solidarity with one or more of the groups. List who you might help, and how.

_____

_____

_____

_____

_____

_____

_____

_____

Create some reminder (like a note or picture on your mirror) to pray for this group every day and suggest that your family add a prayer for them at dinner.

Group Action

Research as a class a variety of groups or programs in other countries that could use your help. Missionary groups like Maryknoll and the Columban Fathers, aid groups like Catholic Relief Services, and the USCCB Offices of Domestic Social Development and International Justice and Peace can be very helpful. Choose one group or program and create a plan to help. Consider sharing your plan with other classrooms, or other groups in your parish or local community, and invite them to help.

Sacrifice and Solidarity

Have the students silently read this section.

- Invite the class to expand upon the ideas in the last paragraph on ways we can work toward solidarity.
- Have a volunteer record the ideas on the board or on chart paper.

> Ask the students to discuss the reflection question with a classmate.

Personal Action

Give the students time to research and respond to the activity.

- Invite volunteers to share with the class some of their findings and/or their ideas for reminders to pray for certain groups.
- Have a student list, on the board or on chart paper, each of the groups that are mentioned.

Group Action

Use the list of groups of people in other countries who are in need of help to transition to the group activity.

- Decide as a class which group to focus on and brainstorm ways that your class and/or your local community and parish can help.
- Follow through with these ideas to reinforce the importance of working as one toward the solidarity of the human family.

ℹ Teacher Background

Living the Principle

The Catholic Church calls us

- to recognize the rights and needs of people throughout the world.
- to respond to these needs both personally and through public policy advocacy.
- to promote peaceful alternatives to war for settling international conflicts.

> **Reflect** In what ways do you foster a sense of solidarity with others around the world in what you read and teach, how you spend your money, how you vote, and how you pray?

About This Principle

The Church teaches that we are to be stewards of God's creation, but the more urban our society and our own lives become, the more cut off from God's creation we seem to be. We tend to take natural resources for granted and focus our lives around things more than around people. The inspiring and healing effects of natural beauty are a powerful antidote to the stresses and struggles of daily life, but we are often too busy to drink deeply of God's incredible gifts in nature.

Care for God's Creation

Introduce the topic. See pages TE56–TE57 for more information on all seven Catholic Social Teaching principles.

Point out the photo at the top of this page.

- *Ask:* What are these people doing? How do you think this helps them and others to appreciate God's creation?

Summarize the first paragraph.

- Invite a volunteer to look up and read Genesis 1:31 and Genesis 1:28b to the class.
- Discuss how these readings connect to the photo.

Read aloud the last two paragraphs.

- Emphasize that we are not only to enjoy and take care of creation, but we must also take the time to recognize God and the beauty in his creation.

Live Your Faith
Catholic Social Teaching

Care for God's Creation

When God created the world—the animals, plants, and all natural things, he looked upon what he had made and called it "very good" (Genesis 1:31). God made people the stewards of the "fish of the sea, the birds of the air, and all the living things that crawl on the earth" (Genesis 1:28b). That means humans have a special responsibility to care for all of God's creation.

Sacred Tradition teaches us that God created the earth and all living things for the common good—the good of everyone. We should work to take care of the environment and all living things, so they can be enjoyed by everyone today and in future generations. The *Catechism* teaches us that we owe animals kindness, because they give glory to God just by being what they were made to be.

Our response to God's sharing all this goodness and beauty with us involves several steps. First, God wants us to enjoy it. God invites us to pause every day to notice the beauty around us and just enjoy it—see it, smell it, touch it, listen to it, taste it. It could be a sunset, a flower, a creek, a bird, a mountain, a sky full of stars, a baby. Just enjoy them! Second, God wants us to realize that he is there in all that beauty and to say "thank you, God." Yes, we are made to live in communion with God in his "garden of paradise" on Earth. This is real happiness. Third, God wants us to take care of this garden, to make it even more beautiful, and to share it with others.

346 Live Your Faith

 Using This Feature

Chapter/Lesson Connection

Use this feature to enhance the following chapters:

Chapter 1, page 51E   **Chapter 17**, page 263E

Chapter 5, page 103E   **Chapter 21**, page 315E

Use this feature to enhance the following seasonal lesson:

The Annunciation, page 31

Generosity and Creation

In the Book of Genesis, God tells us to "have dominion" over the Earth. This doesn't mean we can do anything we want to the Earth. Even if something is "our property," we are not free to destroy it or harm it. We have to take care of the beauty and resources of the Earth for future generations and to share it with others now. God made it for everyone.

Just because God meant his creation to be for everyone doesn't mean we have the right to take property from someone else. That would be stealing, which is against the Seventh Commandment. But it means that if we see that someone has been kept from enjoying God's blessings, either because their property has been stolen or because they have been unfairly kept from having anything, we should try to help them. God calls us to be generous and fair. He wants us to make a difference in the way the world operates by speaking up for others and helping all people to enjoy his blessings together.

> How do you say "thank you, God" when you enjoy his gifts of beauty?

Personal Action

Take a trip around your neighborhood (or a special place in your community) and make a list of the forms of natural beauty you find.

_____

_____

_____

_____

Choose your favorite and spend ten minutes enjoying it with all your senses. Say a prayer of thanks to God for this beauty. Then decide what you can do to protect this place. List your ideas here.

_____

_____

_____

_____

RECYCLED TIRE BELT

Group Action

Discuss with your classmates different ways that your school could improve its recycling program (or other ways that the area around your school or neighborhood could be made more beautiful) or another project that honors God's creation. You may want to organize a group to promote the recycling efforts or ask a speaker to explain its use. Then create a plan for putting your group's work into practice.

Generosity and Creation

Have the students silently read this section.

- As a class, discuss the main points the students have read.
> Read aloud the reflection question.
- Invite volunteers to share or, if there are no volunteers and time allows, let the students reflect and write their answers. Remind them that they do not have to share their personal responses with the class.

Personal Action

Review the instructions with the class.

- Invite the students to share some of their favorite things in nature.
- Assign a due date on which they will need to be prepared to share their lists and their ideas on how they can protect their favorite places.

Group Action

Talk about this activity as a class.

- Brainstorm ideas and have a volunteer list them on the board or on chart paper.
- Arrange the students in small groups where they will consider ways to fulfill one of the options that they have listed.
- Vote, as a class, for the group that comes up with the best plan, and follow their plan of action.

Teacher Background

Living the Principle

The Catholic Church calls us

- to praise our Creator and to celebrate creation as part of our observance of the Lord's Day.
- to recover our partnership with God in caring for God's creation.
- to turn our dominion over the Earth into a blessing for all creatures and generations to come.

> **Reflect** As a teacher, how can you make daily and weekly time for savoring creation, praising the Creator, and sharing this joy with others?

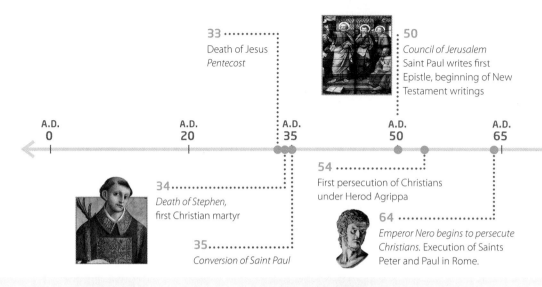

33 ··········
Death of Jesus
Pentecost

50
Council of Jerusalem
Saint Paul writes first
Epistle, beginning of New
Testament writings

A.D.
0

A.D.
20

A.D.
35

A.D.
50

A.D.
65

34 ··········
Death of Stephen,
first Christian martyr

54 ·········
First persecution of Christians
under Herod Agrippa

35 ··········
Conversion of Saint Paul

64 ·········
*Emperor Nero begins to persecute
Christians.* Execution of Saints
Peter and Paul in Rome.

● **Pentecost,** A.D. 33

A most astonishing event occurred around the year 30 during Shavu'ot, the Jewish harvest Festival of Weeks, so called because it took place fifty days—or a week of weeks—after Passover. The Greek name for Shavu'ot was Pentecost, a word that means "fiftieth day."

Many people gathered in Jerusalem for this feast. A small group of Jesus' Apostles and disciples were meeting in an upper room of a house there and suddenly the Holy Spirit entered the room and filled them with the power and grace to begin boldly preaching the Gospel message. This event is said to mark the beginning of the Church.

Go to the Source

Read Acts 2:2-4 to find out more about the events of Pentecost.

● **Death of Stephen,** A.D. 34

Stephen was a deacon, or assistant, of the Apostles. In addition to preaching and serving the needs of widows and the poor, he also worked miracles. The Jewish leaders denounced him as a blasphemer and when he reproached them for their part in putting Jesus to death, the crowd stoned him to death. Saul, later to become Saint Paul, took part in the stoning.

Go to the Source

Read Acts 6—7 to learn more about Stephen's martyrdom.

● **Conversion of Saint Paul,** A.D. 35

Saul, a member of the Pharisees, was an ardent persecutor of early Christians. As he traveled to Damascus to obtain authority to arrest followers of Jesus, a light from Heaven blinded him and he heard a voice saying, "Why do you persecute me?" When the voice revealed himself to be Jesus, Saul converted, changed his name and became one of the great leaders of the early Church. He is noted especially for his missions to the Gentiles and the many letters, called Epistles, that he wrote to churches he helped found throughout Asia Minor.

Go to the Source

Read Acts 9:3-6 for the events of Paul's conversion.

● **Council of Jerusalem,** A.D. 50

An account of the meeting Peter had with other Christians is often called the Council of Jerusalem. This meeting occurred because some Christian Jews at Antioch taught that Gentile converts had to be circumcised. Paul, Barnabas, and others traveled to Jerusalem to consider this matter with the Apostles and presbyters ("elders") there. The leaders of the Church announced the decision to free the Gentiles from this Jewish regulation and other Jewish dietary laws.

Go to the Source

Read Acts 15:28-30 to read more about the Council of Jerusalem.

348 Church History Timeline

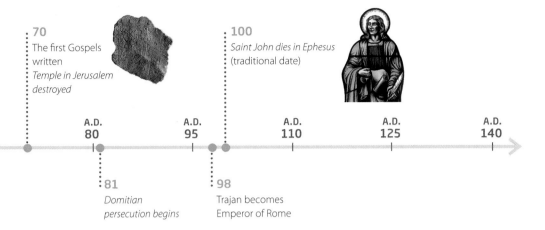

70
The first Gospels written
Temple in Jerusalem destroyed

100
Saint John dies in Ephesus (traditional date)

| A.D. 80 | A.D. 95 | A.D. 110 | A.D. 125 | A.D. 140 |

81
Domitian persecution begins

98
Trajan becomes Emperor of Rome

● **Emperor Nero's Persecution**, A.D. 64-67

On July 19, 64, a huge fire destroyed much of Rome. Although Emperor Nero may have set the fire himself in order to rebuild the city, when he realized how angry the citizens were, he blamed the new religion of Christianity and began a massive persecution of Christians. Saints Peter and Paul are believed to have died during this period. Saint Peter was crucified head-down and Saint Paul was beheaded.

● **Temple in Jerusalem Destroyed,** A.D. 70

In A.D. 70, the Roman army, under the command of the future Emperor Titus, attacked and conquered the city of Jerusalem, laying waste to the Jewish Temple. Before his Death, Jesus predicted the destruction, saying, "Do you see all these great buildings? Not one stone here will be left on another; everyone will be thrown down."

📖 **Go to the Source**

Mark 13:1-2 relates Jesus' prophecy regarding the Temple.

● **Domitian Persecution,** A.D. 81-96

The Emperor Domitian began an empire-wide persecution of all those who did not worship him as "lord and god." Many accounts of the early Church persecutions of Christians come from this period. He also taxed the Jews and then claimed that Christians pretended not to be Jews to avoid taxation.

● **Saint John dies in Ephesus,** A.D. 100

Saint John the Evangelist was a follower of John the Baptist and a fisherman before Jesus called him to be an Apostle. Saint John was with Jesus for three years and was the only Apostle known to have been present at the Crucifixion. John is said to be the author of the Book of Revelation, the final book of the Bible, as well as the Gospel according to John and three Epistles.

140
*First lists of
New Testament
writing begin*

155
Martyrdom of Polycarp

A.D.	A.D.	A.D.	A.D.	A.D.
140	**155**	**170**	**185**	**200**

150
Earliest atlas
(Ptolemy's
Geography)
is created

161
Persecutions under Marcus Aurelius

● **First lists of New Testament writing begin,** A.D. 140

Beginning approximately 50 years after Jesus' Death, Gospels, letters (called Epistles), memoirs, teachings, and other documents were shared among Christian churches to help explain the saving work of Jesus and the mission of early Church leaders. Over the next century, more Epistles were written. A list of these writings became part of the canon of Scripture, joining the Old Testament writings as a New Testament. The order of New Testament books is consistent in the Roman Catholic, Orthodox, and Protestant churches. The first translations of the New Testament had already been made by the end of the Second Century.

● **Martyrdom of Polycarp,** A.D. 155

Saint Polycarp is considered one of the "apostolic fathers of the Church," one of the first- and second-century writers who give us information about the early Christian Church. They are called apostolic because it is believed they had a historical connection to the Apostles. Polycarp was the author of the Epistle of Barnabas and the Didache, which contains several important teachings of the early Church. He was martyred after refusing to burn incense in honor of the Roman Emperor. Though he had been sentenced to be burned at the stake, it is said that the fire would not touch him, and he was stabbed to death.

● **Persecutions under Marcus Aurelius,** A.D. 161–180

Marcus Aurelius was the Emperor of Rome between 161 to 180. He was known as a strong proponent of Stoicism, a philosophy which conflicted with the Christian teachings of the time. In the early years of his reign as Emperor, Marcus Aurelius continued a policy of allowing Christian to worship, but after a time he upheld that the Church's belief in an immortal soul and life after death was dangerous to the state, and began persecutions of Christians in A.D. 161.

350 Church History Timeline

249–251
*Problem of the lapsi,
Christians who denied the
faith under persecution*

258
*Emperor
Valerian's
persecution*

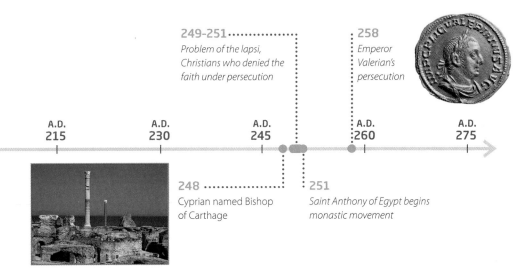

A.D. 215   A.D. 230   A.D. 245   A.D. 260   A.D. 275

248
Cyprian named Bishop
of Carthage

251
*Saint Anthony of Egypt begins
monastic movement*

● Problem of the *lapsi*, A.D. 249-251

In the first years of Christianity, people expected the immediate return of Jesus. As time wore on and the Second Coming didn't happen, some people began to fall away from the faith and resume old pagan practices or deny the faith under the pressure of persecution. When these people wanted to return at a later date, the Church was forced to decide how to handle the situation. Sanctions ranged from severe penance to denial of absolution until the time of death.

● Saint Anthony of Egypt begins monastic movement, A.D. 251-356

The first monk in the Catholic Church was Saint Anthony of Egypt. He was inspired by two passages in Scripture to sell all he had and give to the poor, and to not be concerned about tomorrow. A brilliant scholar, he lived as a hermit in modern-day Libya. Eventually, his reputation for holiness attracted many to him and he was convinced to establish a community of monks. Preferring to live alone, he visited the community now and then to be sure they were following his rules.

Go to the Document

Read *Life of Saint Anthony* by Athanasius, Bishop of Alexandria.

● Emperor Valerian's persecution, A.D. 258

During his reign as Emperor of Rome, Valerian first ordered Christian clergy members to make sacrifices to Roman gods under threat of banishment from the empire. A year later, he demanded that Christian leaders be executed, and forced Roman Christians in authority to renounce their faith or lose their positions. Cyprian, the Bishop of Carthage and an early Christian writer, was executed under Valerian's order for refusing to worship the Roman gods.

Church History Timeline   **351**

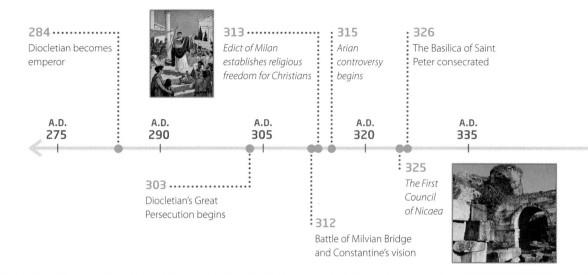

284 ········
Diocletian becomes
emperor

313 ········
*Edict of Milan
establishes religious
freedom for Christians*

315
*Arian
controversy
begins*

326
The Basilica of Saint
Peter consecrated

A.D.
275

A.D.
290

A.D.
305

A.D.
320

A.D.
335

303 ········
Diocletian's Great
Persecution begins

325
*The First
Council
of Nicaea*

312
Battle of Milvian Bridge
and Constantine's vision

● **Edict of Milan establishes religious freedom for Christians,** A.D. 313

One of the most important events in the life of the Church occurred in 313 when the Emperor Constantine issued the Edict of Milan granting religious freedom to Christians. This edict allowed Christians to practice their faith openly without fear of persecution. In addition, it meant that Christians could be involved in secular affairs, Christian worship became public, and Christian missionaries would help spread both the faith and the Roman civilization throughout the Empire.

● **Arian controversy begins,** A.D. 315

One of the first major threats to Christianity began shortly after the Edict of Milan, when an Alexandrian priest named Arius taught that Jesus was not of the same substance as the Father, and while he was like the Father, Jesus was not truly God. Arius' teachings became popular because they reflected earlier pagan beliefs about the gods. Debate over the nature of Jesus got so heated, riots even broke out in Egypt and the Emperor became embroiled in the controversy.

Go to the Document

Read more about early heresies in the *Catechism of the Catholic Church*, 464-465.

● **The First Council of Nicaea,** A.D. 325

In order to address the controversy created by Arius, Emperor Constantine brought all Church leaders together in Nicaea, a town outside present-day Istanbul, Turkey. This gathering is considered the first ecumenical council or meeting of Catholic bishops. At this council, the bishops combated the Arian heresy by formulating the Nicene Creed, which is used in Catholic masses to this day. In it, we affirm that Jesus is truly divine by proclaiming that he is "the Only Begotten Son of God, born of the Father before all ages. God from God, Light from Light, true God from true God, begotten, not made, consubstantial with the Father; through him all things were made."

Go to the Document

Read more about the Creed in the *Catechism of the Catholic Church*, 198.

© Our Sunday Visitor

352 Church History Timeline

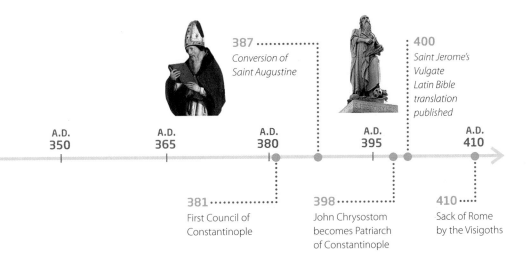

387 .... Conversion of Saint Augustine

400 Saint Jerome's Vulgate Latin Bible translation published

| A.D. 350 | A.D. 365 | A.D. 380 | A.D. 395 | A.D. 410 |

381 .... First Council of Constantinople

398 .... John Chrysostom becomes Patriarch of Constantinople

410 ..... Sack of Rome by the Visigoths

● **Conversion of Augustine,** A.D. 387

Saint Augustine was the bishop of Hippo, located in present-day Algeria. One of the most important early Church Fathers, his early youth was marked with a libertine lifestyle. His mother, Saint Monica, prayed for his conversion and, at age 32, he became a Christian. Augustine was heavily influenced by Saint Ambrose, Bishop of Milan. Through his writings, Augustine challenged Christians to see a deeper spiritual meaning in everything, reassuring his readers that eternal life is more important than anything happening in the present day. This perspective became a dominant worldview in the medieval period. Saint Augustine's writings continue to inspire and influence theologians to the present time. Pope Boniface VIII named him a Doctor of the Church in 1298.

Go to the Document

Read Augustine's most important works: *City of God* and *Confessions*.

● **Jerome's Vulgate Latin Bible translation published,** A.D. 400

In 382, Pope Damasus I commissioned Saint Jerome to begin work on a Latin version of Scripture. He corrected earlier Latin text of the New Testament and in 390 began translating the Old Testament from the original Hebrew. By the 13th century, his Bible became known as the *versio vulgata,* "commonly used translation," generally referred to as the Vulgate. It was the official Latin text of Scripture in the Church and was often used until more modern translations were made in the 20th century. One of Jerome's most famous sayings is, "Ignorance of the Scriptures is ignorance of Christ."

© Our Sunday Visitor

Church History Timeline **353**

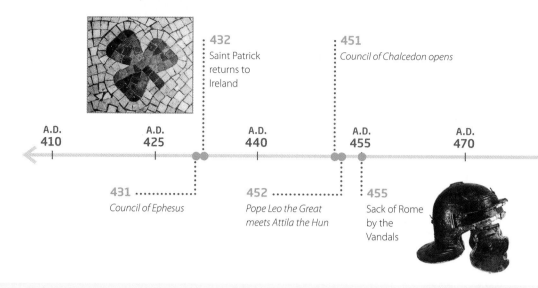

432
Saint Patrick returns to Ireland

451
Council of Chalcedon opens

A.D. **410**   A.D. **425**   A.D. **440**   A.D. **455**   A.D. **470**

431 ············
Council of Ephesus

452 ··············
Pope Leo the Great meets Attila the Hun

455
Sack of Rome by the Vandals

● **Council of Ephesus,** A.D. 431

The third ecumenical council, the Council of Ephesus, was convened by the Roman Emperor Theodosius II. It reconfirmed the wording of the Nicene Creed, forever establishing that Jesus is both God and man. It also affirmed Mary's title as the *Theotokos,* "Mother of God." Approximately 250 bishops took part in the gathering, which was held in the Church of Mary in Ephesus in present-day Turkey.

● **Council of Chalcedon,** A.D. 451

The Council of Chalcedon, the fourth ecumenical council, declared Christ's two natures were unmixed, unchanged, undivided and inseparable in refutation of the heresy of Monophysitism, which said the human nature of Jesus was lost in the Divine. The Council was held near modern-day Istanbul.

Go to the Document

Read more about the teachings of the Council in *Catechism of the Catholic Church,* 467.

● **Pope Leo I (the Great) meets Attila the Hun,** A.D. 452

Attila the Hun invaded Italy, sacking cities on his way to overtake the city of Rome. The Emperor sent an envoy that included Pope Leo to try to prevent Attila from attacking the Eternal City. Although the exact details of the negotiations are lost, historians agree that as a result of Pope Leo's intervention, Attila agreed to withdraw. Three years later, when Genseric did occupy Rome, Leo was able to mitigate the effects of the invasion, persuading the Vandals not to harm the citizens or plunder the city.

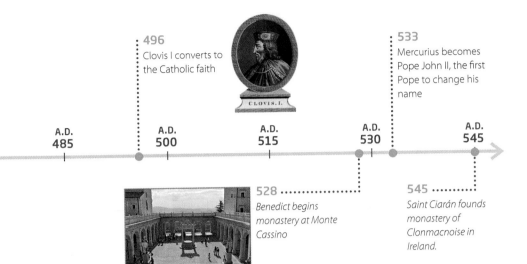

496
Clovis I converts to the Catholic faith

533
Mercurius becomes Pope John II, the first Pope to change his name

A.D. **485**　　A.D. **500**　　A.D. **515**　　A.D. **530**　　A.D. **545**

528 ·············
Benedict begins monastery at Monte Cassino

545 ············
Saint Ciarán founds monastery of Clonmacnoise in Ireland.

● Benedict begins monastery at Monte Cassino, A.D. 528

Saint Benedict of Nursia is widely recognized as the father of Western monasticism. He founded 12 monasteries in Subiaco, before finally settling at Monte Cassino. His twin sister, Saint Scholastica, lived in a nearby convent. He is best known for his "Rule of Saint Benedict," a list of guidelines for monastic life that continues to guide and influence monastic life today with its principles of moderation and reasonableness. He is the patron Saint of Europe and of students.

Go to the Document

Find the original Rule of Saint Benedict and read about three of the guidelines.

● Saint Ciarán founds monastery of Clonmacnoise, A.D. 545

Saint Ciarán is considered one of the Twelve Apostles of Ireland, early monastic Saints of the country. Ciarán studied as a monk on Aran Island in Ireland, where he was eventually ordained as a priest. After some traveling he settled in the area of Clonmacnoise and founded a monastery whose ruins are still visible today. He was known as a humble man whose monastery became renowned as a place of spiritual and intellectual learning. The site served as a monastery until 1552, when it was dissolved under the rule of King Henry VIII of England and his Suppression of the Monasteries. Pope Saint John Paul II visited the site of the monastery during his visit to Ireland in 1979.

553
Second Ecumenical Council of Constantinople

571
The Monophysites reject the Council of Chalcedon, causing a further schism in the Church

596
Saint Augustine of Canterbury evangelizes the English

| A.D. **545** | A.D. **560** | A.D. **575** | A.D. **590** | A.D. **605** |

569
John of Ephesus completes *Biographies of Eastern Saints*

590
Pope Saint Gregory the Great elected

● **Pope Saint Gregory the Great,**
A.D. 590

Pope Saint Gregory, one of the Doctors of the Church, was a strong supporter of monasticism and an organizer of missionary activity, especially to England. During his reign, he reformed the liturgy and clarified doctrines. Although he would have personally preferred to remain a monk, he willingly agreed when he was elected Pope. The Gregorian chant is named after him because he promoted its use and even wrote some chants for parts of the Mass, although it probably existed as an earlier musical form. He was the first Pope to call himself "Servant of the Servants of God." His *Dialogues,* a collection of four books, including a biography of Saint Benedict, are still read today.

Go to the Document
Read Pope Saint Gregory's *Dialogues* for insight into sixth-century Italian religious life.

● **Saint Augustine of Canterbury evangelizes the English,** A.D. 596

A Benedictine monk, Saint Augustine is considered the "Apostle to the English." In 595, Pope Saint Gregory the Great chose him to lead a band of missionaries to Britain to bring the Gospel message to King Æthelberht and his kingdom. Augustine, along with Laurence of Canterbury, and a group of about 40 companions, landed on Isle of Thanet in 597. Their missionary activity met with success and thousands were baptized. Saint Augustine was named the first Archbishop of Canterbury. He died in 604 and was soon afterwards declared a Saint.

Go to the Document
Some of the early history of the missions to the English is recorded in Venerable Bede's *Ecclesiastical History of the English People.*

356 Church History Timeline

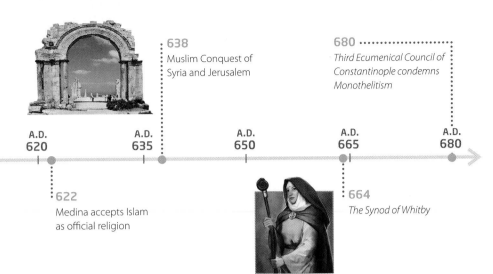

638
Muslim Conquest of
Syria and Jerusalem

680
*Third Ecumenical Council of
Constantinople condemns
Monothelitism*

A.D. **620**   A.D. **635**   A.D. **650**   A.D. **665**   A.D. **680**

622
Medina accepts Islam
as official religion

664
The Synod of Whitby

● **The Synod of Whitby,** A.D. 664

The Celtic priest Saint Aidan introduced some practices into the English church that were different from those in Rome. The Synod of Whitby determined that the Pope was appointed to head the entire Church and that the English Church would follow Rome in matters such as the date for the celebration of Easter. This decision cleared the way for the whole English Church to be united in doctrine and practice under one head. Saint Hilda, who was a pupil of Saint Aidan and had founded a double monastery for men and women at Whitby in 657, had a prominent role during this Synod, supervising the discussions. Though she had initially followed Saint Aidan, Hilda accepted the decision of the Synod in favor of Rome. Following the Synod, the Church in England flourished, and monks from Rome brought many famous manuscripts to English monasteries, where they were copied and made available to many.

● **Third Ecumenical Council of Constantinople condemns Monothelitism,** A.D. 680

Convened by Emperor Constantine IV, this Council further clarified the nature of Jesus by declaring that monothelitism, the teaching that Jesus has two natures but only one will, is heretical. It affirmed that Jesus has two wills (human and Divine) that correspond to his two natures, although his human will was "in subjection to his divine and all-powerful will."

711 ....
Muslim armies
invade Spain

716–718
*Saint Boniface
evangelizes the
Germans*

732
*Battle
of Tours*

A.D.
680

A.D.
695

A.D.
710

A.D.
725

A.D.
740

731 ....
Venerable Bede writes
The Ecclesiastical
History of the English
People

● **Saint Boniface evangelizes the Germans,** A.D. 716–718

Boniface, also known as Winifred, was an English Benedictine priest. He traveled to what is now present-day Germany to convert the native peoples to Christianity. The story is told that when Boniface started to chop down an oak that was sacred to the pagan population, a great wind finished the job. When Boniface was not punished by the god, the townsfolk converted and Boniface used the wood to build a chapel dedicated to Saint Peter.

Go to the Document

Some of Boniface's works include: *Collection of Letters; Poems and Riddles; Poenitentiale; Compendium of the Latin Language* and *Compendium of Latin Prosody.*

● **Venerable Bede writes** *The Ecclesiastical History of the English People,* A.D. 731

An author and scholar, Venerable Bede was given the title of "The Father of English History" based on his most famous writing, *The Ecclesiastical History of the English People,* which he wrote to demonstrate the growth and history of the English Catholic Church. About 160 manuscript copies of his work still exist today. A skilled linguist and translator of both Latin and Greek, he was named a Doctor of the Church by Pope Leo XIII in 1899, the first native Briton to be so designated.

● **Battle of Tours,** A.D. 732

By this time in history, the Muslims ruled much of Spain and were beginning to make inroads into the rest of Europe. Charles Martel, a Christian prince who had already united the kingdom of the Franks after two centuries of weakened rulers, defeated a Muslim force that had invaded present-day France as far as Tours. Most historians agree that if Martel hadn't defeated the Muslim army, all of Europe might have fallen under Islamic rule, effectively ending the Christianization of Europe. Because of his role in the battle, Charles was given the nickname *Martellus,* "The Hammer." He was the father of Pepin the Short, king of the Franks, and the grandfather of Emperor Charlemagne.

358 Church History Timeline

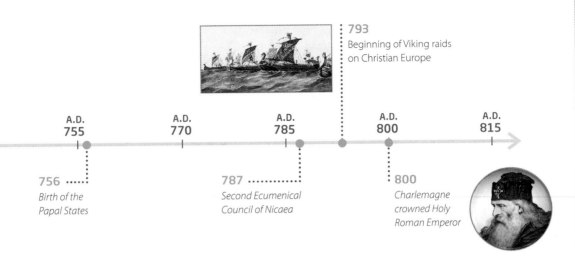

793
Beginning of Viking raids
on Christian Europe

| A.D. **755** | A.D. **770** | A.D. **785** | A.D. **800** | A.D. **815** |

756 ·····
*Birth of the
Papal States*

787 ··········
*Second Ecumenical
Council of Nicaea*

800
*Charlemagne
crowned Holy
Roman Emperor*

● Birth of the Papal States, A.D. 756

In 751, Pepin the Short (the son of Charles Martel) was crowned King of the Franks, beginning the Carolingian dynasty. Five years later, in the Donation of Pepin, he gave Pope Stephen III control over the middle part of Italy, founding the Papal States, which existed until 1870. Today Vatican City is all that remains. It is a separate city-state, independent from Italy, even though it lies in the heart of Rome.

● Second Ecumenical Council of Nicaea resolves iconoclasm, A.D. 787

Iconoclasm refers to the destruction of religious images. Around 730, the Byzantine Emperor Leo III ordered the removal of an image of Jesus over the ceremonial entrance to the Great Palace of Constantinople to be replaced by a cross. This began a systematic removal of holy images and a quarrel between those who venerated "icons" and those who wanted them removed. The Second Council of Nicaea ended the conflict by stating: "we decree with full precision and care that, like the figure of the honoured and life-giving cross, the revered and holy images, whether painted or made of mosaic or of other suitable material, are to be exposed in the holy churches of God, on sacred instruments and vestments, on walls and panels, in houses and by public ways; these are the images of our Lord, God and saviour, Jesus Christ, and of our Lady without blemish, the holy God-bearer, and of the revered angels and of any of the saintly holy men…"

● Charlemagne crowned Holy Roman Emperor of the West, A.D. 800

On Christmas Day, 800, Pope Leo III crowned Charlemagne, or Charles the Great, Holy Roman Emperor of the West. Possessing both great political power and enormous personal charisma, Charlemagne was accepted as ruler of Europe from the Baltic to the Mediterranean. He is sometimes called the "second Constantine" because he united all of Europe under the Catholic faith. Believing he ruled by divine right, Charlemagne refused to be subject to the Pope, and actively involved himself in Church affairs, even instituting rules for members of the clergy and enacting laws against heresy. His coronation symbolized the union of Church and state in Western Europe, leading to a growing discontent between the Western Church and the emperor in the East, which eventually led to the split between Eastern and Western Christianity.

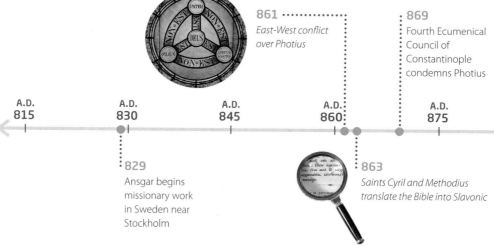

861 ....
East-West conflict
over Photius

869
Fourth Ecumenical
Council of
Constantinople
condemns Photius

A.D.
815

A.D.
830

A.D.
845

A.D.
860

A.D.
875

829
Ansgar begins
missionary work
in Sweden near
Stockholm

863
*Saints Cyril and Methodius
translate the Bible into Slavonic*

● **East-West conflict over Photius,**
   A.D. 861

Photius I was a layman who was named the Patriarch
of Constantinople from 858 through 867, and then
again from 877 through 886. Photius was first named
Patriarch after the Emperor deposed the previous
man in the position, the Patriarch Ignatius. At first the
reigning Pope Nicholas expressed support for the
new Patriarch, but then Photius declared he could
not accept the Pope's supremacy over the Catholic
Church in the East. Separate synods were held in
Rome and Constantinople (now Istanbul), and what
became known as the Photian Schism between the
Church in the East and in the West was created.

Go to the Document
Read more about the Church's definition of *schism* in
the *Catechism of the Catholic Church,* 2589.

● **Saints Cyril and Methodius
translate the Bible into
Slavonic,** A.D. 863

The Byzantine Greek brothers Cyril and Methodius
were sent by the Patriarch of Constantinople as
missionaries to the Slavic people in what is now near
present day Hungary, Slovakia, Bosnia, Herzegovina
and the Czech Republic. Given the title "Apostles to
the Slavs," they helped devise the Glagolitic alphabet
whose descendant script, Cyrillic, is still used today.
They translated the Bible into Slavonic and were
quite successful in their efforts to promote their new
translation. Pope Saint John Paul II named them
co-patrons of Europe, along with Saint Benedict
of Nursia.

360   Church History Timeline

Alive in Christ

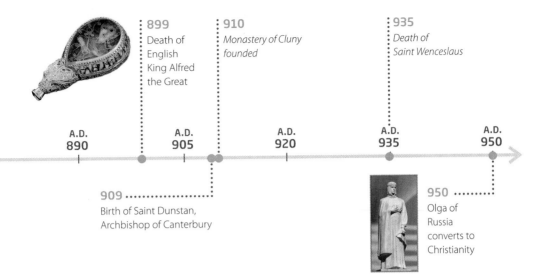

899
Death of
English
King Alfred
the Great

910
*Monastery of Cluny
founded*

935
*Death of
Saint Wenceslaus*

A.D.
890

A.D.
905

A.D.
920

A.D.
935

A.D.
950

909 ········
Birth of Saint Dunstan,
Archbishop of Canterbury

950 ········
Olga of
Russia
converts to
Christianity

● **Monastery of Cluny Founded,**
A.D. 910

William the Pious, Duke of Aquitaine, donated land
in Cluny, France to a monk named Berno to found a
Benedictine monastery with the proviso that it would
report directly to the Pope, although the monks
would choose their own abbot. This centralization
under the Pope was the beginning of a campaign
to address abuses that had crept into the monastic
system. The monks at Cluny emphasized prayer over
all else, praying the Divine Office or Liturgy of the
Hours five or six times a day. The Cluniac reform, as
it came to be known, spread throughout France,
England, Italy, and Spain. New monasteries sprang
up all over Europe, with the result that after the pope
himself, the Abbot of Cluny was the most important
Church figure in the Western world. By the twelfth
century the Congregation of Cluny included more
than a thousand monasteries.

● **Death of Saint Wenceslaus,** A.D. 935

Wenceslaus was one of two grandsons of Saint
Ludmilla. His twin brother was known as Boleslaus
the Cruel, but Wenceslaus was influenced to such an
extent by his grandmother Ludmilla that he became
a Christian. He became ruler of Bohemia when he
was eight years old, and as he grew older, he helped
spread Christianity throughout Bohemia. It is still
the major religion of the region, located primarily in
the Czech Republic. Wenceslaus was murdered by
supporters of his brother when he was on his way
to church. Though in his lifetime he was known as a
Duke, after his death he was given the title King by
Holy Roman Emperor Otto I. He is the king referred to
in the Christmas carol "Good King Wenceslaus."

962
Otto I crowned Holy Roman Emperor by Pope John XII

966
Mieszko I of Poland converts to Catholicism

1009
Muslims destroy Holy Sepulchre in Jerusalem

| A.D. **950** | A.D. **965** | A.D. **980** | A.D. **995** | A.D. **1010** |

982
Eric the Red establishes first Viking colony in Greenland

988
Saint Vladimir I the Great becomes the first Christian Grand Duke of Kiev

● **Otto I crowned Holy Roman Emperor by Pope John XII,** A.D. 962

Otto I was a German king who founded the Holy Roman Empire. Otto was known for associating himself with Catholic Church leaders, often placing bishops in positions of secular leadership rather than allowing other men who disagreed with him to come to power. Otto considered himself a protector of the Church, but many believed that by controlling Church leaders, Otto was establishing more power for himself. He also became known for appointing men who had little ecclesiastical background as leaders of monasteries and churches. After helping protect the city of Rome and the Papal States from an attack by Berengar II, Otto was eventually crowned Emperor by Pope John XII, and this event joined the kingdoms of Germany and Italy as the Holy Roman Empire. This Empire lasted from 962 until 1806.

● **Muslims destroy Holy Sepulchre in Jerusalem,** A.D. 1009

Although Jerusalem was under Muslim rule, most Christian places of worship were left alone. That changed on October 18, 1009 when Fatimid Caliph Al-Hakim bi-Amr Allah ordered the destruction of the Church of the Holy Sepulchre, long believed to be built over the burial place of Jesus. One Christian writer wrote at the time that everything was destroyed "except those parts which were impossible to destroy or would have been too difficult to carry away." A few repairs were attempted but restoration would take decades. Ultimately this act of desecration gave fuel to the later Crusades.

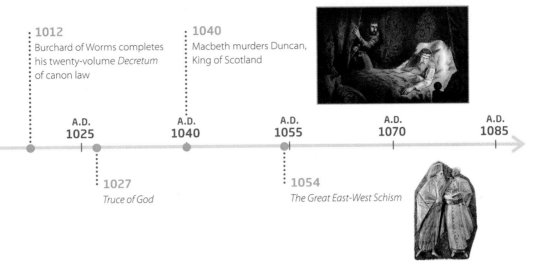

1012
Burchard of Worms completes his twenty-volume *Decretum* of canon law

1040
Macbeth murders Duncan, King of Scotland

A.D.
1025

A.D.
1040

A.D.
1055

A.D.
1070

A.D.
1085

1027
Truce of God

1054
The Great East-West Schism

● Truce of God, A.D. 1027

One of the world's first "peace movements," the Peace of God, or *Pax Dei,* used spiritual sanctions to limit violence against those who could not defend themselves, beginning with peasants and clergy. The Truce of God, or *Treuga Dei,* was an extension of the movement that asked Christian soldiers to abstain from fighting on Sundays, holy days, Lent and eventually all Fridays. Its goal was to reduce the private wars and fighting that had become rampant in feudal society.

● The Great East-West Schism, A.D. 1054

Over the first 1,000 years of Church history, differences began to develop between the Western and the Eastern Churches. For instance, Western bishops added the words "from the Father *and the Son*," to the Creed over the objections of Eastern leaders. Other conflicts, including the use of icons and sacred images, as well as some doctrinal points continued to foment until finally, in 1054 both the Eastern and the Western Church excommunicated each other. The Eastern Churches, which were no longer in union with Rome, are known as the Orthodox Churches. Those Eastern Churches that remained in communion with the Pope are known as Eastern Rite Catholic Churches. In 2013, the Ecumenical Patriarch Bartholomew, head of the Orthodox Churches, attended Pope Francis' installation as Bishop of Rome, something that had not happened since the Great East-West Schism.

Scripture

Catholic Bibles

Catholic Bibles have seven Old Testament books or parts of books not included in other Christian Bibles. When these books are included in a Protestant Bible, they are usually found in a section called the Apocrypha or Deutero-canonical Books. The word *apocrypha* comes from a Greek word that means, "hidden things."

Catholic translations of the Bible include The New American Bible Revised Edition and The New Jerusalem Bible. Some translations, such as The New Revised Standard Version, are accepted by Catholics and Protestants.

Senses of Scripture

There are many layers, or senses, of Scripture.

- The **literal** sense of Scripture refers to the actual words recorded. We understand the literal sense by studying the culture in which the words were written and the meaning of the words at that time.
- The **allegorical** sense of Scripture shows how certain events pointed to Christ, even before his birth. The crossing of the Red Sea, for example, is a sign of Christ's victory over death.
- The **moral** sense of Scripture gives instruction on how to live justly before God.
- The **anagogical** sense of Scripture shows how human events and realities are signs of our heavenly future. The word *anagogical* comes from the Greek word *anagoge*, which means "leading." The Church, for example, is understood as leading to the New Jerusalem of Heaven.

364 Our Catholic Tradition

You should always rely on the guidance of the Holy Spirit and the Church to help you understand the Word of God in Scripture.

Gospel Formation

The Gospels according to Matthew, Mark, Luke, and John announce the Good News of Jesus to Christians today. These books were formed in three stages:

1. **The life and teaching of Jesus**
   Jesus' whole life and teaching proclaimed the Good News.

2. **Oral tradition**
   After the Resurrection, the Apostles preached the Good News. Then the early Christians passed on what Jesus preached. They told and retold the teachings of Jesus and the story of his life, Death, Resurrection, and Ascension.

3. **The written Gospels**
   The stories, teachings, and sayings of Jesus were collected and written in the Gospels according to Matthew, Mark, Luke (the synoptic, or similar Gospels), and John.

The Apostles

You can find the names of the Twelve Apostles in Matthew 10:1−4, Mark 3:13−19, and Luke 6:12−16.

Simon Peter: The leader of the Apostles, Simon was renamed "Peter" by Jesus. A fisherman from Galilee, he was introduced to Jesus by his brother Andrew. Peter was the first to proclaim Jesus as "the Christ, the Son of the Living God." He is said to have been crucified upside down in Rome under the Emperor Nero. Considered the first Pope, he is believed to be buried under St. Peter's Basilica at the Vatican.

© Our Sunday Visitor

Andrew: Andrew was originally a follower of John the Baptist. A fisherman like his brother Simon Peter, he is the disciple who brought the young boy with the loaves and fishes to Jesus to feed the crowds. According to tradition, he founded the church in Constantinople, present day Istanbul, Turkey, and was martyred in Southern Greece.

James: Considered the first Apostle to be martyred, he was a son of Zebedee and Salome and brother of John. He and his brother were called *Boanerges* or "Sons of Thunder" by Jesus, perhaps because of their tempers.

John: Traditionally known as the author of the Fourth Gospel, John is the brother of James. Jesus entrusted his mother Mary to John's care during the Crucifixion. He is the only Apostle to live into old age and not be martyred.

Philip: Originally from the town of Bethsaida, Philip introduces Nathanael (Bartholomew) to Jesus. At the Feeding of the 5,000, Jesus tested him, asking, "Where can we buy enough food for them to eat?" At the Last Supper, he asks Jesus to show them the Father, prompting Jesus' teaching about the Father and the Son being one. He was martyred in what is now Turkey.

Bartholomew: Often identified as Nathanael, he was a friend of Philip. When he learned about Jesus, he had a hard time believing the Messiah could come from Nazareth, saying, "Can anything good come out of Nazareth?" He is said to have traveled to India and was later killed in Armenia.

Matthew: Matthew calls himself "the tax collector" in his Gospel and the Gospel according to Mark says his name was "Levi." After Jesus called him, he went to Matthew's house and shared a meal with him.

Nothing specific is known about the end of Matthew's life.

Thomas: The Gospel according to John calls Thomas "Didymus," which means "the twin." He is sometimes called "Doubting Thomas" because he said he would not believe Jesus had risen from the dead unless he could put his fingers in Jesus' wounds. When Jesus appeared and invited him to do just that, Thomas proclaimed, "My Lord and my God." He is believed to have been martyred in India.

James: Some called him the "son of Alphaeus" to show he is a different James from John's brother. Sometimes he is called "James the Lesser." His name appears four times in the New Testament, in lists of the Apostles. Tradition says that he was martyred in Egypt where he was preaching the Gospel.

Simon: Matthew and Mark calle him "the Cananean," and Luke called him a "Zealot," to make sure we know he is not Simon Peter. Other than that, nothing specific is known about him. He is traditionally believed to have traveled and preached with Saint Jude Thaddeus and been martyred with him in the area around present-day Lebanon.

Thaddeus: He is also called "Jude Thaddeus." He is not to be confused with Judas, who betrayed Jesus. Jude Thaddeus is the patron Saint of lost or hopeless causes. According to legend, he was the son of a cousin of the Virgin Mary and a close friend of Simon the Zealot.

Judas Iscariot: Judas handed Jesus to the authorities to be crucified for 30 coins. He is said to have hanged himself in remorse for his betrayal. Matthias was later chosen to take his place among the Twelve Apostles.

The Holy Trinity

God is a communion of three Divine Persons: Father, Son, and Holy Spirit. God the Father is the Creator and source of all things. God the Son, Jesus, is the Savior of all people. God the Holy Spirit guides and makes holy all people and the Church.

The Holy Trinity is honored in the Sign of the Cross, in the Doxology, and in the liturgy of the Church. Christians are baptized "In the name of the Father, and of the Son, and of the Holy Spirit." In the blessings and in the Eucharistic Prayer of the Mass, prayers are directed to God the Father, through the Son, in the Holy Spirit.

God the Father

The First Person of the Holy Trinity, God the Father, is Creator of all that is. He is all-powerful and all-knowing. He is the one who journeys with you. He is the faithful and compassionate God who freed his People from slavery. He is as revealed to Moses, "I am who I am." God is gracious and merciful and steadfast in his love.

He is a God whom you can call Father, as Jesus taught in the Lord's Prayer. And, as Jesus also taught, God is love.

God the Son

Through the power of the Holy Spirit, the Second Person of the Trinity took on human nature and was born of the Virgin Mary. This is known as the Incarnation. Jesus is both true God and true man.

The Paschal Mystery includes Jesus' suffering, Death, Resurrection, and Ascension. By the Paschal Mystery, Jesus completed the work of salvation and won for all people the promise of eternal life. The Paschal Mystery is celebrated in each of the Sacraments, particularly in the Mass, and in Lent, the Triduum, and Easter. Jesus' whole life can be said to be a Sacrament, a sign of God, a sign of God's salvation and love. At the Last Supper, Jesus said, "Whoever has seen me has seen the Father. . . . Believe me that I am in the Father and the Father is in me. . ." (John 14:9, 11).

- In each Sacrament, Jesus is priest. For example, in the Eucharist, Jesus brings the people's prayers to God and offers himself as a sacrifice.
- Jesus is prophet because he speaks for God. Jesus announced the Good News of God's mercy and forgiveness. He calls people to love God and one another, to be sorry for their sins, and to live justly.
- Jesus is King, the judge of everything in Heaven and on Earth. His judgments are merciful and just.

God the Holy Spirit

The Third Person of the Trinity, the Holy Spirit, is the guide who helps people to know God as he is revealed in Sacred Scripture and the living Word, Jesus. It is through the power of the Spirit that you come to know the Father and the Son.

The Spirit makes the Paschal Mystery real and present in the Sacraments and the Mass. At Mass it is the Spirit who is called on to transform the bread and wine into the Body and Blood of Jesus. Finally, in the Eucharist, the Spirit unites the faithful with one another and with God in Christ. The Holy Spirit brings joy, peace, and reconciliation into the lives of the faithful.

© Our Sunday Visitor

Creed

A creed is a summary of the Christian faith. The word *creed* means "I believe." There are two main creeds in the Church: The Nicene Creed and the Apostles' Creed.

Nicene Creed

This creed which is prayed at Mass was written over a thousand years ago by leaders of the Church who met at a city named Nicaea. It is a summary of basic beliefs about God the Father, God the Son, and God the Holy Spirit, the Church, and other teachings.

I believe in one God,
the Father almighty,
maker of heaven and earth,
of all things visible and invisible.

I believe in one Lord Jesus Christ,
the Only Begotten Son of God,
born of the Father before all ages.
God from God, Light from Light,
true God from true God,
begotten, not made, consubstantial with
   the Father;
through him all things were made.
For us men and for our salvation
he came down from heaven,

At the words that follow up to and including and became man, *all bow.*

and by the Holy Spirit was incarnate of the
   Virgin Mary,
and became man.

For our sake he was crucified under
   Pontius Pilate,
he suffered death and was buried,
and rose again on the third day
in accordance with the Scriptures.
He ascended into heaven
and is seated at the right hand of the Father.
He will come again in glory
to judge the living and the dead
and his kingdom will have no end.

I believe in the Holy Spirit, the Lord,
   the giver of life,
who proceeds from the Father and the Son,
who with the Father and the Son is adored
   and glorified,
who has spoken through the prophets.

I believe in one, holy, catholic and
   apostolic Church.
I confess one Baptism for the forgiveness
   of sins
and I look forward to the resurrection
   of the dead
and the life of the world to come. Amen.

Apostles' Creed

This summary of Christian beliefs has been taught since the time of the Apostles. It is used in the celebration of Baptism and is often used at Mass during the Season of Easter and in Masses with children. This creed is part of the Rosary.

I believe in God,
the Father almighty,
Creator of heaven and earth,
and in Jesus Christ, his only Son, our Lord,

At the words that follow, up to and including the Virgin Mary, *all bow.*

who was conceived by the Holy Spirit,
born of the Virgin Mary,
suffered under Pontius Pilate,
was crucified, died and was buried;
he descended into hell;
on the third day he rose again from the dead;
he ascended into heaven,
and is seated at the right hand
   of God the Father almighty;
from there he will come to judge
   the living and the dead.
I believe in the Holy Spirit,
the holy catholic Church,
the communion of saints,
the forgiveness of sins,
the resurrection of the body,
and life everlasting. Amen.

The Church

The Catholic Church is the Church founded by Christ and his Apostles. There are four marks, or essential characteristics, that distinguish Christ's Church and her mission: one, holy, catholic, and apostolic. These marks are mentioned in the Nicene Creed.

Marks of the Church

One means all the members are united as the Body of Christ, given life by the one Spirit. They acknowledge one Lord, one faith, one Baptism.

Holy means the Church is centered in God. It is Christ who, by his sacrifice, makes the Church holy.

Catholic means universal. The Church has the fullness of faith and is the means of salvation for all. The Church is for all times and all people.

Apostolic means the Church is built on the foundation of the Apostles. It teaches the doctrine of Jesus as it has been handed down through the Apostles and their successors, the Pope and bishops.

The Church's Mission

The Church's mission is to proclaim and further God's Reign in the world. She continues the mission, or work, of Christ through the Holy Spirit, according to God's plan until Jesus comes again in glory. This work is done by all Catholics—clergy, laity, and religious.

Ecumenism is a movement that seeks to bring about the unity of all Christian churches. The word *ecumenism* comes from a scriptural phrase in Greek that means "the whole household of God."

The Pope

The Pope's title of "Servant of the Servants" began with Pope Gregory the Great. It is stated that "[W]hoever wishes to be first among you will be the slave of all" (Mark 10:44).

The many titles for the Pope include: Bishop of Rome, Vicar of Christ, Supreme Pontiff of the Universal Church, Patriarch of the West, Primate of Italy, Successor of Saint Peter, Prince of the Apostles, Servant of the Servants of God, and Sovereign of Vatican City.

The Church as Community

The church is a building in which God's people come together to worship. But the Church is the community of people. It was the plan of God the Father to call together those who believe in Christ. The Church is a gift from God, brought into being by the Holy Spirit to serve the mission of Jesus. The Church, in Christ, can be called a Sacrament, a sign of the communion of the Trinity, the union of all people with God, and the unity among people that will reach completion in the fullness of the Kingdom of God.

The Catholic Church is united in her faith, leadership structure, and Seven Sacraments. She is made up of Eastern Rite Catholics (Middle East and Eastern Europe) and Latin Rite Catholics (Rome and Western Europe).

The Catholic Church is governed by the Pope in union with all the bishops. Through the Sacrament of Holy Orders, bishops, priests, and deacons are ordained to serve the Church. Between fifteen and twenty days after the death of a Pope, the cardinals who are under the age of 80 meet in the Sistine Chapel in Rome to vote for a new Pope. Each cardinal writes on a sheet of paper the name of the man (usually one of the cardinals) he wishes to elect. If a candidate does not receive a majority of votes, the papers are burned with straw to produce black smoke. If a new Pope has been chosen, the papers alone are burned, producing white smoke.

The resignation of Pope Benedict XVI in 2013 was the first papal resignation in nearly 600 years. Following his resignation, Benedict XVI's official title became Pope Emeritus (a word that means retired but retaining a title). His successor, Cardinal Jorge Maria Bergoglio, took the name Pope Francis. Because he was the Cardinal Archbishop of Buenos Aires, Argentina, Pope Francis became the first Pope from the New World.

The Saints

The Saints are holy people who loved God, did his work on Earth, cooperated with his grace, and are now with him in Heaven. Catholics honor the Saints for their virtue and try to imitate them. They also ask that the Saints join with them in praying to God for special blessings. Saints are remembered in the Eucharistic Prayer and in the Litany of the Saints at Baptisms. Statues and images of the Saints on medals and holy cards are reminders that these "friends of God" can help believers grow in their own friendship with God.

Mary is honored above all other Saints. She is the Mother of God because she is the mother of the Son of God who became a human being. When the Angel Gabriel told Mary that she would be the mother of the Son of God, Mary believed and accepted God's plan. Her "yes" sets the example for all believers.

Throughout the liturgical year, the Church celebrates Mary's place in Christian history. Among different cultures and traditions, devotion to Mary takes many forms.

Life after Death

At the end of the Nicene Creed we profess, "and I look forward to the resurrection of the dead and the life of the world to come." The Church sometimes refers to teaching about this topic as the Last Things.

The Particular Judgment is the judgment made at the moment of a person's death. At this judgment the soul is rewarded with the blessings of Heaven, given a time of purification, or condemned to Hell.

- Heaven is the state in which souls of the just experience the full joy of living in God's presence forever.

- Purgatory is a time after death for those who are in God's friendship but need to be purified to be with him in Heaven. It is a state of final cleansing after death and before entering into Heaven.

- Hell is the state of eternal separation from God because of a choice to turn away from him and not seek forgiveness

The Last Judgment is also called the General Judgment. This refers to God's final triumph over evil that will occur at the end of time when Christ returns and judges all the living and the dead. Then, all will fully see and understand God's plan for creation.

The new Heaven and new Earth is the Kingdom of God (or new Jerusalem) that will come in its fullness at the end of time.

The Seven Sacraments

The Sacraments of Initiation

The Sacraments of Initiation—Baptism, Confirmation, and Eucharist—celebrate membership into the Catholic Church.

Through the words and waters of **Baptism**, God forgives all sin and gives new life in Christ.

In emergencies and other times of necessity, anyone can baptize another person. The person baptizing must intend to do what the Church does in this Sacrament. He or she needs to pour water over the head of the person being baptized while saying, "I baptize you in the name of the Father, and of the Son, and of the Holy Spirit."

Confirmation completes the baptismal grace and strengthens a person to be a witness to the faith through the power of the Spirit.

Catholics in different dioceses in the United States receive the Sacrament of Confirmation at different ages. In the Roman, or Latin, Rite candidates for Confirmation must meet certain criteria. They must believe in the faith of the Church, be in a state of grace, and want to receive the Sacrament. Candidates must be prepared and willing to be a witness to Christ in their daily lives and take an active part in the life of the Church.

Eucharist completes the Sacraments of Initiation, nourishing the baptized with Christ's own Body and Blood and uniting the new Christians with God and one another in Jesus.

The Eucharist is known by several different names. These include the Blessed Sacrament, Holy Communion, the Bread of Heaven, Breaking of Bread, the Lord's Supper, Holy Sacrifice, Holy Mass, and the Body of Christ.

The Sacraments of Healing

In the Sacraments of Healing—Penance and Reconciliation and Anointing of the Sick— God's forgiveness and healing are given to those suffering physical and spiritual sickness.

In **Penance and Reconciliation**, through the words of absolution, personal sins are forgiven and relationships with God and the Church are healed.

In the **Anointing of the Sick**, one who is sick or dying is anointed with oil and with the laying on of hands. The person unites his or her suffering with that of Jesus. The Sacrament gives spiritual strength and God's grace. Physical healing also may take place.

The Sacraments at the Service of Communion

The Sacraments at the Service of Communion— Holy Orders and Matrimony—celebrate people's commitment to serve God and the community and help build up the People of God.

In **Holy Orders**, the bishop lays hands on a man and anoints him with Sacred Chrism. The man is empowered to serve the Church as deacon, priest, or bishop.

In **Matrimony**, a baptized man and a baptized woman, through their words of consent, make a covenant with God and one another. Marriage is for the sake of their love and any children God blesses them with.

© Our Sunday Visitor

Order of Mass

Introductory Rites

Entrance Chant

Greeting

Rite for the Blessing and Sprinkling of Water

Penitential Act

Kyrie

Gloria

Collect

Liturgy of the Word

First Reading

Responsorial Psalm

Second Reading

Gospel Acclamation

Dialogue at the Gospel (*or* Gospel Dialogue)

Gospel Reading

Homily

Profession of Faith (*or* Creed—Nicene Creed or Apostles' Creed)

Prayer of the Faithful

Liturgy of the Eucharist

Preparation of the Gifts

Invitation to Prayer

Prayer over the Offerings

Eucharistic Prayer

> Preface Dialogue
>
> Preface
>
> Preface Acclamation
>
> Consecration
>
> Mystery of Faith
>
> Concluding Doxology
>
> Amen

Communion Rite

The Lord's Prayer

Sign of Peace

Lamb of God

Invitation to Communion

Communion

Prayer after Communion

Concluding Rites

Solemn Blessing or Prayer over the People

Final Blessing

Dismissal

Order of Rite for Reconciliation of Individual Recipients

1. Reception of the Penitent (Welcome)

2. Reading of the Word of God

3. Confession of Sins and Acceptance of Satisfaction (a Penance)

4. Prayer of the Penitent (beginning with the Act of Contrition; see page 387)

5. Absolution, including the words of absolution from the priest:

> God, the Father of Mercies,
> through the death and resurrection of
>   his Son
> has reconciled the world to himself
> and sent the Holy Spirit among us
> for the forgiveness of sins;
> through the ministry of the Church
> may God give you pardon and peace,
> and I absolve you from your sins
> in the name of the Father, and of
>   the Son,
> and of the Holy Spirit.

6. Closing Prayer

The Liturgical Year

The liturgical year celebrates Jesus' life and work for the salvation of the world. During Advent and Christmas, the Church celebrates the Incarnation. The Seasons of Lent, Triduum, and Easter explore the Paschal Mystery. Easter is the high point of the liturgical year because it is the greatest celebration of the Resurrection. The life and ministry of Jesus are the focus of Ordinary Time. Mary and the Saints are also remembered throughout the year in what is known as the sanctoral cycle.

Holy Days of Obligation

Catholics must attend Mass on Sunday unless a serious reason prevents their doing so. They must also go to Mass on certain holy days. United States Holy Days of Obligation are

- Mary, Mother of God (January 1)
- Ascension (forty days after Easter or the Sunday nearest the end of the forty-day period)
- Assumption (August 15)
- All Saints Day (November 1)
- Immaculate Conception (December 8)
- Christmas (December 25)

Fasting and Abstinence

To help prepare spiritually for the Eucharist, Catholics fast for one hour before Holy Communion. They take no food or drink except water. (Exceptions are made for those who are sick and for those of advanced age.)

To fast means to eat only one full meal and two smaller meals during the course of a day. All Catholics, from their eighteenth birthday until their fifty-ninth birthday, are required to fast on Ash Wednesday and Good Friday unless a serious reason prevents them from doing so. Another discipline of self-denial is abstinence. Catholics who are fourteen years of age or older are expected to abstain from eating meat on Ash Wednesday, Good Friday, and, in the United States, on all of the Fridays in Lent.

Examination of Conscience

Examining your conscience should be done daily and especially in preparation for the Sacrament of Penance and Reconciliation.

1. Pray to the Holy Spirit to help you examine your conscience.

2. Look at your life in light of the Beatitudes, the Ten Commandments, the Great Commandment, and the Precepts of the Church.

3. Ask yourself:
   Where have I fallen short of what God wants for me?
   Whom have I hurt?
   What have I done that I knew was wrong?
   Have I done penance and tried as hard as I could to make up for past sins?
   Am I working to change my bad habits?
   With what areas am I still having trouble?
   Am I sincerely sorry for all my sins?

4. In addition to confessing your sins, you may wish to talk with the priest about one or more of the above questions.

© Our Sunday Visitor

The Law

Divine law is the eternal law of God. It includes:

physical law: the law of gravity is an example of physical law.

natural moral law: a moral law is one that humans understand through reasoning (stealing is wrong) and through Divine Revelation (keep holy the Lord's Day).

Natural moral law refers to the precepts about goodness that are written by God in our hearts and accessible through our God-given reason. For example, people everywhere understand that no person may kill another unjustly. Everyone must obey natural moral law because everyone is created by God. God's Commandments are based on natural moral law.

© Our Sunday Visitor

The Ten Commandments

1.	I am the Lord your God. You shall not have strange gods before me.
2.	You shall not take the name of the Lord your God in vain.
3.	Remember to keep holy the Lord's Day.
4.	Honor your father and your mother.
5.	You shall not kill.
6.	You shall not commit adultery.
7.	You shall not steal.
8.	You shall not bear false witness against your neighbor.
9.	You shall not covet your neighbor's wife.
10.	You shall not covet your neighbor's goods.

The Great Commandment

"You shall love the Lord, your God, with all your heart, with all your being, with all your strength, and with all your mind, and your neighbor as yourself." **(Luke 10:27)**

The New Commandment

"Love one another. As I have loved you, so you also should love one another." **(John 13:34)**

Precepts of the Church

The Precepts of the Church are some of the minimum requirements given by Church leaders for deepening our relationship with God and the Church. They name specific actions that all Catholics are obligated to carry out.

1. Take part in the Mass on Sundays and holy days. Keep these days holy and avoid unnecessary work.

2. Celebrate the Sacrament of Penance and Reconciliation at least once a year if there is serious sin.

3. Receive Holy Communion at least once a year during the Easter Season.

4. Fast and/or abstain on days of penance.

5. Give your time, gifts, and money to support the Church.

The Beatitudes

The Beatitudes are Jesus' eight teachings about the meaning and path to true happiness. They depict the way to live in God's Kingdom now and always, working toward the eternal holiness to which God calls all people. Jesus spoke them during his Sermon on the Mount, and his words lead us on a new path of discipleship, explaining how we are to live with each other.

Blessed are the poor in spirit,
for theirs is the kingdom of heaven.
Blessed are they who mourn,
for they will be comforted.
Blessed are the meek,
for they will inherit the land.
Blessed are they who hunger and thirst for righteousness,
for they will be satisfied.
Blessed are the merciful,
for they will be shown mercy.
Blessed are the clean of heart,
for they will see God.
Blessed are the peacemakers,
for they will be called children of God.
Blessed are they who are persecuted for the sake of righteousness,
for theirs is the kingdom of heaven.
Matthew 5:1–12

The Corporal and Spiritual Works of Mercy

The Works of Mercy are "charitable actions by which we come to the aid of our neighbor in his spiritual and bodily necessities" (CCC, 2447). The Corporal Works of Mercy are actions the show care for the physical needs of people, while the Spiritual Works of Mercy are actions that address the needs of the heart, mind, and soul.

The Works of Mercy	
Corporal (for the body)	**Spiritual (for the spirit)**
Feed the hungry.	Warn the sinner.
Give drink to the thirsty.	Teach the ignorant.
Clothe the naked.	Counsel the doubtful.
Shelter the homeless.	Comfort the sorrowful.
Visit the sick.	Bear wrongs patiently.
Visit the imprisoned.	Forgive injuries.
Bury the dead.	Pray for the living and the dead.

© Our Sunday Visitor

Gifts of the Holy Spirit

The Gifts of the Holy Spirit are seven powerful gifts God gives us to follow guidance of the Holy Spirit and live the Christian life. We are sealed with these gifts at the Sacrament of Confirmation, and they strengthen the gifts we receive at Baptism.

Wisdom helps you see yourself as God sees you and act as God wants you to act. Wisdom allows you to live in the image and likeness of God.

Understanding allows you to get to know God, yourself, and others better, and to see how your sometimes make the wrong choices in life. With understanding comes help to make better choices and forgive more freely.

Right judgment (Counsel) helps you give good advice to others and hear the Holy Spirit, who speaks to you through the good advice and good example of others.

Courage (Fortitude) helps you stand up for what is right even doing so it difficult, and allows you to face and overcome your fears, which sometimes lead you to making the wrong choices or failing to love others.

Knowledge allows you to be open to God's loving communication and know God in the way that you come to know someone you love and someone who loves you.

Reverence (Piety) helps you show faithful love and honor to God, and allows you to recognize the importance of spending time talking and listening to God in prayer.

Wonder and awe (Fear of the Lord) allows you to know that God is greater and more wonderful than any created thing, and reminds you to be open to his surprising and powerful goodness.

Fruits of the Holy Spirit		
The Fruits of the Spirit are qualities that can be seen is us when we allow the Holy Spirit to work in our hearts.		
Charity	Faithfulness	Gentleness
Joy	Modesty	Generosity
Peace	Kindness	Self-control
Patience	Goodness	Chastity

Grace and Sin

Sanctifying grace allows you to share in God's own life. It is a permanent gift that builds your friendship with God and assures you of eternal life.

Actual grace is a temporary gift that helps you think or act according to God's will for you in a particular situation. Actual grace helps you understand what is right and strengthens you to turn away from sin.

Sacramental grace is the gift that comes from the Sacraments. Each Sacrament gives its own particular grace.

Sin

Sin is a turning away from God and a failure to love. Sin affects both the individual and the community. A person may be sorry for his or her sin, ask forgiveness for it, accept punishment for it, and resolve to do better. In this case, the experience may actually help the person develop as a Christian and avoid sin in the future. However, a person who makes a habit of sin will harm his or her development, set a poor example, and bring sorrow to others. Society suffers when people disobey God's law and the just laws of society. There are many types of sin.

Original Sin is the sin that the first humans committed by choosing to disobey God. This sin describes the fallen state that caused the human condition of weakness and tendency toward sin. Baptism restores the relationship of loving grace in which all people were created by God.

Personal sin is any thought, word, act, or failure to act that goes against God's law. Sin is a choice, not a mistake.

Mortal sin separates you from God. For a sin to be mortal, it must be a serious matter done with full knowledge and complete consent.

Venial sin weakens or wounds your relationship with God. Continual venial sin can lead to mortal sin.

Social sin results from the effect that personal sin has on a community. People who have been sinned against may sin in return. Violence, injustice, and other wrongs may develop within the community. God created humans in his image and likeness. Because of this, you have dignity and therefore need to respect your dignity and that of others.

Asking forgiveness, accepting punishment, and resolving not to sin again helps a person develop as a Christian. However, one who habitually sins neglects Christian development, sets a poor example, and harms others. When individuals disobey God's law and just civil laws, the entire community suffers.

Virtue

Living a virtuous life is living a holy life. Virtues make it possible for us to relate to God and grow in our understanding of being made in his image and likeness. Virtues are lasting habits or attitudes that lead us to make good decisions and act appropriately. Virtues lead the way to holiness. They strengthen our character, which is uniquely ours but built on the foundation of God's grace and his help.

The Theological Virtues of faith, hope, and charity (love) are gifts from God. These virtues help you live in a loving relationship with God.

The Cardinal Virtues are the principal moral virtues that help you lead a moral life. They help us live as children of God. We strengthen these virtues through God's grace and our own efforts.

Prudence is careful judgment. This virtue helps you be practical and make the right decisions on what is morally good, with the help of the Holy Spirit and an informed conscience.

Fortitude is courage, especially in the face of evil and temptation. Fortitude gives you strength to get through difficulties and helps you not give up when you have chosen to do good.

Justice is giving to God and to each person what is due to them. Justice helps you build up the community by respecting rights and promoting the common good, the conditions that allow people to become who God wants them to become (see page 379).

Temperance means keeping a balance in life. It allows us to use moderation, be disciplined, and have self-control.

Human Dignity

Human dignity is the worth each person has because he or she is made in the image of God. We are all equal in dignity, each and every one of us worthy of respect and love. Because our common human dignity, people have basic human rights, such as food, clothing, and shelter. No government or social group should fail to recognize those rights.

God's image is his likeness that is present in you because you are his creation. You are called to respect the dignity of all people because everyone is made in God's image.

- Freedom means you are able to choose and act with few limitations. We are given freedom by God that we may choose to good things.

- Free will is the gift from God that allows humans to make their own choices. Because you are free to choose between right and wrong, you are responsible for your choices and actions.

- Conscience is a gift from God that helps us judge whether actions are right or wrong. It is important for us to know God's laws so our conscience can help us make good decisions. Conscience helps you choose what is right. It involves free will and reason working together. You must form your conscience properly. If not formed properly, your conscience can lead you to choose what is wrong.

Forming your conscience is a lifelong process. It involves practicing virtues and avoiding sin and people or situations that may lead you to sin. You can turn to good people for advice, to Church teachings for guidance, and to God for help in educating your conscience. It is recommended that Catholics practice an Examination of Conscience (see page 372) before receiving the Sacrament of Penance and Reconciliation.

© Our Sunday Visitor

Justice and Peace

Justice is a Cardinal Virtue. It is the habit and practice of giving God what is due him. It also means to give each person what he or she is due because that person is a child of God.

Social justice is a part of this Cardinal Virtue. It is the part that urges individuals to seek the common good of the whole group rather than just his or her individual good.

Peace is a state of calm and harmony when things are in their proper order and people settle problems with kindness and justice. In the Catholic tradition, peace is not just the absence of conflict. It is the result of right relationships with God and with your neighbor.

Common Good

The common good refers to the good of everyone, with particular concern for those who might be most vulnerable to harm. It means all the conditions that allow people to become who God wants them to become. The common good includes peace, development of groups of people, and respect for every person. These conditions vary from society to society, which is why the Church does not recommend any one country's political or economic system. The Church evaluates each system on the basis of whether or not it provides the conditions for human fulfillment.

Catholic Social Teaching

The Catholic bishops of the United States have named seven themes of Catholic Social Teaching that embrace the Gospel message on how we are to treat others and live in community. For more on each of these themes, read the Live Your Faith section of your book, beginning on page 334.

Life and Dignity of the Human Person: All policies and personal decisions must show a value for human dignity.

Call to Family, Community, and Participation: The well-being of individuals depends on community and family. All people have the right and a duty to participate in society.

Rights and Responsibilities of the Human Person: Human rights must be respected, and responsibilities to others must be met.

Option for the Poor and Vulnerable: Actions must be evaluated in terms of how they affect those who are most vulnerable. A basic moral test is to ask whether an act will help those who are poor or in need.

Dignity of Work and the Rights of Workers: Workers deserve the right to a just wage, to form unions, to hold private property, and to act independently of outside influence or control.

Solidarity of the Human Family: We must be committed to the common good globally as well as locally.

Care for God's Creation: To practice social justice, we must take care of the Earth's natural resources.

Vocations

God calls all of us to share in the life and mission of Jesus. A vocation is the purpose for which God made us, and a particular way to answer his call to service. The word vocation comes the Latin word *vocare*, which means "to call." Our vocation helps us see how everything fits together in our lives. It shows us how God created us to love, serve, and work with each other. Our vocation comes from the grace we receive in the Sacrament of Baptism. Every one of us must answer our call from God to work with him to build up his Kingdom on Earth.

There are three ways you can serve God through your vocation: as a layperson, or member of the laity (see page 295), as a member of a religious community, or as a member of the ordained ministry.

The Laity

The laity is all of the baptized people in the Church who share in God's mission but are not priests or consecrated sisters and brothers. Members of the laity can be single people or married couples. They can perform various roles in the Church, such as lector, altar servers, and musicians at Mass, and also serve their parish by acting as good Catholic role models in their daily lives.

Members of Religious Communities

There are many kinds of communities of religious sisters and brothers. The members of these communities teach, care for the sick, work as missionaries, or do other good works as part of their call from God. Consecrated religious brothers and sisters dedicate their lives to serving God by following the charism, or special grace, of their community and its founder.

Ordained Ministry

Some men are called to ordained ministry through the Sacrament of Holy Orders. This Sacrament gives a sacred power, through the laying on of hands by a bishop, for serving the faithful by teaching, leading people in worship, and pastoral care. Bishops, priests, and deacons share in this Sacrament. A bishop serves the Church as the pastor and teacher of his diocese. They work with other bishops and the Pope for the good of the whole Catholic Church. Priests assist the bishop within a diocese and celebrate the Sacraments with their parish community. Deacons are ministers who serve by helping in liturgical roles and doing works of charity.

You may not know yet about the vocation to which God is calling you. As you get older, you can continue to think about the gifts God has given you, and through them, you will better understand his plan and purpose for you.

Charisms

Charisms are special gifts or graces of the Holy Spirit which benefit the Church and help us lead a Christian life. These gifts build up the community and also help us share Christ's message with others, and serve the common good. Members of religious communities follow the specific charisms given to that community and its founder. For example, some communities are devoted to prayer, because their founders built the foundation of the community's spirituality on the power of this special communication with God. Saint Benedict followed a motto of *prayer and work*, and the Benedictans continue to model their ministry on those things. Other communities may be devoted to service, health care, or missions.

Vows

Members of religious communities profess, or promise aloud, to live three vows, or sacred promises made to or before God, that are found in the Gospel: poverty, chastity, and obedience. These vows are also evangelical counsels that lead to the perfection of the Christian, and therefore apply to all of us.

- **Poverty:** living a simple life and sharing material possessions in community. This helps one free one's self from undue attachment to material things and to rely on God to care for their needs while they provide for others.
- **Chastity:** exercising discipline over sexuality and maintaining the right balance of body and spirit in human sexuality. This shows that for consecrated religious, their love for God is the most important thing in their lives.
- **Obedience:** following and obeying God's will, expressed through the guidance of the community's leaders, the charism of the community, and the person's conscience. Consecrated religious find peace in discerning and following God's will for them.

We are called to live out these counsels, but men and women religious do so in a radical way.

Forms of Prayer

Prayer is talking and listening to God. In prayer, we raise our hearts and minds to God. One of the first prayers we learn in the Church is the Lord's Prayer, which Jesus taught his followers. Jesus prayed when he needed help, when he wanted to help other people, and when he wanted to praise God his Father. Prayer should be an important part of your life as well. You can pray a prayer you have heard before in church or school, or create one yourself with your own words. You can pray out loud or in silence. Your prayers will always be heard by God.

On the next pages, you will find several common prayers of the Catholic Church. You will have heard many of them at Mass, and they fit under the categories of these five principal forms of prayer:

Blessing and Adoration

In this prayer form, we show that we understand God is the Creator of all things, and that we need him. We give him respect and honor his greatness. We bless God, who blesses us. We also bless others who are made in God's image. A blessing is a response to God's gifts. Adoration means giving respect to God by honoring his greatness.

Praise

In this prayer form, we give God honor and thanks because he is God. We give him glory not for what he does, but simply because he is. When we praise God in prayer, we give him glory as his children. Praise holds together all of our prayers, and prayer forms, and raises them toward God, who is the source and goal of all prayer.

Intercession

Intercession, or intercessory prayer, is a form of prayer that involves praying to God on behalf of someone else. We can pray for people who are close to us; for people around the world who suffer from hunger, poverty, disease, war, or other problems; and for those who have died and are not yet with God in Heaven. We use intercessory prayer on behalf of others as Jesus intercedes for us with his Father. Because praying for other is a Work for Mercy, intercessory prayer is vital to the Church and our relationship with God.

Petition

In this prayer form, we ask God for what we need. We turn to God and ask for his help, and recognize that we need him. In prayers of petition, we might pray for God's mercy, forgiveness, and guidance when we are sad, sick, troubled, confused, or in a state of sin. We also ask God to help others.

Thanksgiving

When we pray a prayer of Thanksgiving, we give thanks to God for all he has given us. We express our gratitude to him for the good things in our lives. When we experience a special reason for happiness, such as good grades or someone feeling better after an illness, or even just for a good day, we can thank God for it in prayer.

Basic Prayers

These are essential prayers that every Catholic should know. Latin is the official, universal language of the Church. As members of the Catholic Church, we usually pray in the language that we speak, but we sometimes pray in Latin, the common language of the Church.

Sign of the Cross

In the name of the Father
and of the Son
and of the Holy Spirit. Amen.

Signum Crucis

In nómine Patris
et Fílii
et Spíritus Sancti. Amen.

The Lord's Prayer

Our Father, who art in heaven,
hallowed be thy name;
thy kingdom come,
thy will be done
on earth as it is in heaven.
Give us this day our daily bread,
and forgive us our trespasses,
as we forgive those who trespass
 against us;
and lead us not into temptation,
but deliver us from evil.
Amen.

Pater Noster

Pater noster qui es in cælis:
santificétur Nomen Tuum;
advéniat Regnum Tuum;
fiat volúntas Tua,
sicut in cælo, et in terra.
Panem nostrum
cotidiánum da nobis hódie;
et dimítte nobis débita nostra,
sicut et nos
dimíttus debitóribus nostris;
et ne nos indúcas in tentatiónem;
sed líbera nos a Malo.

Glory Be

Glory be to the Father
and to the Son
and to the Holy Spirit,
as it was in the beginning
is now, and ever shall be
world without end.
Amen.

Gloria Patri

Gloria Patri
et Filio
et Spíritui Sancto.
Sicut erat in princípio,
et nunc et semper
et in sæ´cula sæ´culorem. Amen.

The Hail Mary

Hail, Mary, full of grace,
the Lord is with thee.
Blessed art thou among women
and blessed is the fruit of thy womb, Jesus.
Holy Mary, Mother of God,
pray for us sinners,
now and at the hour of our death.
Amen.

Prayer to the Holy Spirit

Come, Holy Spirit, fill the hearts of
   your faithful.
And kindle in them the fire of your love.
Send forth your Spirit and they shall
   be created.
And you will renew the face of the earth.
Let us pray.
Lord, by the light of the Holy Spirit you
   have taught the hearts of your faithful.
   In the same Spirit help us to relish
   what is right and always rejoice in
   your consolation.
We ask this through Christ our Lord.
Amen.

Ave, Maria

Ave, María, grátia plena,
Dóminus tecum.
Benedícta tu in muliéribus,
et benedíctus fructus ventris tui, Iesus.
Sancta María, Mater Dei,
ora pro nobis peccatóribus,
nunc et in hora mortis nostræ.
Amen.

Memorare

Remember, most loving Virgin Mary,
never was it heard that anyone who turned
   to you for help was left unaided.
Inspired by this confidence, though
   burdened by my sins, I run to your
   protection for you are my mother.
Mother of the Word of God, do not despise
   my words of pleading but be merciful
   and hear my prayer.
Amen.

Hail, Holy Queen

Hail, holy Queen, Mother of mercy,
hail, our life, our sweetness, and our hope.
To you we cry, the children of Eve;
to you we send up our sighs,
mourning and weeping in this land of exile.
Turn, then, most gracious advocate,
your eyes of mercy toward us;
lead us home at last
and show us the blessed fruit of your womb,
Jesus:
O clement, O loving, O sweet Virgin Mary.

Prayers from the Sacraments

Holy, Holy, Holy Lord

Holy, Holy, Holy Lord God of hosts.
Heaven and earth are full of your glory.
Hosanna in the highest.
Blessed is he who comes in the name of
  the Lord.
Hosanna in the highest.

Sanctus, Sanctus, Sanctus

Sanctus, Sanctus, Sanctus
Dominus Deus Sabaoth.
Pleni sunt coeli et terra gloria tua.
Hosanna in excelsis.
Benedictus qui venit in nomine Domini.
Hosanna in excelsis

Lamb of God

Lamb of God, you take away the
  sins of the world,
    have mercy on us.
Lamb of God, you take away the
  sins of the world,
    have mercy on us.
Lamb of God, you take away the
  sins of the world,
    grant us peace.

Agnus Dei

Agnus Dei, qui tollis peccata mundi:
miserere nobis.
Agnus Dei, qui tollis peccata mundi:
miserere nobis.
Agnus Dei, qui tollis peccata mundi:
dona nobis pacem

Gloria

Glory to God in the highest,
and on earth peace to people of good will.

We praise you,
we bless you,
we adore you,
we glorify you,
we give you thanks for your great glory,
Lord God, heavenly King,
O God, almighty Father.

Lord Jesus Christ, Only Begotten Son,
Lord God, Lamb of God, Son of the Father,
you take away the sins of the world,
    have mercy on us;
you take away the sins of the world,
    receive our prayer;
you are seated at the right hand of the
Father,
    have mercy on us.

For you alone are the Holy One,
you alone are the Lord,
you alone are the Most High,
Jesus Christ,
with the Holy Spirit,
in the glory of God the Father.
Amen.

Confiteor

I confess to almighty God
and to you, my brothers and sisters,
that I have greatly sinned,
in my thoughts and in my words,
in what I have done
and in what I have failed to do,
through my fault, through my fault,
through my most grievous fault;
therefore I ask blessed Mary ever-Virgin,
all the Angels and Saints,
and you my brothers and sisters,
to pray for me to the Lord our God.

Prayers from the Liturgy of the Hours

The Canticle of Zechariah

This hymn is sung during the Liturgy of the Hours, Morning Prayer.

Blessed be the Lord, the God of Israel;
he has come to his people and set them free.

He has raised up for us a mighty savior,
born of the house of his servant David.

Through his holy prophets he promised of old
that he would save us from our enemies,
from the hands of all who hate us.

He promised to show mercy to our fathers
and to remember his holy covenant.

This was the oath he swore to our father
    Abraham:
to set us free from the hands of our enemies,
free to worship him without fear,
holy and righteous in his sight
all the days of our life.
Based on Luke 1:68–75

The *Magnificat* (Mary's Canticle)

This hymn is sung during the Liturgy of the Hours, Evening Prayer.

My soul proclaims the greatness of the Lord,
my spirit rejoices in God my Savior;
for he has looked with favor on his lowly
servant.
From this day all generations will call me
blessed:
the Almighty has done great things for me,
and holy is his Name.

He has mercy on those who fear him
in every generation.
He has shown the strength of his arm,
he has scattered the proud in their conceit.
He has cast down the mighty from their
thrones,
and has lifted up the lowly.
He has filled the hungry with good things,
and the rich he has sent away empty.
He has come to the help of his servant Israel
for he has remembered his promise of mercy,
the promise he made to our fathers,
to Abraham and his children for ever.
Based on Luke 1:46–55

Personal and Family Prayers

Morning Prayer

God be in my head, and in my
understanding;
God be in my eyes, and in my looking;
God be in my mouth, and in my speaking;
God be in my heart, and in my thinking;
God be at my end, and at my departing.
Amen.

Evening Prayer

Lord, from the rising of the sun to its
setting, your name is worthy of all praise.
Let our prayer come like incense before
you. May the lifting up of our hands be
as an evening sacrifice acceptable to you,
Lord our God.
Amen.

Act of Faith

O God, we firmly believe that you are one God in three divine Persons, Father, Son, and Holy Spirit; we believe that your divine Son became man and died for our sins, and that he will come to judge the living and the dead. We believe these and all the truths that the holy Catholic Church teaches because you have revealed them, and you can neither deceive nor be deceived.

Act of Hope

O God, relying on your almighty power and your endless mercy and promises, we hope to gain pardon for our sins, the help of your grace, and life everlasting, through the saving actions of Jesus Christ, our Lord and Redeemer.

Act of Love

O God, we love you above all things, with our whole heart and soul, because you are all-good and worthy of all love. We love our neighbor as ourselves for the love of you. We forgive all who have injured us and ask pardon of all whom we have injured.

Act of Contrition

My God, I am sorry for my sins with all my heart.
In choosing to do wrong
and failing to do good,
I have sinned against you
whom I should love above all things.
I firmly intend, with your help,
to do penance,
to sin no more,
and to avoid whatever leads me to sin.
Our Savior Jesus Christ
suffered and died for us.
In his name, my God, have mercy.

The Jesus Prayer

Lord Jesus Christ, Son of God, have mercy on me, a sinner.

Eternal Rest

Eternal rest grant to them, O Lord,
and let perpetual light shine upon them.
May they rest in peace.
Amen.

Devotional Practices

When we pray with the Saints, we ask them to pray to God for us and to pray with us. The Saints are with Christ. They speak for us when we need help.

As the Mother of Jesus, the Son of God, Mary is called the Mother of God, the Queen of all Saints, and the Mother of the Church. There are many prayers and practices of devotion to Mary. One of the most revered is the Rosary. It focuses on the twenty mysteries that describe events in the lives of Jesus and Mary.

How to Pray the Rosary

1. Pray the Sign of the Cross and say the Apostles' Creed.

2. Pray the Lord's Prayer.

3. Pray three Hail Marys.

4. Pray the Glory Be.

5. Say the first mystery; then pray the Lord's Prayer.

6. Pray ten Hail Marys while meditating on the mystery.

7. Pray the Glory Be.

8. Say the second mystery; then pray the Lord's Prayer.

Repeat 6 and 7 and continue with the third, fourth, and fifth mysteries in the same manner.

9. Pray the Hail, Holy Queen (see page 384).

The Mysteries of the Rosary

The Joyful Mysteries
The Annunciation
The Visitation
The Nativity
The Presentation in the Temple
The Finding in the Temple

The Sorrowful Mysteries
The Agony in the Garden
The Scourging at the Pillar
The Crowning with Thorns
The Carrying of the Cross
The Crucifixion and Death

The Glorious Mysteries
The Resurrection
The Ascension
The Descent of the Holy Spirit
The Assumption of Mary
The Coronation of Mary in Heaven

The Luminous Mysteries
The Baptism of Jesus
The Wedding at Cana
The Proclamation of the Kingdom
The Transfiguration
The Institution of the Eucharist

The Chaplet of Divine Mercy

1. Begin with the Sign of the Cross

2. Pray the Our Father.

3. Pray the Hail Mary.

4. Say the Apostles' Creed.

5. Then pray, on the large bead before each decade on the Rosary:

Eternal Father,
I offer you the Body and Blood,
Soul and Divinity,
Of Your Dearly Beloved Son,
Our Lord, Jesus Christ,
in atonement for our sins
and those of the whole world.

6. One the small beads of each decade, say:

For the sake of his sorrowful Passion,
have mercy on us and on the whole world.

7. Then say three times:

Holy God,
Holy Mighty One,
Holy Immortal One,
have mercy on us,
and on the whole world.

© Our Sunday Visitor

Stations of the Cross

The devotional practice of the Stations of the Cross began in the early Church. Pilgrims would visit the various sites in Jerusalem that were associated with Christ's suffering and death. The Stations of the Cross focus on fourteen scenes of Christ's Passion.

First Station: Jesus is condemned to death on the Cross.

Second Station: Jesus accepts his Cross.

Third Station: Jesus falls the first time.

Fourth Station: Jesus meets his sorrowful mother.

Fifth Station: Simon of Cyrene helps Jesus carry his Cross.

Sixth Station: Veronica wipes the face of Jesus.

Seventh Station: Jesus falls the second time.

Eighth Station: Jesus meets and speaks to the women of Jerusalem.

Ninth Station: Jesus falls the third time.

Tenth Station: Jesus is stripped of his garments.

Eleventh Station: Jesus is nailed to the Cross.

Twelfth Station: Jesus dies on the Cross.

Thirteenth Station: Jesus is taken down from the Cross.

Fourteenth Station: Jesus is placed in the tomb.

Angelus

V. The angel spoke God's message to Mary,
R. and she conceived of the Holy Spirit.
Hail, Mary. . . .
V. "I am the lowly servant of the Lord:
R. let it be done to me according to
    your word."
Hail, Mary. . . .
V. And the Word became flesh,
R. and lived among us.
Hail, Mary. . . .
V. Pray for us, holy Mother of God,
R. that we may become worthy of the
    promises of Christ.
Let us pray.
Lord,
fill our hearts with your grace:
once, through the message of an angel
you revealed to us the incarnation of your Son;
now, through his suffering and death
lead us to the glory of his Resurrection.
We ask this through Christ our Lord.
R. Amen.

Litany of Saint Joseph

Lord, have mercy.	Lord, have mercy.
Christ, have mercy.	Christ, have
mercy.	
Lord, have mercy.	Lord, have mercy.
Good Saint Joseph,	pray for us.
Descendant of the House of David	pray for us.
Husband of Mary,	pray for us.
Foster father of Jesus,	pray for us.
Guardian of Christ,	pray for us.
Support of the holy family,	pray for us.
Model of workers,	pray for us.
Example to parents,	pray for us.
Comfort of the dying,	pray for us.
Provider of food to the hungry,	pray for us.
Companion of the poor,	pray for us.
Protector of the church,	pray for us.

Merciful God,
grant that we may learn from Saint Joseph
to care for the members of our families
and share what we have with the poor.
We ask this through Christ our Lord. Amen.

A

abba the Aramaic word with the English equivalent of "daddy" or "papa" (**81**)

abortion the deliberate termination of a pregnancy by killing an unborn child. It is a grave sin. (**229**)

absolution words spoken by the priest during the Sacrament of Penance and Reconciliation to grant forgiveness of sins in God's name (**280**)

Advocate literally means "he who is called to one's side." The Holy Spirit is our Advocate, guiding and comforting us, strengthening us to know and live by the truth. (**118**)

Anointing of the Sick one of the Sacraments of Healing for people who are seriously ill or in danger of dying. In the Sacrament, the person's forehead and hands are anointed with the blessed oil of the sick. (**283**)

Annunciation the Angel Gabriel's announcement to Mary that she would be the Mother of God and give birth to the Savior (**109**)

Apostles the twelve men Jesus chose to be his closest followers and to share in his work and mission in a special way (**177**)

apostolic a Mark of the Church. The Church is apostolic because her teaching authority comes directly from Jesus and his chosen Apostles, handed down through the bishops of the Church, who are direct successors of the Apostles. (**177**)

B

Baptism the Sacrament of in which a person is immersed in water or has water poured on him or her. Baptism takes away Original Sin and all personal sin, and makes a person a child of God and member of the Church. (**199**)

Beatitudes Jesus' eight teachings about the meaning and path to true happiness; they depict the way to live in God's Kingdom now and always, working toward the eternal holiness or blessedness to which God calls all people (**150**)

C

canon of Scripture the Church's complete list of inspired books included in Sacred Scripture (**6, 66**)

Cardinal Virtues the four principal moral virtues—prudence, temperance, justice, and fortitude—that help us live as children of God and from which the other moral virtues flow. We strengthen these good habits through God's grace and our own efforts. (**240**)

catholic a Mark of the Church. The Church is catholic because she is universal, meant for all people in all times and in all places. (**200**)

Church the community of all baptized people who believe in the Holy Trinity and follow Jesus. The word is often used for the Catholic Church because we trace our origins back to the Apostles. (**177**)

Confirmation the Sacrament of Initiation through which the spiritual life received in Baptism is strengthened and the person is sealed with the Gifts of the Holy Spirit (**269**)

consecrated religious life a state of life lived by religious sisters, brothers, and priests in community and characterized by the vows of poverty, chastity, and obedience (**298**)

conscience the God-given ability that helps individuals judge whether actions are right or wrong (**214**)

contrition true sorrow for disobeying God and the commitment to try to avoid sin in the future (**279**)

covenant a sacred promise or agreement between humans or between God and humans (**79**)

D

discernment the process by which a person reflects, discusses, and prays about how God might be calling him or her to live out a particular vocation (**297**)

disciples people who learn from and follow the example of a teacher. The disciples of Jesus are those who believe in him, follow his teachings, and put them into practice. (**175**)

discipleship accepting Jesus' invitation to believe in and follow him by studying his ways and putting them into practice (139)

Divine Inspiration the gift of the Holy Spirit which assisted the human authors in writing the Bible to ensure it contained the truths God wanted us to know (66)

Divine Revelation the process by which God makes himself known. The chief sources of revelation are Sacred Scripture and Sacred Tradition. (55)

doctrine official Church teachings on matters of faith and morals. Catholics are obligated to believe these truths. (177)

domestic Church a name for the Catholic family, because it is the community of Christians in the home. God made the family to be the first place we learn about loving others and following Christ. (295)

Emmanuel the name given to the Messiah by the prophet Isaiah, meaning "God is with us" (109)

eternal the term that means "God is" and "has always been," even before the beginning of time, and will be forever (58)

eternal life life forever with God for all who die in his friendship (200)

Eucharist the Sacrament of Initiation during which the bread and wine become the Body and Blood of Christ and all who receive him in Holy Communion are brought closer to him and one another (270)

euthanasia the deliberate action or inaction which causes the death of someone who is sick, dying, or suffering because of disabilities or a debilitating condition. It is a grave sin. (229)

Evangelists the four inspired human authors of the Gospels: Matthew, Mark, Luke, and John (69)

faith the Theological Virtue that makes it possible for us to believe in God and the things that he has revealed to us. Faith leads us to obey God. It is both a gift from God and a free, human choice. (95)

free will the God-given freedom and ability to make choices. God created us with free will so we can have the freedom to choose good. (199)

Gifts of the Holy Spirit seven powerful gifts God gives us to follow guidance of the Holy Spirit and live the Christian life. We are sealed with the Gifts of the Holy Spirit at Confirmation. (269)

Gospel a word that means "Good News." The Gospel message is the Good News of God's Kingdom and his saving love. (69)

grace God's free, loving gift of his own life and help to do what he calls us to do. It is participation in the life of the Holy Trinity. (98)

Heaven the state, or experience, of the full joy of living eternally in God's presence (321)

Hell the state, or experience, of eternal separation from God because of a choice to turn away from him and not seek forgiveness (321)

hierarchy the organization of the Church into different levels of leadership and membership (186)

Holy Trinity the mystery of one God in three Divine Persons: Father, Son, and Holy Spirit (8, 96)

human dignity the worth each person has because he or she is made in the image of God (227)

© Our Sunday Visitor

392 Catholic Faith Words

image of God the Divine likeness in all human beings that comes from being made by God and includes the ability to think, choose, be free, love, and be in relationship with God and others (**57**)

Incarnation the truth that the Second Divine Person of the Holy Trinity, the Son of God, assumed human nature in order to save all people; Jesus Christ is both true God and true man (**106**)

intellect the God-given ability which makes it possible for humans to think, reason, and judge (**215**)

intercession a form of prayer that involves praying to God on behalf of another; also called intercessory prayer (**121**)

J – L

justice the constant and firm desire to give God and other people what is their due as children of God, made in his image and possessing equal human dignity (**306**)

Kingdom of God God's rule of peace, justice, and love that exists in Heaven, but has not yet come in its fullness on Earth (**147**)

laity all baptized members of the Church who share in Jesus' mission and witness to him and his message but are not priests or consecrated sisters or brothers; sometimes called lay people (**295**)

Last Judgment God's final triumph over evil that will occur at the end of time when Christ returns and judges all the living and the dead. Then, all will fully see and understand God's plan for creation. (**322**)

Mediator the title given to Jesus because, as true God and true man, he alone is able to reconcile all people to God the Father, bringing us closer to God the Father by his words and saving actions (**136**)

miracle an event for which there is no scientific explanation because it happened by the power of God. Jesus worked miracles to help us see the presence of the Kingdom of God. (**110**)

mortal sin a grave (very serious) sin by which someone turns completely away from God and breaks his or her relationship with God (**215**)

murder the deliberate killing of another person when the killing is not in self-defense. It is always gravely sinful. (**227**)

mystery a truth of faith that cannot be fully understood but that is believed because God has shown it in Scripture, in the life of Jesus, or in the teachings of the Church (**55**)

Mystical Body of Christ a name for the Church, whose baptized members are all united to Christ and one another through the Holy Spirit, forming one holy people with Christ as her head (**186**)

natural moral law precepts about goodness that are written by God in our hearts and accessible through our God-given reason (**83**)

New Commandment Jesus' command for his disciples to love one another as he has loved us (**83**)

one a Mark of the Church. The Church is one because the power of the Holy Spirit unites all the members through one faith and one Baptism (**188**)

Original Holiness the state of goodness that humanity enjoyed before our first parents, Adam and Eve, chose to sin against God (**159**)

Original Sin the sin of our first parents that wounded human nature and introduced sin, suffering, and death into the world; all humans are born with Original Sin and are thus tempted to sin (**159**)

parable a short story Jesus told using examples from everyday life or nature to illustrate moral or spiritual truths (147)

Particular Judgment the individual judgment by God at the time of a person's death; when God decides, after a person's death, where that person will spend eternity according to his or her faith and works (321)

Paschal Mystery Christ's work of redemption through his Passion, Death, Resurrection, and Ascension (162)

peace a state of calm and harmony when things are in their proper order and people settle problems with kindness and justice (309)

penance the name for the prayer, offering, or good work the priest gives you in the Sacrament of Reconciliation (280)

Penance and Reconciliation the Sacrament of Healing that celebrates God's mercy and forgiveness and a sinner's reconciliation with God and the Church through absolution from a priest (279)

personal sin a deliberate thought, word, deed, or omission that violates the law of God (159)

Purgatory a state of final cleansing after death and before entering into Heaven that removes any remaining personal obstacles to eternal union with God. Purgatory frees the person from temporal punishment (being deprived of the entrance into Heaven for a time) due to sin. (321)

Real Presence a phrase used to describe the Catholic teaching that Jesus is really and truly with us in the Eucharist—Body, Blood, Soul, and Divinity (258)

S

Sacraments at the Service of Communion Holy Orders and Matrimony. They celebrate people's commitment to serve God and the community and help build up the People of God. (257)

Sacraments of Healing Penance and Reconciliation and the Anointing of the Sick. In these Sacraments, God's forgiveness and healing are given to those suffering physical and spiritual sickness. (257)

Sacraments of Initiation the three Sacraments that celebrate membership into the Catholic Church: Baptism, Confirmation, and Eucharist (257)

Sacred Scripture the Word of God written by humans acting under the Holy Spirit's inspiration and guidance; another name for the Bible (5, 66)

Saints those whom the Church declares led holy lives and are enjoying eternal life with God in Heaven (121)

salvation the loving action of God's forgiveness of sins and the restoration of friendship with the Father brought by Jesus Christ (160)

scandal the destructive behavior by which a person deliberately leads, through his or her own action or inaction, another person to sin (230)

Seven Sacraments effective signs of God's grace instituted by Christ and given to his Church. In the celebration of each Sacrament, there are visible signs and Divine actions that give grace and allow us to share in God's work. (255)

Sermon on the Mount the summary of key teachings of Jesus found in the Gospel according to Matthew (149)

solidarity a Christian principle that motivates believers to share their spiritual gifts as well as their material ones (310)

soul the spiritual principle of a human person that is individual, created by God, and will exist forever (215)

394 Catholic Faith Words

Ten Commandments the ten fundamental moral laws given by God to Moses, and recorded in the Old Testament, to help his People live by the covenant (**82**)

Theological Virtues gifts from God that help us believe in him, trust in his plan for us, and love him as he loves us; they are faith, hope, and charity (**239**)

transubstantiation the process by which, through the power of the Holy Spirit and the words and actions of the priest, the bread and wine are transformed into the Body and Blood of Christ (**270**)

venial sin a sin that weakens, but does not destroy, a person's relationship with God (**215**)

virtue a good spiritual habit that strengthens you and enables you to do what is right and good (**239**)

Visitation the event of Mary, who was pregnant with Jesus, visiting her cousin Elizabeth, who was pregnant with Saint John the Baptist (**135**)

vocation the purpose for which God made us and the particular way to answer and live out his call, whether as a lay person (married or single), a member of a religious community, or a member of the ordained ministry (**297**)

wisdom the spiritual gift that helps us to see God's purpose and plan for our lives. Wisdom is also one of the seven Gifts of the Holy Spirit. (**147**)

Works of Mercy actions that show care for the physical and spiritual needs of others (**322**)

© Our Sunday Visitor

© Our Sunday Visitor

The Subcommittee on the Catechism, United States Conference of Catholic Bishops, has found this catechetical series, copyright 2014, to be in conformity with the *Catechism of the Catholic Church.*

Nihil Obstat
Rev. Fr. Jeremiah L. Payne, S.Th.L.
Censor Librorum, Diocese of Orlando

Imprimatur
✠ Most Rev. John Noonan
Bishop of Orlando
January 20, 2014

Alive in Christ Grade 7 Student Book
ISBN: 978-1-61278-018-4
Item Number: CU5108

1 2 3 4 5 6 7 8 015016 18 17 16 15 14
Webcrafters, Inc., Madison, WI, USA; June 2014; Job# 113686

400 Credits

ALIVE IN CHRIST

Chapter Test Answer Key Preview

CHAPTER 2 · Test

Name _____   Date _____

Circle the letter of the choice that best completes each sentence.

1. ___ is another name for the Bible, the Word of God written by humans acting under the Holy Spirit's inspiration and guidance.
   a. Sacred Tradition
   b. Sacred Scripture
   c. Divine Tradition
   d. Divine Scripture

2. The ___ sense of Scripture refers to the actual words that have been recorded.
   a. analogical
   b. allegorical
   c. literal
   d. spiritual

3. Catholics respond to God and commit themselves to follow God's Word during ___.
   a. Mass
   b. the Gospels
   c. the Epistles
   d. Tradition

4. Divine ___ is the process by which the Holy Spirit assisted the human authors in writing the Bible.
   a. Revelation
   b. Inspiration
   c. Proclamation
   d. Annunciation

Complete each sentence with the correct term.

5. The ___Gospel___ message is the Good News of God's Kingdom and his saving love.

6. God's Word helps us develop a ___conscience___, which helps us judge between right and wrong.

7. In the Bible, the literary form of ___narrative stories___ helps people recall, in a straightforward way, something about God's relationship with the world.

8. The ___moral sense___ of Scripture explains how to live justly and humbly before God.

Write a response on the lines below.

9. What is the canon of Scripture? ___The canon of Scripture is the Church's official collection of inspired books of Sacred Scripture.___

10. Name the four Evangelists and describe their work. ___The four Evangelists are Matthew, Mark, Luke, and John. They are the inspired human authors of the Gospels who helped to spread Jesus' Good News to people of many nations.___

CHAPTER 1 · Test

Name _____   Date _____

Match each description in Column A with the correct term in Column B by filling in the appropriate letter.

Column A	Column B
c 1. Steadfast love, truth, almighty	a. intellect
b 2. Choosing to turn from God	b. sin
d 3. God is, was, and always will be	c. attributes of God
a 4. The ability to think and make connections	d. eternal

Circle the letter of the choice that best completes each sentence.

5. Created in the image of God, humans have the ability to think, ___, be free, love, and be in a relationship with God and others.
   a. hate
   b. choose
   c. protest
   d. change

6. A(n) ___ is a truth of faith that cannot be fully understood but is believed because God has shown it to us through Scripture, his Son, or the Church.
   a. mystery
   b. account
   c. canon
   d. truth

7. The story of God's relationship with his Chosen People is recorded in the ___.
   a. Tradition
   b. Gospels
   c. Old Testament
   d. New Testament

8. Through ___, God wants to reconcile creation to himself.
   a. the Old Testament
   b. his attributes
   c. his Son
   d. his blessings

Write a response on the lines below.

9. What is Divine Revelation? ___Divine Revelation is the process by which God makes himself known.___

10. Why do humans need the salvation of Jesus Christ? ___Possible response: Because of the actions of our first parents, all humans have the tendency to sin; Jesus came to turn us back to God the Father and restore us to the original state of goodness for which we were created.___

Name _____ Date _____

Circle the letter of the choice that best completes each sentence.

1. God has offered us the free gift of _____ so that we can share in his life.
   a. love
   b. hope
   c. grace
   d. courage

2. When we are baptized, we become members of God's family, the _____.
   a. Holy Trinity
   b. Church
   c. baptized
   d. confirmed

3. Faith is a belief or trust in God and the things he has revealed to us; it is both a gift from God and a _____.
   a. Sacrament
   b. free choice
   c. Mark of the Church
   d. sacrifice

4. Jesus asked the Apostles to go and make _____ of all nations.
   a. brothers and sisters
   b. fathers
   c. disciples
   d. friends

Complete each sentence with the correct term.

5. The ___Holy Trinity___ is the mystery of one God in three Divine Persons—Father, Son, and Holy Spirit.

6. The ___love___ between the Father, Son, and Holy Spirit is central to the mystery of the Trinity.

7. The ___Holy Spirit___ is a counselor for the Church.

8. Christ established the ___Church___ through the Apostles.

Write a response on the lines below.

9. In God's plan for us, how do our best and most loving family and community relationships resemble the relationships of the Holy Trinity?
   Possible response: A loving family works together. In the Trinity, the Father asked his Son to come to us, the Son acted in obedience to the Father, and the Holy Spirit helps us build a loving relationship as members of the Church.

10. Explain how the gift of faith can be like a compass.
   Possible response: If we keep faith in God as the direction home, where we want to end up, our life will move in God's direction.

Name _____ Date _____

Complete each sentence with the correct term.

1. In the ___Resurrection___, Jesus makes it known that God's Reign and Divine life can be part of our existence.

2. The beginning of the Lord's Prayer refers to God as ___Abba___, the English equivalent of "daddy" or "papa."

3. Jesus was God the Father's new ___covenant___ with us so that we would be reconciled with him.

4. Precepts about goodness that are written by God in our hearts and accessible through our God-given reason are called ___natural moral law___.

Indicate whether the following statements are true or false. Rewrite the false statements to make them true.

5. A commandment is a sacred promise or agreement between humans or between God and humans. True/**False** ___A covenant is a sacred promise or agreement between humans or between God and humans.___

6. When we are baptized, we become adopted children of God. **True**/False

7. The Ten Commandments are the fundamental moral laws given by God to Jesus. True/**False** ___The Ten Commandments are the fundamental moral laws given by God to Moses.___

8. Christians are called to live holy lives because of the law of love that exists within their hearts. **True**/False

Write a response on the lines below.

9. How does God's revealed law lead us to him? ___God's revealed law helps us live in a covenant relationship with him and one another, drawing us closer to him.___

10. What is the New Commandment that Jesus gave us and how does it connect us to God? ___This is Jesus' command for his disciples to love one another as he has loved us. We try to do this because Christ poured out his life and love for us, and his Holy Spirit dwells within us. Through loving our neighbor, we show our love for God.___

CHAPTER 6 Test

Name _____ Date _____

Complete each sentence with the correct term.

1. The Church is the Body of Christ alive in the world; the **Holy Spirit** is the soul.

2. The Holy Spirit is our **Advocate** , guiding and comforting us, strengthening us to know and live by the truth.

3. **Prayer** is when we raise our minds and hearts to God.

4. The liturgical feast celebrating the descent of the Holy Spirit upon the Apostles is known as **Pentecost** .

Circle the letter of the choice that best completes each sentence.

5. In a prayer of _____ you pray to God on behalf of another person.
   a. petition   c. thanksgiving
   b. blessing   **d.** intercession

6. The Holy Spirit acts through the _____ of the Church to teach and form us as disciples.
   a. Sacred Scripture   c. Precepts
   b. Sacred Tradition   d. Marks

7. When we pray a prayer of _____ we give respect to God by honoring his greatness.
   a. blessing   c. thanksgiving
   b. intercession   d. praise

8. A(n) _____ is a person whom the Church declares led a holy life and is enjoying eternal life with God in Heaven.
   a. Advocate   c. disciple
   b. Saint   d. member of the Church

Write a response on the lines below.

9. Why do you think we need the Holy Spirit? Possible responses: to guide and build up the community of faith, to help people in the Church be faithful, to sanctify the Church, to be our Advocate, to unite us

10. Explain this statement: "Neglecting the time and effort for prayer will produce a withered spiritual garden." Possible response: If we don't take time to pray we are not taking time to raise healthy hearts and minds to God, just like not taking time to care for a garden will result in weeds or dying from neglect.

Alive in Christ, Grade 7: Chapter 6   115F

CHAPTER 5 Test

Name _____ Date _____

Match each description in Column A with the correct term in Column B.

Column A	Column B
d **1.** The truth that Jesus Christ is both true God and true man	a. Jesus
c **2.** An event that can't be explained scientifically because it happened through the power of God	b. Annunciation
b **3.** The visit of the angel Gabriel to Mary to tell her she would be the Mother of God	c. miracle
a **4.** The eternal Word of God	d. Incarnation

Indicate whether the following statements are true or false. Then rewrite the false statements to make them true.

5. The Holy Spirit was acting in Mary even before she was born so that through her the Son of God could become man. True/**False**

   _____

6. Jesus is like us in all things but sorrow. True/**False**

   Jesus is like us in all things but sin.

7. The name Jesus literally means "God lives." True/**False**

   The name Jesus literally means "God saves."

8. God the Father speaks directly to us in Christ through the power of the Incarnation. **True**/False

Write a response on the lines below.

9. What is the significance of God the Father's promise to send his Son, who would be named "Emmanuel," which means "God is with us"? Possible response: God used to send his prophets to speak with us, but he promised to send his Son to actually be with us. Jesus changed our relationship to God.

10. In your own words, explain how Jesus is fully God and fully man. Possible response: Jesus was born human from a human woman, and he died a human death. But he was also God's only Son, the eternal Word, conceived by the Holy Spirit.

Alive in Christ, Grade 7: Chapter 5   103F

Name _____ Date _____

Match each description in Column A with the correct term in Column B by filling in the appropriate letter.

Column A	Column B
c **1.** Summary of key teachings of Jesus found in the Gospel according to Matthew	**a.** parables
d **2.** God's rule of peace, justice, and love that exists in Heaven, but is yet to come on Earth	**b.** Beatitudes
a **3.** Short stories Jesus told to illustrate moral or spiritual truths	**c.** Sermon on the Mount
b **4.** Jesus' eight teachings about the meaning and path to true happiness	**d.** Kingdom of God

Circle the letter of the choice that best completes each sentence.

5. Jesus used The Parable of the Good Samaritan to illustrate the idea of _____.
   a. discipleship
   b. an eye for an eye
   c. love of neighbor
   d. peace

6. Jesus compared living according to his words to _____.
   a. safe sailing on a stormy sea
   b. preaching from a mountaintop
   c. building a house on solid rock
   d. ignoring stereotypes of others

7. In the Beatitudes, Jesus says we will find true happiness when _____.
   a. we experience much good luck
   b. God's Kingdom becomes real
   c. we read the parables
   d. we change our point of view

8. _____ is the Gift of the Holy Spirit that helps us to see God's purpose and plan for our lives.
   a. Fortitude
   b. Apostolic
   c. Piety
   d. Wisdom

Write a response on the lines below.

9. Why do you think Jesus used parables? **Answers will vary, but might mention that Jesus used examples from everyday life to illustrate moral or spiritual truths.**

10. How do accounts of the Beatitudes differ in the Gospels according to Matthew and Luke? **Answers will vary, but should include some of the information from page 150.**

Name _____ Date _____

Match each description in Column A with the correct term in Column B by filling in the appropriate letter.

Column A	Column B
c **1.** Name for disciples of Jesus	**a.** Nativity
d **2.** Special prayer that focuses on the events in the lives of Jesus and Mary	**b.** Mediator
b **3.** Title given to Jesus because he alone is able to bring us closer to God the Father	**c.** followers of the Way
a **4.** The birth of Jesus	**d.** Rosary

Complete each sentence with the best term or phrase.

5. Jesus is the Second Person of the **Holy Trinity** .

6. Becoming the person God calls you to be is reaching your **full potential** .

7. Jesus is known as the **Substantial Image** of the Father.

8. The **Visitation** is the event in which Mary, who was pregnant with Jesus, visited her cousin Elizabeth, who was pregnant with John the Baptist.

9. **Discipleship** is accepting Jesus' invitation to believe in and follow him by studying his ways and putting them into practice.

Write a response on the lines below.

10. Jesus is "true God" and "true man." What did Jesus show us by being human? What did Jesus show us by being Divine? **Through his humanity, Jesus showed us how to live a full life, how to reach our full potential, and how to become children of God. Through his divinity, Jesus helps us become closer to the Father and shows us a visible image of the true nature of God. He shows us God's infinite mercy, love, and healing.**

_____

_____

CHAPTER 9 Test

Name _____ Date _____

Circle the letter of the choice that best completes each sentence.

1. Jesus made eternal life with God the Father possible by ___.
   - a. the Sacrament of Reconciliation
   - (c.) the Paschal Mystery
   - b. the practice of fasting
   - d. Original Sin

2. The Paschal Mystery is Christ's work of ___ through his Passion, Death, Resurrection, and Ascension.
   - a. Original Sin
   - c. suffering
   - b. healing
   - (d.) Redemption

3. We call ___ the Messiah because he was sent by God the Father to fulfill his promise to redeem his People.
   - (a.) Jesus
   - c. Peter
   - b. John the Baptist
   - d. Martha

4. The Church has the power to forgive our sins committed after Baptism through ___.
   - a. the Old Testament prophecies
   - c. Mosaic Law
   - (b.) the Sacrament of Reconciliation
   - d. the Book of Genesis

Write the word or phrase that best completes each sentence.

5. The term "Anointed One" refers to the Greek word __Christ__.

6. __Original Sin__ is the sin of our first parents that introduced sin, suffering, and death into the world.

7. Because Jesus, in his humanity, remained faithful to God the Father, he is called the __new Adam__.

8. __Salvation__ is the loving action of God's forgiveness of sins and the restoration of friendship with the Father brought by Jesus Christ.

9. A deliberate thought, word, deed, or omission that violates the law of God is called __personal sin__.

Write a response on the lines below.

10. Describe the Original Holiness of the first humans.
    __Original Holiness is the state of goodness that humanity enjoyed before__
    __our first parents chose to sin against God.__

CHAPTER 10 Test

Name _____ Date _____

Match each description in Column A with the correct term in Column B.

Column A

C **1.** Official Church teachings on matters of faith and morals

d **2.** All the laws of the Church

a **3.** People who learn from and follow the example of a teacher

b **4.** The Old and New Testaments of the Bible

Column B
- a. disciples
- b. Sacred Scripture
- c. doctrine
- d. Code of Canon Law

Circle the letter of the choice that best completes each sentence.

5. The ___ are the twelve men Jesus chose to be his closest followers and to share in his work and mission in a special way.
   - a. disciples
   - c. Gospels
   - (b.) Apostles
   - d. followers of John the Baptist

6. Jesus told his disciples to "travel light" because he wanted them to ___.
   - (a.) have total dependence on God the Father to take care of them
   - b. get away quickly if there was trouble
   - c. find out how hard it is to be poor
   - d. go without things

7. The ___ is the community of all baptized people who believe in the Holy Trinity and follow Jesus.
   - a. Apostles
   - (c.) Church
   - b. Magisterium
   - d. Communion of Saints

8. The Church is ___ because her teaching authority comes directly from Jesus and his chosen Apostles.
   - a. catholic
   - b. holy
   - c. Papal
   - (d.) apostolic

Write a response on the lines below.

9. What do you think attracted people to following Jesus? __Answers will vary, but should__ __mention that Jesus taught people in a way that drew them to him.__

10. How is the Church our guide in all parts of our lives and in everything we do?
    __Answers will vary, but should include that the Church teaches us how to__
    __keep God's law and live as Jesus did.__

Name _____ Date _____

Match each description in Column A with the correct term in Column B.

	Column A	Column B
a	**1.** Purification, on Earth or in Purgatory, frees us from this consequence of sin	**a.** temporal punishment
c	**2.** The Church is universal, for all people in all times	**b.** Baptism
d	**3.** The God-given freedom and ability to make choices	**c.** catholic
b	**4.** Takes away Original Sin and all personal sin	**d.** free will

Circle the letter of the choice that best completes each sentence.

5. Along with faith in God, we need to be _____ into new life in Christ and experience the gift of salvation.

  (a.) baptized   **b.** saved   **c.** signed up   **d.** forced

6. The _____ explains that "all salvation comes from Christ the Head through the Church which is his Body."

  a. First Vatican Council   (c.) Second Vatican Council

  b. parish bulletins   **d.** Liturgy of the Eucharist

7. The _____ builds the Church, brings her to life, and makes her holy.

  a. Lord's Prayer   **b.** Eucharist   **c.** Pope   (d.) Holy Spirit

8. The Church's treasury is _____.

  a. a collection of money

  (b.) all the holiness and goodness from Jesus, Mary, and the Saints

  c. the many people who are members of the Church

  d. jewels and works of art

Write a response on the lines below.

9. Provide some examples of the universal nature of the Church.
Responses will vary, but should include that the Church is all over the world and has existed for centuries, that all are welcome as members, that she is missionary, and that she was sent by Christ to all people.

10. What is eternal life?
Eternal life means life forever with God for all who die in his friendship.

Name _____ Date _____

Circle the letter of the choice that best completes each sentence.

1. The Church is _____ because the power of the Holy Spirit unites all her members through one faith and one Baptism.

  a. apostolic   (c.) one

  b. communal   **d.** catholic

2. The organization of the Church into different levels of leadership and membership is the _____.

  (a.) hierarchy   **c.** Mystical Body of Christ

  b. vine and the branches   **d.** Communion of Saints

3. In the Beatitudes, Jesus asks us to recognize his presence in _____.

  a. our parish priest   (c.) people who are poor or persecuted

  b. the Church hierarchy   **d.** the prayer of great Saints

4. Saul (Paul) became a believer and wrote that the Church is _____.

  a. always going to be persecuted   **c.** people in a building

  (b.) the Body of Christ   **d.** sad that Jesus died

Complete each sentence with the correct terms.

5. Because of the different _____gifts_____ of her members, the Church is able to help build God's Kingdom in many ways and places.

6. The _____Mystical Body of Christ_____ is the Church, united to Christ and one another through the Holy Spirit, forming one holy people with Christ as her head.

7. Acts that meet people's physical needs are the _____Corporal Works of Mercy_____.

8. A word that means a "gathering" or an "assembly" is _____Church_____.

Write a response on the lines below.

9. Why do we need both the physical and spiritual parts of the Church?
Responses will vary, but should include the ideas that we are both physical and spiritual beings, that Christ was both human and Divine, and that we are his Body on Earth.

10. How do you think you can make a difference in the Church? Why is each member important?
Answers will vary.

CHAPTER 13 Test

Name _____ Date _____

Match each description in Column A with the correct term in Column B by filling in the appropriate letter.

Column A

Column B

b **1.** A sin that weakens a person's relationship with God

d **2.** The God-given ability that makes it possible to think, reason, and judge

c **3.** The spiritual principle of humans that is individual, created by God, and exists forever

a **4.** A grave sin by which someone turns completely away from God

a. mortal sin

b. venial sin

c. soul

d. intellect

Indicate whether the following statements are true or false. Then rewrite false statements to make them true.

5. It is all right to do evil if a good result will come from it. **True**/**False**
We are never allowed to do evil, even if good might come from it.

6. Conscience is the God-given ability that helps individuals judge whether actions are right or wrong. **True**/**False**

7. We do not need to do anything to form our conscience. **True**/**False**
We must read the Bible and seek guidance from the Church and Holy Spirit.

8. Follow these steps to make a good moral decision: **1)** Think about possible consequences, **2)** Compare your options to the Commandments and Beatitudes, **3)** Talk with someone who can advise you, **4)** Pray to the Holy Spirit, and **5)** Act with confidence that you have made the right decision. **True**/**False**

Write a response on the lines below.

9. Why is it important to have a well-formed conscience?
Answers will vary, but should include a reference to how a well-formed conscience helps us to choose good and avoid sin.

10. Explain the three elements that determine the morality of a human action.
The object, the action itself; the intention, the reason for doing the action; and the circumstances, what is going on around the decision-maker.

CHAPTER 14 Test

Name _____ Date _____

Complete each sentence with the correct term.

1. _____Scandal_____ is the destructive behavior by which a person leads another person, either through action or inaction, to sin.

2. _____Abortion_____ is the deliberate termination of a pregnancy by killing an unborn child.

3. To deliberately cause the death of someone who is sick, dying, or suffering either through action or inaction is called _____euthanasia_____.

4. The Fifth Commandment says that _____murder_____, the deliberate killing of another person when the killing is not in self-defense, is always a grave sin.

Circle the letter of the choice that best completes each sentence.

5. The sacredness of all human life comes directly from ____.

a. how people think

b. the kind of work they do

c. their heredity

d. being created by God

6. Of all the creatures made by God, humans are the only ones who have the capacity to ____.

a. recognize God's presence

b. help others

c. learn

d. communicate

7. When Jesus taught about the Fifth Commandment, he widened the understanding of "You shall not kill" to include ____.

a. anger and vengeance

b. accidental killing

c. suicide

d. lying

8. When Jesus was arrested, he ____.

a. ordered his Apostles to fight to defend him

b. upheld and honored every human life, including those who were harming him

c. expressed his anger at those arresting him

d. practiced passive resistance

Write a response on the lines below.

9. Explain your understanding of the "consistent ethic of life." Answers should include that this Catholic teaching states we must honor, respect, and defend all life.

10. What is human dignity? Human dignity is the worth each person has because he or she is made in the image of God.

CHAPTER 16 Test

Name _____ Date _____

Circle the letter of the choice that best completes each sentence.

1. The ____ are effective signs of God's grace instituted by Christ and given to his Church.
   - a. Saints
   - c. Precepts
   - (b.) Seven Sacraments
   - d. Real Presence

2. Jesus is the perfect ____ between God the Father and humanity because he is fully God and fully man.
   - (a.) Mediator
   - c. image
   - b. Sacrament
   - d. Messiah

3. The Sacraments of Healing bring God's ____ to those who are physically and spiritually sick.
   - a. justice and healing
   - (c.) forgiveness and healing
   - b. forgiveness and sacrifice
   - d. sacrifice and healing

4. Jesus followed the ____ customs of prayer and worship.
   - (a.) Jewish
   - c. Roman
   - b. Christian
   - d. European

Indicate whether the following statements are true or false. Then rewrite false statements to make them true.

5. God gives us grace when we do something to earn it. True/(False)
   Grace is a free gift from God. There is nothing we can do to earn it.

6. The three Sacraments of Initiation celebrate membership into the Church. (True)/False

7. Jesus Christ is called the first Sacrament. (True)/False

8. Pentecost describes that Jesus is really and truly with us in the Eucharist. True/(False)
   Real Presence describes that Jesus is really and truly with us in the Eucharist.

Write a response on the lines below.

9. What are the two Sacraments at the Service of Communion and what do they celebrate?
   They are Holy Orders and Matrimony and they celebrate people's
   commitment to serve God and the community.

10. Where is Jesus when we celebrate the Sacraments?
    Jesus is present and acting in each Sacrament.

Alive in Christ, Grade 7: Chapter 16   **251F**

CHAPTER 15 Test

Name _____ Date _____

Match each description in Column A with the correct term in Column B by filling in the appropriate letter.

Column A	Column B
_b_ 1. Good spiritual habit that strengthens and enables you to do what is right and good	a. Cardinal Virtues
_d_ 2. Faith, hope, and charity (love)	b. virtue
_a_ 3. Prudence, temperance, justice, and fortitude	c. fortitude
_c_ 4. Courage to do what is right, even if others disagree	d. Theological Virtues

Complete each sentence with the correct term.

5. Giving God and others what is due to them is the virtue of ____justice____.

6. The virtue of ____temperance____ helps us keep our desires from ruling our lives.

7. ____Chastity____ helps us maintain the right balance of body and spirit in human sexuality.

8. When we are discreet in the way we dress and speak, we are practicing the virtue of ____modesty____.

Write a response on the lines below.

9. List two of the four behaviors that can damage our integrity and keep us from living a life of excellence. Why are these behaviors sinful?
   Responses should include lying, slander/calumny, revenge, and/or not
   living up to our promises. These behaviors are sinful because they hurt
   the person committing the sin as well as others who are involved. These
   behaviors are the opposite of the virtue of truth.

10. Why is it not always easy to live a virtuous life? What can we do to get help?
    Responses will vary but might include a reference to challenges created
    by the culture we live within, and should refer to help coming from
    Catholic teaching, Sacred Scripture, the lives of Saints, and people who
    exemplify virtuous living.

Alive in Christ, Grade 7: Chapter 15   **235F**

CHAPTER 17 Test

Name _____ Date _____

Match each description in Column A with the correct term in Column B.

Column A	Column B
c 1. We are brought closer to Jesus through his Body and Blood	a. Baptism
d 2. Adults receive Baptism, Confirmation, and Eucharist in the same celebration	b. Confirmation
a 3. The Sacrament that is always celebrated first	c. Eucharist
b 4. Seals a person with the Gifts of the Holy Spirit	d. Rite of Christian Initiation

Circle the letter of the choice that best completes each sentence.

5. _____ is the Sacrament of new life in Christ through the forgiveness of sins and incorporation into the Church.
   - a. Confirmation
   - b. Eucharist
   - **c. Baptism**
   - d. Initiation

6. In Confirmation the bishop anoints candidates with the oil of _____.
   - a. catechumens
   - **b. Sacred Chrism**
   - c. Initiation
   - d. transubstantiation

7. When the bread and wine are transformed into the Body and Blood of Christ in the Eucharist, this change is called _____.
   - **a. transubstantiation**
   - b. reconciliation
   - c. a Mystery of the Faith
   - d. transfiguration

8. After we are fed at the Lord's table, we must go out and _____.
   - a. clean up
   - **b. feed others**
   - c. sing a hymn
   - d. meet people

Write a response on the lines below.

9. What do the Gifts of the Holy Spirit do for us? They help us to follow the guidance of the Holy Spirit and live the Christian life.

10. Why can we only receive Baptism and Confirmation once? Both Sacraments give us a special seal or character that is permanent.

CHAPTER 18 Test

Name _____ Date _____

Circle the letter of the choice that best completes each sentence.

1. A turning away from sin and back to God is _____.
   - a. sorrow
   - b. confession
   - c. Eucharist
   - **d. conversion**

2. The Church celebrates Jesus' forgiveness and healing in the two Sacraments of _____.
   - a. Initiation
   - **b. Healing**
   - c. Service
   - d. children

3. True sorrow for disobeying God and committing to try to avoid sin in the future is called _____.
   - a. reparation
   - b. conversion
   - **c. contrition**
   - d. regret

4. The Anointing of the Sick unites those who are seriously ill or dying with Christ's _____.
   - **a. suffering**
   - b. teachings
   - c. birth
   - d. Mother

Indicate whether the following statements are true or false. Then rewrite false statements to make them true.

5. The Sacrament of the Eucharist celebrates a sinner's reconciliation with God and the Church. True **False**
   This happens in the Sacrament of Penance and Reconciliation.

6. When we confess our sins to a priest, we are actually talking to Christ. **True** False

7. Contrition is the prayer, offering, or good work given by the priest in Reconciliation. True **False**
   This is called penance.

8. Jesus taught us that God's compassion will end if we don't turn back to him. True **False**
   God's compassion will never end.

Write a response on the lines below.

9. What is absolution? the words spoken by the priest during the Sacrament of Reconciliation that grant forgiveness of sins in God's name

10. Why do you think it is important for people who are ill or in danger of death to receive the Anointing of the Sick? Responses will vary, but they should mention the grace given to help strengthen the person.

CHAPTER 19 Test

Name _____ Date _____

Match each description in Column A with the correct term in Column B.

Column A

Column B

<u>d</u> 1. A sweet-smelling oil used at Baptism

a. laity

<u>e</u> 2. A process by which one reflects, discusses, and prays about how God might be calling him/her

b. domestic Church

<u>a</u> 3. All baptized members of the Church who share in Jesus' mission but are not priests or consecrated brothers or sisters

c. vocation

<u>b</u> 4. The Catholic family; a community of Christians in the home

d. Sacred Chrism

<u>c</u> 5. Our purpose; the way we answer and live out God's call

e. discernment

Circle the letter of the choice that best completes each sentence.

6. A man who has received Holy Orders is known as a ____.
   a. lay person
   b. religious brother
   c. lector
   (d.) priest

7. At a Baptism, parents and godparents are called to bring the baptized up in ____.
   a. a vocation
   b. communion
   (c.) the practice of the faith
   d. consecrated religious life

8. Consecrated religious life is a communal life characterized by the vows of poverty, chastity, and ____.
   (a.) obedience
   b. fortitude
   c. fear of the Lord
   d. right counsel

9. Children should first learn about God from their ____.
   (a.) family members
   b. parish priest
   c. school teachers
   d. friends

Write a response on the lines below.

10. Why do you think vocations to the religious life are important? Possible response: because they involve work and sacrifice out of love for God and the community

11. Describe the role of lay people as priests, prophets, and kings. Answers should include content from the graphic organizer on page 297.

CHAPTER 20 Test

Name _____ Date _____

Match each description in Column A with the correct term in Column B.

Column A

Column B

<u>d</u> 1. The sin that the Tenth Commandment warns us about

a. justice

<u>a</u> 2. The desire to give what is due to God and and what is due to others as children of God

b. peace

<u>b</u> 3. A state of calm and harmony when things are in order and people settle problems with kindness

c. solidarity

<u>c</u> 4. Christian virtue that motivates believers to share their spiritual and material gifts

d. envy

Circle the letter of the choice that best completes each sentence.

5. The Kingdom of God will be complete when ____.
   (a.) Jesus comes again
   b. we recite the Lord's Prayer
   c. everyone has enough food
   d. the Bible is finished

6. By supporting workers in Poland, Pope Saint John Paul II showed ____.
   a. hope
   b. pride
   (c.) solidarity
   d. charity

7. ____ is called the perfect prayer because it sums up the message of the Gospels.
   a. The Mass
   (b.) The Lord's Prayer
   c. The Hail Mary
   d. The Glory Be

8. Jesus compares the Kingdom of God to a mustard seed that ____.
   a. withers in the sun
   b. becomes food for everyone
   (c.) grows and spreads
   d. falls on poor soil

Write a response on the lines below.

9. What opportunities to further justice do you see in your everyday life? Responses will vary, but should center on helping those who are victimized by poverty, prejudice, or other social injustices.

10. Why is it important for everyone to work for the Kingdom of God? Possible response: It is important for everyone to work for the Kingdom of God because the job is too big for any one person to do it.

Name _____   Date _____

Complete each sentence with the correct term.

1. The Theological Virtue that helps us look forward to the future is _____**hope**_____.

2. _____**Hell**_____ is eternal separation from God because of a choice to turn away from him and not seek forgiveness.

3. _____**Purgatory**_____ is a state of final cleansing after death and before Heaven.

4. The _____**Last Judgment**_____ is God's final triumph over evil when Christ will return to judge all of the living and the dead.

Circle the letter of the choice that best completes the sentence or answers the question.

5. The full joy of living eternally in God's presence is _____.
   - **a.** Heaven
   - **b.** Purgatory
   - **c.** Hell
   - **d.** Earth

6. The _____ are actions that show care for the physical and spiritual needs of others.
   - **a.** Sacraments
   - **b.** Sacred Chrism
   - **c.** Works of Mercy
   - **d.** Cardinal Virtues

7. Which will NOT happen at the Second Coming of Jesus?
   - **a.** the dead will rise
   - **b.** all humanity will be judged
   - **c.** bodies and souls will be united
   - **d.** God will recreate the world

8. Which person was raised from the dead by Jesus?
   - **a.** Mary
   - **b.** Lazarus
   - **c.** Martha
   - **d.** Paul

Write a response on the lines below.

9. Why should knowing about Heaven make us hopeful?
   Possible response: Knowing about Heaven should make us hopeful because it shows that our earthly efforts will be rewarded and gives us something to look forward to.

10. What happens during Particular Judgment?
   After a person's death, God decides where that person will spend eternity according to his or her faith and works.

Activity Master Answer Key Preview

Ordinary Time: The King Returns Activity Master, p. 18B

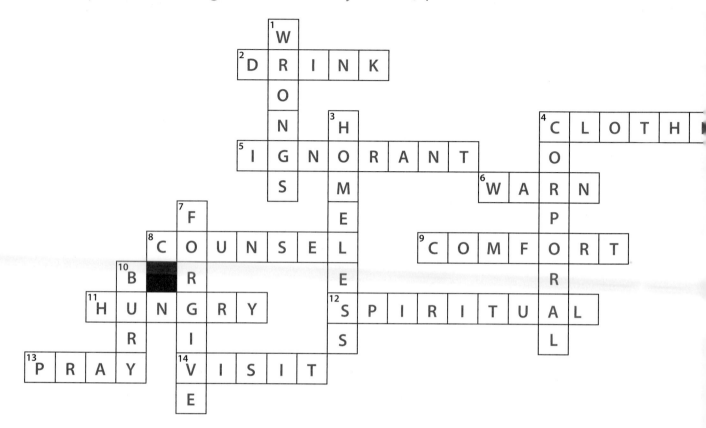

Advent: Being Ready Activity Master, p. 22B

Answers will vary. Check that the students fully completed the activity.

Christmas: Our Gift Activity Master, p. 26B

Answers will vary. Check that the students fully completed the activity.

Lent: The Annunciation Activity Master, p. 30B

Answers will vary. Check that the students fully completed the activity.

Lent: Conquering Temptation Activity Master, p. 34B

Answers will vary. Check that the students fully completed the activity.

Easter: Triduum Activity Master, p. 38B

1. Answers will vary, but might include taking part in an anti-bullying campaign.
2. Answers will vary, but might include researching to reduce the amount of food wasted and/or helping to create a connection between school cafeterias and homeless shelters/food banks.
3. Answers will vary, but might include helping to create awareness of the problem and/or being an example to others.
4. Answers will vary, but might include making donations or working with organizations that help this cause.
5. Answers will vary, but might include creating awareness and donating time or money to the cause.

Easter: Meeting Jesus with Joy Activity Master, p. 42B

Check that the students fully completed the activity.

Easter: Ascension Activity Master, p. 46B

Answers will vary. Check that the students fully completed the activity.

Chapter 1 Activity Master, p. 51G

Check that the students have completed this activity as assigned.

Chapter 2 Activity Master, p. 63G

Check that the students have completed this assignment.

Chapter 3 Activity Master, p. 75G

Answers will vary. Check that the students fully completed the activity.

Chapter 4 Activity Master, p. 91G

Check that the students have completed the activity as assigned.

Chapter 5 Activity Master, p. 103G

Check that the students have fully completed the activity.

Chapter 6 Activity Master, p. 115G

Check that the students have completed the activity as assigned.

Chapter 7 Activity Master, p. 131G

Answers will vary. Check that the students fully completed the activity.

Chapter 8 Activity Master, p. 143G

Check that the students have fully completed the activity.

Chapter 9 Activity Master, p. 155G

Answers will vary. Possible responses: Being reconciled with God means that we are presented before him as "holy, without blemish, and irreproachable before him." We are reconciled with God through Jesus' "making peace by the blood of his Cross." Jesus helps us to be "reconciled . . . through his death."

Chapter 10 Activity Master, p. 171G

1. <u>J</u> <u>O</u> <u>H</u> <u>N</u> the <u>B</u> <u>A</u> <u>P</u> <u>T</u> <u>I</u> <u>S</u> <u>T</u> was a popular preacher in Jesus' time.
   6   13   18

2. Philip invited his friend to meet Jesus by saying "<u>C</u> <u>O</u> <u>M</u> <u>E</u> <u>A</u> <u>N</u> <u>D</u> <u>S</u> <u>E</u> <u>E</u>."
        2   11   22

3. Zebedee's sons were also called the "<u>S</u> <u>O</u> <u>N</u> <u>S</u> <u>O</u> <u>F</u> <u>T</u> <u>H</u> <u>U</u> <u>N</u> <u>D</u> <u>E</u> <u>R</u>."
         24   27

4. Thomas was called <u>D</u> <u>I</u> <u>D</u> <u>Y</u> <u>M</u> <u>U</u> <u>S</u>, which means "the twin."
       20   3

5. In the Gospel according to Mark, Matthew is called <u>L</u> <u>E</u> <u>V</u> <u>I</u>.
        8   21 26

6. Jesus told his disciples not to carry <u>M</u> <u>O</u> <u>N</u> <u>E</u> <u>Y</u> or a <u>W</u> <u>A</u> <u>L</u> <u>K</u> <u>I</u> <u>N</u> <u>G</u> stick.
       14 23   10   7   19

7. If a town didn't welcome them, they were to shake the dust of that town from their <u>S</u> <u>H</u> <u>O</u> <u>E</u> <u>S</u>.
                    4

8. Jesus gave <u>S</u> <u>I</u> <u>M</u> <u>O</u> <u>N</u> the new name, <u>P</u> <u>E</u> <u>T</u> <u>E</u> <u>R</u>.
         9   28

9. Don't <u>C</u> <u>O</u> <u>N</u> <u>F</u> <u>U</u> <u>S</u> <u>E</u> Jude <u>T</u> <u>H</u> <u>A</u> <u>D</u> <u>D</u> <u>E</u> <u>U</u> <u>S</u> with
      1   5 25 12   15
   Judas <u>I</u> <u>S</u> <u>C</u> <u>A</u> <u>R</u> <u>I</u> <u>O</u> <u>T</u>.
      16

10. <u>M</u> <u>A</u> <u>T</u> <u>T</u> <u>H</u> <u>E</u> <u>W</u> called himself "the tax collector."
              17

THE MESSAGE:

<u>C</u> <u>O</u> <u>M</u> <u>E</u> <u>F</u> <u>O</u> <u>L</u> <u>L</u> <u>O</u> <u>W</u> <u>M</u> <u>E</u> <u>A</u> <u>N</u> <u>D</u> <u>I</u> <u>W</u> <u>I</u> <u>L</u> <u>L</u>
1 2 3 4   5 6 7 8 9 10   11 12   13 14 15   16   17 18 7 8

<u>G</u> <u>I</u> <u>V</u> <u>E</u> <u>Y</u> <u>O</u> <u>U</u> <u>L</u> <u>I</u> <u>F</u> <u>E</u>.
19 20 21 22 23 24 25 7 26 27 28

Chapter 11 Activity Master, p. 183G

Check that the students have completed the activity as assigned.

Chapter 12 Activity Master, p. 195G

Check that the students fully completed the activity.

Chapter 13 Activity Master, p. 211G

Moral Dilemma #1
Object: reading of six books over the summer; Intention: to find an easy and fast way to complete the work; Circumstances: procrastinating left little time for the work; Decision: Answers will vary.

Moral Dilemma #2
Object: a birthday present for your mom; Intention: to make your mom happy without having to spend money on a gift; Circumstances: being in stores owned by wealthy corporations makes you feel less immoral about stealing a birthday present for your mom; Decision: Answers will vary.

Moral Dilemma #3
Object: a person who is being picked on in your class; Intention: to stop a group's bullying actions toward another student; Circumstances: you don't have a direct connection to the student who is being picked on, or the bully, but you feel obligated to help make it stop; Decision: Answers will vary.

Chapter 14 Activity Master, p. 223G

Answers will vary. Check that the students fully completed the activity.

Chapter 15 Activity Master, p. 235G

Answers will vary. Check that the students fully completed the activity.

Chapter 16 Activity Master, p. 251G

Check that the students have completed the activity as assigned.

Chapter 17 Activity Master, p. 263G

Answers will vary. Check that the students fully completed the activity.

Chapter 18 Activity Master, p. 275G

Check that the students have completed the activity as assigned.

Chapter 19 Activity Master, p. 291G

Check that the students have completed the activity as assigned.

Chapter 20 Activity Master, p. 303G

Answers will vary. Check that the students fully completed the activity.

Chapter 21 Activity Master, p. 315G

Check that the students have completed the activity as assigned.